Oligopoly Pricing

Oligopoly Pricing

Old Ideas and New Tools

Xavier Vives

The MIT Press
Cambridge, Massachusetts
London, England

© 1999 Massachusetts Institute of Technology

All rights reserved. No part of this book may be reproduced in any form by any electronic or mechanical means (including photocopying, recording, or information storage and retrieval) without permission in writing from the publisher.

This book was set in Palatino by Asco Typesetters, Hong Kong.

Printed and bound in the United States of America.

Library of Congress Cataloging-in-Publication Data

Vives, Xavier.
  Oligopoly pricing : old ideas and new tools / Xavier Vives.
    p.   cm.
  Includes bibliographical references and index.
  ISBN 0-262-22060-1 (hc : alk. paper)
  1. Oligopolies. 2. Pricing. 3. Competition. 4. Game theory.
I. Title.
HD2757.3.V58   2000
338.5′23—dc21
                                              99-32864
                                                  CIP

Al Santiago que ens va deixar massa aviat i al Jaume que tenia pressa per arribar.

Contents

Preface

The "oligopoly problem" has proved to be one of the more resilient problems in the history of economic thought. The debate over whether or not pricing in conditions of oligopoly is determinate has gone through different phases but has never disappeared from the academic scene. The question remains: How are prices formed when there are only a few competitors in the market?

This book reviews the theory of oligopoly pricing from the perspective of modern game theory. It builds on the ideas of the founding fathers of the field. The focus is on models of pricing, from a partial equilibrium perspective. This approach is biased by this author's own work in the field. It includes some consideration of entry and industrial structure issues, and the study of the evolution of state variables that condition pricing, but the main concentration is on short-run supply theory, both from a dynamic and a static perspective. Competition in non-price variables such as advertising and R&D, or issues related to price discrimination, vertical relations, switching and search costs, and network externalities are not explicitly addressed.

The book also attempts to cover in some depth a selection of important topics which are dispersed in the literature. Some of the results gathered here may not be surprising to the insiders in the field but may not be so well known in the profession at large. Several chapters include new results, particularly in the applications of supermodular game theory to oligopoly.

This book evolved mostly from graduate-level lectures pertaining to second- and third-year doctorate courses, and including courses at the advanced undergraduate level, delivered over time at the University of Pennsylvania, the University of California at Berkeley, Universitat Autònoma de Barcelona, Universitat Pompeu Fabra, and Harvard University. Its contents are therefore advanced but presented in a self-contained way. Readers are expected to be conversant with basic microeconomic theory and to have some mathematical background and maturity. The exposition is rigorous, but to allow for a smooth reading, it does not emphasize the technical details. The text is suitable for graduate industrial organization, applied game theory, and specialized oligopoly courses. It can be used as well to complement graduate microeconomics and advanced theory courses on imperfect competition. Advanced undergraduates with mathematical training should also be able to profit from it. Some advanced topics and exercises should prove challenging for researchers at large.

Chapter 1 reviews the key ideas of the classical contributors to the field, Cournot, Bertrand, Edgeworth, Chamberlin and Robinson, and Stackelberg, and relates them to modern game theory. Chapter 2 presents some basic game-theoretic tools needed for the analysis in a self-contained way. Results on the characterization of Nash equilibrium (existence, uniqueness, and stability) as well as Bayesian Nash equilibrium form the central part of the chapter. Emphasis is given to recent developments in the theory of supermodular games. The reader with a good working knowledge of game-theoretic tools can pick and choose topics from chapter 2, or refer back to it when necessary. Chapter 3 provides a foundation for partial equilibrium analysis, where oligopoly theory is typically developed. This includes a rationalization of downward-sloping demand schedules and of the use of consumer surplus as a welfare measure. Chapter 3 can be skipped without loss of continuity.

Chapters 4 to 6 provide an in depth treatment of classical static models: quantity (Cournot) competition in chapter 4, price competition (Bertrand and Edgeworth) in chapter 5, and product differentiation in chapter 6 (Chamberlin and Robinson). Chapter 5 provides also the foundations for the Cournot model when firms compete in prices. Chapter 6 compares Cournot and Bertrand equilibria and studies monopolistic competition. Each chapter provides specialized existence results, characterizations of equilibria, extensions to large markets and, in most instances, to entry, and an analysis of comparative statics with a view toward applied work.

Chapter 7 summarizes some of the attempts to deal with the oligopoly problem, including conjectural variations and supply functions, and it introduces the study of commitment with two-stage games starting from the Stackelberg model. Topics covered include entry deterrence and the advantages of incumbency. The concept of subgame-perfect equilibrium is introduced formally in this chapter because it provides the appropriate tool with which to study commitment issues.

Chapter 8 concentrates on a few topics of the vast literature on the modeling of competition under asymmetric information and briefly surveys other important material. It presents the basic competition models with incomplete information and includes a complete analysis of information sharing and strategic information transmission. Furthermore, mechanism design theory is used to explain the constraints faced by cartels and trade associations in an incomplete information environment. Finally the chapter studies the manipulation of information flows, re-examines the value of commitment under uncertainty and incomplete information, and characterizes the effects of signaling distortions on pricing policies. Basic tools of analysis are provided by the concepts of Bayesian (Nash) equilibrium and of perfect Bayesian (Nash) equilibrium. The latter is introduced in this chapter.

Chapter 9 develops the basic elements of the theory of repeated and dynamic games in order to explain the sustainability of collusion and dynamic patterns of pricing. It studies the factors that hinder or foster collusion and extends the analysis to incorporate uncertainty and private information as well as imperfect monitoring. The dynamics of commitment are analyzed using a state space restriction on strategies in both discrete and continuous time (differential) games. The concept of Markov perfect equilibrium provides the appropriate tool to study dynamic commitment; it is introduced in this chapter, which also contains a discussion of differential games. The chapter develops a taxonomy of strategic behavior in dynamic games.

Every chapter includes exercises which range from easy to difficult to solve. Starred exercises are the more difficult ones and/or require more work. Exercises with a double star can be viewed as small research projects.

Some of the material has been adapted from previously published articles in the following journals: the *European Economic Review* (1989, 1993) for chapter 1, the *Journal of Mathematical Economics* (1990a) for several sections of chapter 2, the *Review of Economic Studies* (1987) for chapter 3, *Economics Letters* (1986a) for section 5.2.4, the *Journal of Economic Theory* (1985a) for sections 6.3 and 6.4, the *International*

Journal of Industrial Organization (1986b) for section 7.2.1, the *Rand Journal of Economics* (1984, a joint paper with Nirvikar Singh) for section 7.2.2, the *European Economic Review* (1988) and the *Review of Economic Studies* (1986, a joint paper with Richard Gilbert) for section 7.4.2, the *Rand Journal of Economics* (1990b) for sections 8.2 and 8.3.4, the *Journal of Economic Theory* (1984) for section 8.3.1, and the *Journal of Economics and Management Strategy* (1992, a joint paper with Richard Kihlstrom) for sections 8.4.2 and 8.4.3.

I owe an intellectual debt to many colleagues and former professors. I would like to mention first my Berkeley colleagues from the early 1980s, especially Gerard Debreu, Drew Fudenberg, Richard Gilbert, and Andreu Mas-Colell, from whom I learned and consolidated my interest in oligopoly theory, and my coauthors in the oligopoly field, Ramon Caminal, Richard Gilbert, Byoung Jun, Richard Kihlstrom, Kai-Uwe Kühn, Carmen Matutes, Nirvikar Singh, and Jacques Thisse with whom I developed several of the models presented in the book. Next I would like to thank my colleagues and visitors at the Institut d'Anàlisi Econòmica in Barcelona for useful comments. The writing of this book was essentially completed while I was a visiting professor at Harvard University enjoying the hospitality of the Department of Economics. I am grateful also to Xavier Martinez and to anonymous reviewers for the MIT Press who provided useful suggestions to improve the manuscript, to Dana Andrus for her careful copyediting, and to Terry Vaughn for his enthusiastic support. I gratefully acknowledge the research support of the Spanish Ministerio de Educación y Ciencia through DGICYT project 93-0679 and of the Fundación ICO. Angela Hernández provided crucial help in the typing and presentation of the manuscript.

Oligopoly Pricing

1   Ideas of the Founding Fathers: Oligopoly Theory and Modern Game Theory

A recurrent theme of oligopoly theory is whether prices are determinate with oligopolistic interaction. Cournot, Bertrand, and Edgeworth established the foundations of modern oligopoly theory and discussed the central issue of how prices would be formed in a market with only a few competitors. In doing so, they preceded modern noncooperative game theory in developing solution concepts for situations of strategic interaction. In fact they raised most of the issues which later would become central in oligopoly theory: the appropriate solution concept, the analysis of equilibria (existence, uniqueness, and stability), and comparative statics and dynamic properties. They also raised concerns about the plausibility of the very concept of equilibrium, although this seems to have been unnoticed in the literature. Later on, Chamberlin, Hotelling, and Robinson stressed the importance of product differentiation. Let us review briefly these contributions in turn.[1]

Cournot (1838) laid out the foundation of oligopoly theory by proposing a solution concept for oligopolistic interaction, examining both the cases of substitute and complementary products and studying the stability of the proposed solution. He discussed also the possibility of collusion and the connection between oligopoly and perfect competition.

Cournot claimed that prices would also be determined under oligopolistic rivalry. He envisioned firms (the celebrated mineral water producers) competing independently and deciding about their production levels. Then firms would bring to the market the output produced, where a price would emerge from the interaction of supply and demand. An equilibrium is reached when the output of any firm is a best response to the other firms' outputs. This occurs when each firm chooses an output level that maximizes profits given the outputs chosen by the rivals. In modern terms this is a Nash equilibrium (Nash 1950) with quantities as strategic variables. As is well known, the equilibrium involves a price above the marginal cost of production. Our author also considered competition of producers of complementary products. Interestingly he assumed that in this case firms would compete via prices and applied the same abstract (Nash) solution concept. Again, an equilibrium is characterized by actions, prices in this case, that are consistent in the sense that the action of a firm is a best response to the actions of the rivals. This is a Nash equilibrium with prices as strategic variables. Furthermore he showed that the equilibrium price with competition in complementary products, and contrary to the case of substitutes, is larger than the monopoly or cartel price.[2] Cournot also hinted at the modern noncooperative foundation of perfect competition when dealing with "unlimited," that is, perfect, competition. Indeed, in order for firms to have no effect in the limit on the market price, Cournot recognized that they have to be small with respect to the market, each one with "inappreciable" production.

Cournot's contribution went largely unnoticed by economists until the review of his book by Bertrand in 1883. Bertrand, after claiming that the obvious choice for oligopolists is to collude, contended that in the homogeneous product market considered by Cournot the relevant strategies for firms were prices and not quantities. In modern language, Bertrand proposed the Nash solution concept in prices. If this suggestion is adopted and unit production costs are constant and equal for all the firms, as in Cournot's mineral water example, price will equal marginal cost, which is the competitive solution.

Edgeworth challenged strongly Cournot's ideas, in particular, the assertion that equilibrium is determinate in oligopoly. Indeed, Edgeworth stated in his article on the pure theory of monopoly (1925, 117–18; first published in 1897):

[Cournot] concludes that a determinate proposition of equilibrium defined by certain quantities of the articles will be reached. Cournot's conclusion has been shown to be erroneous by Bertrand for the case in which there is no cost of production; by Professor Marshall for the case in which the cost follows the law of increasing returns; and by the present writer for the case in which the cost follows the law of diminishing returns.

Edgeworth's central idea is that in situations of fewness in numbers, in oligopoly, and in contrast with monopoly or perfect competition, equilibrium is *indeterminate*. He illustrated his theory examining price competition in a duopoly with substitute or complementary products x and y. Positing a utility function $U(x, y)$ for the consumer commensurable with money (i.e., linear in money), Edgeworth defines the goods to be rival if $\partial^2 U / \partial x \partial y < 0$ for all consumers (or at least on average), and complementary if the cross derivative is positive.[3] From the utility specification inverse and direct demands are derived and their properties analyzed (e.g., noting that concavity of the utility function and rival goods imply gross substitutability).[4]

For *substitute* goods Edgeworth considered the case of a homogenous product supplied by a duopoly with increasing marginal costs, either in the extreme form of capacity constraints (1925) or with quadratic costs of production (1922). He concluded in both cases that prices would never reach an equilibrium position and would oscillate, cycling indefinitely. Edgeworth also pointed out that the "extent of indeterminateness" diminishes as the goods become more differentiated, in the limit being the firms independent monopolies. A main insight of his analysis is that a firm will not have an incentive to supply more than its competitive supply (as determined by its marginal cost schedule) at any given price. According to Edgeworth, the analysis must take into account this *voluntary trading* constraint. Indeed, in the case of capacity constraints the firm simply cannot supply more than the available capacity. The consequence is that the competitive equilibrium, which is the only possible equilibrium in pure strategies in the Edgeworth duopoly (see Shubik 1959), may be destabilized: A firm by *raising* its price can increase its profit given that the rival firm may not be able (or may not want) to supply the whole market at the competitive price. This fact together with the traditional price-cutting Bertrand argument yields nonexistence of a price equilibrium (in pure strategies) for plausible ranges of firms' capacities or cost specifications. His model has given rise to what now is termed *Bertrand-Edgeworth competition*, where firms compete in prices but also where no firm is required to supply all the forthcoming demand at the set price. In this type of competition, existence of equilibrium, according to the game-theoretic modern analysis, can be guaranteed only in mixed strategies, with firms randomizing over a certain range of prices.

For *complementary* goods Edgeworth thought it "at least very probable," in contrast to the case of rival products where he thought it "certain," that "economic equilibrium is indeterminate." The illustration provided considers perfectly complementary products produced by (price) competing suppliers and also the fanciful competitors Nansen and Johansen "dragging their sledge over the Artic plains (all their dogs having died)." The reason for the indeterminacy may be, as in the case of rival commodities, that the shape of profit functions is such that a (Nash) equilibrium does not exist. Nevertheless, even if it exists, this equilibrium may not obtain even if both firms are "perfectly intelligent and aware of each other's motives."[5] Indeed, if only one firm is perfectly intelligent and foreseeing while the other is myopic, the equilibrium proposed by Edgeworth is the point later proposed by Stackelberg (1934) in his leader-follower model. The (Stackelberg) point, in the words of Edgeworth, "will not be a stable equilibrium, except on the extreme supposition that Nansen is perfectly intelligent and foreseeing, while Johansen, as the saying is, 'can not see beyond his nose.'"[6] If both firms are forward-looking, then they may try to outsmart each other and the candidate (Nash) equilibrium may be unsettled by accident or by a player foreseeing a future move of the rival away from the equilibrium.

Edgeworth seems to be pointing at a modern criticism of Nash equilibrium: "Rationality" (utility maximization given some beliefs) and payoffs being common knowledge is not sufficient to explain (Nash) equilibrium behavior. The *rationalizability* literature (Bernheim 1984; Pearce 1984; see section 2.6.1) has pointed out that Nash equilibrium is not the only outcome of common knowledge of payoffs and rationality. Equilibrium strategies are rationalizable, but in general, the rationalizable set is much larger. For example, in a Cournot linear demand oligopoly with more than two firms and constant marginal costs, any price between the competitive and the monopoly levels is rationalizable.

In summary, Edgeworth thought that the oligopoly problem was essentially *indeterminate* and that prices would never reach an equilibrium position in markets characterized by fewness in numbers, as opposed to what happens in competitive markets. For substitute products, his line of attack is to point out nonexistence of price equilibria (in pure strategies). For complementary products, the attack can be seen to be more fundamental, since he questions the very concept of (Nash) equilibrium.

A recent development taking off from an oligopoly theory focus, the theory of supermodular games,[7] provides conditions bounding the extent of indeterminacy in strategic behavior, a central concern of Edgeworth. As stated before, Edgeworth was the first to consider a utility function of the general type $U(x, y)$ and to introduce assumptions on its cross second derivatives. Indeed, the assumption $\partial^2 U / \partial x \partial y > 0$ is referred to sometimes as "Edgeworth complementarity." In modern terminology, when the marginal payoff of action x of an agent is increasing in the action y (which may be an action of the same agent or of another), we say that actions x and y are *strategic complements*.[8] The theory of supermodular games provides the theoretical framework in which to study strategic complementarities and has a bearing on the Edgeworthian indeterminacy theme. Indeed, supermodular games have always equilibria in pure strategies, the equilibrium set has nice order and stability properties, and rationalizable behavior can be confined within some bounds.

Hotelling (1929), Chamberlin (1933), and Robinson (1933) emphasized product differentiation in the study of imperfect competition. They all thought in terms of firms competing in prices. The Hotelling location model incorporates heterogeneous tastes in consumers and provides the foundation for location theory. Chamberlin (1933) and Robinson (1933) advanced the monopolistic competition model. In Chamberlin's "large group" model firms are small relative to the market but retain some monopoly power. This is the basis of the monopolistic competition model in which, although an individual firms faces a downward-sloping demand for its variety, it cannot influence market aggregates.

Two other issues have deserved attention in oligopoly theory: The stability of equilibria and the tendency of oligopolists to collude.

Cournot thought that his proposed solution would be stable in the sense that a departure from it would be self-correcting through a series of reactions of the firms. The disequilibrium dynamics would be governed by the best-response functions of the firms, that is, by the functions that yield the optimal output of a firm in terms of the outputs of the rivals. This concept of stability has been criticized, since Cournot's firms in the adjustment process to equilibrium see how their expectations are systematically falsified by the evidence. They expect rivals to maintain their outputs while in fact they are changing constantly. Only at the equilibrium point expectations are not falsified. This led Fellner (1949) to state that Cournot was "right for the wrong reasons." However, the criticism does not apply to the solution concept. In a Cournot equilibrium firms anticipate correctly the production levels of rivals and optimize accordingly. Furthermore the Cournot adjustment process is now seen, from an evolutionary perspective, as a rudimentary way of modeling the behavior of boundedly rational agents.

The possibility of *collusion* among producers has been a permanent concern of oligopoly theory. Cournot evoked the question of why firms do not come to an understanding and agree on sharing the market at the monopoly price. He thought that from the point of view of a firm, if the rivals follow the agreement, it is in the interest of the firm to depart from it, and this way increase its profits. In other words, there is an incentive to cheat. Cournot thought that monopoly or cartel type agreements could only be maintained by "means of a formal engagement" (1938, p. 83). The tendency toward collusion in oligopoly was argued forcefully by Chamberlin (1929). He thought that while in the "large-group" case the monopolistically competitive model was appropriate, in the "small-group" case firms would realize their interdependence and would act (implicitly) to maximize joint profits, taking into account the possible use of retaliation strategies against defectors. This "tacit collusion" view has been endorsed by many influential economists, including Fellner (1949), Samuelson (1967), and Stigler (1964), and has been popularized in industrial organization textbooks like Scherer and Ross (1990). Stigler (1964) advanced the idea that a major obstacle to the stability of collusive agreements is secret price cutting. When a firm observes a low level of sales, it is not sure whether this is because there is an adverse shock to the demand for its product or whether rivals are cheating on the cartel agreement.

The "oligopoly problem" is centered around the potential indeterminateness of prices with a few number of competitors. Cournot's contention that prices would be determinate under conditions of oligopoly was strongly challenged by Edgeworth, who thought that prices were essentially indeterminate. Bertrand's opinion on this account falls on the Cournot side, while Chamberlin's leans toward Edgeworth's.[9] The appropriate solution concept and its properties (existence, unicity, stability and comparative statics) have remained concerns of modern analysis using the tools of game theory. Von

Neumann and Morgenstern's *Theory of Games and Economic Behavior* was published in 1944, and Nash's articles on noncooperative games in 1950 and 1951. Although their influence was felt by some researchers in the oligopoly field (i.e., Shubik 1959), the massive application of game theory to the analysis of competition among firms had to await until the late seventies.

It is precisely the interaction between game theory and oligopoly theory what made possible the formalization of important ideas about competition in industrial organization contexts. I have described the contributions of oligopoly theory to static noncooperative game theory, including the more recent developments of supermodular games. From the theory of games, important tools have been contributed to the analysis of commitment, dynamic interaction, and situations of incomplete information. For dynamic games of complete information, subgame-perfect equilibrium (SPE), a refinement of Nash equilibrium due to Selten (1965), is central. For games of incomplete information, Harsanyi (1967–68) introduced the concept of Bayesian Nash equilibrium (BNE). For dynamic games of incomplete information the concept of perfect Bayesian equilibrium (PBE), a refinement of Nash equilibrium, combines the ideas behind SPE and BNE with the rules from Bayesian updating. Stronger refinements of Nash equilibrium in dynamic games of incomplete information have been proposed by Selten (1975) with perfect equilibrium and by Kreps and Wilson (1982a) with sequential equilibrium.

The leader-follower model proposed by Stackelberg (1934) incorporates the idea of commitment, the leader setting its output first and anticipating the reaction of the follower. The Stackelberg equilibrium is an instance of Selten's subgame-perfect equilibrium in which incredible threats are ruled out. In the Stackelberg model, for example, the follower cannot threaten to flood the market if the leader does not produce a certain output. This would be an empty threat because the follower would have no incentive to carry out the threat in case the leader does not comply.

Stackelberg (1952, pp. 194–95) thought that his leader-follower solution, which he called asymmetrical duopoly, "is unstable, for the passive seller can take up the struggle at any time.... It is possible, of course, that the duopolists may attempt to supplant one another in the market so that 'cut-throat' competition breaks out." This is what has been termed the "Stackelberg warfare point" where each firm in a duopoly attempts to be leader in a quantity setting game.[10] Stackelberg (1952; section 4.3.2) thought that duopoly was an unstable regime and equilibrium would be restored only with "collective monopoly or State regulation."

Schelling (1960) pioneered the analysis of situations in which a supposed weakness, like the restriction of allowable strategies for a player, can be turned into a source of strength or a strategic advantage. In a more general setting the restriction to Markov strategies, that is, strategies that depend only on payoff-relevant variables, has proved useful to understand the dynamics of commitment whenever state variables, like capacities, condition short-run competition. Incumbency advantages in markets subject to entry provide a leading illustration of the phenomena. Markov perfect equilibrium (Maskin and Tirole 1997) provides then the appropriate solution concept. Using the tools provided by differential games, the analysis can be extended to competition in continuous time. The result is a rich theory which explains a variety of dynamic patterns of pricing and in which intertemporal strategic complementarity or substitutability plays a key role.

The theory of repeated games, pioneered by Friedman (1971), Aumann and Shapley (1976), and Rubinstein (1979), provides an appropriate tool to analyze the mechanisms to sustain collusion using threats that are credible. An extension of the theory, initiated by the oligopoly model of Green and Porter (1984), allowing for imperfect monitoring of the actions of firms can explain the role of price wars in sustaining collusion and what is needed to prevent secret price cutting.

The developments brought forward by the analysis of games of incomplete information have contributed in a major way to the study of pricing when firms have private information and to explain phenomena like information sharing and strategic information revelation. Mechanism design, an application of the theory of games with incomplete information, illuminates the incentive constraints that firms face when trying to reveal their information, for example, for collusive purposes. Dynamic games of incomplete information allow the study of investment in an intangible variable as information or misinformation. The use of pricing to manipulate information with its associated signaling distortions helps in building theories about limit pricing and the free-rider problem in entry deterrence, market share inertia, introductory pricing, and predatory behavior.

In summary, oligopoly theory has foreshadowed (noncooperative) game theory with the basic equilibrium concept, the Cournot-Nash equilibrium, as well as its characterization in terms of existence and stability properties. In turn, game theory has contributed valuable tools, developed sometimes hand in hand with oligopoly applications like supermodular games and repeated games with imperfect monitoring, which have proved essential in the analysis of dynamics and of situations of incomplete information.

2   Game Theory Tools

Noncooperative game theory analyzes situations in which (economic) agents' payoffs (utilities) depend on the actions of other agents and in which the agents/players cannot, in principle, sign binding agreements enforceable by third parties about what course of action to follow. In most situations arising in economic competition, binding contracts are rarely possible, and therefore *noncooperative* game theory provides the appropriate tools for analysis. Indeed, the equilibrium concepts and analysis developed by Cournot, Bertrand, and Edgeworth can be seen as precursors of modern game-theoretic developments like Nash equilibrium (Nash 1950) and even non-equilibrium analysis as rationalizability (Bernheim 1984; and Pearce 1984).[1]

This chapter develops the game theory tools appropriate for the study of games in normal or strategic form. We start by reviewing the theory of Nash equilibrium and the basic existence result in section 2.1. Section 2.2 is devoted to the theory of supermodular games incorporating results from lattice programming and monotone comparative statics. Section 2.3 deals with related existence results in pure strategies in cases where best replies need not be increasing. Mixed strategies are considered in section 2.4. Section 2.5 approaches the issue of uniqueness of equilibria, and section 2.6 reviews results on stability of equilibria. Section 2.7 examines situations of incomplete information and develops the concept of Bayesian Nash equilibrium. It includes also the study of monotone comparative statics under uncertainty and the modeling of information structures and signals. The tools presented for the study of games in normal form will be enough for most of the rest of the chapters except for parts of chapters 7, 8, and 9. Refinements of Nash equilibrium for dynamic games (subgame-perfect equilibrium for games of complete information and perfect Bayesian equilibrium for games of incomplete information in particular) will be introduced as needed. Section 2.1 discusses briefly also the extensive form of a game and introduces some terminology to be used when studying dynamic games.

2.1 Games in Normal Form and Nash Equilibrium

Let us start by describing briefly the basic concept of the extensive form of a game, since it provides the formal representation of a situation of strategic interdependence among a given set of players.

A game in *extensive form* specifies the order of play or moves of the players, the choices available to each player, the information each player has available when making a choice, the outcomes that follow from the choices made by the players, and the payoffs to each player for each possible outcome. The specification is summarized in a tree structure (the *game tree*) with decision and terminal nodes, and information sets (to this moves by "nature" can be added according to a known probability distribution). A decision *node* is a point in the tree where a player has to make a move. An *information set* for a player who has to move consists of all the decision nodes that the player can not distinguish.[2] A list of all the information sets of a player provides a list of all possible events (that the player can distinguish) in which he may have to make a move. The payoff to a player is the amount of profit (or utility) that the player obtains at every terminal node of the game tree.

A *subgame* is the part of the game that starts at a singleton information set (i.e., an information set that contains only one decision node), preserves the information sets of the general game, and is closed under succession. The study of subgames is important in dynamic games.

Games can be classified according to the information players have when it is their turn to move. A *perfect information game* is one where every player, when he has to move, knows the moves of the players that have played before (i.e., if all information sets are singletons). A game is of *imperfect information* if at least a player has one information set which is not a singleton. In a game of perfect information at every node, a subgame starts.

A *strategy* is a complete description of the actions to be taken by a player at every information set. That is, a strategy is a complete contingent plan of action for any possible distinguishable circumstance that the player may have to act upon. Given a profile of strategies for the players, the payoff for each player can be obtained. This leads us to the normal or strategic form of a game.

A game in *normal* or *strategic form* G consists of a triplet $(A_i, \pi_i; i \in N)$, where N is the set of players $N = \{1, \ldots, n\}$; A_i the (pure) strategy space of player i; and $\pi_i : A \to R$, with $A = A_1 \times \cdots \times A_n$, the payoff function of player i. All these elements are *common knowledge* to the players. That is, every player knows them and knows that other players know and knows that other players know that he knows, and so on ad infinitum (see Aumann 1976; Milgrom 1981a).

For any extensive form representation of a game, there is (essentially) a unique associated normal form but not conversely. However, in a simultaneous move game (where players move only once and at the same time) the normal form representation is equivalent to the extensive form representation (in which each player makes a choice without observing the choices of rivals). In the rest of this chapter we confine attention to simultaneous move games.

Each player tries to maximize its payoff by choosing an appropriate strategy knowing only the structure of the game: Strategy spaces and payoffs of other players. Therefore each player must conjecture the strategies that the rivals are going to use. In an equilibrium situation, the conjectures of the players must be correct, and no player must have an incentive to change his strategy given the other players' choices. In a Nash equilibrium, both conditions are fulfilled.

A *Nash equilibrium* is a set of strategies $a^* = (a_1^*, \ldots, a_n^*)$ such that $\pi_i(a^*) \geq \pi_i(a_i, a_{-i}^*)$ for all a_i in A_i, where, as usual, a_{-i} denotes the vector a with the ith component deleted. For example, in the Cournot case the strategies are quantities, and in the Bertrand case, prices. The Nash equilibrium concept is central in oligopoly theory, let us briefly try to understand why.

Noncooperative game theory tries to obtain "rational predictions" of how a game would be actually played. Nash equilibrium seems to be then a necessary condition or a consistency requirement for any prediction of rational behavior of players who decide independently on the best course of action. Indeed, suppose, to the contrary, that a suggested solution is not a Nash equilibrium. Then it is not consistent in the sense that if the players think it is an accurate description of the game, then someone is not behaving rationally (not maximizing utility). In other words, a theory that would recommend a solution other than a Nash equilibrium would be self-defeating. It is worth noticing that this argument relies heavily on the common knowledge assumption.

Once accepted that the Nash equilibrium concept is a minimal consistency requirement of any proposed solution, we still are faced with the problem of how do players get to play it. We can distinguish two situations according to whether there is preplay communication or not. With preplay communication, a Nash equilibrium is a self-enforcing agreement between the players: It is in the interest of any player to follow it given that the others comply. Without preplay communication, given common knowledge assumptions on the structure of the game and on Nash behavior, Nash equilibria are the only consistent description of play that rational players can imagine. To this end each player has to "see" the game from the point of view of other players. In the words of Nash (1950b): "We proceed by investigating the question: What would be a 'rational' prediction of the behavior to be expected of rational playing the game in question? By using the principles that a rational prediction should be unique, that the players should be able to deduce and make use of it, and that such knowledge on the part of each player of what to expect the others to do should not lead him to act out of conformity with the prediction, one is led to the concept of a solution defined before."

This describes what Nash termed the "rationalistic and idealizing interpretation" of his equilibrium concept.[3] It is worth noting that it requires the players to know not only the game but also its solution. It requires, on top, that the solution be unique, since otherwise a player will not know the strategies used by the other players. What happens then when there is multiplicity of equilibria, how will players coordinate on one of them? In this case players will have to use information that is not included in the formal description of the game in order to coordinate their expectations. In fact Nash already observed that sometimes heuristic reasons can be found to narrow down the set of equilibria. One possibility is the theory of focal points developed by Schelling (1960). Equilibria are selected according to prominence, convention, past experiences, or cultural background of the players when there is no arbitrator with authority to choose a solution. It has been proposed also that a Pareto dominant equilibrium should be chosen by the players whenever it exists. However, two objections have been raised against this plausible idea. The first is that without preplay communication the Pareto

Table 2.1
Payoffs of 2×2 game

	U	D
U	7, 7	8, 0
D	0, 8	9, 9

dominant equilibrium may be too "risky" for the players. Harsanyi and Selten (1988), while developing a complete theory of equilibrium selection in games, have proposed the concept of risk dominance to select among equilibria. With preplay communication Aumann (1990) has also raised objections to select according to the Pareto criterion.

Consider the two by two game in table 2.1. The potential problem is that a player may have the incentive to say that he will play the strategy corresponding to the Pareto dominant equilibrium (D, D) even if he intends not to do so. However, there is some experimental evidence that suggests that communication helps in attaining efficient equilibria.[4]

Another justification for Nash equilibrium does not insist on the rationality of players, minimizes their informational requirements, and sees equilibrium points as the outcome of the repeated interaction of a large population of players who are matched at random. This was termed the "mass-action" interpretation by Nash (1950b; more on this approach in section 2.4 on mixed strategies and in section 2.6 on stability).

In the rest of this section we will analyze conditions under which Nash equilibria exist and later on (in section 2.5) under which the equilibrium set is a singleton. Nonexistence of Nash equilibria in pure strategies (and nonuniqueness when they exist) is pervasive in oligopoly models. Apart from the Edgeworth model, examples of duopoly models where firms can produce at no cost and where demands arise from well-behaved preferences in which no Nash equilibrium (in pure strategies) exists are easily produced (e.g., see Roberts and Sonnenschein 1977 and Friedman 1983, pp. 67–69).

Consider an n-player game $(A_i, \pi_i; i \in N)$, and let Ψ_i be the best-response correspondence[5] of player i, that is,

$$\Psi_i(a_{-i}) = \left\{ a_i \in A_i : a_i \in \arg\max_{b \in A_i} \pi_i(b, a_{-i}) \right\}.$$

$\Psi_i(a_{-i})$ assigns a set of best replies for player i to any combination of strategies of the other players a_{-i}.

We have then that a^* is a Nash equilibrium (in pure strategies)[6] if and only if

$$a^* \in \Psi(a^*) \equiv (\Psi_1(a^*_{-1}) \times \cdots \times \Psi_n(a^*_{-n})).$$

The standard existence result derives from the theorem of Nash (1950; e.g., see Debreu 1952):

THEOREM 2.1   Consider the game $(A_i, \pi_i; i \in N)$. If the strategy sets are nonempty convex and compact subsets of Euclidean space and the payoff to firm i is continuous in the actions of all firms and quasiconcave in its own action, then there is a Nash equilibrium.

The proof of the theorem follows applying Kakutani's fixed point theorem to the best-reply map Ψ. Continuity of payoffs and compactness of strategy sets imply that best-response correspondences are upper hemicontinuous,[7] and quasiconcavity of payoffs and convexity of strategy sets that they are convex-valued. It also follows that the equilibrium set is compact.

Nonexistence examples typically fail the quasiconcavity test. Without quasiconcavity best replies have jumps (that is, they are not convex-valued). Lack of continuity of payoffs may not be a problem per se. Dasgupta and Maskin (1986) show that existence in pure strategies with weak continuity requirements is guaranteed provided that payoffs are quasiconcave.

There are several recent results available in the literature showing existence without requiring quasiconcavity. A first type of approach is based on nontopological methods and exploits monotonicity properties of optimization problems using lattice-theoretical results. This approach, which defines the class of *supermodular games*, will be expounded with some detail given its recent introduction in economic analysis. A second type of approach restricts attention to symmetric games and uses a one-dimensional fixed point theorem. Still a third approach uses constructive methods applied to the Cournot model with homogeneous product.[8]

2.2   Supermodular Games and Lattice Programming

The class of supermodular games was introduced by Topkis (1979) and further studied by Vives (1985b and 1990a) and Milgrom and

Roberts (1990).[9] The machinery needed to study supermodular games is lattice theory, Tarski's fixed point theorem, and monotonicity results in lattice programming. The methods used are non-topological, and they exploit order properties. A rough idea of the attack on the existence problem is as follows: Tarski's theorem shows the existence of a fixed point for increasing functions. We can use it then when best-reply correspondences of players have a monotone increasing selection. This monotonicity property is guaranteed when the marginal benefit of increasing the strategy of a player raises with the levels of the strategies of rivals (i.e., when the game exhibits "strategic complementarity") and when, in games with multidimensional strategy spaces, the marginal benefit of increasing the strategy of a player raises with the levels of the other strategies of the player. The result of the analysis is not only to show existence of equilibrium without requiring quasiconcavity of payoffs but also to obtain order properties of the equilibrium set like the existence of a largest and a smallest equilibrium point. Furthermore the monotonicity of solutions to optimization problems under supermodularity (complementarity) conditions proves to be the right approach to characterize monotone comparative statics without making unnecessary assumptions. Below I survey first the basics of the theory of lattices and Tarski's theorem. I then go on to define the concept of supermodularity and develop the results on monotonicity of solutions of programming in lattices. Finally, I study supermodular games.

2.2.1   Lattices and Tarski's Theorem

Let $\geq$ be a binary relation on a nonempty set S. The pair $(S, \geq)$ is a *partially ordered set* if $\geq$ is reflexive, transitive, and antisymmetric.[10] A partially ordered set $(S, \geq)$ is *(completely) ordered* if for x and y in S either $x \geq y$ or $y \geq x$.

A *lattice* is a partially ordered set $(S, \geq)$ in which any two elements x and y have a least upper bound (supremum), $\sup_S(x, y) = \inf\{z \in S : z \geq x, z \geq y\}$, and a greatest lower bound (infimum), $\inf_S(x, y) = \sup\{z \in S : z \leq x, z \leq y\}$, in the set. For example, any interval of the real line with the usual order is a lattice, since any two points have a supremum and a infimum in the interval. However, the set $S \subset R^2$, $S = \{(1,0), (0,1)\}$, is not a lattice with the vector ordering (the usual componentwise ordering: $x \leq y$ if and only if $x_i \leq y_i$ for any component i of the vectors), since $(1,0)$ and $(0,1)$ have

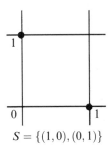

$$S = \{(1,0),(0,1)\}$$

Figure 2.1a

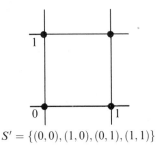

$$S' = \{(0,0),(1,0),(0,1),(1,1)\}$$

Figure 2.1b

no joint upper bound in S. The set $S' = \{(0,0),(1,0),(0,1),(1,1)\}$ is indeed a lattice with the vector ordering. (See figure 2.1a and b.)

Similarly the simplex in R^n (again with usual vector ordering), $\{x \in R^n : \Sigma_i x_i = 1, x_i \geq 0\}$, is not a lattice while the box $\{x \in R^n : 1 \geq x_i \geq 0\}$ is. (See figure 2.2.a and b.)

A lattice $(S, \geq)$ is *complete* if every nonempty subset of S has a supremum and an infimum in S. Any compact interval of the real line with the usual order is a complete lattice while the open interval (a,b) is a lattice but is not complete (indeed, the supremum of (a,b) does not belong to (a,b)). Cubes in R^n, formed as the product of n compact intervals, are complete lattices with the usual vector ordering.

A subset L of the lattice S is a *sublattice* of S if the supremum and infimum of any two elements of L belong also to L. That is, a sublattice L of the lattice S is a subset of S that is closed under the operations "supremum" and "infimum." The sublattice L of S is *complete* if every nonempty subset of L has a supremum and a infimum in L. A lattice is always a sublattice of itself, but a lattice need not

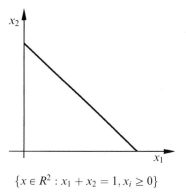

$$\{x \in R^2 : x_1 + x_2 = 1, x_i \geq 0\}$$

Figure 2.2a

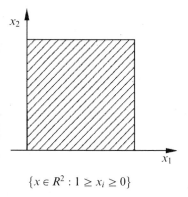

$$\{x \in R^2 : 1 \geq x_i \geq 0\}$$

Figure 2.2b

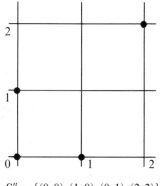

$$S'' = \{(0,0), (1,0), (0,1), (2,2)\}$$

Figure 2.2c

be a sublattice of a larger lattice. The reason is that the operations "supremum" and "infimum" have to be referred to the larger lattice. I will index *sup* and *inf* with the reference set only when there is danger of confusion. In this case, when $T \subset S$, where S is lattice, I denote the least upper bound of T in S by $\sup_S T$, and the greatest lower bound of T in S by $\inf_S T$ whenever they exist. Consider the following example: If in the set $S' = \{(0,0),(1,0),(0,1),(1,1)\}$ we replace $(1,1)$ by $(2,2)$ to obtain $S'' = \{(0,0),(1,0),(0,1),(2,2)\}$, then S'' is still a lattice under the vector ordering in R^2 (e.g., since, $\sup_{S''}\{(1,0),(0,1)\} = (2,2)$, but it is not a sublattice of R^2 because $\sup_{R^2}\{(1,0),(0,1)\} = (1,1)$ does not belong to S''. (See figure 2.2c and remark 2 below, and figure 2.4 for another example.)

Let $(S, \geq)$ be a partially ordered set. A function f from S to S is *increasing* (decreasing) if for x, y in S, $x \geq y$ implies that $f(x) \geq f(y)$ $((f(x) \leq f(y))$. We are now ready to state the following lattice-theoretical fixed point theorem due to Tarski (1955).

THEOREM 2.2 (Tarski)   Let $(S, \geq)$ be a complete lattice, f an increasing function from S to S, and E the set of fixed points of f; then E is nonempty and $(E, \geq)$ is a complete lattice. In particular, this means that there is a largest and a smallest fixed points (respectively, $\sup_S E = \sup\{x \in S : f(x) \geq x\}$ and $\inf_S E = \inf\{x \in S : f(x) \leq x\}$).

Proof   We show first that $u = \sup_S X$, where $X = \{x \in S : f(x) \geq x\}$, is the largest fixed point. Note that X is nonempty, since $\inf_S$ belongs to X, and that u exists, since S is a complete lattice. We have that $x \leq u$ and $f(x) \leq f(u)$ for x in X because f is increasing. Consequently $x \leq f(u)$ for x in X and $f(u)$ is an upper bound of X. Therefore $u \leq f(u)$, since u is the least upper bound of X in S. Now, since f is increasing, $f(u) \leq f(f(u))$, $f(u)$ belongs to X and therefore $f(u) \leq u$. We conclude that $u = f(u)$ and u belongs to E. Therefore $\sup_S E \geq u$. Since $E \subset X$, we have that $\sup_S E \leq u$ and $\sup_S E = u$. One shows similarly that $\inf_S E = \inf\{x \in S : f(x) \leq x\}$ is the smallest fixed point. Consider now $P \subset E$. We show that there is a least upper bound of P in E. The set $Z = \{x \in S : \sup S \geq x \geq \sup P\}$ is a complete lattice, since S is complete. It is easy to check that the function f restricted to Z, denoted by f', is increasing. Denote by E' the set of fixed points of f'. We know that $v = \inf_Z E'$ belongs to E'. We have then that v belongs to E and that it is the least fixed point of f which is an upper bound for any element of P. Therefore $v = \sup_E P$. Similarly one shows the existence of a greatest lower bound of P in E.   ◆

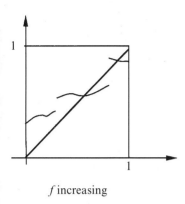

f increasing

Figure 2.3a

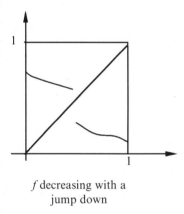

f decreasing with a
jump down

Figure 2.3b

The theorem is visualized easily thinking of a function f from $[0, 1]$ to $[0, 1]$. The set of fixed points of f is just the intersection of the graph of f with the 45° line. An increasing function f can have many jumps up, but it cannot avoid crossing the 45° line. This is not the case for a decreasing function and a similar theorem unfortunately does not hold for decreasing functions. If f is decreasing, it may jump down, miss the 45° line, and no equilibria will exist. (See figure 2.3a and b.)

Remark 1 It is noteworthy that no topological properties (like compactness, continuity, etc.) are involved in the result, only order properties.

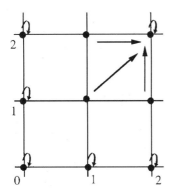

Figure 2.4

Remark 2 Tarski's theorem is not asserting that the set E of fixed points of $f : S \to S$ is a sublattice of S. That is, if x and y belong to E, it is not necessarily true that $\sup_S\{x, y\}$ and $\inf_S\{x, y\}$ also belong to E. What is true is that x and y have a supremum and an infimum in E. The following example will clarify the issue and will illustrate again the fact that a lattice need not be a sublattice of a larger lattice: Let S be a finite lattice in R^2 consisting of the nine points (i, j) where i and j belong to $\{0, 1, 2\}$. Let $f : S \to S$ be such that all points are fixed points except $(1, 1)$, $(1, 2)$, and $(2, 1)$ which are mapped into $(2, 2)$. S is a complete lattice and f is increasing. Consider $H = \{(0, 1), (1, 0)\}$, $H \subset E$; $\sup_S H = (1, 1)$ is not a fixed point of f. Therefore E is not a sublattice of S, but certainly $\sup_E H = (2, 2)$ does belong to E. (See figure 2.4.)

Remark 3 The conclusion in Tarski's theorem that the set of fixed points E of f is a complete lattice is stronger than the assertion that $\inf_S E$ and $\sup_S E$ belong to E. Suppose that in our previous example all points in S are fixed points with respect to a certain function g except $(1, 1)$ which gets mapped into $(2, 2)$. Then E would *not* be a complete lattice, although $\inf_S E = (0, 0)$ and $\sup_S E = (2, 2)$ belong to E, since $(0, 1)$ and $(1, 0)$ have no supremum in E. Actually $(2, 2)$, $(1, 2)$, and $(2, 1)$ are all upper bounds of $(0, 1)$ and $(1, 0)$, but there is no least upper bound of $(0, 1)$ and $(1, 0)$ in E, since $(1, 1)$ is not a fixed point of g. Clearly g is not increasing since $g((1, 1)) = (2, 2)$ but $g((1, 2)) = (1, 2)$.

2.2.2 Monotonicity of Optimal Solutions, Lattice Programming, and Complementarity

Consider the following family of optimization problems indexed by a parameter t, $t \in T$:

$$\max_{x \in S}\{g(x,t)\},$$

where $g : X \times T \to R$, X is a lattice, T a partially ordered set and $S \subset X$. For simplicity (although it is not necessary) consider all sets to be subsets of Euclidean space endowed with the usual component-wise ordering. Let $\phi(t)$ be the set of optimal solutions to the problem (i.e., $\phi(t) = \arg\max_{x \in S}\{g(x,t)\}$).

We define now an ordering on sets (introduced by Veinott) denoted by $\geq^P$. Consider the lattice $(S, \geq)$ and two subsets of S, B, and C. We say that B "is higher than" C, $B \geq^P C$ if, for each $b \in B$ and $c \in C$, we have that $\sup(b,c) \in B$ and $\inf(b,c) \in C$. The order $\geq^P$ is consistent with the underlying order $\geq$: If $B = \{b\}$ and $C = \{c\}$, then $B \geq^P C$ if and only if $b \geq c$.[11] When $S \subset R$, the definition says that $B \geq^P C$ if whenever $b \in B$, $c \in C$, and $c \geq b$, then b and c belong to $B \cap C$.

We say that the correspondence ϕ from T to S is *increasing* if when $t \geq t'$, $t \neq t'$, then $\phi(t) \geq^P \phi(t')$ (it is decreasing if the conclusion is that $\phi(t) \leq^P \phi(t')$). This definition is consistent with the definition of an increasing function (just think of the case in which ϕ is a function).

The correspondence ϕ from T to S is *strongly increasing* if $t \geq t'$, $t \neq t'$, implies that for each s in $\phi(t)$ and each s' in $\phi(t')$, $s \geq s'$. The correspondence ϕ is strongly increasing if and only if all selections[12] of ϕ are increasing. For example, let $\phi(t)$ be the interval $[\underline{\phi}(t), \bar{\phi}(t)]$ of the reals. If $\bar{\phi}(t)$ and $\underline{\phi}(t)$ are increasing in t, then ϕ is increasing. Figure 2.5 depicts a thick band ϕ from $[0,1]$ to $[0,1]$ with increasing boundaries: ϕ is increasing but not strongly increasing. Topkis (1978) examines the monotonicity properties of ϕ with respect to t. This subsection provides a summary of the results he obtains and some extensions.

A function $g : X \to R$ on the lattice X is *supermodular* if for all x, y in X,

$$g(\inf(x,y)) + g(\sup(x,y)) \geq g(x) + g(y).$$

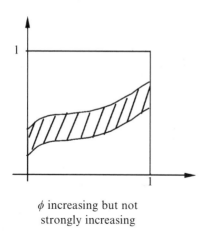

ϕ increasing but not
strongly increasing

Figure 2.5

The function g is *strictly supermodular* if the inequality is strict for all pairs x, y in X which cannot be compared with respect to $\geq$.[13] A function f is (strictly) *submodular* if $-f$ is (strictly) supermodular.

Remark 4   A function of one variable is trivially supermodular.

Let X be a lattice and T a partially ordered set. The function $g : X \times T \to R$ has (strictly) *increasing differences* in its two arguments (x, t) if $g(x, t) - g(x, t')$ is (strictly) increasing in x for all $t \geq t'$ $(t \geq t', t \neq t')$. Decreasing differences are defined replacing "increasing" by "decreasing."

Remark 5   The concepts of supermodularity and increasing differences are closely related. They both formalize the idea of complementarity: In the usual case of X being a product set, increasing one variable raises the return to increase another variable.[14] The complementarity idea can be made more apparent by thinking of the square in R^n with vertices $\{\min(x, y), y, \max(x, y), x\}$ and rewriting the definition of supermodularity as $g(\max(x, y)) - g(x) \geq g(y) - g(\min(x, y))$. Consider, for example, points in R^2, $x = (x_1, x_2)$ and $y = (y_1, y_2)$ with the usual order. Then going from $\min(x, y) = (x_1, y_2)$ to y, for given y_2, increases the payoff less than going from x to $\max(x, y) = (y_1, x_2)$, for given $x_2 \geq y_2$. (See figure 2.6.)

Remark 6   Supermodularity is a stronger property than increasing differences. If g is (strictly) supermodular on $X \times T$, then it has

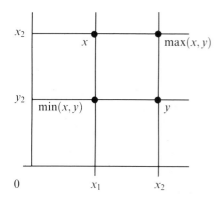

Figure 2.6

(strictly) increasing differences on $X \times T$ and, obviously, g is (strictly) supermodular on X for any t in T.[15] Supermodularity is more convenient to work with mathematically while increasing differences is often more easily recognizable.

Remark 7 For a function defined on a product of ordered sets, the two concepts coincide. For example, if $g : R^n \to R$ is twice-continuously differentiable, then g is supermodular if and only if $\partial^2 g(x)/\partial x_i \partial x_j \geq 0$ for all x and $i \neq j$. This characterization can be directly linked to a standard formulation of cost complementarities in production. Indeed, a submodular cost function in R^n, that is, with $\partial^2 g(x)/\partial x_i \partial x_j \leq 0$, exhibits weak cost complementarities according to Baumol, Panzar, and Willig (1988). If $\partial^2 g(x)/\partial x_i \partial x_j > 0$ for all x and $i \neq j$, then g is strictly supermodular. The equivalence between the condition $\partial^2 g(x)/\partial x_i \partial x_j \geq 0$ and supermodularity for smooth functions can again be motivated by thinking of the square with vertices $\{\min(x, y), y, \max(x, y), x\}$ and rewriting the definition of supermodularity as: $g(\max(x, y)) - g(x) \geq g(y) - g(\min(x, y))$.

Remark 8 Supermodularity is unrelated to convexity, concavity or returns to scale. Indeed, consider the case of a twice-continuously differentiable function g. According to the previous remark supermodularity only puts restrictions on the cross partials of g; the other concepts impose restrictions also on the diagonal of the matrix of second derivatives. (The reader is invited to think about examples of supermodular functions that are convex, concave, with increasing or decreasing returns, or with neither of these properties.)

Remark 9 The complementarity properties of a family of functions $g_n : X \times T \to R$ are preserved under several elementary transformations like positive linear combinations, pointwise limits and maximization. As we will see in section 2.7, an important observation for comparative statics under uncertainty and Bayesian games is that supermodularity is preserved under integration (Vives 1990a).[16]

The complementarity properties of the function $g : X \times T \to R$, supermodular on X and with increasing differences on $X \times T$, yield the monotonicity of the solutions $\phi(t)$ to the optimization problem $\max_{x \in S} g(x, t)$ with respect to the parameter t (the correspondence ϕ is increasing). Furthermore the supermodularity of g on X implies an order property for the set of maximizers $\phi(t)$ (it is a sublattice of X). When the complementarity properties are strict, then ϕ is strongly increasing and $\phi(t)$ ordered. The following theorem states the monotonicity results on optimal solutions. A proof is added for completeness.

THEOREM 2.3   Let $g : X \times T \to R$ be supermodular on the lattice X for each t in the partially ordered set T. Let S be a sublattice of X.

(i) Then $\phi(t)$ is a sublattice of S for all t.

(ii) If g has increasing (decreasing) differences in (x, t), then ϕ is increasing (decreasing).

(iii) If g is strictly supermodular on X for each t in T, then $\phi(t)$ is ordered for all t.

(iv) If g has strictly increasing differences in (x, t), then ϕ is strongly increasing.

Proof   We show first (ii) and then (i), (iii), and (iv).

(ii) Consider the case of increasing differences first. Let $x \in \phi(b)$ and $y \in \phi(t)$, $t \geq b$, we claim that min $(x, y) \in \phi(b)$ and $\sup(x, y) \in \phi(t)$. Consider the following string of inequalities:

$$0 \geq g(\sup(x, y), t) - g(y, t) \geq g(\sup(x, y), b) - g(y, b)$$

$$\geq g(x, b) - g(\inf(x, y), b) \geq 0.$$

The first and the last inequalities hold, respectively, since $y \in \phi(t)$ and $x \in \phi(b)$ and S is a sublattice (and therefore $\sup(x, y)$ and $\inf(x, y)$ belong to S); the second, since g has increasing differences on $S \times T$; the third, since g is supermodular on S. The claim follows.

With decreasing differences the proof is analogous. Notice that the claim above follows if $b \geq t$.

(i) Let now $b = t$. It follows then from supermodularity of g that $\inf(x, y)$ and $\sup(x, y)$ belong to $\phi(t)$. Thus $\phi(t)$ is a sublattice of S.

(iii) Suppose now that g is strictly supermodular on S. Let x and y belong to $\phi(t)$, and suppose that they are not comparable with respect to $\geq$. Since g is strictly supermodular on S, we have

$$0 \geq g(\sup(x, y), t) - g(x, t) > g(y, t) - g(\inf(x, y), t) \geq 0,$$

which is a contradiction. Therefore $\phi(t)$ is ordered for all t.

(iv) We show that $t \geq b$, $t \neq b$ implies $y \geq x$ for $x \in \phi(b)$ and $y \in \phi(t)$. Suppose it is not true that $y \geq x$. Then $\sup(x, y) \geq y$ and $x \neq y$. Therefore the second inequality in the string considered in the proof of the claim in (ii) is strict because of strictly increasing differences, which provides the desired contradiction.   ◆

Some intuition on the result is gained in the case where $g : R^2 \to R$ is twice-continuously differentiable and supermodular on R^2 (note that this implies that g has increasing differences in (x, t)). Suppose first that g is strictly concave (or quasiconcave) in x with $\partial^2 g / (\partial x)^2 < 0$ and that the solution to the maximization problem $\phi(t)$ is interior. Then, using the implicit function theorem on an interior solution, for which $\partial g(\phi(t), t)/\partial x = 0$, ϕ is continuously differentiable and $\phi' = -(\partial^2 g / \partial x \partial t)/(\partial^2 g / (\partial x)^2)$. Obviously the sign of ϕ' is the same as the sign of $\partial^2 g / \partial x \partial t$. The solution is increasing (decreasing) in t if there are increasing (decreasing) differences. That is, depending on whether the marginal return to x increases, $\partial^2 g / \partial x \partial t \geq 0$, or decreases, $\partial^2 g / \partial x \partial t \leq 0$, with increases in t. When g is not strictly concave (quasiconcave) in x, then $\phi(t)$ need not be a singleton or convex-valued. But, provided that $\partial^2 g / \partial x \partial t$ does not change sign, theorem 2.3 asserts that the solution $\phi(t)$ will be monotone increasing in t.

When X is multidimensional, then the restriction that g be super-modular on X has bite. It ensures that for any components i and j, changes in the variable x_j raise the marginal return of variable x_i. This in turn, coupled with increasing differences on $X \times T$, guarantee the monotonicity of the solution. Consider $g : R^{k+1} \to R$ twice-continuously differentiable and supermodular on R^{k+1}. That is, $\partial^2 g(x, t)/ \partial x_i \partial x_j \geq 0$ for all (x, t) and $i \neq j$, and $\partial^2 g(x, t)/\partial x_i \partial t \geq 0$ for all (x, t) and all i. If g is strictly concave in x (with the Jacobian of $\nabla_x g = (\partial g / \partial x_1, \ldots, \partial g / \partial x_k)$ with respect to x, H_x, negative definite) and the solution to the optimization problem $\phi(t) = (\phi_1(t), \dots, \phi_k(t))$ is interior, then $\phi(t)$ is continuously differentiable and $\phi'(t) = -H_x^{-1} \nabla_{xt} g$, where $\phi'(t) = (\partial \phi_1 / \partial t, \dots, \partial \phi_k / \partial t)$, and $\nabla_{xt} g = (\partial^2 g / \partial x_1 \partial t, \dots, \partial^2 g / \partial x_k \partial t)$. If the off-diagonal elements of H_x are nonnegative, then all the elements of $-H_x^{-1}$ are nonnegative and the diagonal elements are positive (McKenzie 1959). A sufficient condition for $\partial \phi_i / \partial t \geq 0$, for all i, is that all the elements of $\nabla_{xt} g$ be nonnegative. If $\partial^2 g / \partial x_i \partial t > 0$ for all i, then $\partial \phi_i / \partial t > 0$ for all i. Again, even if H_x is not negative definite, the assumptions that its off-diagonal elements and that all elements of $\nabla_{xt} g$ are nonnegative ensure that $g(x, t)$ is supermodular, theorem 2.3 applies, and the solution set $\phi(t)$ has the monotonicity properties stated in the theorem. (See below for an application to a classical monopoly problem and to the best-response correspondence of players in games with one-dimensional and multidimensional strategy spaces.)

Remark 10 Sometimes in applications we are also interested in comparative statics with respect to the constraint set S. One example is where S is parametrized also by $t : S(t)$. Theorem 2.3 is easily extended to encompass this situation. We make explicit the dependence of the set of maximizers on $S : \phi(t, S)$. For example, theorem 2.3 (ii), under the same maintained assumptions, would read now: If g has increasing differences in (x, t), then ϕ is increasing in (t, S) where S is given the set ordering $\geq^p$ introduced before. If S is parametrized by t and $S(t)$ is increasing in t (according to the set ordering $\geq^p$), then ϕ is increasing in t.

Remark 11 The basic insight of this theorem is that to obtain monotone comparative static results on the solutions to an optimization problem, the complementarity conditions (supermodularity and increasing differences) are the key ingredient. In particular, no convexity or concavity conditions on the optimized function g are needed. The complementarity conditions are not preserved by arbitrary increasing transformations (i.e., they are cardinal properties), but the solutions to our family of optimization problems are indeed invariant to strictly increasing transformations of the objective function. A particularly useful transformation is the logarithmic one. The (nonnegative) function $g : X \to R_+$ is *log-supermodular* if for all x, y in X, $g(\inf(x, y)) \, g(\sup(x, y)) \geq g(x) g(y)$. If $g(\cdot)$ is positive, then it is log-supermodular if and only if $\log(g(\cdot))$ is supermodular. The interpretation is again straightforward. Think of the square in R^n with vertices $\{\min(x, y), y, \max(x, y), x\}$ (figure 2.6), and rewrite the definition of log-supermodularity, for positive $g(y)$ and $g(\min(x, y))$, as $(g(\max(x, y))/g(x)) \geq (g(y)/g(\min(x, y)))$. Then going from $\min(x, y)$ to y increases relatively the payoff less than going from x to $\max(x, y)$. Log-supermodularity requires thus, with X a product set, that an increase in one variable raises the relative returns to other variables.

A relaxation of the complementarity conditions provides necessary and sufficient conditions for monotone comparative statics. Theorem 2.3 can be extended to purely ordinal complementarity conditions ("quasisupermodularity" and "single crossing property") providing then necessary and sufficient conditions for the monotonicity result (Milgrom and Shanon 1994).

Let X be a lattice, the function $f : X \to R$ is *quasisupermodular* if for x and y in $Xf(x) \geq f(\inf(x, y))$ implies that $f(\sup(x, y)) \geq f(y)$, and $f(x) > f(\inf(x, y))$ implies that $f(\sup(x, y)) > f(y)$. This property expresses a weak complementarity between the variables. Think again of the square in R^2 with vertices $\{\min(x, y), y, \max(x, y), x\}$ in figure 2.6: If going from $\min(x, y)$ to x increases the value of f, then the same must be true when going from y to $\max(x, y)$. A sufficient condition for a function f to be quasisupermodular is that there is a strictly increasing function h such that $h \circ f$ is supermodular.

Let X be a lattice, T a partially ordered set and $g : X \times T \to R$. Then g satisfies the *single crossing property* in (x, t) if for $x' > x$ and $t' > t$, $g(x', t)) \geq g(x, t)$ implies that $g(x', t')) \geq g(x, t')$, and $g(x', t)) > g(x, t)$ implies that $g(x', t')) > g(x, t')$. The function g satisfies the strict *single crossing property* in (x, t) if for $x' > x$ and $t' > t$, $g(x', t)) \geq g(x, t)$ implies that $g(x', t')) > g(x, t')$.[17]

Let $S \subset X$. The Milgrom-Shanon result states that $\phi(t, S) \equiv \arg\max_{x \in S} g(x, t)$ is increasing in (t, S) if and only if $g : X \times T \to R$ is quasisupermodular in x and satisfies the single crossing property in (x, t). If S is a sublattice of X, then $\phi(t, S)$ is a sublattice of S. If in addition the constraint set $S(t)$ is increasing in t and g satisfies the strict single crossing property in (x, t), then $\phi(t, S(t))$ is strongly increasing in t.

Suppose now that $g : R^2 \to R$ is twice-continuously differentiable and "strongly" quasiconcave in x (i.e., strictly quasiconcave with $\partial g / \partial x = 0$, implying that $\partial^2 g / (\partial x)^2 < 0$) and that the (unique) solution to the maximization problem $\phi(t)$ is interior. Then

$$\phi'(t) = -\frac{\partial^2 g(\phi(t), t)/\partial x \partial t}{\partial^2 g(\phi(t), t)/(\partial x)^2}$$

and $\phi'(t) \geq 0$ if and only if $\partial^2 g(\phi(t), t)/\partial x \partial t \geq 0$. That is, $\phi'(t) \geq 0$ if and only if $\partial^2 g/\partial x \partial t \geq 0$ whenever $\partial g/\partial x = 0$.[18] We obtain therefore an easy way to check the necessary and sullicient condition for monotone comparative statics where g is strongly quasiconcave and solutions are interior.

For the moment we have not considered the issue of the existence of solutions to our maximization problem. Indeed, no topological concepts have been introduced so far. Nevertheless, a complete lattice has a direct (topological) compactness counterpart. Recall first that if $(S, \geq)$ is a lattice, its *interval topology* is defined by taking the sets of the type $\{z \in S : z \leq x\}$ and $\{z \in S : x \leq z\}$ to form a subbasis for closed sets. Now, a lattice is compact in its interval topology if and only if it is complete (a result due to Frink 1942; see also Birkhoff 1967, thm. 20)). In R^n a lattice is compact (in the usual topology) if and only if it is complete. The following theorem ensures the existence of solutions and the compactness of solution sets (recall that for simplicity we work in Euclidean space).

THEOREM 2.4   Let $g : X \times T \to R$ be supermodular on S, a compact sublattice of the lattice X, for each t in T. If g is upper semi-continuous[19] (u.s.c.) on X for any t, then $\phi(t)$ is a nonempty compact sublattice of S for all t.

COROLLARY   The set of solutions $\phi(t)$ has a largest $\bar{\phi}(t)$ and a smallest element $\bar{\phi}((t)$ for any t in T (i.e., $\bar{\phi}(= \sup \phi)$ and $\underline{\phi}(= \inf \phi)$ are selections of ϕ; $\sup \phi(t) \in \phi(t)$ *and* $\inf \phi(t) \in \phi(t)$). If g has increasing differences in (s, t), then $\bar{\phi}$ and $\underline{\phi}$ are increasing.

Proof $\phi(t)$ is nonempty and compact, since g is u.s.c. on S and S is compact. We know $\phi(t)$ is a sublattice from theorem 2.3 (i). Furthermore ϕ is complete, since it is compact; therefore $\phi(t)$ has a largest $\bar{\phi}(t)$ and a smallest element $\underline{\phi}(t)$ for any t in T. From theorem 2.3 (ii) we know that if g has increasing differences in (s, t), then ϕ is increasing. It follows immediately that $\bar{\phi}$ and $\underline{\phi}$ are increasing.   ◆

A familiar monopoly example will illustrate the use of the monotonicity results obtained (theorems 2.3 and 2.4). Consider a single-product monopolist facing a revenue function $R(x)$ and a cost function $C(x, t)$, where x is the output and t a cost reduction parameter. Suppose that the output space is a compact interval of the real line, on which $R(\cdot)$ is upper semicontinuous and $C(\cdot, t)$ lower semicontinuous, and suppose that C displays decreasing differences in

(x, t). If C is smooth, then $\partial^2 C / \partial x \partial t \leq 0$; that is, an increase in t reduces marginal costs. Then the largest $\bar{\phi}(t)$ and the smallest $\underline{\phi}(t)$ monopoly outputs are increasing in t. If C displays strictly decreasing differences in (x, t) ($\partial^2 C / \partial x \partial t < 0$ for C smooth), then the set of monopoly outputs $\phi(t)$ is strongly increasing in t (i.e., if $t > t'$, $\underline{\phi}(t) \geq \bar{\phi}(t')$).

It is worth noting that no concavity assumption is made on the profit of the firm. In fact suppose that the profit of the firm $g(x, t) = R(x) - C(x, t)$ is smooth in (x, t) and strictly concave (or quasi-concave) in x with $\partial^2 g / (\partial x)^2 < 0$. Then there is a unique monopoly output for each parameter t, $\phi(t)$. Suppose that it is interior; then ϕ is continuously differentiable, and the usual comparative static analysis yields

$$\phi'(t) = -\frac{\partial^2 g / \partial x \partial t}{\partial^2 g / (\partial x)^2} = \frac{\partial^2 C / \partial x \partial t}{\partial^2 g / (\partial x)^2}.$$

Therefore the monopoly output will be increasing or decreasing with t according to whether $\partial^2 C / \partial x \partial t \leq 0$ or $\partial^2 C / \partial x \partial t \geq 0$. What we have shown is that the monotonicity result is also true (in the appropriate way when ϕ is a correspondence) when profit is not quasiconcave. The general result can also be obtained directly using a revealed preference argument (see exercise 2.2).

A similar result is obtained for a multiproduct firm (e.g., with outputs in a cube X, the product of k compact intervals) provided that the profit function $g(x, t)$ is supermodular on X (R supermodular and C submodular on X is sufficient) and C displays decreasing differences in (x, t). Then, as before, the largest $\bar{\phi}(t)$ and the smallest $\underline{\phi}(t)$ vectors of monopoly outputs are increasing in t. If C displays strictly decreasing differences in (x, t), then if $t > t'$, $\underline{\phi}(t) \geq \bar{\phi}(t')$. What is needed for the result are revenue and cost complementarities among outputs (in the differentiable case, for all $i \neq j$, $\partial^2 R / \partial x_i \partial x_j \geq 0$ and $\partial^2 C / \partial x_i \partial x_j \leq 0$, respectively), and $\partial^2 C / \partial x_i \partial t \leq 0$ for all i (with strict inequality to obtain strictly decreasing differences in (x, t)).

2.2.3 Supermodular Games

We now introduce the class of supermodular games that exploits the monotonicity results associated to payoffs fulfilling complementarity properties. For convenience in applications, we introduce also the class of smooth supermodular games. In short, a supermodular game is a game with strategic complementarities.

The game $(A_i, \pi_i; i \in N)$ is (strictly) *supermodular* if for each i, A_i is a compact lattice, π_i is upper semicontinuous and supermodular in a_i for fixed a_{-i} and displays (strictly) increasing differences in (a_i, a_{-i}).[20] The game $(A_i, \pi_i; i \in N)$ is *smooth supermodular* if each A_i is a compact cube in Euclidean space, π_i is twice continuously differentiable, and $\partial^2 \pi_i / \partial a_{ih} \partial a_{ik} \geq 0$ for all $k \neq h$ and $\partial^2 \pi_i / \partial a_{ih} \partial a_{jk} \geq 0$ for all $j \neq i$ and for all h and k.[21] Strict inequalities for the second set of derivatives will yield strictly increasing differences in (a_i, a_{-i}) and a smooth strictly supermodular game.

The reader is invited to keep in mind a Bertrand oligopoly with differentiated substitutable products (studied further in sections 6.1 to 6.3). In this case strategy sets are compact intervals of prices, and the marginal profitability of an increase of a price of a firm is increasing in the prices of rivals (i.e., payoffs display increasing differences), and in the other prices charged by the same firm if its offer is multiproduct (this is the supermodularity restriction on own strategies). Alternatively, one could consider the case of a Cournot oligopoly with complementary products (studied further in the appendix to chapter 6). In this case the strategy sets are compact intervals of quantities.

The strategy of the analysis is very simple. The aim is to apply Tarski's theorem to a selection of the best-reply map Ψ. Consider the supermodular game $(A_i, \pi_i; i \in N)$, and denote by $\bar{\Psi}_i(a_{-i})$ the largest best-response function of player i, $\sup \Psi_i(a_{-i})$, and by $\underline{\Psi}_i(a_{-i})$ the smallest one, $\inf \Psi_i(a_{-i})$. Both exist and are well defined in a supermodular game according to theorems 2.3 and 2.4. Indeed, given the strategies of the rivals a_{-i}, player i has a nonempty set of best responses $\Psi_i(a_{-i})$, a compact sublattice of A_i because A_i is a compact lattice and its payoff π_i upper semicontinuous and supermodular (theorem 2.4). Since $\Psi_i(a_{-i})$ is a sublattice of A_i, it follows that both $\bar{\Psi}_i(a_{-i}) = \sup \Psi_i(a_{-i})$, and $\underline{\Psi}_i(a_{-i}) = \inf \Psi_i(a_{-i})$ are themselves best responses. Furthermore, since π_i has increasing differences in (a_i, a_{-i}), from theorem 2.3 (ii) we know that $\Psi_i(a_{-i})$ is increasing. It is immediate then (corollary to theorem 2.4) that both $\bar{\Psi}_i(a_{-i})$ and $\underline{\Psi}_i(a_{-i})$ are increasing. Let $\bar{\Psi} = (\bar{\Psi}_1, \ldots, \bar{\Psi}_n)(\underline{\Psi} = (\underline{\Psi}_1, \ldots, \underline{\Psi}_n))$ be the largest (smallest) best-reply map. We have seen that $\bar{\Psi}$ is an increasing function (from the product of the strategy spaces A into itself, which is a compact lattice and therefore complete), so we can apply Tarski's theorem to conclude that $\bar{a} = \sup\{a \in A : \bar{\Psi}(a) \geq a\}$ is a fixed point of $\bar{\Psi}$. For any Nash equilibrium a, $\bar{\Psi}(a) \geq a$, and consequently $\bar{a}$ is the largest equilibrium. A similar argument can be made that $\underline{a} = \inf\{a \in A : \underline{\Psi}(a) \leq a\}$ is the smallest equilibrium. We have therefore shown the following theorem about equilibria in supermodular games:

THEOREM 2.5 (Topkis)   In a supermodular game the equilibrium set E is nonempty and has a largest, $\bar{a} = \sup\{a \in A : \bar{\Psi}(a) \geq a\}$, and a smallest, $\underline{a} = \inf\{a \in A : \underline{\Psi}(a) \leq a\}$, element.

In summary, compactness of strategy sets and upper semicontinuity of payoffs yield well-defined best responses; payoffs with the complementarity conditions (supermodular and with increasing differences) and lattice strategy spaces yield monotone increasing best responses. Tarski's theorem can be applied then to the best-reply map.

Remark 12   Zhou (1994), extending a result of Vives (1990a), shows that the set of Nash equilibria of a supermodular game is a complete lattice. This follows, since the conclusion of Tarski's theorem can be extended to increasing complete sublattice-valued correspondences and the best-reply correspondence Ψ of a supermodular game has these properties according to theorems 2.3 and 2.4. In case the game is strictly supermodular and payoffs are strictly supermodular in a_i for fixed a_{-i}, then, according to theorem 2.3, Ψ_i is strongly increasing, $\Psi_i(a_{-i})$ is ordered for all $a_{-i} \in X_{j \neq i}A_j$, and an increasing selection g of Ψ can be constructed such that $E = \{a \in A : a = g(a)\}$. The result follows directly then from Tarski's theorem (Vives 1990a, thms. 4.1(ii), 4.2(ii) and ex. 2.4).[22]

Remark 13   If $n = 2$ and π_i is supermodular on A_i and has decreasing differences in (a_i, a_j), $j \neq i$, $i = 1, 2$ (with the maintained assumptions: A_i a compact lattice, and π_i upper semicontinuous in a_i for fixed a_{-i}), then an equilibrium exists. From theorems 2.3, 2.4, and its corollary, we know that $\bar{\Psi}_i$ will be a decreasing selection of Ψ_i. Tarski's theorem can be used on the composite best-reply map $f : A_2 \to A_2$, $f = \bar{\Psi}_2 \circ \bar{\Psi}_1$. The function f will be increasing, since it is the composition of two decreasing functions. Therefore the function f will have a fixed point, say $\bar{a}_2$, and $(\bar{\Psi}_1(\bar{a}_2), \bar{a}_2)$ will be the desired fixed point of

$\bar{\Psi}$ (Vives 1990a; thm. 4.2 (iii)). (An alternative derivation in Euclidean space defines a new equivalent game which is supermodular. Just define new strategies $s_1 = a_1$ and $s_2 = -a_2$, reversing the natural order in firm's 2 strategy set; then the transformed payoffs display increasing differences.) In consequence duopoly games with decreasing best responses (and lattice strategy spaces) can be guaranteed to have equilibria. The typical application of this result is to a Cournot duopoly, since in many instances then the marginal revenue of a firm is decreasing in the quantity produced by the rival (yielding payoffs with decreasing differences; see section 4.1). The result does not extend to the general oligopoly case.

Remark 14 (Welfare) In a supermodular game if the payoff to a player is increasing in the strategies of the other players then the payoffs associated to the largest, $\bar{a}$, and smallest, $\underline{a}$, equilibrium points provide bounds for equilibrium payoffs for each player. Indeed, $\bar{a}$ is the Pareto best and $\underline{a}$ the Pareto worst equilibrium. Tighter bounds on payoffs associated to any subset of equilibria, $T \subset E$, may be provided by $\sup_E T$ and $\inf_E T$, which are themselves equilibria since E is a complete lattice. For example, in the Bertrand oligopoly case the profits associated with the largest price equilibrium are also the highest for every firm. This will be the equilibrium preferred by the firms. Similarly, if for some players payoffs are increasing in the strategies of rivals, and for some others they are decreasing, then the largest equilibrium is best for the former and worst for the latter. This is the case, for example, in the Cournot duopoly of remark 13 (with the strategy transformation yielding a supermodular game). The preferred equilibrium for a firm (highest profits) is the one in which its output is largest and the output of the rival (as well as its profits) lowest.

Remark 15 In a symmetric supermodular game (exchangeable against permutations of the players) symmetric equilibria exist. Indeed, $\bar{a}$ and $\underline{a}$ are symmetric. A corollary is that if the game has a unique symmetric equilibrium then the equilibrium is unique, since $\bar{a} = \underline{a}$.

Comparative Statics
Supermodular games provide a natural frame to derive monotone comparative static properties (Lippman et al. 1987; Sobel 1988;

Milgrom and Roberts 1990; and Topkis 1995). Consider a supermodular game with parametrized payoffs: $\pi_i(a_i, a_{-i}; t)$ with t in a partially ordered set T. If $\pi_i(a_i, a_{-i}; t)$ has increasing differences in (a_i, t) (or in the smooth version $\partial^2 \pi_i / \partial a_{ih} \partial t \geq 0$ for all h and i), then the largest and smallest equilibrium points are increasing in t. The proof of the fact is straightforward. According to theorems 2.3, 2.4, and its corollary, the largest best reply of agent i, $\bar{\Psi}_i(a_{-i}; t)$, is increasing in t. This means that $\bar{\Psi}(a; t)$ is also increasing in t. Now $\bar{a}(t) =$ $\sup\{a \in A : \bar{\Psi}(a; t) \geq a\}$ is the largest equilibrium, and it is increasing in t, since $\bar{\Psi}(a; \cdot)$ is increasing. The proof for the smallest equilibrium point is analogous. The analysis can be used, for example, to check the effect on equilibrium prices of the imposition of an excise tax in a Bertrand supermodular oligopoly (see section 6.2).

As an example consider an application to a duopoly game where each player has a compact interval as strategy space. The payoff to player 1 is $\pi_1(a_1, a_2; t)$ and to player 2, $\pi_2(a_1, a_2)$. If the game is supermodular and $\pi_1(a_1, a_2; t)$ has increasing differences in (a_1, t), then it is immediate again that extremal equilibria are increasing in t. If the game is submodular (with π_i with decreasing differences in (a_i, a_j)), then extremal equilibrium strategies for firm 1 (2) are increasing (decreasing) in t. For example, $\bar{a}_1$ is increasing and $\underline{a}_2$ decreasing in t. If $\pi_1(a_1, a_2; t)$ has decreasing differences in (a_1, t), then the results are reversed. When the game is supermodular, extremal equilibria are decreasing in t. When the game is submodular, then extremal equilibrium strategies for firm 1 (2) are decreasing (increasing) in t. This application generalizes the Fudenberg and Tirole (1984) taxonomy of strategic behavior, taking t to be the premarket investment of incumbent firm 1, without imposing unnecessary regularity assumptions (see section 7.4.3 and exercise 2.13, where the reader is asked to derive a formal proof of the results).

The results can be extended to the class of ordinal supermodular games replacing the (cardinal) assumptions that π_i is supermodular in a_i and displays increasing differences in (a_i, a_{-i}) by the (ordinal) assumptions that π_i is quasisupermodular in a_i and satisfies the single crossing property in (a_i, a_{-i}). The basic idea is that what drives the results in supermodular games is the monotonicity of best responses to the strategies of the rivals or to exogenous parameters and the ordinal conditions are sufficient for the monotonicity results. This extension allows further applications to oligopoly as we will see in the Cournot homogeneous product case (section 4.1) and in differentiated oligopolies (section 6.2). Further results on supermodular games can be found in section 2.6 on stability of equilibria. The comparative static results can be similarly generalized replacing the "increasing differences" assumption by the appropriate single crossing property.

In order to gain some further intuition on supermodular games, let us consider in turn examples with one-dimensional and multidimensional strategy spaces.

Example (One-dimensional Strategy Sets)

Consider a smooth game with strategy sets being compact intervals. Suppose, for the moment, that the ith player best reply to a_{-i} is unique, interior, and equal to $r_i(a_{-i})$. We know then that the first-order condition for profit maximization will be satisfied:

$$\frac{\partial \pi_i}{\partial a_i}(r_i(a_{-i}), a_{-i}) = 0.$$

Furthermore, if $\partial^2 \pi_i / (\partial a_i)^2 < 0$ then r_i is continuously differentiable and

$$\frac{\partial r_i}{\partial a_j} = -\frac{\partial^2 \pi_i / \partial a_i \partial a_j}{\partial^2 \pi_i / (\partial a_i)^2}, \qquad j \neq i.$$

Therefore the best reply of player i will be increasing or decreasing according to the sign of $\partial^2 \pi_i / \partial a_i \partial a_j$. It turns out that this result also holds when π_i is *not* quasiconcave. Indeed, we have seen that if $\partial^2 \pi_i / \partial a_i \partial a_j \geq (>)0$, $j \neq i$, that is, when the payoff has (strictly) increasing differences in (a_i, a_{-i}), then the best-reply correspondence of player i is (strongly) increasing in the actions of the rivals.

This implies that the maximum and minimum selections (all the selections in the strict case) of the best replies are increasing. It is instructive to prove directly these results in a typical oligopoly situation. Suppose that the payoff function of agent i, π_i, can be expressed as the sum of a twice-continuously differentiable revenue function R_i and a lower semicontinuous cost function $C_i : \pi_i(a) = R_i(a) - C_i(a_i)$. We claim that if $\partial^2 R_i / \partial a_i \partial a_j \geq (>)0$ for all a, and $i \neq j$, then $\max \Psi_i$ and $\min \Psi_i$ are decreasing (increasing) selections of Ψ_i (Ψ_i is strongly increasing). We show that $x_{-i} \geq y_{-i}$ implies that $\max \Psi_i(x_{-i}) \geq \max \Psi_i(y_{-i})$. Let $\bar{y}_i = \max \Psi_i(y_{-i})$. We check that

$\pi_i(\bar{y}_i, x_{-i}) \geq \pi_i(y_i, x_{-i})$ if $y_i \leq \bar{y}_i$, which implies that $\max \Psi_i(x_{-i}) \geq \bar{y}_i$. Indeed,

$$R_i(\bar{y}_i, x_{-i}) - R_i(y_i, x_{-i}) = \int_{y_i}^{\bar{y}_i} \frac{\partial R_i(z_i, x_{-i})}{\partial a_i} dz_i,$$

$$R_i(\bar{y}_i, y_{-i}) - R_i(y_i, y_{-i}) = \int_{y_i}^{\bar{y}_i} \frac{\partial R_i(z_i, y_{-i})}{\partial a_i} dz_i.$$

The first expression is larger or equal than the second, since $\partial^2 R_i / \partial a_i \partial a_j \geq 0$ and $x_{-i} \geq y_{-i}$. Furthermore $R_i(\bar{y}_i, y_{-i}) - R_i(y_i, y_{-i}) \geq C_i(\bar{y}_i) - C_i(y_i)$, since $\bar{y}_i \in \Psi_i(y_{-i})$ (revealed preference). We conclude that $R_i(\bar{y}_i, x_{-i}) - R_i(y_i, x_{-i}) \geq C_i(\bar{y}_i) - C_i(y_i)$ or $\pi_i(\bar{y}_i, x_{-i}) \geq \pi_i(y_i, x_{-i})$. If $\partial^2 R_i / \partial a_i \partial a_j > 0$, one shows similarly that $\pi_i(\bar{y}_i, x_{-i}) > \pi_i(y_i, x_{-i})$ if $y_i < \bar{y}_i$; this means that if $x_i \in \Psi_i(x_{-i})$, then $x_i \geq \bar{y}_i$. Therefore $x_i \geq y_{-i}$ and $x_{-i} \neq y_{-i}$ imply that $\min \Psi_i(x_{-i}) \geq \max \Psi_i(y_{-i})$ and Ψ_i is increasing.

In a strictly supermodular game with compact intervals as strategy spaces some further properties of the equilibrium set can be derived. First of all, if the game is symmetric, then only symmetric equilibria can exist.[23] Second, with two or three players ($n = 2$ or 3), it is easily seen that the equilibrium set is in fact ordered (Vives 1985b; see exercise 2.5). For $n = 2$ just think that the intersections of two increasing best-reply maps in R^2 are necessarily "nested" according to the usual order. Starting from any equilibrium to find another, we have to move to the northeast. (See figure 2.7.)

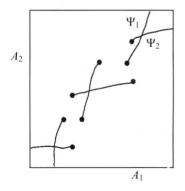

E is ordered for $n = 2$

Figure 2.7

Example (Multidimensional Strategy Sets)
Let the strategy space of player i, A_i, be a product of k_i compact intervals, $A_i \subset R^{k_i}$, and suppose, for the moment, that π_i is twice-continuously differentiable and that the Jacobian of $\nabla_i \pi_i$ with respect to a_i, D_{i1}, is negative definite ($\nabla_i \pi_i$ is the gradient of marginal profitability of player i, $\partial \pi_i / \partial a_{ih}$, $h = 1, \ldots, k_i$). In this case the ith player best reply to a_{-i} is unique. Denote it by $r_i(a_{-i})$, and suppose that it is interior. It will satisfy then the first-order condition

$$\nabla_i \pi_i(r_i(a_{-i}), a_{-i}) = 0,$$

and according to the implicit function theorem, r_i is continuously differentiable and its Jacobian equals

$$Dr_i = -D_{i1}^{-1} D_{i2},$$

where D_{i2} is the Jacobian of $\nabla_i \pi_i$ with respect to a_{-i}. If the off-diagonal elements of D_{i1} are nonnegative, it follows that all the elements of $-D_{i1}^{-1}$ are nonnegative and the diagonal elements positive (See McKenzie 1959). A sufficient condition for the elements of Dr_i to be nonnegative (nonpositive) is that all the elements of D_{i2} be nonnegative (nonpositive). Note that if the elements of D_{i2} are (strictly) positive, then the elements of Dr_i will be also (strictly) positive. Now, even if D_{i1} is not negative definite, the assumptions that off-diagonal elements of D_{i1} and all elements of D_{i2} be nonnegative are exactly the characterization in the smooth context of supermodularity and therefore the best-reply correspondence of any player is increasing. If the elements of D_{i2} are (strictly) positive, then payoffs exhibit strictly increasing differences and therefore the best-reply correspondence of any player is strongly increasing. If profits are given, as it is usual in oligopoly games, by revenue minus cost, $\pi_i(a) = R_i(a) - C_i(a_i)$, the assumptions on D_{i2} involve only the revenue function, and this applies to D_{i1} also if costs are separable (of the form $C_i(a_i) = \sum_{h=1}^{k_i} C_{ih}(a_{ih})$, with $C_{ih} = A_{ih} \to R_+$, $h = 1, \ldots, k_i$, and where a_{ih} is the hth component of firm i's strategy; Vives 1985b).

In summary, the new box of tools to analyze Nash equilibria provided by lattice theory and supermodularity proves to be powerful and simple, having strong implications in terms of the characterization of equilibria. The applications to oligopoly theory are immediate, and some will be developed in subsequent chapters. The examples with one-dimensional and multidimensional strategy spaces above provide indications on how to apply the results. The essential requirement is the strategic complementarity of strategies. As stated, a leading example is a Bertrand oligopoly with differentiated products (section 6.2); another example is a Cournot duopoly with substitute products (section 4.1) or a Cournot oligopoly with complementary products (appendix to chapter 6). However, the reader is warned that important oligopoly pricing games are not supermodular (e.g., the Bertrand-Edgeworth game and the Hotelling game when firms are located close together; see section 6.2). Games with strategic complementarities arise naturally in macroeconomics under imperfect competition (Cooper and John 1988), search (Diamond 1982), bank runs (Diamond and Dybvig 1983; Postlewaite and Vives 1987), banking competition (Matutes and Vives 1998), network and adoption externalities (Dybvig and Spatt 1983; Farrell and Saloner 1986; and Katz and Shapiro 1986).[24]

2.3 Existence Results for Quasi-increasing and Decreasing Best Replies

2.3.1 Quasi-increasing Best Replies in Symmetric Games

For one-dimensional strategy spaces existence of symmetric equilibria can be obtained relaxing the monotonicity requirement of best responses (which characterizes supermodular games). It is enough that all the jumps in the best reply of a player be up.

The result follows from an *intersection point theorem* of Tarski where $(S, \geq)$ is a completely and densely ordered lattice. That is, we have a completely ordered lattice for which for all x, y in S with $x < y$, there is a z in S such that $x < z < y$.[25] A function f from S to S is *quasi-increasing* if for every nonempty subset X of S, $f(\sup X) \geq \inf f(X)$ and $f(\inf X) \leq \sup f(X)$, where $f(X) = \{y \in S : y = f(x), x \in X\}$. If a function is quasi-increasing, it cannot jump down; all the jumps must be up. A somewhat simplified version of theorem 3 in Tarski (1955, p. 250; see Vives 1990a) follows. As usual denote the set of fixed points of f by E.

THEOREM 2.6 (Tarski) Let $(S, \geq)$ be completely and densely ordered lattice and f a quasi-increasing function from S to S. Then E is nonempty and $(E, \geq)$ is a completely ordered lattice. In particular, $\bar{x} = \sup\{x \in S : f(x) \geq x\}$ and $\underline{x} = \inf\{x \in S : f(x) \leq x\})$ are, respectively, the largest and the smallest fixed points of f.

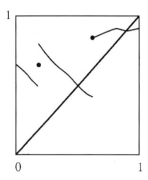

Figure 2.8a

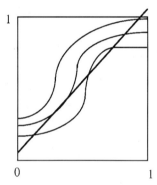

Figure 2.8b

In applications S is typically a compact interval of the real line with the usual order. In order to gain some intuition, let $S = [0,1]$, and consider a function which when discontinuous only jumps up. The function must cross then the 45° line at some point. Indeed, suppose that it starts above the 45° line (otherwise, 0 is a fixed point), then it either stays above it (and then 1 is a fixed point) or it crosses the 45° line. (See figure 2.8a.)

A version of theorem 2.6 for S a compact interval is the following (Amir 1996): Let S be a compact interval and φ a correspondence of S into itself such that its slope is bounded below (i.e., if $x_1 \neq x_2$, $y_1 \in \varphi(x_1)$, and $y_2 \in \varphi(x_2)$, then $(y_1 - y_2)/(x_1 - x_2) \geq -k$ for some $k > 0$). Then φ has a fixed point. Indeed, a correspondence with slope bounded below has no jumps down (and it will have a quasi-increasing selection).

Remark 16 Comparative statics analysis is trivial when the function f is (strictly) increasing in a parameter t (for t in a partially ordered set T). Then $\bar{x}(t)$ and $\underline{x}(t)$ are (strictly) increasing in t. This follows since $\bar{x}(t) = \sup\{x \in S : f(x; t) \geq x\}$, $\underline{x}(t) = \inf\{x \in S : f(x; t) \leq x\}$), and f is (strictly) increasing in t. It is worth to remark that as t varies, the number of equilibria may change, but still the largest and the smallest equilibrium will be increasing in t. (See figure 2.8b, where it is shown that as t increases, the number of equilibria goes from three to two to one.)

Analogous theorems to theorem 2.6 have been used to show existence of equilibria in a certain class of symmetric Cournot games by McManus (1962, 1964) and Roberts and Sonnenschein (1976) (although these authors were not aware of the theorem by Tarski and proved versions of the existence result directly).[26] The comparative static result can be used to determine how Cournot quantities move with changes in market parameters. (See sections 4.1 and 4.3; see also exercise 2.20 for an application to R&D competition which generalizes results for the standard memoryless patent race model; Reinganum 1989.)

Consider a symmetric game with compact intervals as strategy spaces and the payoff to player i depending on a_i and the aggregate strategy of the rivals $\sum_{j \neq i} a_j$ (as in a Cournot game with homogeneous product). Existence of symmetric equilibria follows then from theorem 2.6 if the best-reply Ψ_i of a player (identical for all i due to symmetry) has no jumps down. We will provide in section 4.1 conditions on demand and costs for this property to hold in a Cournot game. The existence of symmetric equilibria follows easily. Indeed, symmetric equilibria are given by the fixed point of the correspondence φ which assigns to $\sum_{j \neq i} a_j$, $(a_i + \sum_{j \neq i} a_j)(n - 1)/n$, where $a_i \in \Psi_i(\sum_{j \neq i} a_j)$, and φ never jumps down because Ψ_i does not either.[27] The fact that φ has no jumps down ensures that it has a quasi-increasing selection. The following corollary to theorem 2.6 states the result:

COROLLARY Consider a symmetric game where the strategy space of each player is a compact interval of R and the payoff to a player depends only on its own strategy and the aggregate strategy of the rivals. If the best reply of a player has no jumps down, then symmetric equilibria exist.

2.3.2   Decreasing Best Replies in n-Player Games

Despite the fact that no *general* n-dimensional fixed point theorem is known for the case of decreasing best replies Bamon and Frayssé (1985) and Novshek (1985a) are able to provide a fixed point argument when the best replies of any player depend only on the aggregate action of the rivals. The proof originates in a observation by Selten (1970) and has as its main application the Cournot model (see section 4.1).

THEOREM 2.7   Let A_i be a compact interval of the reals, and suppose that best replies are upper hemicontinuous strongly decreasing correspondences of the type $\Psi_i(\sum_{j \neq i} a_j)$ for all i. A fixed point of the best reply map exists then.

Selten's idea consists of reducing the problem of finding an equilibrium to finding the fixed point of a certain real-valued function. This is accomplished considering the *cumulative* best reply of player i, Φ_i, which gives the optimal action of player i which is consistent with a given level of *aggregate* action $\hat{a} = \sum_{i=1}^{n} a_i$. That is,

$$\Phi_i(\hat{a}) = \{ a_i \in A_i : a_i \in \Psi_i(\hat{a} - a_i) \}.$$

(Φ_i could be empty, and the appropriate domain has to be specified.) It follows immediately that there is an equilibrium if and only if the correspondence $\sum_{i=1}^{n} \Phi_i$. has a fixed point. Bamon and Frayssé (1985) consider the case where Ψ_i is (strongly) decreasing and has at most one jump down. In this case (noting that a vertical jump in Ψ_i corresponds to a "45° jump" in Φ_i) they show by induction the existence of a fixed point of $\sum_{i=1}^{n} \Phi_i$. The general result (Novshek 1985a; Frayssé 1986, 58–63) can be shown approximating uniformly the strongly decreasing correspondence Ψ_i by decreasing step-correspondences once the existence result has been checked valid for the latter.

Uniqueness of equilibrium will be treated in section 2.5 in the context of smooth games. We note here that by adding a requirement to Ψ_i in theorem 2.7, we obtain a uniqueness result. Denote $\sum_{j \neq i} a_j$ by $\hat{a}_{-i}$. The requirement is that for all i, Ψ_i must have slopes strictly above -1 or, in other words, all selections of $\Psi_i(\hat{a}_{-i}) + \hat{a}_{-i}$ must be strictly increasing in $\hat{a}_{-i}$.[28] Note that under this assumption $\Psi_i(\hat{a}_{-i})$ cannot jump down. Together with the requirement in theorem 2.7 that Ψ_i be strongly decreasing, it implies that Ψ_i cannot jump at all.

A proof of the uniqueness result is offered (an alternative proof considering the cumulative best reply of player i, Φ_i is proposed in exercise 2.8).

THEOREM 2.8 Consider a game as in theorem 2.7 with the added requirement that for all i Ψ_i has slopes strictly above -1. Then the equilibrium is unique.

Proof Suppose that there are two fixed points of the best-reply map (at least there is one according to theorem 2.7) a and a', and without loss of generality, suppose that $\sum_i a_i' \geq \sum_i a_i$. I claim that $\hat{a}'_{-i} \geq \hat{a}_{-i}$ for all i. Indeed, if for some i $\hat{a}'_{-i} < \hat{a}_{-i}$, then $\hat{a}'_{-i} + a_i' < \hat{a}_{-i} + a_i$, for $a_i' \in \Psi_i(\hat{a}'_{-i})$ and $a_i \in \Psi_i(\hat{a}_{-i})$ because all selections of $\Psi_i(\hat{a}_{-i}) + \hat{a}_{-i}$ are strictly increasing in $\hat{a}_{-i}$. This contradicts the fact that $\sum_i a_i' \geq \sum_i a_i$. I claim also that for all $a_i' \leq a_i$ for all i. This follows, since $\hat{a}'_{-i} \geq \hat{a}_{-i}$ and Ψ_i is strongly decreasing. We have then that $\sum_i a_i' \leq \sum_i a_i$ and $\hat{a}'_{-i} \leq \hat{a}_{-i}$. In consequence $a_i' = a_i$ for all i.   ◆

Remark 17 In a symmetric game of the class we are considering (with one-dimensional strategy spaces and with best replies of the type $\Psi_i(\sum_{j \neq i} a_j)$, identical for all i) only symmetric equilibria can exist if Ψ_i has slopes strictly above -1. This follows immediately, since the condition implies that for any aggregate action $\hat{a} = \sum_{i=1}^{n} a_i$, there is a unique cumulative best-reply $\Phi_i(\hat{a})$ identical for any player by symmetry.

Summarizing the existence arguments (in pure strategies and without requiring quasiconcavity) and under mild conditions on strategy spaces we have the following:

1. In supermodular games (for which best replies are increasing) existence is guaranteed and the equilibrium set has certain order properties. For example, there is a largest and a smallest equilibrium point. The basic tool is Tarski's fixed point theorem (theorem 2.2).

2. When best replies are decreasing, existence is guaranteed for two-player games (using the same tools as in 1) but not in general. In the particular case of one-dimensional strategy sets where the best reply of a player depends only on the aggregate actions of others existence can be shown for any number of players.

3. In symmetric games with one-dimensional strategy sets and with the best reply of a player depending only on the aggregate actions of others existence of symmetric equilibria can be shown provided best

replies never jump down. The basic tool is Tarski's intersection point theorem (theorem 2.6).

In the first two instances the existence results are based on monotonicity properties of the best replies that follow in turn from the supermodularity or submodularity properties of the payoffs.

2.4 Mixed Strategies

We have seen in chapter 1 that in the Edgeworth model, where firms use price strategies and face capacity limits, there may be no Nash equilibrium (in pure strategies). Nevertheless, an equilibrium can be found if firms choose price *distributions*. Existence can be restored this way in many situations where no pure-strategy equilibrium exists. Nash (1951) showed existence of mixed-strategy equilibria for games with finite pure-strategy spaces. In fact the proof of this result is analogous to the proof of the standard existence result.

The formalization of mixed-strategy equilibria is similar to the pure strategy case. Consider a game $(A_i, \pi_i, i \in N)$ where A_i is a compact subset of Euclidean space and π_i is a bounded and (Borel) measurable function. The *mixed extension* of the game is defined by the strategy space $D(A_i)$, the set of all (Borel) probability measures on A_i, and the payoff $V_i(\mu) = \int \pi_i(a) d\mu(a)$ where $d\mu(a) = (d\mu_1(a_1) \times \cdots \times d\mu_n(a_n))$ and $\mu = (\mu_1, \ldots, \mu_n)$, $\mu_i \in D(A_i)$ for all i. Player i chooses now a probability measure on his (pure-) strategy space A_i. Players randomize independently, and this is the reason why expected payoffs are computed using the product measure $\mu_1 \times \cdots \times \mu_n$. A mixed-strategy equilibrium of the game $(A_i, \pi_i; i \in N)$ is then a Nash equilibrium of its mixed extension $(D(A_i), V_i; i \in N)$.

The basic existence theorem with mixed strategies is due to Gliksberg (1952).

THEOREM 2.9   Consider the game $(A_i, \pi_i; i \in N)$. If the (pure-) strategy sets are nonempty compact subsets of Euclidean space and payoffs are continuous there is a mixed-strategy Nash equilibrium.

Remark 18   It is worth noticing that no quasiconcavity requirement on payoffs and no convexity requirement on strategy spaces are necessary due to the convexifying effect of mixed strategies on best responses. The payoffs and strategy spaces of the mixed extension have the appropriate convexity properties. The proof of the theorem proceeds by showing that the strategy sets of the mixed extension, $D(A_i)$, are convex and (sequentially) compact (endowing the set with the topology of weak convergence). Furthermore the expected payoff of player i, V_i, is linear (and therefore quasiconcave) in μ_i, and continuous in μ. Existence follows then from standard fixed point theorems as in theorem 2.1.

A potential problem with the application of Gliksberg theorem to economic games is that sometimes, as in Edgeworth's model, payoffs are not continuous. When a firm undercuts the price of a rival in a homogeneous product market, it increases discontinuously its profits. Dasgupta and Maskin (1986) have shown nevertheless that for the types of discontinuities usually encountered in economic games mixed-strategy equilibria can be shown to exist. More precisely, consider a game $(A_i, \pi_i; i \in N)$ where A_i is a closed interval and π_i is bounded and continuous, except maybe on a subset of a continuous manifold of dimension less than n, and satisfies a weak lower-semicontinuity condition in a_i. Then if $\sum_{i=1}^{n} \pi_i(a)$ is upper semicontinuous the game has a mixed-strategy equilibrium. The upper semicontinuity requirement on $\sum_i \pi_i$ can be substituted by the condition that at any point where one player's payoff falls, another's rises. The result by Dasgupta an Maskin can be used to show existence of mixed-strategy equilibria in Edgeworth-type models and also in Cournot-type models even when no pure-strategy equilibrium is known to exist. Indeed, in the Edgeworth duopoly game profits are discontinuous only when the two firms charge the same price, that is, along the "diagonal" in price space. The basic idea of the Dasgupta-Maskin result is to provide sufficient conditions to ensure that the limit of equilibria of any sequence of finite games that approximates the original game is an equilibrium. Simon (1987) relaxes these conditions by requiring that at least one limit be an equilibrium.

The use of mixed strategies for economic modeling is somewhat controverted. Indeed, decision makers do not seem to flip coins usually to choose optimal actions.[29] Further in a mixed-strategy equilibrium all actions in the support of the equilibrium distribution of a player are best responses to the distributions used by the rivals. Therefore in equilibrium players have no strict incentive to use the prescribed mixed strategy. A potential answer to this criticism is that players in fact do not randomize but use pure strategies in a larger (unmodeled) game with private information. More specifically, players choices may depend on random factors that are not payoff-relevant as, for example, on what side of the bed they woke up in the morning. However, the following question can still be raised: Why is it that the type of incomplete information introduced in the model is such that it supports *precisely* the original mixed-strategy equilibria? One step further is provided by Harsanyi (1973) who argues that at a mixed-strategy equilibrium each player uses a pure strategy that is contingent on a small random disturbance to the payoff known only to him. For example, in the model of Edgeworth, a firm could know its own cost but have slight uncertainty about the costs of the rivals. According to Harsanyi as the amount of uncertainty vanishes, the pure-strategy equilibria of the incomplete information game converge to the mixed-strategy equilibria of the original formulation. (See section 2.7.3 for a description of games of incomplete information and Bayesian Nash equilibrium.)

Furthermore mixed-strategy equilibria have a *regret property* which is absent in pure-strategy equilibria. Suppose that we have two firms in the Edgeworth market and that they play a mixed-strategy price equilibrium. Any firm would like to wait and see what price the rival firm has charged and respond in an optimal way. In general, this optimal response will not correspond to the price charged by the firm according to its mixed strategy. In other words, once a firm has set its price, it regrets it. In a pure-strategy equilibrium this does not happen since the price chosen by the firm is a best response to the rival's price. In a mixed-strategy equilibrium the price *distribution* of the firm, and therefore any price in its support is a best response to the price distribution of the rival firm.

There is still another justification for mixed-strategy equilibria based on Nash's "mass-action" interpretation of equilibrium points (Nash 1950b). As stated in section 2.1, in this interpretation players need not be rational or know the structure of the game, which is played repeatedly by participants. Then a mixed-strategy over the pure-strategy set A_i can be interpreted as a population distribution over A_i. An n-tuple of players is drawn randomly, one for each player population, to play the game. The suggestion then is that (mixed-strategy) equilibrium points could be seen as the outcome of dynamic interaction among boundedly rational players in large populations. This theme has been developed in the evolutionary approach to Nash equilibrium.[30]

2.5 Uniqueness

Nash equilibria are not unique in general, although uniqueness is certainly a desirable property from an applied point of view (e.g., to perform comparative static analysis). Three basic approaches have been used in the literature. We will term them "contraction," "univalence," and "index theory" approach, respectively. They are ordered from more to less used in practice and from more to less restrictive in their assumptions when cast in a differentiable framework. The first is based on the contraction principle, the second, on the Gale-Nikaido univalence theorems, and the third on the Poincaré-Hopf index theorem.

Consider a game $(A_i, \pi_i; i \in N)$ where for all i, A_i is a product of k_i compact intervals and π_i is smooth on A and strictly quasiconcave in a_i. Under these conditions the best reply of player i to actions a_{-i} of rivals is unique and given by a function. Denote this function by $r_i(\cdot)$.

The *contraction* approach is based on showing that the best-reply map $r(\cdot) \equiv (r_1(\cdot), \ldots, r_n(\cdot))$ is a contraction. Then there is a unique fixed point of $r(\cdot)$, that is, a unique equilibrium, according to the contraction principle.[31] When A_i is one-dimensional, a sufficient condition for $r(\cdot)$ to be a contraction is

$$\frac{\partial^2 \pi_i}{(\partial a_i)^2} + \sum_{j \neq i} \left| \frac{\partial^2 \pi_i}{\partial a_i \partial a_j} \right| < 0 \qquad \text{for all } a \in A. \tag{$*$}$$

Similar dominant diagonal conditions on the second derivatives of π_i yield the result in the multidimensional case.

The contraction condition is the easiest to check, but it is also the strongest. It is quite restrictive for Cournot games (see section 4.2) but less so for Bertrand games with differentiated products (see section 6.2).

Suppose now that all candidate equilibria are interior, and therefore they are determined by the solution to the set of first-order conditions:

$$g_i(a) \equiv \nabla_i \pi_i(a) = 0, \qquad i \in N,$$

where $\nabla_i \pi_i$ is the gradient of marginal profitability of player i, $\partial \pi_i / \partial a_{ih}$, $h = 1, \ldots, k_i$. The *univalence* approach finds conditions under which the map $g : A \to R^k$ is one-to-one (where $k = \sum_{i=1}^{n} k_i$). The Gale-Nikaido theorem asserts that this is the case provided that A is convex and that the Jacobian of g, Dg, is negative (or positive) semi-definite (Gale-Nikaido 1965). Consequently, if $Dg(a)$ is negative quasi-definite for all a in A, the equilibrium will be unique. Rosen (1965) also takes a similar approach to uniqueness. The contraction condition $(*)$ is a sufficient condition for Dg to be negative definite in the one-dimensional strategy space case, since it means that Dg has a negative dominant diagonal.

The univalence approach proves useful in ensuring the global invertibility of inverse demand systems (see sections 3.1 and 6.1).

The *index theory* approach is based on the Poincaré-Hopf index theorem[32] which implies that if $g : A \to R^k$, where A is a compact cube in R^k, satisfies a boundary condition and the determinant of $D(-g(a))$ is positive whenever $g(a) = 0$, then there is a unique solution to $g(a) = 0$. Notice that if $Dg(a)$ is negative definite for all a in A (the Gale-Nikaido condition), then the determinant of $D(-g(a))$ is positive. The index approach only requires information about $Dg(a)$ at the candidate equilibria that satisfies $g(a) = 0$, and therefore it is very general. In fact the condition of the theorem is "almost" necessary for uniqueness in general, and necessary for models with non-vanishing $D(-g(a))$ at equilibrium points. When $k = 1$, the intuition of the result is easily seen. Let $A = [0, 1]$, then if $g(0) > 0$, $g(1) < 0$ (boundary conditions) and $g(a) = 0$ implies that $g'(a) < 0$, there is a unique fixed point of g. (See figure 2.9; section 4.2 provides a characterization of uniqueness of the Cournot equilibrium using the index theory approach.)

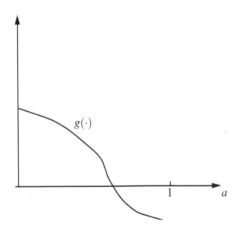

Figure 2.9

2.6 Stability

Cournot proposed an adjustment or tatônnement process to reach equilibrium. In this process firms in a duopoly take turns in adjusting their outputs, each firm reacting optimally to the rival's last period output. According to this dynamic process players respond myopically to the choices of other firms, that is, without trying to anticipate their behavior. Although this adjustment process can (and has) been criticized for being ad hoc, it can also be interpreted as a crude way of expressing the *bounded rationality* of agents. Indeed, several learning mechanisms for agents to play a Nash equilibrium can be understood as refinements of the basic tatônnement. The Cournot tatônnement has a close connection with equilibria of some dynamic games when agents are very impatient.[33] Furthermore, as we will see, best-reply dynamics and Cournot stability have important connections with solution concepts for games as dominance solvability and rationalizability, as well as implications for comparative statics.

2.6.1 Dominance Solvability and Rationalizability

As hinted by Edgeworth, even in a situation where there is common knowledge of payoffs and rationality, Nash behavior is not compelling. A much weaker requirement is for agents not to play strictly dominated strategies. A (pure) strategy a_i is strictly dominated by another (pure) strategy b_i if for all a_{-i}, $\pi_i(a_i, a_{-i}) < \pi_i(b_i, a_{-i})$. It is weakly dominated if the inequality is weak (with strict inequality for some a_{-i}). Similarly we could consider domination by a mixed strategy. A rational player will not play a strictly dominated strategy. *Serially undominated strategies* are those that survive after iterated elimination of strictly dominated strategies. A game is *dominance solvable* if the set remaining after iterated elimination of strictly dominated strategies is a singleton (Moulin 1984). In this case the surviving strategy profile is a Nash equilibrium.

The related *rationalizability* literature (Bernheim 1984; Pearce 1984) has pointed out that Nash equilibrium is not the only outcome of common knowledge of payoffs and rationality. Under the assumptions, in general, it is possible to rule out more strategies than by iterated elimination of strictly dominated strategies. Rationalizable strategies are those that rational players could play. A strategy is rationalizable if it is a best response to some beliefs about the play of opponents. Since the opponents are also rational, and payoffs are common knowledge, the beliefs cannot be arbitrary. More formally, the sets of strategies $B_1, B_2, \ldots, B_n$ (with B_i a subset of the strategy set A_i of player i) are *rationalizable* if any strategy of player i in B_i is optimal for some beliefs about the strategies played by opponents with support on the rationalizable set B_{-i} (B_{-i} denotes $(B_1, B_2, \ldots, B_n)$ except the ith component). In other words, rationalizable strategies are those that survive iterated elimination of strategies that are never a best response. A (mixed) strategy for a player is never a best response if there does not exist a (mixed-) strategy profile for the rivals such that the strategy is a best response. Rationalizable strategies are necessarily serially undominated, but the converse is not true in general. The reason is that a strictly dominated strategy is never a best response, but the converse is not true in general.[34] Nash equilibrium strategies are rationalizable, but in general, the rationalizable set is much larger. For example, in a Cournot linear demand oligopoly with more than two firms and constant marginal costs, any price between the competitive and the monopoly levels is rationalizable.

It is worth noting that in supermodular games (adding the requirement that the payoff of a player be continuous in the strategies of the rivals) strategic, including nonequilibrium, behavior can be bounded between the largest and the smallest equilibrium points. Indeed, in a supermodular game the largest and the smallest equilibrium points constitute also (respectively) the largest and smallest profiles of serially undominated strategies (see the remarks after theorem 2.10). As it is well-known, the set of serially undominated strategies contains the sets of Nash equilibria (pure or mixed), correlated equilibria (e.g., see Aumann 1987), and rationalizable strategies.[35] Two interesting consequences are derived from this. First, all *rationalizable* strategies lie between the smallest and largest equilibrium points. Second, if the game has a unique equilibrium, it is *dominance solvable*. In this case there are no other equilibria in mixed or correlated strategies (Milgrom and Roberts 1990).

2.6.2 Tatônnement Stability

Consider the smooth game $(A_i, \pi_i; i \in N)$ (with A_i a compact cube for all i) where the best reply of player i is given by the continuous function $r_i(\cdot)$. A Nash equilibrium a^* will be (*globally*) *stable* if for any initial position the system converges to it. It will be *locally stable* if there exists a neighbourhood of a^* such that stability holds.

A simultaneous *discrete* tatônnement with a^0 as initial point, $a^0 \in A$, is a sequence $\{a^t\}$, $t = 0, 1, \ldots$ such that $a^t = r(a^{t-1})$. In a *sequential* discrete process, as the one envisioned by Cournot, the players alternate in taking actions. For example, with two players, player 1 could move in even periods and player 2 in odd periods. Moulin (1984) shows that dominance solvability implies Cournot stability, but the converse need not hold. The converse does hold, however, for two-player games with one-dimensional strategy spaces and strictly quasiconcave payoffs. Furthermore the author shows that if strategy spaces are one-dimensional and the contraction condition $(*)$ holds, then the game is dominance solvable and therefore Cournot (globally) stable. In fact Gabay and Moulin (1980) show that if strategy spaces are one-dimensional (and not necessarily compact) and the contraction condition $(*)$ holds, then both the simultaneous and the sequential discrete adjustment processes converge to the (unique) Nash equilibrium for any initial position. This can be generalized in the natural way to multidimensional strategy spaces.

Gabay and Moulin (1980) and Moulin (1982, p. 124) show also that if a^* is a locally stable regular Nash equilibrium, then the spectral radius of the Jacobian of the best-reply map, $Dr(a^*)$, is no more than one.[36] And conversely, if this spectral radius is less than one, then a^* is locally stable.

A corollary of this result is the following: Consider a two-player game with one-dimensional strategy spaces. If a^* is a regular Nash equilibrium, then it is locally stable if at a^*:

$$\left| \frac{\partial^2 \pi_1}{(\partial a_1)^2} \frac{\partial^2 \pi_2}{(\partial a_2)^2} \right| > \left| \frac{\partial^2 \pi_1}{\partial a_1 \partial a_2} \frac{\partial^2 \pi_2}{\partial a_1 \partial a_2} \right|,$$

or, equivalently, $|r_1'| \, |r_2'| < 1$.

The equilibrium will not be locally stable if the inequalities are reversed. (See figure 2.10.) The intuition for the result can be gained considering that an equilibrium is also a fixed point of the composite map $r_2 \circ r_1$ from A_2 into itself. The condition for stability then is transparent (exercise 2.9). Note that the contraction condition implies that $|r_i'| < 1$ for $i = 1, 2$ (because $|r_i'| = |\partial^2 \pi_i / \partial a_i \partial a_j| / (\partial^2 \pi_i / (\partial a_i)^2)$, $j \neq i$).

Continuous adjustment processes have also been treated in the literature. The conditions for stability being in general less restrictive

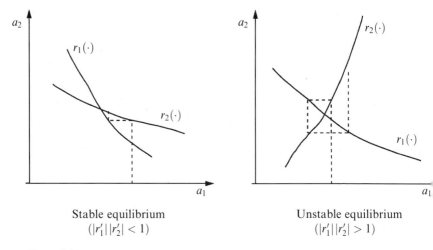

Figure 2.10

than for the discrete processes. One version of the continuous adjustment has an evolutionary (replicator dynamics) flavor,[37] players changing strategies at a rate proportional to the gradient of marginal profitability:

$$\frac{da_i(t)}{dt} = \alpha_i \nabla_i \pi_i(a(t)),$$

with adjustment speeds $\alpha_i > 0$, $i \in N$.

Rosen (1965) shows that such a process is (globally) stable if the Jacobian of g (where $g_i(a) \equiv \nabla_i \pi_i(a)$), $Dg(a)$, is negative definite for all a in A. That is, starting from any initial position, the system converges to the unique equilibrium of the game.

In summary, restrictive assumptions are needed to insure the stability of the adjustment processes considered (see sections 4.2, 4.3, and the proposed exercises of chapter 4 for applications to the Cournot case and relations of stability with comparative statics).[38] Further, as shown by Rand (1978) (see also Dana and Montrucchio 1986), simple duopoly games with nonmonotone best responses generate easily "chaotic" dynamics in discrete time. In contrast, we will see now that supermodular games have nice stability properties. Indeed, the outcomes of the Cournot tatônnement will be bounded by the largest and smallest equilibrium points of the game. If the equilibrium is unique, then it will be globally stable. Similarly learning processes need not settle in Nash equilibria (Fudenberg and Levine 1998); meanwhile in supermodular games a broad class of adaptive learning processes will converge to a subset of the serially undominated strategies, which are bounded above and below by the extreme Nash equilibrium points (Milgrom and Roberts 1990).[39]

We will say that the (continuous or discrete) dynamic system with initial condition $a^0\{a(t;a^0)\}$ *approaches* the set S if its omega limit set $\omega(\{a(t;a^0)\})$ is contained in S. Let us recall that $\omega(\{a(t;a^0)\}) = \{a \in A : a(t_k;a^0) \to a$ for some (sub)sequence $t_k \to \infty\}$.

Consider first the discrete (simultaneous) *Cournot tatônnement* in a supermodular game G. Recall that it is defined by the process $a^0 \in A$, $a^t \in \Psi(a^{t-1})$, $t = 1, 2, \ldots$, where, as before, Ψ is the product of the best-reply correspondences of the players.

Let

$$A_i^+ = \{a \in A : a_i \geq \bar{\Psi}_i(a_{-i})\}, \quad A_i^- = \{a \in A : a_i \leq \underline{\Psi}_i(a_{-i})\}, \quad \text{and}$$

$$A^+ = \bigcap_{i=1}^{n} A_i^+ \quad \text{and} \quad A^- = \bigcap_{i=1}^{n} A_i^-,$$

where, $\underline{\Psi}_i$ and $\bar{\Psi}_i$ are, respectively, the smallest and largest best response function of player i. Let $[\underline{a}, \bar{a}] = \{a \in A : \underline{a} \leq a \leq \bar{a}\}$.

The following theorem, which is a variation of theorem 5.1 in Vives (1990a), establishes that any Cournot tatônnement in a supermodular game approaches the cube $[\underline{a}, \bar{a}]$ defined by the largest and smallest equilibrium points. Furthermore, if the tatônnement starts "below" or "above," all the best-reply correspondences of the players, that is, whenever $a^0 \in A^-$ or $a^0 \in A^+$, convergence to an equilibrium point that is monotone under mild assumptions. (See figure 2.11. What are the implied dynamics when $a^0 = (\underline{a}_1, \bar{a}_2)$?)

THEOREM 2.10   Let G be a supermodular game with continuous payoffs:

(i) Then any Cournot tatônnement $\{a^t\}$ approaches the set $[\underline{a}, \bar{a}]$, where $\underline{a}$ and $\bar{a}$ are, respectively, the smallest and the largest equilibrium points of the game.

(ii) Then, if the players always select the largest (or the smallest) best response (or, alternatively, if G is strictly supermodular—and we make the convention that if the rivals of player i choose the same strategies in t and $t + 1$, then player i also chooses the same strategy in $t + 2$ as in $t + 1$),[40] then a Cournot tatônnement starting at any

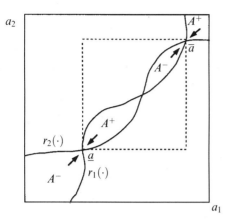

Cournot tatônnement in a supermodular game,
with best reply functions $r_1(\cdot)$, $r_2(\cdot)$

Figure 2.11

a^0 in $A^+(A^-)$ converges monotonically downward (upward) to an equilibrium point of the game.

COROLLARY If the equilibrium of a supermodular game with continuous payoffs is unique, it is globally stable.

Proof We show first (ii). Let $a^0 \in A^+$, then for any i, $a_i^0 \geq \bar{\Psi}_i(a_{-i}^0)$, and the Cournot tatônnement defines a monotone decreasing sequence. Because the game is supermodular $\underline{\Psi}$ and $\bar{\Psi}$ are increasing. If players always select the largest best response, then it is immediate, reasoning by induction, that the sequence $\{a^t\}$ with $a^t = \bar{\Psi}(a^{t-1})$ is decreasing, since $a^0 \geq a^1 = \bar{\Psi}(a^0)$ and $\bar{\Psi}$ is increasing. If they always select the smallest best response, the same is true, since $a^0 \geq \bar{\Psi}(a^0) \geq a^1 = \underline{\Psi}(a^0)$. Now, if G is strictly supermodular, then any best-reply correspondence is strongly increasing, since payoffs show strictly increasing differences. Again we have that $a^0 \geq \bar{\Psi}(a^0) \geq a^1$ since $a_i^1 \in \Psi_i(a_{-i}^0)$ for all i. It follows that $a_i^1 \geq a_i^2$, since $a_i^1 \in \Psi_i(a_{-i}^0)$, $a_i^2 \in \Psi_i(a_{-i}^1)$, and $a_{-i}^0 \geq a_{-i}^1$, where $a_{-i}^0 \neq a_{-i}^1$ or $a_{-i}^0 = a_{-i}^1$ and then $a_i^1 = a_i^2$ according to our convention. We have therefore $a^0 \geq a^1 \geq a^2$. Thus the Cournot tatônnement defines, in any case (reasoning by induction), a monotone decreasing sequence $\{a^t\}$, $a^t \geq a^{t+1}$ for all t. This decreasing sequence defines in turn a nested sequence of (nonempty) closed sets $C^t = \{a \in A : a \leq a^t\}$ in the compact space A which satisfies the finite intersection property. Therefore the intersection of the collection of closed sets C^t is nonempty and equal to the infimum of the sequence. The point $\hat{a} = \inf\{a^t\}$ is a limit point of the sequence $\{a^t\}$. This point must also be an equilibrium point, $\hat{a} \in \Psi(\hat{a})$, by continuity of the payoffs. For any t, $\pi_i(a_i^t, a_{-i}^{t-1}) \geq \pi_i(a_i, a_{-i}^{t-1})$ for all a_i in A_i, since $a_i^t \in \Psi_i(a_{-i}^{t-1})$. Since π_i is continuous on A and $a^t \to \hat{a}$, we have that $\pi_i(\hat{a}_i, \hat{a}_{-i}) \geq \pi_i(a_i, \hat{a}_{-i})$ for all a_i in A_i, and therefore $\hat{a}_i \in \Psi_i(\hat{a}_{-i})$. If $a^0 \in A^-$, the proof follows along the same lines.

We now show (i). Let $\{\bar{a}^t\}$ and $\{\underline{a}^t\}$ be, respectively, the tatônnement starting at $\bar{a}^0 = \sup A$ and $\underline{a}^0 = \inf A$, with $\bar{\Psi}$ and $\underline{\Psi}$. Obviously $\bar{a}^0 \in A^+$ and $\underline{a}^0 \in A^-$. According to the reasoning in the proof of (ii), $\{\bar{a}^t\}$ and $\{\underline{a}^t\}$ converge to an equilibrium point of the game. It is immediate that $\bar{a}^t$ converges to $\bar{a}$ and $\underline{a}^t$ to $\underline{a}$. Indeed, consider any equilibrium a. Suppose that $\bar{a}^t \geq a$ for some t (recall that $\bar{a}^0 = \sup A$). Then $\bar{a}^{t+1} = \bar{\Psi}(\bar{a}^t) \geq \bar{\Psi}(a) \geq a$. This implies that the limit of $\bar{a}^t$ is no smaller than a. Result (i) says that the omega limit set of any Cournot tatônnement $\{a^t\}$ is contained in the set $[\underline{a}, \bar{a}]$. This follows from the observation that $\underline{a}^t \leq a^t \leq \bar{a}^t$ for any t. To see that the inequalities hold, consider the tatônnement starting at a^0. Obviously $\bar{a}^0 = \sup A \geq a^0 \geq \inf A = \underline{a}^0$. Since $a^1 \in \Psi(a^1)$, we have that $\underline{a}^1 = \underline{\Psi}(\inf A) \leq \underline{\Psi}(a^0) \leq a^1 \leq \bar{\Psi}(a^0) \leq \bar{\Psi}(\sup A) = \bar{a}^1$ and, by induction, $\underline{a}^t \leq a^t \leq \bar{a}^t$ for any t.   ◆

Remark 19   A similar argument was used in Vives (1985a).[41] Topkis (1979) obtains related results. Global (i.e., starting from an arbitrary initial point) convergence can be established for the sequential two-player tatônnement in supermodular games with one-dimensional strategy spaces (see Krisnha 1992 and exercise 2.11).

Remark 20   For the case of two players, if best replies are decreasing, then the theorem applies just by reversing the order of the strategy set of one player. The extremal equilibria are now the ones involving the largest (smallest) equilibrium strategy for player i ($j, j \neq i$), $i = 1, 2$. (See figure 2.12.)

Furthermore a similar argument to the proof of the theorem shows that the largest and smallest equilibrium points are the largest and smallest serially undominated strategies (Milgrom and Roberts 1990). Indeed, consider the set of strategy profiles $[{}_*a, a^*]$, and let $U([{}_*a, a^*])$ denote the set of undominated responses by the players given $[{}_*a, a^*]$. Then it should be clear that $\sup U([{}_*a, a^*]) = \bar{\Psi}(a^*)$ and $\inf U([{}_*a, a^*]) = \underline{\Psi}({}_*a)$. As in the proof of theorem 2.10, letting

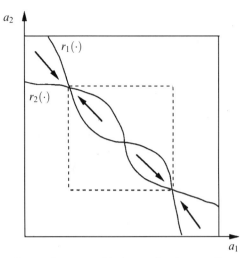

Duopoly game with decreasing best replies

Figure 2.12

$\bar{a}^0 = \sup A$ and $\underline{a}^0 = \inf A$, the tatônnement with $\overline{\Psi}$ and $\underline{\Psi}$, respectively, defines two monotone decreasing sequences $\{\bar{a}^t\}$ and $\{\underline{a}^t\}$ which bound the sets $U([\underline{a}^{t-1}, \bar{a}^{t-1}])$. We know also that $\{\bar{a}^t\}$ and $\{\underline{a}^t\}$ converge, respectively, to the largest $\bar{a}$ and smallest $\underline{a}$ equilibrium points of the game and that therefore they are serially undominated profiles. This means, in particular, that if the equilibrium is unique, then the supermodular game is dominance solvable.

Results developed by Hirsch for (continuous) monotone dynamic systems apply readily to supermodular games (Vives 1990a, sec. 5). Consider a continuous dynamic system with state space X, an open convex subset of Euclidean space, and initial condition x^0, $x(t; x^0)$ such that

$$\frac{dx(t)}{dt} = g(x(t)).$$

The system is *monotone* if $x^0 \geq y^0$ implies that $x(t; x^0) \geq x(t; y^0)$ for all t. It is *strongly monotone* if $x(t; x^0) \gg x(t; y^0)$ for all $t > 0$ when $x^0 \geq y^0$ and $x^0 \neq y^0$.[42] Let E be the set of rest points or equilibria of the system: $E = \{x \in X : g(x) = 0\}$. Hirsch (1985; see also 1988) shows that the set of initial conditions for which bounded forward trajectories[43] of a strongly monotone system does not approach the equilibrium set E is of (Lebesgue) measure zero (Hirsch 1985, thm. 4.1,

1988, thm. 0.1(b)). If furthermore E is countable (Hirsch 1985, thm. 4.4), or totally ordered (Hirsch 1985, thm. 4.1 and cor. to thm. 2.3), then convergence to an equilibrium point for almost all initial conditions obtains. If there is a unique equilibrium then a global convergence result obtains: All trajectories converge to it (Hirsch 1988, thms. 0.5 and 10.3).

A sufficient condition for the system to be monotone when g is differentiable is $\partial g_i/\partial x_j \geq 0$, $j \neq i$ (i.e., the system should be "cooperative" in the words of Hirsch). If the Jacobian of g, Dg, is also irreducible,[44] then the system is strongly monotone (Hirsh 1985, thm. 1.7).

It follows then that in smooth strict supermodular games gradient dynamics converge to an equilibrium point from almost all initial conditions a^0 in A provided that E is countable or (totally) ordered.[45] The same result holds for best-reply dynamics

$$\frac{da_i(t)}{dt} = r_i(a_{-i}(t)) - a_i(t), \qquad i = 1, \ldots, n$$

(or in a more compact form: $da(t)/dt = r(a(t)) - a(t)$) provided that the Jacobian of marginal profitability $\nabla_i \pi_i$ with respect to a_i, D_{i1}, is negative definite.

In both cases the system is cooperative and irreducible. For gradient dynamics the result follows because in a smooth strict supermodular game $\partial^2 \pi_i/\partial a_{ih}\partial a_{jk} > 0$ for all $j \neq i$, and for all h and k and $\partial^2 \pi_i/\partial a_{ih}\partial a_{ik} \geq 0$ for all i and $h \neq k$. When D_{i1} is negative definite, best replies are continuously differentiable and strictly increasing, $\partial r_{ih}/\partial a_{jk} > 0$, for all $j \neq i$, all h and k (see the example on multidimensional strategy sets at the end of section 2.2). When there is a unique equilibrium then it is globally stable (note that this result for the continuous dynamic system is consistent with the one obtained for the discrete Cournot tatônnement). The following theorem summarizes the results obtained:

THEOREM 2.11   In a smooth strict supermodular game the gradient dynamics converge to an equilibrium point for almost all initial conditions provided that E is countable or (totally) ordered. The same result holds for best-reply dynamics provided that the best replies are smooth and strictly increasing (as is the case in a smooth strictly concave strict supermodular game). In both cases if the equilibrium is unique, then it is globally stable.

Remark 21 With one-dimensional strategy spaces and two players, convergence everywhere, as opposed to almost everywhere, obtains (Hirsch 1985, cor. 2.8) for both gradient and best-reply dynamics, with payoffs either with increasing or decreasing differences and, correspondingly, with increasing or decreasing best replies. This result can be generalized to arbitrary slopes of best replies provided that the Jacobian of g, Dg, is nonsingular at any equilibrium. With three players, and no restriction on the slopes of best replies, chaotic behavior is easily generated (see Corchón and Mas-Colell 1996).

A natural application of the stability analysis of supermodular games is the Bertrand oligopoly with differentiated products (see section 6.2) and Cournot markets with complementary products (see the appendix to chapter 6).

2.7 Incomplete Information and Bayesian Nash Equilibrium

In many situations of strategic interaction the presence of uncertainty and private information are crucial in the analysis. In this section I indicate briefly the main ingredients of the extension of the lattice programming methods to uncertainty and private information and then introduce Bayesian games.

2.7.1 Lattice Programming under Uncertainty

As we have seen in section 2.2.2, lattice programming delivers monotone comparative static results without making unnecessary assumptions. Under uncertainty we are typically concerned about the monotonicity properties of optimal solutions with respect to a parameter or vector of parameters. We know that this mononote comparative statics result will depend on the properties of the expected payoff in relation to the actions and parameters. We present here three types of results.

Consider an optimization problem indexed by a parameter y in the partially ordered set Y of the form: $\max_{x \in X} \int g(x, y, \theta) \, d\mu(\theta)$, where X is a lattice and μ is a measure on (the Borel subsets of) the set Θ. The sets X, Y, and Θ are subsets of Euclidean space. The set of optimal solutions $\phi(y)$ will be monotone increasing in y if $G(x, y) = \int g(x, y, \theta) \, d\mu(\theta)$ is supermodular in x for each y and if it displays increasing differences in (x, y) (theorem 2.3). A fortiori, the result is true if $G(x, y)$ is supermodular in (x, y), and we also know that it will hold if log $G(x, y)$ is supermodular in (x, y) (or G log-supermodular in (x, y)).

It is worth noting that supermodularity of the objective function will yield monotone comparative static results robust to additively separable terms like $G(x, y) + \sum_i h_i(x_i)$. Log-supermodularity of the objective function will yield monotone comparative static results robust to multiplicative terms like $G(x, y)(\prod_i h_i(x_i))$ for nonnegative functions h_i.

The first result is that $G(x, y)$ fulfills the complementarity conditions (G supermodular in x for each y and with increasing differences in (x, y) or G supermodular in (x, y)) whenever $g(x, y, \theta)$ does for any θ. This a consequence of the linearity property of the integral and the fact that the properties of supermodularity and increasing differences are preserved by summation.[46] The result holds for any distribution of uncertainty. Furthermore there are no weaker conditions that ensure that G satisfies the complementarity conditions or that ensure supermodularity irrespective of the distribution of θ. Indeed, consider a degenerate distribution concentrating its mass at a point where g does not fulfill the complementarity conditions (is not supermodular) in (x, y). Then obviously G cannot fulfill them either. The result has important applications. For example, it implies that a basic supermodular game to which uncertainty and private information are added is still supermodular (Vives 1990).

Let $z = (x, y)$. The second result states that if g is a nonnegative function log-supermodular in (z, θ) (μ almost everywhere), then $G(z) = \int g(z, \theta) d\mu(\theta)$ is log-supermodular in z. The result is an immediate corollary of the following theorem in statistics (see Karlin and Rinott 1980 for a proof): If we have four nonnegative functions $f_i : R^n \rightarrow R_+$, $i = 1, \ldots, 4$, for which $f_1(\theta)f_2(\theta') \leq f_3(\min\{\theta, \theta'\}) \cdot f_4(\max\{\theta, \theta'\})$ (μ almost everywhere), then $(\int f_1(\theta) d\mu(\theta))(\int f_2(\theta) \cdot d\mu(\theta)) \leq (\int f_3(\theta) d\mu(\theta))(\int f_4(\theta) d\mu(\theta))$.[47] The result is remarkable because the sum of log-supermodular functions (as opposed to the product) does not need to be log-supermodular. The result can be applied to situations where the parameter y affects the distribution of uncertainty (Athey 1997a; Jewitt 1987). Suppose, for example, that the measure μ admits a density $f(\theta, y)$ parametrized by y. Then expected utility $\int u(x, \theta)f(\theta, y) d\mu(\theta)$ will be log-supermodular in (x, y) whenever the (nonnegative) utility function and the density are log-supermodular (μ-a.e.).[48]

The results can be extended to encompass conditional expectations (Athey 1997a). Suppose that $u(x, \theta)$ is supermodular in (x, θ_i) for all i and that the distribution μ admits a parametrized density $f(\theta; y)$ that is log-supermodular in (θ, y). Then the conditional expected utility $E(u(x, \theta)|S; y) = \int_S u(x, \theta) f(\theta; y|S) d\mu(\theta)$ is supermodular in (x, y). (In fact it is supermodular in (x, y, S) when comparing sets according to the set order $\geq^p$.)

For problems involving a single decision and a single random variable, there are available variations of the results presented.[49] For example, if $u(x, \theta)$ satisfies the SCP in (x, θ) and $f(\theta, y)$ is log-supermodular in (θ, y) (with x, θ, and y real numbers), then expected utility satisfies the SCP in (x, y).[50] Log-supermodularity of the density is equivalent to requiring that the probability distribution fulfills the monotone likelihood ratio property (MLRP). This means that for a distribution F with support independent of y, the likelihood ratio $f(\theta, y')/f(\theta, y)$ is increasing in θ on the support of F for all $y' > y$. A larger realization of θ is to be interpreted as news that the underlying distribution is more likely to be $F(\theta; y')$ rather than $F(\theta; y)$.[51] If expected utility satisfies the SCP in (x, y), we know then that optimal solutions to the expected utility maximization problem are monotone increasing in y (see section 2.2.2). Similarly, given that whenever $u(x, \theta)$ satisfies the SCP we know that the optimal solutions to the (certainty) optimization problem, $\arg\max_x u(x, \theta)$, are monotone in θ, we have found that when the distribution of θ changes with y according to the MLRP, the monotone comparative static result is preserved. The MLRP is therefore the right condition to extend monotone comparative static results from the certainty to the uncertainty case (see exercise 2.16 for a simple illustration).

The results can be applied to derive monotone comparative static conclusions in classical problems of investment under uncertainty (like the amount of risky investment or risk choice as a function of a risk aversion parameter (see, respectively, Eeckhoudt and Gollier 1995 and Jewitt 1987). We will see below another application to pricing games with incomplete information.

The third type of result finds conditions for expected utility $\int u(x, \theta) f(\theta; y) d\theta$ to be supermodular in (x, y). This is assured by supermodularity of the payoff in (x, θ) and by the ordering of the distribution $F(\theta; y)$ by y according to first-order stochastic dominance. For a single random variable, this means that $F(\theta; y)$ is decreasing in y. For multivariate uncertainty (assuming that θ is a vector of independent random variables), each marginal $F_i(\theta; y)$ must be decreasing in y. (For a single random variable, the result is shown by Hadar and Russell 1978 and Ormiston and Schlee 1992. See Athey 1995 for the multivariate extension.)

2.7.2 Information Structures and Signals

In this section we review briefly the formalization of the information received by an agent in an uncertain context. We explain why information has value for a Bayesian decision maker (with no interaction with other agents), state informally Blackwell's theorem about the informativeness of signals, and provide examples of noisy information structures used in applications (in particular, the linear information structure model).[52]

Consider a (measurable) space of states of nature (Θ, E), where E is the set of events, endowed with a prior probability measure μ. The information available to an agent can be described by a partition of the state space Θ. Equivalently, by a (measurable) function ϕ from Θ to a space of signals S (indeed, the corresponding partition of Θ is given by the elements $\phi^{-1}(s)$, $s \in S$). When the agent receives a signal he knows in which partition element lies the state of nature. A partition is more informative than another if it is finer (if each element of the latter can be obtained as the union of elements of the former). With a finer partition a decision maker cannot do worse (indeed, with the finer partition available he can always make decisions based only on the coarser one). In fact any decision maker (for any utility function and prior distribution on Θ) will prefer one information structure to another if and only if the former is finer than the latter. As we will see, this need not be the case in a situation of multiagent interaction. Then an improvement in information can make everyone worse off.

Typically the signals received by the agent are noisy. In this case for every state of the world, a distribution is induced on the signal space. Formally the function ϕ assigns to each element of Θ a probability measure on S. A typical case is to have for each θ in Θ a conditional density $h(s|\theta)$ defining the likelihood function of the signals received by the agent. The information structure $(S, h(\cdot|\cdot))$ defines thus a random variable, experiment, or signal s with values on the set S.[53] The precision of a signal s about θ is given by $(E\,\mathrm{var}(s|\theta))^{-1}$. Sometimes the precision of a signal is given in terms of the posterior distribution of θ given s as $(E\,\mathrm{var}(\theta|s))^{-1}$.

We have here also the result that any decision maker (for any utility function and prior distribution on Θ) will prefer information structure $(S, h(\cdot|\cdot))$ to $(S', h'(\cdot|\cdot))$ if and only if the former is "finer" than the latter. "Finer" has to be taken in the sense of Blackwell "more informative" (Blackwell 1951; see also Kihlstrom 1984).[54] Signal s is more informative than signal s' if s is sufficient for signal s'. Intuitively a signal s is sufficient for s' if, independent of the value of θ, s' can be obtained from s by adding noise. More formally, for continuously distributed signals, we say that signal s is sufficient for signal s' if there exists a stochastic transformation from s to s' (i.e., a function $g : S' \times S \to R_+$ such that $\int_{S'} g(s', s)\, ds' = 1$ for any s in S) such that $h'(s'|\theta) = \int_S g(s', s) h(s|\theta)\, ds$ for any θ in Θ and s' in S' (for technical convenience it is also assumed that g is integrable, with positive value, with respect to s for any s').[55] Note that a realization s' can be generated by a randomization using $g(\cdot, s)$ given that $\int_{S'} g(s', s)\, ds' = 1$ for any s in S, and therefore $g(\cdot, s)$ is a probability density function for any s in S. A similar definition can be given for the case of discrete signals. If the number of possible states and signals in any information structure is finite, then an information structure is characterized by (S, L), where S has a finite number of elements and L is a likelihood matrix (with entries of the type $Pr\{s_k|\theta_j\}$). The information structure (S, L) is more informative than (S', L') if and only if there is a (conformable) Markov matrix M (i.e., a matrix with nonnegative elements with columns adding up to 1) such that $L' = ML$. A simple example of the discrete information structure is a two-state space, with $\Theta = \{\underline{\theta}, \bar{\theta}\}$, and two-point support signals. The agent may receive a low $(\underline{s})$ or a high $(\bar{s})$ signal about θ with likelihood $\Pr(\bar{s}|\bar{\theta}) = \Pr(\underline{s}|\underline{\theta}) = q$, where $\frac{1}{2} \leq q \leq 1$. If $q = \frac{1}{2}$, the signal is uninformative; if $q = 1$, it is perfectly informative. It is easily checked that s is more informative than s' if and only if $q > q'$.

The likelihood matrix associated to s', $L' = \begin{bmatrix} q' & 1 - q' \\ 1 - q' & q' \end{bmatrix}$, can be obtained with a stochastic transformation of the likelihood matrix associated to s, $L = \begin{bmatrix} q & 1 - q \\ 1 - q & q \end{bmatrix}$. Indeed, $L' = ML$ where

$$M = \frac{1}{q - (1 - q)} \begin{bmatrix} q' - (1 - q) & q - q' \\ q - q' & q' - (1 - q) \end{bmatrix}$$

is a Markov matrix.

An example, with the reals as state space (and the Borel subsets as events) has both prior and likelihood being normally distributed. Let θ be normally distributed with mean $\bar{\theta}$ and variance σ_θ^2 ($\theta \sim N(\bar{\theta}, \sigma_\theta^2)$), and let the likelihood be given by $s|\theta \sim N(\theta, \sigma_\varepsilon^2)$. Provided that the signal is unbiased (i.e., $E(s|\theta) = \theta$) the signal can be interpreted as being the sum of the true θ plus (orthogonal) noise: $s = \theta + \varepsilon$, with $\varepsilon \sim N(0, \sigma_\varepsilon^2)$ and $\text{cov}(\theta, \varepsilon) = 0$.[56] The precision of the signal is thus $(\sigma_\varepsilon^2)^{-1}$ (note that $\text{var}(s|\theta) = \sigma_\varepsilon^2$ is nonrandom because of normality of the distributions). The signal can be thought of coming from a sample of (conditionally) independent observations from $N(\theta, \sigma^2)$. A sufficient statistic for θ is the sample mean. Therefore for a n-sample we have that $\sigma_\varepsilon^2 = \sigma^2/n$. The precision of the signal s (the sample mean) is therefore proportional to the size of the sample. We will denote $(\sigma_y^2)^{-1}$ by τ_y. In terms of the posterior distribution, it is immediate then that the precision of the signal is given by $\tau_\theta + \tau_\varepsilon$ (i.e., $\text{var}(\theta|s) = (\tau_\theta + \tau_\varepsilon)^{-1}$). Therefore the (posterior) precision of the signal is given by the sum of the precision of the prior, τ_θ, and the precision of the signal, τ_ε. This information structure is particularly useful in applications because it yields linear conditional expectations.[57] Indeed, it is immediate from normal theory[58] that $E(\theta|s) = ts + (1-t)\bar{\theta}$, where $t = \tau_\varepsilon/(\tau_\theta + \tau_\varepsilon)(= \sigma_\theta^2/\text{var}\,s)$. That is, the conditional expected value of θ is a weighted average of the signal and the prior mean with the weights according to their relative precisions.

The pair of prior and likelihood normal-normal is only one example of the class for which conditional expectations are linear.[59] In fact, with prior and likelihood with finite variances, if the signal is unbiased (i.e., if $E(s|\theta) = \theta$) and $E(\theta|s)$ is linear, say $E(\theta|s) = A + ts$, then $t = \sigma_\theta^2/\text{var}\,s$ (or, equivalently, $t = r/(\tau_\theta + r)$, where $r = (E\,\text{var}(s|\theta))^{-1}$) and $A = (1-t)\bar{\theta}$. Under the assumptions the (posterior) precision of the signal, $(E\,\text{var}(\theta|s))^{-1}$, is given by $\tau_\theta + r$, and therefore the "additive property" of precisions of the normal case is preserved.[60] Letting $\varepsilon = s - \theta$ we have also that $\text{cov}(\varepsilon, \theta) = 0$ and $\text{var}\,\varepsilon = E\,\text{var}(s|\theta)$.[61] Therefore the precision of the signal is given by τ_ε. A more precise signal implies a smaller mean squared prediction error, $E\{\theta - E(\theta|s)\}^2$.

The typical example of a linear information structure is for the prior and the likelihood densities to be normal. As stated before, the signal s may be the (sample) average of a variable number of observations n from a normal distribution with mean θ and fixed variance (or the average of a fixed number of independent observations from a normal distribution with variable variance). The precision of the information is proportional to the number of observations n. Other examples where the sample mean is a sufficient statistic for θ and a linear information structure obtains include cases in which the observations are conditionally independent binomial, negative, binomial, Poisson, gamma, or exponential when assigned natural conjugate priors.[62] The pairs of prior-likelihood beta-binomial and gamma-Poisson have the linear conditional expectation property. If the prior is beta(α, β) on $(0, 1)$ (where $\alpha > 0$ and $\beta > 0$) and the signal the average of n independent Bernoulli trials with parameter θ, then the likelihood of the signal is $1/n$ binomial (n, θ) with $r = \tau_\theta n/(\alpha + \beta)$ and the posterior distribution is beta $(\alpha + ns, \beta + n(1 - s))$.[63] If the prior is gamma $\Gamma(\alpha, \beta)$ and the likelihood Poisson, $P(n\theta)/n$, then $r = \beta n/\alpha$ and the posterior distribution is $\Gamma(\alpha + ns, \beta + n)$. In these examples, as well as in the normal case, s is more precise (weakly) than s' if and only if s is more informative than s' in the Blackwell sense (since a more precise signal means a larger sample). The precision of the signal r is proportional to the size of the sample. The examples provided are important when the unbounded support assumption of the normal distribution is unreasonable. For example, if θ is the demand intercept, then a nonnegativity constraint may want to be imposed and the gamma-Poisson model is appropriate. In other instances, θ a cost parameter for example, the support may need to be bounded and then the beta-binomial model is suitable.

If n unbiased conditionally independent signals $(s_1, \ldots, s_n)$ about θ are received, with signal s_i of precision $r_i = (E \operatorname{var}(s_i|\theta))^{-1}$, and if the posterior expectation is linear, then it is easily seen that $E(\theta|s_i) = E(s_j|s_i)$, $j \neq i$, and that $\tilde{s} = \sum_{i=1}^{n}(r_i / \sum_{j=1}^{n} r_j)s_i$ is sufficient for θ.[64]

The preceding results can be generalized to the case of a multidimensional state of the world and multidimensional signals. For example, suppose that θ is a random n-dimensional vector, with finite variances $\operatorname{var} \theta_i = \sigma_i^2$ and with linear conditional expectations and $\partial E(\theta_i|\theta_{-i})/\partial \theta_j \geq 0$, $j \neq i$, indicating positive correlation. Then we have that $E(\theta_i|\theta_j, j \in K \subset N)$, $N = \{1, 2, \ldots, n\}$, is linear in θ_j.[65] With a symmetric joint distribution for the random vector θ, then

$$E(\theta_i|\theta_j, j \in K \subset N) = \bar{\theta} + \frac{\rho}{1 + (k - 1)\rho} \sum_{j \in K}(\theta_j - \bar{\theta}),$$

where $\bar{\theta}$ is the common mean, ρ the correlation coefficient between θ_i and θ_j and k the cardinality of K. (See section 8.1 for applications and further examples of linear information structures.)

2.7.3 Bayesian Equilibrium

Up to now we have considered games of complete information where each player knows the payoffs (as well as the action spaces) of the other players. In many instances, however, a player does not know some characteristic (the "type") of the payoff or strategy space of other players. For example, a firm may not know the costs of production of the rival or may have private information about demand conditions. Those are games of incomplete information. A fundamental insight to deal with such situations was provided by Harsanyi (1967–68) who proposed a method to transform a game of incomplete information into a game of imperfect information. The latter is a game where some players do not observe some of their opponents' actions. For example, a simultaneous move game is a game of imperfect information: Just think that one player chooses before the other and that the second does not observe the move of the first.[66]

In an incomplete information game the characteristics of each player are known to the player, but from the point of view of other players they are drawn from some probability distribution, which is common knowledge among the players. The idea of Harsanyi is to introduce a move of "nature" at the beginning of the game choosing the types of the players and then only player i is informed about his type. Players have thus imperfect information about the move of "nature." A Bayesian Nash equilibrium, according to Harsanyi, is then just a Nash equilibrium of the imperfect information version of the game.

The type of a player embodies all the relevant private information in order to make his decisions.[67] Following Harsanyi, it is assumed that the types of the players are drawn from a common prior distribution (probability measure) μ on (the Borel subsets of) T, the cartesian product of the sets of types of the players, $T = X_{i=1}^{n} T_i$, where T_i is the set of types of player i (a nonempty complete separable metric space). The type of player i, t_i, is observed only by him. The measure μ_i will represent the marginal on T_i. Under our assumptions there exists a regular conditional distribution on T_{-i} given t_i.[68] For example, if each T_i has a finite number of elements then we can denote by $p(t_{-i}|t_i)$, the conditional probability of player i about the types of the rivals t_{-i} given the type t_i of the player. Assume in this case, without loss of generality, that the marginal on each type is strictly positive: $p_i(t_i) > 0$.

Let the action space of player i, A_i, be a compact subset of Euclidean space and his payoff be given by $\pi_i : A \times T \to R$, (Borel) measurable and bounded. (Recall that $A = X_{i=1}^n A_i$.) The payoff to player i when the vector of actions is $a = (a_1, \ldots, a_n)$ and the realized types $t = (t_1, \ldots, t_n)$ is $\pi_i(a; t)$. It is assumed that action spaces, payoff functions, type sets, and the prior distribution are common knowledge. The Bayesian game (one-shot simultaneous move game of incomplete information) is then fully described by $(A_i, T_i, \pi_i; i \in N)$.

A (pure) strategy for player i is a (Borel measurable) map $\sigma_i : T_i \to A_i$ which assigns an action to every possible type of the player. Let $\Sigma_i(\mu_i)$ denote the strategy space of player i when we identify strategies σ_i and τ_i if they are equal μ_i almost surely (a.s.).[69] Then the expected payoff to player i, when agent j uses strategy σ_j, $j \in N$, and $\sigma = (\sigma_1, \ldots, \sigma_n)$, is given by

$$P_i(\sigma) = \int_T \pi_i(\sigma_1(t_1), \ldots, \sigma_n(t_n); t)\, d\mu(t).$$

A Bayesian Nash equilibrium is a Nash equilibrium of the game where player i's strategy space is Σ_i and its payoff function P_i. At a Bayesian Nash equilibrium (BNE) each player correctly anticipates the (type contingent) strategies of the other players and optimizes accordingly. Given the strategies $\sigma_j(\cdot)$, $j \neq i$, denote by $\sigma_{-i}(t_{-i})$ the vector $(\sigma_1(t_1), \ldots, \sigma_n(t_n))$ except the ith component. Let the expected payoff to player i conditional on t_i when the other players use σ_{-i} and player i uses a_i be $E\{\pi_i(a_i, \sigma_{-i}(t_{-i}); t)|t_i\}$. Then the profile of strategies σ is a BNE if and only if for every i the action $\sigma_i(t_i)$ maximizes over A_i the conditional payoff $E_{t_{-i}}\{\pi_i(a_i, \sigma_{-i}(t_{-i}), t)|t_i\}$ (μ_i almost surely T_i). With a finite number of types $E_{t_{-i}}\{\pi_i(a_i, \sigma_{-i}(t_{-i}), t)|t_i\} = \sum_{t_{-i}} p(t_{-i}|t_i)\pi_i(a_i, \sigma_{-i}(t_{-i}); t)$.

It is worth noting that in a Bayesian game a player behaves as if he were confronting mixed strategies of the other players. For example, in a two-player game suppose that player 2 has two types, $\underline{t}$ and $\bar{t}$ (independent of the types of player 1), and two actions available, a and a'. Then, when player 2 uses strategy σ_2 with $\sigma_2(\underline{t}) = a$ and

$\sigma_2(\bar{t}) = a'$, it is as if he were using a mixed strategy: a with probability $\Pr(t = \underline{t})$ and a' with probability $1 - \Pr(t = \underline{t})$. This observation provides the starting point of Harsanyi's idea of justifying mixed-strategy equilibria as the limits as uncertainty vanishes of pure-strategy equilibria of nearby incomplete information games (see the discussion in section 2.4). The existence of BNE follows from the standard existence theorem (theorem 2.1) when the number of types as well as the number of actions for each player are finite. Indeed, then the n-player game can be reinterpreted as a game with $\sum_{i=1}^{n}(\#T_i)$ players. Now player i is transformed into $\#T_i$ players. The game is then one of a finite number of players and a finite number of actions and, consequently, an equilibrium (possibly in mixed strategies) exists. Things are more complicated when there are a continuum of types and/or actions. Milgrom and Weber (1985) state conditions under which an equilibrium in distributional strategies exists. A distributional strategy is a joint distribution on $T_i \times A_i$ with a marginal on T_i equal to μ_i. The authors assume that the payoff to player i can be written as $U_i(a; t_0, t)$ where t_0 (belonging to T_0, a complete, separable metric space) is an environmental variable. The type of player i is given by t_i as before (and $t = (t_1, \ldots, t_n)$).[70] Sufficient conditions for existence of a BNE are as follows: Each A_i is compact, U_i is uniformly continuous on $A \times T_0 \times T$ (or each A_i finite), and the information structure is continuous (the measure over $T_0 \times T$ absolutely continuous with respect to $\mu_0 \times \mu_1 \times \cdots \times \mu_n$).[71] Under these conditions the Gliksberg theorem can be applied (theorem 2.9) to ensure the existence of a fixed point.

The authors find conditions also under which pure-strategy equilibria exist (a "purification" result). Sufficient conditions are that conditional on t_0 the types of the players are independent, the payoff to player i can be written as $U_i(a; t_0, t_i)$, each A_i as well as T_0 are finite, and μ_i atomless for $i = 1, \ldots, n$. (See also Aumann et al. 1982; Radner and Rosenthal 1982.[72])

Existence in pure strategies can also be obtained from the theory of supermodular games. The basic idea is to establish the super-modularity of the Bayesian game derived by adding uncertainty and private information to a basic supermodular game (Vives 1990a). With this approach the conditions for existence in the basic game translate, without distributional restrictions, into existence of pure-strategy Bayesian equilibria. As explained in section 2.2.2, a basic observation to obtain the result is that the properties of super-modularity and increasing differences are preserved by integration. Consider our original Bayesian game described by $(A_i, T_i, \pi_i; i \in N)$, and assume that for any t in T the game is supermodular. That is, for each i, A_i is a compact lattice, π_i is upper semicontinuous and super-modular in a_i for fixed a_{-i}, and it displays increasing differences in (a_i, a_{-i}) for any t in T. Then the game $(\Sigma_i, P_i, i \in N)$ is supermodular with a natural order for $\Sigma_i : \sigma_i \leq \sigma_i'$ if $\sigma_i(t_i) \leq \sigma_i'(t_i)$ for μ_i-a.s. T_i. That is, Σ_i is a complete lattice for the natural order, and $P_i(\sigma)$ is super-modular on $\Sigma = \Sigma_1 \times \cdots \times \Sigma_n$.

In order to show that the strategy space $\Sigma_i(\mu_i)$ is a complete lattice under the natural ordering, a potential difficulty is that the supremum of an uncountable set of functions need not be measurable. However, the result can be shown to hold (see lemma 6.1 in Vives 1990a). Furthermore, if $\pi_i(a; t)$ is supermodular in a_i and displays increasing differences in (a_i, a_{-i}) for all t, and since both super-modularity and increasing differences are preserved by integration, then $P_i(\sigma)$ is also supermodular in σ_i and displays increasing differ-ences in (σ_i, σ_{-i}). Existence of (pure strategy) largest and smallest equilibrium points follows (as in theorem 2.5). An equivalent way to check the result is the following. Let $\psi_i(\sigma_{-i})$ be the set of best responses of player i to the strategy profile of the other players, σ_{-i}. Now $E\{\pi_i(a_i, \sigma_{-i}(t_{-i}); t) | t_i\}$ is upper semicontinuous on A_i, since π_i is bounded and upper semicontinuous on A_i.[73] Furthermore it is supermodular on A_i (again since $\pi_i(a; t)$ is supermodular in a_i for all t and all a_{-i} and supermodularity is preserved by integration). In ad-dition $E\{\pi_i(a_i, \sigma_{-i}(t_{-i}); t) | t_i\}$ displays increasing differences in (a_i, σ_{-i}) for any t_i (again, because $\pi_i(a_i, a_{-i}; t)$ displays increasing differences in (a_i, a_{-i}) for all t and because increasing differences are preserved by integration).[74] Therefore, for a given t_i, the set of optimal best responses $(a_i's)$ is increasing in σ_{-i} (with respect to the set order $\geq^p$ introduced in section 2.2.2, see theorem 2.3 (ii)). It follows that ψ_i is increasing. We have then, from theorem 2.4 and its corollary, that $\sup \psi_i(\sigma_{-i})$ and $\inf \psi_i(\sigma_{-i})$ belong to $\psi_i(\sigma_{-i})$ and that they are increasing. Tarski's theorem can be applied to obtain the result.

The existence result extends to the case where the basic game is a duopoly submodular game. In that case recall that changing the order of the action set of one player the game is supermodular.

These results can be applied to basic supermodular oligopoly games as we will see in chapter 8 (e.g., Bertrand and Cournot type games). Other examples include supermodular games like the Diamond search model (1982) and a certain class of arms race models when uncertainty and private information are added (see Milgrom and Roberts 1990).

Another approach based also on lattice programming (and on our second type of result in 2.7.1) finds conditions under which the best response to an increasing strategy (with respect to type) of a rival is also increasing. Suppose that both actions and types for a player are compact subsets of the real line. Suppose also that given that rivals use increasing strategies, the payoff to player i $E\{\pi_i(a_i, \sigma_{-i}(t_{-i}); t)|t_i\}$ is log-supermodular or has increasing differences (or, in general, fulfills the single crossing property) in (a_i, t_i). Then, if the action space is discrete and the type space continuous and atomless, a pure-strategy equilibrium can be shown to exist in increasing strategies. The result follows, noting first that an increasing strategy will have to be a step function. This puts strategies in the realm of finite-dimensional Euclidean spaces. Second, under the assumed single crossing property, the best-response correspondence is convex valued. We can apply then Kakutani's fixed point theorem to show existence of (pure-strategy) equilibria. The existence result holds also for games with a continuum of actions (in a compact interval) provided that payoffs are continuous in actions (and integrable). This follows because under the assumption made, the strategies for any discrete version of the game are of bounded variation (indeed, they are increasing)[75] and therefore sequences of equilibria of finite games will have (almost everywhere) convergent subsequences,[76] whose limits will be equilibria of the continuous action limit game (by continuity of payoffs). Some games with discontinuous payoffs, like first-price auctions, can also be accommodated in the theory. The results can be applied to common value two asymmetric bidder, or n-bidder symmetric auctions, as well as to Bertrand pricing games with private cost information (see section 8.1 and Athey 1997a, b; see also exercise 2.19 for a basic characterization of Bayesian equilibrium in an auction).

Summary

This chapter provides an overview of some basic game-theoretic tools for oligopoly analysis. After reviewing the basics of Nash equilibrium, it develops a self-contained exposition of the theory of supermodular games and monotone comparative statics. The chapter supplies also a unified treatment of existence results of Nash equilibrium in pure strategies, uniqueness, and stability of equilibria. It also develops the tools needed to study games of incomplete information, including monotone comparative statics under uncertainty, information structures and signals, and the theory of Bayesian Nash equilibrium. Major results in the chapter include the classical existence theorem for Nash equilibrium (theorem 2.1), the basic monotonicity result for optimizers (theorem 2.3), the existence result and characterization of equilibria in supermodular games (theorem 2.4 and remarks, including comparative statics of extremal equilibria), the existence result for symmetric games with quasi-increasing best replies (theorem 2.6), the existence and uniqueness result for games with decreasing replies and one-dimensional strategy spaces (theorems 2.7 and 2.8), the general existence result with mixed strategies (theorem 2.9), the three approaches to uniqueness (contraction mapping, univalence conditions and index theory approach), and the stability properties of supermodular games (theorems 2.10 and 2.11). The monotonicity results in optimization problems are extended to allow for uncertainty and applied to find conditions for the existence of (pure-strategy) Bayesian Nash equilibria.

Exercises

2.1. Construct a duopoly example with no Nash equilibrium. (*Hint:* If unsuccessful, turn to Friedman 1983 and Roberts and Sonnenschein 1977 for inspiration.)

2.2. Consider a single product monopolist facing a revenue function $R(x)$ and a cost function $C(x, t)$, where x is the output and t a cost reduction parameter. Suppose that the output space is a compact interval of the real line, on which $R(\cdot)$ is upper semicontinuous and C is smooth with $\partial^2 C / \partial x \partial t < 0$. Prove directly, using a revealed preference argument, that the set of monopoly outputs $\phi(t)$ is strongly increasing in t (i.e., if $t > t'$, $\underline{\phi}(t) \geq \bar{\phi}(t')$).

2.3. Consider a monopoly facing an inverse demand function $P(Q/m)$, where Q is total output and m the number of customers, and cost function $C(Q)$. $P(Q/m) = 0$ for $Q/m \geq k$. Inverse demand (when positive) and costs are smooth. How do optimal outputs per customer depend on m? (*Hint:* It depends on the properties of the cost function. See Milgrom and Shanon 1994.)

2.4. Show that the equilibrium set of a strictly supermodular game is a complete lattice. (*Hint:* Show that if the best-reply correspondence of any player is strongly increasing and ordered, then an increasing selection g of Ψ can be constructed such that $E = \{a \in A : a = g(a)\}$. See Vives 1990a.)

2.5. Consider a strictly supermodular game with two or three players and one-dimensional strategy spaces. Show that the equilibrium set must be (totally) ordered.

*2.6. Examine the set of coalition-proof equilibria (in the sense of Bernheim, Peleg, and Whinston 1987) in a supermodular game with the payoff to any player increasing in the actions of the other players. (See Milgrom and Roberts 1996.)

2.7. Show directly that a function from $[0, 1]$ to $[0, 1]$ which when discontinuous only jumps up has a fixed point.

2.8. Provide an alternative proof to theorem 2.8 using the concept of the cumulative best reply of player i, Φ_i. (*Hint:* Show that Φ_i, is strongly decreasing under the assumptions, and conclude that $\sum_{i=1}^{n} \Phi_i$ has at most one fixed point.)

2.9. Consider a two-player game with one-dimensional strategy spaces. Prove that if a^* is a regular Nash equilibrium, then it is locally stable if at $a^* |r_1'| \, |r_2'| < 1$. Prove that the equilibrium will not be locally stable if the inequalities are reversed. (See section 2.6.2 and Moulin 1982.)

*2.10. Consider a smooth game $(A_i, \pi_i; i = 1, \ldots, n)$ with A_i a compact interval for each i, and suppose that $\partial^2 \pi_i / (\partial a_i)^2 + \sum_{j \neq i} |\partial^2 \pi_i / \partial a_i \partial a_j| < 0$ for all $a \in A$. Show that there is a unique Nash equilibrium of the game and that it is globally stable. (*Hint:* Show that the best-reply map is a contraction by finding bounds on its derivative.)

2.11. Consider a two-player supermodular game with one-dimensional strategy spaces and continuous payoffs. Show that the sequential Cournot tatônnement converges to an equilibrium from any initial position.

2.12. Consider a two-player game with strategy sets $[0, 1]$. Player i has the best-reply function $r_i(a_j) = a_j$, $j \neq i$. Describe explicitly the dynamics induced by the discrete and continuous versions of the Cournot (best-response) tatônnement.

*2.13. Consider a duopoly game where each player has a compact interval as strategy space. The payoff to player 1 is $\pi_1(a_1, a_2; t)$ and to player 2, $\pi_2(a_1, a_2)$. Show that if the game is supermodular and $\pi_1(a_1, a_2; t)$ has increasing (decreasing) differences in (a_1, t), then extremal equilibria are increasing (decreasing) in t. Show that if the game is submodular, then extremal equilibrium strategies for firm 1(2) are increasing (decreasing) in t if $\pi_1(a_1, a_2; t)$ has increasing differences in (a_1, t), and that the result is reversed if $\pi_1(a_1, a_2; t)$ has decreasing differences in (a_1, t). How would you extend the results to multidimensional strategy spaces? (*Hint:* For the submodular game consider the transformed game $s_1 = a_1$ and $s_2 = -a_2$.)

*2.14. Consider a rent-seeking game in which agent i, $i = 1, \ldots, n$, expends a nonnegative amount x_i and obtains the "rent" (normalized to be one) with probability $p_i = f_i(x_i)/(\sum_{j=1}^{n} f_j(x_j))$, where each f_i is smooth with $f_i' > 0$, $f_i'' < 0$, and $f_i(0) = 0$. Show that there is a unique Nash equilibrium of the game. (*Hint:* Get inspiration from theorem 2.7 and exercise 2.8. Note also that letting $q_i = f_i(x_i)$, the game can be interpreted as a Cournot game with inverse demand function $P(Q) = Q^{-1}$, $Q = \sum_{j=1}^{n} q_j$ and strictly convex costs for firm i, $C_i(q_i) = f_i^{-1}(q_i)$. See Szidarovszky and Okuguchi 1997.)

2.15. Consider the parametrized smooth demand function $D(p; \alpha)$. Find a necessary and sufficient condition for D to be log-supermodular in $(p; \alpha)$ in terms of its price elasticity.

2.16. Let $\phi(y|f) = \arg\max_x \int u(x, \theta) f(\theta; y) \, d\theta$ and (the corresponding problem under certainty) $x^*(\theta) = \arg\max_x u(x, \theta)$. Suppose that both problems are strictly quasiconcave and differentiable and that the optima are interior. Show that for all f which fulfill the MLRP, $\phi(y|f)$ is increasing in y if and only if $x^*(\theta)$ is increasing in θ. (See Ormiston and Schlee 1993.)

2.17. Suppose that with prior and likelihood with finite variances, a signal s about an unknown parameter θ is unbiased (i.e., $E(s|\theta) = \theta$). Then, if $E(\theta|s)$ is linear in s (e.g., $E(\theta|s) = A + ts$), show that $t = \sigma_\theta^2/\text{var}\,s = r/(\tau_\theta + r)$, where $r = (E\,\text{var}(s|\theta))^{-1}$ and $A = (1 - t)\bar{\theta}$. (See Ericson 1969.)

2.18. Consider a bivariate normal random pair (θ_1, θ_2) with nonnegative correlation, and let $\mu_i = E\theta_i$. Show that $Eg(\theta_1, \theta_2)$ is supermodular in (μ_1, μ_2) provided that g is supermodular in (θ_1, θ_2). (See Athey 1995 for a general method of proof.)

**2.19. Consider an auction with n risk neutral bidders for an object. Bidder i has valuation θ_i for the object and receives a private signal s_i

correlated with the unknown θ_i. The density of $(\theta_1, \ldots, \theta_n, s_1, \ldots, s_n)$ is log-supermodular with support on a compact $2n$ dimensional cube and the bidders are ex ante symmetric. A strategy for bidder i is a function that selects a bid $b_i(s_i)$ for every signal s_i. Characterize the symmetric Bayesian equilibrium (BNE) of the auction $b(\cdot)$ when the winner is the highest bidder and pays the second highest bid (second-price auction). Compute by how much a bidder would shade his bid from the benchmark of the second-price auction if the object is auctioned in a first-price auction (you have to characterize the BNE of the auction when the winner is the highest bidder and pays his bid, this is a more difficult task). Explain intuitively the bid shading result. (See Milgrom and Weber 1982.)

*2.20. Suppose that n firms are engaged in a memoryless patent race and have access to the same R&D technology. If a firm spends x, the (instantaneous) probability of innovating and obtaining the prize V (losers obtain nothing) is given by $h(x)$, where h is a smooth function with $h(0) = 0$, $h' > 0$ for x in $(0, \bar{x})$, $h'(0) = \infty$ and $h'(x) = 0$ for $x \geq \bar{x} > 0$. Without innovating the normalized profit of firms is zero. Under these conditions the expected discounted profits (at rate r) of firm i investing x_i if rival j invests x_j is given by $\pi_i = (h(x_i)V - x_i)/(h(x_i) + \sum_{j \neq i} h(x_j) + r)$ (see Reinganum 1989). Show that the game is strictly log-supermodular and that all equilibria are symmetric. Show that at extremal equilibria the expenditure intensity x^* is increasing in n.

3

Foundations of Partial Equilibrium Analysis

Oligopoly theory has been developed mostly in the context of partial equilibrium analysis.[1] Indeed, competition among firms has been studied in a market or group of interrelated markets abstracting from connections with the rest of the economy. Furthermore it has been typically assumed, starting from the pioneering work of Cournot, that firms face a downward-sloping demand curve, and welfare changes have been measured by changes in consumer surplus since the contribution of Dupuit (1844). In the following chapters we will consider a single market or a group of commodities in isolation from the rest of the economy.

This chapter will try to clarify when is partial equilibrium analysis warranted and when it can be safely assumed that demand is downward sloping and that consumer surplus is an appropriate measure of welfare change. Section 3.1 presents a canonical model of partial equilibrium analysis based on quasilinear utility and no income effects on the industry under study. Section 3.2 provides conditions under which income effects are small based on the Marshallian idea that if the expenditure share on any good is small the income effects should be small. This case is important because the share of consumer expenditure devoted to a typical oligopolistic industry is small. In the appendix to the chapter the implications of the results for consumer surplus analysis are derived. Section 3.2 and the appendix closely follow Vives (1987).

3.1 A Canonical Partial Equilibrium Model

Consider a demand system derived from the optimization problem of a representative consumer with quasilinear utility[2]

$$\max W(q_o, q) = q_o + U(q) \quad \text{subject to} \quad q_o + pq \leq I,$$

where U is an increasing and concave function of the vector of n (differentiated) goods $q = (q_1, \ldots, q_n)$ which compose the industry or market being studied, with associated price vector p; q_o is the numéraire good (or "money") which represents the rest of the economy, and I is the income of the consumer. The solution to the problem, for large enough income, is equivalent to the solution to

$$\max_q U(q) - pq,$$

yielding a demand system $q = D(p)$ which is independent of income. In this formulation all the income effects are being captured by the numéraire good.[3]

Suppose that U is smooth and its Hessian, H_U, negative definite. Inverse demands follow from the first-order conditions of the maximization problem:

$$p_i = \frac{\partial U_i}{\partial q_i} \quad \text{for } q_i > 0.$$

The properties of symmetry of cross effects, $\partial P_i/\partial q_j = \partial P_j/\partial q_i$, $j \neq i$, and downward-sloping demand, $\partial P_i/\partial q_i < 0$, are obtained immediately from the fact that the Jacobian of the inverse demand system P just equals the Hessian of U (which is negative definite and symmetric).

Global invertibility of inverse demands on a convex region is assured, since the Jacobian of the inverse demand system is negative definite according to the univalence approach (see section 2.5). Inverting the inverse demand system, we obtain direct demands. The demands will be downward sloping and with symmetric cross effects because the Jacobian of the direct demand system D is just the inverse of the Hessian of the utility function H, and therefore it will be negative definite and symmetric.

The surplus of the consumer will be a convex decreasing function of prices $CS(p) = U(D(p)) - pD(p)$. This follows immediately noting that the optimization problem of the consumer is formally identical to a firm's maximization problem, finding the optimal input mix at prices p to maximize profit, with U as a production function and normalized output price. Indeed, we have then that $\partial CS/\partial p_i = -D_i(p)$ and convexity of CS follows from standard production theory.

In the special case in which $U(q)$ is additive separable, $U(q) = \sum_{i=1}^n u_i(q_i)$, with smooth and concave subutility functions u_i, then

$p_i = u_i'(q_i)$ for $q_i > 0$,

and there are no cross-price effects.

If there are several consumers all with quasilinear utility $W^h(q_0^h, q^h) = q_0^h + U^h(q^h)$, $h = 1, \ldots, H$, then aggregate demand (for large enough incomes) can be obtained from the solution to a representative consumer problem. Indeed, the indirect utility function for consumer h is just $V^h(p, I^h) = CS^h(p) + I^h$. This has the Gorman form $V^h(p, I^h) = a^h(p) + b(p)I^h$ with $b(p) = 1$. It follows then that the aggregate demand can be derived from the aggregate indirect utility function $CS(p) + I = \sum_{h=1}^{H} CS^h(p) + \sum_{h=1}^{H} I^h$. In this respect, with quasilinear utility, the assumption of a representative consumer is not restrictive.

With this approach we isolate the industry object of study from the rest of the economy, obtain downward-sloping demands, and the consumer surplus is an appropriate measure of welfare change (because it corresponds directly to the indirect utility function). When is it justified to use such a shortcut? The idea of Marshall (1920) is that the partial equilibrium approach will be justified when the industry under study represents only a small part of the budget of each consumer. In this case income effects in the industry of interest should be small, and changes in the industry should not provoke significant changes in other markets (in particular, in the relative prices of the goods in other markets). This justifies, in the limit, the assumption of a utility function linear in the numéraire, the (Hicksian) composite good representing the aggregate of the rest of the goods in the economy, which captures all the income effects.

In the next section we provide a rigorous foundation for these ideas. We find conditions on preferences under which expenditure shares on any good, as well as income effects, are small. We give an approximation result to check when are income effects going to be small enough to justify the use of quasilinear utility as an (approximate) solution and, in consequence, to obtain downward-sloping demand and consumer surplus as an appropriate measure of welfare change.

3.2 Small Expenditure Shares and Small Income Effects

Two related ideas have been proposed in the literature to obtain small income effects. Consider the Slutsky equation in elasticity terms:

$$\eta_i = \eta_i^C + \frac{p_i D_i}{I} \eta_i^I,$$

where $\eta_i = -(p_i/q_i)(\partial D_i/\partial p_i)$ is the elasticity of demand, η_i^C the elasticity of compensated (or Hicksian demand), and $\eta_i^I = (I/q_i)(\partial D_i/\partial I)$, the income elasticity of demand. Now, if the proportion of income spent on the good $p_i D_i/I$ is small, then, ceteris paribus, the income effect on that good should be small also. This is the position of Hicks (1946, p. 35), who, when discussing the "law of demand," states that even if a good is inferior, "the demand curve will still behave in an orthodox manner so long as the proportion of income spent upon the commodity is small, so that the income effect is small." Indeed, when the income effect is small, demand is downward sloping because the compensated demand is downward sloping.

An obvious problem with this type of reasoning is the ceteris paribus assumption: What happens to the income elasticity of demand when the expenditure share on the good becomes small? It is easy to construct examples with two goods for which as the expenditure share of one good tends to zero the income effect on the same good remains bounded away from zero (see exercises 3.1 and 3.2).

Marshall provided a related approach to consumer surplus and downward-sloping demand. He discussed these topics in his principles of economics on the supposition that "the marginal utility of money to the individual purchaser is the same throughout," and he based this supposition "on the assumption, which underlies our whole reasoning, that his expenditure on any one thing, as, for instance, tea, is only a small part of his whole expenditure" (Marshall 1920, p. 842). Obviously a "constant" marginal utility of money means that income effects are absent. It is worth noting nevertheless that the marginal utility of money, the Lagrange multiplier in the consumer's optimization problem, can not be independent of prices and income.[4] Therefore, when assuming a constant marginal utility of income implicitly, we are keeping constant something, be it income or the price of a good (numéraire).

We will make now rigorous the Marshallian notion that when any good represents a small part of the expenditure of a consumer, income effects are negligible (for a full development of the model and details of the proofs, see Vives 1987).

In our model we have a countable infinity of potential commodities, and our consumer has well-defined preferences for any finite subset of n of them according to some utility function U with domain in the positive orthant of R^n. When the consumer consumes n goods, we normalize income to be of the same order, equal to n for simplicity, so that for n large small shares of expenditure on any commodity are associated to nonnegligible consumptions of the commodity.[5] In other words, under our assumptions and using the budget constraint, average expenditure per good is constant, and normalized to 1, independent of n.

With n goods in the market with prices $p \in R_{++}^n$ the optimization program of our consumer is

$$\max U(q) \quad \text{subject to} \quad pq \leq n, \quad q \in R_+^n.$$

In order to fix ideas, suppose, for the moment, that U is a symmetric (interchanging the amounts consumed of any two goods i and j the level of utility remains constant), strictly quasiconcave, and increasing utility function. Let all the prices equal p, $p > 0$. In this completely symmetric situation the demand for good i is $1/p$, its expenditure share $1/n$, and the income derivative of demand is $1/np$. The income effect on good i (the consumption of good i times the income derivative of demand) equals $1/np^2$, which tends to zero as n tends to infinity at a rate of $1/n$. The consumer spreads his income over all the goods, and expenditure shares and the income effect dissipate as the number of goods grows because prices are bounded always from zero.[6]

We provide conditions on preferences that generalize this result. What is needed is preferences that are not very asymmetric (so as to avoid any good picking up most of the income effects) and no two goods being close to perfect substitutes (so as to avoid any good picking up most of the demand). Furthermore a curvature condition on the utility function must be imposed to avoid unbounded income derivative of demands. Under these conditions, when the consumer consumes a large number of goods, expenditure shares on any good and income effects will be small.

Very asymmetric preferences give rise easily to significant income effects even when the consumer consumes a large number of goods. For example, let $U(q) = \sum_{i=1}^n 2^{-i} \log q_i$, and fix a sequence of prices $\{p_i\}_{i=1}^\infty$, $p_i > 0$. Demand for good i is $n2^{-i}/(p_i \sum_{i=1}^n 2^{-i})$, its expenditure share, $2^{-i}/\sum_{i=1}^n 2^{-i}$, and the income derivative of demand is $2^{-i}/(p_i \sum_{i=1}^n 2^{-i})$. The marginal utility of income is $\sum_{i=1}^n 2^{-i}/n$. Because $\sum_{i=1}^\infty 2^{-i} = 1$, as n tends to infinity, the demand for good i tends to infinity, its expenditure share to 2^{-i}, the income derivative of demand to $2^{-i}/p_i$, and the marginal utility of income to zero. We will consider preferences satisfying some regularity conditions, the uniform Inada property, and the curvature property. For any number of goods n the assumed properties will define a class of utility functions U^n.

- *Regularity conditions.* Let $U : R^n_{++} \to R$ be smooth (twice continuously differentiable) with strictly positive gradient, $\nabla U(q) \gg 0$, and negative definite Hessian, $H_U(q)$, for all $q \in R^n_{++}$.
- *Uniform Inada property* (UIP). There exist decreasing positive functions which are bound above and below the marginal utility of any good, which depend only on the quantity of the good considered (in particular, they are independent of n), and which satisfy the Inada requirement for marginal utility (as the consumption of the good ranges from zero to infinity, marginal utility ranges from infinity to zero).[7]
- *Curvature property.* The absolute values of the eigenvalues of H_U are bounded above and away from zero (uniformly in n) provided that the consumption of each good lies in a compact set bounded away from zero.

Given the regularity conditions stated, a utility function satisfying the UIP formalizes the idea that preferences are not "very asymmetric" and that we never have two goods being close to perfect substitutes. In the monopolistic competition literature we find assumptions similar in spirit to our uniform Inada property.[8] This property is a strong one. It means that no good has a "neighbor" no matter how many goods there are in the market. Think intuitively of the assumption as bounding the elasticity of substitution between any two goods. For this to happen, we have to think in terms of goods being drawn from an unbounded space of characteristics. Indeed, with a compact space of characteristics, most of the goods would eventually become very close substitutes as the number of goods n grows. The UIP implies that expenditure shares will be small for n large. In fact demands will be uniformly bounded above and away from zero provided that prices are not of different orders of magnitude.

A sufficient condition for the curvature property to hold is that for utilities in the class U^n, H_U be strongly dominant diagonal and that the terms on its diagonal be bounded. That is, $|\partial^2 U/(\partial q_i)^2|$ bounded above, and $\partial^2 U/(\partial q_i)^2 + \sum_{j \neq i} |\partial^2 U/\partial q_i \partial q_j| < 0$ and bounded away from zero for all goods (uniformly in n) for consumptions of any good in a compact and positive interval. In other words, the aggregation of the interaction terms $\sum_{j \neq i} |\partial^2 U/\partial q_i \partial q_j|$ should not overwhelm the own effect $|\partial^2 U/(\partial q_i)^2|$.

The curvature property allows us to obtain bounds on the income derivative of demand in terms of the number of goods once demands are in a compact set. It implies also that the slopes of the Hicksian demand curves are nondegenerate (or, more in general, the Slutsky matrix, is nondegenerate) no matter the number of goods.[9] The following theorem summarizes the result:

THEOREM 3.1 Consider utility function in the class U^n which satisfies the regularity conditions, the uniform Inada property, and the curvature property. Let prices for any good be in a compact and positive interval.

(i) The demand for any good and the marginal utility of income are uniformly bounded above and away from zero.

(ii) The order of magnitude of the (Euclidean) norm of the income derivative of demand of any good is $1/\sqrt{n}$. If preferences are representable by additive separable or homothetic utility functions, then the order of magnitude of the income derivative of demand of any good is $1/n$.

(iii) The associated Slutsky matrix is nondegenerate.

The theorem implies that when the consumer consumes a large number of goods:

(i) The expenditure share on any good is small (and positive).

(ii) The income effects are small. More precisely, the order of magnitude of the income derivative of demand of any good is at most $1/\sqrt{n}$ ($1/n$ if preferences are representable by additive separable or homothetic utility functions). While:

(iii) The substitution effects are nondegenerate.

A sketch of the proof of the result is as follows (for a complete proof, see Vives 1987): The uniform Inada property guarantees that demands are uniformly bounded above and away from zero. This implies that (i) is true. (Under our assumptions, if demand for any good were unbounded, then demand for all goods would be unbounded, which is a contradiction because from the budget constraint average demand has to be bounded.) Similarly it is possible to show that demands are bounded away from zero. Once demands are in a compact set, bounds on the norm of the income derivative of demand in terms of the number of goods are easily derived from the bounds on the Hessian of the utility function through the effect of the expansion of the price vector. Part (iii) follows similarly. The norm of the income derivative of demand is seen to be of the order $1/\sqrt{n}$, which means that the order of magnitude of individual income derivatives of demand is at most $1/\sqrt{n}$. When preferences are representable by additive separable utility functions with strictly concave components, all goods are normal, and from the bounds on second derivatives, it follows that all individual income derivatives are of the same order of magnitude, which must be $1/n$ because of the budget constraint. If preferences are homothetic, then uniform bounds on demand imply the result, since with income I the demand for good i is given by $D_i(p, I) = Ig_i(p)$, where g_i is an appropriate positive function. Therefore $\partial D_i/\partial I = g_i(p)$ is of the order of q_i/I, which is $1/n$, since $I = n$ according to our normalization.

Two examples of classes of utility functions satisfying the assumptions of the theorem follow.

Example
Let

$$U(q) = \sum_{i=1}^{n} \alpha_i \log q_i + \sum_{k=1}^{n-1} \frac{1}{2^{k+1}} \sum_{i=1}^{n-k} \frac{q_i}{1 + q_i} \frac{q_{i+k}}{1 + q_{i+k}},$$

where $\bar{\alpha} \geq \alpha_i \geq 1$ for all i. It is easily seen that it satisfies the UIP and that H_U is strongly dominant diagonal and that the terms on its diagonal are bounded. Therefore it satisfies the curvature property. The functions which bound marginal utility can be taken to be

$$\bar{\phi}(z) = \frac{\bar{\alpha}}{z} + \frac{1}{(1+z)^2} \quad \text{and} \quad \underline{\phi}(z) = \frac{1}{z}.$$

Note that the weights given to the interaction between good i and j decrease as the goods become farther apart, that is as $|i - j|$ increases.

Example

Let $U(q) = \sum_{i=1}^{n} \alpha_i q_i^{\rho_i}$ with $0 < \underline{\alpha} \le \alpha_i \le \bar{\alpha}$ and $0 < \underline{\rho} \le \rho_i \le \bar{\rho} < 1$ for all i.

Remark 1   The theorem applies to preferences that are *representable* by utility functions satisfying the stated assumptions. The boundedness result on the marginal utility of income applies only to the utility functions satisfying the stated assumptions. For example, the theorem applies to the preferences given by utility functions of the type $U(q) = \Pi_{i=1}^{n} q_i$, since $V(q) = \sum_{i=1}^{n} \log q_i$ is an increasing transformation of U which satisfies the required assumptions.

Remark 2   The theorem has immediate consequences for consumer surplus analysis and downward-sloping demand, since for n large the slope of the (Marshallian) demand function $\partial D_i / \partial p_i$ will be close to the slope of the Hicksian (or compensated) demand function $\partial h_i / \partial p_i$. Indeed, from the Slutsky equation we have

$$\frac{\partial h_i}{\partial p_i} - \frac{\partial D_i}{\partial p_i} = q_i \frac{\partial D_i}{\partial I},$$

and for n large the income effect is small. As a corollary we obtain that for large n demand will be downward sloping because the slope of the Hicksian demand is negative (and nondegenerate for any n). Our results concern *individual* demand. If all consumers satisfy our assumptions, it follows that *market* demand must be downward sloping too.[10] (See exercise 3.2 for an example of a Giffen good which when replicating appropriately the number of goods, demand becomes downward sloping.)

Furthermore the Marshallian consumer surplus will be a good approximation of the true measure of welfare change, the Hicksian consumer surplus. More precisely, under the assumptions of theorem 3.1, suppose that only the price of good i changes, then the order of magnitude of the percentage error in approximating the Hicksian consumer surplus (or the Hicksian deadweight loss) by its Marshallian counterparts is at most of the order of $1/\sqrt{n}$. In the additively separable case the order of magnitude of the percentage error is $1/n$. For multiple price changes the Hicksian measures are well approximated by the Marshallian surplus independently of the order of prices with respect to which integration takes place. (See the appendix to the chapter for details.)

Remark 3 A particular case of the theorem with preferences additively separable by groups, $U(q) = \sum_{i=1}^{N} U^i(q^i)$, with $q^i \in R_+^l$, yields an order of magnitude of the income derivative of demand for any good of $1/N$ (N is the number of groups and the normalized income).[11] Under the assumptions the indirect utility function of each group (as a function of income I^i), $V_i(I^i) = \max\{U^i(q^i) : p^i q^i = I^i, q^i \in R_+^l\}$, satisfies the regularity conditions, the UIP and the curvature property. Consider the demand functions as arising from a two-step procedure: First, given the income I^i allocated to group i, the demands are derived, $D^i(p^i, I^i)$; second, income I is distributed optimally among the N groups using the indirect utility function for each group and solving $\max\{\sum_{i=1}^{N} V_i(I^i) : \sum_{i=1}^{N} I^i = I, I^i \geq 0\}$. Denote the solution to the latter problem by $\theta^i(I)$. The demands in group i are given by $D^i(p^i, \theta^i(I))$ With $I = N$ the order of $\partial \theta^i / \partial I$ is $1/N$ according to theorem 3.1 (b) with additive separable preferences. The result then follows applying the chain rule to the income derivative of demand of good j in group $i : \partial D_j^i / \partial I = (\partial D_j^i / \partial I_i)(\partial \theta^i / \partial I)$ because $\partial D_j^i / \partial I_i$ is bounded and $\partial \theta^i / \partial I$ is of order $1/N$ when $I = N$.

We establish now some direct connections with partial equilibrium analysis. Suppose that preferences are additively separable, $U(q) = \sum_{i=1}^{n} u_i(q_i)$, in the class fulfilling the assumptions of theorem 3.1. Fix a sequence $\{u_i\}_{i=1}^{\infty}$ and a sequence of prices $\{p_i\}_{i=1}^{\infty}$, with $p_i \in [\underline{p}, \bar{p}]$, $\underline{p} > 0$. Assume furthermore that there is a well-defined limit demand for any good as n tends to infinity. Then for n large the consumer problem can be approximated by the solution to

$$\max_q \sum_{i=1}^{n} u_i(q_i) - \hat{\lambda} pq, \quad q \in R_+^n.$$

These "marginal utility of money constant" demand functions (sometimes called Frisch demands; see Browning et al. 1985) show no income effects. For n large the consumer acts approximately as if he had a fixed constant marginal utility for income, $\hat{\lambda}$.[12] The result follows immediately, noting that if the demand for good i with n goods, q_i^n, tends to q_i as n tends to infinity, this means that the associated Lagrange multiplier λ^n tends to $\hat{\lambda} = u_i'(q_i)/p_i$ since $u_i'(q_i^n) = \lambda^n p_i$. Given our assumptions, $\hat{\lambda} > 0$. For example, if preferences correspond to the linear expenditure system, $U(q) = \sum_{i=1}^{n} \log(q_i - \beta)$, with $0 < \beta < 1$ and $\bar{p} < 1$, then $\lambda^n = 1 - \beta \tilde{p}^n$, where $\tilde{p}^n$ is the average price. If the average price converges as n tends to infinity (e.g., to $\bar{p}$), then demands converge also. In this case for n large, the demand for good i can be approximated by $q_i = \beta + (1 - \beta\tilde{p})^{-1}p_i^{-1}$.

Similarly suppose that preferences are additively separable by groups as in remark 3 above, $U(q) = \sum_{i=1}^{N} U^i(q^i)$, with $q^i \in R_+^l$. Fix a sequence $\{U_i\}_{i=1}^{\infty}$ and a sequence of price vectors $\{p^i\}_{i=1}^{\infty}$, $p^i \in R_{++}^l$ with $p_j^i \in [\underline{p}, \bar{p}], \underline{p} > 0$ for $j = 1, \ldots, l$ and all i. Assume as before that there is a well defined limit demand for any good as N tends to infinity and denote by $\hat{\lambda}$ the limit Lagrange multiplier of the consumer problem. Then, also as before, for a large number of groups N, the consumer problem can be approximated by the solution to

$$\max_q \sum_{i=1}^{N} U^i(q^i) - \hat{\lambda} \sum_{i=1}^{N} p^i q^i, \qquad q^i \in R_+^l \quad \text{for all } i.$$

In consequence, for additive separable preferences, the partial equilibrium approach to a subset of the goods is warranted. In this case the marginal utility of income can be taken to be "constant" when the number of goods is large. The price of the numéraire in the partial equilibrium approach is then $p_0 = 1/\hat{\lambda}$, and the demands for the industry under consideration, say, group i, come from the solution to the program

$$\max_{q^i} U^i(q^i) - \hat{\lambda} p^i q^i, \qquad q^i \in R_+^l.$$

Appendix: Consumer Surplus Analysis

Consumer surplus has been controversial ever since its introduction by Jules Dupuit (1944). Marshall (1920), Hotelling (1969), and Hicks (1941, 1946) used it, but Samuelson (1947) was very critical of the concept. (See Chipman and Moore 1976 for a good exposition of the issue.) More recently Willig (1976) has tried to make the case for the use of consumer surplus "without apology" based on approximation results.

Consider a consumer with utility function $U(\cdot)$ on R_+^n and income I facing prices p. Let $D(p, I)$ denote the (Marshallian) demand and $h(p, u)$ the Hicksian demand for utility level u. Suppose that our consumer faces a change from (p^0, I^0) to (p^1, I^1).

An acceptable measure of welfare change based on integrating demand functions, like the consumer surplus, must fulfill two requirements:

1. It should be path independent. That is, it should not depend on the path of integration when going from (p^0, I^0) to (p^1, I^1).

2. The ranking according to the welfare measure should agree with the ranking derived from the indirect utility function.

The consumer surplus, in general, is not an acceptable measure of welfare change. More precisely, with no restrictions on the end points (p^0, I^0) and (p^1, I^1), there are no conditions on preferences under which the consumer surplus measure fulfills requirements 1 and 2.

Suppose that k prices change (for simplicity suppose these are the k first goods) and that $I^0 = I^1$. We are contemplating a price change from p^0 to $p^1 = (p_1^1, \ldots, p_k^1, p_{k+1}^0, \ldots, p_n^0)$. Suppose that prices are changed sequentially, each price being changed only once. We restrict attention to this type of *simple* sequences and denote by π_1 the ordering where p_1 is changed first, then p_2, and so on. The (Marshallian) consumer surplus (MCS) is given by

$$\text{MCS}(p^0, p^1, I; \pi_1) = \sum_{i=1}^{k} \int_{p_i^0}^{p_i^1} D_i(p^{(1)}, I) \, dp_i,$$

where $p^{(i)} = (p_1^1, \ldots, p_{i-1}^1, p_i, p_{i+1}^0, \ldots, p_n^0)$.

The problem is that the MCS depends on what particular sequence of price changes we are considering. This is so since, in general, $\partial D_i / \partial p_j$ does not equal $\partial D_j / \partial p_i$ for $i \neq j$. Furthermore the MCS does not need to accord with the indirect utility function. For example, for a single price change, say p_i, MCS is given by the integral

$$\text{MCS}(p^0, p^1, I) = \int_{p_i^0}^{p_i^1} D_i(p, I) \, dp_i.$$

Using Roy's identity we have that $D_i(p, I) = (-\partial V(p, I)/\partial p_i)/(\partial V(p, I)/\partial I) = -(\partial V/\partial p_i)/\lambda$. The MCS is then equal to $(V(p^1, I) - V(p^0, I))/\lambda$, where λ is the marginal utility of income if λ is independent of p_i. In this case the MCS accords with the indirect utility function, but in general, λ does depend on p_i.

We know already of a restriction on preferences and end points which makes the MCS acceptable as a measure of welfare change: The quasilinear case with a numéraire good (as in section 3.1). Then the marginal utility of income depends only on the price of the numéraire and cross-price effects are symmetric, since demands come from the solution to the program $\max_q U(q) - pq$. Another instance is when preferences are homothetic and $I^0 = I^1$. Then the marginal utility of income depends only on income, which is constant, and cross-price effects are symmetric as it is well known.

In contrast with the consumer surplus, the Hicksian measures of welfare change, the compensating and the equivalent variations, do not depend on the path of integration of the Hicksian demands. Let us review these measures and how well they are approximated by the consumer surplus (MCS).

Let $e(p, u)$ and $V(p, I)$ denote, respectively, the expenditure and the indirect utility functions. Suppose that our consumer faces a price change form p^0 to p^1. According to Hicks the compensating variation of a price change, CV, is the amount of income the consumer must receive at prices p^1 to leave utility unaffected by the price change:

$$CV(p^0, p^1, I) = e(p^1, u^0) - I, \qquad \text{with } u^0 = V(p^0, I).$$

The equivalent variation of a price change, EV, is the amount of income that should be taken away from the consumer at prices p^0 to make him as well off as with prices p^1:

$$EV(p^0, p^1, I) = I - e(p^0, u^1), \qquad \text{with } u^1 = V(p^1, I).$$

It is easily seen that the EV is an acceptable measure of welfare change, since, apart from being path independent, it accords with the indirect utility function. That is, for all p^0, p^1, p^2, and I, $EV(p^0, p^1, I) \gtreqless EV(p^0, p^2, I)$ if and only if $V(p^1, I) \gtreqless V(p^2, I)$. This is not the case, in general, for the CV. (See Chipman and Moore 1980.)

We define the Hicksian consumer surplus (HCS) corresponding to the price change to be the equivalent variation. HCS may be computed by integrating the Hicksian demand function evaluated at u^1:

$$HCS(p^0, p^1, I) = \sum_{i=1}^{k} \int_{p_i^0}^{p_i^1} h_i(p^{(i)}, u^1) \, dp_i$$

where, as before, $p^i = (p_1^1, \ldots, p_{i-1}^1, p_i, p_{i+1}^0, \ldots, p_n^0)$.

However, in economics more often we are interested in the deadweight loss (DL) of a price change. For example, in estimating the distortion introduced by monopoly pricing, it is not the entire loss to the consumer we are interested in but rather the loss in excess of the profit accrued to the monopolist. That is, from our consumer surplus measure we have to subtract a transfer payment (see Auerbach 1985; Mohring 1971). We may define the Hicksian deadweight loss (HDL) from monopoly pricing with constant marginal production costs (a price change from the competitive price p^0, equal to the constant marginal cost, to the monopoly price p^1) as the difference between the equivalent variation and the profit collected when prices are p^1:

$$\text{HDL}(p^0, p^1, I) = \text{EV}(p^0, p^1, I) - (p^1 - p^0) \cdot D(p^1, I).$$

Or, more generally, we may define the HDL as the difference between the EV and an appropriate transfer payment T:

$$\text{HDL}(p^0, p^1, I) = \text{EV}(p^0, p^1, I) - T(p^0, p^1, I).$$

Willig (1976) has claimed that under plausible parameter configurations the consumer surplus is a good approximation of the "true" welfare change as measured by the Hicksian equivalent and compensating variations. Let us consider a single price change (of good i). The author provides bounds on the percentage error made when approximating the true welfare indicator HCS by the MCS. These bounds depend on the income elasticity of demand and on the expenditure share of the good in question. However, even when the percentage error in approximating HCS by MCS is small, it may be the case that the percentage error of approximating the Hicksian deadweight loss by its Marshallian counterpart is very large. Hausman (1981) provides an example where while the first error is 3 percent, the second is 30 percent. For instance, consider, as before, a monopoly distortion of t units on good i. Its price goes from p_i^0 to $p_i^0 + t$, and the amount demanded from q_i^0 to q_i^1 (see figure 3.1, where good i is assumed to be normal). We have that $\text{MCS} = T + B + C$ and $\text{HCS} = T + B$. $\text{MDL} = B + C$ and $\text{HDL} = B$, since T is the profit collected by the monopolist. Notice that $\text{MCS} - \text{HCS} = \text{MDL} - \text{HDL}$, and denote it by Δ. It should be clear that at the same time that Δ/HCS is small, Δ/HDL may be large. In our case $\Delta = C, C/(T + B)$ may be small, while C/B may be large.

In order to obtain the percentage error of approximation small we need that the slopes of the Hicksian and Marshallian demand curves be close. This is an immediate consequence of our theorem for a large enough number of goods. From the Slutsky equation and with n goods,

$$\frac{\partial h_i}{\partial p_i} - \frac{\partial D_i}{\partial p_i} = q_i \frac{\partial D_i}{\partial I},$$

and theorem 3.1 provides conditions under which q_i stays bounded and $\partial D_i/\partial I$ becomes small, while $\partial h_i^n/\partial p_i$ does not degenerate to 0 or

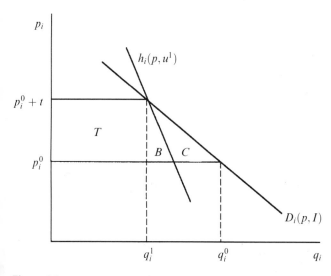

Figure 3.1

infinity as n grows. The order of magnitude of $|\partial D_i/\partial I|$ can be at most $1/\sqrt{n}$. When preferences are representable by additive separable utility functions, we know that the order of magnitude of $\partial D_i/\partial I$ is $1/n$.

The upper bound on the income effect in terms of the number of goods translates easily into an upper bound on the difference between the Marshallian and the Hicksian measure with n goods, Δ^n. This is done by integrating twice and using the Slutsky equation to obtain a bound on Δ^n of the type $d(\Delta p_i)^2/2\sqrt{n}$, where d is an appropriate constant and $\Delta p_i = |p_i^1 - p_i^0|$. On the other hand, the Hicksian deadweight loss is bounded below by $(\Delta p_i)^2 b/2$, where b is a lower bound on the slope of the Hicksian demand function. We conclude that the order of magnitude of $\Delta^n/|\mathrm{HDL}^n|$ is at most $1/\sqrt{n}$. Obviously this applies to $\Delta^n/|\mathrm{HCS}^n|$ also, since $|\mathrm{HCS}^n| \geq |\mathrm{HDL}^n|$. In the additively separable case, and under the assumptions of the theorem, all goods are normal, and it is possible to show that the order of magnitude of Δ^n is $1/n$. Proposition 3.1 states the results. (See exercise 3.7 for an example.)

PROPOSITION 3.1   Under the assumptions of theorem 3.1, suppose that only the price of good i changes. Then the order of magnitude of the percentage error in approximating the HDL by MDL($\Delta^n/|\mathrm{HDL}^n|$) is at most $1/\sqrt{n}$. In the additively separable case the order of magnitude of the percentage error is $1/n$.

When *multiple prices* change, it is well known that the Marshallian consumer surplus depends on what particular sequence of price changes one considers. Restricting attention to simple sequences, we show that for any ordering of the sequence of price changes the order of magnitude of the approximation error done in measuring the Hicksian consumer surplus by its Marshallian counterpart is at most $1/\sqrt{n}$. Proposition 3.2 states the results.

PROPOSITION 3.2   Under the assumptions of theorem 3.1, suppose that only k prices change. It follows then that the approximation error done in measuring the HCS (or the HDL), using any simple sequence π of price changes to compute the MCS, is bounded above by $\Delta p^\tau E \Delta p d/\sqrt{n}$, where d is an appropriate positive constant $\Delta p = |p^0 - p^1|$ and E is a matrix of ones. If preferences are additively separable, one can use $1/n$ instead of $1/\sqrt{n}$.

Summary

This chapter provides the foundation for the partial equilibrium analysis in which oligopoly theory is typically developed. It reviews the canonical partial equilibrium model for a group of differentiated products and supplies a rationale for it based on the idea of small expenditure shares and small income effects. The basic result is theorem 3.1, which provides conditions on preferences for income effects to be small giving bounds in terms of the number of goods. The conditions are that preferences cannot be very asymmetric and two goods can never be close to perfect substitutes, plus a curvature property of the utility function. As a corollary to this theorem, we have conditions under which demand is downward sloping and the Marshallian consumer surplus is, approximately, an acceptable measure of welfare change. The appendix to the chapter contains the basics of consumer surplus analysis.

Exercises

3.1. Consider a consumer with CES preferences over two goods. Find a sequence of budget sets such that as the market share on one good tends to zero the income effect stays constant. (*Hint:* Consider the cases of complement and substitute goods separately.)

*3.2. Consider the example of the Giffen good by Wold and Juréen (1953, p. 102) in which the consumer has a utility function over two goods given by $U(x, y) = \ln(x - 1) - 2\ln(2 - y)$, with domain $\{(x, y) \in R^2_{++} : x > 1, y < 2\}$. Let p_x and p_y be the prices of the goods x and y, respectively, let the income of the consumer be 1 and assume that $(p_x, p_y) \in P$ with $P = \{(p_x, p_y) \in R^2_{++} : 2p_y + p_x > 1 > p_x + p_y\}$.

a. Show that good x is Giffen if $1 > 2p_y$.

b. Find a sequence of prices for which good x remains Giffen even though its budget share tends to zero.

c. Check that when all expenditure shares are small (by replicating appropriately the number of goods available to the consumer) demand becomes downward sloping. (*Hint:* Suppose that there are N groups of two goods (x_i, y_i), total utility is given by $\sum_{i=1}^{N} -e^{-tU(x_i, y_i)}$ with $t > 1$ and the income available to the consumer in the N-group program is N. The prices of the x goods equal p_x and the prices of the y goods equal p_y with $(p_x, p_y) \in P$. The budget restriction is therefore $\sum_{i=1}^{N}(p_x x_i + p_y y_i) = N$. Show that the derivative of the demand function for good x_i with respect to its own price p_{x_i} equals (evaluated at $p_{x_i} = p_x$ and $p_{y_i} = p_y$ for all i) $\dfrac{1}{p_x}\left(\dfrac{2 - x}{N} - \dfrac{2t - 1}{t - 1}(x - 1)\left(1 - \dfrac{1}{N}\right)\right)$, where $x = 2 + (2p_y - 1)/p_x$. As N tends to infinity the slope of the demand function for good x converges to $-\dfrac{2t - 1}{t - 1}\dfrac{x - 1}{p_x}$.)

d. Does the UIP hold for the sequence of utility functions $\sum_{i=1}^{N} -e^{-tU(x_i, y_i)}$?

*3.3. Prove theorem 3.1 when preferences are additively separable.

3.4. A consumer has the following CES utility function: $U(q) = \sum_{i=1}^{n} \alpha_i q_i^{\rho}$ with $0 < \underline{\alpha} \le \alpha_i \le \bar{\alpha}$ for any i and $1 > \rho > 0$ for all i and n. Consider the optimization program $\max U(q)$ subject to $pq \le n$ with any price in the compact positive interval $[\underline{p}, \bar{p}]$. Find explicitly bounds on demands for any good (independent of n) and an upper bound for the income derivative of demand (as a function of n).

*3.5. Consider a particular case of theorem 3.1 with preferences additively separable by groups, $U(q) = \sum_{i=1}^{N} U^i(q^i)$, with $q^i \in R^l_+$. Show that the order of magnitude of the income derivative of demand for any good is $1/N$, where N is the number of groups and the normalized income. (*Hint:* See remark 2 in section 3.2 on the two-step procedure, and note that V'_i equals the marginal utility of income in the program $\max\{U^i(q^i) : p^i q^i = I^i, q^i \in R_+^l\}$. Go through the two-step procedure for the case $U^i(x, y) = x^{\alpha_i} y^{\beta_i}, (x, y) \in R_+^2$ and with (α_i, β_i) belonging to a compact subset of $\{(\alpha, \beta) \in R_{++}^2 : \alpha + \beta < 1\}$. Find explicit bounds for demands (independent of N) and for the income elasticity of demand for any good.

3.6. Consider the canonical partial equilibrium model with a concave utility function U for the differentiated sector. Show that gross surplus $U(D(p))$ is decreasing in prices whenever the differentiated goods are normal (with respect to the utility function U). (*Hint:* Consider $U(D(p))$ as the solution to $\max_u \{u - e(p, u)\}$, where $e(p, u)$ is the expenditure function associated to U.)

3.7. A consumer has utility function $U(q) = \sum_{i=1}^{n} \log q_i$. Firms produce goods at constant marginal cost equal to 1 and prices are competitive except for the first good. All the prices except the price for the first good equal 1. The initial price of good one p_1 is 2. Evaluate the welfare gain of having p_1 decreased to the competitive level using the Marshallian and the Hicksian measures. Show that the difference between them is of the order of $1/n$. Check that for $n = 3$ the percentage error in approximating the Hicksian consumer surplus (deadweight loss) by its Marshallian counterpart is about 11 percent (31 percent). For $n = 10$ the numbers are 3 percent (11 percent). (See Vives 1987.)

4   Quantity Competition: The Cournot Model

The classical model of oligopoly proposed by Cournot concerns a finite, and typically small, number of producers competing in a homogeneous product market. Consumers are assumed to be passive and are described by an aggregate demand function or by an inverse demand function. In *Cournot competition* firms select independently the quantities of production to bring to the market. These output levels jointly determine the market price according to the inverse demand function. The process by which the market clears is left unspecified or assumed to be done by an auctioneer. We delay until chapters 5 and 7 a discussion of alternative interpretations of Cournot competition. A Cournot market defines a game with strategy spaces being quantities of production and with payoffs as revenues minus costs. A Cournot equilibrium is just a Nash equilibrium of the described game.

In section 4.1 we describe formally the model and the existence of equilibrium is addressed together with a discussion of the character of competition (in terms of the slope of best replies) in Cournot markets. Section 4.2 studies smooth Cournot games and deals with uniqueness and stability properties of equilibria. Comparative static and entry results are provided in section 4.3. Section 4.4 reviews briefly large markets.

4.1 The Model and Existence of Equilibrium

Let inverse demand be given by $P : R_+ \to R_+$, a continuous decreasing function of total output Q with $P(Q) = 0$ for all Q large enough. Denote by $D(\cdot)$ the demand function. Firm $i, i = 1, \ldots, n$, can produce according to the cost function $C_i(\cdot)$, where $C_i : R_+ \to R_+$ is increasing and lower semicontinuous.[1]

The strategy space of firm i is an interval of possible outputs. A Cournot equilibrium is just a Nash equilibrium of the game where the payoff to firm i is $\pi_i = P(Q)q_i - C_i(q_i)$, with q_i denoting the output of firm i and $Q = \sum_{i=1}^{n} q_i$. The payoff to firm i depends on its own output, q_i, and on the aggregate output of rivals, $Q_{-i} : \pi_i(q_i, Q_{-i}) = R(q_i, Q_{-i}) - C_i(q_i)$, where $R(q_i, Q_{-i}) = P(Q)q_i$ is the revenue of the firm. In the differentiable case denote by MR_i the marginal revenue of firm i, $P(Q) + q_i P'(Q)$. It is worth noting that with positive costs firm i may lose money for some choice of output if other producers bring to the market an aggregate output high enough.

In order to use the standard existence theorem (theorem 2.1), profits π_i have to be quasiconcave with respect to q_i. This is quite restrictive, particularly because nonconvexities in costs are not uncommon and very convex demand functions cannot be ruled out. Examples of duopoly models in which no Cournot equilibrium (in pure strategies) exists are easily produced. (See Roberts and Sonnenschein 1977 and Friedman 1983, pp. 67–69, for examples where firms can produce at no cost and where demands arise from well-behaved preferences.) The lack of quasiconcavity of payoffs introduces discontinuities in the best-response functions of firms and makes possible the nonexistence of equilibrium. Nevertheless, as we saw in section 2.3, there are three types of existence results which may apply to the Cournot model and which do not require quasiconcave payoffs.

First, the Bamon/Fraysée-Novshek existence result allows for general cost functions but requires demand to be well behaved in order to obtain (strongly) decreasing best replies and use the fixed point theorem 2.7. Strongly decreasing best replies are implied by π_i displaying strictly decreasing differences in (q_i, Q_{-i}) for all i. With smooth revenues this is implied by the usual downward-sloping marginal revenue condition: $\partial MR_i / \partial Q_{-i} = P'(Q) + q_i P''(Q) < 0$ (assume that P is twice-continuously differentiable with $P' < 0$ whenever $P > 0$). Costs are unrestricted (and need to be only lower semicontinuous).[2] The (strictly) decreasing marginal revenue assumption is a common assumption which implies, as we have argued in section 2.2, that best replies Ψ_i are (strongly) decreasing. A weaker sufficient condition (see exercise 4.2 based on Amir 1996) implying that Ψ_i is strongly decreasing for all i is that $P(\cdot)$ be strictly decreasing and log-concave (and C_i strictly increasing for each i).[3] In conclusion, under either set of assumptions, the best-reply correspondences Ψ_i are upper hemicontinuous and strongly decreasing for all i, and theorem 2.7 implies then the existence of an equilibrium. The second approach to existence deals with the cases in which the Cournot game is a supermodular game. The following assumptions turn a n-firm Cournot game into a log-supermodular game (Amir 1996): Firm i has constant unit cost c_i up to capacity k_i and the net price $P(\cdot) - \max_i\{c_i\}$ is log-convex in the range $[0, \Sigma_i k_i]$.[4] Best replies are increasing under these conditions, although this is not considered to be the "normal" case in Cournot games. To gain some intuition for this result, suppose that inverse demand is log-convex and that there are no costs. Then demand is so convex that higher outputs of the rivals enhance the marginal revenue of the own output of the firm. Furthermore a duopoly Cournot game with decreasing best replies, when one firm's strategy set is given the reverse order, is a supermodular game. (Alternatively, as stated in remark 13 of section 2.2.3, to obtain existence, apply Tarski's theorem—theorem 2.2—to the composite best-reply map.) Decreasing best replies are implied by π_i exhibiting decreasing differences in (q_i, Q_{-i}). With smooth revenues this is in turn implied by the usual downward-sloping marginal revenue condition: $\partial MR_i/\partial Q_{-i} = P'(Q) + q_i P''(Q) \le 0$. Costs are unrestricted (and need to be only lower semicontinuous). As stated above a weaker sufficient condition implying decreasing best replies is that $P(\cdot)$ be strictly decreasing and log-concave (with C_i strictly increasing for each i).

Finally, the Tarski-Mac Manus-Roberts/Sonnenschein result allows for a general (upper-semicontinuous) downward-sloping inverse demand[5] $P(\cdot)$ but restricts the cost functions to be identical and convex.[6] The symmetry assumptions imply that the best replies of firms are identical. The homogeneity of the product yields that the best reply of a firm, $\Psi_i(\cdot)$, depends only on the aggregate production of rivals. It follows then from the assumptions that all the jumps in the best reply of a firm must be up (i.e., best replies are quasi-increasing).[7] Existence of symmetric equilibria follows then from Tarski's intersection point theorem (theorem 2.6) and its corollary (see section 2.3.1).[8] In a smooth symmetric market with $P' < 0$ (and with firms facing a capacity constraint), existence of a symmetric equilibrium can be obtained under the weaker requirement that $C'' - P' > 0$ in the relevant range (Amir and Lambson 1996). This is accomplished by showing that the correspondence φ, which assigns to Q_{-i}, $(q_i + Q_{-i})(n-1)/n$, where $q_i \in \Psi_i(Q_{-i})$, is strongly increasing and then using Tarski's theorem. As stated in section 2.3.1, symmetric equilibria are given by fixed points of this correspondence. The assumptions imply that Ψ_i has slopes larger than -1 (exercise 4.5), and this means that all selections of $\Psi_i(Q_{-i}) + Q_{-i}$, are (strictly) increasing. In fact, under the assumptions no asymmetric equilibrium can exist, according to the remark following theorem 2.8, because Ψ_i has slopes larger than -1.

A discussion of the slope of best replies in Cournot markets seems in order. In Cournot games best replies are typically thought to be decreasing, but this need not be the case always (although it holds with concave demand). Indeed, with demand of constant elasticity, a classical example, the output of a firm is first increasing and then decreasing in the output of the rival (see Bulow et al. 1985b and exercise 4.3 for other examples). We have even seen above that best replies can be monotonically increasing for all firms in a Cournot game. For example, consider a Cournot duopoly with $P(\cdot) = (Q + 1)^{-\alpha}$, for $\alpha > 2$ and zero costs with no capacity limits. Then the Cournot game is log-supermodular, and best-reply functions are increasing and have a unique (symmetric) intersection. However, introducing linear costs makes best replies nonmonotonic (and consequently the game no longer is log-supermodular). Introducing costs may change an "unusual" strategic complements Cournot game into a "usual" strategic substitutes Cournot game (Amir 1996). The presence of costs (even constant unit costs) biases best replies into being decreasing, even though from the revenue side strategic complementarity would prevail. From the revenue side, $\log P(\cdot)$ convex (concave) implies increasing (decreasing) differences of log-revenue $\log P(Q)q_i$ in (q_i, Q_{-i}).[9] However, $\log P(\cdot)$ convex is easily transformed into $\log(P(\cdot) - c_i)$ concave (implying decreasing differences of log-profit $\log(P(Q) - c_i)q_i$ in (q_i, Q_{-i})) for $c_i > 0$.[10] The slope of best responses has important implications for comparative static analysis (see section 4.3) and stability of equilibria (see section 4.2 and exercise 4.3).

4.2 Characterization of Smooth Cournot Games

Let us consider a Cournot market where both inverse demand and costs are smooth (both of class C^2), $P' < 0$ (in the interval for which $P > 0$), the decreasing marginal revenue property $(P' + q_iP'' \leq 0)$

holds, and $C_i'' - P' > 0$ for all i. Under these conditions the profit of firm i is strictly concave in q_i.[11] The best reply of firm i to Q_{-i} is the unique solution to the first-order condition:

$$\frac{\partial \pi_i}{\partial q_i} = P(Q) + q_i P'(Q) - C_i'(q_i) = 0,$$

whenever the solution is positive and it is zero otherwise. It follows that the best-reply function of firm i, $r_i(\cdot)$, is smooth when positive and its slope is in the interval $(-1, 0]$:

$$r_i'(Q_{-i}) = -\frac{\partial^2 \pi_i / \partial q_i \partial Q_{-i}}{\partial^2 \pi_i / (\partial q_i)^2} = -\frac{P'(Q) + q_i P''(Q)}{2P'(Q) + q_i P''(Q) - C_i''(q_i)}.$$

Under these conditions the best-reply map $r(\cdot) \equiv (r_1(\cdot), \dots, r_n(\cdot))$ is not necessarily a contraction. For this to be the case a sufficient condition (see section 2.5) is that

$$\frac{\partial^2 \pi_i}{(\partial q_i)^2} + (n-1) \left| \frac{\partial^2 \pi_i}{\partial q_i \partial Q_{-i}} \right| < 0 \qquad \text{for all } i.$$

Or equivalently, given that $P' + q_i P'' < 0$, $P' + (n-2)|P' + q_i P''| < C_i''$, for all i. This is a very strong assumption (which, as we know, would ensure dominance solvability of the Cournot game and, consequently, uniqueness and global stability). For example, with concave demand and constant marginal costs it requires $(3-n)P' + q_i P''(2-n) < 0$, and therefore it is satisfied only for $n = 2$ (see also exercise 4.7).[12] If the Cournot game is supermodular, then the stability results obtained for the discrete Cournot tâtonnement hold (theorem 2.10).[13]

However, uniqueness of equilibrium follows under our assumptions from theorem 2.8 given that the best-response function for any firm has nonpositive slope larger than -1. A direct proof of this result following Selten's idea of the cumulative best reply is presented here (see also Szidarovszky and Yakowitz 1977). Let $\emptyset_i(Q)$ be the optimal output of firm i which is consistent with an aggregate output Q.[14] It is the unique solution, given our assumptions, to $q_i = r_i(Q - q_i)$. (See figure 4.1.)

When positive $\emptyset_i$ is smooth and $\emptyset_i' \leq 0$ because $\emptyset_i' = r_i'/(1 + r_i')$ and $-1 < r_i' \leq 0$. Therefore $\sum_{i=1}^{n} \emptyset_i$ will be decreasing in Q and will intersect only once the $45°$ line.[15] This will give the total aggregate equilibrium output Q^* which determines the Cournot equilibrium.

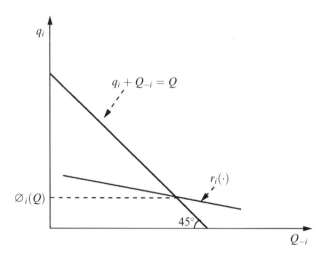

Figure 4.1

We have seen therefore that $P' + q_iP'' \leq 0$ and $C''_i - P' > 0$ for all i are sufficient conditions to ensure uniqueness of equilibrium. In particular, costs need not be convex. However, to require that $P' + q_iP'' \leq 0$ holds globally is strong and unnecessary. All that is needed for the result to obtain is for $P' + q_iP'' \leq 0$ to hold along the best reply $r_i(\cdot)$ of the firm (or what amounts to the same, along the first-order condition $\partial \pi_i/\partial q_i = 0$). This is true if $P(\cdot)$ is log-concave. We have then that sufficient conditions for uniqueness of equilibrium (and π_i being strictly quasiconcave in q_i) are $P' < 0$, $P(\cdot)$ log-concave, and $C''_i - P' > 0$ for all i.[16]

As should be clear from our discussion in section 2.7, the above is not the most general approach to uniqueness. The conditions given for uniqueness are sufficient but not necessary. Restricting attention to regular and interior Cournot equilibria of a smooth market where profit functions are quasiconcave, there is a unique Cournot equilibrium if and only if the Jacobian determinant of minus marginal profits, $|J|$, is positive at all candidate equilibria. This follows directly from the index approach to uniqueness. Kolstad and Mathiesen (1987) show the result allowing for noninterior equilibria. We have that

$$|J| = \left\{ 1 - \sum_i \frac{P' + q_iP''}{C''_i - P'} \right\} \prod_{i=1}^n (C''_i - P'),$$

where the sum is over firms with positive output (say, n). For example, assuming that

$$C_i'' - P' > 0 \qquad \text{for all } i \text{ with } q_i > 0, \tag{4.1}$$

a sufficient condition for $|J| > 0$ is that

$$\frac{P' + q_i P''}{C_i'' - P'} < \frac{1}{n} \qquad \text{for all } i. \tag{4.2}$$

If (4.1) and (4.2) hold at all candidate equilibria then equilibrium must be unique. With (4.1) holding condition (4.2) is just

$$\frac{\partial^2 \pi_i}{(\partial q_i)^2} + (n-1)\frac{\partial^2 \pi_i}{\partial q_i \partial Q_{-i}} = P' - C_i'' + n(P' + q_i P'') < 0;$$

that is, the own effect on marginal profitability of a change in q_i dominates (in algebraic terms) the sum of the cross effects of similar changes of other firms' output.

The conditions $P' + q_i P'' \leq 0$ and $C_i'' - P' > 0$ for all i were identified by Hahn (1962) to ensure the (local) stability of the equilibrium with respect to continuous best-reply dynamics. This requires best replies to be downward sloping. Conditions (4.1) and (4.2) are sufficient to ensure (local) stability if best replies are upward sloping, $P' + q_i P'' \geq 0$ for all i, but if inequality (4.1) is reversed, with (4.2) holding, then the equilibrium is unstable. Unstable equilibria obtain when the own effect on marginal profitability of a change in q_i is dominated by the sum of the cross effects of changes of other firms' output. The equilibrium can also be stable with firms with different signs for the slope of best responses. This happens provided that for all i $((P' - C_i'')/(n-2)) < P' + q_i P'' < (|P' - C_i''|/n)$ (see Seade 1980a and exercise 4.6).[17] It is worth noting also that if the Cournot game we consider is strictly supermodular, then the global stability results for continuous systems obtained in theorem 2.11 hold. In particular, if the equilibrium is unique it will be (globally) stable.

In the smooth Cournot market which we are considering, let us suppose that there is a unique and interior equilibrium characterized by the FOC $(\partial \pi_i / \partial q_i) = 0$. This equation can be expressed in the usual form

$$\frac{p - C_i'}{p} = \frac{s_i}{\eta},$$

where s_i is the share of firm's i in total output, q_i/Q, and η is the elasticity of demand ($\eta = -p/QP'$).

One of the reasons why the Cournot model has been so popular and has survived its critics is that it provides reasonable and intuitive economic implications for pricing in oligopolistic markets. Another main reason is its tractability.

The margin over marginal cost of firm i increases with the firm's market share and decreases with the market elasticity of demand. In fact η/s_i can be understood as the elasticity of the perceived or residual demand of firm i. The markup over marginal cost is decreasing with η/s_i. Firms enjoy market power in the Cournot model in relation to their size, which is directly related to their productive efficiency. Nevertheless, as is usual with Nash equilibria, firms do not attain a Pareto optimal outcome in equilibrium. That is, the Cournot equilibrium is not efficient from the point of view of the firms. It induces firms to produce too much. The reason is that a firm, when considering to change its output, does not take into account that the resulting change in price will affect other firms. If firms where to maximize joint profits, the usual monopoly formula would apply:

$$\frac{p - C_i'}{p} = \frac{1}{\eta}.$$

The Cournot pricing formula is derived equating the *Lerner index* of monopoly power of firm i, $L_i = (p - C_i')/p$, with the inverse of its perceived elasticity of demand, s_i/η. At the market level we can relate an aggregate Lerner index with the Herfindahl index of concentration, $H = \sum_{i=1}^{n} s_i^2$. Indeed, weighting the Lerner indexes by market shares and aggregating over firms, we obtain

$$\sum_{i=1}^{n} s_i L_i = \frac{H}{\eta}.$$

The Cournot model therefore gives support to the idea that concentrated markets will have more important departures from marginal cost. It is worth noting that H may increase both because the number of active firms decreases and because firms have more unequal shares. This is so since the shares of the firms are squared and larger firms carry more weight. Both "inequality" and "numbers" affect the departures of Cournot pricing from marginal costs. When all firms are identical, the pricing formula can be restated as

$$\frac{p - C'}{p} = \frac{1}{n\eta},$$

since the (assumed) unique equilibrium will be symmetric. For a given demand elasticity, the more firms there are in the market, the more the price is closer to marginal cost. Indeed, only numbers matter here, $H = 1/n$. From the preceding analysis it does not follow that a higher concentration, as measured by H, will translate into lower welfare, as measured by the total (Marshallian) surplus $TS = \int_0^Q P(Z)\,dZ - \sum_{i=1}^n C_i(q_i)$, the sum of consumer surplus and profits (see chapter 3). The inverse relationship between concentration and welfare holds, for example, with identical firms with constant marginal costs but does not need to hold in the presence of economies of scale or asymmetric costs. Indeed, in the former case TS is increasing in n and $H = 1/n$. However, with firms of different efficiencies welfare is enhanced if low-cost firms gain market share at the expense of high-cost firms. This redistribution of total output raises both welfare and concentration. Farrell and Shapiro (1990a) show that a small change in total output Q raises total surplus TS if and only if $\Delta Q/Q + \frac{1}{2}(\Delta H/H) > 0$ (exercise 4.8). This means that for a given percentage change in total output, welfare is more likely to rise if H increases. Furthermore it is possible to show also that small output changes Δq_i induce movements of H and TS of opposite sign if and only if $0 \leq (\sum_{i=1}^n s_i \Delta q_i)/\Delta Q \leq H$ (Farrell and Shapiro 1990b; see exercise 4.8). This holds, for example, when the market share of the only firm which output changes is small. In fact, for any redistribution of output among the oligopolists, H and TS move together. It is easy to construct examples of Cournot markets in which dropping one (inefficient) firm welfare is improved by lowering Q and increasing H (exercise 4.9).[18]

4.3 Comparative Statics and Entry

4.3.1 Comparative Statics

The smooth Cournot model has comparative static properties that accord to intuition provided that some regularity conditions hold. Suppose that the costs of firm i are affected by a parameter θ_i, $C_i(q_i; \theta_i)$ in such a way that an increase in its level increases the total and marginal cost of the firm of producing any output. This parameter could be a tax rate on the firm's output or (its inverse $1/\theta_i$) could be the result of the firm's investment in cost reduction or R&D. Suppose that at all candidate equilibria conditions (4.1) and (4.2) of section 4.2 are met (which ensure uniqueness of equilibrium). Dixit (1986) shows that provided that the equilibrium is locally stable (e.g., this holds if locally for all i best replies are decreasing, increasing, or the contraction condition holds), then an increase in θ_i, which affects negatively firm's i marginal profitability, in equilibrium decreases the firm's output as well as total output while increasing the profits of rival firms. Furthermore, if the best-response function of firm j is decreasing (increasing), an increase in θ_i increases (decreases) the output of firm j; if best responses for all firms other than i are decreasing, then the profits of firm i decrease with θ_i. (See exercise 4.10.)

Stability-type assumptions are needed to ensure "natural" comparative statics. The reason why intuitive comparative statics results and stability properties tend to be associated (although not always, as we will see later) is easily understood graphically in a duopoly example. An increase in θ_i will shift inward the best-response function of firm i and produce the described effects provided that best responses are decreasing and have a "stable" intersection (see figure 4.2a). The slope of the best reply of firm i is irrelevant in terms of the effects on q_j (upward-sloping best replies for firm i are depicted with discontinuous lines in the figure).

If $r_j(\cdot)$ were to be increasing, then q_j would decrease rather than increase when θ_i increases (see figure 4.2b). If $r_i(\cdot)$ and $r_j(\cdot)$ were not to have a stable intersection, then the increase in θ_i would increase q_i and reduce q_j (see figure 4.3). What yields "intuitive" comparative statics in the Cournot model is the conjunction of stability conditions and downward-sloping best responses. It is worth to remark that downward-sloping best responses are not necessary for stability.[19]

Let us restrict attention now to symmetric models. Assuming that the profit function of a firm is smooth and strictly quasiconcave in its own action, we have a well-defined best-response function $r_i(\cdot; \theta)$ for any firm. In this framework it is easy to show uniqueness of equilibrium if a symmetric version of condition (4.2) holds. Symmetric equilibria will be then the solution to $f(q) \equiv r_i((n-1)q) - q = 0$. Since $f(0) = r_i(0) > 0$ and $f(q) < 0$ for q large enough, the equilibrium will be unique (according to the uniqueness analysis of section

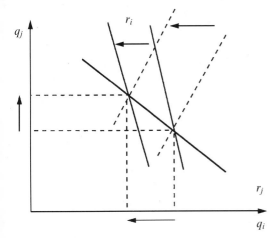

Figure 4.2a

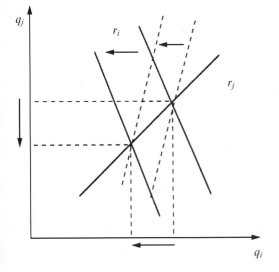

Figure 4.2b

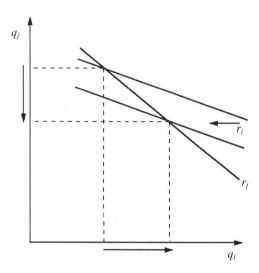

Figure 4.3

2.7) if $f = 0$ implies that $f' < 0$. That is, $r_i'((n-1)q^*) < 1/(n-1)$ if q^* is a symmetric equilibrium. This is easily seen equivalent to a symmetric version of condition (4.2),

$$P'(nq^*) - C''(q^*) + n(P'(nq^*) + q^*P''(nq^*)) < 0.$$

This condition is compatible with upward-sloping best responses, that is, with $P' + qP'' > 0$.

Let $E = -QP''(Q)/P'(Q)$ (the elasticity of the *slope* of inverse demand). Condition (4.2) reads then $E + C''/P' < 1 + n$. Whenever condition (4.2) holds together with condition (4.1) of section 4.2, $1 - C''/P' > 0$, at any symmetric equilibrium q^*, then there is a unique and locally stable symmetric equilibrium.[20] I will assume these conditions to hold at any symmetric equilibrium q^*. Furthermore the global version of condition (4.1) implies that no asymmetric equilibria can exist (section 4.1).

Suppose now that costs depend on a parameter θ, $C(q; \theta)$ and, to be more concrete, that θ represents an excise tax on the product of any firm: $C(q; \theta) = c(q) + \theta q$. Seade (1987) shows that if the stability conditions are met, (4.1) and (4.2), an increase in θ decreases the individual output of a firm and increases the market price as expected. (This result is obviously consistent with the result obtained above about comparative statics on extremal equilibria when allowing for multiple symmetric equilibria.) If $E + C''/P' > 1$, then tax overshifting occurs. That is, the price increases by more than the tax increase. This should come as no surprise in an oligopoly context where firms enjoy market power. In fact, with demand of constant elasticity, we have that $E = 1 + 1/\eta$, and therefore tax overshifting occurs *always* if marginal costs are constant.

What seems less intuitive, or perhaps even "perverse," is that a tax increase may lead to an increase in the profits of all firms. This will happen if (and only if) $E + C''/P' > 2$. In the constant elasticity-constant marginal cost case the condition amounts to demand being inelastic $\eta < 1$. The economic explanation of this result is that the tax increase causes a positive externality effect for firms, since it raises the market price substantially. The perverse profit result is consistent with (locally) decreasing best replies at the equilibrium point q^*, that is, $P'(nq^*) + q^* P''(nq^*) < 0$. This inequality is easily seen to be equivalent to $E < n$, and therefore it is consistent with $E > 1$ for $1 < E < n$. A sufficient condition to rule out the "perverse" profit result is to assume an elasticity of the *slope* of inverse demand strictly less than one $(E < 1)$. Then $E > 2 - C''/P'$ and $E < 1$ would imply $0 > 1 - C''/P'$, contradicting the first stability condition (4.1).[21]

Another illustration of the principle that both stability conditions and decreasing best replies are needed to confirm the common intuitions about the Cournot model is provided by the comparative static analysis with respect to the number of firms. Still assuming that the stability conditions hold, Seade (1980b) shows that increasing the number of firms *increases* the output per firm if (and only if) $n + 1 - C''/P' > E > n$. In the constant elasticity (η) and constant marginal cost case this amounts to $n^{-1} < \eta < (n-1)^{-1}$. This perverse result is not possible if $E < 1$. In fact the result is not compatible with (locally) decreasing best replies $(E < n$ or, equivalently, $P' + qP'' > 0)$. In order for further entry to increase, the equilibrium output per firm is necessary that a firm responds to an aggregate output increase by rivals increasing production itself. When $E < n$ (i.e., with locally decreasing best responses), Ruffin (1971) had shown already that individual output would decrease with new entry when $E < n$. Seade (1987) also shows that as expected, total output (strictly) increases, and profits per firm (strictly) decrease with new entry if equilibria are stable. (See exercise 4.11.)

The previous comparative static results have been obtained with the usual approach imposing strong regularity conditions like concavity or quasiconcavity of payoffs as well as conditions ensuring the uniqueness of equilibrium. This approach may obscure sometimes the results with the use of unnecessary assumptions or even mislead the reader. For example, in the presence of multiple equilibria, some ambiguity is introduced in the previous comparative static analysis with the number of firms n because increasing n either may make disappear the equilibrium considered or introduce more. This ambiguity is eliminated performing a global analysis with "monotone comparative statics/supermodular" methods as described below. With these methods comparative statics results on (symmetric) extremal equilibria are easily derived. In asymmetric games we need to work with a supermodular game. We describe first the case of (potentially asymmetric) supermodular games and then turn to the analysis of symmetric Cournot equilibria.

For the case of two firms and decreasing best replies, we know that the Cournot game is supermodular (reversing the sign in the strategy space of one firm). In this case an increase in θ_i decreases (increases) output and profits for firm i (j, $j \neq i$) at the extremal Cournot equilibria (best (worst) for firm i and worst (best) for firm j ($j \neq i$)). This follows immediately, noting that an increase in θ_i increases marginal costs of firm i. This means that the cost function $C(q_i; \theta_i)$ displays increasing differences in (q_i, θ_i), and therefore the profit function $\pi_i(q_i; \theta_i)$ displays decreasing differences in (q_i, θ_i). The result for outputs follows then from the comparative static analysis of supermodular games in section 2.2.3 (see exercise 2.13 in particular). The results for profits is immediate given that profits of a firm decrease with the output of the rival. We have argued in section 4.1 why decreasing best replies tend to be considered the normal case under Cournot competition. However, we presented also a class of cases for which a n-firm Cournot game was (log-)supermodular. In this case, if θ is a parameter that raises marginal revenue or decreases marginal cost for any firm, then the largest and smallest Cournot equilibrium output vectors will be increasing in θ (because for all i π_i will display increasing differences in (a_i, θ) or, in the smooth version, $\partial^2 \pi_i / \partial q_i \partial \theta \geq 0$; see the comparative statics discussion in section 2.2.3).

Let us turn attention now to symmetric models. We know from section 4.1 that in a smooth market a symmetric equilibrium (and no asymmetric equilibrium) exists when $P' < 0$ and $C'' - P' > 0$ in the relevant range. Under these assumptions we know also that all selections from the correspondence φ, which assigns to Q_{-i}, $(q_i + Q_{-i})(n-1)/n$, where $q_i \in \Psi_i(Q_{-i})$, are increasing. Comparative statics on extremal equilibria follow easily. The largest (smallest) equilibrium output for $n - 1$ firms, $(n - 1)\bar{q}((n - 1)\underline{q})$, is given by the largest (smallest) fixed point of the largest (smallest) selection of φ, $\bar{\varphi}(\varphi)$. Suppose that θ is a parameter that decreases marginal cost (i.e., $C(q_i, \theta)$ has decreasing differences in (q_i, θ)). Then the largest, $\bar{\Psi}_i(Q_{-i}; \theta)$, and the smallest, $\underline{\Psi}_i(Q_{-i}; \theta)$, best replies of any firm are increasing in θ (see theorem 2.3 and the monopoly example at the end of section 2.2.2). The same holds therefore for the largest and smallest selections of φ, $\bar{\varphi}$, and $\underline{\varphi}$, respectively. It follows then that the largest and the smallest symmetric Cournot equilibrium outputs are increasing in θ (see remark 17 in section 2.3.1). Suppose now that we have a well-defined best-response function $r_i(\cdot; \theta)$ for any firm and that $\partial^2 C / \partial q_i \partial \theta < 0$. Then r_i is strictly increasing in θ, and extremal equilibrium outputs are strictly increasing in θ.

One can similarly derive comparative static results with respect to the number of firms (Amir and Lambson 1996). Indeed, the total output at extremal Cournot equilibria is increasing in n. This follows because $\bar{\varphi}$ and $\underline{\varphi}$ are increasing in n, and therefore $(n - 1)\bar{q}(n)$ and $(n - 1)\underline{q}(n)$ are increasing in n. Now, since from the assumptions made the slopes of $\bar{\Psi}_i$ and $\underline{\Psi}_i$ are larger than -1, we have that the total largest (smallest) equilibrium output $(n - 1)\bar{q} + \bar{\Psi}_i((n - 1)\bar{q})$ $((n - 1)\underline{q} + \underline{\Psi}_i((n - 1)\underline{q})$ is increasing in n. It can also be shown that profits per firm decrease with n at extremal equilibria (exercise 4.11). Individual output at extremal equilibria, however, can increase or decrease with n. For example, if P is log-concave, then there is a unique symmetric equilibrium (see section 4.2) and extremal individual outputs are decreasing in n. The explanation in this case (the profits of a firm are strictly quasiconcave in its own output and) is that the best-reply function of a firm is decreasing (see section 4.2), and we know that $(n - 1)\bar{q}(n)$ and $(n - 1)\underline{q}(n)$ are increasing in n. Conversely, if P is log-convex and costs are zero, then we know that the game is log-supermodular (see section 4.1). It follows that extremal best replies are increasing and that consequently extremal individual outputs are increasing in n.

4.3.2 Entry

Another question is how many firms will enter a market when there is a fixed cost of entry $F > 0$? Suppose that for any n there is a unique, symmetric equilibrium with associated profits per firm π_n.

At a free-entry equilibrium with n^* firms in the market, each firm makes nonnegative profits, $\pi_{n^*} \geq F$, and further entry would result in negative profits, $\pi_{n^*+1} < F$. Under the first condition, a firm that decides to enter the market does at least as well as staying out (and making zero profits). Under the second, a firm that stays out is (strictly) worse off than by choosing to enter. More formally, the free-entry equilibrium is the (pure-strategy subgame-perfect equilibrium) outcome of a two-stage game where first firms decide whether or not to enter (and pay the entry cost), and then there is Cournot competition. In a subgame-perfect equilibrium (SPE), given any decisions at the first stage, a Nash equilibrium follows at the second stage. This rules out incredible threats. A SPE requires strategies to form a Nash equilibrium starting at any subgame. Nash equilibria only require optimizing behavior along the equilibrium path. (See section 4.4.1 for more on two-stage games and applications of the SPE concept.) With stable equilibria we know that π_n is (strictly) decreasing in n, and therefore, at most, there is one free-entry equilibrium (there will be one, indeed, if π_n tends to 0 as n tends to infinity). (See exercise 4.12 for a linear example.)

Will the market provide the right amount of entry from a welfare (total surplus) point of view? We will assume that the planner can control the entry of firms but not their pricing behavior (this is called sometimes second best structural regulation). For a given (symmetric) Cournot equilibrium q_n we have that $TS_n = \int_0^{nq_n} P(Q)\,dQ - n(C(q_n) + F)$. The welfare benchmark is then given by any n that maximizes TS_n. Two forces related to the external effects provoked by entry are at work. On the one hand, firms do not capture the entire consumer surplus generated by their production because they can not price discriminate. This means that firms will be too cautious when entering. On the other hand, there is typically a business-stealing effect: When a new firm enters the output of each incumbent diminishes (i.e., q_n is decreasing in n). This fact, with prices above marginal costs, provides a tendency toward excess entry. Mankiw and Whinston (1986) and Suzumura and Kiyono (1987) find that the latter force tends to dominate, resulting in excess entry (see also von Weizsäcker 1980 and Perry 1984). According to Mankiw and Whinston (1986), if $P' < 0$ and costs are convex, there is business stealing and total output increases with n, we have too little entry at most by one firm (i.e., $n^* \geq n^s - 1$, where n^* is the equilibrium number of firms and n^s the optimal one).[22] This means that ignoring the integer constraint, there is always excess entry. Indeed, treating n as a continuous variable, $\pi_{n^*} = F$ at the free-entry equilibrium, while at the optimum $\partial TS_{n^s}/\partial n = 0$. It is easily seen that $\partial TS_n/\partial n = \pi_n - F + (P(nq_n) - C'(q_n))n\partial q_n/\partial n$. Now, at a Cournot equilibrium, $P(nq_n) - C'(q_n) > 0$, and if there is business stealing, $\partial q_n/\partial n < 0$. It follows that at the optimum $\pi_{n^s} > F$. But for stable equilibria π_n is (strictly) decreasing with n. We conclude that $n^s < n^*$.

The previous argument shows that the marginal contribution to surplus of the entry of a firm consists of its profits $\pi_n - F$ (direct contribution) plus the negative impact of the output reduction $n\partial q_n/\partial n$ (due to business stealing) times the margin over marginal costs $p - C'$. At the free-entry equilibrium $\pi_{n^*} = F$, and therefore $\partial TS_{n^*}/\partial n < 0$.

It is worth remarking that increases in the size of the market tend to increase the (free-entry) equilibrium number of firms n^*, and as the size of the market grows without bound, n^* tends to infinity. For example, if demand has constant elasticity $P(Q) = A/Q$. with $A > 0$, and marginal costs are constant with $c > 0$, we have that $n^* = (A/F)^{1/2}$. Increasing the size of the market A, n^* increases less than proportionately because of the increased pressure on margins when there are more firms in the market. (The next section develops this theme further.) It is not always true that increasing the size of the market concentration diminishes. Indeed, in the constant demand elasticity example, if costs for any firm are concave, $C(q) = q^{1/r}$ with $1 < r \leq 2$, then n^* is bounded above by $r/(r-1)$. This means that the market is a "natural oligopoly"; that is, no matter how large the market is, only a finite number of firms can survive. This situation tends to arise also when firms compete in fixed outlays to gain market share and when the latter is very sensitive to the effort of the firms. (See Sutton 1991; exercise 6.15 provides an example in a product differentiated context.)

The excess entry result has been obtained in a context of symmetry, but one of the potentially beneficial effects of competition is the selection of efficient firms and the weeding out of inefficient ones. If cost asymmetries are taken into consideration, it can be seen that the entry externality is more favorable for welfare. For example, there is now a business-shifting effect of entry that goes from high-cost to low-cost incumbents provided that demand is convex. Similarly the effects of asymmetries between the cost level of the entrant and incumbents, the effects of entry on the distribution of costs in the industry, and, in the extreme, the inducement to exit for inefficient incumbents tend to improve the entry externality (see Vickers 1995 and exercise 4.13). (The issue of optimal entry with product differentiation will be pursued in section 6.6 in a monopolistically competitive context and in the appendix to chapter 6 in relation to complementary products.)

4.4 Large Markets

One of the attractive properties of the Cournot model is that the margins over marginal costs tend to decrease with decreases in the concentration of the markets. In fact, if all firms are identical in a symmetric Cournot equilibrium, the margin over marginal cost is inversely related to the number of firms. This suggests that in the limit a price-taking outcome should prevail, price equaling marginal cost. Nevertheless, the argument is only valid under nonincreasing returns to scale. As n grows with fixed demand, the output of each firm must tend to zero at a symmetric equilibrium. If average costs are U-shaped, for example, then price can not approach marginal cost (Novshek 1980).

With convex costs the typical rate of convergence of the price-cost margin to zero as the number of firms grows is $1/n$. Under our maintained assumptions demand is bounded by $D(0)$ and therefore at a symmetric equilibrium, $(D(0)/n) \geq q_n$. It follows that the order of magnitude of a firm's output will be at most $1/n$. This translates, given an inverse demand with bounded slope, into the same order of magnitude for the price-cost margin $(1/n)$. The result is obtained from the first-order condition for a symmetric interior equilibrium:

$$P(nq_n) - C'(q_n) = -q_n P'(nq_n).$$

Under what conditions the Cournot outcome approaches price-taking behavior or, in a more classic vein, yields approximately zero (economic) profits?

Novshek (1980) showed the existence and approximate competitiveness of (free-entry) Cournot equilibria in large markets characterized by U-shaped average costs or always declining average costs.[23] The key idea is to realize that what matters is not the absolute size of firms but the relative size with respect to the market. In this sense the "competitiveness" of the Cournot outcome is not so much an issue of large numbers of firms but an issue of smallness of firms in relation to the market. Sometimes smallness will require a large number of firms, but it need not be so.

It is worth noting that Cournot equilibria in large markets exist under very mild conditions on demand and costs (downward-sloping demand and no essential restriction on costs). Existence follows using the Bamon/Frayssé-Novshek fixed point result for decreasing best replies. Consider a market with m identical consumers with demand function $D(p)$. This yields the m-replica market with inverse demand function $p = P(Q/m)$. The declining marginal revenue condition for firm i (which implies that best replies must be decreasing) is given by $(P' + q_i m^{-1} P'')m^{-1} < 0$. The inequality will hold in a large market for which the production of each firm is small relative to the market size, that is, $q_i m^{-1}$ small (provided that $P' < 0$).

Two approaches may be distinguished in the literature. In the first, conditions for the approximate efficiency of large Cournot markets are found. In the second, conditions for convergence of the Cournot outcome to a well-defined competitive limit are sought.

Consider a market with m identical consumers (which determine the size of the market) and n_m identical firms. Under mild conditions on demand and costs, Ushio (1985) shows that the per capita welfare loss due to Cournot pricing tends to zero as the economy is replicated (1) if the choke-off price for demand is no more than average cost for very large outputs and, otherwise, (2) if and only if n_m tends to infinity with m. That is, if approach 1 holds, Cournot equilibria in large markets are approximately efficient independently of the number of firms. A typical case would be U-shaped average costs (Novshek 1980). The result is easy to understand considering the extreme case of a market with linear demand and a single firm facing a capacity limit, say, equal to the monopoly output of the market with one consumer ($m = 1$) but otherwise with zero production costs. In this case the efficient and the monopoly outcome coincide for any replica m of the economy! If approach 1 does not hold, Cournot equilibria in large markets are approximately efficient if, and only if, the numbers of firms is large. The typical example would be always decreasing average cost (see the results by Novshek 1980 and Ushio 1983). In this case the rate of convergence to the efficient outcome is $1/\sqrt{m}$, while in case (1) typically the rate will be $1/m$. Increasing returns pose a more serious problem for efficiency than the case of bounded productive capacities. In fact in this case even under free-entry conditions, profits of Cournot firms may be bounded away from zero for any degree of "competitiveness" (or replica) of the market. This is so because even if price approaches average cost, firms have an incentive to produce a very large output under increasing returns.

The results presented have an immediate application for the efficiency of large markets with free entry. For example, in the regular case in which demand is downward sloping, variable costs are strictly convex and firms face a positive setup cost, replicating the market prices converge to the minimum average cost (or "long-run" competitive price) and the per capita welfare loss tends to zero. (See exercise 4.14.)

The second approach approximates Cournot equilibria in large markets by perfectly competitive equilibria of a well-defined limit market. Novshek (1985b) shows that if the Cournot markets converge smoothly to the limit market in terms of the underlying demand and costs characteristics (otherwise, costs are basically unrestricted), then all the Cournot equilibria converge to the competitive equilibrium of the limit market. These Cournot equilibria will be approximately efficient when close to the competitive limit. (See exercise 4.15 for an example where a unique Cournot equilibrium does not converge to a competitive equilibrium.)

What can we say about dominance solvability in a large Cournot market? Consider a well-defined limit market with a unique competitive equilibrium. It follows then that if this competitive equilibrium is globally stable with respect to cobweb dynamics, then the approximating large Cournot markets are dominance solvable (Börgers and Janssen 1995). Note that a very different result holds if there is no well-defined limit market. Indeed, if demand is not replicated as the number of firms n grows, then many output choices survive iterated elimination of dominated strategies (see Bernheim 1984 for the linear Cournot model).

Summary

This chapter provides an in-depth analysis of the Cournot model with an exhaustive account of results on the existence of equilibrium, characterization, uniqueness, and comparative statics, completed with an analysis of entry and large markets. The methods developed in chapter 2 have been applied here. The topics covered include the three approaches to existence of equilibrium (with decreasing, increasing, and, in symmetric games, quasi-increasing best replies), a characterization of uniqueness in smooth Cournot games, and its relationship to stability conditions, and properties of Cournot pricing, market concentration, and welfare. The results in the chapter attempt to provide minimal conditions on demand and costs to ensure existence and/or uniqueness of equilibrium as well as desired comparative statics results. It is explained why downward-sloping best replies is considered the normal case in Cournot competition and the sometimes counterintuitive relationships between market concentration and welfare. The analysis provides a link between "intuitive" comparative static results, in terms of shifts in demand and costs or entry, and the assumptions on basic market parameters. In this respect the role of the character of competition (strategic substitutes versus strategic complements) and of stability conditions is highlighted. Finally we examine the links between equilibria in large Cournot markets and competitive outcomes. The key issue here is the relative size of firms with respect to the market.

Exercises

4.1. Suppose that inverse demand is a continuous decreasing concave function $P(\cdot)$, which is twice-continuously differentiable and strictly decreasing on the interval where it has positive value. Suppose that the costs of the firm are given by $C : R_{++} \to R$, continuous and increasing. (*Note:* One may have $C(0) \neq C(0+)$.) Derive the continuity and monotonicity properties of the best-response correspondence of the firm (to an aggregate output of other firms of Q_{-i}). Can you weaken the concavity requirement of demand while preserving the derived properties?

*4.2. Consider a n-firm Cournot game with $P(\cdot)$ strictly decreasing and log-concave (plus your favorite boundary assumption for large outputs) and C_i strictly increasing for each i. Show that the best-reply correspondence of any player is strongly decreasing. Check that the convex demand function $P(Q) = (\max\{a - Q, 0\})^2$ for $a > 0$ fulfills the requirements but not the downward-sloping marginal revenue condition. What happens if $P(Q) = e^{-aQ}$? (*Hint:* Use the ordinal extension of payoff submodularity due to Milgrom and Shanon 1994. See Section 2.2.2 and Amir 1996.)

*4.3. Consider a Cournot duopoly game with inverse demand $P(Q) = (Q + a)^{-1}$, $a > 0$, and constant unit costs c_i, with $a^{-1} > c_1 \geq c_2 > 0$. Characterize the best-reply functions depending on the parameter constellation ($c_1 < (4a)^{-1}$ and $c_1 \geq (4a)^{-1}$). What can you say of best-reply dynamics in the different cases? Consider both continuous and discrete versions of the Cournot tâtonnement. (See Dana and Montrucchio 1986.)

4.4. Is it possible in a Cournot game for the payoff to firm i to display increasing differences in (q_i, Q_{-i}) for all pairs (q_i, Q_{-i})? Is your answer compatible with having a Cournot game with (globally) increasing best responses?

4.5. Consider a smooth symmetric Cournot market with $P' < 0$, $C'' - P' > 0$, and firms facing a capacity constraint. Show that the slopes of the best-reply correspondence of any firm, Ψ_i, are larger than -1. (*Hint:* Write profits of firm i as $F(Q, Q_{-i}) = (Q - Q_{-i})P(Q) - C(Q - Q_{-i})$, note that $\partial^2 F / \partial Q \partial Q_{-i} = C'' - P'$, and consider the correspondence φ in section 4.1. See also Section 2.3.1 and Amir and Lambson 1996.)

*4.6. Consider a smooth n-firm Cournot market, with inverse demand $P(\cdot)$ and cost function $C_i(\cdot)$ for firm i. Show that if the contraction condition on profits is fulfilled in a rectangular neigbourhood of a Cournot equilibrium then the equilibrium is locally stable with both versions of the continuous adjustment process (i.e., gradient dynamics and best-reply dynamics). Repeat the argument for the cases of downward- (respectively, upward-) sloping best responses for all firms, assuming that $P' - C_i'' < 0$ for all i. (*Hint:* Study the stability of the linearized dynamical system around the equilibrium. All the eigenvalues of the appropriate matrix must have negative real parts.)

4.7. Consider a Cournot market with inverse linear demand $P(\cdot)$ and zero costs for all n firms. Examine the stability of the unique Cournot equilibrium with respect to the discrete tâtonnement. (*Hint:* Look at the cases $n = 2$, $n = 3$, and $n \geq 4$ separately). Do the results change if the adjustment is according to the continuous version of the Cournot tâtonnement (best-response dynamics)?

*4.8. Consider a smooth n-firm Cournot market. Show the following:

a. A small change in total output Q raises total surplus if and only if $\Delta Q / Q + \frac{1}{2}(\Delta H / H) > 0$, where H is the Herfindahl index of market concentration. (See Farrell and Shapiro 1990a.)

b. Small output changes Δq_i induce movements of H and TS of opposite sign if and only if $0 \leq (\sum_{i=1}^{n} s_i \Delta q_i)/\Delta Q \leq H$, where s_i is the market share of firm i. (See Farrell and Shapiro 1990b.)

4.9. Display a Cournot duopoly example in which dropping one of the firms total surplus increases.

*4.10. Consider a smooth n-firm Cournot market in which the costs of firm i are affected by a parameter θ_i, $C_i(q_i; \theta_i)$ such that $\partial C_i/\partial \theta_i > 0$ and $\partial^2 C_i/\partial \theta_i \partial q_i > 0$. Assume that there is a unique Cournot equilibrium q_i^*, $i = 1, \ldots, n$. The equilibrium is interior with $\{1 - \sum_i (P' + q_i P'')/(C_i'' - P')\} > 0$ and $C_i''(q_i^*) - P'(Q^*) > 0$ for all i. Show that an increase in θ_i (1) decreases total output and increases the profits of rival firms and (2) increases (decreases) the output of firm j if the best-response function of firm j is decreasing (increasing). Display further assumptions needed to show that an increase in θ_i decreases the firm's output and, if best responses for all firms other than i are decreasing, its profits. What relation do they have to stability conditions (with respect to the continuous Cournot adjustment process)? (*Hint:* See sections 4.2 and 4.3.)

*4.11. Consider a n-firm symmetric smooth Cournot market (with $P' < 0$ when positive). Confine attention first to symmetric equilibria fulfilling the stability conditions (4.1) and (4.2) in the text (section 4.3). Can there be multiple equilibria? Treat n as a continuous variable (how would you justify it?). Derive the following expressions: Elasticity of individual output with respect to n : $(E - n)/(n + 1 - E - C''/P')$; elasticity of total output with respect to n : $(1 - C''/P')/ (n + 1 - E - C''/P')$; and $\operatorname{sign}(d\pi/dn) = \operatorname{sign}[n(2 - C''/P') - E]/ [n + 1 - E - C''/P']$. Sign them using conditions (4.1) and (4.2). Suppose now that we only know that condition (4.1), $C'' - P' > 0$, holds globally. What statement can be made about how equilibrium profits per firm vary with n? (*Hint:* Look at extremal equilibria. See section 4.3).

4.12. Consider a Cournot market with linear demand, $p = a - bQ$, $a > 0, b > 0$, and zero marginal costs for all the firms. Find the free-entry equilibrium if there is a fixed cost of entry F. (The answer is n^* equal to the largest integer no larger than $a(bF)^{-1/2} - 1$.) Compare the free-entry equilibrium with the first-best (the planner controls n and pricing) and the second-best (the planner controls n only) socially optimal number of firms. (See von Weizsäker 1980.)

*4.13. Consider a n-firm Cournot market with linear demand, $p = a - bQ$, $a > 0, b > 0$, and constant, but possibly unequal, marginal costs for all the firms. Define the entry externality as the net effect of entry of a new firm on consumers and incumbent firms (the difference in total surplus between the pre-entry situation and the postentry one excluding the profits of the entrant). Suppose that entry does not cause any incumbent to exit the market. Relate the entry externality with the incumbent's cost variance. Would your answer change if demand were strictly convex? Allow now for entry to induce exit. Show that unless the entrant is much more efficient than the surviving incumbents the inducement to exit will tend to improve the entry externality. (See Vickers 1995)

*4.14. Consider a Cournot market with downward-sloping demand $P(Q/m)$ and free entry. Suppose that all firms have access to the same strictly convex variable cost function $V(\cdot)$ and face a positive entry cost $F > 0$. Show that the equilibrium price tends to the minimum average cost and the per capita welfare loss tends to zero as the market is replicated (m grows).

4.15. Consider a n-firm Cournot industry with downward-sloping demand in which n_1 firms have constant unit cost c_1 and n_2 firms have unit cost $c_2 > c_1$ ($n = n_1 + n_2$). Suppose that best replies are decreasing and that $P(0) > c_2$. Examine the limit properties of the Cournot equilibrium as the number of firms tends to infinity distinguishing the cases in which n_1 or n_2 tend to infinity. Compute explicitly the cases of linear and isoelastic demand. (See Campos and Padilla 1996.)

5

Price Competition: The Models of Bertrand and Edgeworth

Bertrand and Edgeworth built models of firms competing by setting prices. Bertrand criticized the Cournot model and Edgeworth pointed at the importance of decreasing returns in the characterization of price competition (see chapter 1). I present first, in section 5.1, *Bertrand competition*, which is price competition with the commitment to supply whatever demand is forthcoming at the set price. In section 5.2, I deal with *Bertrand-Edgeworth competition*, which is competition with a voluntary trading constraint according to which firms are not obliged to supply completely the residual demand they face. In order to do so, I discuss rules for rationing demand (section 5.2.1) and analyze the equilibrium problem resorting to mixed strategies (sections 5.2.2 and 5.2.3). Afterward I deal with the relationship of price competition with the Cournot model (section 5.2.4), and with large markets (section 5.2.5). I conclude with a comment on the use of mixed strategies (section 5.2.6).

5.1 Bertrand Competition

As stated *Bertrand competition* will be taken to mean that firms select independently the prices they charge for the product and that every firm has to supply *all* the forthcoming demand at the price it is setting. With a homogeneous product all demand will go to the producer charging the lowest prices. If more than one firm charge the lowest price, then a sharing rule must be assumed. The strategy space of firm i is an interval of possible prices to charge, and a Bertrand equilibrium is a Nash equilibrium of the associated game. Notice that firm i would not like to supply all the forthcoming demand at a certain price p_i when this demand is larger than the competitive supply of the firm at that price, that is, larger than $MC_i^{-1}(p_i)$. Nevertheless the firm *must* supply it under the Bertrand assumption. This can be rationalized assuming that when a firm sets a price p_i, this represents a commitment with customers to supply the forthcoming demand. The Bertrand assumption is plausible when there are large costs of turning customers away. This may be the case in regulated industries (e.g., in the supply of electricity or telephone) or the result of consumer protection laws. For example, it is typical of "common carrier" regulation to require firms to meet all demand at the set prices.[1] In the case where the supply of a product is exhausted, the customer may take a "rain check" (a coupon to purchase the good at the posted price at a later date).

Consider a smooth homogeneous product market with (strictly) downward-sloping demand $D(\cdot)$ when positive, cutting both axes, and n firms with increasing (identical) cost functions $C(\cdot)$.

In Bertrand competition firms set prices, and in equilibrium each firm maximizes profit given the prices set by the other firms. Let $N = \{1, 2, \ldots, n\}$ be the set of firms. We suppose that the firms that set the lowest price split the demand and that the remaining firms do not sell anything. That is, given $(p_i)_{i \in N}$, the sales of firm i are

$$x_i = \frac{D(p_i)}{l} \quad \text{if } p_j \geq p_i \quad \text{for all } j \in N,$$

where $l = \#\{j \in N : p_j = p_i\}$, and equal to 0 otherwise.

If marginal costs are constant and equal to c, then the price vector $(p_i)_{i \in N}$ is a Bertrand equilibrium if and only if $p_j \geq c$ for all firms and at least two firms set the price equal to marginal cost. When $n = 2$, the unique Bertrand equilibrium is $p_i = c$, $i = 1, 2$.[2] In any case, the unique symmetric equilibrium is $p_i = c$ for all firms. When $n \geq 3$, if a firm sets a price larger than marginal cost in equilibrium, it gets no demand, and consequently it does not produce anything. Therefore the only equilibrium where all the firms are producing a positive amount is the symmetric one. Under mild conditions, fulfilled under our assumptions but not necessarily with constant elasticity demand, the zero-profit Bertrand outcome is the unique possible outcome even if mixed price strategies are allowed. (See exercise 5.1.)

With increasing returns Bertrand competition yields somewhat surprising outcomes. Indeed, add an avoidable fixed production cost F to the common constant marginal cost of the firms ($C(q) = F + cq$ if $q > 0$ and $C(0) = 0$), and suppose that a monopoly would be strictly viable. With a positive fixed cost of production the entry decision (or

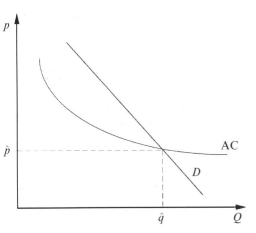

Figure 5.1

the decision to be active) has important consequences. It is assumed here that firms decide simultaneously about entry and price. Then with $n \geq 2$ and the sharing rule, which splits demand in case of a price tie, there is no equilibrium. Indeed, with at least two active firms in the market equilibrium would require price to be equal to marginal cost for those firms, but then they would make negative profits. Furthermore it is easily seen that there cannot be an equilibrium with only one active firm either.

However, if we change the sharing rule in such a way that in case of a price tie a firm is selected (randomly) to serve the whole market, then the unique Bertrand equilibrium is for all firms to name the least break even monopoly price $\hat{p}$ (the least price that equates the monopoly profit, $(p - c)D(p) - F$ to zero; see figure 5.1). Indeed, a firm that undercuts this price would make negative profits and a higher price entails no sales. Uniqueness is checked easily (exercise 5.2). This outcome has the following properties: (1) All firms make zero profits, (2) the industry configuration is cost-efficient (i.e., only one firm produces), and (3) the outcome, with price equal to average cost, is constrained efficient (i.e., it maximizes total surplus subject to the constraint that firms make no losses). Baumol, Panzar, and Willig (1982) have studied markets with those properties. More precisely, they define an industry configuration (a set of outputs and a price p charged by the incumbents or active firms) to be *sustainable* if no entrant (nonactive firm) can make a profit by cutting prices and make a profit supplying no more than market demand at those prices (i.e., for $p^e \leq p$ and $q^e \leq D(p^e)$ we have that $p^e q^e \leq C(q^e)$). A (perfectly) *contestable* market is a market in which sustainability is a necessary condition for equilibrium. The story that accompanies these definitions is one of "hit-and-run" entry where an entrant can enter and exit the market to undercut the incumbent without costs (and before the incumbent can respond). In the example considered, the unique sustainable configuration is to have one firm producing $\hat{q}$ and charging $\hat{p}$, and this coincides with the Bertrand equilibrium. In general, however, both solutions concepts need not coincide.

It is worth noting that a very different outcome obtains if firms have to decide first whether to enter the market and pay the fixed cost F or whether to stay out, and then price competition follows. In this case the (pure strategy) outcome is monopoly. Indeed, if more than one firm were to enter, profits would be negative.[3] The harsh competition at the price-setting stage results in a monopolistic outcome. This contrasts with the outcome of the same game with quantity competition at the second stage (see section 4.3.2). A softer postentry competition induces more entry. The difference between the simultaneous and the sequential entry/price decision structures is that in the former an entrant takes as given the price charged by the incumbent and therefore can "steal" his market without fear of retaliation.

With (strictly) decreasing returns there are typically multiple equilibria.[4] Suppose all firms have a strictly increasing smooth convex cost function $C(\cdot)$. Without loss of generality, let $C(0) = 0$. Demand is smooth with $D' < 0$ in the range in which it is positive (i.e., for p no larger than the choke-off price for demand $\bar{p}$). Let $\pi_n(p)$ be a firm's profit when they split the market at price p. That is, $\pi_n(p) = pD(p)/n - C(D(p)/n)$. Let $\bar{p}_n = \{p \in [0,\bar{p}) : \pi_1(p) = \pi_n(p)\}$ and $\underline{p}_n = \{p \in [0,\bar{p}) : \pi_n(p) = 0\}$. Both $\underline{p}_n$ and $\bar{p}_n$ are well defined (with $\underline{p}_n < \bar{p}_n$ and are unique), and they are decreasing in n for $n \geq 2$.[5] Figure 5.2 depicts $\pi_1, \pi_n, \underline{p}_n$, and $\bar{p}_n$ for the case where the functions are strictly concave in p (let p^m denote the monopoly price).[6] Let w_n denote the Walrasian or competitive equilibrium of the market. That is, the (unique) solution to $D(p) = S_n(p)$, where $S_n(p) = nMC^{-1}(p)$. It is easy to check that it must be a Bertrand equilibrium, and therefore it necessarily lies in the interval $[\underline{p}_n, \bar{p}_n]$. (See exercise 5.3.) At $\underline{p}_n$ price equals average cost and at w_n price equals marginal cost (see figure 5.3, where $\underline{p}_1, w_n$, and $\underline{p}_n$ are depicted). Similarly all firms charging a

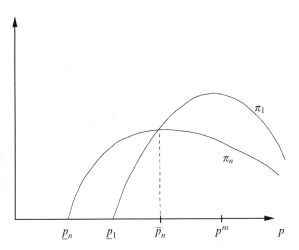

Figure 5.2

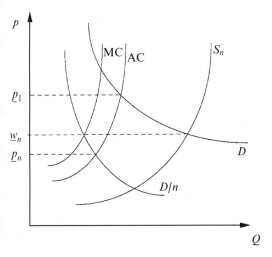

Figure 5.3

common price in the interval $[\underline{p}_n, \bar{p}_n]$ will be a Bertrand equilibrium. Indeed, if all firms except i set a common price in this interval, then firm i by raising the price obtains no demand, and by lowering it and serving the whole market decreases its profit (see figure 5.2). High prices are sustained because for a firm to cut prices is very costly when by doing so it becomes the sole server of the market beyond its competitive supply. It is worth noting that profits are increasing in the interval $[\underline{p}_n, \bar{p}_n]$, starting with zero profits at the lower end. The following proposition states the result:

PROPOSITION 5.1 Suppose that demand is smooth with $D' < 0$, in the range in which it is positive, and the n firms in the market have a strictly increasing smooth convex cost function $C(\cdot)$. Let $\pi_n(p) = pD(p)/n - C(D(p)/n)$, $\bar{p}_n = \{p \in [0, \bar{p}) : \pi_1(p) = \pi_n(p)\}$, and $\underline{p}_n = \{p \in [0, \bar{p}) : \pi_n(p) = 0\}$. Then $\underline{p}_n < \bar{p}_n$, and all firms charging a common price in the interval $[\underline{p}_n, \bar{p}_n]$ is a Bertrand equilibrium. The competitive price belongs to the interval of equilibria.

Example
With demand $D(p) = a - bp$ and costs $C(q) = cq^2/2$, we have that $\underline{p}_n = ac/(2n + bc)$ and $\bar{p}_n = ac(1 + n^{-1})/(2 + bc(1 + n^{-1}))$. The Walrasian equilibrium is $w_n = ac/(n + bc)$. As the number of firms grows, all prices in the range $[0, ac/(2b + c)]$ are equilibria, since $\underline{p}_n$ tends to 0 and $\bar{p}_n$ to $ac/(2b + c)$ as n tends to infinity. Replicating demand induces a greater multiplicity of equilibria. As the number of firms grows, all prices that do not choke off demand are equilibria. That is, as the number of firms increase, the equilibrium set expands to all relevant prices. Suppose that demand is given by $D(p) = n(a - bp)$, then $\underline{p}_n = ac/(2 + bc)$ for all n, and now $\bar{p}_n$ tend to a/b as n tends to infinity (in this case the Walrasian equilibrium equals $ac/(1 + bc)$ for any n). Furthermore the largest Bertrand price $\bar{p}_n$ can be larger than the Cournot price $p^C = a(1 + c)/(n + 1 + c)$ (letting $b = 1$). For example, for $n = 2$, $\bar{p}_2 > p^C$ if $c > 2$. That is, under decreasing returns, a Bertrand price can be larger than the Cournot equilibrium price. In fact, if $c > 4$, then $\bar{p}_2(= 3ca/(4 + 3c))$ is larger than the cartel price $(p^m = (2 + c)a/(4 + c))$! (In section 5.2 we will compare systematically Cournot and Bertrand equilibria in differentiated product markets.)

The results can be readily extended to asymmetric cost functions C_i. Suppose that marginal costs are strictly increasing (or that there are capacity limits). In this case and with asymmetric costs, it is more reasonable to assume that when firms set the same price demand is split in proportion to capacity. Capacity is understood as the competitive supply of the firm, $S_i(p) = MC_i^{-1}(p)$. Now, if l firms set the lowest price p, firm i (among them) has to fulfill a demand of $x_i = D(p)(S_i(p)/S(p))$, where $S(p) = \sum_{j=1}^{l} S_j(p)$. Again there is typically a range of Bertrand equilibria with firms quoting the same price in an interval around the competitive price (see also exercise 5.3).[7]

If marginal costs are constant but different and there are at least two firms with lowest cost c, then the result with symmetric costs holds. If there is only one firm with lowest cost, then this firm prices at the next to the lowest cost or at the monopoly price, whichever is lowest, and obtains the whole market.[8] All firms other than the lowest cost firm earn zero profits.

In summary, the idea that with Bertrand competition and homogeneous products prices are competitive holds only when marginal costs are constant and are identical for all firms. Even with constant returns, with firms with different efficiencies Bertrand competition will not yield the competitive outcome (price equal to the lowest marginal cost) but a higher price (equal to the second lowest marginal cost). With increasing returns, equilibrium (in pure strategies) may fail to exist or may yield somewhat surprising outcomes, and with decreasing returns there are typically multiple equilibria (with the competitive outcome being one of them). As a general rule firms with positive sales charge the same price in equilibrium.

5.2 Bertrand-Edgeworth Competition

In Bertrand-Edgeworth (B-E) competition firms compete with prices realizing that competitors may not be able or may not want to supply all the forthcoming demand at the set prices. Firms announce simultaneous and independently prices, and production decisions follow the realization of the demands for the firms. Each firm takes into account that its rivals will not sell more than their competitive profit-maximizing supplies at the announced prices. In this sense there is voluntary trading. The quantity that each firm sells, given the vector of prices, is the minimum of its residual demand and its competitive supply.

5.2.1 Rationing Rules and Contingent Demand

Consider a duopoly market characterized by a downward-sloping demand function $D(\cdot)$ with finite maximum demand $D(0)$. Firms have costs given by the continuous increasing functions $C_i(\cdot)$, $i = 1, 2$. The competitive supply of firm i is in the set

$$\arg\max_{q_i \in [0, D(0)]} \{ pq_i - C_i(q_i) \}.$$

Define the competitive supply of firm i at the price p, $S_i(p)$, to be the maximum element of this set. Obviously, if $C_i(\cdot)$ is strictly convex, the set of maximizers is a singleton.

It is possible to think of B-E competition as firms choosing price-quantity (p, q) pairs that specify the maximum quantity q that the firm is willing to supply at the price p and with $q = S(p)$, where $S(p)$ is the competitive supply of the firm.

Suppose that firm 1 puts a price higher than firm 2, $p_1 > p_2$. The residual or contingent demand for firm 1, $\tilde{D}_1(p_1; p_2)$, may well be positive, unlike in the Bertrand competition case, since firm 2 may not supply the whole market at the price p_2. If $S_2(p_2) < D(p_2)$, we have to specify a *rationing rule* for unsatisfied demand. Two leading rules have been proposed: *proportional* and *surplus-maximizing*. Edgeworth considered the first (see also Beckmann 1965), and Levitan and Shubik (1972) the second.

Let there be a unit mass of identical consumers in the market, each one with preferences with no income effects on the homogenous good, giving rise to a demand function $D(\cdot)$. Total (average) demand therefore coincides with individual demand. With the surplus-maximizing rule the lower-priced firm (firm 2) places a limit equal to $S_2(p_2)$ to the amount of the good each consumer can buy. Consequently the residual demand for firm 1 is $\max\{0, D(p_1) - S_2(p_2)\}$. It is just a parallel displacement of $D(\cdot)$ to the left by the amount $S_2(p_2)$. Notice that with this method the high-priced portion of the demand curve is supplied first, and therefore it is a surplus-maximizing rationing scheme. It would arise if consumers could engage in costless arbitrage. With the proportional rule, rationing at the lowest price is made through a queuing system. Consumers in front of the line obtain their entire demand while others obtain nothing. Output is sold thus on a first-come–first-served basis. Resale is assumed impossible. The lower-priced firm, firm 2, will satisfy a proportion

$\alpha \equiv S_2(p_2)/D(p_2)$ of consumers; therefore the demand left for firm 1 is $\max\{0, (1 - \alpha)D(p_1)\}$. In this case the consumers left for firm 1 are a random sample of the consumer population.

The rationing rules considered are extreme in the following sense: The surplus-maximizing (SM) one yields the *worst* possible (in a context of costless rationing) contingent demand for the high-priced firm (firm 1). This is so because the top portion of the demand curve of every consumer is captured by the low-priced firm. The proportional (P) rule yields the *best* possible contingent demand to firm 1 among the rules that place a limit to what each consumer may purchase with supply on a first-come–first-served basis. (See Davidson and Deneckere 1986.)

The rationing schemes could also be interpreted in terms of a heterogeneous population of consumers with inelastic demands and different reservation prices. In the SM case high reservation price consumers are served first. In the P case customers would arrive at random to firms.

Summarizing, the contingent demand for firm 1 is given by

$$\tilde{D}_1(p_1; p_2) = \begin{cases} D(p_1) & \text{if } p_1 < p_2, \\[2ex] \max\left\{\dfrac{D(p)}{2}, D(p) - S_2(p)\right\} & \text{if } p_1 = p_2 = p, \\[2ex] \begin{array}{l} SM : \max\{0, D(p_1) - S_2(p_2)\} \\[2ex] P : \max\left\{0, \left(1 - \dfrac{S_2(p_2)}{D(p_2)}\right)D(p_1)\right\} \end{array} & \text{if } p_1 > p_2. \end{cases}$$

When the quoted prices are the same, demand is split equally if both firms can satisfy its share. Otherwise, the residual demand goes to the competitor. Alternatively, demand could be split in proportion to the (competitive) supplies of the firms when $p_1 = p_2 = p : \tilde{D}_1(p; p) =$ $\max\left\{\dfrac{S_1(p)}{S_1(p) + S_2(p)}D(p), D(p) - S_2(p)\right\}$. Still another possibility would be to split randomly the demand when there is a price tie.

In a parallel fashion the contingent demand for firm 2, $\tilde{D}_2(p_2; p_1)$, and the generalization of residual demands to the case of n firms can be given. (See exercise 5.4.)

At prices (p_1, p_2) the quantity sold by firm i will be $q_i = \min\{S_i(p_i), \tilde{D}_i(p_i; p_j)\}$, and its payoff $\pi_i(p_i, p_j) = p_i q_i - C_i(q_i)$. Many of the results in the B-E model depend on the rationing rule used. Let us consider what determines which one is in effect.

The surplus-maximizing rule has in its favor that it is robust to the presence of the possibility of resale. Resale will not affect the analysis given above, since according to the SM rule the higher reservation price consumers (or the top portion of the demand curve) will be served first. In contrast, resale would affect the analysis with the P rule, since then a sample of the population is served by the low-priced firms. There would be incentives for low reservation price consumers who have obtained the good to resell it to higher reservation price consumers.

Assuming that the resale of goods is not feasible, Davidson and Deneckere (1986) provide an argument in favor of the proportional rule. If rationing rules are chosen first by firms and price competition follows, then the P rule is likely to emerge in equilibrium. The reason is that any firm by choosing the P rule (by not setting a limit on consumer purchases) leaves a better residual demand for the rival firm as we have seen, and consequently the rival will be induced to charge higher prices. This clearly benefits the first firm.

5.2.2   Equilibria: The Existence Problem

A Bertrand-Edgeworth equilibrium is a Nash equilibrium of the game with price strategy spaces and payoffs as above. The problem is that as pointed out by Edgeworth, an equilibrium (in pure strategies) in such a game may not exist.

A particular case of the duopoly market is when firms face capacity limits (k_1 and k_2, respectively) but otherwise have zero production costs. Then the maximum possible supply of firm i is k_i. Edgeworth considered the P rationing rule and showed that pure-strategy equilibria may not exist unless demand is highly elastic. It is easily shown that no equilibrium exists if $D(\cdot)$ is inelastic at the competitive price provided that $0 < \min\{k_1, k_2\} < D(0)$. The competitive price cannot be an equilibrium since firms will have an incentive to increase prices if demand is inelastic. Indeed, a firm charging a price higher than the competitive level will face a residual demand of the type $(1 - \alpha)D(p_i)$ and the marginal revenue price of firm i will be increasing in p_i if demand is inelastic.

It must be pointed out nevertheless that if firms' strategies are price-quantity (p, q) pairs, which specify the maximum quantity q

that the firm is willing to supply at the price p with $q > S(p)$, then existence in pure strategies may be restored. For example, with symmetric firms with strictly convex costs and rationing according to the P rule (and if firms set the same price demand is shared equally) the competitive price (which is the only candidate for a pure strategy equilibrium) is supported as a Bertrand-Edgeworth equilibrium by threatening to supply the whole market at the competitive price (Allen and Hellwig 1986b, n. 8).[9] The result can be refined to allow a no-bankruptcy constraint according to which no firm can commit to sell an output that would make the firm incur in losses. A sufficient condition for existence then is that $n - 1$ firms must be able to supply all demand at the competitive price (without losing money). The condition is met, for instance, in a duopoly market with quadratic costs (Dixon 1992). (See exercise 5.5.)

It is instructive to compare the regions of nonexistence of pure-strategy equilibria with the SM and P rules in a simple model with concave downward-sloping demand, $D(p)$, and, for simplicity, firms producing at no cost. In this case there is a unique symmetric Cournot equilibrium determined by the intersection of the Cournot best replies $r(\cdot)$. Denote by p^m the (unique) monopoly price. Two observations are immediate. First, with either rationing rule, the only possible candidates for pure-strategy equilibria are competitive equilibria. That is, at a pure-strategy equilibrium firms sell to capacity whenever this does not flood the market. Second, with the SM rule a firm would never charge a price below the one induced by its optimal response to the rival selling at capacity. That is, $p_i \geq P(k_j + r(k_j))$, for $i = 1, 2$ and $i \neq j$. It is a simple matter to check then (exercise 5.6) that under the SM rule pure-strategy equilibria exist if and only if capacities belong to the set

$$E^{SM} \equiv \{k \in R_+^2 : k_i \leq r(k_j), j \neq i, i = 1, 2\} \cup \{k \in R_+^2 : k_i \geq D(0), i = 1, 2\}.$$

Under the P rule they exist if and only if capacities belong to the set

$$E^P \equiv \{k \in R_+^2 : D^{-1}(k_1 + k_2) \geq p^m\} \cup \{k \in R_+^2 : k_i \geq D(0), i = 1, 2\}.$$

In any case the pure-strategy equilibrium equals the competitive equilibrium:

$$p = \begin{cases} D^{-1}(k_1 + k_2) & \text{if } k_1 + k_2 \leq D(0), \\ p = 0 & \text{otherwise.} \end{cases}$$

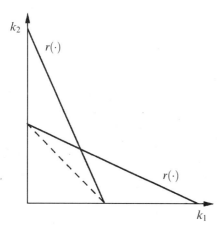

Figure 5.4

The set E^P is a strict subset of E^{SM}. (See figure 5.4 where a linear case is depicted.) This is clear since the output combinations that yield the monopoly price (the "contract curve" for the firms given by the dotted line in figure 5.4) are always closer to the origin than the Cournot best replies. Under both rules equilibria exist when the competitive price is zero. Otherwise, under the *SM* rule the existence region is bound by the Cournot best replies $r(\cdot)$, and under the *P* rule by the condition that the competitive price be no smaller than the monopoly price p^m. In particular, the capacities corresponding to the Cournot equilibrium will yield a pure-strategy equilibrium with the *SM* rule but not with the *P* rule. With the latter, the Cournot price cannot be an equilibrium, since at that price demand is inelastic, and any firm would like to increase its price. With the former it is an equilibrium, since by increasing its price a firm would sell less and move away from its best response to the quantity sold by the rival firm; by decreasing its price it would sell the same at a lower price. This explains why E^P is strictly included in E^{SM}: Upward deviations from candidate equilibria are more heavily penalized with the *SM* rule.

5.2.3 Mixed Strategies

It is clear then that we should look for mixed-strategy equilibria in B-E competition. Under what conditions will an equilibrium in mixed strategies exist?

If firms face capacity limits or have identical convex costs, then the Dasgupta-Maskin theorem (see section 2.4) applies for both types of rationing rules under mild assumptions on the demand function. $D(\cdot)$ should be continuous, downward sloping, and equal to zero for large prices. In fact, even non-downward-sloping demands can be allowed (Maskin 1986; Allen and Hellwig 1986a). The assumptions of the Dasgupta-Maskin theorem are met, since discontinuities in profits happen only when there are price ties, profits are bounded and satisfy the weak lower semicontinuity requirement, and the sum of payoffs is upper semicontinuous. Nevertheless, if firms have non-identical convex costs, a potential problem arises: The sum of the profits of the firms need not be upper semicontinuous, since a demand shift and an increase in production in favor of less efficient firms may decrease total profit. This difficulty can be overcome nevertheless assuming strictly convex costs (see Maskin 1986).

Existence of mixed-strategy equilibria in B-E competition is thus guaranteed under relatively weak assumptions. Another story is the characterization and computation of the equilibria.

In the context of our simple concave demand duopoly with capacity constraints, when there is no equilibrium in pure strategies, firms charge prices on an interval using continuous distribution functions, except for the (strictly) larger firm; this firm names the highest price with positive probability. When firms' capacities are equal, both distributions are continuous and identical. The lowest price charged is larger than the competitive price. All this holds both under the P and the SM rules. Obviously equilibria are different under each rule.

Under the P rule the highest price charged is always the monopoly price, p^m. This is easily understood. Suppose that firm 1 is the larger firm $(k_1 > k_2)$. Firm 1, when naming the highest price, will surely be undercut by firm 2. In this case firm 1 does not lose any customers in raising its price, since firm 2 serves an expected fraction of consumers $\bar{x}$ and firm 1 has a "captive" fraction $1 - \bar{x}$. The optimal price for firm 1 will be thus p^m, since this maximizes $(1 - \bar{x})pD(p)$ (the factor $(1 - \bar{x})$ not affecting the elasticity of demand). Notice that p^m is independent of k_2, the capacity of the smaller firm. Similarly there are no incentives for the smaller firm to name prices above the monopoly price.

Under the SM rule the highest price in the market is the monopoly price on the residual demand of the larger firm when this firm is undercut. This is $\bar{p} = \arg\max_p\{p(D(p) - k_2)\}$. Note that $\bar{p}$ is decreasing with k_2. Equilibria with this rule have been explored extensively. In the mixed-strategy region (the complement of E^{SM}), Kreps and Scheinkman (1983) show that firms randomize according to price distributions with common support $[\underline{p}, \bar{p}]$ (which may have an atom at $\bar{p}$). Given $k_1 \geq k_2$, and $\bar{p}$ as above, the expected revenue of firm 1 is given by $\bar{p}(D(\bar{p}) - k_2) = \underline{p}\min\{k_1, D(\underline{p})\}$ and of firm 2 by $\underline{p}k_2$. The expected revenue of the larger firm equals its minmax level. This is the profit of a firm faced with a rival that will sell k_2 for sure. In other words, it is the profit obtained by a firm with an optimal production response to the capacity of the rival.[10]

The characterization of expected revenues in the capacity constrained price games serves as a building block to consider two-stage games in which firms choose first capacities and then prices are set. In particular, a useful result is that in the mixed strategy region the expected revenue of the largest firm (firm 1) is equal to $P(r(k_2) + k_2)r(k_2)$ (see exercise 5.6). As we will see in section 5.2.4, this serves as a foundation for Cournot equilibrium in a context where firms compete in capacities first and then set prices (with demand rationed according to the surplus maximizing rule).

The price distribution of the larger firm $(\varnothing_1)$ strictly dominates stochastically (in terms of first-order dominance) the price distribution of the smaller firm $(\varnothing_2)$. Formally, if $k_1 > k_2$, $\varnothing_1(p) < \varnothing_2(p)$ for all prices in the interior of the support of the distributions. In other words, the larger firm charges higher prices in a stochastic sense. This may seem surprising at first glance. One could think that the firm with the larger capacity would gain by undercutting the rival, but also the penalty to the larger firm of charging high prices is diminished by the fact that the rival cannot sell very much. In equilibrium the second effect dominates. Think, for example, of the extreme case where the capacity of the second firm is very small; then the first firm will have an incentive to set high prices (close to the monopoly price). In fact as the capacity of the small firm converges to zero the equilibrium converges to the monopoly price.

Equilibria with the SM rule are easily computable. For example, in the symmetric case, $k_i = k$, $i = 1, 2$ and in the range $D(0) > k > q^c$, at the mixed-strategy equilibrium each firm uses the continuous distribution function $\varnothing(p; k) \equiv (k - \bar{\pi}/p)/(2k - D(p))$ with support on $[\bar{\pi}/k, \bar{p}]$, where $\bar{p} \equiv \arg\max_p\{p(D(p) - k)\}$ and $\bar{\pi} \equiv \bar{p}(D(\bar{p}) - k)$ (see Vives 1986a). To compute the mixed-strategy equilibrium, we take as given that there is an atomless mixed-strategy equilibrium with support in a compact interval. We have necessarily that the supremum of the interval will be given by $\bar{p} \equiv \arg\max_p \{p(D(p) - k)\}$. Expected profits $\bar{\pi}$ will be constant in the interval $[p, \bar{p}]$ and equal to $\bar{p}(D(\bar{p}) - k)$. Therefore $\underline{p} = \bar{\pi}/k$, because at $p = \underline{p}$ the firm will be capacity constrained. Now the expected profits of firm 1 of naming a price in the interior of the support will be given by $\bar{\pi} = (1 - \emptyset(p))pk + \emptyset(p)p(D(p) - k)$ (note that ties do not matter because the equilibrium is atomless). Solving for $\emptyset(p)$, we obtain the desired result. It is a simple matter to check that the equilibrium price distributions are ordered by the capacity level $k : \emptyset(\cdot; k)$ (first order) stochastically dominates $\emptyset(\cdot; k')$ if $k \leq k'$ (i.e., $\emptyset(\cdot; k) \leq \emptyset(\cdot; k')$ for all p if $k \leq k'$). Dominance is strict on the intersection of the interior of the supports of the strategies if $k < k'$. In other words, in a market with larger capacities of production (relative to demand) prices are stochastically lower.

When total market revenue is not concave the characterization of mixed-strategy equilibria is more complex both with the P and the SM rules. Allen and Hellwig (1986a) analyze the properties of n-firm B-E equilibria under the P rule without requiring demand to be downward sloping. In their model there may be several competitive and monopoly prices. They show that at any B-E equilibrium there is positive probability that firms charge prices close to or even above the lowest monopoly price. Osborne and Pitchik (1986) analyze a B-E duopoly under the SM rule with general downward-sloping demand. When the revenue function is not concave, they find equilibrium strategies that can have holes in their supports. They obtain several comparative static results. Among them, they show that by reducing the capacity of the small firm, the equilibrium profit of the large firm always increases but the one of the small firm may increase or decrease. This happens because the reduction in the capacity of the small firm tends to raise equilibrium prices and therefore it may compensate the decrease in size of the firm.

In summary, it is not easy in general to obtain comparative static results on B-E equilibria, since functional strategies are involved and closed form solutions typically do not exist. Nevertheless, the results obtained conform to intuition and stylized facts about industry competition. For example, we have seen that the B-E model predicts that markets where firms have high capacities (relative to demand) will tend to have (stochastically) low prices and that larger firms will tend to set higher prices. These predictions could have been obtained also from models of the Cournot type.

5.2.4 Price Competition and the Cournot Model

There are circumstances where the basic structure of the market dictates the relevant strategic variables for the firms. For example, in some agricultural markets quantities emerge as the natural strategic variables. Firms make production decisions in advance of the market period and then bring whatever is produced to the market place where a market-clearing price obtains (maybe through an auction-type mechanism). We could think in similar terms of fishermen bringing the catch of the day to the market, or street vendors stocking up on perishables to sell during the day. On the other hand, markets characterized by production to order will fit the Bertrand model. Prices are set first, orders by customers are taken, and production follows. Discount brokerage may be an example. With capacity constraints, this would naturally give rise to Bertrand-Edgeworth-type competition.

These examples suggest that the timing of decisions about prices and quantities will be very important in determining the market outcome. Firms, indeed, make decisions about prices and quantities and the Cournot and Bertrand models perhaps are better viewed as reduced forms of some dynamic process where decisions are made about both type of variables. The variable that is more difficult to adjust would be the dominant strategic variable. For example, in a car factory the production run is fixed in advance and costly to change while prices are easily adjusted. Quantities thus would be the main strategic variables. This gives more of a medium-term perspective to Cournot competition as a choice of the scale of operation, capacity, or the short-run cost function with which to engage in price competition.[11] It is also compatible with the short-run perspective according to which first stocks are obtained and then they are sold in the market among competing price offers.

This idea is naturally modeled in a two-stage game where firms make production decisions (or capacity choices) first and then compete in prices subject to their supply limits. We know then from section 5.2.2 that for given capacities, firms will use mixed strategies in prices unless capacities are so small that competitive pricing constitutes a Bertrand-Edgeworth equilibrium. Now small capacities will obtain if capacity is costly enough. In this case any capacity choice that firms would consider to make will involve pure strategy Bertrand-Edgeworth equilibria equal to the (capacity-constrained) competitive price. For example, consider the linear demand model, $p = a - Q$, with two firms. The monopoly profit (with no production cost) is $a^2/4$. Firm i will never consider setting a capacity for which $(a^2/4) - ck_i < 0$ (indeed, such a strategy is strictly dominated by setting $k_i = 0$ and guaranteeing zero profits). This bounds capacities, $k_i \leq a^2/4c$. If $c \geq 3a/4$, then $k_i \leq a/3$. In this range of capacities, we know (section 5.2.2) that under the surplus-maximizing rationing rule for unsatisfied demand, Bertrand-Edgeworth equilibria are in pure strategies and equal to the competitive price $p = a - (k_1 + k_2)$ (note that $a/3$ is precisely the Cournot equilibrium output with no production costs). Therefore, for set capacities k_1 and k_2, $\pi_i = (a - (k_1 + k_2) - c)k_i$. This is exactly the form of profits assumed in the quantity competition model. This justifies the interpretation of the quantity-setting model as the reduced form of capacity choices followed by (simultaneous) price competition when the cost of capacity is large.

Kreps and Scheinkman (1983) extend this interpretation to any cost of capacity characterizing the revenues that firms earn in the region of capacities for which mixed-strategy Bertrand-Edgeworth equilibria obtain under the surplus-maximizing rationing rule. Assuming smooth concave demand, that unsatisfied demand is rationed according to the surplus-maximizing rule, and that the cost of capacity is given by a smooth convex function $C(\cdot)$ with positive marginal cost at zero, they show that the unique equilibrium outcome of the two-stage game involves productions at the Cournot level (under the assumptions there is a unique Cournot equilibrium; see chapter 4). What is surprising is that the Cournot outcome is the unique equilibrium outcome. Indeed, it is easy to see that the Cournot outcome must be an equilibrium. Just let firms choose the Cournot price; if each firm chooses in the first stage the Cournot quantity and if one firm does not, then let the rival set a zero price at the second stage. With these pricing strategies no firm has an incentive to deviate from the Cournot equilibrium because the deviant would face the residual demand corresponding to the Cournot quantity. However, the strategies proposed do not constitute a subgame-perfect equilibrium because they involve the incredible threat of naming a zero price after a defection.

Let us check that there is a subgame-perfect equilibrium (SPE) of the two-stage game which yields the Cournot outcome. In order to do this, we have to characterize first the (expected) revenues arising from Bertrand-Edgeworth competition for any capacity choices in the first stage. This will yield the reduced form first-stage payoffs once we take into account the cost of capacity. The Cournot outcome must be then a Nash equilibrium associated to these payoffs. As we know, Bertrand-Edgeworth competition with capacity limits in the region bounded above by the Cournot best-response functions associated to zero production costs yields pure-strategy price equilibria corresponding to the market-clearing price (see figure 5.4). Obviously the Cournot equilibrium q^C (with production costs given by $C(\cdot)$) belongs to this region, since the Cournot best-response functions shift inward with increases in the marginal cost of production. It is possible to show that if a rival sets the Cournot equilibrium capacity, then the global best response of a firm is to set also the Cournot equilibrium capacity. This is the best strategy not only in the region where pure-strategy equilibria obtain—which should be clear since then reduced form profits are exactly as in Cournot competition—but also considering capacities, yielding mixed-strategy equilibria. Indeed, if firm j sets a capacity equal to the Cournot equilibrium q^C, firm i by setting $k_i > r(q^C)$, where $r(\cdot)$ denotes the Cournot best-response function with no costs. Now, by inducing pricing in the mixed-strategy region, one obtains $P(r(q^C) + q^C)r(q^C) - C(k_i)$.[12] This is clearly dominated by setting $k_i = q^C$, since q^C is precisely a Cournot equilibrium with costs $C(\cdot)$. If production at the second stage is costly, then the Cournot outcome associated to the sum of the capacity and the production costs functions obtains as a unique equilibrium of the two-stage game. The only requirement is for capacity to be costly at the margin.

A problem with the result is that it depends on the rationing rule being used. Davidson and Deneckere (1986) show that the Kreps-Scheinkman result is not robust to departures from the SM rule if the cost of capacity is zero. If it is small, then the Cournot equilibrium cannot be an equilibrium outcome of the two-stage game if the rationing rule is sufficiently different from the efficient one (see Tirole 1988, sec. 5.7.2.3). Davidson and Deneckere show, furthermore, that with the proportional rationing rule (and otherwise similar assumptions to Kreps and Scheinkman) the equilibrium tends to be more competitive than Cournot. For small costs of capacity there are two asymmetric equilibria, at which the capacity of each firm exceeds the Cournot level. For larger costs of capacity there is a symmetric equilibrium with capacity also exceeding the Cournot level. In all cases, except for very large costs of capacity, the equilibrium involves mixed strategies in prices at the second stage. Let us recall that with the proportional rationing rule and capacities at the Cournot level, the price equilibrium is in mixed strategies. Still considering the proportional rule, it is worth noting that if demand is uniformly elastic and there are no production costs at the second stage, then for any first stage capacities the market clearing price will be an equilibrium of the second stage (Madden 1995). This holds since with elastic demand a firm has no incentive to raise its price at the market-clearing solution (and cannot gain anything by decreasing it). Elastic demand is not contradictory with the existence of a Cournot equilibrium with positive production costs.[13] The implication is that the Cournot outcome (associated to the corresponding costs of capacity) obtains for any rationing rule (given that the proportional is the most favorable to induce upward price deviations).

The models presented suggest that even when firms choose prices, if they make irreversible production decisions first, a quantity-setting reduced form model may be appropriate.[14] That is, payoffs would depend on quantities incorporating already the effects of ensuing price competition. Furthermore the Cournot outcome emerges as the equilibrium outcome in the particular case of the surplus-maximizing rationing rule. This rule is the more pessimistic one for firms that set high prices. The proportional rule is very optimistic.[15] This indicates that the Cournot outcome would be the least competitive one in this class of two-stage games using intermediate rules between the surplus-maximizing and the proportional (Davidson and Deneckere 1986).

Holt and Scheffman (1987) also obtain the result that the quantity-setting model may be a good description of the behavior in the market even if firms choose prices. The authors show that the use of facilitating practices like most-favored-customer and meet-or-release clauses, transform a price-setting game into a quantity-setting one. This happens because with the meet-or-release clause if one firm makes a discount, the rivals maintain their sales by matching the discount, and with the most-favored-customer clause, the discount has to be made to all customers. Holt and Scheffman consider a two-stage game where firms announce list prices for the homogeneous product first, and then they may introduce discounts. They show that if firms are identical and discounts are nonselective, any list price above marginal cost, which is no larger than the Cournot price, and offering no discounts at the second stage, constitutes an equilibrium of the game. Notice that, again, the Cournot outcome provides the least competitive benchmark.

5.2.5 Large Bertrand-Edgeworth Markets

Do the equilibria of *large* B-E markets are close to the competitive outcome?

First of all, existence of pure strategy equilibria is not restored in a large B-E market but approximate (ε) price equilibria do exist and are close to competitive equilibria if ε is small enough (see Dixon 1987 for a model with convex costs). Similarly, when there are costs to turn away customers the competitive price is an equilibrium in a large B-E market (see Dixon 1990). Second, as argued below, mixed-strategy equilibria can be seen to be close to the competitive outcome in a large market.

In order to fix ideas consider a n-firm market with concave demand where each firm has capacity limit $k_n = K/n$ for some total capacity K such that $D(0) \geq K > 0$. By fixing total capacity at the level K when the number of firms is increased each one of them is made smaller with respect to the market. With the proportional rationing scheme an equilibrium in pure strategies will exist if and only if the competitive price equals the monopoly price given the aggregate capacity K (or, $p^m = \arg\max_p p \min\{K, D(p)\}$). Otherwise, there is a symmetric atomless mixed strategy equilibrium in which the highest price charged is p^m, which is independent of n. This means that whatever the number of firms in the market, however small they are in relation to the market, the monopoly price is always named by firms. The reason is simple, and we follow the same logic as when we explained equilibrium behavior under the P rule. The residual demand of a firm naming the highest price in the market has the *same* elasticity as market demand. Nevertheless, the mixed-strategy equilibrium converges in distribution to the competitive price as n tends to infinity. The reason is that the incentives to undercut other firms relative to exploiting monopolistically the own captive clientele increase as there are more firms in the market (Allen and Hellwig 1986a, b). Things are different with the SM rule. It is easily seen that if $K < D(0)$, eventually (for n large enough) all firms charge the competitive price $D^{-1}(K)$. If $K = D(0)$, then for any n there is a symmetric atomless mixed-strategy equilibrium in which the supremum of the support of the price distribution converges monotonically to zero at a rate $1/n$. The reason is that the residual demand left for a firm naming the highest price is $D(p) - (n-1)k_n$, which depends on the aggregate capacity of the rivals. This residual demand tends to zero as n grows, since the quantity sold by the rival firms, $(n-1)K/n$ approaches the competitive level $K = D(0)$ (Vives 1986a).

We see that in both cases prices converge in distribution to the competitive level but with the SM rule convergence is "stronger," since the supports of the equilibrium price distributions also converge to the competitive price. In fact, the rate of convergence to the competitive outcome in the latter case is the same as for Cournot markets under similar assumptions. Allen and Hellwig (1986 a) show weak convergence of B-E equilibria to the competitive limit under very general assumptions on the demand when the P rule is used. They later show (Allen and Hellwig 1989) that the highest competitive price or generically, any competitive price at which demand is downward sloping, can always be approximated by a sequence of B-E equilibria. Interestingly Börgers (1992) has shown that *iterated elimination of dominated strategies* yields prices close to the competitive price for the large B-E model if the SM rule is used but not with the P rule. In order for one to successfully use iterated elimination of dominated strategies, the mixed strategies must converge not only in distribution but also in support.

5.2.6 Concluding Remark: The Rationale for Mixed Strategies

Mixed strategies have been introduced as a solution to the existence problem in the B-E model. What is the economic rationale for firms to randomize when choosing prices?

In section 2.4 I mentioned the Harsanyi (1973) defense of mixed strategies. The pure strategies in this case are of an incomplete information game. For example, a firm could know its own cost but have slight uncertainty about the costs of the rivals. Mixed strategies, however, include a regret property. Each firm in B-E competition at a mixed-strategy equilibrium would rather wait and see what the rival has done before deciding on its price (see section 2.4).

Another line of reasoning, proposed by Varian (1980), interprets randomized equilibria in prices as a way for firms to price discriminate between informed and noninformed customers through a mechanism of sales. Shilony (1977) already showed the existence of a mixed-strategy equilibrium in prices in a model where consumers incur a cost in checking the prices of stores outside its neighborhood. Varian's motivation is to explain persistent price dispersion over time. The problem with the usual explanations of the phenomenon is that they imply that some stores consistently price above others. Over time consumers learn about this. In contrast, where stores follow random price strategies, that is, have random sales, consumers cannot learn anything from experience.[16]

Summary

This chapter examines the classical models of Bertrand and Edgeworth. The implications of Bertrand competition are analyzed not only for the case of constant returns but also in the case of decreasing and increasing returns. The role of the sharing rule for demand in the case of price ties is highlighted. With increasing returns connections are drawn with the theory of contestable markets. With decreasing returns Bertrand outcomes, typically there are a continuum of them, include the competitive equilibrium. Bertrand-Edgeworth competition is analyzed paying attention to the role of rationing rules, characterizing the regions of existence of equilibria in pure strategies according to the rationing rule used, and characterizing equilibria in mixed strategies including some comparative static properties. Conditions are provided also under which Cournot competition can be interpreted as the outcome of two-stage capacity competition followed by price competition. The conditions are restrictive and depend on the rationing rule used. The Cournot outcome tends to emerge as the least competitive outcome possible of the two-stage capacity-price games. Large Bertrand-Edgeworth markets are analyzed and their outcomes compared to competitive equilibria. Again results are sensitive to the rationing rule used. Finally the use of mixed strategies is discussed.

Exercises

*5.1. Consider a n-firm Bertrand oligopoly with a homogeneous product and a continuous (strictly) downward-sloping demand $D(\cdot)$

when positive, and choke-off price $\bar{p}$. Firms have constant and equal marginal costs c with $\infty > D(c) > 0$. In the case of a price tie, demand is shared among the low-price firms. Show that at the unique symmetric Bertrand equilibrium price equals marginal cost. Describe nonsymmetric equilibria. Consider the case, $n = 2$, and show that there is no mixed-strategy equilibrium different from (the degenerate) price equal to marginal cost. What happens if $D(p) = p^{-\eta}$ with $\eta > 0$? (*Hint:* Distinguish the cases $\eta < 1$ and $\eta \geq 1$. When $\eta < 1$, there is a continuum of symmetric atomless mixed-strategy equilibria with positive expected profits; see Baye and Morgan 1996).

5.2. Consider a n-firm homogeneous product market with a downward-sloping demand $D(\cdot)$ that cuts both axes. Each firm has the cost function $C(q) = F + cq$ if $q > 0$ and $C(0) = 0$. Suppose that a monopoly would be strictly viable and that in the case of a price tie, a single firm is selected (randomly) to serve the whole market. Show that the *unique* Bertrand equilibrium is for all firms to name the least break even monopoly price $\hat{p}$. Does the result hold if we allow for mixed strategies? Show that the market outcome maximizes total surplus given that firms cannot make losses. Is this true if we allow the planner to use mixed (price) strategies?

5.3. Consider a smooth n-firm homogeneous product market with a downward-sloping demand $D(\cdot)$ that cuts both axes. Firms have identical strictly convex cost functions. Show that the competitive (Walrasian) equilibrium of this market is also a Bertrand equilibrium (where, as defined, firms cannot refuse to serve consumers). Show the result if cost functions are allowed to be different, supposing that in a price tie, demand is shared according to capacity (competitive supply).

5.4. Consider a Bertrand-Edgeworth n-firm game with capacity constraint k_i for firm i. Show that residual demands can be written for $i = 1, \ldots, n$ as

$$\tilde{D}_i^{SM}(p) = \max\left\{0, \left(D(p_i) - \sum_{j \in J} k_j\right) \frac{k_i}{\sum_{j \in J^0} k_j}\right\}$$

for the surplus-maximizing rationing scheme and as

$$\tilde{D}_i^{P}(p) = \max\left\{0, \left(1 - \sum_{j \in J} \frac{k_j}{D(p_j)}\right) D(p_i) \frac{k_i}{\sum_{j \in J^0} k_j}\right\}$$

for the proportional rationing scheme, where $J = \{j : p_j < p_i\}$, and

$J^0 = \{j : p_j = p_i\}$, whenever, at price ties, demand is shared according to capacity. Check that with downward-sloping demand $\tilde{D}_i^{SM}(p) \le \tilde{D}_i^P(p)$.

*5.5. Consider a Bertrand-Edgeworth duopoly game with linear demand $D(p) = a - bp$. Suppose that costs of production are quadratic $C(q) = cq^2$. Suppose that if firms set the same price, demand is shared equally and that rationing is according to the proportional rule.

a. Is the competitive price a B-E equilibrium?

Modify now the game in the sense that firms' strategies are price-quantity (p,q) pairs which specify the maximum quantity q that the firm is willing to supply at the price p with $q > S(p)$, where S is the competitive supply at price p.

b. Answer the question above again. Is the answer the same in the case where firms set the same prices and demand is split randomly among the firms?

c. Introduce now a no-bankruptcy constraint according to which no firm can commit to sell an output that would make the firm incur in losses. Show that a sufficient condition for existence of a B-E equilibrium in pure strategies in a n-firm oligopoly is that $n - 1$ firms must be able to supply all demand at the competitive price (without losing money). Show that the condition is met in the example with quadratic costs. (See Dixon 1992.)

**5.6. Consider a Bertrand-Edgeworth duopoly game with concave downward-sloping demand $D(p)$. Suppose that firm i faces a capacity constraint k_i but otherwise zero costs of production. Without loss of generality assume that $k_1 \ge k_2$. Suppose that rationing is according to the surplus-maximizing rule.

a. Show that pure-strategy equilibria (equal to the competitive equilibria) exist in the region $E^{SM} \equiv \{k \in R_+^2 : k_i \le r(k_j), j \ne i, i = 1, 2\} \cup \{k \in R_+^2 : k_i \ge D(0), i = 1, 2\}$, where $r(\cdot)$ is the Cournot best-response function of a firm with no costs.

b. Characterize the support of the price distributions that firms use in the mixed-strategy region. Characterize expected revenues. Show, in particular, that firm 1 (the largest) has an expected revenue equal to $P(r(k_2) + k_2)r(k_2)$, where $P(\cdot)$ is the inverse demand function.

c. Suppose that $k_1 = k_2 = k$, and compute explicity the mixed-strategy equilibria. (See the results in the text; see also Levitan and Shubik 1972; Kreps and Scheinkman 1983.)

5.7. Consider a Bertrand-Edgeworth oligopoly game with linear demand $D(p) = 1 - p$. There are n firms, each with capacity equal to k and zero marginal cost. Rationing is according to the surplus-maximizing rule. Find the range of values of k for which there is no pure-strategy equilibrium. Let $k = 1/n$. Compute the (symmetric) mixed-strategy equilibrium and study its behavior as n tends to infinity. Compare your results with the asymptotics of the Cournot equilibrium.

6 Product Differentiation

Product differentiation and imperfect substitution among products was already considered by Edgeworth. Nevertheless, it was Hotelling (1929) who emphasized the softening effect of differentiation on price competition. The popular Hotelling location model lays the foundation of demand systems with product differentiation based on heterogeneous tastes of consumers. Indeed, the location model of Hotelling has also a product differentiation interpretation in terms of location of the products of firms in the space of characteristics that define them (see Gabszewicz and Thisse 1992 for a survey of location models). The characteristics approach to product differentiation has been developed by Lancaster (1966, 1971, 1979) and assumes that consumers have preferences over all potential products.

Chamberlin (1933) and Robinson (1933) studied extensively imperfect competition with product differentiation starting from a demand system. They modeled firms competing in prices and considered situations of oligopoly, or competition among a few, and monopolistic competition, or competition among many firms. In Chamberlin's "large group," model firms are small relative to the market and retain some monopoly power. Price competition according to these authors is à la Bertrand but in a product differentiation environment. The Edgeworth problem, that is, the fact that with increasing marginal costs firms may not be willing to supply all the forthcoming demand, is not considered. A firm is committed to supply whatever demand it faces at the set price.

In the present chapter we will follow the Chamberlin-Robinson approach, considering a demand system for differentiated products. In this framework we will derive the implications for price and quantity competition models. The only foundation we will offer for demands will be a representative consumer with a taste for variety (Spence 1976a, b; Dixit and Stiglitz 1977). The representative consumer approach is also consistent with other approaches that start from the heterogeneity of consumer tastes, like the characteristics approach and discrete choice models. In the latter, firms treat unobservable taste differences as a random variable, and consumers choose the variant of the differentiated product which maximizes their utility. (See Anderson et al. 1992; Caplin and Nalebuff 1991; Dierker 1991 for results using these approaches.) Equivalences between representative consumer models, characteristics models, and discrete choice models are derived in Anderson et al. (1992). Endogenous differentiation is not treated in this chapter except in connection with the optimal number of products in monopolistic competition (section 6.6) and product selection with complementary products (appendix).

Section 6.1 provides the basic properties of the demand systems considered, a rationalization in terms of a representative consumer, and some leading examples. Section 6.2 examines the existence and uniqueness of price and quantity equilibria, and section 6.3 characterizes and compares those equilibria. Large markets are dealt with in section 6.4, and the Edgeworth problem is considered in section 6.5 (under the heading Bertrand-Edgeworth-Chamberlin competition). Section 6.6 deals with the monopolistic competition model and optimal product diversity. The appendix addresses product selection for complementary products.

6.1 Demand Systems

Consider an industry with n differentiated products, each produced by a different firm. The demand for product i is given by $q_i = D_i(p)$ where p is the price vector. We will assume that demand is smooth, at least in the region of prices for which it is strictly positive and downward sloping, $\partial D_i/\partial p_i < 0$. If the Jacobian of the demand system $D(\cdot) = (D_1(\cdot), \ldots, D_n(\cdot))$ is negative definite, then the system can be inverted (on a convex region, see section 2.5 and inverse demands are obtained: $p_i = P_i(q)$ with $\partial P_i/\partial q_i < 0$ for all i.[1] If the goods are gross substitutes, $\partial D_i/\partial p_j \geq 0$, $j \neq i$, then $\partial P_i/\partial q_j \leq 0$, $j \neq i$. If the goods are complements, in the sense that $\partial P_i/\partial q_j \geq 0$, $j \neq i$, then they must be gross complements, $\partial D_i/\partial p_j \leq 0$, $j \neq i$.[2] In this chapter the maintained assumption on demand will be as follows:

ASSUMPTION For any good i, $D_i(\cdot)$ is smooth whenever positive, and the Jacobian of $D(\cdot)$ is negative definite.

The demand system can be obtained from the optimization problem of a representative consumer. Furthermore, as we have seen in chapter 3, partial equilibrium analysis of the industry can be justified if the representative consumer has utility linear in income (or in an aggregate numéraire sector representing the rest of the economy). Let us recall that in this case the demands for the differentiated product sector, with subutility $U(q)$ and for a large enough income, are derived from the solution to the program

$$\max_q U(q) - pq.$$

Suppose that U is smooth and strictly concave (the Hessian of U, H_U, is negative definite). Inverse demands follow from the first-order conditions of the maximization problem: $p_i = \partial U_i/\partial q_i$ for $q_i > 0$. They have the properties of symmetry of cross effects, $\partial P_i/\partial q_j = \partial P_j/\partial q_i$, $j \neq i$, and downward-sloping demand, $\partial P_i/\partial q_i < 0$. If goods are substitutes, $\partial^2 U/\partial q_j \partial q_i = \partial P_i/\partial q_j \leq 0$, $j \neq i$, and if they are complements, $\partial^2 U/\partial q_j \partial q_i = \partial P_i/\partial q_j \geq 0$, $j \neq i$.

Inverting the inverse demand system we obtain direct demands, downward sloping and with symmetric cross effects. Nevertheless, it is worth pointing out that except for the case of two goods, even if goods are substitutes according to the utility function, $\partial^2 U/\partial q_j \partial q_i \leq 0$, we cannot tell whether they are gross substitutes, $\partial D_i/\partial p_j \geq 0$, $j \neq i$.[3]

We do not require as a maintained assumption that demands come from a representative consumer except when dealing with welfare analysis. In consequence cross-price effects need not be symmetric in general. Some examples of demand systems follow.

Example 1. Quadratic Utility Function and Linear Demands
Consider first a duopolistic industry with a representative consumer with U given by

$$U(q) = \alpha_1 q_1 + \alpha_2 q_2 - \tfrac{1}{2}(\beta_1 q_1^2 + 2\gamma q_1 q_2 + \beta_2 q_2^2),$$

with all the parameters positive expect possibly γ and with $\beta_1 \beta_2 - \gamma^2 > 0$. These assumptions ensure that U is strictly concave. Furthermore we assume that $\alpha_i \beta_j - \alpha_j \gamma > 0, i \neq j, i = 1, 2$. The goods are substitutes, independent, or complements according to whether $\gamma \gtreqless 0$.

When $\alpha_1 = \alpha_2$, and $\beta_1 = \beta_2 = \gamma$, then the goods are perfect substitutes. When $\alpha_1 = \alpha_2$, $\gamma^2/\beta_1\beta_2$ expresses the degree of product differentiation, ranging from 0 for independent goods to 1 for perfect substitutes. The inverse demand system is given by

$$p_1 = \alpha_1 - \beta_1 q_1 - \gamma q_2,$$

$$p_2 = \alpha_2 - \beta_2 q_2 - \gamma q_1,$$

on the region $\{q \in R_+^2 : \alpha_1 - \beta_1 q_1 - \gamma q_2 > 0, \alpha_2 - \beta_2 q_2 - \gamma q_1 > 0\}$. Direct demands are given by

$$q_1 = a_1 - b_1 p_1 + c p_2,$$

$$q_2 = a_2 - b_2 p_2 + c p_1,$$

in the cone-shaped region of price space

$$\{p \in R_+^2 : a_1 - b_1 p_1 + c p_2 > 0, a_2 - b_2 p_2 - c p_1 > 0\},$$

where $a_1 = (\alpha_1\beta_2 - \alpha_2\gamma)/\Delta$, $b_1 = \beta_2/\Delta$, $c = \gamma/\Delta$, $\Delta = \beta_1\beta_2 - \gamma^2$, and similarly for a_2 and b_2.

The demand for firm 1 is given by

$$D_1(p_1, p_2) = \max\left\{0, \min\left\{a_1 - b_1 p_1 + c p_2, \frac{\alpha_1 - p_1}{\beta_1}\right\}\right\},$$

and similarly for firm 2. The demand of the firm has a kink at a critical p_1 for which the firm becomes a monopoly, with demand $(\alpha_1 - p_1)/\beta_1$. In a symmetric case this price is given by $p_1 = \gamma^{-1}(\beta p_2 - \alpha(\beta - \gamma))$.

The example is easily generalized to n products. With a symmetric (strictly concave) utility function we have (see exercise 6.9 for the general asymmetric version):

$$U(q) = \alpha \sum_{i=1}^{n} q_i - \frac{1}{2}\left(\beta \sum_{i=1}^{n} q_i^2 + 2\gamma \sum_{j \neq i} q_i q_j\right),$$

where $\beta > \gamma > 0$ and $\alpha > 0$. Then for positive demands and $i = 1, \ldots, n$,

$$P_i(q) = \alpha - \beta q_i - \gamma \sum_{j \neq i} q_j,$$

$$D_i(p) = a_n - b_n p_i + c_n \sum_{j \neq i} p_j,$$

where $a_n = \alpha/(\beta + (n-1)\gamma)$, $b_n = (\beta + (n-2)\gamma)/((\beta + (n-1)\gamma)(\beta - \gamma))$, and $c_n = \gamma/((\beta + (n-1)\gamma)(\beta - \gamma))$.

Example 2. Constant Elasticity
Consider a n-good industry with representative consumer with U given by

$$U(q) = \left(\sum_{i=1}^{n} q_i^{\beta} \right)^{\theta}.$$

The function $U(\cdot)$ is homogeneous of degree $\beta\theta$. To ensure (strict) concavity, we need $0 < \beta\theta < 1$. We assume that $\theta < 1$ and $1 \geq \beta$. The function displays a constant elasticity of substitution between the (differentiated) goods: $\sigma = 1/(1 - \beta)$. Goods are substitutes, independent, or complements, according to whether β is larger, equal, or smaller than 0. For $\beta = 1$ goods are homogenous. See figure 6.1.
    Inverse demands are given by

$$P_i(q) = \beta\theta \left(\sum_{j=1}^{n} q_j^{\beta} \right)^{\theta-1} q_i^{\beta-1}$$

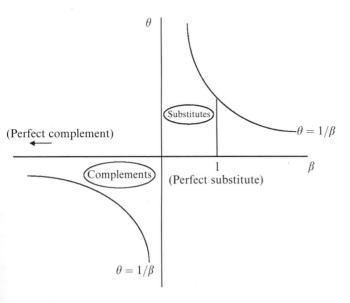

Figure 6.1

for any strictly positive vector of quantities q. Demand is downward sloping, $\partial P_i/\partial q_i < 0$, and $\partial P_i/\partial q_j \leq 0$, $j \neq i$ if the goods are substitutes, $\beta \geq 0$ ($\partial P_i/\partial q_j \geq 0$, $j \neq i$, if they are complements, $\beta \leq 0$). Direct demands are given by

$$D_i(p) = (\beta\theta)^{1/(1-\beta\theta)} \frac{p_i^{1/(\beta-1)}}{\left(\sum_j p_j^{\beta/(\beta-1)}\right)^{(1-\theta)/(1-\beta\theta)}}$$

for any strictly positive price vector p. Note that $1 > \theta > 0$ and $0 < \beta < 1$ imply that $(1-\theta)/(1-\beta\theta) \in (0,1)$.

Under the assumptions, demand is downward sloping and the goods are gross substitutes (complements) if $\beta \geq 0$ (≤ 0).

Example 3. Logit
For all $p \geq 0$,

$$D_i(p) = \frac{k_i e^{\lambda p_i}}{\sum_j k_j e^{\lambda p_j}}, \qquad \text{with} \quad \lambda < 0 \text{ and } k_j > 0.$$

Example 4. Constant Expenditure

$$D_i(p) = \frac{1}{p_i} \frac{g(p_i)}{\sum_j g(p_j)},$$

with $g(p) > 0$ for all $p \geq 0$, g is smooth with $g' < 0$. This system has a (normalized) constant expenditure $\sum_i p_i D_i = 1$. Particular examples are CES demands, with $g(p) = p^r$ and $r < 0$, and exponential with $g(p) = e^{-\beta p}$, and $\beta > 0$. In this system, demand is downward sloping and goods (strict) gross substitutes.

Remark 1 The logit and CES demands can be derived from three different approaches: A representative consumer, a discrete choice model, or a characteristics model (see Anderson et al. (1992, ch. 5). This provides three different interpretations or microfoundations of these demand systems.

6.2   Quantity and Price Competition

Quantity (Cournot) and price (Bertrand) competition are defined as in chapters 4 and 5, respectively. In the Cournot case profits are given, as a function of quantities supplied to the market, by $\pi_i =$

$P_i(q)q_i - C_i(q_i)$, and in the Bertrand case, as a function of prices set, by $\pi_i = p_i D_i(p) - C_i(D_i(p))$.

Suppose that strategy sets (quantities or prices) are compact intervals (this could be extended to the closed half-line) and that cost functions are lower semicontinuous. The demand system fulfills the maintained assumption of the last section. Then whenever profits are a quasiconcave function of the strategy of the firm, existence is guaranteed according to the classical existence theorem (theorem 2.1). As we know, quasiconcavity is a restrictive assumption.

With Cournot competition, if $P_i(q)$ is log-concave (and downward sloping) in q_i (whenever $P_i(q) > 0$) and $\partial P_i/\partial q_i - C_i'' < 0$, then π_i is strictly quasiconcave in q_i. Indeed, considering a smooth market, log-concavity of $P_i(q)$ in q_i is equivalent to $p_i\partial^2 P_i/(\partial q_i)^2 - (\partial P_i/\partial q_i)^2 \leq 0$, and then $\partial^2 \pi_i/(\partial q_i)^2 < 0$ when evaluated at a critical point $\partial \pi_i/\partial q_i = 0$.[4] (If π_i is monotone, then it is obviously quasiconcave.)

With Bertrand competition and with constant marginal costs, c_i for firm i, a sufficient condition for $\pi_i = (p_i - c_i)D_i(p)$ to be quasiconcave in p_i is that $1/D_i(p)$ be convex in p_i (whenever $D_i(p) > 0$).[5] This provides a weaker condition than concavity of $D_i(p)$ with respect to p_i to ensure existence of price equilibria. Indeed, it is easy to check that concavity of $D_i(p)$ with respect to p_i implies that $1/D_i(p)$ is convex in p_i. Examples where $1/D_i(p)$ is convex in p_i but concavity of demand cannot be ascertained are the logit, and constant expenditure systems with CES or exponential functions. Strengthening the requirement on the demand function (and with the maintained assumption of downward-sloping demand) the result can be extended: If $D_i(p)$ is log-concave in p_i (whenever $D_i(p) > 0$) and costs are convex, then π_i is strictly quasiconcave in p_i (see exercise 6.4).[6]

Another sufficient condition for π_i to be quasiconcave whenever profits are strictly positive in p_i is that $\log D_i(p)$ be concave in $\log p_i$ whenever demand is strictly positive (Caplin and Nalebuff 1991, prop. 11). Indeed, to demonstrate the result, it is sufficient to note that, under the assumption, $\log \pi_i(= \log(p_i - c_i) + \log D_i(p))$ is concave in $\log p_i$ whenever profits are strictly positive. The condition is equivalent to the elasticity of demand for good i, $\eta_i = -(p_i/q_i)(\partial D_i/\partial p_i)$, being increasing in p_i. This holds, for example, in the logit and CES cases.

In regard to the uniqueness issue, the standard theorems of section 2.5 can be applied. A difference between the Cournot and Bertrand cases is that the contraction condition $\partial^2 \pi_i/(\partial a_i)^2 + \sum_{j \neq i} |\partial^2 \pi_i/\partial a_i \partial a_j|$ < 0 tends to be more easily fulfilled in the latter case.

With Cournot competition the assumption is particularly strong when goods are close to perfect substitutes. Indeed, it is worth to recall that with homogeneous products, concave demand, and constant marginal costs, the assumption is only fulfilled for the case of two firms. For example, in the linear and symmetric demand system with substitute goods (example 1 with $\beta > \gamma > 0$), the contraction condition for the Cournot case boils down to $2\beta - (n-1)\gamma > 0$, which holds always only with two or three firms. Furthermore, for given utility parameters β and γ, it never holds for n large. The closer the γ is to β, the harder it is to meet the condition. In contrast, in the Bertrand case the condition is $2b - (n-1)c > 0$, which holds always (under the assumption of a negative definite Jacobian for $D(\cdot)$, we have that $b - (n-1)c > 0$). Sufficient conditions for the contraction condition to hold in the (gross substitutes) price game is that $(1 - (\partial D_i/\partial p_i)C_i'') > 0$, $\sum_{j=1}^{n}(\partial D_i/\partial p_j) < 0$, and $\partial^2 D_i/(\partial p_i)^2 + \sum_{j \neq i} |\partial^2 D_i/\partial p_i \partial p_j| < 0$. The latter two conditions mean that the own effect of a price change dominates the cross effects both in terms of the level and slope of demand. Indeed, we have that

$$\frac{\partial^2 \pi_i}{(\partial p_i)^2} + \sum_{j \neq i} \left| \frac{\partial^2 \pi_i}{\partial p_i \partial p_j} \right|$$

$$= \frac{\partial D_i}{\partial p_i} + \left(1 - \frac{\partial D_i}{\partial p_i} C_i'' \right) \sum_{j=1}^{n} \frac{\partial D_i}{\partial p_j} + (p_i - C_i') \left(\frac{\partial^2 D_i}{(\partial p_i)^2} + \sum_{j \neq i} \left| \frac{\partial^2 D_i}{\partial p_i \partial p_j} \right| \right).$$

Unlike the Cournot case, these sufficient conditions do not become more restrictive as the number of firms increases.[7] We will later see other examples in which the contraction condition holds for the price game. For Cournot markets the other approaches to uniqueness must be used. When inverse demand for good i depends only on its own quantity q_i and the aggregate of the quantities of the rivals $\sum_{j \neq i} q_j$, then a sufficient condition for uniqueness of equilibrium is that Cournot best-response functions have negative slopes larger than -1. The proof of this fact is similar to the case of homogeneous products (see exercise 6.2).

Using the theory of supermodular games, we can do away with the quasiconcavity assumption to ensure existence, and we can obtain further results on the structure of the equilibrium set in several instances. Let us discuss the Cournot case first and the Bertrand one afterward.

In the Cournot case we can dispose of the quasiconcavity assumption for the duopoly case when goods are strategic substitutes (the revenue $R_i(q_i, q_{-i})$ displays decreasing differences or $\partial^2 R_i/\partial q_i \partial q_j \leq 0$; that is, $-R_i(q_i, q_{-i})$ displays increasing differences), or when goods are strategic complements ($R_i(q_i, q_{-i})$ displays increasing differences or $\partial^2 R_i/\partial q_i \partial q_j \geq 0$). The first case is more likely to arise when goods are substitutes. Indeed, $\partial^2 R_i/\partial q_i \partial q_j = \partial P_i/\partial q_j + q_i(\partial^2 P_i/\partial q_i \partial q_j)$ is more likely to be nonpositive if the goods are substitutes, $\partial P_i/\partial q_j \leq 0, j \neq i$. The second, when they are complements, $\partial P_i/\partial q_j \geq 0, j \neq i$. In the case of strategic complementarity (according to theorem 2.5), there is a smallest and a largest equilibrium. If $\partial^2 R_i/\partial q_i \partial q_j > 0$ and $n = 2$ or 3, the equilibrium set is ordered.

In fact, to obtain decreasing best responses, it is enough that $\pi_i(q_i, q_{-i})$ fulfills a dual (strict) single crossing property in (q_i, q_{-i}): $\pi_i(x_i, y_{-i}) \leq \pi_i(y_i, y_{-i})$ implies that $\pi_i(x_i, x_{-i}) \leq (<) \pi_i(y_i, x_{-i})$ for $x_i > y_i$ and $x_{-i} \geq y_{-i}, x_{-i} \neq y_{-i}$. The strict version of the single crossing property holds when $\log P_i$ is submodular in (q_i, q_{-i}), costs are strictly increasing, and goods are strict substitutes. Then best-response correspondences are strongly decreasing (i.e., every selection is decreasing). Similarly best-response correspondences are strongly increasing when $\log P_i$ is supermodular in (q_i, q_{-i}), costs are strictly increasing, and goods are strict complements. These latter set of assumptions is fulfilled, for instance, in the constant elasticity case (example 2) when $\beta < 0$ and with constant marginal costs.[8] (See exercise 6.5 and sections 2.2.2 and 2.2.3. See exercise 6.6 for a smooth version of the results.)

With Bertrand competition and substitute goods, the assumption that the game is supermodular is a natural, although not a universal one. Indeed, suppose that the game is smooth, then the profit function will exhibit increasing differences if $\partial^2 \pi_i/\partial p_i \partial p_j = [1 - (\partial D_i/\partial p_i)C_i''](\partial D_i/\partial p_j) + (p_i - C_i')(\partial^2 D_i/\partial p_i \partial p_j) \geq 0$. The first term will be positive if the goods are gross substitutes and costs are convex, and the second, if demand shows increasing differences $\partial^2 D_i/\partial p_i \partial p_j \geq 0$ (and price is above marginal cost). The conditions are met if demand is linear ($\partial^2 D_i/\partial p_i \partial p_j = 0$) and costs are convex. Considering increasing transformations of payoffs the theory of supermodular games can be extended (see sections 2.2.2. and 2.2.3). With constant marginal costs, c_i for firm i, it is sufficient that the logarithm of demand displays increasing differences for the log-transformed game to be supermodular.[9] Indeed, in this case $\pi_i = (p_i - c_i)D_i(p)$ and $\partial^2 \log \pi_i / \partial p_i \partial p_j \geq 0$ whenever $\partial^2 \log D_i / \partial p_i \partial p_j \geq 0$. The latter holds when the elasticity of demand for good $i (\eta_i)$ is increasing in the price of the rival goods. This is the case for the constant elasticity, logit, and constant expenditure examples. Equilibrium exists in those cases.

In fact, in the CES and logit cases the contraction condition holds for the transformed payoffs, and therefore the equilibrium is unique and stable $(\partial^2 \log \pi_i / (\partial p_i)^2) + \sum_{j \neq i} |(\partial^2 \log \pi_i) / \partial p_i \partial p_j| < 0$, see sections 2.5 and 2.6). In the general constant expenditure system if the elasticity of g, $\eta_g = -pg'(p)/g(p)$, is increasing with p, then for equal marginal costs there is a unique and symmetric price equilibrium (see exercise 6.7).

Equilibria in pure strategies in supermodular price games with substitute products will always exist and will be bounded between a largest and a smallest equilibrium price vectors (which will coincide with the Pareto best and the Pareto worst equilibria from the point of view of firms since the profit of a firm is increasing in the prices of the rivals for prices above marginal cost because the goods are gross substitutes. (See remark 14 in section 2.2.3.) Typically the equilibrium set has more order structure. For example, with two or three single-product firms, equilibrium prices are ordered if the game is strictly supermodular (Vives 1985b; see section 2.2.3). The order structure of the equilibrium set is not only useful in welfare analysis but also in comparing Bertrand (price competition) and Cournot (quantity competition) outcomes. As we will see, the fact that there is a smallest Bertrand equilibrium can be used to show that, under regularity conditions, all Cournot prices must be above it (Vives 1990a).

Even if equilibrium analysis is not found palatable, supermodular price games will typically narrow down possible strategic outcomes. Indeed, if the equilibrium is unique, the game will be dominance solvable and consequently stable according to the Cournot tâtonnement. If there are multiple equilibria, all possible strategic (rationalizable) outcomes will lie in the cube determined by the largest and the smallest price equilibrium vectors. In a supermodular price game the Cournot tâtonnement will approach this set of prices starting from any initial position. These results contrast, for example, with nonsupermodular oligopoly games for which, in general, a wide array of outcomes between the monopoly and the competitive solution are possible. Further smooth supermodular games give rise to monotone systems, yielding global convergence from almost all initial conditions for both continuous best-reply or gradient dynamics provided that the equilibrium set is countable or (totally) ordered. (See section 2.6, in particular, theorems 2.10 and 2.11.)

As claimed in section 2.2.3, comparative statics results follow easily. For example, the imposition of an excise tax t on a Bertrand supermodular oligopoly with a unique equilibrium will increase necessarily equilibrium prices, since the marginal profitability of a firm increases with t ($\pi_i = (p_i - t)D_i(p) - C_i(D_i(p))$ and $\partial^2 \pi_i / \partial p_i \partial t = -\partial D_i / \partial p_i > 0$). If there are multiple equilibria, then the largest and smallest price equilibrium vectors are increasing in the parameter t.

It is worth to remark nevertheless that Bertrand games need not be supermodular. For example, Roberts and Sonnenschein (1977) and Friedman (1983) provide nonexistence examples of price-setting differentiated duopolies with no costs. In the first instance the best-reply map of one of the firms slopes down (pp. 109–10), and in the second the best-reply correspondence of one of the firms jumps down (p. 69). Another example is provided by the presence of avoidable fixed costs, which will make best replies jump down and may imply the nonexistence of a price equilibrium (in pure strategies). Indeed, consider the duopoly game arising from example 1 with two firms with zero marginal costs and firm 2 having an avoidable fixed cost F. When the price of firm 1 is low, demand for firm 2 is also low and revenues are not enough to cover the fixed cost. Firm 2 then decides to stay out of the market (charging a price such that chokes off demand). As p_1 increases revenues for firm 2 also increase, and at the point where they cover the fixed cost F, the firm is indifferent between staying out or entering the market by charging a *lower* price. This jump down of the best reply of firm 2 will cause the nonexistence of a Bertrand equilibrium when F is large enough so that an interior Bertrand equilibrium (with positive production for both firms) is not profitable for firm 2. But it is small enough so that whenever it is optimal for firm 1 to price firm 2 out of the market, this is not feasible (see figure 6.2).

In the classical *Hotelling model* there is no equilibrium in prices if firms are located close to each other. In that case firm 1 sets a low

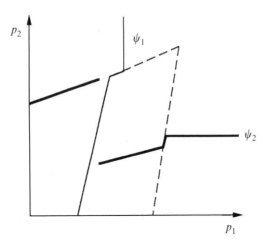

Figure 6.2

price when firm 2 sets a low price too. As p_2 increases firm 1 raises its price up to a point where it pays to undercut firm 2's price. Firm 1 lowers p_1 discontinuously to price firm 2 out of the market (see D'Aspremont et al. 1979). This is another instance of a well-known price game that is not supermodular. This is not to say that we cannot obtain monotone best responses in price games in location models. For example, best responses are increasing in the Hotelling model when firms are located at the extremes of the segment (see exercise 6.8 for an instance of discontinuous but increasing best response in a location game studied by Thisse and Vives 1992).

6.3 Characterization and Comparison of Cournot and Bertrand Equilibria

Suppose now that demand and costs are smooth, that goods are (strict) gross substitutes and let us restrict attention to interior equilibria.[10] Both Cournot and Bertrand equilibria will fulfill first-order necessary conditions. In the Cournot case this will yield

$$\frac{p_i - C_i'}{p_i} = \varepsilon_i,$$

where ε_i is the elasticity of inverse demand $\varepsilon_i = -(q_i/p_i)(\partial P_i/\partial q_i)$. In the Bertrand case

$$\frac{p_i - C_i'}{p_i} = \frac{1}{\eta_i},$$

where η_i is the elasticity of demand $\eta_i = -(p_i/q_i)(\partial D_i/\partial p_i)$.

In both cases firms price according to the monopoly price formula with respect to their residual demand. It is important to notice that the residual demand is not the same in the Cournot and in the Bertrand cases. That is, $\varepsilon_i \neq 1/\eta_i$. This is in contrast to a homogeneous product market where the elasticity of inverse demand equals the inverse of the demand elasticity. In fact it is easily seen that if goods are gross substitutes, then for any price vector the perceived elasticity of demand is larger under price competition $\varepsilon_i \geq 1/\eta_i$.

PROPOSITION 6.1   For any price vector and any good $\varepsilon_i \geq 1/\eta_i$ whenever goods are gross substitutes or complements.[11]

Proof   The result follows by differentiating the identity $p_i = P_i(D_1(p), \ldots, D_n(p))$ with respect to p_i to obtain

$$1 = \frac{\partial P_i}{\partial q_i}\frac{\partial D_i}{\partial p_i} + \sum_{j \neq i} \frac{\partial P_i}{\partial q_j}\frac{\partial D_j}{\partial p_i}.$$

If the goods are gross substitutes then $\partial D_i/\partial p_j \geq 0, j \neq i$, and $\partial P_i/\partial q_j \leq 0, j \neq i$. If the goods are complements then $\partial P_i/\partial q_j \geq 0, j \neq i$, and $\partial D_i/\partial p_j \leq 0, j \neq i$. Therefore in both cases $(\partial P_i/\partial q_j)(\partial D_j/\partial p_i) \leq 0$ and $(\partial P_i/\partial q_i)(\partial D_i/\partial p_i) \geq 1$. This is equivalent to $\varepsilon_i \geq 1/\eta_i$. Notice that any negative product $(\partial P_i/\partial q_j)(\partial D_j/\partial p_i) < 0$ will make the inequality strict.   ◆

A corollary to the proposition is that at a Cournot equilibrium with price vector p^C firms would have always incentives to cut prices, that is, $\partial \pi_i(p^C)/\partial p_i \leq 0$ for any i (where π_i are profits as a function of prices). Similarly, at a Bertrand equilibrium, firms would have an incentive to decrease output. That is, at quantity vector q^B, $\partial \pi_i(q^B)/\partial q_i \leq 0$, for any i (where π_i are profits as a function of quantities).[12] In Cournot competition each firm expects the others to cut prices in response to price cuts, while in Bertrand competition the firm expects the others to maintain prices. The consequence is that Cournot competition penalizes price cuts more and tends to be less competitive. The following two propositions formalize the intuition. The first follows from Vives (1985a, prop. 2; 1990a, prop. 7.2).

PROPOSITION 6.2   In a market with gross substitute—or complementary—products if the price game is (smooth ordinally) supermodular and quasiconcave (i.e., π_i is quasiconcave in p_i) then any interior Cournot equilibrium will involve higher prices than the smallest Bertrand equilibrium price vector.

Proof   Consider the Cournot price equilibrium vector p^C. It follows then from quasiconcavity and the fact that $\partial \pi_i(p^C)/\partial p_i \leq 0$ that $p_i^C \geq \Psi_i(p_{-i}^C) = \inf \Psi_i(p_{-i}^C)$ for any i, where $\Psi_i(\cdot)$ is the Bertrand best-reply correspondence of firm i. Consider now the dynamic process $p^0 = p^C, p^1 = \Psi(p^C), \ldots$ This defines a decreasing sequence, since $p^C \geq \Psi(p^C)$ and $\Psi(\cdot)$ is an increasing function (see section 2.6). The sequence is bounded below and therefore converges to a price vector p^B which must be a Bertrand equilibrium by continuity of the payoffs in prices. Since the game is (ordinally) supermodular there is a smallest Bertrand equilibrium $\underline{p}^B$ and certainly $\underline{p}^B \leq p^C$.   ◆

Remark 2   Sufficient conditions for the price game with gross substitute goods to be ordinally supermodular and (strictly) quasiconcave are as follows: Each firm has an increasing convex cost function $C_i, D_i(p)$ is log-concave (and downward sloping) in p_i when positive, and $\partial^2 \log D_i/\partial p_i \partial p_j \geq 0, i \neq j$. (See exercise 6.4.)

Remark 3   A dual argument establishes the following result for quantity comparisons in a market with gross substitute or complementary products: If the quantity game is (smooth ordinally) supermodular and quasiconcave (i.e., π_i is quasiconcave in q_i), then any interior Bertrand equilibrium will involve higher outputs than the smallest Cournot equilibrium quantity vector. The quantity game will be naturally supermodular when goods are complementary. Sufficient conditions for the quantity game with complementary goods to be ordinally supermodular and (strictly) quasiconcave are as follows: Each firm has an increasing convex cost function $C_i, P_i(q)$ is log-concave (and downward sloping when positive) in q_i, and log-supermodular in (q_i, q_{-i}). (See exercise 6.6.)

In the constant elasticity case (example 2) with constant and equal marginal costs, best-response functions are well-defined and increasing when $\beta < 0$, although then $P_i(q)$ is log-convex in q_i. In fact in this case there is a unique symmetric Cournot equilibrium, and there are no asymmetric equilibria (because best replies are increasing and the game is symmetric with one-dimensional strategy spaces, only symmetric equilibria can exist; see the comments at the end of the example on one-dimensional strategy spaces in section 2.2.3). Suppose that the demand system is symmetric. That is, interchanging the prices of the rival goods does not affect the demand for any good, as a function of its own price, and any two goods which sell at the same price have the same demand. Formally, the demand system can be described by a unique demand function for any good depending on its own price and the prices of rivals, $D_i(p_i; p_{-i}) = D(p_i; p_{-i})$ for all i. We can define the demand for simultaneous price movements as $G(p) = D(p; p, \ldots, p)$ which corresponds to the Chamberlinian DD curve. It follows from our assumptions that demand is downward sloping, $G' < 0$. This just means that the own price effect dominates the cross-price effects when all firms charge the same price:[13]

$$G' = \frac{\partial D_i}{\partial p_i} + \sum_{j \neq i} \frac{\partial D_i}{\partial p_j} < 0.$$

Now, if firms have identical cost functions $C(\cdot)$ and the contraction condition $(\partial^2 \pi_i / (\partial p_i)^2) + \sum_{j \neq i} |\partial^2 \pi_i / \partial p_i \partial p_j| < 0$ (see section 2.5) holds for the price game, then $\phi(p) = \partial \pi_i(p, \ldots, p)/\partial p_i$ will be downward sloping in p and $\phi(p) = 0$ will define the unique (interior) Bertrand equilibrium. At a symmetric interior Cournot equilibrium $\phi(p^C) \leq 0$, and therefore the Bertrand price will be lower. Since $G' < 0$, it follows also that a Cournot equilibrium the quantity produced must be smaller than the Bertrand one. Further, provided that $pG(p) - C(G(p))$ is concave in p, it is easy to see that Bertrand profits will be lower than Cournot profits (in turn lower, obviously, than monopoly profits; Vives 1985a). The welfare ranking with Bertrand dominating Cournot in terms of total surplus TS easily follows. At a symmetric solution q, $TS(q) = U(q, \ldots, q) - nC(q)$, which is concave provided that costs are convex under our maintained assumption on utility for the substitute goods (negative definite Hessian of U with nonpositive off-diagonal elements). At the Bertrand solution $TS'(q^B) > 0$, since $p^B > C'(q^B)$ (and $TS' = n(p - C')$) while at the optimum $p = C'(q^0)$. It follows then that $TS(q^0) > TS(q^B) \geq TS(q^C)$. In summary, we have (Vives 1985a, prop. 1):

PROPOSITION 6.3   If the market for the gross substitute products is symmetric (in terms of demand and cost structure across firms which satisfy regularity assumptions guaranteeing interior equilibria) and the contraction condition holds for the price game, the unique Bertrand equilibrium displays lower prices and profits, and higher total surplus, than any symmetric Cournot equilibrium.

Let us analyze now in more detail a few examples: an asymmetric linear duopoly, and symmetric, respectively, linear, constant elasticity, and constant expenditure oligopolies.

Consider the linear duopoly of example 1 with firms with constant marginal costs $m_i < \alpha_i, i = 1, 2$. In this case Cournot (Bertrand) competition with substitute products is the dual of Bertrand (Cournot) competition with complementary products. This duality was first pointed out in a nondifferentiated framework by Sonnenschein (1968). The duality result in our linear duopoly follows immediately from the profit expressions. For example, with zero marginal costs, in the Cournot case firm's 1 profit is $(\alpha_1 - \beta_1 q_1 - \gamma q_2)q_1$, and in the Bertrand case $p_1(a_1 - b_1 p_1 + c p_2)$. The expressions are perfectly dual (and recall that $\gamma > 0$ if the goods are substitutes and $\gamma < 0$ if they are complementary). We can obtain one expression from the other by identifying q_i with p_i, α_1 with a_1, β_1 with b_1 and γ with $-c$. A practical implication is that the computations made for one type of competition provide the result immediately for the other type. With positive marginal costs just let $\hat{\alpha}_i = \alpha_i - m_i, \hat{a}_i = a_i - b_i m_i + c m_j$, and $\hat{p}_i = p_i - m_i$. Then in the Cournot case firm's 1 profit is $(\hat{\alpha}_1 - \beta_1 q_1 - \gamma q_2)q_1$, and in the Bertrand case $\hat{p}_1(\hat{a}_1 - b_1 \hat{p}_1 + c \hat{p}_2)$.

Cournot and Bertrand equilibria are unique. The equilibrium levels of prices and quantities are given in table 6.1 (Singh and Vives 1984). It is easily checked that

$$p_i^C - p_i^B = \frac{\hat{a}_i}{4(\beta_1\beta_2/\gamma^2) - 1} \quad \text{and} \quad q_i^B - q_i^C = \frac{\hat{a}_i}{4(b_1 b_2/c^2) - 1}.$$

Table 6.1
Equilibrium levels of prices and quantities

	Price	Quantity
Bertrand	$\dfrac{2\hat{a}_1 b_2 + \hat{a}_2 c}{4b_1 b_2 - c^2}$	$b_1 \hat{p}_1^B$
Cournot	$\beta_1 q_1^C$	$\dfrac{2\hat{\alpha}_1\beta_2 - \hat{\alpha}_2\gamma}{4\beta_1\beta_2 - \gamma^2}.$

The first difference is strictly positive by assumption and the second also provided that when firms price at marginal cost both firms have positive demand ($\hat{a}_i > 0$). The last condition is needed to ensure interior equilibria for all possible demand systems. Then with substitute products Cournot competition involves higher prices and profits and lower outputs than Bertrand equilibria. However, when $\hat{a}_i < 0$, which means that when firms price at marginal cost firm i cannot sell anything, then $q_i^B - q_i^C < 0$, and this situation may arise with interior solutions for both types of equilibria.[14] The difference between the Cournot and the Bertrand price increases the less differentiated the products are (i.e., the smaller $\beta_1\beta_2/\gamma^2$ is). It is worth noting that the profit result holds in an asymmetric situation.

Under the maintained assumption on the demand system (negative definite Jacobian) the result for prices and quantities ($q_i^B - q_i^C > 0$ and $p_i^B - p_i^C < 0$) is also true for complementary products.[15] Nevertheless, with complementary products Cournot prices may be lower than Bertrand prices when the demand assumptions do not hold (e.g., when cross price effects dominate own price effects; see Okuguchi 1987). The profit ranking between Cournot and Bertrand equilibria is reversed with complementary products.

The welfare implications for consumers of lower prices are immediate: Consumer surplus is higher. In the linear duopoly example consumer surplus is higher under Bertrand competition irrespective of whether the goods are substitutes or complements (obviously, if the goods are independent both equilibria are identical and equal to the monopoly outcome). Total surplus (given by $U(q) - m_1q_1 - m_2q_2$) increases with q, and therefore whenever both outputs are higher under Bertrand competition, we can guarantee that total surplus will be higher also than under Cournot competition.

For the n-firm symmetric case equilibria are easily computed also (example 1). Assuming for simplicity that marginal costs are constant and equal to zero, Cournot and Bertrand equilibria are unique. Linearity and the parameter restrictions assure global invertibility of the first-order conditions in both instances according to the univalence approach (see section 2.5). In fact, as we have seen before, in the price game the contraction condition for payoffs holds if and only if $2b - (n-1)c > 0$, and our assumptions on demand imply that $b - (n-1)c > 0$. The Cournot price is given by $p^C = \alpha\beta/(2\beta + (n-1)\gamma)$ and the Bertrand price by $p^B = a/(2b - (n-1)c)$. The regularity assumptions of proposition 6.3 are fulfilled and the results hold with strict inequality. Furthermore the difference $p^C - p^B$ is increasing in the degree of substitutability of the products γ/β. The Chamberlinian DD demand function is given by $G_n(p) = (\alpha - p)/ (\beta + (n - 1)\gamma)$. (See exercise 6.9.)

Let us consider now the constant elasticity case (example 2). Suppose that marginal costs are constant and equal to m. It is easily seen that there is a unique symmetric Cournot equilibrium with price $p^C = nm/(\beta(\theta + n - 1))$ and a unique symmetric Bertrand equilibrium with price $p^B = n(1 - \beta\theta) + \beta(\theta - 1))m/(\beta n(1 - \beta\theta) + \beta(\theta - 1))$. (See exercise 6.10.) The price game is log-supermodular, and therefore the symmetric equilibrium is the unique one. The comparison of prices, quantities, and welfare is as in proposition 5.3, and the difference $p^C - p^B$ is increasing with the degree of substitutability of the products β. As β tends to 1 (perfect substitutes), p^C tends to the Cournot price with homogeneous products, $nm/(\theta + n - 1)$, and p^B to marginal cost m (the competitive price). The Chamberlinian DD demand function is given by $G_n(p) = (\beta\theta)^{1/(1-\beta\theta)} p^{-1/(1-\beta\theta)} n^{-(1-\theta)/(1-\beta\theta)}$.

In the constant expenditure case (example 4) with $g(p) = e^{-\beta p}$, $\beta > 0$, and constant marginal costs m, the unique Bertrand equilibrium of the game is given by

$$p^B = \frac{m + \sqrt{m^2 + 4mn/[\beta(n - 1)]}}{2}$$

(see exercise 6.7). As before, $p^B \to m$ as goods become perfect substitutes ($\beta \to \infty$) provided that there are at least two firms.

Remark 4 It should be clear how to extend the results presented to multiproduct competition using the general results of chapter 2. The theorems stated there about existence, unicity, and stability of equilibria apply typically to firms having as strategy sets compact cubes in Euclidean space. For examples of analysis of multiproduct Bertrand oligopolies with product differentiation, see Spady (1984), who uses a modified logit model yielding increasing best responses and unique equilibria, and Anderson et al. (1992, sec. 7.7), considering a multinomial nested logit model (see also exercise 6.11).

6.4   Large Markets and Monopolistic Competition

What happens as we increase the number of firms in a differentiated product environment? Two possibilities arise depending on whether the residual elasticity of demand faced by a firm remains bounded or not. If it increases without bound, then the outcome will be competitive (price will equal marginal cost in the limit). If it remains bounded, the outcome will be monopolistically competitive. That is, a firm will retain some monopoly power in the limit even if it is negligible with respect to the market. This corresponds to the Chamberlinian large group case. The crucial determinant of the final outcome (and therefore of the competitiveness of the market) is the degree of substitutability of the products. Indeed, we know from Mas-Colell (1975) that increasing the number of goods with a compact space of characteristics will make the goods more substitutable and the outcomes closer to competitive. On the other hand, if goods, no matter how many there are, have no "neighbors" (as in Spence 1976a, b; Dixit and Stiglitz 1977; Hart 1985; or Vives 1987; see the uniform Inada property in section 3.2), then even in the limit firms retain monopoly power, that is, face a downward-sloping demand.

Consider a symmetric (both in terms of demand and costs) differentiated market satisfying our maintained assumptions. Interior symmetric equilibria will be characterized by $(p - C')/p = 1/\eta$, in the Bertrand case, where η is the elasticity of demand of a firm. Price will approach marginal cost as the number of firms n increases if η tends to infinity with n. Following Bennassy (1989), suppose now that demands come from a representative consumer with (strictly quasiconcave) utility function $U(q_0, q)$, where q is the vector of differentiated commodities and q_0 is the numéraire (this a generalization of the quasilinear case, for which $W(q_0, q) = q_0 + U(q)$; see section 3.1). For a symmetric allocation denote by σ the (Allen-Hicks) elasticity of substitution between any pair of differentiated goods,[16] by σ_0 the elasticity of substitution between the numéraire and a differentiated good, and by η^I the income elasticity of the demand for a differentiated good. Assuming that the latter is bounded, it is easy to see that at a symmetric Bertrand equilibrium,

$$\eta = \mu\sigma_0 + (1 - \mu)\sigma(n - 1)n^{-1} + (1 - \mu)\eta^I n^{-1},$$

where μ is the expenditure share of the numéraire good. It follows then that for $n \geq 2$, η tends to infinity as σ tends to infinity, and that for a given finite σ, η remains bounded as n tends to infinity. The result is that for $n \geq 2$, a large substitutability implies prices close to marginal cost, but for a limited degree of substitutability, prices will be bounded away from marginal cost whatever large n is. This is so because, as we have seen, when σ grows large the perceived elasticity of demand for the firms also grows large, while if σ is bounded the elasticity of demand will also be bounded even if the number of firms increases. Therefore the competitive outcome will only obtain if by increasing without bound the number of firms the degree of substitutability of the products also increases unboundedly. Related results are presented in Vives (1985a). Consider a symmetrically differentiated market satisfying our maintained assumptions. Suppose that there is a limited market for the differentiated sector, in the sense that $nG_n(p)$ remains bounded for any n and p, and that inverse demands have bounded slopes at symmetric solutions. These are sufficient conditions for both (symmetric) Cournot and Bertrand price equilibria to converge to marginal cost at the rate of $1/n$. This follows immediately from the first order conditions,

$$p_n - C'(q_n) = \frac{q_n}{|\partial D_i/\partial p_i|}, \qquad \text{in the Bertrand case,}$$

$$p_n - C'(q_n) = q_n \left| \frac{\partial P_i}{\partial q_i} \right|, \qquad \text{in the Cournot case.}$$

Indeed, from the assumptions, $nq_n = nG_n(p)$ and $|\partial P_i/\partial q_i|$ are bounded above. It follows also that $1/(|\partial D_i/\partial p_i|)$ is bounded above, since from the proof of proposition 6.1 we know that for any given price vector, $|\partial P_i/\partial q_i| \geq 1/(|\partial D_i/\partial p_i|)$. In consequence $n(p_n - C'(q_n))$ is bounded above. Obviously, q_n is at most of the order $1/n$. The following proposition summarizes the results.

PROPOSITION 6.4   Consider a n-firm symmetrically differentiated market for gross substitute products. If there is a limited market for the differentiated goods and the slopes of inverse demand at symmetric solutions are bounded, then as n tends to infinity, both (symmetric) Cournot and Bertrand prices, p_n^C and p_n^B, respectively, tend to marginal cost at least at the rate of $1/n$.

Remark 5   If the demand system comes from a representative consumer with (symmetric) utility U^n, defined on R_+^n, then a sufficient condition for the demands to have bounded slope is that $|\partial^2 U^n(q, \ldots, q)/(\partial q_i)^2|$ be bounded for symmetric consumptions and any n (Vives 1985a, prop. 3).

Example 1 (quadratic utility function) with constant and equal marginal costs m fulfills the assumptions in proposition 6.4. Then

$|\partial P_i / \partial q_i| = \beta$ for all n, and $|\partial D_i / \partial p_i| = b_n$, which tends to $1/(\beta - \gamma)$ as n tends to infinity. It is easily obtained (see exercise 6.9) that $n(p_n^C - m) \xrightarrow{n} \beta(\alpha - m)/\gamma$, and $n(p_n^B - m) \xrightarrow{n} (\beta - \gamma)[(\alpha - m)/\gamma]$. It is worth noting that the constant of convergence is smaller with Bertrand competition.[17] This means that convergence to the competitive outcome is faster in this case (although in both cases convergence obtains at the rate $1/n$).

Having a limited market for the monopolistic industry is not enough for our result if the slopes of the inverse demand functions are unbounded. An example (a modification of example 1 illustrates this point; see Shubik and Levitan 1971).

Let

$$U^n(q) = \frac{\alpha}{\beta} \sum_i q_i - \frac{1}{2\beta} \left(\sum_i q_i \right)^2 - \frac{n}{2\beta(1+\gamma)} \left[\sum_i q_i^2 - \frac{\sum_i q_i}{n} \right],$$

where α, β, and γ are positive constants. Then for positive demands and $i = 1, \dots, n$,

$$P_i(q) = \frac{\alpha}{\beta} - \frac{n+\gamma}{\beta(1+\gamma)} q_i - \frac{\gamma}{\beta(1+\gamma)} \sum_{j \neq i} q_j,$$

$$D_i(p) = \frac{1}{n} \left(\alpha - \beta \left[p_i + \gamma \left(p_i - \frac{1}{n} \sum_j p_i \right) \right] \right).$$

Note that $|\partial P_i / \partial q_i| = -(n+\gamma)/\beta(1+\gamma)$ tends to infinity and that $|\partial D_i / \partial p_i| = -\beta(1+\gamma(1-1/n))/n$ tends to zero as $n \to \infty$. Furthermore $nG_n(p) = \alpha - \beta p$, which means that we have a limited market. Certainly q_n^C and q_n^B tend to zero as n tends to infinity but the corresponding prices do not tend to the constant marginal cost m. Instead, they tend to $((1+\gamma)m + \alpha/\beta)(2+\gamma)^{-1}$. It is easily seen that the demand elasticity for any good does not tend to infinity as n increases. We are thus in the Chamberlinian situation, where although there are many "small" firms each one of them has some market power and prices are above marginal cost.

Another example with a monopolistically competitive outcome in the limit is example 2 (constant elasticity). In this case the market for the differentiated goods is not limited. It is easily checked that both the Cournot and the Bertrand prices converge to m/β as n tends to infinity at a rate of $1/n$. The price m/β is the monopolistically competitive price, which is above marginal cost provided that products are not homogeneous, $\beta < 1$. Indeed, $n(p_n^C - m/\beta)$ tends to $(1 - \theta)m/\beta$, and $n(p_n^B - m/\beta)$ tends to $((1 - \beta)/(1 - \beta\theta))(1 - \theta)m/\beta$ as n tends to infinity (see exercise 6.10). Again, convergence is faster in the Bertrand case since $(1 - \beta)/(1 - \beta\theta) < 1$. It is worth pointing out that $nG_n(p)$ tends to infinity with n. Similarly, in example 4 (constant expenditure) with $g(p) = e^{-\beta p}$ for $\beta > 0$ and constant marginal costs m, we have also a Chamberlinian outcome: $p_n^B \rightarrow \frac{1}{2}[m + \sqrt{m^2 + (4m/b)}] > m$ as $n \rightarrow \infty$.

In the last examples we have seen how as n grows both Cournot and Bertrand prices tend to a price above marginal cost given the behavior of elasticities. That is, firms in the limit maintain some market power. This is so since in these examples, as n grows, the elasticity of substitution between the goods remains bounded. It is easy to see that for symmetric solutions (with demands arising from the maximization of a quasilinear utility function) the (direct) elasticity of substitution is given by $\sigma = (\varepsilon_{ij} + \varepsilon_i)^{-1}$, where ε_{ij} is the cross elasticity of inverse demand, $\varepsilon_{ij} = (q_j/p_i)(\partial P_i/\partial q_j)$.[18] In the constant elasticity example the elasticity of substitution between the goods is $1/(1 - \beta)$ no matter the value of n. As n grows, ε_i tends to $1 - \beta$ and ε_{ij} tends to zero. The price of a single firm influences less and less the demand of any other firm when n increases. A similar phenomenon occurs in other cases where the monopolistically competitive outcome obtains.

6.5   Bertrand-Edgeworth-Chamberlin Competition

We saw in chapter 5 that *capacity constraints* (or increasing marginal costs) induce nonexistence of pure-strategy equilibria with Bertrand-Edgeworth competition. As noted by Edgeworth, product differentiation, in general, does not restore existence of pure-strategy equilibria (see also Shapley and Shubik 1969; Vives 1985a; Benassy 1989). Nevertheless, it is true that the existence problem in pure strategies is less severe the more differentiated the products are.

Suppose that we have a n-firm market with increasing marginal production costs and that demand comes from a representative consumer with utility function U for the differentiated products. With voluntary trading firm i will not supply more than its competitive supply $S_i(p_i)$ at the set price p_i (as before, $S_i(p_i)$ could just be the capacity constraint of the firm, say, k_i). We will speak of $S_i(p_i)$ as the capacity of the firm. The residual or contingent demand for firm i, given the prices charged by the rival firms p_{-i} and the capacities of the rivals S_{-i}, is denoted by $D_i(p_i, p_{-i}; S_{-i})$. It will be the solution for q_i to

$$\max_q \{U(q) - pq\} \quad \text{subject to} \quad q_j \leq S_j(p_j) \quad \text{for } j \neq i.$$

The system of contingent demands that arises is akin to residual demands with the surplus-maximizing rule in the homogeneous product case.

Firm i solves for p_i,

$$\max p_i q_i - C_i(q_i) \quad \text{subject to} \quad q_i \leq D_i(p_i, p_{-i}; S_{-i}).$$

It is not difficult to see that under regularity conditions, if a pure-strategy equilibrium exists in the Bertrand-Edgeworth-Chamberlin (B-E-C) game with product differentiation, it will be a Bertrand-Chamberlin equilibrium. Bennassy (1989) shows this result under our maintained assumption on demand, smooth strictly convex costs and strictly quasiconcave profits functions for the Bertrand-Chamberlin price game. The key to the result is to show that at a B-E-C equilibrium in pure strategies demand is not rationed.

Consider a symmetric product differentiation market. A sufficient condition for a symmetric Bertrand-Chamberlin equilibrium to be a B-E-C equilibrium is that at equilibrium competitors of any firm display an excess capacity in the aggregate larger than individual firm production, that is, $(n - 1)(S(p^B) - q^B) \geq q^B$. The intuition is the following: The problem for existence of a price equilibrium in pure strategies in the B-E-C game is typically that at a candidate Bertrand-Chamberlin equilibrium a firm has incentives to raise its price. Now, under the assumption, if a firm deviates by raising its price, the rivals will be willing to absorb the increased demand forthcoming to them (which will not be larger than their "capacities"). This destroys the incentives of the firm to raise prices. In the case of constant elasticity (elastic) demand functions ($\eta > 1$) and with constant elasticity cost functions ($\beta \geq 1$), the inequality $n - 1 \geq (\beta - 1)\eta$ implies the sufficient condition. For constant marginal costs ($\beta = 1$) the condition is always satisfied, and there is no existence problem. For increasing marginal costs ($\beta > 1$) existence is guaranteed for large n and low η. In particular, for products close to substitutes, which will have η large, the condition is satisfied only if the number of firms is large (see Benassy 1991).

Nevertheless, pure-strategy equilibria need not exist. In a symmetric product differentiation market with n firms producing under
(identical) increasing marginal costs (and with further regularity
conditions)[19] Benassy (1989) shows that:

1. Given a finite n, a sufficiently large degree of substitutability σ
entails nonexistence.

2. For a given σ, a sufficiently large n entails existence.

3. High substitutability *and* large numbers (with n large enough to
guarantee existence) imply that equilibria are close to competitive.

As an example consider the linear duopoly arising from a (symmetric) quadratic utility function for substitute goods (example 1) with
firms facing capacity constraints (k_1, k_2), and zero marginal costs up
to the capacity limit. The contingent demand for firm 1 is given by
$D_1(p_1, p_2; k_2) = \max\{(\alpha - \gamma k_2 - p_1)/\beta, \min\{a - bp_1 + cp_2, (\alpha - p_1)/\beta\}\}$,
and similarly for firm 2.[20] This demand is nonconcave in p_1 and
gives rise to a failure of quasiconcavity for the profit function of the
firm and a discontinuous best reply. Indeed, the capacity constraint
for firm 2 makes the best-reply correspondence of firm 1 to jump
down at some critical level. When firm 2 charges a low price, the firm
is capacity constrained, and then the best reply of firm 1 is to charge
the monopoly price on the residual demand $D_1(p_1, p_2; k_2)$. As firm 2
keeps raising its price, there is a point where firm 1 is indifferent between charging the monopoly price or *lowering* its price and making
firm 1 no longer capacity constrained. This can cause easily the nonexistence of equilibria (see figure 6.3). This example shows, indeed,
that the B-E-C game is not supermodular, since the best replies may
jump down.

The regions of existence of a pure-strategy price equilibrium are
easily characterized. Let $\beta = 1$ and $k_i = k$, for $i = 1, 2$ to simplify
notation. Pure-strategy equilibria exist if $k \geq k(\gamma) = \alpha(1 - 2(1 - \gamma)^{1/2}/
(2 - \gamma)(1 + \gamma)^{1/2})/\gamma$, in which case the Bertrand-Chamberlin equilib-
rium $p^B = a/(2b - c)$ obtains, or if $k \leq q^C = \alpha/(2 + \gamma)$, in which case
firms are so capacity constrained that a competitive equilibrium
obtains. The boundary $k = k(\gamma)$ is computed equating profits at the
candidate Bertrand-Chamberlin equilibrium ($\pi^B = b(p^B)^2$) with monopoly profits on the residual demand $D_i = (\alpha - \gamma k - p_i)$ of a firm
(equal to $(\alpha - \gamma k)/2)^2$). It is easily checked that k increases with γ and
that $k(0) = \alpha/2$. In (k, γ) space the region of existence expands as

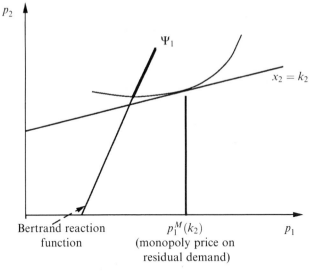

Firm 2 is capacity constrained

Figure 6.3

goods become more differentiated (see figure 6.4). In summary, as conjectured by Edgeworth, product differentiation does not solve the existence problem but it makes it less severe.[21]

6.6 Monopolistic Competition and Entry

We consider in this section the Chamberlinian large group case. We start with a market with a large (and fixed) number of firms. Each firm produces a different variety and is negligible in the sense that its actions alone can not influence the profits of any other firm. Nevertheless, the firm keeps some monopoly power, facing a demand curve with finite elasticity. More formally, suppose that there is a continuum of firms indexed in the interval $[0, 1]$ (endowed with the Lebesgue measure).[22] Furthermore the inverse demand for firm i is given by

$$p_i = P_i(q_i, \tilde{q}),$$

where $\tilde{q}$ is a vector of statistics which characterizes the output distribution of firms, q_i the individual output, and p_i the price set by firm i. The direct demand of the firm is given by

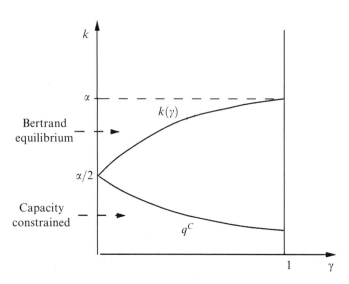

Figure 6.4

$$q_i = D(p_i, \tilde{p}),$$

where $\tilde{p}$ is a vector of statistics which characterizes the distribution of prices. In fact, in a monopolistically competitive industry, only aggregate statistics of firms' actions should be payoff relevant when consumers use search strategies based only on a few moments of the distribution of actions of firms. For example, $\tilde{q}$ and $\tilde{p}$ could be unidimensional and have an additive form: $\tilde{q} = \int f(q_j)\, dj$ and $\tilde{p} = \int g(p_j)\, dj$. When f and g are the identity function then $\tilde{q}$ is the average quantity and $\tilde{p}$ the average price, respectively. When $f(q_j) = q_j^{\beta}$ and $g(p_j) = p_j^{\beta/(1-\beta)}$ we are in the constant elasticity case (example 2 in section 6.1).

In contrast with the oligopoly case, in the monopolistically competitive limit we have always that the price elasticity of demand for a firm, $\eta_i = -(p_i/q_i)(\partial D/\partial p_i)$, equals the inverse of the quantity elasticity of inverse demand, $\varepsilon_i = -(q_i/p_i)(\partial P_i/\partial q_i)$, that is, $\varepsilon_i = 1/\eta_i$. This is so because in monopolistic competition an individual firm is negligible and can not affect market aggregates. A firm takes the action distribution of the other firms as given and behaves as a monopoly on the residual demand. By changing its action (be it price or quantity) a firm does not the affect the residual demand of other firms. This is a general property of the monopolistic competition model which implies that Cournot and Bertrand equilibria coincide.[23]

With marginal costs for firm i given by the function $MC_i(\cdot)$, the first-order condition for a Nash equilibrium (in prices or quantities) will yield

$$\frac{p_i - MC_i}{p_i} = \frac{1}{\eta_i} \,(= \varepsilon_i).$$

An example is provided by the following linear demand system (which can be obtained as the limit of the Shubik quadratic utility example when the number of firms tends to infinity):

$$p_i = \alpha_i - (1 - \delta)q_i - \delta\tilde{q} \quad \text{with } \delta \in [0, 1],$$

$$q_i = \beta_i - (1 + \gamma)p_i + \gamma\tilde{p} \quad \text{with } \gamma \geq 0,$$

where (p_i, q_i) is the price-output pair of firm i, and tildes denote averages. We can obtain the second equation by inverting the first and letting $\beta_i = (\alpha_i - \delta\tilde{\alpha})/(1 - \delta)$ and $\gamma = \delta/(1 - \delta)$. (Making the appropriate restriction on the support of the distribution of α_i to ensure that $\beta_i > 0$ for all i.) Notice that when $\delta = 0$ each firm is an isolated monopoly and when $\delta = 1$, it is a perfect competitor (the product is homogeneous). The parameter δ represents thus the degree of product differentiation.

If firms have constant unit costs, equal to zero for simplicity, then Cournot and Bertrand equilibria are given by (note that $\tilde{\beta} = \tilde{\alpha}$)

$$q_i = \frac{1}{2(1 - \delta)}(\alpha_i - \tilde{\alpha}) + \frac{1}{2 - \delta}\tilde{\alpha}, \quad \text{with average output } \tilde{q} = \frac{1}{2 - \delta}\tilde{\alpha},$$

$$p_i = \frac{1}{2(1 + \gamma)}(\beta_i - \tilde{\beta}) + \frac{1}{2 + \gamma}\tilde{\beta}, \quad \text{with average price } \tilde{p} = \frac{1}{2 + \gamma}\tilde{\beta}.$$

What type of preferences will give rise to the demand system in the monopolistic competition model? We have already seen examples where by increasing the number of goods the limit was monopolistically competitive and not competitive.[24] A common thread of these examples is that a good must not have close neighbors no matter how many goods there are in the market. A class of preferences satisfying this property was provided in section 3.2 (see also Hart's Chamberlinian model; Hart 1985). Spence (1976a, b) and Dixit and Stiglitz (1977) provided representative consumer models giving rise to monopolistically competitive demand systems. Let us consider the Spence version, which corresponds to our canonical partial equilibrium model with quasilinear utility (section 3.1). The utility function for the differentiated goods is given by

$$G(\tilde{q}) \quad \text{with } \tilde{q} = \int_0^N f(q_i)\, di$$

where q_i is the amount consumed of variety i. There is a mass N of potential varieties. The utility function G is smooth, strictly increasing, and strictly concave in $\tilde{q}$. The function $f : R_+ \to R_+$, is continuous, increasing and concave, and smooth on $R_{++} : f'(q) \geq 0$ and $f''(q) \leq 0$ for all $q > 0$, with $f(0) = 0$. An example is the constant elasticity case, $G(\tilde{q}) = \tilde{q}\theta$ and $f(q) = q^\rho$ with $1 > \theta > 0$ $1 \geq \rho \geq 0$. When $f'' < 0$ the indifference curves of the consumer are strictly convex and the consumer prefers variety. The inverse demand of product i (the Chamberlinian dd inverse demand function) is given by $P(q_i, \tilde{q}) = G'(\tilde{q})f'(q_i)$. We will follow here the analysis in Kühn and Vives (1995b).

The degree of preference for variety is given by $v(q) = 1 - \rho(q)$, where $\rho(q) = qf'(q)/f(q)$. This represents the proportion of social benefits not captured by revenues when introducing a new variety $(1 - G'f'q/G'f = 1 - \rho = v)$. The degree of preference for variety is between 0 and 1. When revenues capture all benefits, goods are perfect substitutes, and $v = 0$. When revenues capture no benefits, there is maximal preference for variety and $v = 1$. It is plausible that v be increasing. That is, when there is a high consumption per variety consumers should desire more variety than when there is a low consumption per variety (this is the view of Spence 1976a, b, but, apparently, not of Dixit and Stiglitz 1977). We will say that there is increasing preference for variety when $v' > 0$ (this is equivalent to $\rho' < 0$). However, the case which has received more attention in the literature is the constant elasticity case, which exhibits constant preference for variety. In that case $\rho(q) = \rho$ is a constant between 0 and 1.

The output elasticity of inverse demand, given that the individual output does not affect the aggregate $\tilde{q}$, is given by

$$\varepsilon_i = -\frac{\partial P(q_i, \tilde{q})}{\partial q_i}\frac{q_i}{p} = -\frac{q_i f''(q_i)}{f'(q_i)}.$$

For symmetric solutions this elasticity just equals the inverse of the (direct) elasticity of substitution between any two goods $1/\sigma$. This relation reflects the fact that $\sigma = (\varepsilon_{ij} + \varepsilon_i)^{-1}$, but in monopolistic competition the cross elasticity of inverse demand is zero, $\varepsilon_{ij} = 0$, because an individual firm has no effect on the price that another rival firm can charge. Now, it is plausible that the elasticity of substitution between two goods, at symmetric solutions, $\sigma(q)$ be decreasing in q. That is, a higher output per variety q, or less varieties for a given total output, should induce a lower σ. Indeed, it is a common assumption that ε is increasing with q (or σ decreasing with q).

Both increasing preference for variety v and increasing inverse elasticity of demand ε with q are to be considered the normal case. At higher outputs per variety we should expect an increased preference for variety together with an increased inverse price elasticity of demand (or decreased elasticity of substitution).[25] We can offer two different results in this regard. First, under a relatively mild assumption[26] it can be shown that the elasticity of ε equals the elasticity of v in the limit as q tends to 0: $\eta_\varepsilon(0+) = \eta_v(0+)$. Therefore $\eta_\varepsilon(0+) > 0$ if and only if $\eta_v(0+) > 0$. Second, if f is of the HARA (hyperbolic absolute risk aversion) class and ε is strictly increasing, then there is strictly increasing preference for variety.[27]

Chamberlin discussed the provision of variety by the market and thought that in both the optimum and market allocations there was a trade-off between providing variety (which consumers like because of preference for variety) and economies of scale (because there is a fixed cost in introducing a new variety; e.g., see in Chamberlin 1933, ch. 5). Nevertheless, the conventional wisdom arising from his famous diagram showing the tangency between the demand facing an individual firm and average cost is that in a monopolistically competitive equilibria there is "excess capacity." This case reflects the fact that the production of a firm at such an equilibrium is smaller than the production that minimizes average cost (whenever a minimum average cost exists). This has been interpreted as an excess entry result, since there would appear to be too many firms in the market producing too little each one. It should be clear, however, that this fact does not translate into a welfare statement about whether the market overprovides or underprovides variety. Indeed, introducing a new product benefits consumers, who like variety. In general there will be two forces which will distort the market solution. First of all, the firms do not appropriate the full surplus generated by the introduction of a product. This will tend to generate too few varieties in equilibrium.

Second, there is a business-stealing effect. A firm by introducing a new product decreases the demand and profits of competitors. This will tend to generate too many varieties. Let us examine more closely the determinants of product diversity in monopolistic competition.

Suppose that a firm to produce a variety must pay a fixed cost F and that there is a constant marginal cost of production m. We make the maintained assumption that in the relevant range, $\varepsilon(q)$ is increasing. Profits of firm i are given by $\pi_i = (P(q_i, \tilde{q}) - m)q_i - F$, and the unique symmetric monopolistically competitive equilibrium (p^*, q^*), with a mass of entrants of n^*, is characterized by

$$\frac{p^* - m}{p^*} = \varepsilon(q^*) \quad \text{(monopolistically competitive pricing)}$$

and

$$(p^* - m)q^* = F \quad \text{(free entry)}.$$

Comparative static results are easily obtained. Output per variety is strictly decreasing in m and strictly increasing in F. The mass of firms in the market n^* is decreasing in both m and F.[28]

At a symmetric allocation welfare (total surplus) is given by

$$W(q, n) = G(nf(q)) - n(mq + F).$$

The first-order conditions for optimization are as follows: Price equal to marginal cost, $p = m$, and optimal entry, $G'f = qm + F$ (the marginal benefit and marginal cost of introducing product i must be equated).[29] Denoting the first best allocation by (q^0, n^0) it is easy to see that both gross and net surplus are strictly lower at the market allocation, $\tilde{q}^0 > \tilde{q}^*$ and $W^0 > W^*$. Furthermore, with increasing preference for variety, we have that $q^* < q^0$, and with decreasing preference for variety, we have that $q^* > q^0$ and $n^* < n^0$. In the case of constant preference for variety the market does not distort output per firm, $q^* = q^0$, but still $n^* < n^0$. The intuition of the results follows from the fact that the degree of preference for variety v measures the proportion of social benefits *not* captured by the firm's revenues when introducing a product. Now, if v decreases (increases) with q, there is too large an incentive to produce a high (low) q. With constant preference for variety, there is no output distortion. Both with decreasing and constant preference for variety, there is insufficient entry.

In the constant elasticity example (see Perry and Groff 1985), $W(n,q) = (n^\theta q^{\rho\theta}/\theta) - ncq - nF$, and we can find explicit expressions for the equilibrium:

$$n^* = \rho^{2/(1-\theta)} \left(\frac{\rho F}{1-\rho}\right)^{(1-\rho\theta)/(1-\theta)} m^{\rho\theta/(1-\theta)} \quad \text{and} \quad q^* = \left(\frac{\rho F}{1-\rho}\right)\frac{1}{m}$$

for the market solution, and

$$n^0 = \rho^{1/(1-\theta)}((1-\rho)/\rho F)^{(1-\rho\theta)/(1-\theta)} m^{\rho\theta/(1-\theta)} \quad \text{and} \quad q^0 = \frac{\rho F}{(1-\rho)m},$$

for the first best.

The first best serves as a benchmark, but it is not attainable in general. Two second-best benchmarks have been proposed in the literature. A "behavioral" second best takes free entry as the constraint and looks at the optimal number of firms given this constraint. This assumes that pricing of firms can be controlled and corresponds to behavioral regulation. A "structural" second best takes the pricing behavior of downstream firms as given and looks at the number of varieties in the market. This assumes that entry can be controlled and corresponds to structural regulation. In more abstract terms the regulator will maximize welfare subject to a constraint $\Psi(n,q) = 0$ or $n = n^\Psi(q)$. In the case of the behavioral second best ($\Psi = B$) this will be $(p - m)q - F = 0$, and in the case of the structural second best ($\Psi = S$), it will be $(p - m)/p = \varepsilon$. Both constraints have the property that at a monopolistically competitive equilibrium $dn^\Psi/dq < 0$.[30]

We will say that there is (locally) excess entry relative to the constraint $\Psi(n,q) = 0$, for a point $(\hat{n}, \hat{q})$ such that $dn^\Psi/dq < 0$, if

$$\left.\frac{dW}{dq}\right|_\Psi (\hat{n}, \hat{q}) > 0.$$

In our model we have

$$\left.\frac{dW}{dq}\right|_\Psi = \frac{n}{q}\left\{(p-m)q + \frac{dn^\Psi}{dq}\frac{q}{n}(G'f - mq - F)\right\}.$$

The equation reflects the tension between the positive first summand inside the brackets, $(p - m)q$, related to the price distortion, and the second, $(dn^\Psi/dq)(q/n)(G'f - mq - F)$, related to the entry distortion. The elasticity of n^Ψ is negative and the term $(G'f - mq - F)$ is positive if price equals average cost. The first summand represents the business-stealing effect and leads to too much entry; the second, the lack of full appropriability of surplus, and leads to too little entry. Taking into account the equilibrium conditions, we can write

$$\frac{dW}{dq}\bigg|_{\Psi=B} = np\frac{v}{1-v}\left[1-v+\frac{qv'}{v}+\frac{dn^{\Psi}}{dq}\frac{q}{n}\right] > 0.$$

At equilibrium (q^*, n^*) we have that $(dn^B/dq)(q/n) = v - 1 < 0$, and therefore for excess entry to arise with respect to the behavioral second best we need

$$\frac{dW}{dq}\bigg|_{\Psi=B} (q^*, n^*) = np\frac{v}{1-v}\left[\frac{qv'}{v}\right] > 0.$$

In consequence we obtain the result of Dixit and Stiglitz (1977): There is excess entry relative to the behavioral second best if and only if there is increasing preference for variety ($v' > 0$ or $\rho' < 0$).

Another way to understand the result is provided noting that

$$\frac{dW}{dq}\bigg|_{\Psi=B} = n\left\{\frac{\partial\pi}{\partial q} + p\left(\frac{p-m}{p} - v\right)\right\}.$$

The Lerner index $(p-m)/p$ represents the business stealing effect and v, as stated before, the proportion of surplus not captured by a firm when introducing a new product.[31] In equilibrium we have that $\partial\pi/\partial q = 0$ and $(p-m)/p = \varepsilon$. Therefore

$$\frac{dW}{dq}\bigg|_{\Psi=B} (q^*, n^*) > 0 \quad \text{if and only if} \quad \varepsilon(q^*) > v(q^*).$$

It is easily seen that $\varepsilon - v = v\eta_v/(1-v)$. For constant preference for variety $\eta_v = 0$, $\varepsilon = v$ and entry is not distorted. For increasing preference for variety we have that $\eta_v > 0$ and $\varepsilon > v$.

In the "structural second best," the constraint schedule in this case has slope

$$\frac{dn^s}{dq} = -\frac{n}{\phi q}\left[\frac{\varepsilon}{(1-\varepsilon)}(1-\varepsilon+\eta_\varepsilon) + (1-v)\phi\right] < 0,$$

where the parameter $\phi = -zG''/G'$. This constraint differs from the "behavioral" constraint only by the first term inside the brackets. Given that $\varepsilon < 1$ and $v < 1$ (and that by assumption $\eta_\varepsilon > 0$) the term in brackets is positive. It is immediate then that

$$\text{sign} \left. \frac{dW}{dq} \right|_{\Psi=S} (q^*, n^*)$$

$$= \text{sign} \left\{ \varepsilon(q^*) - v(q^*) - \frac{1}{\phi(z^*)} \frac{\varepsilon(q^*)}{1 - \varepsilon(q^*)} (1 - \varepsilon(q^*) + \eta_\varepsilon(q^*)) \frac{v(q^*)}{1 - v(q^*)} \right\}.$$

It follows that to obtain excess entry under the structural second best constraint is more difficult than under the behavioral constraint. For example, in the constant preference for variety case there is insufficient entry with respect to $\Psi = S$ (see Spence 1976a, b) while entry is not distorted with $\Psi = B$.[32]

However, for small fixed costs the (limit) behavior of η_ε (or, equivalently, of η_v) at the origin determines whether there is excess entry according to both second best benchmarks. Indeed, the previous characterizations yield a general excess entry result for the case of small fixed costs.

PROPOSITION 6.5   If $\eta_v(0+) > 0$, then for F small but positive there is excess entry both with respect to the behavioral and to the structural second best.

Proof   We claim first that as F tends to 0, q^* tends to 0 also. Combining the pricing and the entry conditions at equilibrium, we have that $pq\varepsilon = F$. We know that q^* is increasing with F. If q were to tend to $\hat{q} > 0$ as F tends to 0, then ε would tend to $\varepsilon(\hat{q}) > 0$ (recall that our maintained assumption is that ε is increasing). This would contradict the equilibrium conditions since as F tends to 0, $pq\varepsilon$ would tend to something positive. Now $\text{sign} \left. \frac{dW}{dq} \right|_{\Psi=B} (q^*, n^*) = \text{sign}\{(\varepsilon(q^*) - v(q^*))/v(q^*)\} = \text{sign}\,\eta_v(q^*)$. Furthermore

$$\text{Sign} \left. \frac{dW}{dq} \right|_{\Psi=S} (q^*, n^*)$$

$$= \text{sign} \left\{ \eta_v(q^*) - \frac{1}{\phi(z^*)} \frac{\varepsilon(q^*)}{1 - \varepsilon(q^*)} (1 - \varepsilon(q^*) + \eta_\varepsilon(q^*)) \right\}.$$

The sign is positive since as F tends to 0, q^* tends to 0, $\eta_v(0+) > 0$, $v(0+) = \varepsilon(0+)$, and $\eta_v(0+) > 0$ implies that $v(0+) = 0$.   ◆

Remark 6   In the limit, as F tends to zero, we obtain that $\varepsilon(0+) = v(0+) = 0$, price equals marginal cost, and there is no entry distortion. This is consistent with the results of Deneckere and Rothschild (1992, prop. 4).

In summary, and contrary to a tradition in the literature, with excessive reliance on the constant elasticity model, excess entry does appear to be a robust phenomenon arising in a range of very plausible situations. First, under the natural assumption of increasing preference for variety, excess entry obtains according to the behavioral second-best benchmark. Second, under mild regularity assumptions and a positive elasticity of preference for variety at zero consumption, when fixed costs are small there is always excess entry. This conclusion is consistent with spatial models where the tendency to excessive entry is strong (see Salop 1979; Tirole 1988). Furthermore a recent paper of Anderson et al. (1995) shows that excess entry obtains in a discrete choice model with a log-concave distribution of consumer's characteristics.

Appendix: Product Selection and Complementary Products

Complementary products tend to be undersupplied in a Cournot equilibrium. Spence (1976b) claims that if products are "strongly complementary" (i.e., strict strategic complements: the marginal revenue of a firm is strictly increasing in the output of the rivals), then there should be an equilibrium in which all quantities are below the optimal quantities and some of the optimal products are not produced. However, Spence did not address the existence of such an equilibrium. Existence follows immediately from the theory of supermodular games (see section 2.2.3). The intuitive reason of the result, according to Spence, is that "when a monopolistically competitive firm holds back output and raises price above marginal cost, it reduces the demand for other complementary products. That induces further quantity cutbacks and possibly the exit of products from the market as well. That cycle reinforces itself and leads to an equilibrium where all outputs are below the optimum and some of the products in the optimal set are not produced at all." (Spence 1976b, p. 220). Another way to put it is that with complementary products the business-stealing effect, responsible for excess entry, is transformed into a business-augmenting effect. Indeed, a firm when entering the market does not take into account the increase in demand it will generate for other producers.

Suppose that our inverse demand system comes from the canonical partial equilibrium model (see section 3.1):

$$\max\{U(q) - pq, q \in R^n_+\},$$

where $U(\cdot)$ is a three times continuously differentiable concave utility function. Each firm produces a single differentiated product. The potential product set is N and the costs to firm i of producing a positive amount q_i are $F_i + V_i(q_i)$, where $F_i \geq 0$ and V_i is a twice-continuously differentiable, increasing, and convex variable cost function. If the firm decides not to produce, F_i is avoidable. Furthermore, assume that revenue net of variable cost for firm i is strictly quasiconcave in q_i, that the goods are complementary, and that the game is supermodular. We have then that the best reply map of firm i is an increasing function of the quantities produced by the rivals whenever the firm produces a positive amount. (See Vives 1985a, b.)

Now, given any welfare optimum, q^0, solving the optimal program

$$\max\left\{U(q) - \sum_{i \in N} C_i(q_i), q \in R^n_+\right\},$$

we can find a Cournot equilibrium with no more products and no more production than the optimum. This is the way to find it. Because the game is supermodular, best replies are increasing. Given that the net revenue function is quasiconcave, then the point q^0 lies in the upper contour set of the best replies. The implication, similarly as in the proof of theorem 2.10, is that a Cournot tatônnement starting from this position defines a monotonic dynamic system which converges to a Cournot equilibrium. This Cournot equilibrium necessarily has less products and less production than the optimum. Furthermore, because the game is supermodular, there is a least equilibrium. At this equilibrium (the infimum of the equilibrium set) there are fewer products and lower production that at any welfare optimum. The following proposition summarizes the result. (See exercise 6.14 for an illustration of the model.)

PROPOSITION 6.6   Under the assumptions above there is a Cournot equilibrium with less products and less production than any welfare optimum.

Summary

The chapter presents basic imperfect competition product differentiation models following the approach of Chamberlin and Robinson. It therefore, starts from a demand system for differentiated products which the firms are facing. Properties and examples of such systems are developed with linear and constant elasticity cases as leading examples. Existence and uniqueness of equilibrium results are presented for quantity and price competition using the tools provided in chapter 2. Those equilibria are characterized and compared in terms of competitiveness and welfare. It is also examined when as the number of firms grows a perfectly competitive or a monopolistically competitive limit is obtained, and at what rate. Edgeworth's problem is considered in the context of product differentiation and the role of supply constraints discussed. The monopolistic competition model, corresponding to Chamberlin's large group, is developed and analyzed and applied to the problem of entry and optimal product diversity. Finally product selection with complementary products is considered. Major results in the chapter include existence and uniqueness results for Cournot and Bertrand equilibria (some of which are new and based on the theory of supermodular games; see also exercises 6.3, 6.5 for existence and exercises 6.2 and 6.10 for uniqueness), the statement of the conditions under which Cournot prices are above Bertrand prices (propositions 6.2 and 6.3), conditions under which Cournot and Bertrand equilibria tend to marginal cost at the rate of $1/n$ (proposition 6.4), the presentation of the fact that product differentiation lessens but does not eliminate the existence problem of price equilibria in Bertrand-Edgeworth-Chamberlin competition, the characterization of the utility foundations of the monopolistic competition model around the concept of preference for variety and the presentation of classical excess entry results together with new results for small fixed costs (proposition 6.5), and a rigourous characterization of the underprovision of goods with complementary products (proposition 6.6).

Exercises

6.1. Compute the unique Bertrand equilibrium of the logit demand system with n goods $D_i(p) = e^{\lambda p_i} / \sum_j e^{\lambda p_j}$, with $\lambda < 0$ and constant marginal costs c. (The answer is $p = c - n/(n-1)\lambda$.)

6.2. Consider a smooth Cournot game with product differentiation in which the payoff to player i depends only on its own production and on the aggregate quantity of the rivals. Show that if best replies have slopes in the interval $(-1, 0]$, then the equilibrium is unique.

6.3. Consider a n-firm Bertrand oligopoly with gross substitute goods such that $\log D_i$ is supermodular in (p_i, p_{-i}). Firm i has an increasing convex cost function C_i. Show that for any i, π_i fulfills the single crossing property in (p_i, p_{-i}).

6.4. Consider a smooth n-firm Bertrand oligopoly where firm i has an increasing convex cost function C_i. Show that if $D_i(p)$ is log-concave (and downward sloping) in p_i when positive then π_i is strictly quasiconcave in p_i (Hint: Show that $\partial \pi_i / \partial p_i = 0$ implies that $\partial^2 \pi_i / (\partial p_i)^2 < 0$.) Suppose now that goods are gross substitutes and that $\partial^2 \log D_i / \partial p_i \partial p_j \geq 0, i \neq j$. Show that if r_i is the best-reply function of firm i (which is well-defined given the assumptions), then $\partial r_i / \partial p_j \geq 0, i \neq j$. (Hint: Show that $\partial^2 \pi_i / \partial p_i \partial p_j \geq 0, i \neq j$, whenever $\partial \pi_i / \partial p_i = 0$.)

*6.5. Consider a n-firm Cournot oligopoly where firm i has a strictly increasing cost function C_i and where goods are strict substitutes (complements) with $\log P_i$ submodular (supermodular) in (q_i, q_{-i}). Show that $\pi_i(x_i, y_{-i}) \leq (\geq) \pi_i(y_i, y_{-i})$ implies that $\pi_i(x_i, x_{-i}) < (>)$ $\pi_i(y_i, x_{-i})$ for $x_i > y_i$ and $x_{-i} \geq y_{-i}$, $x_{-i} \neq y_{-i}$, and conclude that the best response of firm i is strongly decreasing (increasing). (Hint: See section 2.2.2.)

6.6. Consider the following variation of problem 6.5: A smooth n-firm Cournot oligopoly with substitute (complementary) goods where firm i has an increasing convex cost function C_i, with P_i downward sloping when positive, log-concave in q_i, and log-submodular (log-supermodular) in (q_i, q_{-i}). Show that if r_i is the best-reply function of firm i (which is well-defined given the assumptions), then $\partial r_i / \partial q_j \leq 0$, $(\partial r_i / \partial q_j \geq 0)$ $i \neq j$. (Hint: Show that $\partial^2 \pi_i / \partial q_i \partial q_j$ $\leq (\geq) 0, i \neq j$, whenever $\partial \pi_i / \partial p_i = 0$.)

6.7. Consider a Bertrand oligopoly with the constant expenditure demand system:

$$D_i(p) = \frac{1}{p_i} \frac{g(p_i)}{\sum_j g(p_j)},$$

with $g(p) > 0$ for all $p \geq 0$, with $g' < 0$. Suppose that $-pg'(p)/g(p)$ is increasing with p and that marginal costs are constant and equal for all the firms. Show that there is a unique and symmetric price equilibrium. Does the condition hold for the case $g(p) = e^{-\beta}, \beta > 0$? (Hint: Show that there is a unique symmetric equilibrium, and note that the log-transformed game is supermodular and symmetric.)

*6.8. Consider a standard Hotelling model where (a) consumers are uniformly distributed over the interval $[0, 1]$ and have inelastic demands of one unit of a homogeneous product, (b) transport costs are linear in distance with rate t, and (c) firms are located at the endpoints of the market (firm A at 0, firm B at 1) and produce at no cost. Suppose that firm B uses FOB pricing (i.e., setting a price at the mill and adding the transport cost) and that firm A uses a modified FOB pricing policy: FOB pricing in its natural market (whenever its mill price plus transport cost is below the rival's) and matching of firm's B total (mill plus transport) price wherever profitable. Characterize the price game by studying the best-response functions of the firms and the equilibrium set. (Thisse and Vives 1988, 1992.)

*6.9. Consider a representative consumer as in example 1 with a quadratic utility function for the n differentiated goods $U(q) = \alpha q - \frac{1}{2} q' \Gamma q$, where α is a n-dimensional vector and Γ a symmetric $n \times n$ positive definite matrix. It is immediate (check it) that for interior price and quantity solutions $P(q) = \alpha - \Gamma q$ and $D(p) = \Gamma^{-1}(\alpha - p)$. Let Λ be the diagonal matrix composed with the diagonal of $-\Gamma$ (i.e., the absolute value of the slopes of inverse demands, the β_i's). Let B be the diagonal matrix composed with the absolute value of the entries in the diagonal of $-\Gamma^{-1}$ (i.e., the absolute value of the slopes of direct demands, the b_i's). Let I be the identity matrix. Suppose that firms have constant marginal costs given by the vector m with $\alpha_i - m_i > 0$. Show that interior Cournot and Bertrand equilibria are given by $q^C = (\Gamma + \Lambda)^{-1}(\alpha - m)$, $p^C = (I + \Gamma\Lambda^{-1})^{-1}(\alpha - m) + m$, $p^B = (I + \Gamma B)^{-1}(\alpha - m) + m$, and $q^B = (\Gamma + B^{-1})^{-1}(\alpha - m)$. Show also that $q^B = B(p^B - m)$ and $p^C - m = \Lambda q^C$ (this generalizes to n firms the relationships between prices and quantities in each type of equilibrium established in table 6.1). Consider now the symmetric version of the problem with

$$U(q) = \alpha \sum_{i=1}^{n} q_i - \frac{1}{2} \left(\beta \sum_{i=1}^{n} q_i^2 + 2\gamma \sum_{j \neq i} q_i q_j \right),$$

where $\beta > \gamma > 0$ and $\alpha > 0$. Give expressions for the inverse and direct demands, as well as the unique Cournot and Bertrand equilibria assuming that marginal costs are constant and equal to m. Derive the limits of $n(p_n^C - m)$ and $n(p_n^B - m)$ as n tends to infinity. Interpret the results. (See Jin 1996 for the first part and the text, and Vives 1985a for the second.)

*6.10. Consider a n-good industry with representative consumer with utility function for the differentiated goods given by

$$U(q) = \left(\sum_{i=1}^{n} q_i^{\beta} \right)^{\theta},$$

with $0 < \theta < 1$ and $1 \geq \beta > 0$. Derive the inverse and direct demands as well as the unique symmetric Cournot and Bertrand equilibria assuming that marginal costs are constant and equal to $m > 0$. Can there be asymmetric equilibria? What happens as n tends to infinity? Characterize the limit equilibria and the rate of convergence. Explain the differences betwen the Cournot and Bertrand cases. (*Hint:* See the text for results. The issue of asymmetric equilibria is resolved in the Bertrand game noting that the price game is log-supermodular. In the Cournot case a change of units transforms the Cournot differentiated market with constant marginal costs into a Cournot homogeneous product market with strictly convex costs. Then the issue is resolved similarly as in exercises 6.5 and 6.2.)

6.11. Consider the following demand system arising from a multinomial nested logit model in which firm i ($i = 1, \ldots, n$) produces m_i varieties of a differentiated product. The price of product k of firm i is given by p_{ki} and demand by

$$D_{ik}(p) = \frac{e^{-p_{ik}/\mu_2}}{\sum_{h=1}^{m_i} e^{-p_{ih}/\mu_2}} \frac{e^{s_i/\mu_1}}{\sum_{j=1}^{n} e^{s_j/\mu_1}},$$

where $s_j = \mu_2 \ln(\sum_{h=1}^{m_i} e^{-p_{jh}/\mu_2})$ and $\mu_1 \geq \mu_2 \geq 0$. (Think of the demand system as consumers choosing probabilistically first the firm and then the variety.) Interpret the parameters μ_1 and μ_2 in terms of interfirm and intrafirm heterogeneity. Suppose firms face constant marginal costs c and a fixed cost per variant F. Find a price equilibrium in the case that all firms produce m varieties. (The result is $p^* = c + n\mu_1/(n-1)$; see Anderson et al. 1992, sec. 7.7.)

6.12. Consider the symmetric version of the linear demand system of example 1 with $n = 3$. Firms have constant marginal costs, equal to zero for firms 2 and 3, and positive for firm 1: $m_1 > 0$. Suppose that if firms price at marginal cost, all firms face a positive demand. Find a range for the marginal cost of firm 1 such that if the goods are substitutes (complements), the Cournot output (price) of firm 1 is larger (lower) than its Bertrand output (price). (See Jin 1996.)

*6.13. Consider the following continuum version of the monopolistic competition model of Dixit and Stiglitz (1977). There is a representative consumer with utility function $V(\cdot)$ over a numéraire good q_0 and a continuum of differentiated products denoted (abusing the notation) by q. The potential product set is $[0, \infty)$. The utility function is given by $V(q_0, u(q)) = q_0^\gamma (u(q))^{1-\gamma}$ where $\gamma \in (0, 1)$ and $u(q) = (\int q_i^\rho \, di)^{1/\rho}$ where $\rho \in (0, 1)$. Firm i produces good i at constant marginal cost c, $c > 0$, and fixed cost $F > 0$.

a. Derive the inverse demand system assuming that the consumer solves $\max V(q_0, u(q))$ subject to $\int_0^m p_i q_i \, di + q_0 = I$, where I is income and $p_i, i \in [0, m]$ when there is a mass of m goods in the market (*Hint:* Do it by analogy to the case of a finite number of goods and replace $\sum$ by $\int$).

b. Find the Cournot equilibrium of the market if there is a mass m of active firms. Give explicit formulas for prices and quantities, and perform comparative static analysis with respect to c, p, m, I, and γ. Would your answers change considering Bertrand competition?

c. Find the free-entry equilibrium. Give an explicit formula for the equilibrium mass of firms m^*.

d. Find the first-best solution, the optimal mass of firms m^o and individual production q^0. Compare them to the market solution m^* and q^*. Interpret the results.

e. What optimality properties, if any, does the market solution have?

*6.14. Consider a duopoly with a demand system arising from a representative consumer who maximizes $U(q) - pq$, $q \in R_+^2$, where

$$U(q_1, q_2) = \alpha_1 q_1 + \alpha_2 q_2 - \frac{\beta_1 q_1^2 + 2\gamma q_1 q_2 + \beta_2 q_2^2}{2}$$

for $\alpha_i > 0$, $\beta_i > 0$, $\beta_1 \beta_2 - \gamma^2 > 0$, $i = 1, 2$. Firm i produces product i with zero marginal cost and fixed cost $F_i \geq 0$, which is avoidable if the firm decides not to produce anything. Suppose that $\gamma < 0$ so that the goods are complements. Firms compete in quantities. We want to compare the Cournot equilibria of the model with the social optimum. Give parameter configurations (α_i, β_i, F_i) such that:

a. The optimum involves producing both products but at the unique Cournot equilibrium only product 1 is provided.

b. Both the optimun and the unique Cournot equilibrium produce both products.

c. No product is provided at the Cournot equilibrium while both are produced at the optimum.

d. Only product 1 is provided at the optimum but both products are provided in a Cournot equilibrium. Can this equilibrium be the unique Cournot equilibrium?

e. Product 1 is produced at the optimum but at the unique Cournot equilibrium only product 2 is produced.

(*Hint:* See section 6.3 for Cournot equilibrium quantities and revenues. Pictures of best-response maps should help. Of the above at least one is not a possible situation.)

*6.15. Consider a differentiated product market in which the demand for product i is given by $D_i(p) = Ap_i^{-\phi}/(\sum_{j=1}^{n} p_j^{-\phi})$ with $A > 0$ and $\phi > 2$. Firms compete in prices, there is free entry, with setup cost $F > 0$, and each firm can produce a different variety at contant marginal cost $c > 0$. Show that at a (symmetric) free-entry equilibrium (the SPE of the two-stage entry-pricing game) the number of firms is given by (the integer part of) $n^* = (c(A/F) + \phi)/(\phi - 1)$. Conclude that as the size of the market A expands unboundedly n^* tends to infinity. Why is n^* decreasing in ϕ? Interpret the parameter ϕ. Suppose now that the price is regulated at the level $p > c$ and that firm i can spend z_i to improve its market share $Az_i^{\phi}/(\sum_{j=1}^{n} z_j^{\phi})$ where $0 < \phi \le 2$. The profit of firm i is thus $\pi_i = (p - c)Az_i^{\phi}/(\sum_{j=1}^{n} z_j^{\phi}) - z_i - F$. Show that at a (symmetric) free-entry equilibrium (the SPE of the two-stage entry-effort game) n^* tends to infinity with A if $\phi \le 1$ but converges to $\phi/(\phi - 1)$ if $1 < \phi \le 2$. Explain the results (*hint:* look at how fast the expenditure z is growing in relation to A in both cases). Would the results hold if the margin $p - c$ were to be positive but decreasing with n because of price competition? (See Schmalensee 1992.)

7

Conjectures, Reactions, and Commitment

We have seen how equilibrium prices differ according to the specification of the strategic variables in the market. Cournot, Bertrand, or Bertrand-Edgeworth competition yield different outcomes in either the homogeneous or the differentiated product settings. From the same market (cost and demand) conditions we obtain different price predictions according to the model used, without even departing from equilibrium analysis or considering the possibility of collusion, making evident the "oligopoly problem." Several attempts have been made in the literature to come to grips with this issue. I have already alluded to, in section 5.2.4, the possibility that quantity or price competition may be seen as reduced forms of multistage games. I will review first briefly the approach provided by conjectural variations (section 7.1). In section 7.2, I will allow firms to choose from a more complex strategy space by studying supply function equilibria. A comment on the possibility of collusive outcomes with one-shot competition follows in section 7.3. The role of commitment in oligopoly pricing is examined in section 7.4 for two-stage games, starting with the classical model of Stackelberg, examining incumbency advantages and entry deterrence, and providing a taxonomy of strategic behavior.

7.1 Conjectural Variations

The *conjectural variations* approach, which goes back to Bowley (1924), attempts what seems impossible—the consideration of dynamics in a static model. It is based on the idea that a firm when choosing its output takes into account the "reaction" of rival firms. Consider a homogeneous product duopoly with inverse demand $p = P(Q)$ and identical costs of production $C(\cdot)$ for any firm. According to the theory, firm i acts as if it would face a residual inverse demand with slope $P'(Q)(1 + r_{ij}(q_i))$, where $r_{ij}(\cdot)$ is the conjectural variation term, $r_{ij}(q_i) = \partial q_j / \partial q_i$. It represents the "reaction" of firm j to a change in the output of firm i. If $r_{ij} = 0$, then firm i expects no reaction to its change in output and we are in the Cournot case. If $r_{ij} = -1$, firm i expects a change in output of firm j which exactly compensates its own, so as to leave the price unchanged (competitive assumption). If $r_{ij} = 1$, then changes in the output of firm i will be matched by firm j and the market shares of the firms will be constant (collusive assumption). At symmetric interior solutions with $r_{ij} = r$, we have

$$\frac{p - C'}{p} = \frac{(1 + r)/2}{\eta}.$$

This yields the Cournot pricing formula for $r = 0$, price equal marginal cost for $r = -1$, and monopoly pricing for $r = 1$.

Letting the conjectural variation be asymmetric, "collusive" for quantity expansions and "Cournot" for quantity contractions, the kinked demand curve (Sweezy 1939) analysis could be reproduced. This theory is based on the presumption that a firm should expect that price reductions will be matched by rivals but not price increases. The conjectural variation model encompasses different types of competition according to the terms $r_{ij}(\cdot)$. The market outcome depends thus on the perceptions of the reactions of the firms. A step further in this type of analysis is to make these perceptions endogenous by requiring the conjectures to be locally consistent. That is, the term $r_{ij}(\cdot)$ should equal, in the neighborhood of the equilibrium point, the slope of the true reaction function of firm j (i.e., the function that gives the best response of firm j, given the choice of firm i).[1]

In any case the problem with the argument is that we are in the context of one-shot simultaneous move games, and therefore there is no opportunity for firm j to react to firm i's move. If we restrict attention to Nash equilibria and strategies are quantities, only Cournot equilibria can be the outcome of the game played by firms.[2] Nevertheless, the conjectural variation approach has proved useful in applied work because it parametrizes the degree of competition in a market (e.g., see Dixit 1986). It makes possible to write in a compact form different types of competition. Obviously the conjectural variation terms only make sense when they correspond to static solution concepts (Cournot, Bertrand, etc.) or are reduced forms of truly dynamic models (e.g., see the models of Riordan 1985 in section 8.5.4, and of Maskin and Tirole 1988 in section 9.2.1).

7.2 Supply Functions

Grossman (1981a) and Hart (1982) proposed the *supply function* approximation to the oligopoly problem. In this approach firms compete in supply functions. The strategy for firm i is a supply function $S_i(\cdot)$, the interpretation being that the firm is committed to select a price-quantity pair (p_i, q_i) satisfying $q_i = S_i(p_i)$. The market outcome is then given by a Nash equilibrium in supply functions.

Let us illustrate this type of competition in the context of a homogeneous product, n-firm oligopoly with (smooth downward-sloping and concave) demand $D(\cdot)$.[3] Given the chosen supply functions of the firms $(S_i(\cdot), i = 1, 2, \ldots, n)$, if there is a unique price that equates demand and supply $(D(p) = \sum_{i=1}^{n} S_i(p))$, the profits of firm i will be $\pi_i = pS_i(p) - C(S_i(p))$. Otherwise, we may assume, to make things easy, that $\pi_i = 0$. With such payoffs and strategies we have a well-defined game. The problem is that there is an enormous multiplicity of equilibria in supply functions. This is easy to understand. Given the chosen supply function by firm j, $S_j(\cdot)$, $j \neq i$, firm i faces a residual demand $D_i^r(p) = D(p) - \sum_{j \neq i} S_j(p)$. The optimal response of firm i is then to choose *any* supply function $S_i(\cdot)$ such that $q_i^* = S_i(p^*)$, where $p^* \in \arg\max\{pD_i^r(p) - C(D_i^r(p))\}$ and $q_i^* = D_i^r(p^*)$.

Obviously there are infinitely many supply functions for firm i that go through the optimal point (p^*, q_i^*). This leaves many degrees of freedom to construct equilibria that yield a predetermined price. Hart (1982) considers the possibility of supply correspondences and restricts them to be closed graph, convex valued, and credible (in the sense that the firms cannot commit to select a price-quantity pair that implies losses). He shows (Hart 1982, prop. 2) that all market-clearing allocations, p and $(q_1, \ldots, q_n)$, $D(p) = \sum_{i=1}^{n} q_i$, that give to any firm at least its minmax payoffs can be supported with a Nash equilibrium in supply functions in the admissible class. The minmax payoff to any firm is the maximum profits the firm can get when the rest of the firms supply according to their average cost function. This payoff is strictly positive in our model. In general, in supply function models any individually rational point can be supported as a supply function equilibrium in the same way as it can be supported with appropriate conjectures in the conjectural variation approach (see Laitner 1980). Similarly supply function competition can be seen equivalent to competing by choosing reaction functions. In turn, models in which the owners of a firm design incentive contracts for the managers as a function of profitability and sales (of the own firm and/or the rivals) and then market competition follows can be viewed, in reduced form, as supply competition models. By restricting the types of incentive contracts the multiplicity of potential outcomes can be narrowed down (see exercise 7.2 and Vickers 1985; Fershtman and Judd 1987; and Sklivas 1987). For example, Faulí-Oller and Giralt (1995) demonstrate that (linear) supply function equilibria can be the reduced form of competition among multidivisional firms which provide (linear) incentive contracts to the division managers. Under uncertainty competition with incentive contracts may not be equivalent to competing in supply functions.[4]

Klemperer and Meyer (1989) introduce demand uncertainty to limit the multiplicity of supply function equilibria. Indeed, uncertainty will induce firms to favor ex ante certain supply schedules over others and limit this way the multiplicity of outcomes. Consider our oligopolistic market with uncertain demand (of the additive type): $D(p, \theta) = D(p) + \theta$, (with $D(0) = 0$ to ease notation) where θ is a random parameter with support in a subset of $[0, \infty)$. Firms commit to (twice-continuously differentiable) supply functions, $S_i(\cdot)$ $i = 1, \ldots, n$, prior to the realization of uncertainty. Once θ is realized a market-clearing price $p(\theta)$ obtains and the profits of firm i are given by $\pi_i = p(\theta)S_i(p, \theta) - C(S_i(p(\theta)))$.[5] Given the supply functions chosen by rival firms, $j \neq i$, firm i will try to choose $S_i(\cdot)$ so as to maximize profits for each realization of θ. For a given θ the residual demand for firm i is $D_i^r(p, \theta) = D(p, \theta) - \sum_{j \neq i} S_j(p)$ and the firm will solve

$$\max_p \{pD_i^r(p, \theta) - C(D_i^r(p, \theta))\}.$$

Assuming that there is a unique solution $p_i(\theta)$ that is invertible, the pair $(p_i(\theta), q_i(\theta)), q_i(\theta) \equiv D_i^r(p, \theta)$, defines a supply function $S_i(\cdot)$ which is a best response to the choices $S_j(\cdot)$, $j \neq i$, of rival firms. The first-order condition of the maximization problem of the firm, substituting $D_i^r(p, \theta)$ by $S_i(p)$, is

$$p - C' = -\frac{S_i}{\partial D_i^r/\partial p},$$

where $\partial D_i^r / \partial p = D' - \sum_{j \neq i} S_j'$ is the slope of the residual demand of firm i. The authors show that if θ has full support ($[0, \infty)$) a symmetric equilibrium in supply functions exists, and is characterized by the differential equation

$$(n - 1)S'(p) = \frac{S}{p - C'(S)} + D'(p),$$

with $0 < S'(p) < \infty$ for all $p \geq 0$. Furthermore no asymmetric equilibria exist, and the equilibrium set is either a singleton or connected (in the sense that for any two solutions of the differential equation all trajectories that lie in between are also equilibria). Uncertainty reduces the multiplicity of supply function equilibria. For given supply functions of firms $j \neq i$ and a given realization of uncertainty θ, firm i has to determine an ex post optimal price-quantity pair which is different for every θ. The crucial difference with the certainty case is that given the strategies of the rivals the firm faces a random residual demand curve and therefore has a profit-maximizing point for each realization of the demand.

It is worth remarking that the supply function equilibria, under the assumptions made (full support for θ), are independent of the distribution of uncertainty. When a supply function equilibrium is unique, it is a natural candidate for equilibrium under certainty. The reason is that as the distribution of uncertainty degenerates to a mass point, the equilibrium remains invariant.

For any given realization of the uncertainty θ, the supply function equilibrium is easily seen to be intermediate between the (full information given θ) Cournot and Bertrand (or competitive) outcomes in terms of prices, quantities, and profits. Given θ, the equilibrium prices and quantities are given by

$$q = \frac{D(p) + \theta}{n} \quad \text{and} \quad p - C'(q) = \frac{q}{(n - 1)S'(p) - D'(p)},$$

where $q = S(p)$ and $S(\cdot)$ is the equilibrium supply function. In the Cournot world $S' \equiv 0$, and in the Bertrand (competitive) world $S' \equiv \infty$ (and $p - C' = 0$). At the supply function equilibrium, $0 < S' < \infty$ and the price-cost margin is between Cournot and Bertrand. Furthermore the order of magnitude of the margin is $1/n^2$ provided that marginal costs have bounded slope. This is easily understood from the FOC since the order of magnitude of individual supply is $1/n$, and the order of magnitude of the (absolute value of the) slope of residual demand $(n - 1)S'(p) - D'(p)$, is n provided S' is bounded away from zero. This is the case if marginal costs have bounded slope at zero ($C''(0) < \infty$) (see Klemperer and Meyer 1989, prop. 8a). A linear example will illustrate the model and its comparative static properties. Let $D(p) = -bp$, $b > 0$, and $C(q) = (cq^2)/2$, $c > 0$. $D(p, \theta) = \theta - bp$, and θ is distributed with support on $[0, \infty]$. The unique equilibrium in supply functions is given by

$$S(n) = d_n p \quad \text{with}$$

$$d_n = \frac{1}{2(n-1)} \left(\frac{n-2}{c} - b + \sqrt{\left(\frac{n-2}{c} - b \right)^2 + \frac{4b(n-1)}{c}} \right).$$

The supply function is steeper (d_n smaller) with steeper marginal costs (c larger), larger willingness to pay of consumers (b smaller), or a smaller number of firms n. The first two effects would already occur in monopoly and are reinforced in oligopoly through the effect on the residual demand of the firms. As the slope of marginal costs c tends to zero or the number of firms tends to infinity, the supply function tends to the inverse of marginal cost.

Choosing the linear equilibrium as the outcome under certainty (exercise 7.1), we see that the equilibrium price will be given by $p_n^* = \theta/(b + nd_n)$. Where the price is higher, the marginal cost is steeper relative to demand (bc is larger) and the number of firms is lower.

7.2.1 Capacity Determining Competitive Supply

Another approach that limits the multiplicity of supply function equilibria is to assume competition in two stages. First is the capacity choice, which fixes the short-run marginal cost schedule of firms and therefore competitive supply, followed by a competitive market-clearing stage where output is auctioned efficiently (Dixon 1985; Vives 1986b).

Consider the same market as before but with a variation in the cost structure and with nonstochastic demand (Vives 1986b). The capacity choice of firm i, k_i, determines a short-run U-shaped average cost curve. Firm i, when choosing a capacity level k_i, is choosing a cost function with minimum average cost equal to c (the constant long-run marginal cost) at an output level equal to k_i. Marginal production cost are zero up to k_i, and afterward they increase with slope proportional to λ, where λ is a positive constant. We can think that the firm buys or contracts for output k_i at unit cost c before the market period. If the firm wants to sell more at the second stage, it has to pay an additional cost over c.

Given k_i, total costs $C(q_i,;k_i)$ are defined as follows: To produce output $q_i \leq k_i$, the firm must pay ck_i; to produce more, it must pay $cx_i + \lambda V(x_i - k_i)$, where $V(\cdot)$ is a convex increasing function with $V(0) = 0$.

Firms choose their capacities strategically. Once chosen, the short-run marginal cost schedules determine the competitive supply of each firm, $S(p; k_i)$, $i = 1, \ldots, n$. This equals k_i if $p \leq c$, and $k_i + \Phi((p-c)/\lambda)$ otherwise, where Φ is the inverse of marginal cost ($\Phi \equiv (V')^{-1}$). Output is auctioned efficiently and the market price is the one that equates total supply with demand: $\sum_{i=1}^{n} S_i(p, k_i) = D(p)$. The market-clearing price Q depends only on the total capacity $\bar{k} = \sum_{i=1}^{n} k_i$.

Profits of firms i are given by $\pi_i = pS_i(p, k_i) - C(S_i(p, k_i))$, which equal $(p - c)[k_i + \Phi((p-c)/\lambda)] - \lambda V[\Phi((p-c)/\lambda)]$ provided $\bar{k} \leq D(c)$. In Vives (1986b) it is shown[6] that there is a unique and symmetric Nash equilibrium of the capacity game, and this equilibrium is characterized by the first-order condition (FOC), which yields

$$p - c = -\frac{S_i(p; k)}{D'(p) - (n/\lambda)\Phi'((p-c)/\lambda)}.$$

This just says that the margin over long-run cost c equals the supply of the firm divided by the absolute value of the slope of the residual demand faced by the firm when choosing its capacity level. The residual demand faced by firm i is given by $D(p) - (\sum_{j \neq i} k_j + n\Phi((p-c)/\lambda))$. Notice that the variable part of the supply of firm i, Φ, is also subtracted since when choosing k_i the firm already knows that it will supply $\Phi((p-c)/\lambda)$ to the market at price p. Alternatively, we can write the FOC in elasticity terms

$$\frac{p - c}{p} = \frac{1}{n(\varepsilon + \eta)},$$

where $\varepsilon (= p\Phi'/\lambda S_i)$ and $\eta(= -D'p/D)$ are, respectively, the supply and demand elasticities. The elasticity of supply can be shown to be monotone decreasing in λ. When λ is large, representing a rigid technology, ε is close to zero and we are close to the Cournot world (with long run constant marginal cost c). For $\lambda = \infty$, we obtain in fact the FOC of the Cournot case $((p - c)/p = 1/n\eta)$. When λ is low, representing a flexible technology, ε is close to infinity and price is close to long-run cost. That is, we are close to the Bertrand world (with long-run constant marginal cost c). The slope of short-run marginal costs governs thus the departure of price from the long run unit cost. Increasing the number of firms decreases the price/long-run cost margin $p_n^* - c$ at a rate of $1/n^2$ provided that short run marginal costs have a bounded slope at $q_i = k_i$. This is so since the perceived elasticity of demand tends to infinity on two counts when marginal cost has bounded slope. First, as a result of individual output tending to zero at a rate $1/n$, that is, as a result of the inward shifting of residual demand for a firm as the number of firms grow (like in the Cournot case). Second, as a result of the slope of residual demand tending to infinity linearly with n (while in the Cournot case we did not have this effect). The latter effect follows because in adding some flexibility to the technology, the slope of residual demand depends on the supply of the other firms getting flatter as the number of firms increases. The long-run margin $p_n^* - c$ equals individual output times the inverse of the slope of residual demand. Each factor is of the order of magnitude of $1/n$. Therefore $p_n^* - c$ is of the order of magnitude of $1/n^2$.

7.2.2 Choice of Strategy Space

Klemperer and Meyer (1986) have also analyzed a simple one stage game where firms can choose only prices or quantities to compete in an uncertain differentiated duopoly market. Under certainty, the four possible types of equilibria—(price, price), (quantity, quantity), and the mixed ones—emerge. Under uncertainty firms again will not be indifferent between setting prices or quantities, since they face an uncertain residual demand. Their results confirm the importance of the marginal cost curve and add to our understanding of the influence of the type of uncertainty and of the curvature of demand. Prices are shown to be preferred as strategic variables when uncertainty relates only to the size of market in contrast to the case where also the distribution of reservation prices is uncertain. Convex (concave) demand tends to favor prices (quantities) instead of quantities (prices) as well. What matters is the variation in ex post optimal prices and quantities relative to the choice (price or quantity) made by the firm. For example, with uncertainty about the market size only and constant marginal costs, the optimal ex post price of a monopolist is independent of the random disturbance. In this case it is clearly optimal to set prices. In general, it is found that firms' preferences over strategic variables are stronger with more elastic demands and greater uncertainty.

Following also a supply-function approach, Singh and Vives (1984) consider a situation where firms can only choose a price-type or a quantity-type supply function. That is, a horizontal or a vertical supply schedule. Competition is modeled in two stages in a differentiated duopoly market with a linear structure (as in example 1 in section 6.1). Assume that the unit costs of production are constant and equal to zero without loss of generality. The results can be extended to nonlinear structures under certain assumptions. Firms commit to a *type* of strategy (price or quantity) and then compete in the market place. The authors show that with substitute products it is a dominant strategy to choose the quantity strategy, while with complementary products it is dominant to choose a price strategy. With substitute goods, for whatever choice of the rival, a firm will want to commit to a quantity strategy, since this way induces the rival to be softer at the market stage. Think of it in terms of best-response functions in price space (see figure 7.1). The price best-response func-

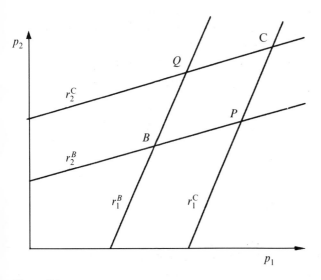

Figure 7.1

tion is the Bertrand one (r_i^B), and the quantity best-response function is the Cournot one translated to price space via the system of demands (r_i^C). When firm i chooses the quantity mode, firm j, $j \neq i$, will be on its Cournot best-response function. The latter yields a higher p_j for any p_i than the Bertrand best-response function. (With complementary products the situation is reversed.) Think of it now in quantity space. Firm i by committing to the price mode induces firm j to be on its Bertrand best response (translated to quantity space). The best response of firm j is more favorable, since for any quantity q_i it yields a higher q_j, which reinforces firm i's market. In summary, with substitute products choosing the quantity mode tends to keep prices high, while with complementary products choosing the price mode tends to keep quantities high.

More formally, denote the Cournot profits of firm i by Π_i^C and the Bertrand profits by Π_i^B. At the second stage, if both firms choose the quantity contract, we have the Cournot outcome. If they choose the price contract, the Bertrand outcome prevails. What happens if firm 1 chooses the price contract and firm 2 the quantity contract?

In that case firm 2 chooses q_2 to maximize its profit $p_2 q_2$ subject to $p_2 = (a_2 + cp_1 - q)/b_2$, taking p_1 as given. This yields the best-response function of firm 2, $q_2 = (a_2 + cp_1)/2$. It is just the quantity q_2 that corresponds to the Bertrand reaction to p_1. Notice that it is upward (downward) sloping for substitutes (complements). Similarly firm 1 chooses p_1 to maximize its profit, taking q_2 as given. Duality gives us the best-response function of firm 1: $p_1 = (\alpha_1 - \gamma q_2)/2$, the price p_1 that corresponds to the Cournot reaction to q_2. We see it slopes down (up) for substitutes (complements). These reaction functions intersect once to yield a Nash equilibrium with prices

$$(p_1^P, p_2^Q) = \left(\frac{2a_1b_2 + a_2c}{E}, \frac{2a_2b_1 + a_1c - a_2c^2/b_2}{E} \right)$$

and quantities

$$(q_1^P, q_2^Q) = \left(\frac{d}{b_2} p_1^P, b_2 p_2^Q \right),$$

where $E = 4b_1b_2 - 3c^2$ and $d = b_1b_2 - c^2$.

If firm 1 chooses the quantity contract and firm 2 the price contract, then firm 1 is on its Bertrand reaction function and firm 2 on its

Cournot reaction function. By a dual argument of the above, we get a Nash equilibrium with prices

$$(p_1^Q, p_2^P) = \left(\frac{2a_1b_2 + a_2c - a_1c^2/b_1}{E}, \frac{2a_2b_1 + a_1c}{E} \right),$$

and quantities

$$(q_1^Q, q_2^P) = \left(b_1 p_1^Q, \frac{d}{b_1} p_2^P \right).$$

Let $\Pi_1^P = p_1^P q_1^P$ and $\Pi_1^Q = p_1^Q q_1^Q$. It is possible to show that $\Pi_1^C > \Pi_1^Q > \Pi_1^B > \Pi_1^P$ if the goods are substitutes, and $\Pi_1^B > \Pi_1^P > \Pi_1^C > \Pi_1^Q$ if they are complements. These inequalities have a clear interpretation. Suppose that the goods are substitutes. If firm 1 sets prices and firm 2 quantities, then firm 1 is in the worst of the possible worlds since it faces a price cutter and takes as given the supply of the rival. Firm 1 would be better off by being a price cutter itself. The outcome would be then the Bertrand equilibrium which yields more profits to firm 1, $\Pi_1^B > \Pi_1^P$. On the other hand, firm 1 would prefer to set quantities and be the price cutter while facing a price-setting rival rather than to face another price cutter, $\Pi_1^Q > \Pi_1^B$. The best of the possible worlds is when both firms set quantities and there is no price cutting. The Cournot outcome dominates in terms of profits the other outcomes. With complements we have the dual inequalities as expected, and the Bertrand equilibrium dominates in terms of profits the others. We have thus firm 1 facing the payoff matrix at the first stage as in table 7.1.

We see that it is dominant for firm 1 to choose the quantity contract if the goods are substitutes, since $\Pi_1^Q > \Pi_1^B$ and $\Pi_1^C > \Pi_1^P$, and to choose the price contract if the goods are complements, since then $\Pi_1^B > \Pi_1^Q$ and $\Pi_1^P > \Pi_1^C$. The same applies to firm 2. With substitute

Table 7.1
First-stage payoff matrix for firm 1

| | Firm 2 | |
	Price	Quantity
Firm 1		
Price	Π_1^B	Π_1^P
Quantity	Π_1^Q	Π_1^C

products, choosing the quantity contract is the best firm 1 can do, regardless of the competitor's choice of contract. This is unfortunate from the welfare point of view, since consumer surplus and total surplus are higher with price competition. It is, however, fortunate from the viewpoint of the firms since Cournot profits are larger than Bertrand profits. With complements, by choosing the price contracts, firms enhance their profits and consumer surplus, and hence general welfare.

7.2.3 Discussion

In the models presented that follow the supply function approach, it has been implicitly assumed that firms can commit to a specific supply function or at least have a choice between price-type and quantity-type strategies. Grossman (1981a) rationalized the approach arguing that firms can establish binding contracts with consumers. Klemperer and Meyer (1986, 1989) argue that internal organizational factors of the firm may explain the commitment to a particular supply function. For example, a management consulting firm may set a fee per hour or a fixed fee per consultation. The first obviously corresponds to setting a price, but the second to setting a quantity since given the capacity constraint of the firm the effective price per hour varies with demand and the time spent with the client. The incentive structure of the firms' workers will have to be adjusted differently in the two cases. Airlines provide another example. The setting of schedules, the reservation system, and the discounts offered can be interpreted as the supply schedule put forward by the firm in advance of knowing precisely market conditions. An extreme case, corresponding to the Bertrand model, is the policy followed on some shuttle routes where a price is set and the airline is committed to meet the forthcoming demand by adjusting the supply of planes. Green and Newbery (1992) use supply functions to model competition in the British electricity spot market.

The supply function approach to the oligopoly problem predicts that the slope of marginal costs is a crucial determinant which indicates whether the Cournot or Bertrand models are more appropriate descriptions of the competitive process. Steep marginal costs, linked to inflexible technologies, are conducive to Cournot-type behavior, while flat marginal costs are conducive to Bertrand behavior. With respect to the departure from efficiency, the magnitude of the price-cost margin is seen to be of the order of $1/n^2$ provided that marginal costs have bounded slope. Supply function competition dissipates quickly the monopoly power of firms in contrast to the Cournot model where the margin is typically of the order of $1/n$. Other factors come also into play. For example, supply functions are flatter with competition among products that are less differentiated. In the product differentiation context when marginal costs tend to be constant, supply functions do not tend to be flat, and correspondingly prices are above Bertrand levels (Klemperer and Meyer 1989).

In summary, the argument about what is the appropriate oligopoly model cannot be separated of the particulars of the market studied. Firms make both production and pricing decisions (leaving aside more medium- or long-run decisions as advertising, R&D, etc.), and which variable emerges as the dominant strategic variable, or which game as the adequate reduced form, depends on structural factors like the commitment power and the temporal structure of the decision variables, and the slope of marginal costs. Obviously there are situations where firms can choose the type of competition; the situation where the competition mode is "dictated" by basic market parameters can be thought as being a special case, once the costs of choosing the mode are taken into account. In a wide range of models the Cournot outcome emerges as the least competitive outcome.

7.3 Collusion and Facilitating Practices

In a static model, collusive Nash equilibria can be supported by appropriate conjectural variations or supply functions. In either case the collusive outcome is one of the multiple equilibria that exist. Similarly competition in contracts for consumers involving *facilitating practices*, as most-favored-consumer or meet-or-release clauses, may induce collusive pricing (Salop 1986). According to the most-favored consumer clause, the buyer receives the lowest price that the seller has offered. According to the meet-or-release clause, the seller must meet the offers made to his customers or release them from the signed contracts. *Best-price* provisions combine both and may support collusive prices. Suppose that all firms are identical and that they post prices and make contracts with consumers. With the best price provisions each firm will price according to the minimum of the posted price and the lowest price announced by the other firms. It will be then for any firm a weakly dominant strategy to quote the monopoly price, and the collusive outcome will prevail. Obviously many other equilibria with lower prices exist. In fact any price between the monopoly price and marginal cost can be supported.[7] It must be noticed nevertheless that facilitating practices are better understood in a dynamic context where there is the possibility of firms reacting to the moves of the rivals.[8]

In summary, collusion can be obtained in static models at the cost of making the strategy space of firms quite complex. These expanded strategy spaces can be thought, explicitly or implicitly, in terms of supply functions.[9]

It can be argued also that the Nash equilibrium solution concept is too restrictive to explain collusion in a static model. In the case where the strategies of the firms are the production levels, is it not possible to improve upon the Cournot equilibrium? After all, if agents are allowed to communicate before the (independent) play of the game, they may decide to build a communication device to correlate their strategies and improve upon the underlying Nash equilibrium outcomes.[10] The players agree to construct a lottery over the possible outcomes of the game. A referee or mediator (which could be a machine) selects an outcome according to the lottery and informs every player (confidentially) what his recommended strategy is. This lottery is a correlated equilibrium if no player has an incentive to deviate from the mediator's recommendation given that the other players follow the recommendations. All pure- and mixed-strategy Nash equilibria of the game are also correlated equilibria, but in general, there are more correlated equilibria and some improve upon the Nash equilibria (see Aumann 1974 and Myerson 1985 for further references). Gerard-Varet and Moulin (1978) have shown, using a slightly different version of correlated equilibrium, that Cournot (with homogeneous products) and Bertrand (with differentiated products) equilibria can be improved upon locally if strategic cross effects loom large in the market interaction.[11] Still a step further may be taken abandoning equilibrium analysis in favor of rationalizable choices (see section 2.6). There is a great multiplicity of rationalizable strategies and this allows for collusion to be supported with such strategies. For example, in a quantity-setting n-firm oligopoly with linear demand and constant (and equal) marginal costs, any nonnegative output up to the monopoly output is rationalizable if $n \geq 3$. For $n = 2$ the unique Nash strategies are the only rationalizable (Bernheim 1984).[12]

Collusion can be sustained with repeated interaction (repeated games will be surveyed in section 9.1). The basic idea is that deviants from a cooperative agreement can be punished when firms compete repeatedly in the marketplace. However, experimental evidence points out that agents tend to cooperate even in encounters which are in fact one-shot.[13] Examples are situations where agents are randomly matched in an anonymous way, so it is impossible to punish the deviators. Cooperation can emerge in this type of settings if players use contagious punishments (i.e., when a deviation by a player provokes a chain reaction of punishments).[14] It must nevertheless be pointed out that strictly speaking, such situations do not correspond to a one-shot game but to one-shot encounters which happen in the context of a larger dynamic game.

7.4 Commitment and Pricing

Up to this point we have considered basically static models, or, at least models with only one strategic stage. We have also considered some two-stage models of competition (e.g., in sections 4.3 and 5.1 on entry into the market, in section 5.2.4 on relating the Cournot model to price competition, and in section 7.2 on certain types of supply function competition). The literature has considered two-stage models as an intermediate step toward dynamics. Those models have provided important insights into the oligopoly problem. In particular, they have illustrated the idea of commitment in oligopoly pricing. In a strategic situation the player who can restrict in a credible way his choices (and can "commit") may gain a strategic advantage. Schelling (1960) has explained this idea with many examples, like burning the ships to commit to a tough fight. In oligopoly theory the idea of commitment goes, at least, back to Stackelberg (1934). Industrial organization analysis has developed many applications of the basic notion. We will review here the Stackelberg model, together with some extensions trying to endogenize the leadership role; we will build also on the model to derive some insights about entry prevention and provide a taxonomy of strategic behavior in two-stage games.

7.4.1   The Stackelberg Model

The simpler model that illustrates the idea of commitment in oligopoly pricing is the celebrated model of Stackelberg (1934). Consider the classical quantity competition model with homogeneous product (chapter 4) with two firms that decide their output in sequence. The leader (e.g., firm 1) chooses it output first, and then the follower (firm 2), having observed the choice of the leader, chooses its output in turn. The leader has the capacity to make an output commitment to which the follower has to adjust. Formally we have a two-stage game of perfect information. The strategy of the leader is a number, its output q_1; the strategy of the follower is a map $h(\cdot)$ from the outputs of firm 1 to the feasible outputs of firm 2. The leader in setting its output anticipates the reaction of the follower. A Stackelberg equilibrium is then a pair $(q_1^S, h(\cdot))$ such that $\pi_2(q_1, h(q_1)) \geq \pi_2(q_1, q_2)$ for all q_1 and q_2, and $\pi_1(q_1^S, h(q_1^S)) \geq \pi_1(q_1, h(q_1))$ for all q_1. The play of the game is then $(q_1^S, h(q_1^S))$. If firm 2 has a unique best reply to any output of firm 1, then $h(\cdot)$ is just the best-reply function of firm 2: $r_2(\cdot)$. In this case q_1^S solves $\max_{q_1} \pi_1(q_1, r_2(q_1))$, and it is clear that the leader must make at least as much profits as at a Cournot equilibrium. (Indeed, firm 1 by setting its output at the Cournot level induces firm 2 to do the same.)

The typical graphical description has the Stackelberg equilibrium at the tangency between the downward-sloping $r_2(\cdot)$ and the isoprofit contour of firm 1 (see figure 7.2a where $a_i = q_i$). This property generalizes to a generic two-stage game under certain conditions. For example, suppose that each firm in the duopoly has a compact interval as action space (be it quantities, prices, or any other action), that payoffs are continuous with the profits of the leader, strictly decreasing in the action of the follower, and that the best-response correspondence of the follower is monotone (increasing or decreasing). Then any interior Stackelberg equilibrium can be found by maximizing the leader's payoff on the graph of the follower's best-response correspondence.[15]

It is important to notice that a Stackelberg equilibrium rules out incredible threats by the follower of the type: "I will flood the market if you do not restrict your output." This is so because it requires the strategy of the follower to be optimal for any output of the leader, not only the equilibrium output. It must be in the interest of the follower to carry out its threats. A Stackelberg equilibrium is just a

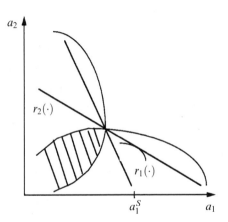

Figure 7.2a

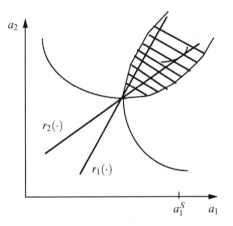

Figure 7.2b

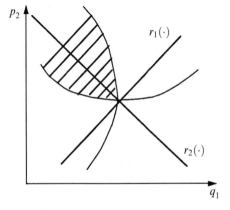

Figure 7.2c

subgame-perfect (Nash) equilibrium (SPE) of the described two-stage perfect information game, where empty threats are not allowed. A SPE requires future strategies to be profit-maximizing choices for whatever inherited history. More formally, a SPE requires strategies to form a Nash equilibrium starting at any subgame. Nash equilibria only require optimizing behavior along the equilibrium path.[16] In contrast, the only requirement Nash equilibria of the two-stage game imposes on the output of the leader is that it is such that it does not generate losses. For example, with linear demand $p = a - Q$ and constant marginal cost m, the only Stackelberg output for the leader is $(a - m)/2$, while any output of firm 1 in the interval $[0, a - m]$ would be sustainable as a Nash equilibrium of the two-stage game.

How do payoffs compare between the simultaneous move Nash equilibrium and the two possible types of Stackelberg equilibria (with firm 1 leading or following, respectively)? Suppose for simplicity that firms have compact intervals as action spaces, that payoffs are continuous, (strictly) quasiconcave in own action, and monotone in the rival's action, and that Nash and Stackelberg equilibria are unique, distinct, and interior. Then we already know, given that each firm has a best-reply *function* to the action of the rival, that the leader in a Stackelberg equilibrium does strictly better than at the Nash equilibrium. Furthermore, if best-response functions are monotone and with slopes of the same sign then either (1) each player prefers his simultaneous Nash payoff to his Stackelberg follower payoff or (2) the opposite happens (each player prefers his Stackelberg follower payoff to his simultaneous Nash payoff). If best-response functions have slopes of different signs, then (3) only one player prefers his Stackelberg follower payoff to his simultaneous Nash payoff (Hamilton and Slutsky 1990; Amir 1995).[17]

A graphical argument checks the results. Under our assumptions (in particular, that the payoff to each firm is monotone in the rival's action) the isoprofit contours of any firm are *functions* of the rival action. The Pareto preferred set (in terms of profits) to the simultaneous Nash equilibrium is bounded by the isoprofit curves and must lie in one of the four quadrants because the isoprofits lines have slopes zero or infinite at the simultaneous Nash equilibrium. Then case 1 corresponds to the situation in which neither best-response function intersects the Pareto preferred set to the Nash equilibrium; case 2 to the situation where both best-response functions intersect the Pareto preferred set to the Nash equilibrium; and case 3 to the situation where only one best-response function intersects the Pareto preferred set to the Nash equilibrium. The usual situation in Cournot competition (see section 4.1) with downward-sloping best responses will yield case 1, since the Pareto preferred set to the Cournot equilibrium does not intersect the best-response functions (figure 7.2a).[18] In this case there is also a first-mover advantage, since a firm will always prefer to be the leader than the follower. A typical case with Bertrand competition and differentiated substitute products is to have upward-sloping best responses (see section 6.2), yielding case 2 (figure 7.2b). Obviously Stackelberg equilibria will lie in the shaded area (respectively) on the follower's best-response function. In this situation, and with symmetric firms, there is in fact a second-mover advantage: A firm makes more profits by following than by leading. The follower sets a lower price than the leader and free rides on the high price of the leader who assumes the role of softening competition (see the depiction of the Stackelberg equilibrium with firm 1 leading in figure 7.2b where $a_i = p_i$).[19] Case 3 arises, for example (see section 7.2), when firm 1 has quantity as a strategic variable and firm 2 price as a strategic variable in a differentiated linear duopoly with substitute products (figure 7.2c). Note that the best-reply function of the quantity-setting (price-setting) firm is upward (downward) sloping because it is responding to the price (quantity) set by the rival. That is, the quantity-setting (price-setting) firm is on his Bertrand (Cournot) best-response function. (See section 7.2.2 and Singh and Vives 1984.) In this case the price-setting player is the only one to prefer his Stackelberg follower payoff to the Nash payoff.

Once payoffs have been compared it is only one step to try to endogenize the order of moves. In fact, a usual criticism of Stackelberg equilibrium is that the order of moves of the players is given exogenously. In some circumstances the asymmetric capacity of commitment of firms is given by technological or market data. For example, an incumbent firm may have the capacity to commit to some actions and make some irreversible decisions. In the next sections we will see how an incumbent may prevent entry of other firms and how, in general, the type of competition in the marketplace interacts with commitment incentives.

A simple game to endogenize the order of moves is to add an initial stage in which players simultaneously decide whether to move in the first period or in the second. The first-period decision is binding for the firms. The characterization of the subgame-perfect equilibria of the extended game is then immediate (Hamilton and Slutsky 1990). In case 1 the Nash equilibrium of the simultaneous move game obtains. In case 2 any of the two Stackelberg equilibria may obtain. In case 3 then only the sequential equilibrium with the follower being the only player who prefers his follower payoff to his Nash payoff obtains. In the usual case in which the slopes of the best responses of both firms have the same sign and changes in the action of one firm affect the profits of the rival in the same direction, then with downward-sloping best replies we are in case 1 and with upward-sloping best replies in case 2. The reason is that under the assumptions the Pareto superior set to the Nash equilibrium lies either in the first or in the third quadrant.

The simple game may be criticized because of its artificial character. Indeed, a more natural two-stage specification for the quantity-setting model would have firms being able to move at any stage with a move implying a commitment to an output. Consider Cournot competition with two production periods before the market for the homogeneous products clears. Firms choose simultaneously outputs in the first period, the choices become observable, and the firms choose again output levels in the second period. The accumulated output determines then the market-clearing price. A strategy for firm i consists then of an output for the first period and a function that specifies the output of the second period contingent on the pair of first-period output choices. A subgame-perfect Nash equilibrium requires that second-period outputs form a Nash equilibrium for any pair of first-period outputs. The first-period outputs must then form a Nash equilibrium anticipating the second-period Nash equilibrium outcomes. Assume that best-reply functions are downward sloping, marginal costs constant, and, as before for simplicity, that Cournot and Stackelberg equilibria are unique. It turns out then that *any* outcome in the outer envelope of the Cournot best-reply functions between the two Stackelberg points (and nothing else) can be sustained as a subgame-perfect equilibrium of the two-stage game. The following strategies sustain any point in the described outer envelope: Produce in the first period according to the desired outcome. In the second period, if first-period outputs lie outside the outer envelope of best-response functions, then stop production. Otherwise, if first-period outputs are less than the Cournot equilibrium, produce up to the Cournot equilibrium level; if my first period output is below the

Cournot level and the rival is not, then produce up to the best response to the rival first-period output, who does not produce in the second period. However, if production in the second period is somewhat cheaper than in the first, then only the Stackelberg outcomes are possible (see exercise 7.5, Saloner 1987, and Pal 1991). Another way to eliminate equilibria other than the Stackelberg outcomes is to add a (vanishingly) small amount of payoff relevant uncertainty which is realized and observed between the first and the second period (see exercise 7.6 and Maggi 1996). The moral of these variations to the model is that Stackelberg outcomes tend to emerge as SPE outcomes whenever it is somewhat more costly to produce in the first period than in the second.[20] In this case the advantage of being a leader compensates the increased cost it has to bear.

7.4.2 Entry Deterrence, Limit Pricing, and Incumbency Advantages

Bain defined a barrier to entry as anything which allows incumbents to earn excess profits. From Stigler on a barrier to entry is viewed as any asymmetry that favors the incumbent and allows him to earn a rent. The simplest model of entry prevention is due to Bain (1956), Modigliani (1958), and Sylos-Labini (1962). It is just the Stackelberg model in which the leader is the incumbent and the follower an entrant who has to pay a fixed cost to enter the market. That is, the incumbent can commit to an output level, and the entrant has to decide whether it is profitable to enter given the output of the incumbent and the fixed cost of entry. Anticipating the behavior of the entrant, the incumbent may decide to accommodate or deter entry, unless by producing according to its monopoly output entry does not occur (in which case it is said that entry is blockaded). Obviously the capacity of the incumbent to prevent entry stems from the existence of the fixed cost of entry. The output that prevents entry is the limit output and the associated price the limit price. This output is typically higher than the monopoly output of the incumbent.

Let us consider a generalized version of this model in which there is a sequence of n potential entrants, each one of which can commit to an output level upon entering the homogeneous product industry.[21] The quantities set by the firms determine the market supply Q, and a market-clearing price obtains according to the demand schedule, $p = a - Q$, with $a > 0$. The costs of the incumbent are sunk and all entrants have access to the same constant returns to scale technology (with zero marginal costs for simplicity) and have to pay entry cost $F > 0$ if they decide to produce a positive amount. Earlier entrants make a quantity commitment and anticipate the behavior of the remaining potential entrants.[22]

We have a game (of perfect information) with $n + 1$ stages. At the initial stage, stage 0, the incumbent firm makes its production decision. At stage k, the kth potential entrant chooses whether or not to enter and if so what to produce, taking as given the outputs produced by earlier firms in the sequence and knowing that there are still $n - k$ potential entrants. Since the product is homogeneous, a firm is only interested in the cumulated output of earlier firms. A strategy for a potential entrant is thus a function that assigns a production level to any possible cumulated output Z of earlier firms in the sequence. At a subgame-perfect equilibrium the strategy of any potential entrant has to yield a best response to any possible cumulated output of already established firms taking into account the reactions of the future entrants. Furthermore the incumbent's output has to maximize profits, taking into account the reactions of the entrants.

Suppose that $q_j(\cdot)$ is the equilibrium strategy for potential entrant j. If the entry cost is zero, $F = 0$, then the equilibrium strategy for any potential entrant is the usual Cournot best-response function $r(Z) = \max\{0, a - Z/2\}$. That is, the optimal best response of a firm when $F = 0$ is the same whether it expects entry or not. In particular, the monopoly output is equal to the Stackelberg output of the incumbent. (This is not a general result but a consequence of linear demand for a homogeneous product and constant marginal costs.) When $F > 0$, the entry preventing output is the solution in Y to $(a - (Y + r(Y)))r(Y) = F$ in $[0, a]$ and equals $\max\{0, a - 2\sqrt{F}\}$. The best-response correspondence of a potential entrant is easily characterized. Assume for convenience that a potential entrant enters if and only if it can make positive profits. An important observation is that an entrant will not allow a downstream firm to enter the industry and prevent entry. The reason is that the entrant makes more profits preventing entry itself since marginal costs are constant and total output will be at least Y anyway. Therefore, if firm j allows entry, it must be the case that everyone else downstream is going to allow entry too.

The last potential entrant produces according to the Cournot best-response function $r(\cdot)$ if it makes positive profits and otherwise it stays out. Consider potential entrant j, $j < n$. If the cumulated output up to firm $j - 1$, Z, is larger than or equal to Y, firm j will stay out. If Z is smaller than Y but larger than a certain number Z_0, firm j will blockade entry by producing $r(Z)$; that is, $r(Z) + Z > Y$. If Z is smaller than Z_0 but larger than Z_{n-j}, where Z_{n-j} is the critical Z for which firm j is indifferent between allowing and preventing entry of the rest of the potential entrants, entry is prevented (producing $Y - Z$).[23] For Z's smaller or equal to Z_{n-j}, entry is allowed and firm j produces $r(Z)$. Then firm $j + 1$ enters and produces $r(Z + r(Z))$ (it can be shown that $Z + r(Z) < Z_{n-j-1}$), and all firms enter similarly producing according to their Cournot best-response function $r(\cdot)$.

The incumbent firm will certainly not allow any potential entrant to enter and prevent or blockade further entry since it makes more preventing entry itself. If Y is smaller than or equal to the monopoly output, $a/2$, the incumbent blockades entry by producing $a/2$. Otherwise, it prevents entry if $Y \leq Y_n$, where Y_n is a critical entry preventing output Y_n, and it allows entry if $Y > Y_n$, in which case it produces $a/2$.[24] In case of entry the total output in the market is given by $(1 - 2^{-(n+1)})a$. A subgame-perfect equilibrium is fully described then by strategies for the potential entrants which are selections of the best-response correspondences and the stated behavior of the incumbent.[25]

Comparative statics with respect to the number of potential entrants n follow easily from the characterization of equilibria. Fix Y, and suppose that entry is not blockaded ($Y > a/2$), then there is a constant $\bar{n}$ ($\bar{n} = -\log(1 - (2Ya^{-1} - 1)^2)/\log 2$) such that for n less than $\bar{n}$ entry is allowed and for n larger than $\bar{n}$ entry is prevented.[26] When there are a lot of potential entrants the incumbent is better off keeping them out, when there are only a few it is too costly (relatively) to prevent entry and they are allowed in. Furthermore it is possible to show that the profits of the incumbent are nonincreasing and that total output and total surplus are nondecreasing in n. Indeed, more potential entrants make the incumbent deter entry, but total output is nondecreasing in n because total output with entry, $Q_n^e = (1 - 2^{-(n+1)})a$, increases with n, and when there is a change of regime, from allowing to preventing entry, total output increases to Y. Total surplus TS is also nondecreasing in n. It increases with n up to $\bar{n}$ (then $TS = aQ_n^e - ((Q_n^e)^2/2) - nF$), and for $n > \bar{n}$ it stays constant at the level $aY - Y^2/2$. Total surplus increases with entry because the increase in consumer surplus more than compensates the decrease in profits induced by the new entrants. Finally the profits of the incumbent decrease in n when entry is allowed, $\pi_0 = (a - Q_n^e)a/2$, and stay constant at the level $(a - Y)Y$ when entry is prevented.

More potential entrants may mean less actual entry in the industry but never lower welfare. This result contrasts with simultaneous entry models where increasing the number of potential entrants may reduce welfare. This comes about because a larger number of potential entrants reduces entry probabilities when looking at symmetric mixed strategy equilibria. If identical players use the same strategy, then firms must randomize the entry decision when there is no room in the market for all the potential entrants.[27]

We have seen in our sequential entry model that when there are many potential entrants the incumbents prefer to keep them out but in order to do so they have to produce a high output. This fact suggests that policies that lower the cost of entry (F) need not be beneficial.[28] Suppose now that F is an entry fee charged by a public authority which wants to maximize total surplus. If there is an infinite number of potential entrants $(n = \infty)$, then the optimal entry fee is zero and the competitive outcome results. If n is finite, then the best policy is not to set a zero entry fee, since by choosing F so that $Y = Y_n - \varepsilon$, for some small enough positive ε, incumbents will prevent entry producing Y which will be larger that the entry output Q_n^e. If there is no other imperfection in the market $(n = \infty)$, then it always pays to lower the entry cost; this is not the case if, for whatever reasons, the number of potential entrants is limited. The moral of the story is that the public authority has to be careful when designing measures to promote competition when there is an incentive for firms to engage in strategic entry deterrence activities.

Several Incumbents and the Free-Rider Problem
We have analyzed the case of an established incumbent facing a sequence of potential entrants. However, as argued in Gilbert and Vives (1986), examples where a single firm has maintained persistent control of a market that is not a natural monopoly are rare. More common are situations where one or a few firms have remained dominant in an industry over significant periods and where industry concentration levels have remained higher than could be justified by technological conditions. Hence a more realistic setting for examining incentives for entry prevention is that of an established oligopoly

facing potential entry where all firms are strategic agents playing a noncooperative game.

The question arises then whether there may be underprovision of entry deterrence from the point of view of the established oligopoly. Indeed, entry-prevention can be seen as a public good. If any firm produces enough to deter entry, all firms are protected from competition. Thus each firm could "free-ride" on the entry-preventing activities of its competitors with the potential implication that there would be little entry deterrence. We will see that this is not the case in a homogeneous product market with constant marginal costs of production. The basic reason is that every incumbent would like to contribute to entry deterrence as much as it can given that entry will be prevented. Indeed, given a price resulting from the entry-preventing output which is above the unit cost, it is in the interest of any incumbent to produce as much as possible. This is in contrast with typical public good provision problems.

Suppose now that instead of a single incumbent, we have an established m-firm oligopoly. The largest entry-preventing output for which to prevent entry is profitable for all incumbents is denoted by $\bar{Y}_{m,n}$. The entry-preventing output that makes incumbent i indifferent between preventing or allowing entry given that the other incumbents produce at Cournot levels is denoted by $\underline{Y}_{m,n}$. It is possible to show that $\bar{Y}_{m,n} \geq \underline{Y}_{m,n} \geq (m/(m+1))a$, the latter being the m-firm Cournot output. The first inequality is strict if $n \geq 1$ and $m \geq 2$; the second is strict if $n \geq 1$.[29]

Provided that entry is not blocked by the m-firm Cournot equilibrium (i.e., if the limit output is larger than the m-firm Cournot output), three regions for the entry-preventing output describe the possible outcomes. If the limit output is small, $Y \leq \bar{Y}_{m,n}$, entry is prevented by incumbents, and typically there is a continuum of entry-preventing equilibria with incumbents producing on the hyperplane $\sum_{i=1}^{m} q_i = Y$. If the limit output is large, $Y \geq \underline{Y}_{m,n}$, entry is allowed by incumbents, and total output is less than the entry-preventing output. For limit outputs in the intermediate region $[\underline{Y}_{m,n}, \bar{Y}_{m,n}]$, both types of equilibria coexist. In this case the entry-preventing equilibria are Pareto dominated in term of profits by the entry equilibrium. (See figure 7.3 where $m = 2$.)[30]

Comparative statics with respect to n are similar than before except that now there are two constants $\bar{n}(Y, m)$ and $\underline{n}(Y, m)$, $\bar{n} > \underline{n} > 0$.

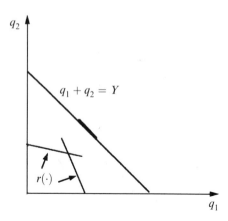

Figure 7.3

Now, if $n < \bar{n}$, to allow entry is an equilibrium, and if $n > \underline{n}$, to prevent entry is an equilibrium provided that entry is not blockaded.[31] If $n \in [\underline{n}, \bar{n}]$, both to allow and to prevent entry are equilibria. However, the interval $[\underline{n}, \bar{n}]$ contains at most one integer, and therefore, if $\hat{n} \in [\underline{n}, \bar{n}]$ at $\hat{n} - 1$, to allow entry is the only equilibrium and at $\hat{n} + 1$ to prevent entry is the only equilibrium. This fact preserves the monotonicity properties of incumbent's profits, total output, and total surplus with respect to the number of potential entrants. When entry is prevented, there is typically a continuum of entry-preventing equilibria, but we know that for $n \in [\underline{n}, \bar{n}]$ the entry equilibrium Pareto dominates in terms of profits the entry-preventing equilibria. Therefore, if for purposes of comparison we take the symmetric entry-preventing equilibria, profits of incumbent i are nonincreasing in n.

In the model considered an established oligopoly never under-invests and may overinvest in entry deterrence. Indeed, at any oligopoly equilibrium where entry is allowed, the profits of incumbents would be lower if entry were prevented. Furthermore there are situations where incumbents' profits are higher, allowing entry, but the unique oligopoly equilibrium calls for entry prevention. In addition, when both types of equilibria coexist, the profits of each incumbent firm are higher when entry is allowed. Thus incumbents may become trapped in a Pareto-dominated arrangement (in terms of profits) by preventing entry. The reason is that even though entry prevention is costly, if entry is to be prevented and there is more than one incumbent, each incumbent firm wants to do the job. Given that the limit output has to be produced to prevent entry and that marginal costs are constant, the profits of any incumbent increase with investment up to the limit output. Furthermore rivalry among incumbents diminishes the value of allowing entry to occur, so that entry prevention becomes relatively more attractive to each firm as the number of incumbents increases.

Waldman (1987) shows that the Gilbert-Vives results are robust to the introduction of uncertainty, in terms of the exact investment needed to prevent entry.[32] Kovenock and Roy (1995) extend the analysis to a product differentiated market. They show then that there may exist underinvestment in entry deterrence in the sense that when both entry-allowing and entry-deterring equilibria coexist the latter may Pareto dominate the former. This happens when products are differentiated enough. The reason is that unlike the homogeneous product case, now there is a cost for an incumbent to increase its participation in the limit output because this increase typically decreases the price that its product fetches (the more so the more differentiated the products are). Then the incumbent's maximum profit from deterring entry, given the outputs of the rival incumbents, may be increasing in the latter. The situation is akin to the case of increasing marginal costs (and homogeneous product) where an incumbent which increases its share in the limit output has to bear an increased unit cost of production. (See exercise 7.10.)

A Reinterpretation of Quantity Commitments

We have seen how quantity commitments give a strategic advantage to incumbents. The key fact to ensure the commitment value of the decision of the incumbent is that it represents a sunk investment. Indeed, if the decision of the incumbent could be reversed, it would lose its commitment value. In this sense the quantity commitment is best understood as a capacity commitment to influence the posterior competition in the marketplace. We will see that under certain assumptions, the quantity commitment model can be understood as a reduced form of a game of capacity commitment followed either by quantity or price competition.

Dixit (1980) and Spence (1977) present an incumbent investing in capacity to gain a strategic advantage at the stage of market competition. Consider the following version of the sequential entry model considered before, in the spirit of Dixit (1980) and analyzed by Ware

(1984) and Eaton and Ware (1987): Maintain the assumption of linear demand. Firms can commit to capacity levels and afterward compete in quantities (contingent on the chosen capacity levels). Suppose that firm i, once it has installed capacity k_i, faces no production costs up to the capacity limit (and infinite otherwise). The costs of installing capacity are c per unit. If potential entrant i now decides to enter, it sinks capacity k_i knowing the capacities already sunk by previous entrants and anticipating the decisions of the firms in the sequence. Once all capacities are installed, a Cournot game is played.

The first thing to note is that given that demand is linear, and therefore marginal revenue for a firm is decreasing in the output of the other firms, implying downward-sloping best responses, we should expect no excess capacity in equilibrium (subgame-perfect equilibrium). Capacity is costly and potential entrants will not be fooled by capacities that will not be used in case entry occurs. Furthermore in case of no entry, an incumbent will produce up to the capacity limit because its best response is downward sloping.[33] It is possible to show that with free entry (i.e., with more potential entrants than actual entrants in equilibrium) the aggregate output in equilibrium is no smaller than the Bain limit output and that when the number of firms is large, for all practical purposes the output is the limit output (Eaton and Ware 1987). This means that for n large, the simple quantity commitment model is a very good approximation of the more sophisticated capacity investment model in terms of predicting the market price.[34] An obvious difference is that in the quantity commitment model entry prevention is carried out by the incumbent only, while in the capacity investment model this may not be feasible in the sense that required capacity to deter entry may not be credible. In this case entry prevention has to be shared with the first entrants in the industry.

If investment in capacity were to lower the marginal cost of production, then "excess capacity" would play an important role. The reason is that established firms would have an incentive to expand capacity to be aggressive at the market stage, to gain market share if entry is to occur or to prevent entry (see the next section).[35]

We can also consider the capacity commitment model with price competition at the market stage. We have claimed (section 5.2.4) that under some assumptions, (simultaneous) capacity competition followed by price competition yields Cournot outcomes. Allen et al. (1995) perform a detailed analysis of the following three-stage model. An incumbent and entrant sequentially set capacities and then at the third stage compete in prices (Bertrand-Edgeworth competition). Firms pay a fixed cost of entry when setting a positive capacity. The unit cost of capacity is constant and equal for both firms. Unit production costs are also constant (up to the capacity limit) and may be different for each firm. There is rationing according to the surplus-maximizing rule. Among the different range of possible (subgame-perfect) equilibria the (quantity-setting) Stackelberg equilibrium emerges when the entry cost is low (so that entry accommodation is optimal for the incumbent) and the cost of capacity high.

7.4.3   A Taxonomy of Strategic Behavior

We have considered only the simplest possible model of entry deterrence with the incumbents having the possibility of committing its output in order to discourage entrants. We have argued also how this output commitment is best viewed as a capacity commitment. The pioneer models of Dixit (1980) and Spence (1977) present an incumbent investing in capacity to gain a strategic advantage at the stage of market competition, but many other investment possibilities are possible (R&D, brand image and advertising, initial production/ sales in the presence of a learning curve or switching costs, product compatibility decisions, product positioning, facilitating practices like price protection provisions, etc.).[36]

The strategic incentives of an incumbent are highlighted in the following very simple model (Fudenberg and Tirole 1984). Consider a two-stage game in which at the first stage the incumbent, firm 1, can make an observable investment k that will affect directly his payoff at the market competition stage $\pi_1(x_1, x_2; k)$. The payoff of the entrant is $\pi_2(x_1, x_2)$, and x_i is the market action of firm i. Assume that at the second stage there are well-defined best-response functions for both firms, and that there is a unique and (locally) stable Nash equilibrium that depends smoothly on k: $x^*(k)$. We will restrict attention to subgame-perfect equilibria of the two-stage game. The first order condition for the maximization problem of firm 1 is $\partial \pi_1 / \partial k + (\partial \pi_1 / \partial x_2)(\partial x_2^* / \partial k) = 0$.[37] The condition $\partial \pi_1 / \partial k = 0$ would correspond to an "open loop" equilibrium where firm 1 would ignore the effect of his investment choice on the market equilibrium. The term $(\partial \pi_1 / \partial x_2)(\partial x_2^* / \partial k)$ corresponds therefore to the strategic effect (taken into account at the SPE). This term will determine whether there is

Table 7.2
Taxonomy of strategic behavior

	Investment makes player 1:	
	Tough	Soft
Strategic substitutes	Overinvest (top dog)	Underinvest (lean and hungry)
Strategic complements	Underinvest (puppy dog)	Overinvest (fat cat)

under or over investment for strategic reasons (i,e., with respect to the "innocent" open loop equilibrium). For example, if an increase in the action of the rival hurts the incumbent, $\partial \pi_1 / \partial x_2 < 0$, then the strategic effect will be positive when $\partial x_2^* / \partial k < 0$. It is immediate that $\partial x_2^* / \partial k = [(\partial^2 \pi_2 / \partial x_1 \partial x_2)(\partial^2 \pi_1 / \partial k \partial x_1)] / D$, where

$$D = \frac{\partial^2 \pi_2}{(\partial x_2)^2} \frac{\partial^2 \pi_1}{(\partial x_1)^2} - \frac{\partial^2 \pi_1}{\partial x_1 \partial x_2} \frac{\partial^2 \pi_2}{\partial x_1 \partial x_2},$$

which is positive at a (locally) stable market equilibrium. The sign of $\partial x_2^* / \partial k$, given a stable intersection of the best-reply functions, depends on the slope of the best response of firm 2 (determined by the sign of $\partial^2 \pi_2 / \partial x_1 \partial x_2$) and on the impact of k on the best response of firm 1 (determined by the sign of $\partial^2 \pi_1 / \partial k \partial x_1$). The sign of the strategic effect is therefore equal to the sign of $(\partial \pi_1 / \partial x_2)(\partial^2 \pi_1 / \partial k \partial x_1) \cdot (\partial^2 \pi_2 / \partial x_1 \partial x_2)$. If $(\partial \pi_1 / \partial x_2)(\partial^2 \pi_1 / \partial k \partial x_1) < 0 (> 0)$, the investment makes firm 1 tough (soft). This provides a taxonomy of strategic behavior in terms of whether market competition is of the strategic substitutes or complements variety and whether the investment makes the incumbent tough or soft (see table 7.2).

Some examples will illustrate the taxonomy. Suppose that the investment reduces marginal costs. In a Cournot market with downward-sloping best-response functions, by investing, the incumbent pushes his best response function to the right and therefore in equilibrium the entrant produces less and the incumbent more (see figure 7.4a). This is a "top dog" strategy by the incumbent in the terminology of Fudenberg and Tirole (1984). The incumbent has a strategic incentive to overinvest to better his position at the market stage. In this case investment makes the incumbent tough (i.e., it raises the marginal profitability of its market action and an increase in this action hurts the entrant), and the market game is of the strategic substitutes type. The situation is very different if at the

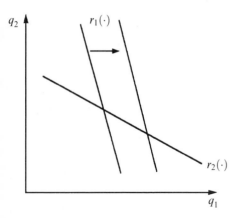

Figure 7.4a

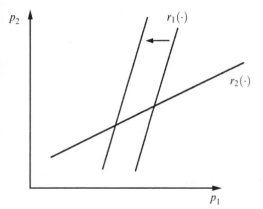

Figure 7.4b

second stage there is price competition with upward-sloping best responses (strategic complementarity). Then the incumbent by investing makes the rival more aggressive at the second stage, since firm 1 pushes firm 2 down his upward-sloping best response. In this case the incumbent has incentives to underinvest. This is the "puppy dog ploy" (see figure 7.4b). If the investment of the incumbent were to make him soft, for example, advertising that pushes his best reply to the right, then the incumbent would look like a "fat cat," overinvesting to induce soft price behavior by the rival. There is still the possibility that competition is of the strategic substitutes type and that the investment makes the incumbent soft. Then there will be incentives by the incumbent to underinvest and look "lean and hungry."

Obviously, if the entrant has to pay a fixed cost to enter, the incumbent may well be able to prevent entry, and then the taxonomy has to be modified. Indeed, in the capacity investment Cournot case the incumbent may be able to push the entrant so far down his best-response function that by entering, it would make negative profits. Indeed, at some point the best-response function of firm 2 jumps to zero when there is a fixed cost of entry. Therefore a top dog strategy is also good to prevent entry. It is important to note that at a SPE the incumbent cannot make incredible threats of flooding the market in case entry occurs. (A threat that would not be in the interest of the incumbent to carry out in case of entry.) The incumbent can only manipulate the equilibrium at the market competition stage. With price competition and strategic complementarity, to overinvest, the top dog strategy again is optimal in case entry must be deterred. In the advertising example with price competition, the incumbent should look "lean and hungry" and underinvest to reduce the profitability of entry.

In order to derive the taxonomy of strategic incentives in the two-stage duopoly games, we have assumed very strong regularity conditions. Among them the existence of well-defined best-reply functions for the firms, as well as a unique and stable market equilibrium. Using the theory of supermodular games, we can uncover the basic properties that drive the results without unnecessary assumptions (see the remarks on comparative statics in section 2.2.3). Consider the basic simple model in which the incumbent, firm 1, can make an observable pre-market investment k. Its payoff is $\pi_1(x_1, x_2; k)$. The payoff of the entrant is $\pi_2(x_1, x_2)$. Assume that action spaces are compact intervals. Suppose first that the market game is supermodular (or ordinally supermodular). That is, π_i has increasing differences (fulfills the SCP) in x_i and x_j for $i = 1, 2$ (this is the strategic complementarity assumption). Now, if $\pi_1(x_1, x_2; k)$ has increasing differences (fulfills the SCP) in x_1 and k, then the extremal equilibria of the market game (which exist because the game is supermodular) will be increasing in k. If $\pi_1(x_1, x_2; k)$ has decreasing differences (fulfills the "dual" SCP) in x_1 and k, then the extremal equilibria of the market game will be decreasing in k. Suppose now that the market game is submodular (or ordinally submodular). This is the strategic substitutability assumption. Now, if $\pi_1(x_1, x_2; k)$ has increasing differences (fulfills the SCP) in x_1 and k, then the extremal equilibrium strategies of the firms in the market game (which exist because the duopoly game is submodular or, equivalently, because the game reversing the order in the strategy space of one player is supermodular) will be increasing (decreasing) in k for player 1 (2). The result is reversed if $\pi_1(x_1, x_2; k)$ has decreasing differences (fulfills the "dual" SCP) in x_1 and k. This yields the comparative static properties of extremal equilibria of the market stage with respect to k. With this we have the crucial ingredient to classify strategic behavior at extremal equilibria based on the minimal assumptions required. In short, the taxonomy holds at extremal equilibria of the duopoly games without any need of regularity assumptions. By the same methods the taxonomy is easily extended in the natural way to cover multiple first-stage investments and multimarket competition at the second stage.

Welfare   Up to now we have made no statement about welfare. As is usual, the effect of the strategic investment of a firm will have an external impact on rival firms and consumers. Typically the effects go in opposite directions. For example, strategic capacity (over)-investment to reduce costs will hurt the rival firm and benefit consumers under Cournot competition/strategic substitutes, while strategic capacity (under)investment to reduce costs will benefit the rival firm and hurt consumers under Bertrand competition (with differentiated products)/strategic complements. In the strategic substitutes case the overall effect is ambiguous, while in the strategic complements case investment tends to be insufficient at the margin.[38] That is, under Bertrand competition consumers are hurt more by the underinvestment incentive than rivals benefit.

Avoidable Fixed Costs   We have seen, as put forward by Dixit (1980), how in the classical Cournot competition case an incumbent enjoys a first-mover advantage when costs are sunk. This is so since in this context the incumbent can commit to be aggressive at the market competition stage, implying that a better market position in case entry is accommodated or the enhanced possibility to deter entry. However, if there are also avoidable fixed costs, then typically there will be multiple equilibria at the market competition stage, including equilibria where the incumbent or the potential entrant do not produce and avoid the fixed cost. It is not obvious, then, that the first-mover advantage remains. Suppose that competition evolves according to the following three-stage game. In the first stage the incumbent invests in capacity. In the second stage the entrant has also an opportunity to invest, once observed the choice of the incumbent, and in the third stage there is market (Cournot) competition contingent on the (observable) capacity choices. In this situation the entrant may be able to capture the market. This is the argument. If the entrant responds to a high level of investment by the incumbent investing heavily also, so heavily that the entrant would make losses at a market-sharing equilibrium, then the incumbent may infer that the entrant intends to produce a very large output and capture the market. The rational response of the incumbent is then to shut down. The argument relies on augmenting the backward-induction logic of subgame-perfect equilibria, which allows a multiplicity of equilibria, by requiring that firms believe not only that future behaviour will be profit maximizing but also that past behavior must have been profit maximizing. Then past behavior, the capacity choices, give information about future market intentions. This type of reasoning is what is termed forward induction. If the entrant is capable of driving the incumbent out, what is the optimal response of the latter? It turns out that typically it will pay the incumbent to reduce its initial investment. (See Bagwell and Ramey 1996.[39])

Adjustment Costs The taxonomy presented above can be extended to consider strategic incentives in general two-stage games. An illuminating case is when the only link between the stages, otherwise identical, is an adjustment cost associated to the actions at the last stage. Production or prices may be costly to adjust. For example, we could have repeated Cournot competition with costly production adjustment in the second stage or a "menu cost" game with Bertrand competition with differentiated products and costly price adjustment. Both asymmetric, where only one firm (e.g., firm 1) faces an adjustment cost and therefore has commitment power, and symmetric situations where both firms have commitment power can be considered. The key element will be, as before, the effect of the first stage action of a firm on the (equilibrium) second-stage action of its rival, and the way this affects the firm's profits. A study of a linear-quadratic adjustment cost duopoly model (linear demand for substitute differentiated products as in example 1 in section 6.1, no production costs for simplicity, and with quadratic adjustment costs) reveals the following pattern for the strategic incentives[40]. With

Cournot competition there is a tendency toward the use of top dog strategies. That is, there is the incentive to overproduce to limit the output of the rival. The exception is when there are symmetric price adjustment costs. In this case the incentives turn out to be of the puppy dog type, and firms benefit from a (credible) joint output reduction. To limit the output of the rival, a firm has to underproduce. Similarly with Bertrand competition there is a tendency toward the use of fat cat strategies. A firm has an incentive to price softly to induce soft pricing behavior of the rival. The exception is when there are symmetric production adjustment costs. In this case the incentives turns out to be of the lean-and-hungry type, and firms get trapped in a joint price reduction. To soften the pricing policy of the rival, a firm now has to be aggressive in the first period. Since both firms do it, the outcome will be a decrease in prices. To derive and understand the results, it is worth noting that by extending the argument in section 6.3 in the linear quadratic model considered, Cournot competition with quantity (price) adjustment costs is the dual of Bertrand competition with price (quantity) adjustment costs. Only the cross effect in demand changes sign in going from one to the other. This way the top dog incentives in Cournot correspond to fat cat incentives in Bertrand except in the symmetric case where what is costly to adjust in the Cournot (Bertrand) case are prices (quantities); then the Cournot puppy dog incentive is transformed into a Bertrand lean and hungry look.

Summary

The chapter provides an overview of different attacks to the problem of oligopolistic price formation. The overview includes conjectural variations, supply functions, and two-stage models of commitment. The conjectural variations approach is criticized on the ground of attempting to perform a dynamic analysis in a static model. Different solutions to the multiplicity of equilibria in supply functions are given in terms of considering uncertainty or restricted competition in certain two-stage games. The supply function approach provides also foundations for the Cournot and Bertrand models of oligopoly. In this respect it is found that the steepness of marginal costs is an important determinant of the competitiveness of the market. The Stackelberg model is analyzed as well as several attempts to endogenize the order of moves of the firms. For this an analysis of first-mover and second-mover advantages is presented. A result is that there is a tendency for the Stackelberg outcome to emerge under classical quantity competition whenever it is somewhat more costly to produce in the first period than in the second. The classical entry prevention model, based on quantity commitments, is analyzed and extended to incorporate sequential entry and the presence of several incumbents. Noncooperative entry deterrence poses the question of who bears the burden and the benefit of preventing entry. The analysis of two-stage models is completed with a taxonomy of strategic behavior according to the type of competition and the effect of strategic variables on incentives. The taxonomy is extended to non-concave games and/or games with multiple equilibria using the theory of supermodular games.

Exercises

7.1. Consider a n-firm oligopoly with linear demand $D(p) = \theta - bp$, $b > 0$, and $C(q) = cq^2/2$, $c > 0$. Compute the equilibrium in linear supply functions. Does your answer change if you allow affine functions?

7.2. Consider a Cournot duopoly with linear demand $p = a - bQ$, with $a > 0$ and $b > 0$, and firm i with constant marginal costs m_i. Suppose that each owner gives its manager an incentive contract that is a linear combination of profits and sales. Managers are paid their (fixed) opportunity cost. Study the two-stage game in which first owners choose the contracts they offer to their managers (i.e., they choose the relative weights to put on profits and sales), and then managers, upon having observed the contracts offered to both of them, compete in the marketplace. Compare the outcome with the Cournot equilibrium and explain the result. Suppose that b is uncertain and unknown ex ante (stage 1) and that managers are risk neutral. How do the results change? What would happen if competition were à la Bertrand (assume a product differentiation context with linear demands)? (See Vickers 1985; Fershtman and Judd 1987; Sklivas 1987.)

*7.3. Show that a Cournot n-firm oligopoly with linear demand and costs has a unique correlated equilibrium (which is the unique Cournot equilibrium of the market). (See Liu 1996, Aumann 1974, and Hart and Schmeidler 1989 for a precise definition of correlated equilibrium.)

7.4. Consider a homogeneous product Cournot duopoly market with firm 1 having marginal cost $m_1 > 0$ and firm 2, $m_2 = 0$. Assume that inverse demand $P(\cdot)$ is strictly decreasing and strictly log-convex but that $P(\cdot) - m_1$ is log-concave. Characterize the best replies of the firms. Show that only firm 2 prefers his Stackelberg follower payoff to his simultaneous Nash payoff. Can you infer that a Cournot equilibrium always exists? (See Amir and Grilo 1994.)

*7.5. Consider a Cournot homogeneous product market with two production periods before the market clears. Firms choose simultaneously outputs in every period with the first-period choices being observable. The total output brought to market determines then the market-clearing price. Assume that best-reply functions are downward sloping, that marginal costs constant (and equal for the firms), and that Cournot and Stackelberg equilibria are unique. Characterize the subgame-perfect equilibria of the game. How does the result change if there are multiple Stackelberg points for each firm? What if production in the second period is somewhat cheaper than in the first? What if production in the second period is a lot cheaper than in the first? Do the results change if the Cournot game is (ordinally) supermodular, that is if best replies are increasing? (See section 7.4.1, Saloner 1987, and Pal 1991.)

*7.6. Consider the basic model in exercise 7.5 with inverse demand depending on a random parameter θ which is realized, and observable, between the production periods. Assume that θ has compact support, that it increases marginal profits, and that with θ at the infimum of its support a Cournot duopoly would not shut down. Show that SPE, in terms of total output per firm, can be taken to be of the of the leader-follower type (with one firm only producing in period 1 and the other only in period 2). Show also that for small uncertainty (e.g., support of θ shrinking to a point) the SPE equilibrium outcomes are close to the Stackelberg outcomes. (See Maggi 1996.)

*7.7. Consider a Bertrand-Edgeworth duopoly market with downward-sloping concave demand, no production costs, and capacity limits $k_1 > k_2$. Rationing is according to the surplus-maximizing rule. Characterize the subgame-perfect equilibria of the two-stage games in which, respectively, firm 1 and firm 2 are price leaders. Suppose that if there is a price tie, the follower sells its capacity first. Show, in particular, that in the range in which in the simultaneous pricing game, there is a mixed-strategy equilibrium where the small firm prefers to be the follower while the large firm is indifferent about leading or following. What consequences do you think may follow from this in terms of an endogenous determination of a price leader? (See section 5.2 and Deneckere and Kovenock 1992.)

*7.8. Consider the quantity-setting sequential entry game of section 7.4.2 with an incumbent facing a sequence of n potential entrants. Inverse demand is given by $p = a - Q$, with $a > 0$. There are no production costs, and entrants have to pay entry cost $F > 0$ if they produce a positive amount. Show that the best-reply correspondence of a potential entrant $j < n$ is given by ($r(\cdot)$ stands for the Cournot reaction function):

$$\Psi_j(Z) = \begin{cases} r(z) & \text{if } Z_{n-j} \geq Z \geq 0, \\ Y - Z & \text{if } Z_0 \geq Z \geq Z_{n-j}, \quad j \in \{1, \ldots, n-1\}, \\ r(Z) & \text{if } Y > Z > Z_0, \\ 0 & \text{otherwise,} \end{cases}$$

where $Z_k = \max\{(2Y - (1 + \Delta_k)a)/(1 - \Delta_k), 0\}$, $k = 0, 1, \ldots, n$, with $\Delta_k = \sqrt{1 - \frac{1}{2^k}}$. Furthermore $Z_{k+1} + r(Z_{k+1}) < Z_k$. For $j = n$, $\Psi_n(Z) = r(Z)$ if $Z < Y$, and zero otherwise.

7.9. Consider a market with inverse demand $p = a - Q$. There are n potential entrants in the market who make simultaneous and independent decisions. If a firm enters and produces one unit at cost c, $a > c > 0$. What is the (welfare) optimal number of entrants in this market? Denote it by n^*. Find the symmetric entry equilibria into this market. (*Hint:* Consider mixed strategies and the cases $n \leq n^*$ and $n > n^*$.) Show that expected total surplus decreases with n for $n \geq n^*$.

*7.10. Examine the issue of the public good aspect of entry prevention considering an established duopoly in a homogeneous product market with linear demand and quadratic (symmetric) production costs. (See section 7.4.2 and Kovenock and Roy 1995.)

**7.11. Consider a two-stage duopoly game with adjustment costs. The payoff to player i is given by $G_i = \pi_i(x^0) + \delta(\pi_i(x^1) + \lambda_i F_i(x^1; x^0))$, where δ is the discount factor, π_i is the profit function, concave and symmetric across players, $x^t = (x_1^t, x_2^t)$ is the strategy vector in period t, $t = 0, 1$, and F_i the adjustment cost in period 1. The parameter λ_i determines the size of the adjustment cost. Period 0 actions are observable and restrict attention to subgame-perfect equilibria of the two-stage game. Assume that for any given actions in period 0, there is a unique and (locally) stable Nash equilibrium at period 1. Let us examine first the asymmetric case $\lambda_2 = 0$ with F_1 a concave function of x_1^1 and x_1^0. For example, $F_1 = -(x_1^1 - x_1^0)^2$. This may arise with Cournot (Bertrand) competition with costly production (price) adjustment. Derive the Fudenberg-Tirole taxonomy of strategic behavior in this framework. Show, in particular, that the sign of the strategic effect (for firm 1) is given by the sign of $(\partial \pi_1 / \partial x_2^1) \cdot (\partial^2 F_1 / \partial x_1^0 \partial x_1^1)(\partial^2 \pi_2 / \partial x_1^1 \partial x_2^1)$. Compute $\partial x_1^0 / \partial \lambda_1 |_{\lambda_1=0}$ and show that its sign equals the sign of the strategic effect. Interpret the result in terms of the described taxonomy noting that for $\lambda_1 = 0$ the SPE of the two-stage game is just the repeated Nash equilibrium of the stage game. Suppose now that $F_i(x^1, x^2) = -(g((x_1^1, x_2^1)) - g((x_1^0, x_2^0)))$, where g is a linear function. Show that now both players have a strategic incentive (why?). Find $\partial x_1^0 / \partial \lambda_1 |_{\lambda_1=0}$ and $\partial x_2^0 / \partial \lambda_1 |_{\lambda_1=0}$ and classify strategic behavior for player 1 and for player 2. Repeat the exercise for the symmetric case $\lambda_i = \lambda, i = 1, 2$. Find $\partial x_i^0 / \partial \lambda |_{\lambda=0}$ and classify again strategic behavior. Apply your results to the linear differentiated duopoly (example 1 in section 6.1) with quadratic adjustment costs. Consider the four possibilities arising from matching Cournot or Bertrand competition with price or quantity adjustment costs. Show the following results. Cournot competition with costly production adjustment yields top dog strategic incentives both in the symmetric and asymmetric cases. With costly price adjustment it yields top dog (puppy dog) strategic incentives in the asymmetric (symmetric) case. Bertrand competition with costly price adjustment yields fat cat strategic incentives both in the symmetric and asymmetric cases. With costly quantity adjustment it yields fat cat (lean-and-hungry) strategic incentives in the asymmetric (symmetric) case. (See Lapham and Ware 1994.)

8 Competition with Asymmetric Information

In the preceding chapters we analyzed competition in a context of complete information where a firm knows the payoff and strategy set of each rival. In practice, this is rarely the case. Indeed, firms have private information about costs and demand, for example. In this way a firm will know his cost but not the cost of the rival, even though he knows the distribution from which it has been drawn. Similarly a firm will know his estimate of demand but will not know the estimates of other firms, although he knows the process by which they have been generated. In this chapter we will review the competition models of Cournot and Bertrand, Chamberlin-Robinson, and Stackelberg when there is incomplete information in sections 8.1, 8.2, and 8.5, respectively. The incentives of firms to exchange information, its welfare consequences, and strategic information revelation are dealt with in section 8.3. Section 8.4 takes a mechanism approach to information transmission and examines the constraints that private information imposes on the design of a cartel scheme as well as the problem of the optimal design of trade associations in large markets. Several dynamic issues arising in an incomplete information context, like signaling distortions and limit pricing, signal jamming and information manipulation are analyzed in section 8.5.

8.1 Static Competition with Incomplete Information

Let us consider first some simple examples of oligopoly games with incomplete information to illustrate Bayesian Nash equilibria before addressing the issue of existence of equilibrium.

Example 1
A first example is a linear Cournot duopoly with uncertain constant marginal costs. Demand is given by $p = a - Q$, and the costs of firm i

are distributed in a compact interval $[\underline{c}_i, \bar{c}_i]$ (with $\bar{c}_i < a$). The costs of the firms are independent. Firm i knows its own cost c_i but only the distribution of costs of the rival (in fact, in this case knowing the expected cost of the rival is enough). A strategy of firm j will depend thus on c_j. We have that $E(\pi_i|c_i) = (a - c_i - Eq_j(c_j) - q_i)q_i$, and the best reply of the firm to the expected output of the rival is $q_i = \max((a - c_i - Eq_j(c_j)/2, 0)$. Equilibrium expected outputs are given by the intersection of the expected best replies of the firms $r_i^e(Eq_j) = \max((a - Ec_i - Eq_j)/2, 0)$ just as in the certainty case equilibrium outputs are given by the intersection of the best replies. This is a certainty equivalent property of the linear model. With identical cost distributions for the firms we have that $Eq_i = (a - Ec_i)/3$ and the (unique) Bayesian Cournot equilibrium is given by $q_i = (2a + Ec_i - 3c_i)/6$ (assume that $2a + Ec_i - 3\bar{c}_i > 0$ to guarantee an interior solution for all cost realizations).

The output of a firm is increasing in the expected cost of the rival (indeed, it is decreasing in the expected output of the rival and the latter is decreasing in its own expected cost). This means that a firm would like to convince the rival that it has low costs. For example, suppose that firm 1 has a level of cost of c and this is common knowledge. Firm 2 can have low ($\underline{c}$) or high costs ($\bar{c}$) with equal probability and only firm 2 knows its realization. The Bayesian Cournot equilibrium is given then by $(q_1^*, (\underline{q}_2, \bar{q}_2))$ with $\underline{q}_2(\bar{q}_2)$ representing the production of firm 2 when costs are low (high). (See figure 8.1.) Firm 2 reacts to the output of firm 1 according to its best-response function for low (or high) costs, $\underline{r}_2(q_1) = \max((a - \underline{c} - q_1)/2, 0)$ (or $\bar{r}_2(q_1) = \max((a - \bar{c} - q_1)/2, 0)$). Firm 1 reacts to the expected output of firm 2, q_2^e, and therefore its equilibrium output is determined by the intersection of its best response function $(r_1(q_2^e) = \max((a - c - q_2^e)/2, 0)$ with the expected best response of firm 2 $(r_2^e(q_1) = \max((a - Ec_2 - q_1)/2, 0))$. If firm 2 manages to convince firm 1 that his expected cost is lower (i.e., that his expected best reply has moved out), then firm 1 will contract its output to the benefit of firm 2. It is an instance of a top dog strategy (see section 7.4.3).

Example 2

Now consider a Bertrand duopoly game with product differentiation. The unique Bayesian Bertrand equilibrium of a linear duopoly (example 1 in section 6.2) with uncertain independent constant mar-

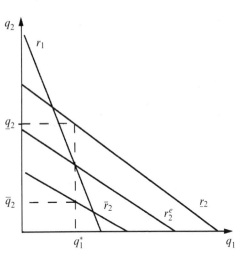

Figure 8.1

ginal costs, m_i for firm i, is easily computed along the same lines as before (exercise 8.1). The best reply of firm i to the expected price of the rival is $p_i = (a + bm_i + cEp_j(m_j))/2b$. Again equilibrium expected prices are given by the intersection of the expected best replies of the firms $r_i^e(Ep_j) = (a + bEm_i + cEp_j)/2b$, yielding, with equal cost distributions, $Ep_i = (a + bEm_i)/(2b - c)$. Equilibrium prices of firm i are now increasing in the expected costs of the rival.

If we consider the same situation as in the Cournot case (firm 1 has a level of cost of c and firm 2 can have low ($\underline{c}$) or high costs with equal probability), then we see that firm 2 would like to convince firm 1 that his costs are high (see figure 8.2). Indeed, this would induce firm 1 to set a higher price and would benefit firm 2. It is an instance of the puppy dog ploy (see section 7.4.3).

Example 3
The case of Bertrand competition with a homogeneous product can be analyzed using techniques from auction theory. Indeed, price competition with incomplete information about costs is analogous to a variable-quantity auction at which the lowest bidder gets to supply the whole market (the demand at the winning price). A firm when setting its price (contingent on its cost level) will take into account the potential profit multiplied by the likelihood of winning the market. A change in price affects the marginal profit (in case of winning)

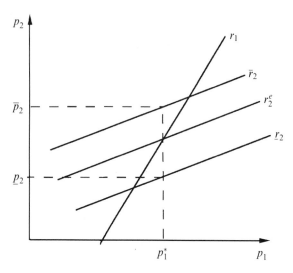

Figure 8.2

as well as the probability of winning the market. There is obviously a trade-off between the two effects. Contingent on winning, the firm would like to charge the monopoly price, but to win, it needs to charge a low price to undercut the rivals. In the standard case of a concave profit function in price, a firm will be risk averse with respect to the price. This explains why the techniques of auctions with risk averse bidders (Maskin and Riley 1984) are relevant in the present case. Spulber (1995) characterizes the Bayesian Bertrand equilibria in a smooth market with downward-sloping demand and (weakly) convex costs parametrized by a variable that raises marginal costs. He assumes that the profit of a monopolist is concave in the price and that the costs parameters are independently and identically distributed with continuous density on a compact interval. It is shown that there is a unique and symmetric (Bayesian) equilibrium in pure strategies. The pricing strategy is increasing (and differentiable) in the cost parameter, prices are always below the monopoly level, and positive expected profits are obtained for any cost realization. Furthermore, if there is a unique positive average cost price, at which monopoly profit is zero, the equilibrium price then converges for any cost parameter realization to the average cost as the number of firms tends to infinity. Therefore, as the number of firms increases, conditional on a cost realization average cost pricing obtains. (See exercise 8.2.) The contrast with the standard certainty case with constant (potentially different) marginal costs is striking. For example, with certainty, only the lowest-cost firm makes a profit, while with asymmetric information on costs, all firms price above their marginal costs and make positive expected profits. However, both in the full and in the incomplete information cases the lowest cost firm wins the market (by setting the lowest price).

8.1.1   Existence of Bayesian Equilibrium

The existence (and uniqueness) of Bayesian Cournot or Bertrand equilibria in the simple examples 1 and 2 is straightforward. In more general cases the results in section 2.7.2 can be used to show existence of a Bayesian Nash equilibrium in pure strategies of the static game considered. We will review their application briefly here.

When the number of actions and types are finite, existence of BNE is guaranteed (although possibly in mixed strategies). With continuous actions and/or type spaces, one needs to put strong assumptions to guarantee the existence of a Bayesian Nash equilibrium in pure strategies. A set of sufficient conditions is that action spaces be finite, and types independent with atomless distribution, and that the payoff to each player depend only on his type. However, if the underlying game is supermodular or some monotonicity properties are fulfilled, then existence in pure strategies can be guaranteed with much weaker assumptions.

Let us recall first that a Bayesian game will be supermodular whenever the underlying certainty game (for any type realization) is supermodular.

Consider a Bayesian Cournot duopoly game with payoff to firm i, $\pi_i(q; t)$ where t is the vector of types of the firms and the outputs of each firm lie in a compact cube. This allows for product differentiation and multiproduct competition. A pure-strategy Bayesian Cournot equilibrium will exist if, conditional on any t, the game is submodular. The types could represent idiosyncratic demand and/ or costs parameters in which case the profits of firm i would depend only on its own type: $\pi_i(q; t_i)$, although obviously the types may be correlated. A Bertrand oligopoly game with product differentiation with payoff to firm i, $\pi_i(p; t)$ will have a pure-strategy Bayesian Bertrand equilibrium if, conditional on any type realization t, the game is supermodular. Again, types could be cost or demand parameters and multiproduct competition is allowed.

With homogeneous product, price competition, and constant marginal costs, θ_i for firm i, it is possible to show existence of a Bayesian Bertrand equilibrium (in pure strategies) in the case of $(\theta_1, \ldots, \theta_n)$ being affiliated (i.e., $(\theta_1, \ldots, \theta_n)$ distributed with log-supermodular joint density). Assume also that the distribution of $(\theta_1, \ldots, \theta_n)$ is atomless with marginals with compact support. To show the result, note first that the expected profit of firm i is the product of $(p_i - \theta_i)D(p_i)$ and $H(p_i; p_{-i}(\cdot)|\theta_i)$, the expected probability of winning conditional on the rivals using strategies $p_j(\theta_j)$, $j \neq i$, and on the firm setting p_i and having cost θ_i. This expected profit is log-supermodular in (p_i, θ_i) if the strategies $p_j(\cdot)$, $j \neq i$, are increasing. First, using the affiliation of the costs, it is possible to check that $H(p_i; p_{-i}(\cdot)|\theta_i)$ is log-supermodular in (p_i, θ_i). Furthermore $(p_i - \theta_i)D(p_i)$ is log-supermodular in (p_i, θ_i) and the product of log-supermodular functions is log-supermodular. This implies that firm i also uses an increasing strategy (according to the set ordering $\leq^p$ if the best reply is a set). It can be shown then than an equilibrium in increasing strategies exists provided D is strictly decreasing, bounded, and continuous (see section 2.7.3 and Athey 1997a, b). It is worth noting that the result allows the distribution of the costs to be asymmetric.[1]

The same methodology can be applied to show existence of pure-strategy Bayesian Bertrand equilibria with a differentiated demand system $D_i(p_i, p_{-i})$. Then $E(\pi_i|\theta_i) = (p_i - \theta_i)E(D_i(p_i, p_{-i}(\theta_{-i}))|\theta_i)$. Expected demand $E(D_i(p_i, p_{-i}(\theta_{-i}))|\theta_i)$ is log-supermodular in (p_i, θ_i) provided both $D_i(p_i, p_{-i})$ and the joint density of $(\theta_1, \ldots, \theta_n)$ are log-supermodular and if the strategies of the rivals, $p_j(\cdot)$, $j \neq i$, are increasing.[2] It follows then that $E(\pi_i|\theta_i)$ is log-supermodular in (p_i, θ_i) and that the best-reply price set of player i is increasing in θ_i. Examples of log-supermodular demands are provided in section 6.2, and they include constant elasticity and logit demand systems. Again existence of a Bayesian equilibrium (in pure strategies) will follow provided D_i is continuous.

8.1.2   The Linear-Normal Model

A class of cases that yields computable (and unique) Bayesian equilibria is provided by the family of linear-quadratic models with uncertainty and signals (types) normally distributed (or with the linear information structure which yields linear conditional expectations, see section 2.7.2). This makes the model very useful for applications as we will see in the next section when studying the incentives to share information. Consider the following general (symmetric) quadratic payoff function for player i in a n-player game[3]:

$$\pi_i(x_i, x_{-i}; \theta_i) = \alpha(\theta_i) + (\kappa + \omega\theta_i - \lambda x_i)\left(\sum_{j \neq i} x_j\right) + (\beta + \gamma\theta_i - \delta x_i)x_i,$$

where $\delta > 0$, $-\delta/(n-1) < \lambda \leq \delta$, $\alpha(\cdot)$ is a function, and θ_i is a random parameter (the other parameters are unrestricted). The action of player j is denoted by x_j. This formulation encompasses Cournot or Bertrand product differentiated markets with linear demand functions (example 1, section 6.1) and constant marginal costs (in the Cournot case quadratic production costs can be accommodated also).[4] Uncertainty can enter in the form of a random demand intercept or random marginal costs. With demand uncertainty, let $\gamma = 1$. In the Cournot model with cost uncertainty, $\gamma = -1$. In all those cases $\omega = 0$. For example, to obtain Cournot competition with demand uncertainty, let also $\alpha = 0, \kappa = 0$. Then (with $x_i = q_i$) $\pi_i = (\beta + \theta_i - \delta q_i - \lambda\sum_{j \neq i} q_j)q_i$. To obtain Bertrand competition with cost uncertainty (with $x_i = p_i$), let $\kappa = 0, \lambda = \omega, \gamma = \delta$, and $\alpha(\theta_i) = -\beta\theta_i$. Then $\pi_i = (p_i - \theta_i)(\beta - \delta p_i - \lambda\sum_{j \neq i} p_j)$, where $\lambda < 0$ for gross substitute goods. Competition is of the strategic substitutes (complements) variety if λ is positive (negative).

The vector of random variables $(\theta_1, \ldots, \theta_n)$ is jointly normally distributed with $E\theta_i = 0$ (for simplicity), $\mathrm{var}\,\theta_i = \sigma_\theta^2$, and $\mathrm{cov}(\theta_i, \theta_j) = \rho_\theta\sigma_\theta^2$ for $j \neq i$, $0 \leq \rho_\theta \leq 1$. The random variables may represent, for example, deviations from the mean of the demand intercepts or of marginal costs.

Firm i receives a signal $s_i = \theta_i + \varepsilon_i$, where $\varepsilon_i \sim N(0, \sigma_{\varepsilon_i}^2)$, and $\mathrm{cov}(\varepsilon_i, \varepsilon_j) = \sigma$, with $\sigma \in [0, \min_i \sigma_{\varepsilon_i}^2]$. Signals can range from perfect ($\sigma_{\varepsilon_i}^2 = 0$ or infinite precision) to pure noise ($\sigma_{\varepsilon_i}^2 = \infty$ or zero precision). The precision of signal s_i is given $\tau_{\varepsilon_i} = (\sigma_{\varepsilon_i}^2)^{-1}$.[5] We make also the technical assumption that the correlation of the error terms of the signals can not exceed the correlation of the parameters ρ_θ. In the symmetric case let $\mathrm{cov}(\varepsilon_i, \varepsilon_j) = \rho_\varepsilon\sigma_\varepsilon^2$, $j \neq i$, with $0 \leq \rho_\varepsilon \leq \rho_\theta$.

Our information structure encompasses the cases of "common value" and of "private values." For $\rho_\theta = 1$ the parameters are perfectly correlated and we are in a *common value* model. When signals are perfect, $\sigma_{\varepsilon_i}^2 = 0$ for all i, and $0 < \rho_\theta < 1$, we will say we are in a *private values* model. Firms receive idiosyncratic shocks, which are imperfectly correlated, and each firm observes its shock with no measurement error. When $\rho_\theta = 0$, the parameters are independent, and we are in an *independent values* model.

Under the normality assumption (as well as with the generalized linear information structure; see section 2.7.2) conditional expectations are linear.[6] Consider the common value case. We have that $E(\theta|s_i) = t_i s_i$ and $E(s_j|s_i) = d_i s_i$, where $t_i = \tau_{\varepsilon_i}/(\tau_\theta + \tau_{\varepsilon_i})$ and $d_i = t_i(1 + \sigma\tau_\theta)$. Note that $E(\theta|s_i)$ equals the weighted average, according to the relative precisions, of the prior mean (equal to 0, with precision τ_θ) and the signal (s_i, with precision τ_{ε_i}). Therefore, as τ_{ε_i} ranges from ∞ to 0, the signal goes from being perfectly informative to being not informative at all and at the same time t_i ranges from 1 to 0. When the information is perfect, $E(\theta|s_i) = s_i$; when there is no information, $E(\theta|s_i) = 0$ (the prior mean). In estimating s_j, the reliance on s_i is increased (with respect to the estimation of θ) because of the correlation between the error terms of the signals.

Firms may receive additional information if they decide, for example, to share information. In this case each firm would have available the vector of signals $(s_1, \ldots, s_n)$. An intermediate situation can be described where each firm receives a noisy version of the signals of others (i.e., firm i receives $\hat{s}_j = s_j + \eta_j$, where $\eta_j \sim N(0, \sigma_{\eta_j}^2)$, $j \neq i$, and the added noise is independently distributed).

Let us denote the information vector available to firm i by I_i. There is common knowledge about payoff functions and distributions of random variables. The only (potential) private information of firm i is its private signal s_i.

The class of normal linear-quadratic models yields unique Bayesian equilibria, and the unique equilibrium strategies are linear in the information the firms have. This is a consequence of the linear structure coupled with the fact that the conditional expectations $E(\theta_i|I_i)$ and $E(s_j|I_i)$ are linear in I_i. Here is a sketch of the argument. Suppose that firm j, $j \neq i$, uses strategy $x_j(\cdot)$. Then the best reply of firm i, $x_i(I_i) = \arg\max_{x_i} E(\pi_i(x_i, x_{-i}(I_{-i}))|I_i)$ is given by $x_i(I_i) = (\beta + \gamma E(\theta_i|I_i) - \lambda \sum_{j \neq i} E(x_j(I_j)|I_i))/2\delta$. The next step is to posit arbitrary linear strategies for the firms other than i and check that the best response of firm i is also linear. Identifying coefficients of the linear strategies, we identify a unique linear Bayesian Nash equilibrium. To show that this is the unique BNE, we check that the BNE of our game are in one-to-one correspondence with person-by-person optimization of an appropriately defined concave team function. In a team agents share the same objective but receive different signals about the underlying uncertainty. A team decision rule $(x_1(I_1), \ldots, x_n(I_n))$ is person-by-person optimal if it cannot be improved by changing only one component $x_i(\cdot)$. This just means that each agent maximizes the team objective conditional on his information and taking as given the strategies of the other agents. In our linear-quadratic model with the type of uncertainty considered and jointly normal random variables the components of the unique Bayesian team decision function of the equivalent team problem are linear (Radner 1962, thm. 5). Now person-by-person optimization is equivalent in our context with global optimization of the team function (since the random term does not affect the coefficients of the quadratic terms and the team function is concave in actions, Radner 1962, thm. 4), so we conclude that the linear BNE is the unique BNE.[7]

The expected profits of firm i at the Bayesian equilibrium are given by $E\pi_i = \bar{\pi}_i + \delta \operatorname{var} x_i(I_i) + \omega K$, where $\bar{\pi}_i$ are the "certainty equivalent" profits of firm i and K is a constant that depends on the responsiveness of firms to their information. In the case where $I_i = \{s_i\}$, $\operatorname{var} x_i(I_i) = (a_i)^2 \operatorname{var} s_i$ and $K = \rho_\theta \sigma_\theta^2 (\sum_{j \neq i} a_j)$, where a_j is the responsiveness of firm j to its signal. With Cournot competition and for Bertrand competition with demand uncertainty, $\omega = 0$ and the variance of the strategy of a firm determines its profitability.

As an example consider a n-firm homogeneous product Cournot market with linear inverse demand $p = \beta + \theta - Q$ and quadratic costs given by $C(q) = \delta' q^2$. Let the information structure be linear with $I_i = \{s_i\}$, with conditionally independent signals, firm i having information precision τ_{ε_i}, and let $t_i = \tau_{\varepsilon_i}/(\tau_\theta + \tau_{\varepsilon_i})$. The payoff to firm i is $\pi_i = (\beta + \theta - \delta q_i - \sum_{j \neq i} q_j)q_i$ with $\delta = 1 + \delta'$. Then the Bayesian-Cournot equilibria of the game are in one-to-one correspondence with the solution to the team problem with objective function $E\{G(q; \theta)\}$, where

$$G(q; \theta) = (\beta + \theta) \sum_j q_j - (1 + \delta') \sum_j q_j^2 - \frac{1}{2} \sum_{i \neq j} q_i q_j.$$

The problem of the team is to choose strategies $q_i(s_i)$, $i = 1, \ldots, n$, to maximize $E\{G(q; \theta)\}$. Note first that the Bayesian-Cournot equilibria of the game are in one-to-one correspondence to person-by-person optimization of the team function G. This is clear since $G = \pi_i(q) + f_i(q_{-i})$, where

$$f_i(q_{-i}) = (\beta + \theta) \sum_{j \neq i} q_j - (1 + \delta') \sum_{j \neq i} q_j^2 - \frac{1}{2} \sum_{\substack{k \neq j \\ k, j \neq i}} q_k q_j.$$

The same outcome obtains by solving $\max_{q_i} E(\pi_i|s_i)$ or $\max_{q_i} E(G|s_i)$, since $f_i(q_{-i})$ does not involve q_i. As argued above, person-by-person optimization is equivalent to global optimization of the team function. Furthermore, with the linear information structure, conditional expectations $E(\theta|s_i)$ are linear in s_i, there is a unique solution to the team problem, and this solution involves strategies linear in the signals. This yields the unique Bayesian Cournot equilibrium with firm i producing according to

$$q_i(s_i) = a_i s_i + b\beta,$$

where

$$a_i = \left(\frac{\gamma_i}{1 + \sum_j \gamma_j} \right), \quad b = \frac{1}{2(\delta' + 1) + n - 1}, \quad \text{and} \quad \gamma_i = \frac{t_i}{2(\delta' + 1) - t_i}$$

for $i = 1, \ldots, n$. In order to check that the candidate strategies form an equilibrium, note that expected profits of firm i, conditional on receiving signal s_i and assuming that firm j, $j \neq i$, uses strategy $q_j(\cdot)$, are

$$E(\pi_i|s_i) = q_i(\beta + E(\theta|s_i) - \sum_{j \neq i} E(q_j(s_j)|s_i) - (1 + \delta')q_i).$$

First-order conditions (FOC) yield then

$$2(1 + \delta')q_i(s_i) = \beta + E(\theta|s_i) - \sum_{j \neq i} E(q_j(s_i)|s_i) \qquad \text{for } i = 1, \ldots, n.$$

Plugging in the candidate equilibrium strategy, it is easily checked that they satisfy the FOC (which are also sufficient given our structure).

8.2 Monopolistic Competition with Private Information

Consider a monopolistic competition model à la Chamberlin with a large (fixed) number of firms. Each firm produces a differentiated commodity, is negligible in the sense that its actions alone do not influence the profits of any other firm, and has some monopoly

power. With no uncertainty, the market equilibrium of our monopolistically competitive industry does not depend on whether firms
use quantities or prices as strategies (see section 6.6). Let us introduce now uncertainty and incomplete information in the model.

Denote the profit function of firm i by $\pi(y_i, \tilde{y}; \theta_i)$, where y_i is the
action of the firm, $\tilde{y}$ the vector of statistics that characterizes the distribution of the firms' actions, and θ_i a parameter drawn from a prior
distribution with finite variance. A strategy for firm i is a measurable
function $y_i(\cdot)$ from the signal space to the action space of the firm,
and the appropriate equilibrium concept is the Bayesian monopolistically competitive equilibrium. Suppose that firm i has available
the (private) information vector I_i. A set of strategies $\{y_i(\cdot): i \in [0,1]\}$
form a Bayesian equilibrium if for any firm (almost surely)

$$y_i(I_i) \in \arg\max_{z_i} E(\pi(z_i, \tilde{y}; \theta_i)|I_i),$$

where $\tilde{y}$ parametrizes the (random) action distribution induced by
the equilibrium strategies. If information is symmetric (e.g., if firms
fully share their information), $\tilde{y}$ is predictable knowing the equilibrium strategies.[8]

The model can accommodate quantity or price competition. It is
worth noting that in the presence of uncertainty, it *does* matter
whether firms use prices or quantities as strategies. This should be
clear since under uncertainty, even though firms still act as monop-
olists on their residual demand, the firm is not indifferent, in general,
between setting prices or quantities.[9]

We will consider a specific quadratic profit function example (a
simplification of the quadratic payoff considered in the last section):[10]

$$\pi(y_i, \tilde{y}; \theta_i) = (\omega_0 + \theta_i)y_i - \omega_1 y_i^2 - \omega_2 \tilde{y} y_i,$$

where $\omega_1 > 0$ to ensure (strict) concavity of π with respect to y_i, and
$\tilde{y} = \int y_j \, dj$ denotes the average action.

As before, we can obtain Bertrand and Cournot competition, with
linear demands and constant unit costs (equal to zero without loss of
generality) by choosing appropriately parameters. The payoffs are
consistent with the following system of demands with random
intercepts:

$$p_i = \alpha_i - (1 - \delta)q_i - \delta \tilde{q} \qquad \text{with } \delta \in [0,1],$$

$$q_i = \beta_i - (1 + \gamma)p_i + \gamma \tilde{p} \qquad \text{with } \gamma \geq 0,$$

where (p_i, q_i) is the price-output pair of firm i; the tildes denote averages. We can obtain the second equation by inverting the first and letting $\beta_i = (\alpha_i - \delta\tilde{\alpha})/(1 - \delta)$ and $\gamma = \delta/(1 - \delta)$. Notice that when $\delta = 0$, the firms are isolated monopolies, and that when $\delta = 1$, they are perfect competitors because then the product is homogeneous. The parameter δ represents the degree of product differentiation. In the quantity competition (Cournot) case, let $\omega_0 + \theta_i = \alpha_i, \omega_1 = 1 - \delta$, and $\omega_2 = \delta$. In the price competition (Bertrand) case, let $\omega_0 + \theta_i = \beta_i$, $\omega_1 = 1 + \gamma$, and $\omega_2 = -\gamma$.

The information structure is as in the last section with firms receiving private signals of symmetric precision and assuming, for simplicity, that the error terms of the signals are uncorrelated. We have thus a symmetric information structure. Ex ante, before uncertainty is realized, all firms face the same prospects. We have then $E(\theta_i|s_i) = ts_i$ and $E(s_j|s_i) = E(\theta_j|s_i) = \rho_\theta t s_i$, where, as before, $t = \tau_\varepsilon/(\tau_\theta + \tau_\varepsilon)$. When signals are perfect, $t = 1$ and $E(\theta_i|s_i) = s_i$, and $E(\theta_j|s_i) = \rho_\theta s_i$. When they are not informative, $t = 0$ and $E(\theta_i|s_i) = E(\theta_j|s_i) = 0$. We can also derive the relationship of θ_i, s_i, and the average parameter $\tilde{\theta} = \int \theta_j \, dj$.[11] Indeed, $E(\theta_i|\tilde{\theta}) = \tilde{\theta}$, $E(\tilde{\theta}|\theta_i) = E(\theta_j|\theta_i)$, $E(\tilde{\theta}|s_i) = E(\theta_j|s_i)$, and $E(\theta_i|\tilde{\theta}, s_i) = (1 - d)\tilde{\theta} + ds_i$, where $d = [\sigma_{\tilde{\theta}}^2(1 - \rho_\theta)]/[\sigma_{\tilde{\theta}}^2(1 - \rho_\theta) + \sigma_\varepsilon^2]$. If signals are perfect, then $d = 1$ and $E(\theta_i|\tilde{\theta}, s_i) = s_i$. If signals are useless or correlation perfect ($\rho_\theta = 1$), then $d = 0$ and $E(\theta_i|\tilde{\theta}, s_i) = \tilde{\theta}$. If both signals and correlation are perfect, then $E(\theta_i|\tilde{\theta}, s_i) = \tilde{\theta} = s_i$ a.s.

We will make the convention that the strong law of large numbers (SLLN) holds in our continuum context. That is, the average of a continuum of uncorrelated random variables ε_i with a common finite mean equals, almost surely, $E\varepsilon_i$. Observe that $\tilde{s} = \tilde{\theta}$ a.s., since $\tilde{s} = \int \theta_i \, di + \int u_i \, di$, and $\int u_i \, di = Eu_i = 0$ according to our convention, since the error terms u_i are uncorrelated and have mean zero.[12]

In the linear-normal model it is very easy to characterize the unique Bayesian equilibrium with linear strategies in either the private or shared information cases (see exercise 8.5). Firms that share information need only to know the average signal $\tilde{s}$ (on top of their signal)—since given the information structure, with linear equilibria $(s_i, \tilde{s})$ is sufficient in the estimation of θ_i by firm i, and with $\tilde{s}(= \tilde{\theta})$ the firm can predict with certainty the aggregate action $\tilde{y}$. The equilibrium strategy of firm i in the private information case is given by $y(s_i) = as_i + b\omega_0$ where $a = t/(2\omega_1 + \omega_2\rho_\theta t)$ and $b = 1/(2\omega_1 + \omega_2)$ and in the shared information case by $z(s_i, \tilde{\theta}) = \hat{a}(s_i - \tilde{\theta}) + b(\omega_0 + \tilde{\theta})$ where $\hat{a} = d/2\omega_1$.

Remark 1 The linear-quadratic model has a certainty-equivalence property. The expected value of an individual (as well as average) action, with either pooling or not pooling of information, equals $b\omega_0$, which is the action firms would choose if they did not have any information. Otherwise, the equilibria when firms share or not their information are different except if $a = \hat{a}$ and $\tilde{\theta} = 0$ a.s. or if $b = a = \hat{a}$. The first case obtains if there is no correlation between parameters, $\rho_\theta = 0$ (independent values); the second, if $2\omega_1(1 - t) = \omega_2 t(1 - \rho_\theta)$. This latter equality obviously holds in the perfect information case, $\rho_\theta = t = 1$. It cannot hold if $\omega_2 < 0$ (strategic complements), or for ω_1 and ω_2 different from zero, in the common value case ($\rho_\theta = 1$, $\in (0, 1)$), or in the private values case ($t = 1, \rho_\theta \in (0, 1)$).

3.3   Information Sharing

We will study in this section the incentives for firms to share information and the welfare consequences of such exchanges. We consider first information exchange in oligopoly and then in a monopolistically competitive context. We end the section by examining the incentive compatibility problem in information revelation.

3.3.1   Information Exchange in Oligopoly

We will consider the linear-normal model introduced in the last section and two different game forms. In the central approach a two-stage game is considered in which each firm decides first about whether it wants to share its private information; then the uncertainty is realized, and private signals are received. The information of a firm is publicly revealed or not depending on whether the firm has decided to share or not and then there is competition in the marketplace (typically of the Cournot or Bertrand variety). In the alternative approach the first stage decision to share information is an industrywide agreement. A firm shares its information if and only if others do too. In both cases firms commit to reveal their information before they receive it, and therefore we are examining the ex ante incentives to share information when this type of commitment is possible.[13]

For example, with uncertain demand an agency, a trade association typically, may collect market data on behalf of each firm. Firm i may allow then part of its private information to be put in a common

pool available to both firms. The signal a firm receives is the bes
estimate of the uncertain demand given its private information and
the information in the common pool. In the central approach the
firms, prior to the market data collection, instruct the agency how
much of their private information to put in the common pool. At the
second stage, market research is conducted, and the agency send
the signals to the firms, which choose an action (quantity or price)
Therefore at the second stage a Bayesian (Cournot or Bertrand) game
is played.

The incentives to share information will depend on some compar
ative static results. Consider the case $\omega = 0$ (Cournot competition o
Bertrand competition with demand uncertainty). Then the expected
profits of firm i at the Bayesian equilibrium are of the form $E\pi_i =$
$\bar{\pi}_i + \delta \operatorname{var} x_i(I_i)$. With no information sharing $I_i = \{s_i\}$, and $\operatorname{var} x_i(I_i) =$
$(a_i)^2 \operatorname{var} s_i$, where a_i is the responsiveness of firm i to its signal. It is
easy to see that $|a_i|$ and $E\pi_i$ are increasing with the precision of its
signal (τ_{ε_i}) and that they are decreasing (increasing) with the preci
sion of the signals of rivals (τ_{ε_j}, $j \neq i$) if competition is of the strategic
substitutes (complements) variety. With symmetric precisions ($\tau_{\varepsilon_i} =$
τ_ε, for all i), $E\pi_i$ increase with a uniform increase in the precision o
the signals for a given signal correlation ($\rho_s = \operatorname{cov}(s_i, s_j)/\operatorname{var} s_i$) and
for given signal precisions, $E\pi_i$ increase (decrease) with increased
correlation of signals with strategic complements (substitutes).

In order to gain intuition about the result consider a duopoly with
common value demand uncertainty with $I_i = \{s_i\}$ and with the error
terms of the signals potentially correlated with covariance equal to σ
The payoff to firm i is given by $\pi_i = (\beta + \theta - \delta x_i - \lambda x_j)x_i$ (with the
constant marginal costs equal to zero for simplicity). Let $x_i = q_i$ with
Cournot competition and $x_i = p_i$ with Bertrand competition. The
Bayesian Nash equilibrium is given by $x_i^*(s_i) = A + B_i t_i s_i$ with $A =$
$\beta/(2\delta + \lambda)$ and $B_i = (2\delta - \lambda d_j)/(4\delta^2 - \lambda^2 d_1 d_2)$. When the firms have no
information at all ($t_i = 0$), the equilibrium strategy is constant (flat)
and equal to $A = \beta/(2\delta + \lambda)$. In the symmetric case, $B = 1/(2\delta + \lambda d)$
and as the information the firms receive improves. In other words,
as t tends toward 1, the slope of the linear strategy increases until
it reaches $1/(2\delta + \lambda)$ (recall that $d = t(1 + \sigma \tau_\theta)$ and $\sigma = \rho_\varepsilon \sigma_\varepsilon^2$, and
therefore σ tends to zero as σ_ε^2 tends to zero). Then $x_i^*(s_i) =$
$(s_i + \beta)/(2\delta + \lambda)$, which is the full information outcome since $s_i = \theta$
a.s. The expected BNE output always equals the Nash certainty

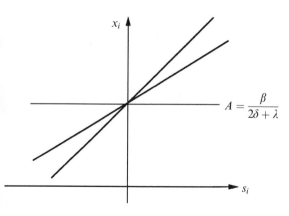

Figure 8.3

output (with $\theta = 0$), since $Es_i = 0$. Note that when $s_i = 0, x_i^*(s_i) = A$, so equilibrium strategies always go through the point $(s_i, x_i) = (0, A)$. (See figure 8.3.)

In the Cournot game (strategic substitutes), it is easy to evaluate the impact of an increased correlation in the signals. If firm 1 observes a high (positive) signal, $s_1 > 0$, it will produce less if the correlation is high than if it is low, since in the former case the probability that the competitor has received a high signal too is larger, and if firm 1 expects a high output of the competitor, it has an incentive to reduce its own output. If firm 1 observes a low (negative) signal, then by the same argument it will tend to increase its output if signals are more correlated. In any case the responsiveness of firm 1 to its information decreases and therefore its expected profits. Similarly for a given covariance of signals, a decrease in the precision of firm 2 will make this firm less responsive to its information and this should increase the responsiveness of firm 1 to its information (and its profits). This so because if, for example, firm 1 observes a high (positive) signal, firm 2 has probably observed a high signal too, but firm 2 will produce less with less precise information. The optimal thing to do for firm 1 is to produce a high output, since in Cournot competition with substitutes, if the competitor is expected to produce low, it is better to produce high.[14]

When firms pool completely their information then $I_i = \{s_1, \ldots, s_n)\}$, for all i. Information sharing with common value increases the correlation of strategies; with independent values or private values (perfect signals), it decreases (increases) the correlation of strategies with strategic substitutes (complements). This holds also for the case $\omega \neq 0$ (i.e., it covers Bertrand competition with cost uncertainty).

We are now ready to state the main result about the incentives for firms to share information. Consider the two-stage game in which firms, before receiving private information, decide whether to unilaterally reveal their forthcoming information, and once the information exchange decisions have taken place, a Bayesian Cournot or Bertrand game follows. That is, "nature" makes its move and firms receive signals according to the information exchange protocol. The first-stage information revelation choices determine a (Bayesian) subgame. The following proposition characterizes the subgame-perfect equilibria of the two-stage game:

PROPOSITION 8.1.   In the two-stage game with n firms (except in the case of Bertrand competition with cost uncertainty) to unilaterally reveal information is a dominant strategy with independent values, with private values (perfect signals), or with common value and strategic complements. With common value and strategic substitutes, not to reveal is a dominant strategy.

The intuition for the result is the following: The unilateral decision about whether to pool information can be understood in terms of the effect on the correlation of strategies and on the precision of information of rivals. With independent values or private values (perfect signals), firm i by sharing information does not improve the rival's information (firm j on θ_j) but only reveals its type to the other firms. This revelation is profitable because it always induces the "right" correlation of strategies. Indeed, in the cases considered, information sharing decreases (increases) the correlation of strategies with strategic substitutes (complements). These are exactly the directions in which expected profits tend to increase (for given symmetric precisions of signals). In the common value case information sharing always increases the correlation of the strategies and the information of rivals. Both effects are good for the expected profits of the firm contemplating to reveal its information with strategic complements and bad with strategic substitutes.

Whenever information revelation by one firm improves the information of other firms about their payoff-relevant parameters, then with strategic substitutes incentives for information sharing may disappear. In the extreme, with common values and strategic substitutes, a firm only looses by unilaterally revealing its information. In general, however, with strategic substitutes in the intermediate imperfect signal situation between independent and common values, firms face a trade-off and will not reveal their information if this improves too much the information of rivals about their own parameters.[15] With strategic complements the trade-off disappears, since having better-informed rivals is good (by itself and because it increases the correlation of strategies).

Another way to understand the results is the following (see Kühn and Vives 1995a). In our framework a monopolist, be it a quantity or a price setter (and as argued in section 8.2, the competition mode matters under uncertainty), increases its expected profits when facing a more variable demand intercept provided that it has some information about it. The reason is that the gain in high demand states is larger than the loss in low demand states. This means that the (private) value of information is increasing in the variance of demand.[16] The key effect to understand therefore is whether a firm that reveals its information to the rivals induces, via an equilibrium mechanism, a more or a less variable residual demand. With common value demand uncertainty and strategic substitutes, unilateral information revelation by firm i decreases the variance of its residual demand. Indeed, by improving the precision of the information of rivals, their outputs are better attuned to the movements in demand (e.g., producing more when demand is high, the effect outweighing the indirect potential decrease in output of the rivals brought about by the news that firm i got a high signal and consequently will produce a relatively high output), and therefore the variance of the residual demand left for firm i is lower. In contrast, with common value demand uncertainty and strategic complements by improving the precision of the information of rivals their prices are better attuned to the movements in demand (pricing higher when demand is high, for example, and the effect being reinforced by the potential increase in price of the rivals brought about by the news that firm i got a high signal and consequently will set a high price) and therefore the variance of the residual demand left for firm i is larger. This same effect will be present with private values (perfect signals) or independent values independently of whether competition is of the strategic substitutes or strategic complements variety. A revelation of a high signal or type by firm i induces rivals to cut back output in Cournot or to increase prices in Bertrand; in both cases the variance of residual demand for firm i increases.

In summary, in the cases considered and from the perspective of firm i, having better-informed rivals about their own payoff-relevant parameters is good or bad, respectively, depending on whether competition is of the strategic complements or substitutes variety. Having rivals being better informed about firm i's payoff-relevant parameter turns out to be always good (because it induces the right correlation of strategies). An exception to the second statement is the case of Bertrand markets with cost uncertainty.

In a Bertrand duopoly for substitute goods and cost uncertainty (with independent and identically distributed marginal costs), it is indeed a dominant strategy not to reveal information (Gal-Or 1986).[17] In this case competition is of the strategic complements variety, and it is still true that information sharing increases the correlation of strategies. However, it does not follow that it pays to pool information. To simplify notation, suppose that we have independent values and perfect signals. The expected profits of firm i equal $E\pi_i = E(p_i - \theta_i)(\beta - \delta p_i) - \lambda E p_i p_j + \lambda E \theta_i p_j$ (where $\lambda < 0$ for gross substitute goods). Information sharing increases $E p_i p_j$ (indeed, both p_i and p_j depend on both θ_i and θ_j), which is good, but it also increases $E \theta_i p_j$, which is bad (because high costs of firm i are associated with high prices of the rival firm and therefore with a higher demand for firm i).

The case of a Bertrand market is more complex because, as we have just seen, information acquisition by rivals of firm i about the payoff of the firm i affects *directly* the expected profits of firm i. The result is that expected profits now depend not only on the variance of the equilibrium strategy but also on a further term based on the covariance of payoff-relevant random parameters.

So far we have examined the unilateral incentives to ex ante share information. However, if firms are able to enter in industrywide agreements of the quid pro quo variety, then what is relevant is whether the information pooling situation increases or reduces expected profits in relation to no pooling of information. Indeed, whenever profits increase with information sharing, all firms can enter into a contract to exchange information on a quid pro quo basis. The following proposition states the result of the profit comparison of regimes:

PROPOSITION 8.2. With the exception of Bertrand competition under cost uncertainty, expected profits in the information-sharing regime are always larger than with no pooling of information with independent values, with private values (perfect signals), and with common value and strategic complements. With common value and strategic substitutes (e.g., Cournot competition with substitute products), information sharing yields higher (lower) expected profits for a high (low) degree of product differentiation or steeply (slowly) rising marginal costs.

The fact that expected profits in the information-sharing regime are always larger with independent or private values follows immediately from the fact that under these conditions the expected profits of firm i are always increased by his unilateral revelation of information and rivals do not learn anything more about themselves. With common value and strategic complements, expected profits of firm i are always increased by his unilateral revelation of information as well as by the revelation of information by rivals. However, with common value and strategic substitutes, firms may end up in a prisoner's dilemma type game in which pooling yields lower profits but is a dominant strategy. In this case, by pooling information, each firm has better information on the uncertain parameter θ, which tends to boost profits, but the correlation of strategies is increased (and the rivals improve their precision), which decreases expected profits. With Cournot competition this is the case if the degree of differentiation of the goods and/or the steepness of marginal costs is low enough. For example, with homogeneous products and constant marginal costs to share information decreases profits.[18] In this situation information sharing increases the precision of the information of firms, which is good, but it also increases the correlation of strategies, which is bad. The latter effect dominates when differentiation and/or the slope of marginal costs are low. The following corollary to proposition 8.2 relates the profit comparison to the outcome of the two-stage information-sharing game:

COROLLARY With independent or private values and with common value and strategic complements, the outcome of the two-stage game is efficient from the point of view of the firms. With common value and strategic substitutes, the outcome of the two-stage game is efficient (inefficient) from the point of view of the firms with a high (low) degree of product differentiation or steeply (slowly) rising marginal costs.

The fact that information sharing raises profits in many situations (in a noncooperative equilibrium) puts in doubt the idea that information sharing may be taken as prima facie evidence of collusion.[19] We will discuss information sharing as a facilitating practice for collusion in section 9.1.5.

Duopoly Example with Common Value Uncertainty
Let us go back to the duopoly common value example and be more specific about the information-pooling process. Suppose that firm i starts with an n_i independent observation sample $(r_{i1}, \ldots, r_{in_i})$ satisfying $r_{ik} = \theta + u_{ik}$, where the u_{ik}'s are i.i.d. normal with mean zero and variance σ_u^2 and are independent of θ. Firm i decides to put $\lambda_i n_i$, $0 \le \lambda_i \le 1$, observations in a common pool. The parameter λ_i is thus the proportion of observations firm i puts in the common pool. $\lambda_i \in \Lambda_i$, where $\Lambda_i = \{0, 1/n_i, \ldots, (n_i - 1)/n_i, 1\}$, $i = 1, 2$. The signal firm 1 receives, s_1, is then the best estimate of θ based on $n_1 + \lambda_2 n_2$ observations, its own sample plus the observations put in the common pool by firm 2. This is just the average, $s_1 = \theta + (1/(n_1 + \lambda_2 n_2)) \cdot (\sum_{k=1}^{n_1} u_{1k} + \sum_{k=1}^{\lambda_2 n_2} u_{2k})$. With this information structure the error terms of the signals $(\varepsilon_1, \varepsilon_2)$ follow a bivariate normal distribution with zero means and covariance matrix $\begin{bmatrix} \sigma_{\varepsilon_1} & \sigma \\ \sigma & \sigma_{\varepsilon_2} \end{bmatrix}$, where $\sigma_{\varepsilon_i} = \sigma_u^2 / (n_i + \lambda_j n_j)$, $i = 1, 2$, $j \neq i$, and $\sigma = ((\lambda_1 n_1 + \lambda_2 n_2)/((n_1 + \lambda_2 n_2)(n_2 + \lambda_1 n_1)))\sigma_u^2$. Note that $\sigma_{\varepsilon_i} \ge \sigma \ge 0$, $i = 1, 2$.

When $\lambda_1 = \lambda_2 = 0$, there is no pooling of information, $\sigma_{\varepsilon_i}^2 = \sigma_u^2 / n_i$, $i = 1, 2$, and $\sigma = 0$. When $\lambda_1 = \lambda_2 = 1$, there is complete pooling, and $\sigma_{\varepsilon_i} = \sigma = \sigma_u^2 / (n_1 + n_2)$, $i = 1, 2$. Information sharing has two effects: It decreases the variance of the error terms, and it increases their correlation (and therefore the correlation of the signals). (More precisely, σ_{ε_i} decreases with λ_j, $j \neq i$, and is independent of λ_i; σ increases with λ_i if $\lambda_j < 1$, $i = 1, 2$, $j \neq i$; otherwise, it is independent of λ_i.)

We can consider now our two-stage game where first firms decide how much information they are going to put in the common pool. An agency, a trade association, for example, collects an $n_1 + n_2$ observation sample and forms the signals according to the instructions of the firms, the λ_i's. At the first stage, then, firm i chooses $\lambda_i \in \Lambda_i$ and communicates it to the agency. At the second stage, firms knowing the selected pair (λ_1, λ_2) play the Bayesian (Cournot or Bertrand) game. For each pair (λ_1, λ_2) we have a well-defined subgame. We are interested in subgame-perfect Nash equilibria of the two-stage game, where equilibrium strategies form a (Bayesian) Nash equilibrium in every subgame.

We have that with strategic substitutes (Cournot competition with substitutes or Bertrand with complements) expected profits of firm i decrease with λ_i. With strategic complements (Bertrand competition with substitutes or Cournot with complements) expected profits of firm i increase with λ_i and with λ_j, $j \neq i$.[20]

The argument is the following: Consider the strategic substitutes case. Increases in λ_i give better information to firm j, $j \neq i$, and increase (maybe weakly) the correlation of the firm's signals. We know that both effects decrease $E\pi_i$. With strategic complements both effects increase $E\pi_i$. This means that at the first stage it is a dominant strategy (not) to share information with strategic complements (substitutes).

To obtain the ranking of profits in the two regimes, note that increases in λ_j, $j \neq i$, give better information to firm i and increase (maybe weakly) the correlation of the firm's signals. With strategic complements both effects increase $E\pi_i$. With strategic substitutes the second effect decreases $E\pi_i$ so that nothing can be said a priori (except if $\lambda_i = 1$, then the covariance of the signals cannot be increased and the first effect dominates). With Cournot competition and substitute products the correlation effect may dominate the increase precision effect when product differentiation is low or marginal costs rise slowly. Then expected profits may be lower with information pooling.

8.3.2   Monopolistic Competition: Trade Associations and Disclosure Rules

The monopolistic competition model is suitable to examine the role that disclosure rules of trade associations (TAs) or information agencies play on the incentives to share information. Institutionally, information-sharing agreements usually take the form of trade associations. At a first stage a firm has to decide whether or not to join the TA, that is, whether or not to reveal its private information. Once the TA gets a hold of the information of firms, typically it discloses an aggregate statistic of the private signals. If the TA follows a non-exclusionary disclosure rule, the information is made available to everyone in the market not just the participants firms; if the TA follows an exclusionary disclosure rule, it discloses the information only to its members.[21]

In our monopolistic competition context (section 8.2), a firm does not need individual nonanonymous data about the rivals (i.e., firm i does not need to know that firm j has received signal s_j) to determine the action distribution in the market provided they know the strategy used by the firms. Individual data are not relevant in a situation where only the distribution of actions is payoff-relevant and firms have the same strategy spaces, that is, in a situation where firms are anonymous. When the distribution of actions affects the payoff of a firm only through an aggregate statistic $\tilde{y}$, then it is typically the case that disclosure of a statistic of firms' signals, say $\tilde{s}$, is sufficient in order to predict the "aggregate action" $\tilde{y}$ of the market. Once the TA has disclosed the statistic $\tilde{s}$, firms compete in the marketplace and a Bayesian-Nash equilibrium results.

The incentives to share information will depend on the disclosure rule used by the TA. With the nonexclusionary disclosure rule, the information-sharing agreement is not stable if joining the TA is costly. This should come as no surprise, since by not joining the TA a firm can ride free and get the market information at no cost, and this does not affect any market aggregate, since the firm is negligible. We make here the natural assumption, in our context with a continuum of firms, that if one firm deviates, the others stick to the agreement.

The oligopoly case is different. Then there are circumstances where a firm would join a costly information-sharing agreement with the nonexclusionary disclosure rule. This is because a firm, by revealing its private information, affects the market outcome in a small numbers situation, and this may be advantageous to the firm. We have seen before that is the case with independent or private values, or with common value and strategic complements.

With the exclusionary disclosure rule information sharing can be a stable arrangement. If everyone shares information, it does not pay to deviate as long as the membership fee is not too high. By deviating, nothing in the market changes except that the deviator does not receive the average signal and therefore is less able to predict the average action.

If all firms participate in the TA and firm i is contemplating to deviate, the firm faces an average market action $\tilde{y} = b\tilde{\theta}$, $b = 1/(2\omega_1 + \omega_2)$. By participating in the TA, the firm obtains the statistic $\tilde{\theta}$ (the average signal $\tilde{s} = \tilde{\theta}$) and therefore predicts $\tilde{y}$ with certainty. Firm i solves $\max_{z_i} E\{\pi_i | s_i, \tilde{\theta}\}$ where $\pi_i = (\omega_0 + \theta_i)z_i - \omega_1 z_i^2 - \omega_2 \tilde{y} z_i$. The solution is $y(s_i, \tilde{\theta}) = \hat{a}(s_i - \tilde{\theta}) + b(\tilde{\theta} + \omega_0)$. (See section 8.2.) If the firm does not participate, then it does not get the TA statistic and solves $\max_{z_i} E\{\pi_i | s_i\}$, where π_i is as before. The solution is easily checked to be $y(s_i) = \bar{a}s_i + b\omega_0$, where $\bar{a} = (1 + \omega_1 - \omega_2 \rho)t/(2\omega_1(2 - \omega_2))$. In solving the second program the firm has to estimate both θ_i and $\tilde{\theta}$ only with s_i, while in solving the first it estimates θ_i with s_i and $\tilde{\theta}$ is known.

It follows from Blackwell's principle of informativeness (see Kihlstrom 1984) that the first program cannot yield lower expected profits than the second, since the signal $(s_i, \tilde{\theta})$ is more informative than s_i in the estimation of θ_i and $\tilde{y} = b\tilde{\theta}$. That is, s_i can be obtained from $(s_i, \tilde{\theta})$ by adding noise (in fact adding an infinite amount of noise to $\tilde{\theta}$). It is possible to check that the first program yields strictly higher expected profits except in two instances in which the aggregate information $\tilde{\theta}$ is irrelevant; then both programs yield the same solution. The instances are the following: First, when there is no correlation between the signals ($\rho_\theta = 0$), then $\tilde{\theta} = 0$ a.s. (i.e., $\tilde{\theta}$ is a degenerate random variable) and $\hat{a} = \bar{a} = t/2\omega_1$. Second, when $2\omega_1(1 - t) = \omega_2 t(1 - \rho)$, then $b = a = \bar{a}$. That is, only when information sharing is irrelevant ($\rho_\theta = 0$) or in the exceptional case where parameters are such that $b = a = \bar{a}$, and therefore both strategies boil down to $y_i = b(s_i + \omega_0)$, the extra information provided by $\tilde{\theta}$ is not used and expected profits from participating and not participating are equated. Otherwise, it pays to participate.

It is worth noting that not to share information is always a stable configuration (Nash equilibrium). Also if no firm shares information, firm i is indifferent between sharing or not sharing, since it makes no difference if membership is free. A fortiori, this holds if membership in the TA is costly.

Again, the situation is very different in an oligopolistic context where the strategic interactions of firms are important. Suppose, for concreteness, that we have an oligopoly with common value uncertainty. A firm, when considering whether to deviate from an information-sharing agreement, has to take into account that its deviation will change the actions of the other firms in the market-place, and therefore its profitability must be evaluated at the new equilibrium. Certainly the deviator will be less able to predict the actions of the other firms and the payoff-relevant parameter, but the strategy of the firm will be less correlated with the strategies of the rivals and this may be beneficial to the firm. In fact this is likely to be the case with Cournot competition if the products are good substitutes as the discussion in the last section shows.

We have not said anything about the relative levels of profit in the no-sharing and sharing cases. Both are self-enforcing configurations under the restricted disclosure rule. In some cases no sharing and in others sharing yield the greatest level of profits; to discuss the factors that influence the profit ranking, we need to add more structure to the model. This we do when considering the linear-normal model.

8.3.3   Welfare Analysis

What are the welfare consequences of information sharing? This is an important question from an applied point of view for the antitrust regulation of information-sharing agreements. A potential scenario is the following: A regulator (e.g., a central bank) collects information about cost or demand data from firms (banks) and ponders whether it is better to disclose the information (perhaps in aggregate form) or not as a matter of policy.

The impact of information exchanges on consumer surplus and general welfare (total surplus) is complex and depends on the type of competition (price vs. quantity) setting, the type of uncertainty (common value vs. private values, and cost vs. demand uncertainty), and on the number of firms in the industry.

We analyze the role of these factors in the welfare analysis of information sharing. We will try to understand first some basic effects of information acquisition under monopoly, then under monopolistic competition, and finally under oligopoly.[22]

To fix ideas, think of a quantity-setting monopolist facing an uncertain demand $p = \alpha + \theta - q$ (and producing without cost for simplicity), and consider giving the firm more information (a more precise signal) about α (with the maintained assumption of joint normality of the random parameter θ and the signals). Because both consumer surplus and profits (in equilibrium) are convex functions of output, ECS $= Eq^2/2$ and $E\pi = Eq^2$, giving the firm more information is good for consumers and total surplus (since then output varies more with the state of the world). Indeed, an informed monopolist will produce more in high-demand states and less in low-demand states. However, the first effect, which reduces the deadweight loss, dominates the second effect, which increases it. The reason is that the gain of an increased production when demand is high is larger than the loss of a reduced production when demand is low. The opposite is true under price setting. Then consumers suffer with a more informed firm because prices tend to be high when demand is high dominating the effect of lower prices when demand is low (reducing ECS $= E(\alpha + \theta - p)^2/2$), and although the firm benefits from better information, expected total surplus decreases. Under quantity setting, ETS $= 3(\alpha + t\sigma_\theta^2)/8$; with price setting, ETS $= (3\alpha + (4 - t)\sigma_\theta^2)/8$. The first is increasing and the second decreasing in $t = \tau_\varepsilon/(\tau_\theta + \tau_\varepsilon)$. This highlights an important difference between price and quantity setting. Giving more information to a quantity-setting monopolist is good, while giving more information to a price-setting monopolist is bad for welfare. Output adjusts to the demand variation more with an informed quantity setter and less with an informed price setter. Price and quantity setting are equivalent when there is no uncertainty ($\sigma_\theta^2 = 0$) or with perfect information ($t = 1$).[23] If there is uncertainty about the constant marginal cost, then the monopolist is indifferent about setting price or quantity (since the demand is nonrandom), and giving the firm more information always reduces the total expected deadweight loss (because output expands in low-cost states and contracts in high-cost ones).

Once we have understood the monopoly case, let us turn to a monopolistically competitive framework. From the monopoly case and with demand uncertainty, we retain that information acquisition leads to more (less) output adjustment in the quantity- (price-) setting mode. Monopolistic competition adds another concern because products are differentiated. Under standard assumptions (convexity of preferences) consumers have a preference for variety and with symmetric product differentiation dislike consuming different quantities of the varieties (see section 6.6). Indeed, consider the following total surplus function (assuming, for simplicity, zero marginal costs of production), which is consistent with the linear demand system posited in section 6.6 and in section 8.2:

Table 8.1
Decomposition of the impact on welfare of information sharing in monopolistic competition under demand uncertainty

	Common value	Private value
Price setting	↓ Output adjustment: −	↓ Output adjustment: −
	↑ Output uniformity: +	↓ Output uniformity: −
	ETS: −	ETS: −
Quantity setting	↑ Output adjustment: +	↑ Output adjustment: +
	↑ Output uniformity: +	↓ Output uniformity: −
	ETS: +	ETS: +

$$TS(q) = \int \alpha_i q_i \, di - \frac{1}{2}\tilde{q}^2 - \frac{1-\delta}{2}\left(\int q_i^2 \, di - \tilde{q}^2\right), \tilde{q} = \int q_i \, di.$$

The last term represents the loss in utility due to output variation across varieties. When $\delta = 1$, the product is homogeneous, and this loss disappears. With common value demand uncertainty $\alpha_i = \alpha$ and the first two terms are as in the homogeneous product case, $\alpha\tilde{q} - \tilde{q}^2/2$.

In terms of prices, total surplus can be written as follows:

$$TS(p) = \frac{(1-\delta)\int \beta_i^2 \, di + \delta\tilde{\beta}^2 - \int p_i^2 \, di - \gamma(\int p_i^2 \, di - \tilde{p}^2)}{2},$$

where, as before, $\beta_i = (\alpha_i - \delta\tilde{\alpha})/(1-\delta)$ and $\gamma = \delta/(1-\delta)$. Note that $\tilde{\beta} = \tilde{\alpha}$.

In the linear-normal model with demand uncertainty, we can perform readily the welfare analysis of information sharing in terms of two effects: output adjustment and output uniformity across varieties (preference for variety). Table 8.1 identifies the change in the two factors due to information exchange (more or less, ↑ or ↓) and their impact on expected total surplus (+ or −) depending on the competition mode and on the type of uncertainty (common values vs. private values). The total effect on ETS (+ or −) is also indicated.

It is worth noting that whenever they conflict, the output adjustment effect dominates the output uniformity effect, and the results are in line with the monopoly case. Information sharing increases output adjustment with quantity setting and decreases it with price setting; it increases output uniformity with common values and decreases it with private values. All this is intuitive given what we know. For example, with quantity setting and private values, information sharing increases Eq_i^2 and decreases $E\bar{q}^2$ and therefore increases expected output variability across varieties $E(\int q_i^2 di - \bar{q}^2)$. The following proposition (Vives 1990b) states the result:

PROPOSITION 8.3 Under demand uncertainty and monopolistic competition with Cournot (Bertrand) competition information sharing always increases (decreases) expected total surplus.

Under Bertrand competition sharing information is good for firms but bad for consumers, and the second effect dominates in terms of total surplus. Under Cournot competition and common value uncertainty expected consumer surplus increases with information sharing. With private value uncertainty the effect of information sharing on consumer surplus is ambiguous, increasing it only for a low enough degree of differentiation (δ high). (For δ high the negative effect of the increase in output variability across varieties brought about by information sharing is minimized.) Information sharing in the Cournot world increases expected profits with private values but may decrease them with a common value if δ is high. (In this case the negative impact of the increase in precision of rivals may dominate the positive impact of the increase in the own precision of information.)[24]

The oligopoly literature on information sharing has obtained several welfare results which are in line with proposition 8.3. In the context of Cournot competition and private value uncertainty, Shapiro (1986) in a homogeneous product world, and Sakai (1989) with differentiated products, have concluded that total welfare and individual firms' profits are always larger with information pooling. With common value demand uncertainty and in a differentiated duopoly context, Vives (1984) has shown that under Cournot competition expected total surplus is larger with information sharing.[25] Under Bertrand competition it will be also larger if the products are good substitutes; otherwise, it is smaller than with no pooling of information. In the same context, but with private value, demand uncertainty results by Sakai indicate a larger total expected surplus with information pooling. The Bertrand result contrasts with the result obtained under monopolistic competition in which, under Bertrand competition, expected total surplus always decreases with information sharing.

Table 8.2
Impact on welfare of information sharing

	Common value	Private value
Demand uncertainty		
Price setting	ECS: −	ECS: −
	ETS: $\begin{cases} - & \text{poor substitutes} \\ + & \text{good substitutes} \end{cases}$	ETS: $\begin{cases} - & \text{monopolistic competition} \\ + & n = 2 \end{cases}$
	(n large: −)	
Quantity setting	ECS: +	ECS: $\begin{cases} - & n \text{ small } (n < 9) \\ ? & \text{otherwise} \end{cases}$
	ETS: +	ETS: +
Cost uncertainty		
Price setting	ECS: ?	ECS: $\begin{cases} - & n \text{ small } (n < 9) \\ ? & n \text{ large} \end{cases}$
	ETS: +	ETS: −
Quantity setting	Same as demand	Same as demand

Cost uncertainty can be accommodated easily with Cournot competition (if m_i is the constant marginal cost of firm i just redefine the intercept α_i net of m_i) but not with Bertrand competition. Nevertheless results obtained by Sakai (1986) in a private value differentiated duopoly context suggest that total surplus is also reduced with information sharing under Bertrand competition (and the effects on firms' profits are ambiguous).

Table 8.2 summarizes the results in the literature (from Kühn and Vives 1995). Despite the complex picture that emerges from the analysis several generalizations hold. Under demand uncertainty, with Cournot competition information sharing is good in term of expected total surplus (ETS) and in Bertrand competition it is bad for consumers (and in monopolistic competition in terms of ETS also). With common values information sharing is always good in terms of ETS except with price competition when goods are poor substitutes and / or the number of firms n is large.

8.3.4 Strategic Information Transmission

Up to now we have assumed that firms can commit to exchange truthfully information before they actually receive it. Our scenario had an information agency collecting private information on behalf of the firms and then pooling and revealing it or not, depending on the instructions (representing a commitment) of the firms. As it should be apparent by now in the absence of such agencies, the incentives to share information at the interim stage, once firm i knows his private signal but not the signals received by rivals, may be different. Indeed, once signals are received, a firm in a Cournot market, for example, may want to convince the rivals that demand is low, or his own costs low, to induce soft behavior on their part. This problem does not arise in the context of monopolistic competition. Indeed, in this case a firm does not affect market aggregates, and therefore there is no incentive to try to mislead rival firms (although there may not be a strict incentive to tell the truth either!). In section 8.4.4 we analyze the large market situation.

In the oligopoly case firms must be provided incentives to reveal truthfully their information. We say then that incentive compatibility is a concern (in section 8.4 we will take a mechanism design approach to the issue). Consider the linear Cournot duopoly with uncertain marginal costs (example 1 of section 8.1). We have seen how in the case in which firm 2 has two possible cost realizations and the costs of firm 1 are known (figure 8.1), it is in the interest of firm 2 to convince firm 1 that it has low costs. The point is obviously more general. Suppose that the costs of firm i are distributed with (prior) positive density over the interval $[\underline{c}_i, \bar{c}_i]$, and that they are independent of the costs of firm j, $j \neq i$, $i = 1, 2$. Consider the general case in which firm j has beliefs given by the distribution function H_i over the possible costs of firm i, $[\underline{c}_i, \bar{c}_i]$. (Those beliefs are independent of the cost realization of firm j and need not coincide with the prior distribution over $[\underline{c}_i, \bar{c}_i]$.) The Bayesian Cournot equilibrium, given those beliefs and the linear structure of the model, will depend on the expected cost of firm i according to the beliefs of firm j, denoted by $E_j c_i$, $j \neq i$, $i = 1, 2$. It is easy to see that in equilibrium, $q_i = (2a + 2E_i c_j - E_j c_i - 3c_i)/6$, $j \neq i$, $i = 1, 2$.[26] It is immediate then that $E(\pi_i|c_i)$ is strictly decreasing in $E_j c_i$, and therefore firm i would like firm j to believe that it has the lowest possible costs. If we interpret the beliefs H_i, $i = 1, 2$, as the outcome of a first stage of information exchange, it should be clear that there will be no truthful revelation of information. The reason is that a firm would always want its rival to believe that it has the lowest possible costs in a situation in which talk is cheap. In a cheap talk situation the messages exchanged are nonbinding, have no costs associated, and are not verifiable.

We will examine in turn under what circumstances can communication be successful in a cheap talk situation and two ways of making communication possible in general: signaling at a cost and verifiable information. Before that we present the basic framework of a signaling game with its natural associated equilibrium solution (perfect Bayesian equilibrium).

Basic Signaling Game and Perfect Bayesian Equilibrium

The basic signaling game consists of player 1 (the sender or leader) who takes an action (sends a message) a_1 in A_1 based on some private information (his type), t_1, lying in some set T_1. A (pure) strategy for player 1 is thus a function $\sigma_1 : T_1 \to A_1$. Player 2 (the receiver or follower) observes the action taken (message send) by player 1 and takes in turn an action a_2 in A_2. A (pure) strategy for player 2 is thus a function $\sigma_2 : A_1 \to A_2$. The payoffs to players 1 and 2 are given, respectively, by $\pi_1(a_1, a_2, t_1)$ and $\pi_2(a_1, a_2, t_1)$. There is a common prior μ on the type of player 1, and as usual, the structure of the game is common knowledge. (With some abuse of notation, we can identify the strategies $\sigma_1(\cdot)$ and $\sigma_2(\cdot)$ as mixed strategies over A_1 and A_2, respectively.)

This game is a simple example of a dynamic game of incomplete information. For this type of game we need to refine Nash equilibrium. The concept of perfect Bayesian equilibrium (PBE) extends the idea of sequential rationality and Bayesian equilibrium to dynamic games of incomplete (or imperfect) information. (Recall that a game of incomplete information can be recast as a game of imperfect information; see section 2.7.3.) The subgame-perfect equilibrium concept may not be enough to embody sequential rationality in an extensive form game with imperfect information. This happens in particular in games in which there are no subgames except the whole game, and therefore SPE has no bite.

The idea behind PBE is to require strategies to form a Bayesian equilibrium at every continuation game once the posterior beliefs of players are specified in a consistent way. More precisely, at a PBE strategies are sequentially rational given beliefs (i.e., at any information set of any player the prescribed strategy is optimal given the beliefs of the player and the strategies used by the rivals), and beliefs are consistent in the Bayesian sense with strategies (i.e., beliefs are derived from strategies using Bayes rule whenever applicable). A PBE is defined thus by a pair formed by a strategy profile and a system of beliefs for the players. A PBE is a refinement of Nash equilibrium because at a Nash equilibrium strategies have to be sequentially rational given beliefs only at the information sets reached with positive probability (i.e., only on the equilibrium path). However, PBE is a relatively weak concept because it allows the players to have any beliefs at information sets not reached with positive probability.[27] This is a source of multiplicity of equilibria, which has called for further refinements of the PBE concept by restricting beliefs derived from out of equilibrium actions to some "reasonable" class.[28] Furthermore a PBE as defined need not be a SPE (although this can be easily fixed by requiring that a PBE must be induced at every subgame).

In the signaling game our weak concept of perfect Bayesian equilibrium is enough as a starting point to study information revelation. A perfect Bayesian equilibrium in the signaling game is a pair of strategies for players 1 and 2, $\sigma_1^*(\cdot)$ and $\sigma_2^*(\cdot)$, and some beliefs for player 2, $\mu(\cdot|a_1)$, such that:

1. The strategy of player 1 is optimal given the strategy of player 2 $\sigma_2^*(\cdot)$ ("Stackelberg" behavior), $\sigma_1^*(t_1) \in \arg\max_{a_1 \in A_1} \pi_1(a_1, \sigma_2^*(a_1), t_1)$, for (almost) all t_1 in T_1.

2. The beliefs of player 2 $\mu(\cdot|a_1)$ are derived from the strategy of player 1 $\sigma_1^*(\cdot)$, the prior μ and a_1, using Bayes's rule whenever applicable (i.e., when the action of player 1 is in the equilibrium range).

3. The action of player 2 is optimal given the action chosen by player 1 and the beliefs player 2 has $\sigma_2^*(a_1) \in \arg\max_{a_2 \in A_2} \int \pi_2(a_1, a_2, t_1) \, d\mu(t_1|a_1)$ for all a_1 in A_1 (Strategies interpreted as mixed payoffs have to be treated as expected payoffs in mixed strategies.)

Signaling games, as many dynamic games of incomplete information, have typically many PBE. The reason is that when Bayes's rule is not applicable, any posterior beliefs are admissible. By choosing appropriate beliefs out of the equilibrium path, different types of equilibria can be supported. Some may reveal fully the type of the sender/leader, and are called "separating" equilibria. Others, do not reveal anything, and are called "pooling" equilibria. In between we may find partially revealing or semipooling equilibria.

When a_1 does not affect directly neither π_1 nor π_2 the message of the sender can matter only if it changes the beliefs of the receiver about the type of player 1. If furthermore messages are not verifiable, we are in a cheap talk situation. When both the type and the action taken by player 1 are directly payoff-relevant to both players, player 1 has costs associated to taking an action (sending a message) a_1. To obtain separating equilibria, the Spence-Mirrlees condition $\partial^2 \pi_1 / \partial t_1 \partial a_1 > 0$ turns out to be important. This is a single-crossing condition (the profit of firm 1 must have strictly increasing differences in (a_1, t_1) for any a_2), and it implies monotonicity of the actions of the leader with respect to his type (see section 2.2.1). It is intuitive that in order for the first mover to be able to signal his information, it must have a different marginal benefit of changing his action for any different type.

The oligopoly case with a first stage of simultaneous action choice (or message exchange) followed by a second stage of competition with updated beliefs, given the observed first-period actions (messages), constitutes an example of simultaneous signaling. Further examples of signaling and simultaneous signaling games, in addition to those presented below, are given in sections 5.2 and 5.3.

Cheap Talk

We have stated that in our duopoly example cheap talk cannot be informative, and cannot matter, when all types of firms always like to be perceived as having low costs. What happens when information is not verifiable and firms have no commitment devices to share information? Let us recall that talk is cheap if messages are non-binding, have no costs associated, and are not verifiable.[29]

Suppose that information transmission is useful, that is, that player 2 prefers different actions depending on the type of player 1. Then necessary conditions for cheap talk between the sender and the receiver to be informative are that different types of sender must have different preferences over the actions of the receiver and that the preferences over actions of sender and receiver must not be completely opposed. Indeed, with completely opposed preferences, if the receiver could do better by not ignoring the sender's message, his response would make the sender worse off. In fact Crawford and Sobel (1982) show that there is more communication through cheap talk when the preferences of sender and receiver are more aligned. More precisely the maximum amount of information that can be conveyed in equilibrium increases as the degree of congruence of the players' preferences increases.[30] There can be perfect information transmission with perfect identification of preferences. This happens, for example, in a pure coordination game. However, it must be pointed out that no communication is always possible and constitutes a PBE of the cheap talk game. Indeed, if player 2 ignores systematically the messages of player 1, then the latter will optimize by choosing the same message for any type (using a "pooling" strategy). Firm 2 in turn will optimize by choosing an optimal strategy according to his prior beliefs: $a_2^* \in \arg\max_{a_2} E_{t_1} \pi_2(a_2, t_1)$. A pooling strategy for the sender, the action a_2^* as defined for the receiver, supported by beliefs that maintain the prior on t_1 both on and out of the equilibrium path, constitute a PBE of the cheap talk game.[31]

Verifiable Information

The question now is whether when information is verifiable incentives to reveal information are restored. With verifiable information, firms cannot lie but may withhold their information. In the framework of the signaling game, the situation to consider is when a_1 does not affect directly π_1 or π_2 but the messages are verifiable. In this context, when the preferences of the sender are monotone in the actions of the receiver, and under some regularity conditions, full revelation obtains in equilibrium.[32]

For a somewhat more complicated example, let us go back to the linear Cournot duopoly (example 1) where the costs of firm 1 (the receiver here) are known and those of firm 2 (the sender here) can be low or high (see figure 8.1). The example is more complicated because now at the second stage there is market competition contingent on the information exchanged. That is, a Bayesian equilibrium obtains once the receiver has revised his beliefs according to the message delivered by the sender. It is clear that the sender has an incentive to reveal his cost when it is low (because this induces at the second stage a low (equilibrium) output of the receiver and the profits of the sender are decreasing in the output of the receiver) but not when it is high. The problem then is that the firm cannot hide cost when it is high. The sender either reveals that its cost is high or says nothing, but the latter will be interpreted, correctly, as implying that the sender has high cost. In short, the private information of the sender unravels. The outcome is then complete revelation of information.

This result generalizes to a class of oligopoly situations (Okuno-Fujiwara, Postlewaite, and Suzumura 1990). The types of the agents are assumed to be independent, with the type of player i, t_i in T_i, a finite and ordered set. The payoff to player i depends on the actions of all the players as well as on all the types realizations, $\pi_i(a, t)$ (see section 2.7.3). The model has two stages with each agent reporting in the first stage a subset of his type space once he knows his type. The assumption is that the reported subsets must be certifiable (or verifiable). That is, the firm must be able to certify that its true type lies in the reported set. Given the information exchange in the first stage, agents update their beliefs about the rivals, and a Bayesian game, contingent on these beliefs, follows.

Suppose that in the two-stage game we consider at the second stage a unique Bayesian equilibrium for any given posterior beliefs that the firms hold. Denote by b_i the common (posterior) beliefs about player i and the (equilibrium) expected payoff to player i of type t_i contingent on the beliefs by $u_i(b_i, b_{-i}, t_i)$. We define a PBE then as a set of reporting strategies of agents (to every type of agent i associate a certifiable subset of T_i) and inference functions (to every potential report about agent i associate a belief) such that (1) beliefs are obtained from reporting strategies via Bayes's rule and they put full probability on the certified reports, and (2) the reporting strategy of agent i maximizes his expected payoff taking into account the way it modifies beliefs about the agent and therefore his expected profits $u_i(b_i, b_{-i}, t_i)$ at the Bayesian equilibrium at the second stage.

Suppose that the following ("positive") payoff belief monotonicity condition holds: Whenever b_i first-order stochastically dominates b_i' (and b_i is not equal to b_i'),[33] then $u_i(b_i, b_{-i}, t_i) > u_i(b_i', b_{-i}, t_i)$ for all b_{-i}, and t_i. This means that firms want to be perceived as being of (stochastically) high types.[34] Suppose furthermore that each type of each agent can certify that his type is at least equal to his true type. Then the unique PBE of the two-stage game yields complete revelation (and with a profile of sceptical inferences). A sceptical inference puts all the weight on the worst possible case for the agent reporting a set. Under the assumptions this is the lowest type in the set.

The following informal unraveling argument explains the full revelation result. Under the assumptions agent i wants the rivals to believe that he is of the highest possible type. This means that the true highest type will reveal itself (it is possible because he can certify that his type is at least equal to his true type). Now the next type cannot pretend to be the highest type and has to separate himself from lower types. This is accomplished by reporting truthfully its type or by reporting that he is of a type no lower that the type he is. In any case the inference will be sceptical, and the other firm will believe he is not of the top type. The unraveling of the types continues to the lowest one. If a firm reports that he is in a set with minimum type (strictly) lower than what he actually is, then the firm is believed to be of the minimum type in the reported set and is made worse off. The equilibrium inference profile must be sceptical. Indeed, suppose that for some disequilibrium report the inference function does not put full weight on the lowest type in the reported set. Then this lowest type is better off by sending the disequilibrium report rather than his equilibrium report which induces a full probability weight on his true type.

The following is sufficient for the payoff belief monotonicity condition to hold in a duopoly. The action space of every agent is a compact interval, π_i is concave and continuously differentiable in a_i, the game is a (strictly) strategic substitutes game (with the payoff to player i strictly decreasing in the action of player j) in which π_i displays strictly increasing differences in (a_i, t_i) and decreasing differences in (a_i, t_{-i}), and for any updated beliefs at the second stage the equilibrium is interior. The payoff belief monotonicity condition also holds with strategic complements competition if for any i, π_i displays strictly decreasing differences in (a_i, t_i) and decreasing differences in (a_i, t_{-i}).

In the strategic substitutes game the best response of a firm shifts (strictly) outward and the best responses of rivals shift inward with increases in his own type. In the strategic complements game the best response of a firm shifts (strictly) inward and the best responses of rivals shift inward with increases in his own type. These assumptions guarantee that if the rivals of firm i believe that the firm is of a higher type, then they will be less aggressive and will believe that firm i is tougher (softer) in the strategic substitutes (complements) game, inducing in turn less aggressive behavior on their part.

It should be clear that if "negative" payoff belief monotonicity holds (reverse the sign of the second inequality in the definition of positive payoff belief monotonicity) and each type of each agent can certify that his type is at most equal to his true type, then complete revelation should obtain. Negative payoff belief monotonicity means that a firm would like to be believed to be of a low type. The property holds in a duopoly if the monotonicity property of best responses with respect to types is reversed. That is, in a (strictly) strategic substitutes game (with the payoff to player i strictly decreasing in the action of player j) π_i displays strictly decreasing differences in (a_i, t_i) and increasing differences in (a_i, t_{-i}). In the standard strategic complements game (with the payoff to player i strictly increasing in the action of player j), π_i displays strictly increasing differences in (a_i, t_i) and increasing differences in (a_i, t_{-i}).

If singleton sets are certifiable, what is needed is a strategic substitutes or complements duopoly game in which best replies move monotonically with the types of agents in such a way that each agent always wants the rival to believe that he is of an extreme type (e.g., lowest possible cost in Cournot or highest possible cost in Bertrand). Once this is the case, then any PBE must involve complete revelation with a sceptical inference profile.

If restrictions in certifiability prevent the reporting of some sets, then the complete revelation outcome may fail. Consider example 2 in section 8.1 in the case where firm 2 has low or high costs and firm 1 known costs. If firm 2 can certify that it has high costs, then complete revelation occurs. Indeed, high-cost type firm 2 induces soft behavior on the part of firm 1, and this cannot prevent the unraveling of the low cost firm 2 (which induces tough pricing by firm 1). Imagine, however, that firm 2 cannot certify that its costs are high, although it can certify low costs (e.g., it may be difficult to convince someone that you are inefficient, although it may easy to proof efficiency by doing something very difficult). Then no revelation of information will occur, since when firm 2 is interested in revealing that it has high costs, it cannot certify its type. Another caveat to the result is that the assumption of a unique interior equilibrium at the second stage is not innocuous. If the equilibrium is not interior then, even under the assumptions made, a firm by revealing his extreme type may not increase its profits with respect to no revelation, and no revelation of information may obtain (see exercise 8.11).

An implication of the analysis is that firms may ex post reveal their information even if ex ante they would like to commit not to do it.[35] Similarly in other contexts we could think of situations where ex ante firms may decide to share information, but after obtaining the private information, a firm may reverse its decision (e.g., if this is feasible by withdrawing from the trade association).

Costly Signaling
Consider again the linear Cournot duopoly mentioned at the beginning of the section (example 1), and suppose that after knowing its

type, firm i can send a message about its cost (m_i in $[0, M_i]$) at a expense given by the smooth increasing function $e_i(m_i)$ with $e_i(0) = 0$. This expense can be interpreted as "burning money," and a firm may incur it by spending the money on uninformative advertising (e.g., as in Milgrom and Roberts 1986). We can let then $e_i(m_i) = m_i$. Once messages have been exchanged, firms compete à la Cournot. The two-stage game is thus a (simultaneous) signaling game (we follow the analysis in Ziv 1993 and Kühn 1993). In Section 8.5.3 below we will examine a simultaneous signaling game in which at the first-stage prices provide the signals and the "cost" associated is the departure from myopic optimization.

At a PBE at the second stage a Bayesian Cournot equilibrium obtains, given the reported messages (m_1, m_2) yielding beliefs for the firms $E_j c_i = E(c_i | m_i)$, $j \neq i$, $i = 1, 2$. We have that $E(c_i | m_i) = E(c_i | c_i \in r_i^{-1}(m_i))$, where r_i is the reporting strategy of firm i if m_i is in the equilibrium range. Otherwise, $E(c_i | m_i)$ is unrestricted in the set $[\underline{c}_i, \bar{c}_i]$. At a separating equilibrium we have that $E(c_i | m_i) = r_i^{-1}(m_i)$ when m_i is in the equilibrium range. The realized revenue of firm i at the Bayesian Cournot equilibrium is given by pq_i, and total profit is $\pi_i(c_i, c_j; m_i, m_j) = (p - c_i)q_i - e_i(m_i)$, where $q_i = (2a + 2E_i c_i - E_j c_i - 3c_i)/6$, and $p = a - (q_1 + q_2)$, $j \neq i$, $i = 1, 2$. Provided that $e_i(M_i)$ is large enough, there is a unique separating equilibrium $r_i(c_i)$, $i = 1, 2$. It can be characterized as follows: From the first-order condition in the first-stage optimization problem of firm i, $E(\partial \pi_i(c_i, c_j; m_i, m_j)/\partial m_i | c_i) = 0$, and noting that at a separating equilibrium $\partial E(c_i | m_i)/\partial m_i = (r_i')^{-1}$, we obtain the differential equation $r_i'(c_i) = -(a + Ec_j - 2c_j)/(9e_i'(m_i))$. With the boundary condition $r_i(\bar{c}_i) = 0$, $i = 1, 2$, and in the case that $e_i(m_i) = m_i$, it is immediate that the (unique) solution is given by $r_i(c_i) = ((a + Ec_j)(\bar{c}_i - c_i) - (\bar{c}_i^2 - c_i^2))/9$.[36]

The highest-cost type in a separating equilibrium will not incur in any signaling cost ($e_i(r_i(\bar{c}_i)) = 0$), while the other types will incur a positive cost. This is a general feature of the signaling cost of the worst type in a separating equilibrium. The reason is that the highest-cost type will be revealed anyway, and therefore it makes no effort to differentiate itself from higher types. In other words, not sending a message and not incurring any cost would strictly dominate sending a message if it had any cost associated. Clearly, $\bar{c}_i$ is already the maximum cost other firms will believe the firm has. If firm i spends in the equilibrium range, Bayesian updating is used by the rival. Otherwise, in the case where it spends more than $e_i(r_i(\underline{c}_i))$, the rival believes firm i to be of type $\underline{c}_i$. (Note that spending nothing means that the firm is believed to be of type $\bar{c}_i$.)

Obviously it is also an equilibrium if firms decide not to send any message (set $m_i = 0$ and incur no signaling cost), then no information is revealed (a "pooling" equilibrium obtains in which all types of firms do the same).[37] The revealing equilibrium may be dominated by the nonrevealing one (no information sharing) in terms of expected profits for the firms. This happens always with symmetric cost distributions with the same upper and lower bounds for both firms. The revealing equilibrium is better than the nonrevealing one if the demand intercept is low and the cost distribution is skewed toward high costs. However, if transfers between firms are allowed, then the signaling cost of one firm can be the payment to another. Now, if firms are symmetric, there will not be a cost to signaling information. (See exercise 8.12.)

More generally, the problem of finding transfers that induce truthful revelation and implement an information-sharing equilibrium is a problem of mechanism design. The expense functions $e_i(\cdot)$ can be chosen to induce truthful revelation of the types by the firms in a revelation game in which m_i is restricted to lie in $[\underline{c}_i, \bar{c}_i]$. Indeed, let $e_i(m_i) = ((a + Ec_j)(\bar{c}_i - m_i) - (\bar{c}_i^2 - m_i^2))/9$.[38] Then, when confronted with the schedule of payment $e_i(m_i)$ and assigned its production at the information-sharing equilibrium according to the revealed messages, a firm would indeed choose to tell the truth when the rival is also telling the truth. (Section 8.4 takes a mechanism design approach to information exchange. See the discussion on the revelation principle and revelation games in section 8.4.1.)

A general implication of the analysis is that if information cannot be exchanged because it is not verifiable, it may still be exchanged with signaling but at a higher social cost. A consequence is that trade associations when disallowed to help exchange information with verifiable documentation information may end up being exchanged anyway but with increased deadweight losses.

8.4 Information Sharing, Collusion, and Mechanism Design

We discussed in section 3.4 the incentive compatibility problem in information exchange. In the absence of commitment devices, firms must be provided incentives to reveal truthfully their information. In this section we will take a mechanism design approach to the issue.

Mechanism design concerns the problem of eliciting private information from agents in order to make a collective decision or implement a certain allocation. This is the problem faced, for example, by colluding firms whose costs are private information or by a trade association or information agency collecting private information from firms. Section 8.4.1 describes briefly the mechanism design approach,[39] section 8.4.2 applies it to the collusion problem under asymmetric information in a Cournot market and section 8.4.3 extends it to large markets. Finally section 8.4.4 models information agencies as information-sharing mechanisms and finds the optimal arrangement from the point of view of the firms.

8.4.1   Mechanism Design and Collusion

When firms try to collude, a problem they face is how to enforce the agreement. For example, how to make each firm abide by its cartel quota. We will discuss in section 9.1 how repeated interaction can help sustain cartel agreements. We consider here a problem that colluding firms face even when enforcement is not an issue. This is often the case when the cartel is legal, such as some agricultural market or export cartels where the courts can enforce the collusive contract.[40] The issue of interest here is asymmetric information. For example, as we have seen, a firm may know only its own costs and not the costs of rival firms.

For collusion to obtain, firms must not reveal their costs truthfully unless they are provided incentives to do so. For example, a high-cost firm may understate its costs in order not to be shut down. Since relative costs determine the distribution of output and profits across firms, more efficient producers are assigned larger production quotas, and side payments from low- to high-cost firms must be introduced. Collusion cannot, in general, be achieved without side payments. (See Roberts 1983, 1985, and exercise 8.13.)

The firms face then a mechanism design problem. They have to devise a side payment scheme to induce each other to reveal its true costs when everyone knows that their cost reports will be used to implement the cartel agreement (the industry profit-maximizing output distribution). Furthermore the side payment scheme has to provide the incentives for firms to participate in the agreement. Under these conditions the allocation, output assignments plus side payments, is said to be incentive compatible, providing incentives to firms to reveal the truth, and individually rational, providing incentives to participate.

A key insight is that according to the revelation principle there is no loss of generality in restricting attention to direct revelation mechanisms in which truth telling is optimal for each agent when trying to implement a contingent allocation of output and side payments.

More precisely, we say that a mechanism (defined by a collection of strategy sets and an outcome function that assigns outcomes to strategies) implements an allocation rule in Bayesian Nash equilibrium (BNE) if there is a BNE of the game induced by the mechanism such that for any type realization of the players the outcomes of the mechanism coincide with the outcome of the allocation rule.

A direct revelation mechanism is a mechanism such that the strategy set of player i is just his type space and the outcome function the allocation rule that wants to be implemented. The revelation principle can be stated as follows: Suppose that there is a mechanism that implements an allocation rule in BNE; then this allocation rule is Bayesian incentive compatible. That is, in the direct revelation mechanism associated to this allocation rule to tell the truth is a BNE. The revelation principle is based in the following simple idea: If in a mechanism player i finds that a certain strategy is a best response to what other players do, then when a mediator asks for his type and assigns him the same strategy the player finds that to tell the truth is optimal provided that the other players also tell the truth.

The cartel agency thus may use a direct revelation mechanism where firms are required to announce their types, and then they are assigned an output and a side payment. The cartel agency induces therefore a communication game among the firms. The result is that in order to find an optimal mechanism, how to implement the cartel rule in our case, it is sufficient to look in the class of incentive compatible mechanisms. To this, we have to add the participation constraint. In summary, the cartel agency has to ensure that the monopoly rule fulfills the incentive compatibility (IC) and the individual rationality (IR) constraints.

8.4.2   Collusion in a Cournot Market

Consider a homogeneous product Cournot market with a given set of firms, which may be finite or infinite.[41] Each firm produces with uncertain independent constant marginal costs. Inverse demand is downward sloping and given by $p = P(Q)$, and cost parameters can take values in the set $\Theta = \{\theta_1, \ldots, \theta_J\}$, where $\theta_1 < \theta_2 < \cdots < \theta_J$. Firm i knows its own cost realization c_i but only the distribution of costs of the rival.[42] The a priori distribution of costs is given by $\mu = (\mu_1, \ldots, \mu_J)$ with the interpretation that the probability that c_i equals θ_j is μ_j.

The firms attempt to collude with the aid of a central agency to whom they report their cost parameters. The role of the agency is to announce and implement a rule for allocating output and making side payments. Formally, the agency announces a mechanism $(q(\cdot), s(\cdot))$ so that when the vector c is reported, $q_i(c)$ is the output to be produced and $s_i(c)$ the side payment to be received by firm i. For each c we assume that the side payments must be balanced; that is, they must add up to zero.

Given cost realizations c, denote by $\hat{q}(c)$ a production rule that achieves the maximum total profits in the industry. This rule exists under mild assumptions, and we suppose for simplicity that it is unique. It allocates all the output to the firms with the lowest marginal cost provided that there is positive mass of such firms. If there is a (positive) mass (or number) of $\underline{n}$ firms with costs equal to $\underline{c} \equiv \min_i c_i$, then

$$\hat{q}_i(c) = \begin{cases} Q^M(\underline{c})/\underline{n} & \text{if } c_i = \underline{c}, \\ 0 & \text{otherwise}, \end{cases}$$

where $Q^M(\underline{c}) = \arg\max_Q [P(Q) - \underline{c}]Q$.

We want to find a transfer system $s(\cdot)$ that implements the monopoly rule $\hat{q}(\cdot)$, making it incentive compatible and individually rational. Given the mechanism $(q(\cdot), s(\cdot))$, the function

$$\Phi(c_i, c^*) \equiv (P(Q(c^*) - c_i)q_i(c^*) + s_i(c^*)$$

relates firm i's income (profits plus side payments) to its true cost parameter c_i and the reported cost parameters c^*. As explained before, the IC constraints require that to tell the truth be a Bayesian Nash equilibrium of the communication game among the firms induced by the mechanism $(q(\cdot), s(\cdot))$. That is, for any firm i, for any possible report $c_i^* \in \Theta$ and for any possible true cost parameter $c_i \in \Theta$,

$$E_{c_{-i}}\{\Phi(c_i, (c_i, c_{-i}))|c_i\} \geq E_{c_{-i}}\{\Phi(c_i, (c_i^*, c_{-i}))|c_i\}, \tag{IC}$$

where the subscript c_{-i} means that the expectation is taken over the cost parameters of the rivals.

Remark 2 We could make the stronger requirement that to tell the truth is a dominant strategy of the direct revelation mechanism. In this case a firm will prefer to report its true cost irrespective of the cost realizations and reports (truthful or not) of the rivals. To tell the truth will be a dominant strategy if $\Phi(c_i, (c_i, c^*_{-i})) \geq \Phi(c_i, c^*)$ for all i, for any possible reports $c^*_i \in \Theta$ and $c^*_j \in \Theta$, $j \neq i$, and any possible true cost parameter $c_i \in \Theta$. Since we confine reports of firms to belong to the set of possible types Θ, this is equivalent to requiring for all i, $\Phi(c_i, c) \geq \Phi(c_i, (c^*_i, c_{-i}))$ for all c_i and c_j in Θ and $c^*_i \in \Theta$.[43] This strong form of incentive compatibility holds if and only if the mechanism is Bayesian incentive compatible for any individual beliefs the players may have.

A positive result with this more stringent requirement holds for the special case of a n-firm industry with constant marginal costs that can be high or low. Then a cartel agreement that promises an (ex post) equal share of the monopoly profits to any firm induces each firm to reveal its true costs as a dominant strategy (exercise 8.13).

The profit that a firm expects to earn if it does not join the cartel depends on the cartel's ability to survive defections. One extreme case is that where unanimous agreement is required for collusion (IR type I). In that case each firm can, by simply refusing to join, prevent the cartel from forming. The other extreme (IR type II) arises if the cartel's formation cannot be prevented by a single firm's refusal to join. The second scenario provides a more stringent test of cartel agreements, since it is easily seen to preclude the stability of a cartel with a large number of participants.[44]

Whatever the circumstances, a firm decides to participate in the cartel agreement once it knows its own costs but not the costs of the rivals (and before it has reported its costs to the cartel manager). This is at the interim stage. A collusive arrangement is interim individually rational if it is acceptable to each firm when knowing his own cost but not knowing the cost of the other firms, and therefore not knowing exactly how the firm will be treated when output is allocated and side payments made. The alternative to participation is Cournot competition, the defector versus the cartel in case II and unrestricted in case I. A firm will agree to participate if the expected profits (computed with the information available at this stage) from participation exceed the expected profits (computed with the same information) associated with nonparticipation.

The expected profits associated with nonparticipation correspond to the Bayesian Cournot equilibria of the duopoly (case II) or oligopoly game (case I). Denote by $\Pi^C(c_i, c_{-i})$ the realized profits, at the (assumed) unique Bayesian Cournot equilibrium, of a firm with costs c_i when its rivals have costs c_{-i}. A cartel contract that specifies the output allocation and sidepayment rules $(q(\cdot), s(\cdot))$ is (interim) individually rational if for all c_i in Θ,

$$E_{c_{-i}}\{\Phi(c_i, (c_i, c_{-i}))|c_i\} \geq E_{c_{-i}}\{\Pi^C(c_i, c_{-i})|c_i\}. \tag{IR}$$

A cartel agreement is implementable when it satisfies both IC and IR.

Remark 3 One could think of alternative ways to introduce the participation constraint. For example, firms may be able to withdraw from the agreement ex post once they receive the cartel manager's recommendations and costs are revealed. A collusive arrangement that is ex post individually rational will be adhered to by each firm even after it learns how it will be treated by the arrangement. The possibility of withdrawal ex post introduces an additional individual rationality constraint and therefore makes more difficult the implementation of the cartel outcome. A collusive arrangement that satisfies both forms of individual rationality—interim and ex post—will be initially acceptable to all firms and will remain acceptable to all even after each knows exactly how its own cost realization compares to that of the other firms. Still another possibility is to have a collusive arrangement to be ex ante individually rational. In this case firms can commit to participate before receiving their private information.

A Duopoly Example
Consider example 1 (in section 8.1), a duopoly with linear demand $p = a - Q$, where firms can have low or high costs, $\Theta = \{\theta_1, \theta_2\}$ with $\theta_1 < \theta_2 < a$. Denote by $\Pi^M(\theta_i)(= ((a - \theta_i)/2)^2)$ the monopoly profits and by $Q^M(\theta_i)(= (a - \theta_i)/2)$ the monopoly output when costs are θ_i.

The monopoly rule $\hat{q}(\cdot)$ assigns all production to the lowest cost firm. If the two firms have the same cost θ_i, then the monopoly output $Q^M(\theta_i)$ is shared. In the present situation it is enough to consider side payments which involve no transfers when both firms are of the same type and a transfer, denoted s, from the low to the high type when they are of different types.

The IC constraints require s to belong to the (non empty) interval $[\underline{f}, \bar{f}]$, where

$$\underline{f} \equiv \Pi^M(\theta_1) - [\theta_2 - \theta_1]Q^M(\theta_1)) \left(\frac{1+\mu_2}{2}\right) - \Pi^M(\theta_2)\frac{\mu_2}{2}, \quad \text{and}$$

$$\bar{f} \equiv \Pi^M(\theta_1)\left(\frac{1+\mu_2}{2}\right) - (\Pi^M(\theta_2) + [\theta_2 - \theta_1]Q^M(\theta_2))\frac{\mu_2}{2}.$$

Indeed, given that the rival firm reports truthfully, a low-type firm will tell the truth if

$$\mu_1 \frac{\Pi^M(\theta_1)}{2} + \mu_2(\Pi^M(\theta_1) - s) \geq \mu_1 s + \mu_2 \frac{\Pi^M(\theta_2) + (\theta_2 - \theta_1)Q^M(\theta_2)}{2}.$$

This yields the upper bound on the side payment $s \leq \bar{f}$. A high type firm will tell the truth if

$$\mu_1 s + \mu_2 \frac{\Pi^M(\theta_2)}{2} \geq \mu_1 \frac{\Pi^M(\theta_1) - (\theta_2 - \theta_1)Q^M(\theta_1)}{2}$$

$$+ \mu_2(\Pi^M(\theta_1) - (\theta_2 - \theta_1)Q^M(\theta_1) - s).$$

This yields the lower bound on the side payment $s \geq \underline{f}$.

The side payment must be large enough for a high type to accept not to produce and low enough not to be profitable for a low type to pretend to have high costs. If the two possible costs are far apart ($\theta_2 - \theta_1$ large) and if the probability of the lowest marginal cost μ_2, is large enough, then no side payment is necessary for incentive compatibility to obtain.

The alternative to collusion at the interim stage for the firms is to play a Bayesian Cournot game. In our linear model there is a unique Bayesian Cournot equilibrium yielding an expected payoff for a firm of type θ_i; $E_{c_j}\{\Pi^C(\theta_i, c_j)|\theta_i\} = ((2a + E_{c_j} - 3\theta_i)/6)^2$, where $Ec_j = \mu_1\theta_1 + \mu_2\theta_2$. The interim individual rationality constraints (IR) require s to be in the interval $[\underline{g}, \bar{g}]$ where

$$\underline{g} \equiv \frac{1}{\mu_1}\left[E_{c_j}\{\Pi^C(\theta_2, c_j)|\theta_2\} - \mu_2\frac{\Pi^M(\theta_2)}{2}\right], \quad \text{and}$$

$$\bar{g} \equiv \frac{1}{\mu_2}\left[\Pi^M(\theta_1)\left(\frac{1+\mu_2}{2}\right) - E_{c_2}\{\Pi^C(\theta_1, c_2)|\theta_1\}\right].$$

To check the result note that a low-type firm will participate in the cartel if

$$\mu_1\frac{\Pi^M(\theta_1)}{2} + \mu_2(\Pi^M(\theta_1) - s) \geq E_{c_j}\{\Pi^C(\theta_1, c_j)|\theta_1\}.$$

This yields the upper bound on the side payments $s \leq \bar{g}$. A high-type firm will participate in the cartel if

$$\mu_1 s + \mu_2 \frac{\Pi^M(\theta_2)}{2} \geq E_{c_j}\{\Pi^C(\theta_2, c_j|\theta_2)\}.$$

This yields the lower bound on the side payment $s \geq \underline{g}$.

The cartel arrangement will be implementable if we can find a side payment s that satisfies IC and IR. That is, if the intersection of $[\underline{f}, \bar{f}]$ and $[\underline{g}, \bar{g}]$ is nonempty. This can be shown to be the case.

Remark 4 When the firms can withdraw ex post form the agreement, then a potential inconsistency arises between the interim and the ex post individual rationality constraints. The inconsistency obtains when the two types of firms are far apart and the odds in favor of low costs are high. In this case the minimum transfer that the high cost firm requires at the interim stage is that the low-cost firm is not prepared to pay ex post. (See exercise 8.14)

8.4.3 Collusion in a Large Market

In this section we consider a large market with a continuum of firms indexed in the interval $[0, 1]$. Average output in the market is now given by $Q(c) = \int_0^1 q_i(c)\,di$ and transfers are balanced: $\int_0^1 s_i(c)\,di = 0$ for every function $c \colon [0,1] \to \Theta$ of reported cost parameters. We restrict attention to anonymous mechanisms, where, given the reports of the firms, the assigned production quota and side payment to any firm depend only on its report and the distribution of reported costs.

In the continuum model there is no aggregate uncertainty, since costs are independent and every firm knows that the distribution of cost parameters in the market corresponds to the proportions given by $\mu = (\mu_1, \ldots, \mu_J)$. This fact has important consequences for the implementation of the cartel outcome via an anonymous mechanism. For example, in a large market, with independent costs, the introduction of a withdrawal possibility ex-post does not lead to a conflict between interim and ex post individual rationality constraints. Indeed, in a large market the ex post Cournot equilibrium and the (interim) Bayesian Cournot equilibrium coincide.

Denote by $\Pi^C(c_i, \mu)$ the Cournot profits of a firm of type c_i when the distribution of costs in the market is μ. Similarly denote by $\Phi(c_i, (c_i^*, \mu))$ the profits of a firm of type c_i when it announces c_i^* and the distribution of costs in the market is μ. In consequence we can write the IR and IC constraints as follows:

$$\Phi(c_i, (c_i, \mu)) \geq \Pi^C(c_i, \mu) \qquad \text{for all } c_i \text{ in } \Theta, \tag{IR}$$

$$\Phi(c_i, (c_i, \mu)) \geq \Phi(c_i, (c_i^*, \mu)) \qquad \text{for all } c_i \text{ and } c_i^* \text{ in } \Theta. \tag{IC}$$

In the analysis of the incentive compatibility constraints in the continuum model, we insist on the truth being a strict Bayesian equilibrium of the communication game induced by the cartel mechanism. That is, we require for any firm to tell the truth to be a unique best response when other firms tell also the truth.

Consider the side payment rule

$$\hat{s}_i(c) = \begin{cases} -\left[\dfrac{1}{\underline{n}} - 1\right]\bar{s}(\underline{c}) & \text{if } c_i = \underline{c}, \\[2mm] \bar{s}(\underline{c}) & \text{if } c_i > \underline{c}, \end{cases}$$

where $\underline{n}$ is the number of firms reporting $\underline{c}$, and $(P(Q^M(\underline{c})) - \underline{c})Q^M(\underline{c}) > \bar{s}(\underline{c}) > (P(Q^M(\underline{c})) - \theta_{j+1})Q^M(\underline{c})$ and j is defined by $\underline{c} = \theta_j$.

When $(\hat{q}(\cdot), \hat{s}(\cdot))$ is implemented, all firms that do not produce (and these are the firms not reporting the lowest costs) receive the same side payment and all firms that do produce make the same side payment. A firm not producing receives an amount larger than the profit a firm with the second lowest marginal cost would receive if it reported the lowest marginal cost and lower than the profit of a low cost firm. With this scheme we have that $(\hat{q}(\cdot), \hat{s}(\cdot))$ is (strictly) incentive compatible.

The argument is as follows: If all firms report truthfully, the firms with marginal costs above the minimum receive the side payment $\bar{s}(\theta_1) > (P(Q^M(\theta_1)) - \theta_2)Q^M(\theta_1)$ and are told not to produce. The μ_1 firms with the lowest marginal cost make the side payment $((1/\mu_1) - 1)\bar{s}(\theta_1)$ and are assigned equal shares of the monopoly output $Q^M(\theta_1)$. Thus each of these low-cost firms produces $Q^M(\theta_1)/\mu_1$. For the μ_2 firms with marginal costs equal to θ_2, the incentive compatibility condition requires that

$$\bar{s}(\theta_1) > (P(Q^M(\theta_1)) - \theta_2)\frac{Q^M(\theta_1)}{\mu_1} - \left(\frac{1}{\mu_1} - 1\right)\bar{s}(\theta_1).$$

This inequality is satisfied by the construction of $\bar{s}(\cdot)$. Since $\theta_j > \theta_2$ implies that $(P(Q^M(\theta_1)) - \theta_2)Q^M(\theta_1) > (P(Q^M(\theta_1)) - \theta_j)Q^M(\theta_1)$, the former inequality implies that the incentive compatibility condition is satisfied for all firms with marginal costs $\theta_j > \theta_2$. The incentive compatibility condition for the μ_1 firms with marginal costs equal to θ_1 is

$$(P(Q^M(\theta_1)) - \theta_1)\frac{Q^M(\theta_1)}{\mu_1} - \left(\frac{1}{\mu_1} - 1\right)\bar{s}(\theta_1) > \bar{s}(\theta_1),$$

or equivalently,

$$(P(Q^M(\theta_1)) - \theta_1)Q^M(\theta_1) > \bar{s}(\theta_1),$$

which holds again by construction of $\bar{s}(\theta_1)$.

Let us recall that if the individual rationality constraint is satisfied when the profit earned by a defecting firm is computed assuming no collusion by other sellers, the cartel agreement is said to satisfy individual rationality type I (IR type I). If the constraint is satisfied when the profit computation assumes collusion by the other firms, the cartel agreement is individually rational type II (IR type II).

It is now easy to see that our mechanism $(\hat{q}(\cdot), \hat{s}(\cdot))$ satisfies IR type I. Indeed, when the cartel does not survive defections by a single firm, defectors will expect to earn zero profits irrespective of its costs, while the mechanism assures every firm a positive income. Because μ_1 firms will have the lowest possible marginal cost, the competitive price will be θ_1. If the defector is one of the μ_1 firms with the lowest possible marginal cost, it will earn zero profits even though it produces because $p = \theta_1$. If the defector is one of the $(1 - \mu_1)$ firms that has marginal cost above θ_1, it will earn zero profits because it doesn't produce. However, it is quite extreme to assume that a cartel with many firms will not survive a defection by a single firm.

When discussing type II individual rationality, it is natural to introduce an assumption that guarantees that each firm is "small" relative to the market. The simplest way of accomplishing this is to assume that each firm faces a capacity constraint k. Assume that $k \geq P^{-1}(\theta_1)/\mu_1$. Since $P^{-1}(\theta_1) \geq Q^M(\theta_1)$, a capacity constraint k satisfying the restriction does not prevent firms with marginal cost θ_1 from producing $Q^M(\theta_1)/\mu_1$ as required by the mechanism when all firms report truthfully. We can extend therefore the implementation results derived thus far to include capacity constraints.[45]

It is immediate that in the presence of the stated capacity constraint, $(\hat{q}(\cdot), \hat{s}(\cdot))$ does not satisfy IR type II. Indeed, if a firm with marginal cost θ_1 defects from the cartel, it can raise its output to the capacity level k without lowering the market price. By defecting, the firm earns more than by adhering to the agreement: $(P(Q^M(\theta_1)) - \theta_1)k > (P(Q^M(\theta_1)) - \theta_1)(Q^M(\theta_1)/\mu_1) - ((1/\mu_1) - 1)\bar{s}(\theta_1)$. This points at the real difficulty in sustaining a cartel in a large market.

The positive implementation results obtained for the constant marginal cost case and IR constraints of type I contrast sharply with the negative result obtained by Cramton and Palfrey (1990). These authors find that for a large enough number of firms the cartel outcome is not enforceable, even with individual rationality constraints of type I, when the cost distribution is uniform. In their model a finite number firms draw (independently) constant marginal costs from a continuous distribution. The problem for implementation is the violation of the IR constraint for the firm with lowest possible marginal cost. It arises when the lowest cost firm does not have enough low-cost firms closeby (i.e., when the distribution of costs is not concentrated enough around the lowest cost firm), and therefore it does not face enough competition when defecting from the cartel agreement. When, as in the setup of this section, there is a mass point at the lowest possible cost, then defection implies zero profits with very high probability in the case of a large number of firms, and zero effectively in the continuum limit. Clearly, it does not pay to defect (according to type I IR).

The positive result obtained in the implementation of the cartel outcome contrasts also with some impossibility results in the mechanism design literature. The problem in our context with independent costs is not incentive compatibility. In fact, d'Aspremont and Gérard-Varet (1979) have shown that it is always possible to find side payments that make an ex post efficient allocation, like the monopoly outcome, Bayesian incentive compatible if utility functions are quasilinear and the types of the agents are independent. Laffont and Maskin (1979), in the context of public goods, and Myerson and Satterwhaite (1983), in the context of bargaining problems, find ex post efficient mechanisms without outside subsides incompatible with incentive compatibility and individual rationality.

In conclusion, the idea that cartel implementation should be more difficult with a larger number of firms is expressed by the strong form of individual rationality constraints (type II). With the weak form of individual rationality constraints (type I), no such incentives exist because defection implies unrestricted market competition.[46]

Up to now we have considered only a restricted class of cartel enforcement problems. More complex models would include different types of competition if the cartel breaks down (e.g., Bertrand), increasing marginal costs, entry, or different requirements than unanimity to approve a cartel. Indeed, in some instances to form a cartel it may be required only that a qualified majority (e.g., two-thirds) approves it. Another problem is that firms may use more sophisticated inference schemes than what has been assumed so far. For example, if a firm withdraws at the interim stage, what are the other firms to believe about its cost level? This will depend obviously on whether the cartel rewards differently firms with different costs. Still in other situations uncertainty may be of the common value type. For example, costs are uncertain but equal for each firm, and firms receive noisy signals about them. Then the implementation of the cartel rule is made easier. Now all firms are equally efficient, and what has to be determined is how much aggregate production must be. Will it be possible now to implement the cartel rule without side payments? It is left as an exercise for the reader to think about these possible extensions (for a discussion of these issues, see Cramton and Palfrey 1990).

8.4.4   Information Sharing in Large Markets

When are information-sharing agreements viable in large markets?

Two conditions are needed for this: First, agents must be honest and report truthfully; second, it must pay to join the agreement. In other words an information-sharing agreement must be incentive compatible and individually rational. We will take thus a mechanism approach to modeling information transmission and will view the information agencies (or trade associations) as mediators that help communicate with the agents in the economy. The objective of the information agency is to implement an information-sharing equilibrium or, even better, the best information-sharing equilibrium possible that fulfills the IC and IR constraints. We restrict the mechanism to be noncollusive because we want to focus on the viability of information agreements in large markets and not on the collusive potential of information agencies (we will comment on the latter in section 9.1.5).

Consider the large market linear-normal model studied in sections 8.2 and 8.3.2. The information structure and payoffs provide the elements of a basic private information game. Agent i faces a payoff $\pi(y_i, \tilde{y}; \theta_i) = (\omega_0 + \theta_i)y_i - \omega_1 y_i^2 - \omega_2 \tilde{y} y_i$, where $\tilde{y} = \int y_j \, dj$ is the average action, and receives a private signal s_i about the uncertain parameter θ_i. On top of that, the information agency/mediator induces a communication game as in the cartel case. The mediator asks each agent to report its type and then recommends (privately) and enforces an action for every agent. One possibility would be to allow the mediator to give random recommendations to the players based on the reported distribution of types. We will follow here a slightly different approach and assume that the mediator forms the recommendations the following way. Once the agents have reported their types, the mediator computes the vector of statistics or moments that summarizes the reported distribution, in this case the average signal $\tilde{s}^*$. If the information-sharing agreement calls for partial pooling of signals, the mediator adds noise to obtain $M = \tilde{s}^* + u$, where u will be normally distributed with zero mean, variance σ_u^2, and zero covariance with the rest of random variables of the model. (These properties of u are common knowledge.) Action recommendations are formed then according to the (linear) function $z(\cdot, \cdot)$ which assigns $z(s_i^*, M)$ to the pair (s_i^*, M), where s_i^* is the reported type by firm i. The mechanism z is anonymous since the recommendation to agent i depends only on the report s_i^* and on the distribution of reported types through M. It does not depend on the "name" of the agent. Further we will require the mechanism to be noncollusive. That is, the function $z(,)$ to be implemented must constitute a Bayesian Nash equilibrium of the game where the information vector available to firm i is $\{s_i, M\}$ and $M = \tilde{\theta} + u$. We identify an information-sharing agreement with a noncollusive anonymous mechanism (NCAM). In the linear-normal model those mechanisms are parametrized by σ_u^2, the noise added to the average signal by the mediator. When $\sigma_u^2 = 0$, the mediator does not add any noise and there is complete pooling of information, when $\sigma_u^2 = \infty$, we are in the private information case.

A NCAM corresponds then to the unique Bayesian equilibrium of the game where the information available to firm i is $\{s_i, M\}$ and $M = \tilde{\theta} + u$. This is just an extension of the Bayesian equilibrium considered in section 8.2. The equilibrium strategy of firm i is given by $z(s_i, M) = As_i + BM + b\omega_0$, where

$$A \equiv \frac{(1-p+\lambda p^{-1})t}{2\omega_1(1-pt)+\lambda(2\omega_1 p^{-1}+t\omega_2)}, \quad B \equiv b\frac{2(1-t)\omega_1-t(1-p)\omega_2}{2\omega_1(1-pt)+\lambda(2\omega_1 p^{-1}+t\omega_2)},$$

$$b \equiv \frac{1}{2\omega_1+\omega_2}, \quad \text{and} \quad \lambda \equiv \sigma_u^2/\sigma_\theta^2.$$

Remark 5 The equilibrium strategy of agent i is independent of σ_u^2 if and only if $C = p(2(1 - t)\omega_1 - t(1 - p)\omega_2) = 0$.[47] In this case information pooling is irrelevant, the coefficient B of shared information M is zero and agents condition only on their private signals. The case of uncorrelated types corresponds to $p = 0$. The Cournot homogeneous product market with constant marginal cost corresponds to $\omega_1 = 0$, $\omega_2 = 1$, and $p = 1$. Direct computation shows then that $A = 1$ and $B = 0$. Firms only condition on their private information, and in any case, they make zero expected profits, since there are constant returns to scale.[48] If $\omega_2 < 0$, then the actions of the agents are strategic complements and $C > 0$ provided that $p > 0$. If $\omega_2 > 0$, the actions of the agents are strategic substitutes, and the information in M may be irrelevant even in the case $p > 0$.[49]

A mechanism z induces a Bayesian communication game among the firms where the strategy of firm i is a reporting function $r_i(\cdot)$ which gives its report contingent on its type, $s_i^* = r_i(s_i)$. Given the strategies of the players $r_j(\cdot)$, for j in $[0, 1]$, the expected payoff to player i is given by $E\{\pi(z(r_i(s_i), M), \tilde{z}; \theta_i)\}$, where $M = \int r_j(s_j)\, dj + u$, and $\tilde{z} = \int z(r_j(s_j), M)\, dj$.

As before, a mechanism z is (Bayesian) incentive compatible if it is a Bayesian equilibrium of the induced communication game for all agents to report their types honestly. In other words, $r_i(\cdot)$ must be the identity function for all i.

We will say that a mechanism z is sensitive to s_i if whenever $s_i \neq s_i^*$, $z(s_i, M) \neq z(s_i^*, M)$ for a positive measure set of M's. This happens in the linear-normal model whenever $A \neq 0$.

We can easily establish the result that a NCAM that is sensitive to s_i is strictly incentive compatible. Indeed, suppose that agents are honest, and player i is considering whether to file a false report. Contingent on his type being s_i, by sending a report s_i^*, he gets $E\{\pi(z(s_i^*, M), \tilde{z}; \theta_i)|s_i\}$ where $\tilde{z} = \int z(s_j, M)\, dj = A\tilde{\theta} + BM + b\omega_0$ and $M = \tilde{\theta} + u$. Telling the truth ($s_i^* = s_i$) is the unique best strategy, since $z(s_i, M) = As_i + BM + b\omega_0$ is the unique best response to $\tilde{z}$ and z is sensitive to s_i, therefore $z(s_i, M) \neq z(s_i^*, M)$ for $s_i \neq s_i^*$.

The individual rationality of participation in an information-sharing agreement will depend on the relative benefits of joining the information agency. We will assume here that if one agent defects from the agreement, the others will stick together (IR type II). The defector then does not send a report and does not get any recommendation provided that the information agency follows a policy of exclusionary disclosure. Similar to the analysis in section 8.4.2, it can be shown that the defector will lose by deviating except in the exceptional cases in which the aggregate information contained in M is irrelevant (and then the deviant is indifferent). The reason is that since an agent's actions are negligible, he does not affect the information-sharing equilibrium. Then, in general, conditional on s_i it is strictly better to receive the information M than not to receive anything. Consequently it is individually rational to participate in an information-sharing agreement.

We conclude that a noncollusive information-sharing agreement in a large market is incentive compatible and individually rational (type II).

We may now view an information agency as an optimal mechanism in the class of incentive compatible and individually rational (type II) mechanisms. The optimal mechanism would maximize the expected payoff of a representative firm among NCAM by choosing appropriately the noise term σ_u^2. The basic question we would like to answer is whether optimal information-sharing agreements involve partial or complete pooling or perhaps no pooling of information at all.

To find the optimal mechanism, we have to optimize the expected profits of a firm with respect to σ_u^2 or, for a fixed σ_θ^2, with respect to $\lambda \equiv \sigma_u^2/\sigma_\theta^2$. The expected payoff of a representative firm is given by

$$\pi(\lambda) = \omega_1 E(z(s_i, M)^2 = \omega_1(A^2(\sigma_\theta^2 + \sigma_\varepsilon^2) + (B^2(1 + \lambda/\rho) + 2AB)\rho\sigma_\theta^2 + b^2\omega_0^2).$$

It is a simple matter, in principle, to find the optimal mechanism in the class we are considering. Mechanisms are parametrized by λ (with σ_θ^2 fixed), and therefore we have to find the maximum of $\pi(\lambda)$. ($\lambda = 0$ corresponds to complete pooling, $\lambda \in (0, \infty)$ to partial pooling, and $\lambda = \infty$ to no pooling of information).

The solution to the problem will depend on whether the actions of the players are strategic complements ($\omega_2 > 0$) or strategic substitutes ($\omega_2 < 0$). Using the expressions for A and B, it is straightforward to check that $A \geq 0$, and provided that $p > 0$, $\text{sign}\{\partial A/\partial \lambda\} = \text{sign}\{-\partial B/\partial \lambda\} = \text{sign}\{B\} = \text{sign}\{2(1-t)\omega_1 - t(1-p)\omega_2\}$. Recall that A and $|B|$ are, respectively, the responsiveness of the action of agent i to its signal and to the aggregate information M.

An increase in λ means that the mediator adds more noise to the aggregate statistic $\tilde{\theta}$. This will always decrease $|B|$. In the strategic complements case and in the strategic substitutes case where $B > 0$, A increases with λ. In the strategic substitutes case when $B < 0$, A decreases with λ.

Using simulations it is possible to show that with strategic complements the optimal mechanism always involves complete pooling of information since $\pi(\lambda)$ is decreasing in λ. With strategic substitutes it either involves no pooling or complete pooling of information depending on the values of p, σ_ε^2, and ω_2. It never pays the mediator to randomize by adding a finite amount of noise to the aggregate information M. M is either used with no garbling ($\lambda = 0$) or not used at all ($\lambda = \infty$).[50]

8.5 Commitment under Uncertainty and Information Manipulation

In section 7.4 we examined the effect of commitment on pricing under conditions of complete information. In this section we will briefly reassess the issue under conditions of uncertainty and private information. The value of commitment under uncertainty and private information will be examined as well as the use of prices to signal information and manipulate inferences of rivals and/or consumers.

8.5.1 Uncertainty, Flexibility, and Commitment

A first issue to confront is whether uncertainty will dilute commitment possibilities. A trade-off that arises in some instances is between commitment and flexibility. A firm may want to stay flexible in order to profit from the resolution of uncertainty, but this may imply that a commitment possibility is forgone. Increased uncertainty would tend then to delay investment in productive capacity, for example.[51] However, we have seen already in section 7.4.1 that the introduction of uncertainty need not eliminate commitment outcomes. In a two-period production duopoly model where firms can move in any period and at the end a market-clearing price obtains

Stackelberg-type outcomes arise when a payoff relevant random parameter with small uncertainty is realized between the two periods (see exercise 7.6).

Furthermore there are many situations where a firm can gain production flexibility if it does not delay decisions about investment. The firm has to invest to stay flexible. Let us take the example of firms faced with uncertainty about demand or prices of inputs where they have to choose between multipurpose technologies and specific technologies. Multipurpose technologies are usually more expensive in terms of capital and maintenance costs, but they give the firm more flexibility in the inputs that may be used in the production process and/or the capacity to meet the changing demand. Often flexibility comes at the cost of not being able to use the most efficient technology for any level of output. Examples of more expensive technologies which give more flexibility to the firm are multipurpose boilers for electric utilities which can use different types of fuel and computer-integrated manufacturing.

To fix these ideas, let us consider a two-stage game in which at the first-period firms can commit an investment, say in capacity which gives production flexibility by lowering the slope of marginal costs, and then Cournot market competition follows. In between firms receive private signals about a payoff-relevant parameter (e.g., the level of demand).[52] A higher investment in the first period yields both more flexibility (a lower slope of marginal costs) and a higher degree of commitment because it lowers marginal costs (and credibly commits to an aggressive production strategy at the market stage). Firms will face more uncertainty whenever the prior variability of the random payoff-relevant parameter increases or whenever they expect to receive more precise signals at the market stage, in which case their beliefs are more variable from the ex ante point of view. Indeed, if a firm expected to receive no information at the market stage, its beliefs would not be variable at all.

An increase in uncertainty will affect then both the desire for flexibility and the desire for commitment. The two effects can be separated by noting that the strategic effect of commitment will be given by the difference between the open loop equilibria (OLE) and the subgame-perfect equilibria (SPE) of the game (as explained in section 7.4.3). In an open loop equilibrium a firm takes as given the capacity positions *and* the output rules of the rival firms and therefore does not try to influence them via its first-stage capacity choice. OLE isolate then the flexibility effect by abstracting from the strategic commitment value of the technology choice. In the game considered after each pair of capacity choices a Bayesian Cournot subgame follows.

Assuming that the n firms in the market are ex ante identical, and that demand for the homogeneous product is linear with random intercept, we restrict our attention to symmetric equilibria and obtain the following results: If the increase in uncertainty comes from an increase in prior variability, both the value of flexibility and the value of strategic commitment are increased, and therefore investment expands. If the increase in uncertainty comes from more variable beliefs (i.e., more precise signals for the firms), then the value of commitment is increased but the change in the value of flexibility is ambiguous. From the point of view of a firm, by increasing the precision of information, we are at the same time improving the precision of the firm and the precision of the rival firms. In the Cournot competition context the first factor tends to increase the value of flexibility for the firm and the second to decrease it (see the discussion in section 8.3.1 after figure 8.3). In fact, if the aggregate precision of the rival firms is high enough, the second factor will overwhelm the first and the value of flexibility will decrease with a general increase in the precision of information. The sign of the total effect on investment depends then on the relative strength of the changes in flexibility and strategic commitment values. (See Vives 1989b and exercise 8.16.) Simulations with examples indicate that the negative change in the value of flexibility may dominate the strategic effect for n as low as 5, in which case the investment in cost reduction as a function of the precision of the information in increasing first and decreasing afterward.

8.5.2   Observability, Commitment, and Private Information

Another relevant issue is whether imperfect observability of the commitment variable will dilute the value of commitment. For example, in the Stackelberg model, what happens if the action of the leader is imperfectly observed by the follower? Suppose that the leader (firm 1) chooses q_1. Then the follower (firm 2) observes a signal s about q_1 distributed according to a positive density with some fixed support S (independent of q_1). Restrict attention to pure strategies. A strategy for the leader is a number (q_1) and a strategy for the follower a function $x_2: S \to R_+$. Suppose, to ease the exposition, that there is a unique best reply of the follower for every action of the leader, $r_2(\bar{q_1})$, and that there is a unique Cournot equilibrium of the simultaneous move game. Then the unique pure-strategy Nash equilibrium outcome of the sequential noisy-leader game is the Cournot equilibrium. That is, under imperfect observability the commitment advantage of the leader disappears. The reasoning is as follows: Let $(q_1, x_2(\cdot))$ be a Nash equilibrium of the sequential game. Then $x_2(s) = r_2(q_1)$ for any s (note that any s is possible for a given q_1 because the support of s is independent of q_1). Firm 2 ignores the signal because in equilibrium it knows the strategy used by firm 1. This implies that a deviation by firm 1 does not affect the action of firm 2. Therefore the leader has to play a best reply to $r_2(q_1) : q_1 \in r_1(r_2(q_1))$. In summary, the leader has to be in its best reply and the Cournot equilibrium is the only possible outcome (Bagwell 1995). The result is robust to the support of s being dependent on q_1 provided that the density of s is continuous over the real line (and therefore, in particular, the density is zero at the boundary of the support; Maggi 1997).

The startling conclusion of the above analysis is that a little bit of noise in the observation of the follower destroys all the commitment possibilities of the leader. However, the Stackelberg outcome can be approximated with small noise considering mixed strategies or introducing private information. With discrete action spaces typically there are two mixed-strategy equilibria. For example, with two actions and two signals one of the mixed-strategy equilibria approximates the Stackelberg outcome as noise becomes small and observability is almost perfect (Bagwell 1995; van Damme and Hurkens 1996).

Private information may restore the commitment power of the action of the leader (Maggi 1997). Suppose that the leader's profit is subject to a privately observed cost shock θ, and specify a linear-normal model as follows: Demand is linear, $p = \alpha - Q$, and the marginal cost of the leader θ is normally distributed $(N(\bar{\theta}, \sigma_\theta^2))$, $s = q_1 + \varepsilon$, and ε is also normally distributed $(N(0, \sigma_\varepsilon^2)$, independently of θ. The marginal cost of the follower is known and equal to $\bar{\theta}$. Now a strategy for the leader is a function of its cost level, $x_1(\theta)$. The follower knows the equilibrium strategy of the leader, $x_1(\cdot)$, but not the output realization. Therefore the signal contains useful information about the realized θ and consequently $x_1(\theta)$. It is possible to show then that there is a Nash equilibrium in linear strategies. In equilibrium, $Ex_1(\theta)$ decreases with $\sigma_\varepsilon^2/\sigma_\theta^2$; $x_1(\theta)$ tends to the (full-information) Stackelberg output as $\sigma_\varepsilon^2/\sigma_\theta^2$ tends to 0 and to the (simultaneous) Bayesian Cournot equilibrium as $\sigma_\varepsilon^2/\sigma_\theta^2$ tends to infinity. We have thus that the leader has regained commitment power, but this power is diminishing as the noise in the signal increases or the prior uncertainty about θ diminishes. Now a little bit of observational noise does not destroy commitment possibilities as long as the costs of the leader are uncertain. The leader can influence the output of the follower while revealing some information about his costs. The latter is beneficial or not for the leader depending on whether costs are low or high. Overall the leader gains from commitment in terms of expected profits (in relation to the simultaneous Bayesian Cournot equilibrium). The value of commitment is decreasing in $\sigma_\varepsilon^2/\sigma_\theta^2$, that is, the more imperfectly observable his action is and/or the less uncertainty there is about the leader's costs. These results generalize under some assumptions for a more general version of the game with nonlinear payoffs and general distributions.

If the private information of the leader is of value to the follower then the leader may in fact have a first mover disadvantage (Gal-Or 1987). Suppose now that demand is uncertain, $p = \alpha + \theta - Q$ and that the follower observes perfectly the output of the leader. Both the leader and the follower observe a private signal about θ: $s_i = \theta + \varepsilon_i$, where $E\varepsilon_i = 0, E\varepsilon_i^2 = \sigma_{\varepsilon_i}^2$ and $\text{cov}(\varepsilon_i, \varepsilon_j) = \text{cov}(\theta, \varepsilon_i) = 0$, $j \neq i$ (and θ is distributed according to some prior density with finite variance and unbounded support). Assume also that $E(\theta|s_i)$ is linear. A strategy for the leader is now a function of his signal, $x_1(s_1)$, and a strategy for the follower a function of his signal and the output choice of the leader, $x_2(s_2, q_1)$.

This game is an example of a signaling game (see section 8.3.4) where the follower has also private information. As usual a multiplicity of PBE exist. A salient PBE of the game considered is separating with the strategy of the leader being invertible.[53] At a separating equilibrium the follower can recover the signal of the leader by observing its output.

It is possible to show that if the strategy of the leader is continuous and unbounded, then it is strictly increasing and linear, and the strategy of the follower is linear also. Provided that $0 < \sigma_{\varepsilon_1}^2 < \infty$ and $\sigma_{\varepsilon_2}^2 < \infty$, there is a unique linear equilibrium.[54] Assume also that $\sigma_{\varepsilon_2}^2 > 0$, which implies that the follower has something to learn from the information of the leader. At this equilibrium and given the unbounded support assumption for θ, all possible outputs observed by the follower fall in the equilibrium range; therefore we do not have to worry about out-of-equilibrium beliefs. At the equilibrium given the strategy of the leader $x_1(\cdot)$, the signal s_2, and the realized output of the leader q_1, the follower chooses q_2 to maximize $E(\pi_2(q_1, q_2, \theta)|s_1 \in x_1^{-1}(q_1), s_2)$. That is, the follower infers that the signal of the leader belongs to the set $x_1^{-1}(q_1)$ and optimizes accordingly. The leader chooses q_1 to maximize $E(\pi_1(q_1, x_2(s_2, q_1), \theta)|s_1)$. The leader therefore anticipates the effect of his output choice on the updating done by the follower, and for a fixed conjecture of the follower about the strategy of the leader $x_1(\cdot)$, he may try to fool the follower into believing that demand is low (i.e., that the leader has received a low signal). To do this, the leader has to distort his output downward. Indeed, a leader of type s_1 by shading his output a little bit below the Stackelberg level when the follower observes s_1 also will suffer a second-order loss (because his profit is at a maximum at the Stackelberg level) but will obtain a first-order decrease in the output of the follower (and consequently and induced first-order increase in his profits). The follower decreases his output because he holds a fixed conjecture about the strategy of the leader, and the leader by shading his output induces the follower to believe that he has observed a lower signal than the actual one. However, in the (separating) equilibrium the follower is not fooled and infers correctly the signal of the leader. The result is that the leader may end up losing from being a first mover in the quantity game and that he would like, if this was possible, to directly reveal his information to the follower. In the latter case the ouput of the leader is strictly larger, for any s_1, than when the follower does not observe s_1. The expected profits of the leader (follower) are strictly larger (smaller) when the follower observes s_1.

It can be checked that at the linear equilibrium the follower's strategy is upward sloping if and only if $\sigma_{\varepsilon_2}^2/\sigma_{\varepsilon_1}^2 > \frac{1}{2}[\sigma_{\theta}^2/(\sigma_{\theta}^2 + \sigma_{\varepsilon_1}^2)]$, in which case $Eq_2 > Eq_1$.[55] It may be then that $E\pi_2 > E\pi_1$. This is certainly the case, for example, if $\sigma_{\varepsilon_2}^2$ is large. Then the leader contracts his output drastically in anticipation of the strong response of the follower to his action.

There may exist also other nonlinear partially revealing equilibria. At those equilibria some types of leader "pool" and produce the same quantity. In a simplified version of the game θ can be low or high with some specified probabilities, and the leader knows θ but not the follower. The follower only observes the output of the leader, and there is a continuum of pooling equilibria. At these equilibria the leader produces the same output no matter what is the value of θ. In this version of the game there is also a continuum of separating equilibria. In both the pooling and separating cases the beliefs used to support the corresponding equilibria are as follows: If the leader were to produce out of the equilibrium range, then the follower would infer that demand is high. In any separating equilibrium the leader in the high demand state makes no effort to separate and therefore produces his Stackelberg perfect information output. The reason is that the high-demand type will be revealed anyway. The leader in the low-demand state produces less than his Stackelberg perfect information output (strictly less provided that the difference between high and low demand is small). Refinements of PBE can be used to select from the equilibrium set. (See exercise 8.17.)

Let us look at an example of a successful application of refinements of PBE to deliver the Stackelberg outcome. In the simple discrete model (with the demand intercept having more than two points in its support to make the problem more interesting) the leader is given the option to move in the first period or to wait until the second period and move simultaneously with the follower (Mailath 1993). A complication in this case is the decision to delay which conveys information about the leaders' type (the state of demand). It is possible to show that the unique PBE, which fulfills a refinement called "strategic stability" (due to Kohlberg and Mertens 1986), involves the informed firm moving first, whatever its type, and a separating equilibrium obtains. This happens despite the fact that the informed firm may increase its ex ante expected profits by moving simultaneously with the follower. The reason is that the delay of the informed firm would be interpreted by the follower as demand being high.[56]

In summary, noisy observability of the action of the leader destroys his commitment possibilities but these may be restored when the leader has private information. However, when the information of the leader is relevant for the follower, a signaling component is introduced, and to be a first mover may be disadvantageous even if in the underlying certainty game it was better to be the leader. In other words, commitment may have negative value because of a signaling distortion.

8.5.3 Limit Pricing and Signaling Distortions

Firms' attempts to signal information to rivals introduce distortions in their behavior and may explain several pricing phenomena. For example, an incumbent may want to convey to the entrant that his costs are low and therefore that rivalry upon entry will be harsh. This idea has been proposed to explain limit pricing when the action of the incumbent, price, or quantity has no commitment value (in section 7.4.2 the entry model with quantity commitments has been examined). Let us consider first in some detail the outcome of simultaneous signaling by price-setting duopolists and then describe some signaling explanations of limit pricing.

Suppose that n firms compete for two periods in prices in our usual differentiated product industry with linear demands arising from a quadratic utility function and allowing for asymmetric varieties (see example 1 in section 6.1 and exercise 6.9). Marginal costs are constant but random and independently distributed across firms. The cost of firm i, θ_i, lies in the compact interval $[\underline{\theta}_i, \bar{\theta}_i]$ and has distribution F_i. Costs are drawn at the beginning of the game, and firm i knows its own cost but not the cost of the rival. Before period 2 firms observe the vector of prices chosen in period 1, p^1. A strategy for firm i is a pair of (measurable) functions (z_i^1, z_i^2) yielding a first-period price $z_i^1(\theta_i)$ and a second-period price $z_i^2(\theta_i, p^1)$ as a function of the information available. Firms maximize the sum of profits of the two periods. Suppose that demands and costs parameters are such that firms always produce positive quantities in both periods. (See Mailath 1989.)

At a PBE the firms' strategies (z_i^1, z_i^2) must be sequentially rational given the beliefs held, and the beliefs must be Bayes-consistent with the strategies whenever possible. At period 2 firm i observes the vector of first-period prices p^1 and knows that the cost of firm j, θ_j, will lie in the set $(z_j^1)^{-1}(p_j^1)$. Firm i will form beliefs about the costs of other firms according to a distribution function $H_j(\cdot|p_j^1)$ Bayes-consistent with the strategies used by the other players: $H_j(\cdot|p_j^1) = F_j(\cdot|\theta_j \in (z_j^1)^{-1}(p_j^1))$ whenever $p_j^1 \in z_j^1([\underline{\theta}_j, \bar{\theta}_j])$. Otherwise, the beliefs in period 2 are unrestricted. For every feasible price vector p^1, period 2 strategies $z_i^2(\theta_i, p^1)$, $i = 1, \ldots, n$, must yield a BNE of the continuation game with the given beliefs. For given θ_i and p^1, denote the expected equilibrium second-period payoffs of firm i by $\bar{\pi}_i^2(\theta_i, p^1)$. Then period 1 strategies must fulfill (almost surely)

$$z_i^1(\theta_i) \in \underset{p_i}{\arg\max}\ E(\pi_i^1(p_i, z_{-i}^1(\theta_{-i}); \theta_i) + \bar{\pi}_i^2(\theta_i, p_i, z_{-i}^1(\theta_{-i}))|\theta_i).$$

A first-period strategy for firm i therefore has to be a best response to the strategies of rivals, taking into account that the rivals invert z_i^1 to infer the type of firm i. At a separating equilibrium first-period strategies are invertible (one to one), and at the second period, on the equilibrium path, we have a game of complete information. A firm in a substitutes industry would like to be perceived to have high costs to induce softer pricing in the second period. This provides incentives to the firms to raise prices in the first period. (Note that if the goods are complements, the incentives to misrepresent work in the same direction because then best replies are downward sloping. To induce the competitor to charge low prices, a firm has to price high in the second period, something it will do if it has high costs.) It is possible to show that there is a unique separating equilibrium outcome path. At a separating equilibrium first-period prices exceed myopic-optimal first-period prices (i.e., abstracting from the signaling effect of prices) except for the lowest possible type (cost) $\underline{\theta}_i$. First-period strategies are differentiable and strictly increasing in the cost level (except for $\theta_i = \underline{\theta}_i$, at which point they have infinite slope). The intuition is as follows: Suppose that a firm, other than the lowest possible cost, were to price at the myopic level. Then by increasing its price a little, the firm would suffer a second-order loss but would make a first-order gain by inducing other firms to believe that it has higher costs. When $\theta_i = \underline{\theta}_i$, there is no finite rate of price increase for firm i which would convince other firms that firm i is of a higher type. Off the equilibrium path beliefs are given as follows: If $p_j^1 < z_j^1(\underline{\theta}_j)$, then firm $i \neq j$ believes that j is of the type $\underline{\theta}_j$; if $p_j^1 > z_j^1(\bar{\theta}_j)$, then firm $i \neq j$ believes that j is of the type $\bar{\theta}_j$. Note that, as before, the worst possible type does not distort his action because at a separating equilibrium he does not need to make any effort to distinguish himself from the other types. Indeed, type θ_i needs to make an effort to distinguish himself from lower types. This applies to all types except the lowest $\underline{\theta}_i$.

Other type of equilibria exist. In fact there is a continuum of semi-pooling equilibria in which different types set the same price.[57]

If we take as benchmark the nonsignaling case in which at the second-period costs are revealed, then one can show that with substitute goods prices are always larger at the separating equilibrium for all cost realizations (but quantities traded need not be always smaller and welfare need not decrease). If we were to have quantity competition in the same industry, then firms would have an incentive to expand output (and this would be unequivocally good for welfare). We see therefore the softening impact on competition of the signaling distortion under Bertrand competition and the reverse result under Cournot competition.

Limit Pricing

Consider the simple Stackelberg model of section 8.5.2 but with the market opening both periods. The first mover (the incumbent) may have high or low costs; he sets a price, produces, and realizes a revenue in the first period. The entrant, whose costs are unrelated to those of the incumbent, observes the price of the incumbent in the first period and decides whether to enter. If he does so, he pays a fixed cost and duopolistic competition (with complete information about costs) follows. Suppose that the entrant would like to enter only if the costs of the incumbent are high. Will the incumbent be able to prevent the entry of the potential entrant? As before we can find in this game both a continuum of separating and pooling PBE. At a separating equilibrium the high-cost type induces entry (and therefore will set the monopoly price in the first period). Typically the low-cost type signals his type by lowering his first-period price from the monopoly benchmark. He has to do so to distinguish himself from the high-cost type. Prices of the incumbent out of the equilibrium range are interpreted as arising from a high-cost type. We have thus a situation in which there is limit pricing (for low-cost types), but the entrant is not fooled and learns the costs of the incumbent. The probability of entry is therefore the same as with full information. There may be also pooling equilibria in which both types of incumbent set the same price. In general, entry may occur more often, equal or less often than with full information (Milgrom and Roberts 1982a).[58]

The model allows for a wide array of behavior, and in fact it is quite sensitive to the assumptions made. For example, suppose (realistically) that the entrant's cost is correlated with the incumbent's cost. Make them equal to simplify. The incumbent knows the cost level but the entrant does not. We will have typically that duopolistic profits after entry are decreasing in the common level of cost of the firms (see section 4.3). Then the incumbent will like to signal that costs are high and, to do so, will have to set a high price (or low output). Now a high price (distorted above the monopoly level) may prevent entry (Harrington 1986).

An interesting issue arises as to whether when there is an incumbent oligopoly there is a free-rider problem in entry deterrence. In section 7.4.2 we established that this was not the case when the output (or capacity) decisions of the incumbents have commitment value. Suppose that n incumbent firms simultaneously choose outputs in the first period and that the common industry marginal cost is constant and random (and follows a differentiable distribution with compact support). The common cost is known to the incumbents but unknown to the entrant, and if entry occurs, a complete information Cournot equilibrium obtains. The potential entrant observes only the first-period market price before making his entry decision. It is possible to show that there is a continuum of BNE of the game which entail strategic entry deterrence (Harrington 1987). In all of these equilibria there is a set of costs for which a limit price is established, involving an aggregate output smaller than the n-firm Cournot equilibrium. Further there is a subset of those costs for which entry that would have occurred under full information is prevented. Underinvestment in entry prevention is possible. The reason is that a low pre-entry output signals high costs, but this is achieved at the cost of reducing short-term profits. Therefore every incumbent would like the rivals to provide the public good (a low pre-entry output). For some cost types both deterring entry and allowing entry are BNE, but incumbents are better off deterring entry. So incumbents may be allowing entry, whereas preventing it would be collectively better (because of the output restriction). (In contrast, recall that in the quantity commitment model of section 7.4.2, we established the possibility of the incumbents preventing entry in equilibrium while they would be better off allowing entry, and the latter is also an equilibrium.)

Several comparative static results can be derived restricting attention to Pareto optimal equilibria for the incumbents that satisfy a plausible monotonicity condition on beliefs off the equilibrium path by analogy with beliefs held on the equilibrium path. This restriction makes expected postentry profits decreasing in out of equilibrium prices set by the incumbents. It is possible then that increasing the number of incumbents increases the probability of entry. This is so because of the negative effect on the incentives to deter entry of increasing the number of firms. Again, as in Gilbert and Vives (1986; see section 7.4.2), increasing the number of incumbent firms may raise the equilibrium price; this occurs when, on increasing n, there is a switch to deter entry (instead of a switch to allow entry as in Gilbert and Vives 1986). If there are multiple potential entrants that choose simultaneously whether to enter, it is found that increasing their number decreases the probability of entry and increases the limit price. With more potential entrants the incumbents find it more costly to allow entry, as in Vives (1988a; see section 7.4.2), and the set of costs for which entry is deterred increases the limit price. The result is that the welfare loss in the (imperfectly competitive) market is increasing in the number of potential entrants. Indeed, for some levels of cost, incumbents raise the price to prevent entry; they also may increase their profits, when potential entry increases.

An interesting case happens when the entrant can observe the prices set by each individual incumbent (Bagwell and Ramey 1991). It can be argued then, using a refinement of PBE, that no distortion occurs in equilibrium and the incumbents play as if there was no entry threat (or as if the entrant had perfect information). At this equilibrium firms are unable to coordinate any attempt to fool the entrant. If in a low-cost duopoly industry an incumbent attempts to signal high costs, the entrant will believe that costs are low because the rival incumbent sticks to his revealing equilibrium strategy. Again, at this equilibrium there is free-riding in providing entry deterrence and signaling high costs is not possible. Needless to say, there are many other equilibria at which distortions typically arise.

8.5.4 Price Setting and Information Manipulation

Firms may have incentives to manipulate the information received by other firms or consumers. In more technical words, some agents may have the incentive to jam the inferences made by other agents. Building a reputation is another instance where the actions of a player try to influence the inferences of rivals. Furthermore lack of knowledge of demand or costs conditions may induce firms to experiment to learn. Obviously experimentation may be costly, in the sense of forcing deviations from short-run optimizing behavior. Let us take these issues in turn.

Signal Jamming, Predation, and Reputation
We have seen how a Cournot firm has incentives to claim to have low costs to induce other firms to produce less, for example. An indirect way of manipulating information occurs when a firm takes an unobservable action which influences the information received by another firm or consumers. We say then that the firm jams the signal received by the other party. Consider a two-period Cournot duopoly (Riordan 1985). Demand is linear with random intercept with some positive correlation across periods. In the first period firms set outputs, and in the second they set outputs contingent only on the observable first period price. If firms maximize the sum of period profits, it is easy to see that there is a PBE in which at the first-period firms produce more than the one-shot Cournot output. This happens because each firm tries to signal jam the inference that the rival is making about the level of demand from the first-period price. If firms were to produce the one-shot Cournot output in the first period, then a firm would have an incentive to produce a little bit more to fool the rival into thinking that demand is lower than what in fact is. Indeed, by doing so, it would incur only in a second-order loss in the first-period but make a first order gain due to the output reduction of the rival in the second period. The rival in updating his beliefs about the level of demand takes as given the candidate equilibrium output of the firm i the Cournot output), and therefore if the firm produces a little bit more, the price will be lower and the rival will tend to think that demand is lower than what in fact is. The outcome is that both firms have incentives to overproduce and no firm is fooled in equilibrium.

Firms can also try to manipulate the beliefs of consumers. For example, consider a two-period monopoly producing with unknown quality and facing different generations of consumers. The quality of the product is unknown to both the firm and the consumers and each consumer receives a private signal about it. The joint information of the consumers reveals the quality of the product. In the first period consumers base their decisions on their private signals only. In the second they can observe also the quantity sold by the monopolist in the first period. This quantity incorporates the aggregate information of consumers but will not reveal perfectly the quality of the product because of the presence of "noise" consumers who purchase at random. That is, the quantity sold is a noisy signal of quality. Now, if the first-period price charged by the monopolist is not observable to second-period consumers (e.g., consumers in the second period observe the number of cars sold in the first period but not if they have been sold at a discount), then the monopolist has an incentive to signal jam the inferences of consumers. Indeed, setting the one-shot monopoly price will not be optimal for a firm maximizing the discounted sum of profits of the two periods. By shading a little the monopoly price, a first-order gain in second-period demand is obtained; then since at the monopoly price static profits are maximized, only a second-order loss is incurred in the first period. This is because in equilibrium consumers will take as given the candidate first-period equilibrium price. Therefore, if the firm cheats and sets a lower price, second-period consumers will attribute the increased demand to a higher quality of the product. In equilibrium the firm sets thus a first-period price lower than the (one-shot) monopoly level and (second-period) consumers are not fooled. (See exercise 8.18.)

If there is price competition among two firms producing products with an uncertain quality differential, then the signal jamming incentive induces first-period prices below the static Bertrand level, and even below marginal costs (Caminal and Vives 1996). This explains patterns of "introductory" pricing and also market share inertia, given that market share conveys information about the quality differential of the products. With a long enough horizon both consumers and firms learn the quality differential and prices settle at the full-information level. However, they do so slowly, and this gives the firms persistent incentives to manipulate the perceptions of consumers (Caminal and Vives 1999). It is also possible to observe price wars in an intermediate phase of the life cycle of a product.

Signal jamming can also explain the possibility of predatory behavior (Fudenberg and Tirole 1986). Predation refers to the efforts of incumbents to drive rivals out of the market by cutting prices in the short run in order to obtain a long-term benefit. An entrant is uncertain about his future profitability and uses his current profits to assess his prospects. The predator can manipulate the profitability of the entrant by secretly cutting prices to induce the exit of the entrant. Although in equilibrium the entrant is not fooled, predation lowers the profitability of entry (and so the welfare effects of predation are ambiguous: lower prices postentry but also lower incentives to enter).

The feasibility and desirability of predatory behavior is a debated issue, and examples and theories abound. Among them there are predation for merger (Saloner 1987), the long purse story (Fudenberg and Tirole 1986; Bolton and Scharfstein 1990), and elaborations on the chain store paradox (Selten 1978). The paradox is the following: A chain store faces competition by n potential entrants each one in a different geographical market. The potential entrants make decisions sequentially, each one knowing the decisions of previous entrants and outcomes. If a potential entrant enters, the incumbent may fight by setting low prices, in which case both get a negative profit. On the other hand, the incumbent may accommodate by setting high prices, in which case the incumbent makes no profit and the potential entrant a positive profit. If the potential entrant stays out, it makes no profit and the incumbent makes a positive profit. It is immediate that the only SPE outcome path of this game has the incumbent accommodating always and any potential entrant entering.[59] Now, with incomplete information about the type of the incumbent, the incumbent may choose to fight at the beginning to establish a reputation for toughness (Kreps and Wilson 1982b and Milgrom and Roberts 1982b). Suppose that with some small probability the incumbent enjoys fighting no matter what and that only the incumbent knows his type. Then for the first entry challenges the entrant would be preyed on because of the reputation concern of the incumbent, so no entry would occur. As long as the incumbent preys on the entrant, he is not revealed to be of a "normal" type. The first time he accommodates, he reveals that he is not of the "always fight" type. When there are fewer markets left, the reputational incentive is weakened, and the "normal" incumbent accommodates. Indeed, a "normal" incumbent will always accommodate entry in the last market because by then reputation is irrelevant. The predation story in the chain store paradox is thus based on reputation effects. The incumbent fights to convey information about his type. (See exercise 8.19 for an example where predation is generated by the lack of common knowledge about the type of the incumbent.)

Experimentation

Firms may also have incentives to use prices to experiment and learn about demand or costs conditions. Experimentation consists of paying a short-term cost in order to gain information that yields a long-term benefit. Due to this trade-off it is not obvious that optimal learning will call for complete learning or even learning enough to obtain the maximum possible payoff ("adequate" learning). Indeed, there are many instances in which there is no complete learning with a single decision maker (Rothschild 1974; McLennan 1984; Easley and Kiefer 1988; Aghion et al. 1991). This happens despite the fact that convergence of actions and beliefs obtains. Aghion et al. (1991) provide conditions in a monopoly framework under which there is complete or incomplete learning. In essence, "adequate" learning obtains if the payoff is regular enough (e.g., smooth and quasi-concave) or if there is no discounting. The idea is that with a regular payoff local experimentation guides the firm towards the global optimum.[60]

Competition introduces other effects. For example, if by producing more a firm gains a better knowledge about its costs, then imprecise prior information provides a mechanism to commit to overproduce in a Cournot market and gain a strategic advantage. Indeed, a less-informed firm will have more incentive to overproduce in order to receive a better signal about its costs (Gal-Or 1988).[61] As another example, price dispersion can be used to learn about the extent of product differentiation. In a market where firms have imperfect information about the degree of product differentiation, demand is noisy, and firms receive cost shocks, it can be shown that firms increase price dispersion with highly substitutable products and reduce it near monopoly (see Harrington 1995; see also Aghion et al. 1993). Suppose that given the cost shocks, which are common knowledge, firms set prices, and demand is realized and observed (together with the price choices). Firms learn from the difference of their realized demands through the price differential they charge. The larger the price differential set, the more informative realized demands are. Incentives are such that when products are very good (poor), substitutes firms want to generate more (less) information. Because the outcome of such experiments is public, a firm may want to limit experimentation (although more experimentation is good) so that it does not benefit its rivals at the same time.[62]

Consumers may have incentives to experiment also, and this will have repercussions in terms of strategic price setting (Bergemann and Valimaki 1996). For example, a new product in a dynamic duopolistic market for experience goods may lead buyers and sellers to try and learn about the value of the new variety, The strategic aspect of learning relaxes competition, and over time market shares converge to full-information levels (Bergemann and Valimaki 1997). A monopolist may set a low initial price to induce consumer experimentation, so that consumers can learn about the quality of the product and repeat purchases in the future at monopoly prices (Milgrom and Roberts 1986). Or, a high-quality products monopolist may set low initial prices, inducing large sales, in order to speed up the word-of-mouth information diffusion (Vettas 1997).

Summary

The chapter introduces incomplete information in the analysis of competition. It starts by providing examples and using the tools about uncertainty, private information, and Bayesian Nash equilibria (BNE) presented in section 8.2.7. Existence results of BNE in oligopoly games are offered. The linear-normal model is developed in full and applied to study the incentives to share information both in oligopoly and monopolistic competition situations. Major results include the conditions under which firms unilaterally or by mutual agreement share their information when they can commit to information exchange ex ante before they know their types and the welfare consequences of such an exchange. Strategic information revelation when firms cannot commit to share information ex ante is analyzed starting from the framework provided by the basic signaling game and using the concept of perfect Bayesian equilibrium. The roles of cheap talk, verifiable information, and costly signaling are addressed. A basic result is that the revelation of nonverifiable information involves a signaling cost. Collusion and optimal information-sharing schemes are analyzed from the perspective of mechanism design based on incentive compatibility and participation constraints that agreements fulfill. The chapter includes new results on the viability and optimality of information-sharing schemes in large markets. Finally, the value of commitment is reexamined in the presence of uncertainty and private information. Issues addressed include the potential trade-off between flexibility and commitment and the dilution of the value of commitment under imperfect observability or because of signaling costs. It is possible then that a first mover cannot take advantage of his commitment power or that he may even lose from it. The consequences of signaling distortions and information manipulation attempts in price formation are used to explain phenomena like limit pricing and the public good aspect of entry deterrence, predation, introductory pricing, market share inertia, and experimentation.

Exercises

8.1. Consider the symmetric linear duopoly model of example 1 in section 6.1 with uncertain independent constant marginal costs m_i for firm i and substitute goods. Compute the unique Bayesian Bertrand equilibrium of the model. (See section 8.1 for results.)

**8.2. Consider a n-firm smooth homogeneous product market with downward-sloping demand $D(p)$. Firm i has (weakly) convex costs $C(q_i; q_i)$, where q_i raises marginal costs. Assume that the profit of a monopolist is concave in the price and that the parameters q_i are independently and identically distributed with continuous density on a compact interval. Characterize the unique and symmetric Bayesian Bertrand equilibrium in pure strategies. Show that pricing is always below the monopoly level and that firms enjoy positive expected profits for any cost realization. Show that if there is a unique positive average cost price (that is, price for which monopoly profits are zero) for any cost parameter realization then the equilibrium price converges to the average cost as the number of firms tends to infinity. Consider the particular case of constant marginal costs and compare systematically the properties of the equilibrium with and without incomplete information. (See Spulber 1995 for answers.)

8.3. In a price-setting duopoly firm i produces product i, with demand given by $q_i = a_i - b_i p_i + c p_j, j \neq i, a_i > 0, b_i > 0, c > 0$, at constant marginal cost m_i. The vector (a_1, a_2, m_1, m_2) has a joint distribution (with finite variances) which is common knowledge, and firm i receives a private signal about (a_1, a_2, m_1, m_2). Assume that for all realizations of the random vector, $a_i - b_i m_i + c m_j > 0, j \neq i, i = 1, 2$.

a. Show that the Bayesian Bertrand equilibria of the duopoly game are in one-to-one correspondence with the solution to a team problem with an appropriate team objective function $F(p_1, p_2; a_1, a_2, m_1, m_2)$. (*Hint:* You have to find $F(\cdot)$ explicitly.)

b. Use the previous result to prove the existence of a unique Bayesian equilibrium of the duopoly game.

8.4. Consider a n-firm oligopoly model with linear demand $p = \alpha - Q$, where α is normally distributed with mean μ and variance σ_α^2. Firm i receives a signal $s_i = \alpha + \varepsilon_i$ about α where ε_i is an error term normally distributed with mean 0 and variance σ_ε^2. Both α and ε_i are uncorrelated, and likewise ε_i and ε_j, are uncorrelated. Firms produce at no cost and conditional on α signals are independent. Compute the (unique) Bayesian Cournot equilibrium of the oligopoly game. Analyze the comparative static properties of the equilibrium with respect to the number of firms, σ_ε^2, and σ_α^2.

8.5. Show that in the linear-normal monopolistically competitive model of section 8.2, there is a unique Bayesian equilibrium in linear strategies in both the private and shared information cases. The equilibrium strategy of firm i in the private information case is given by $y(s_i) = as_i + b\omega_0$ where $a = t/(2\omega_1 + \omega_2\rho_0 t)$ and $b = 1/(2\omega_1 + \omega_2)$ and in the shared information case by $z(s_i, \bar\theta) = \hat{a}(s_i - \tilde\theta) + b(\omega_0 + \tilde\theta)$ where $\hat{a} = d/2\omega_1$.

8.6. In section 8.3.2 we have argued that with monopolistic competition it will pay to join a trade association (with exclusionary disclosure) formed by all firms in the industry. Will this still be the case for a "small" TA? Will an industrywide TA (the grand coalition) be stable against defections by smaller coalitions of firms? (*Hint:* It will matter whether competition is of the strategic substitutes or strategic complements variety.)

*8.7. Consider a price-setting differentiated duopoly where firm i produces product i, with demand given by $q_i = a - bp_i + cp_j$, $j \neq i$, $a > 0, b > c > 0$, at constant random marginal cost m_i. Costs are independently distributed on a compact interval with $Em_i = \bar{m}$, $i = 1, 2$. Firm i knows its type m_i but not the type of the rival. We assume that $a - bm_i + cm_j > 0$, $j \neq i$, $i = 1, 2$ for all cost realizations.

a. Compute the unique Bayesian equilibrium of the Bertrand duopoly game.

b. Examine the incentives to (ex ante) share information about costs. Would the incentives change if $c < 0$? How about if firms were to compete in quantities? Explain carefully the intuition behind the results.

c. Suppose that now firm i can announce an interval where his cost lies and its announcement is verifiable. How would the incentives to share information change if information was exchanged ex post, that is, after firms have received their private signals? Compare the equilibria of information exchange ex ante and ex post.

*8.8. (Warning: The algebra of this exercise is tedious.) Consider the linear-normal monopolistic competition model with private information of section 8.2 and section 8.2.3 with $\delta \in (0, 1)$. Compare profits and consumer surplus with (s) and without (ns) sharing of information. Show that under Bertrand competition $ECS^{ns} > ECS^s$ and $E\pi^{ns} < E\pi^s$ always. Under Cournot competition, with common values, $ECS^{ns} < ECS^s$ and $E\pi^{ns} \gtrless E\pi^s$ if and only if $\delta \gtrless [2(1 - \sqrt{t})]/(2 - t - \sqrt{t})$; with private values, $ECS^{ns} \gtrless ECS^s$ if and only if $\delta \gtrless (4 - 2\sqrt{\rho_\alpha}/(4 - \rho_\alpha)$ and $E\pi^{ns} < E\pi^s$. Explain the results. (*Hint:* Use the fact that $ECS(q) = (\delta E\tilde{q}^2 + (1 - \delta)Eq_i^2)/2$,

$$ECS(p) = [\{\text{constant}\} + (1 + \gamma)Ep_i^2 - \gamma E\tilde{p}^2 - 2E\beta_i p_i\}/2,$$

$$E\pi_C = (1 - \delta)Eq_i^2, E\pi_B = (1 + \gamma)Ep_i^2.$$

See Vives 1990b.)

8.9. Reconsider exercise 8.4, with $n = 2$ allowing the error terms of signals to have positive or negative correlation. Assume that $-\sigma_\varepsilon^2 < \text{cov}(\varepsilon_1, \varepsilon_2) < \sigma_\varepsilon^2$. Examine the profitability of information exchange. Explain your results.

8.10. Consider a homogeneous product Cournot duopoly facing a linear demand. Firms have constant random marginal costs of production which are potentially correlated following a symmetric joint normal distribution. Firm i knows its own cost level but not the cost level of the rival. Show that the (ex ante) unilateral revelation of firm i of its cost level to the rival j reduces firm j's expected profits (from the base level of the Bayesian Cournot equilibrium with private cost information) provided that the correlation of costs levels is large enough. What do you conclude about the value of information for a player in a noncooperative game? (See Sakai 1985.)

8.11. In a Cournot market firm 1 has zero costs (and this is common knowledge); firm 2 can have low (zero) or high (positive) costs, but the firm does not know it. It is firm 1 that gets to know whether the costs of firm 2 are low or high. The parameters are such that the expected cost of firm 2 is so high that it does not produce and firm 1 is a monopoly. If firm 2 learns that it has low costs, then a symmetric Cournot equilibrium obtains. If firm 2 learns that it has high costs, then obviously the firm is out of the market. Examine the incentives of firm 1 to reveal (ex post) the costs of firm 2. (See Okuno, Postlewaite, and Suzumura 1990.)

8.12. Consider the linear Cournot duopoly of example 1 in section 8.1 with an information exchange stage appended before market competition in which firms can send messages at a cost and where information is not verifiable (as in the model at the end of section 8.3.4). Compute directly the "signaling costs" necessary to induce truthful revelation. Compare the expected signaling costs for each firm with the benefits from information sharing (the difference in expected profits for the firm between the information-sharing situation and the no-sharing one). How does the comparison depend on the parameters of the model (and the variances of costs, in particular)? What happens when firms have symmetric distributions over costs? (See section 8.3.4; see also Ziv 1993 and Kühn 1993.)

8.13. Consider a Cournot duopoly with downward-sloping demand and firms having constant marginal costs that can be high or low. The costs of firm i are private to the firm but the probabilities of cost being high or low are common knowledge.

a. Show that the monopoly outcome can be supported even without side payments if firms' costs are sufficiently far apart.

b. Consider now the same industry with n firms. Show that a cartel agreement that promises an (ex post) equal share of the monopoly profits to any firm induces truthful cost revelation as a dominant strategy. Does the arrangement violates individual rationality? Can the result be extended to the case of more than two types of firms? (See section 8.4, and Kihlstrom and Vives 1992, for answers.)

8.14. Consider the duopoly model of section 8.4.2 with the possibility of withdrawal from the cartel agreement ex post. Discuss whether this possibility of withdrawal should modify the incentive compatibility constraints. Derive the ex post individual rationality constraints, and check the potential conflict with the interim individual rationality constraints. Discuss the results obtained. (See Kihlstrom and Vives 1992 for answers.)

8.15. Consider a duopoly model with linear demand for (symmetrically) differentiated products. Firms can produce at no cost and the demand intercept α is random. Suppose that firm i obtains a private signal about α. Signals are conditionally independent, the information structure is linear, and precision can be purchased according to a convex cost function $(C(\tau_i)$ where τ_i is the precision of the signal of firm i). At the first stage firms acquire information (the precision of the signals); at the second they compete in the marketplace upon having received their private signals. Show that at the information acquisition stage (when followed by a Bayesian Nash equilibrium in the marketplace) the strategies are strategic substitutes (comple ments) if and only if the underlying certainty duopoly game is sub modular (supermodular). (See Vives 1988b for the submodular case.

**8.16. Consider the two-stage investment competition game of sec tion 8.5.1. There are n firms in the market. Demand is linear and given by $p = \alpha - \beta Q$, where α is random, $\beta > 0$, and Q is total output Firm i receives a private signal $s_i = \alpha + \varepsilon_i$ about the uncertain α where $E\varepsilon_i = 0, E\varepsilon_i^2 = \sigma_\varepsilon^2$ and $\mathrm{cov}(\varepsilon_i, \varepsilon_j) = \mathrm{cov}(\alpha, \varepsilon_i) = 0, j \neq i$. The in tercept α is distributed according to some prior density with finite variance. Assume that $E(\alpha|s_i)$ is linear. Firms are ex ante identical all face the same technological prospects and receive signals of the same precision. The sequence of events is as follows: Firms make their capacity choice first, receive their private signals, and finally compete in quantities. The total cost function of a firm is then $C(q; \lambda) = \gamma \lambda^{-\eta} + \lambda q^2$, where $\gamma > 0$ and $\eta > 0$. Show that there is a unique symmetric subgame-perfect equilibrium of the two-stage game if η is large enough. Show that equilibrium investment $\gamma(\lambda^*)^{-}$ is increasing in σ_α^2 (provided that $\sigma_\varepsilon^2 < \infty$) and in $(\sigma_\varepsilon^2)^{-1}$ if $2\lambda^* \geq \beta[(\sigma_\alpha^2/(\sigma_\alpha^2 + \sigma_\varepsilon^2))(n - 1) - 2]$. How do you interpret this result? Obtain expressions for the value of commitment and the value of flexibility comparing OLE with SPE. (See Vives 1989b.)

*8.17. Consider the Stackelberg game of section 8.5.2 in which the demand intercept α is uncertain and can be low or high with some specified probabilities. The leader knows α but not the follower who only observes the output of the leader. Characterize the continuum of separating and pooling PBE of the game. Do you find all the equilibria equally plausible? Propose possible criteria to selec among them. (*Hint:* Consider the elimination of weakly dominated strategies to select from the separating equilibria.) What happens to the separating equilibria if α is continuously distributed over an interval? Why?

**8.18. Consider a price-setting monopoly selling a product of un known quality indexed by θ to one-period-lived consumers in a two period market. The monopolist produces at no cost and maximizes total expected discounted profits (with discount factor δ). There is a continuum of consumers in each generation, indexed in the unit interval. The demand of consumer i of generation $t = 0, 1$ is given by $q_i^t = a + E(\theta|I_i^t) - p^t$, where I_i^t is the information of the consumer and p^t the price charged by the firm in period t. Total demand is given by $Q^t = \int q_i^t \, di + u^t$, where u^t is the random demand of "noise" consumers in period t. It is assumed that $I_i^0 = \{s_i^0, p^0\}$ and $I_i^1 = \{s_i^1, p^1, Q^0\}$, where $s_i^t = \theta + \varepsilon_i^t$. The monopoly does not know θ and in period 1 has available the information $I_M^1 = \{Q^0, p^0\}$. The random variables $\varepsilon_i^t, \varepsilon_j^\tau, \theta, u^1$, and u^2 are mutually independent and normally distributed (with finite variances) for any i, j in $[0, 1]$ and $t, \tau = 0, 1$. Assume that in every period the aggregate signal of the consumers reveals θ. Examine the PBE of this model, assuming that the beliefs of consumers are unchanged when they observe an out-of-equilibrium price. (Why does this restriction make sense?) Give an expression for the weight λ given by a consumer in period 1 to the aggregate output Q^0 in the estimation of θ. Provide a sufficient condition (and interpret it) in terms of δ and λ that ensures that there is a unique PBE (in pure strategies) and that the monopoly follows the price policy: $p^0 = \{1 - \lambda\delta/4\}a/2$, and $p^1 = (a + \theta_1)/2$, where θ_1 is the monopoly's estimate of θ in period 1. Compare period 0 prices with myopic monopoly pricing and perform a comparative static analysis of p^0 with respect to the parameters of the model. Can period 0 prices be below cost?

8.19. Consider the chain store model of section 8.5.4 with two potential entrants, $j = 1, 2$ (with the convention that $j = 2$ is the first potential entrant). Suppose that there are three possible (and equally likely) states of the world: A, B, and C. In state A the incumbent is a predator (always preys). In states B and C the payoffs for the incumbent (π_I) and entrant j (π_j) in market $j = 1, 2$ are as follows: If the potential entrant enters and the incumbent preys, $(\pi_I, \pi_j) = (-0.2, 0)$, whereas if he accommodates, $(\pi_I, \pi_j) = (0, 1)$. If the potential entrant stays out, then $(\pi_I, \pi_j) = (1, 0.8)$. Suppose now that entrant 2 has perfect information about the state of the world but that entrant 1 cannot distinguish A from B while the incumbent cannot distinguish B from C. Display a PBE with an outcome path in which entrant 2 does not enter because of the threat of predation. (*Hint:* When the true state is B or C, the incumbent does not know whether entrant 1 knows that he is not a predator. (See Milgrom and Roberts 1982b.)

9   Repeated Interaction and Dynamics

Dynamic interaction is at the heart of two important issues in oligopoly theory: Collusion and commitment. As emphasized by Chamberlin (1929) and Stigler (1964) (see chapter 1, section 1.7.3), the maintenance of collusive agreements, explicit or tacit, needs repeated interaction that allows firms to punish the deviants from the agreement. The concept of repeated games is used to analyze this issue. Commitment has been treated in the context of two-stage games. Two-stage games provide valuable insights into the oligopoly-pricing problem, but the inherent dynamics are limited. Firms compete repeatedly in the marketplace making quantity, price, and inventory decisions that affect short-term prospects and investment decisions that affect long-term prospects. It is very difficult to build dynamic models that take into account all the relevant factors. Two-stage games are manageable and illustrate the effects of a state variable (typically the decision variable in the first stage) in the overall competition process. However, the results obtained should be checked by fully dynamic games. More appropriately the commitment issues in dynamic games may be analyzed by turning to state-contingent (Markov) strategies. Section 9.1 provides an overview of the contribution of the repeated games theory in explaining collusion. Section 9.2 analyzes several discrete and continuous time (differential) games using the Markovian strategy restriction in order to illuminate issues in dynamic commitment and pricing.[1]

9.1   Repeated Interaction and Collusion

Repeated interaction in the marketplace motivates firms to reach agreements that sustain collusive prices. These agreements may be explicit or implicit (tacit) and may be sustained with the threat of punishment in case of noncompliance. In a repeated game (super-game), a one-shot static game—a Cournot game, for example—is repeated with a finite or infinite horizon. As we will see, the outcomes of the repeated game are quite responsive to the specification of the horizon. We will begin with the finite horizon case (section 9.1.1) and follow with the infinitely repeated game (section 9.1.2). Afterward we will study uncertainty and imperfect monitoring of the actions of firms (section 9.1.3), collusive pricing and demand fluctuations (section 9.1.4), and the effect of privately observed signals and the role of communication (section 9.1.5). A discussion of the repeated game framework (section 9.1.6) completes our review.

The analysis of repeated games (and, in general dynamic games) calls for a refinement of the Nash equilibrium in order to rule out incredible threats. As was argued earlier, the appropriate analytical tool for games of complete information is the subgame-perfect Nash equilibrium (SPE). Subgame perfection requires threats and promises (out-of-equilibrium strategies) to be credible in the sense that starting at any subgame they must constitute an equilibrium of the continuation game.

9.1.1 Finite Horizon

Interestingly, when a Cournot game with a unique single-stage equilibrium is repeated finitely many periods, the only possible SPE is just the repetition of the unique one-shot Cournot equilibrium. We can use a backward recursion argument to establish the result immediately, since at the final stage the only possible equilibrium is the Cournot equilibrium for any chosen outputs at the previous stages. At the next to the last stage then, we can apply the same argument, and the result follows. This outcome can be contrasted to the wide range of first-period outputs that can be sustained in a Nash equilibrium of, for example, the twice repeated game. Then different first-period outputs can be sustained with the not credible threat of flooding the market in the second period (see exercise 9.1). In this instance, therefore, subgame perfection narrows down dramatically the possible outcomes.

The unique SPE prediction of the play of the game may seem surprising in light of experimental findings that cooperation emerges in a finite but long-term repeated game with a unique one-shot Nash quilibrium (Axelrod 1984). Three ways have been proposed to break the backward recursion argument.

In the first approach the firms are ε-optimizers instead of classical optimizers. An optimal strategy gets ε close to the profit-maximizing strategy. (The optimal response may be more costly to discover and use for a firm that has a close alternative nearby.) For a large enough horizon, and with firms desiring average profits, outcomes other than a repetition of the single-stage equilibrium can be sustained as ε-SPE (Radner 1980). Suppose that the continuation payoff of a strategy in a subgame is the average of a firm's profits in all periods (and not just in the remaining periods; see exercise 9.2 for this alternative formulation). Consider a linear Cournot market with inverse demand given by $p = a - Q$ and n firms producing at no cost. The game is repeated T periods. This is how the cartel output can be sustained for T periods. Firms use "trigger strategies" according to which a firm cooperates and produces his cartel quota provided that everyone has done so in the past. If someone cheats, then there is reversion to Cournot behavior. In the last period firm i will not cheat if the payoff from cooperating, the share of the firm in monopoly profits $a^2/4n$, is larger than the (average) payoff from defecting, $((T - 1)(a^2/4n) + (a(n + 1)/4n)^2)/T$, where $(a(n + 1)/4n)^2$ are the profits that the firm obtains by deviating and responding optimally to the aggregate cartel output of other member firms. It follows that the incentive to cheat is $(a(n - 1)/4n)^2/T$, which is decreasing in T. If this result is no larger than ε, the firm has no incentive to deviate in the last period (nor in any other period). In summary, for any $\varepsilon > 0$, we can find $T_\varepsilon = (a(n - 1)/4n)^2/\varepsilon$ such that there is an ε-SPE for $T \geq T_\varepsilon$ which supports the cartel outcome. The same strategies support collusion for any number of periods $k = 0, 1, \ldots, T$. The reason why the cartel outcome can be supported at all is that for a long enough horizon T, the incentive to cheat in the final period will be less than ε. This breaks the logic of backward recursion.

The second approach allows for multiple single-stage equilibria. The firm can credibly (subgame-perfect) threaten to revert to a less favorable Nash equilibrium at the final stage(s) if the desired strategies are not followed (see Friedman 1985; Fraysse and Moreau 1985; Benoit and Krishna 1985). For example, let us take a Cournot oligopoly with two (strictly) Pareto-ranked (from the point of view of the firms) one-shot equilibria. Trigger strategies support collusion except in the last period provided that T is large enough and th discount rate low enough, and they take the following form: Coop erate for periods $t = 1, \ldots, T - 1$ as long as there has been coopera tion; otherwise, revert to the inferior one-shot Nash equilibrium Play the strategy corresponding to the superior one-shot Nash equ librium in period T if there has been cooperation; otherwise, play th strategy corresponding to the inferior one-shot Nash equilibrium. is worth noticing that the punishment corresponding to the inferic one-shot Nash equilibrium is credible. Indeed, it prescribes Nas behavior in a subgame induced by a deviation. Furthermore it possible to show (Benoit and Krishna 1985) that provided that th static game has two equilibria that are strictly Pareto ranked an that the dimension of the feasible set is equal to the number c players, any feasible and strictly individually rational payoff[2] can b approximated by a SPE of the finitely repeated game if the horizon long enough (and the discount rate low enough is there is discoun ing).[3] This is a "folk theorem" stating essentially that almost an outcome, under the assumptions, is supportable as an SPE in th finitely repeated game. Different versions of the folk theorem will b presented below.

It is possible also to support cooperation, at least for several pe riods, in a finitely repeated game with a unique one-shot equilibriur introducing a small amount of the right kind of incomplete informa tion or "craziness." For example, suppose that in a duopoly, wit small probability, each player uses a predetermined "nice" strateg and cooperates as long there has been cooperation in the past bu otherwise defects (see Kreps et al. 1982). For a sufficiently long (ye finite) horizon and a high-discount factor, players will cooperate a the beginning because it is in their interest not to contradict that the are of the "nice" type. That is, they want to keep a reputation fo being nice (see also the analysis of reputation in section 8.5.4). Th value of such a reputation is the possible future cooperative out comes if the rival is of the "nice" type. The cost of maintaining th reputation is to be cheated and face a noncooperative rival. When th horizon is long (and the discount factor high) enough, the benefi outweighs the cost. Close to the end of the horizon, the opposite true and cooperation breaks down. However, by choosing the righ kind of incomplete information ("craziness"), a folk theorem hold Essentially any outcome (feasible and strictly individually rationa for the "normal" players can be approximated and supported as perfect Bayesian equilibrium of the finitely repeated game with an arbitrarily small amount of "craziness" if the horizon (and the discount factor) is large enough (Fudenberg and Maskin 1986).

9.1.2 Infinite Horizon

A great multiplicity of subgame-perfect equilibria of the infinitely repeated game obtains even when there is a unique equilibrium in the one-shot game. Consider a single-stage game in which firm i has a convex and compact subset of Euclidean space A_i as the action set and a continuous payoff $\pi_i(a_i, a_{-i})$. Firms compete repeatedly over an infinite horizon with complete information and discount the future with discount factor δ ($\delta = 1/(1+r)$, where r is the discount rate). Each firm observes the whole history of actions. In the present context a strategy for firm i is a sequence of functions $\sigma_i = (\sigma_{it})_{t=0}^{\infty}$, where $\sigma_{it}(\cdot)$ assigns an action to every possible history of actions of firms up to $t - 1$. The strategy profile $(\sigma_i)_{i=1}^{n}$ is a SPE if for any date t and history up to t the strategies form a Nash equilibrium of the continuation subgame starting at t.[4] Let $\hat{\pi}_i$ denote the profits of firm i at the one-shot Nash equilibrium, and consider a "cooperative" action profile a^* with $\pi_i^* = \pi_i(a^*) > \hat{\pi}_i$ for all i. Let $\bar{\pi}_i = \max_{a_i \in A_i} \pi_i(a_i, a_{-i}^*)$ denote the profits attained by an optimal deviation from the cooperative agreement.

Friedman (1971) showed that any vector of payoffs that give every firm (strictly) more than the static Nash profits, $\pi_i^* > \hat{\pi}_i$ for all i, can be supported as a (subgame-perfect) Nash equilibrium of the repeated game if the firms do not discount the future too much (i.e., δ is close to one). The desired outcome is supported with trigger strategies: Firm i cooperates, playing a_i^* until there is a defection, in which case there is reversion to Nash (one-shot) behavior forever. To check that the described strategies form a SPE, it must be shown that the prescribed play after any deviation is a Nash equilibrium in the continuation subgame, and this needs to be checked only when there has been no previous deviation. Indeed, after a deviation, the one-shot Nash equilibrium is played forever, and this itself constitutes a SPE. The incentive compatibility condition for firm i to sustain cooperation is that the payoff from cooperation, $\pi_i^*/(1-\delta)$ must be no less than the payoff from defection $\bar{\pi}_i + [\delta/(1-\delta)]\hat{\pi}_i$, which consists of the gain form deviating one period $\bar{\pi}_i$ plus the discounted payoff of inducing Nash reversion forever. It follows that cooperation can be sustained if firms are patient enough: $\delta \geq \underline{\delta}$ where $\underline{\delta} = (\bar{\pi}_i - \pi_i^*)/(\bar{\pi}_i - \hat{\pi}_i)$. The inequality always holds if δ is close to one because $\pi_i^* > \hat{\pi}_i$. The critical discount factor above which the cooperative outcome can be sustained, $\underline{\delta}$, corresponds to a critical discount rate which is just the ratio of the collusion benefit over the deviation gain, $(\pi_i^* - \hat{\pi}_i)/(\bar{\pi}_i - \pi_i^*)$. It is easy to see that more collusion is supportable, that is, a higher π_i^*, if defection is less profitable (a lower $\bar{\pi}_i$), the punishment more severe (a lower $\hat{\pi}_i$), or the future more important (a higher discount factor). Paradoxically, a very competitive market (in the one-shot game) may foster collusion by making credible harsh punishments (with very low $\hat{\pi}_i$).[5]

The infinite repetition of the one-shot Nash equilibrium constitutes a SPE of the supergame, and therefore (infinitely) repeated competition expands the set of equilibria with respect to the one-shot situation.

Factors That Influence Collusion

The theory of supergames provides a framework to use in assessing the factors that influence collusion. Among them are the horizon of the firms, number of competitors, type of competition, presence of capacity constraints and product differentiation, effect of asymmetries, and multimarket contact. We can think that collusion is easier when the critical discount factor above which collusion can be sustained is lower. Less patient firms can collude then. Let us turn briefly to some examples.[6]

First, the discount factor δ may be interpreted more broadly than the weight given to the future by the firms. For example, δ may be related directly to the *reaction lag* to a potential deviation. Indeed, suppose that τ is the length of a period and r the interest rate. Then the discount factor is given by $\delta = e^{-r\tau}$. Therefore the shorter the period (τ small) is, the larger is δ and the fastest the detection and punishment of deviants. As before, the lower r is, the easier it is to collude because more weight is given to the future. Another interpretation is to think about a game with a random final date. This is effectively equivalent to an infinite horizon with discounting, noting that if μ is the *hazard rate* (the probability that the game continues at any period given that it is still going on), we have $\delta = \mu e^{-r\tau}$. Still δ could be related to the rate of growth of demand in a given market.

In order to illustrate the results, let us consider a homogeneous product market with downward-sloping demand and constant identical) marginal costs of production c for each of the n firms. Suppose for simplicity that the monopoly price p^m is unique. We can characterize tightly when collusion can be sustained with price competition (a Bertrand market). In a duopoly with $\delta \geq \frac{1}{2}$, any price in the interval $[c, p^m]$ is supported as a SPE by Bertrand reversion. However, when $\delta < \frac{1}{2}$, at any SPE outcome path price equals marginal cost. In an oligopoly any price in $(c, p^m]$ is supported as a (stationary) SPE outcome path by Bertrand reversion if and only if $\delta \geq \delta_n^B$, where $\delta_n^B = 1 - (1/n)$. Denoting by π^m the monopoly profit, the incentive compatibility constraint for collusion requires that $\pi^m/(n(1-\delta)) = \pi^m$ (by undercutting slightly the monopoly price the deviant firm obtains the monopoly profit and faces zero profits hereafter). This yields the desired inequality $\delta \geq 1 - (1/n)$ or $n \leq (1-\delta)^{-1}$.

What is the critical number of firms above which collusion cannot be sustained for reasonable values of the discount factor? Suppose a monthly detection lag and an annual discount rate of $r = 12$ percent. We then have that $\tau = 1/12$ and $e^{-r\tau} = 0.99$. If we assume a hazard rate of $\mu = 0.85$, we obtain $\delta = \mu e^{-r\tau} = 0.84$, and the critical n the largest integer smaller than $(1-\delta)^{-1}$) equals 6 firms. If $\mu = 1$, then the critical n is 100 firms. However, it is reasonable to assume a hazard rate less than one given the uncertainty surrounding business conditions. This represents effectively a finite but uncertain horizon for the game.

In a Cournot market, with linear demand $p = a - Q$ and constant marginal costs, the critical discount factor above which the cartel quota can be sustained as a SPE with Cournot reversion is given by $\delta_n^C = (1 + (4n/(n+1)^2))^{-1}$. For two firms we have that $\delta_2^B < \delta_2^C$, whereas for $n > 2$, $\delta_n^B > \delta_n^C$. Clearly, according to this critical discount factor it is easier for two firms to sustain collusion in a Bertrand market, whereas it is easier for more than two firms to sustain collusion in a Cournot market. With Bertrand reversion the deviant firm has a larger one-period gain but faces a harsher punishment. The punishment effect is prominent in the duopoly case, while the one-period gain effect predominates as the number of firms rises.[7] In a duopoly therefore it is easier to collude when one-shot market competition is harsher.

Both critical discount factors, δ_n^B and δ_n^C, are increasing in n. This means that it becomes harder to collude with more firms. A larger n has the uniform effect of decreasing the individual collusive profits in any regime, while not modifying the payoff of cheating in Bertrand and diminishing the profits of a deviant in Cournot (both the one-shot gain and the capitalized punishment). In the Bertrand case therefore there is only one effect, working against collusion with more firms, while in the Cournot case there is a countervailing effect in so far as the benefit of a deviation diminishes with n.

However, the level of cooperation need not, in general, decrease monotonically with the number of firms in the market. This is easily understood in the (symmetric) Bertrand-Edgeworth model. That is, price competition with capacity constraints (with constant marginal cost up to the capacity limit for every firm; see section 5.2). It is possible to show then that using trigger strategies, the maximum sustainable cartel price (and per capita profit) is not monotonic in terms of the number of firms n (Brock and Scheinkman 1985). A uniform increase in the capacity of firms increases the retaliation possibilities (the threat of punishment) but also the individual incentive to deviate.

The theory of supergames provides also insights on whether symmetry helps collusion. It is generally thought that asymmetries in costs functions and even product differentiation hinder collusion. The general idea is that *asymmetries* make coordination more difficult (e.g., see Scherer and Ross 1990, ch. 8). There is some experimental evidence that in duopoly games collusion is more likely when firms have symmetric production costs (Mason, Phillips, and Nowell 1992). A confirmation of the idea that symmetry may help collusion is provided in Compte, Jenny, and Rey (1997).[8] Those authors find in a repeated price game with *capacity constraints* that the introduction of asymmetric capacities hinders collusion when aggregate capacity is low but can foster it when it is large. In their model the sustainability of collusion depends on the capacity of the largest firm and on the aggregate capacity of the rest of the firms. An increase in the capacity of the largest firm tends to hurt collusion because it increases the incentives of this firm to deviate. A decrease in collusion possibilities occurs if the firm cannot cover the whole market. In contrast, an increase of capacity of small firms (which together do not cover the market) increases their retaliatory capacity over and above their increased incentive to deviate. The result is that collusion is helped. However, if the small firms can cover the market, an increase in their capacity only augments their incentive to deviate, hurting collusion possibilities. In short, to help collusion, the retaliation capabilities of small firms should be maximized.

The effect of the degree of *product differentiation* on the critical discount factor above which collusion can be sustained is typically ambiguous.[9] The reason should be clear. Think of the typical trigger strategy. More product differentiation reduces the gain from deviating from the collusive agreement but also diminishes the strength of the punishment following a deviation. Indeed, profits at a Bertrand one-shot equilibrium are typically increasing in the degree of product differentiation. In the symmetric linear price competition product differentiation model (see section 6.1), it can be shown that when the degree of substitutability is low, an increase in its level (as well as an increase in the number of firms) makes collusion more difficult; when the degree of substitutability is high, it can go either way (Deneckere 1983). Asymmetry can be introduced in the same symmetric model in a multiproduct context where firms produce different numbers of products (Motta 1998). It can be shown then that the smallest firm tends to have the strongest incentive to deviate. The reason is that the monopoly profit per product is independent of the size of the firm, but both deviation profits and punishment profits tend to be higher for small firms. Indeed, a firm producing a low number of varieties will tend to set lower prices because it has fewer substitute products to internalize in its optimization, and this makes both the profits of a deviation and the profits of the one-shot multiproduct Bertrand equilibrium larger (see exercise 9.5).

The effect of asymmetries on collusion possibilities has obvious implications for merger policy. For example, a merger that implies a more symmetric distribution of capacities in the industry may be facilitating collusion, although it may induce a decrease in the Herfindahl index of concentration (see section 4.2). Therefore a less concentrated market according to the standard Herfindahl index may imply a higher possibility of colluding successfully.

Multimarket contact may help collusion. This happens, for example, when firms compete repeatedly in independent markets that differ in the number of firms or the effective discount rate (e.g., one market may meet more frequently than another). In this situation, when firms can cartelize one of the markets in isolation, a slack in the incentive constraint in this market can be used to establish collusion everywhere. This is accomplished by pooling the incentive constraints of the different markets: The potential loss of collusion in the easily cartelized market looms large in the overall incentive constraint (see Bernheim and Whinston 1990 and exercise 9.6).[10]

In summary, the theory of supergames can illuminate factors that foster or hinder collusion. A higher weight to the future, a shorter reaction lag, or a higher frequency of interaction tends to facilitate collusion. In general, given constant marginal costs, the level of sustainable cooperation will depend monotonically on the number of firms (more firms make it harder to collude because the firms have a smaller market share at any price). In contrast, the presence of capacity constraints, asymmetries in the distribution of capacity or size constraints on firms in the number of varieties produced will tend to hurt collusion, although product differentiation per se can have an ambiguous impact on collusion possibilities. Multimarket contact will help collusion under some conditions. It is worth noting that price-setting models tend to support more collusive outcomes than quantity-setting models. This is precisely because credible punishments can be more severe in the former (although also the countervailing factor must be taken into account, that it is generally more profitable to deviate from a collusive agreement under Bertrand than under Cournot competition).

Collusion and Commitment
Collusive pricing may change the strategic incentives of firms when they have available some long-run commitment variable, like capacity. An application of the repeated game analysis with a bearing on this topic is provided by Benoit and Krishna (1987; and Davidson and Deneckere 1990) who extend the Kreps-Scheinkman model (see section 5.2.4) to many periods. Benoit and Krishna consider firms choosing capacities of production first, and then competing repeatedly in prices. This allows for collusive pricing equilibria to emerge, inducing capacity choices at the first stage different from the Cournot levels identified by Kreps-Scheinkman. In any case the Cournot capacities and the Cournot price (for all market periods) constitute also an equilibrium. An interesting result of the analysis is that all equilibria of the game, except the Cournot one, involve excess capacity. Davidson and Deneckere (1990) assume that firms cannot collude in capacity but strive to set the maximum possible price sustainable and enforce the agreement with the threat of reversion to the static Nash equilibrium. For linear market demand they show that if the cost of capacity and the discount rate are low, the best response of a firm in capacity space is increasing in the capacity choice of the rival provided the capacities of the firms are

larger than the monopoly output. (The reason is that larger capacity choices of the rival firm will make higher prices sustainable by increasing its share of collusive profits and reducing its temptation to cheat.) This contrasts with the Cournot analysis where capacity choices followed by competitive pricing involve decreasing best responses (with linear demand). We see thus that collusive pricing changes the strategic incentives of the capacity investment or quantity-setting game. Furthermore the authors show (again in the linear demand case) that all equilibria involve capacity choices larger than the Cournot levels.

Optimal Punishments

In general, the threat of Nash reversion does not provide the most severe credible punishment to deviants to a collusive agreement.[11] This fact is important because the more severe the punishment is, the more "cooperative" outcomes can be sustained.

Apart from Friedman's result there are several theorems available (folk theorems) displaying the multiplicity of equilibria in infinitely repeated games (see Aumann and Shapley 1976; Rubinstein 1979; Fudenberg and Maskin 1986). The folk theorem states that any feasible and strictly individual rational outcome (strictly above the minmax payoff or security level for every player) can be supported as a SPE with low enough discounting provided that the dimension of the set of feasible payoffs equals the number of players (Fudenberg and Maskin 1986). The strategies that support the proposed outcomes typically specify punishments for the deviant (e.g., being held at the security level for a period) and rewards for the firms punishing a deviator.[12] The maximum payoffs that firms can attain in the repeated game, the maximal degree of collusion, will be achieved when defectors are punished in the most severe (credible) way possible. This is accomplished by punishing a deviant with the worst possible SPE from its perspective.

By showing the existence of worst player–specific SPE, Abreu (1986, 1988) identifies optimal punishment strategies in Cournot games. He also shows that optimal symmetric punishments have a simple two-phase stick-and-carrot structure in which a deviation is met by an expanding output for one period to revert to the most collusive sustainable output. In a symmetric punishment, firms play in the same way after an asymmetric history. Consider a symmetric (one-stage) Cournot game. Denote by $\pi(q)$ the payoff to each firm when all the firms produce output q. Under mild regularity conditions (e.g., that $\pi(q)$ decreases without bound as q tends to infinity and that the maximal payoff from a deviation when each other firm plays q, $\bar{\pi}(q)$, is decreasing in q) it is possible to characterize easily the best (symmetric) collusive sustainable output q^* as well as the one-period punishment output $\hat{q}$. The best collusive sustainable output q^* corresponds to the best symmetric SPE (with symmetric punishments), yielding a payoff $\pi(q^*)$. The punishment output $\hat{q}$ is part of the worst possible symmetric SPE (with symmetric punishments) in which firms attain the (average) payoff $w = (1 - \delta)\pi(\hat{q}) + \delta\pi(q^*)$. At this worst SPE, players play $\hat{q}$ first and switch to the SPE with payoff $\pi(q^*)$ if there are no deviations. If there is a deviation, players again revert to $\hat{q}$, and so on. The most collusive outcome is attained by playing q^* as long as there are no deviations and switching to the worst possible SPE in case of a deviation. The outputs q^* and $\hat{q}$ can be found as follows: To ensure that it does not pay to deviate from the worst SPE, it must be true that $w \geq (1 - \delta)\bar{\pi}(\hat{q}) + \delta w$, or $w \geq \bar{\pi}(\hat{q})$. Equivalently $\delta(\pi(q^*) - \pi(\hat{q})) \geq \bar{\pi}(\hat{q}) - \pi(\hat{q})$. At an optimal scheme the inequality will hold as equality. Furthermore, to ensure no deviation from the cooperative phase, it is sufficient that $\pi(q^*) + \delta\pi(q^*) \geq \bar{\pi}(q^*) + \delta\pi(\hat{q})$ (it is enough to look one period ahead because, in any case, the strategies prescribe return to the cooperative mode after the one-period punishment), or equivalently, $\delta(\pi(q^*) - \pi(\hat{q})) \geq \bar{\pi}(q^*) - \pi(q^*)$. If full collusion is not sustainable, then again the inequality must hold as equality in the optimal scheme.

In order to support Pareto optimal payoffs (on the frontier of the feasible set), it is necessary and sufficient that there exists a symmetric SPE (with symmetric punishments) that leaves the firms at their minmax values. In the Cournot case it is possible to construct an SPE in which firms earn an average payoff of zero (the minmax value) for a large enough δ. In this case Cournot reversion does not provide the most severe credible punishment. However, in the price game with constant and equal marginal costs, the static Bertrand equilibrium gives the firms zero profits, and therefore Nash reversion provides the most severe credible punishment. Optimal punishments in the presence of capacity constraints are more complex. For example, credible optimal punishments involve firms obtaining their minmax profits as long as firms are similar enough (Lambson 1987, 1995). In general, though, the firm with the largest capacity obtains only its minmax profit in the optimal punishment phase (Lambson 1994).

The discussion of the factors that foster or hinder collusion should be reviewed at the light of the optimal punishments schemes.

9.1.3   Uncertainty and Imperfect Monitoring

Up to now only games with perfect monitoring of actions have been considered. A consequence of this is that punishment phases or "price wars" are never observed in equilibrium. In practice, however, firms often cannot monitor perfectly the actions of rivals but must infer them from market data. Indeed, a major obstacle to collusion is secret price cutting (Stigler 1964). A firm facing low demand does not know whether this is due to a state of low demand in the market or due to secret price cutting by the rival. The consequence is that price wars may be observed.

Green and Porter (1984) and Porter (1983a) introduce imperfect monitoring of the actions of the members of the cartel, assuming that outputs are not observable but the (random) market price is. It is worth noting, however, that this does not match exactly the secret price-cutting story because in the Green-Porter model firms are quantity setters and observe a public signal (the price). Furthermore the firms have no private information. Using trigger price strategies, and reversion to Cournot behavior for a certain number of periods (finite or infinite), the authors characterize the sustainable collusive outcomes (typically bounded away from full collusion). In these models, price wars (reversion to Cournot behavior) occur in states of low demand, despite the fact that no defection occurs in equilibrium, precisely to provide incentives to sustain the prescribed outcome. This is how the model works.

Consider a infinitely repeated Cournot market, $t = 0, 1, 2, \ldots$, with n firms producing a homogeneous product facing a random inverse demand in period $t, P(Q_t, \theta_t) = p(Q_t)\theta_t$, where θ_t is a shock, independently and identically distributed across periods with (differentiable) distribution function $F(\cdot)$ with mean 1, and the function $p(\cdot)$ takes nonnegative values. In the model every price has positive density for every profile of feasible outputs. Firm i produces according to the cost function $C_i(\cdot)$ and maximizes expected discounted profits. The firm observes prices but cannot observe θ_t nor the quantities set by rivals. A strategy for firm i is an infinite sequence of functions $\sigma_i = (\sigma_{it})_{t=0}^{\infty}$ such that in period t, $\sigma_{it}(\cdot)$ assigns an output to the sequence of past price observations $\{p_0, \ldots, p_{t-1}\}$. A strategy profile determines then a stochastic process of prices. A strategy profile is a Nash equilibrium if it maximizes expected discounted profits for any firm over all feasible strategies (taking expectations by fixing the candidate strategy profile for all rival firms). Let $\pi_i^e(q)$ denote the expected single-period profits when firms produce the output vector q.

A collusive arrangement $q^* = (q_1^*, \ldots, q_n^*)$, yielding (strictly) higher profits than the one-shot Cournot equilibrium profile q^C, $\pi_i^e(q^*) > \pi_i^e(q^C)$ for any i, can be sustained in the following way: Firm i plays initially q_i^* until the first time that the price p_t goes strictly below a trigger price $\bar{p}$. When this happens, all firms revert to the one-shot Cournot output for $T - 1$ periods, go back to the collusive output afterward, and the process starts all over. The expected present discounted value of firm i when setting "collusive" output q_i while other firms set q_{-i}^* is given by $V_i(q_i, q_{-i}^*) = \pi_i^e(q_i, q_{-i}^*) + (1 - \gamma(q_i, q_{-i}^*)) \cdot \delta V_i(q_i, q_{-i}^*) + \gamma(q_i, q_{-i}^*) \left(\sum_{t=1}^{T-1} \delta^t \pi_i^e(q^C) + \delta^T V_i(q_i, q_{-i}^*) \right)$, where $\gamma(q_i, q_{-i}^*) = F(\bar{p}/p(q_i + \sum_{j \neq i} q_j^*))$ denotes the probability of a reversionary episode. Rearranging terms, we have that V_i equals the value if firms produce at Cournot levels plus the expected discounted gain of collusion:

$$V_i(q_i, q_{-i}^*) = \frac{\pi_i^e(q^C)}{1 - \delta} + \frac{\pi_i^e(q_i, q_{-i}^*) - \pi_i^e(q^C)}{1 - \delta + (\delta - \delta^T)\gamma(q_i, q_{-i}^*)}.$$

Note that if $\gamma = 0$, then $V_i(q_i, q_{-i}^*) = \pi_i^e(q_i, q_{-i}^*)/(1 - \delta)$. A Nash equilibrium is characterized by a triple $(q^*, \bar{p}, T)$ such that $V_i(q^*) \geq V_i(q_i, q_{-i}^*)$ for all q_i and i. No firm will deviate from the punishment phase because q^C is a Nash equilibrium in the one-shot game. The Cournot equilibrium is indeed a trigger price equilibrium.

The first-order condition for firm i in the case in which $T = \infty$ is given by

$$\frac{\partial \pi_i^e(q^*)}{\partial q_i} = \delta \frac{\partial \gamma(q^*)}{\partial q_i} \left(\frac{\pi_i^e(q^*) - \pi_i^e(q^C)}{1 - \delta + \delta\gamma(q^*)} \right).$$

This condition equates the marginal gain from cheating (and increasing output beyond q_i^*) with its discounted marginal cost (the product of the discounted marginal increase in triggering a reversionary episode times the cost of punishment). In general (allowing for the possibility that $T < \infty$), the equation must be fulfilled with an inequality $\leq$ (firm i should not be able to increase its profits by expanding output beyond q_i^*) yielding the incentive compatibility constraint for collusion to be sustained.

Considering a symmetric market and firms trying to enforce a symmetric tacit collusion agreement, the optimal trigger strategy equilibrium is given then by the triplet $(q^*, \bar{p}, T)$ which maximizes $V(q^*)$ subject to the incentive compatibility constraint. This constraint in fact yields the smallest output that is sustainable as a function of $(\bar{p}, T)$. Then V can be optimized with respect to $(\bar{p}, T)$. In principle, a lower trigger price $\bar{p}$ lowers the probability of a reversionary episode but requires a longer punishment length T to sustain a given amount of collusion. Under regularity conditions and in a linear model (see Porter 1983a and exercise 9.7), it is possible to show that provided uncertainty is not too large (and $\delta < 1$), the best sustainable collusive output q^* is (strictly) between the Cournot q^C and the monopoly level q^m and is decreasing with decreases in the amount of uncertainty (and as the variance of the demand noise tends to zero, q^* tends to q^m). With some noise in the demand, we have that $q^* > q^m$ because increasing the output from the joint profit-maximizing level q^m has no first-order effect in the collusive phase and decreases the gains from cheating. There is an incentive for the firms then to reduce the frequency and/or duration of price wars by expanding output beyond q^m. Similarly, at q^C, there is an incentive to decrease output a little bit because this increases the payoff in the cooperative phase with little incentive to deviate (which is zero in the first order, since $\partial \pi_i^e(q^C)/\partial q_i = 0$). When the optimal length of the reversionary period is finite, then as the number of firms increases, the best sustainable output q^* decreases as total output nq^* increases and the optimal trigger price decreases. For n large enough only the Cournot output is sustainable. A related result by Kandori (1992b) shows that when the public outcome (the price) becomes a (strictly) more informative signal about the actions (the outputs) of the players, the set of equilibria strictly expands. In particular, this implies that when firms receive a more precise public signal about the random demand, the possible range of sustainable collusive outputs increases.

Several features of the equilibrium are worth noting. No firm ever defects from the cartel, and therefore so-called price wars happen only to maintain incentives. Periods of low demand trigger price wars, and collusive phases occur at interval of random length in general. The observation of market prices never induces a firm to believe that another firm has cheated. This is because under no circumstances can a firm infer with full probability from the price that another has cheated. The trigger price strategy equilibrium is a Nash equilibrium, and has a perfection property because for any date and history at any point the prescribed strategies (which are based only on public information, i.e., the sequence of past prices) yield a Nash equilibrium from that date on.[13]

The effect of product differentiation on collusion may be reconsidered when there is imperfect monitoring. Raith (1996) considers a differentiated product model with random demand in which there may be secret price cutting but the quantities sold are public information (and the occurrence of price wars is conditioned on this public information). If the products become more differentiated then the demand shocks are less correlated, and it becomes difficult to distinguish between cheating and random demand shocks. This provides a rationale behind the idea (e.g., see Scherer and Ross 1990, ch. 8) that collusion is harder to sustain in the presence of product differentiation.

The analysis is generalized by Abreu, Pearce, and Stacchetti (1986). In the Green-Porter approach punishments more severe than Cournot are not allowed. It can be shown that under mild assumptions and restricting attention to symmetric equilibria, the best collusive scheme involves alternation between two output levels depending on whether the price falls into a reward or punishment region. The approach allows the consideration of general forms of uncertainty also.[14]

Abreu, Milgrom, and Pearce (1991) demonstrate some counterintutitive effects of changes in the frequency of moves and in information lags in supporting collusion when there is imperfect monitoring. For example, reducing the reaction lag, or more frequent information release, may diminish collusion possibilities. The reason is that the quality of the information received by players may depend positively on the length of the observation period. The benefit of a delayed information release is an increase in the precision of the information received.

9.1.4   Collusive Pricing and Fluctuations

Introducing demand uncertainty in a regime of perfect monitoring yields interesting insights into collusive pricing and the cycle.

Rotemberg and Saloner (1986) consider observable (i.i.d.) shifts in demand, and they argue, using a model with constant marginal costs and no capacity constraints, that incentives to cheat in a price-setting supergame are greater during economic booms. The inverse demand faced by the n firms in the market suffers a shock θ_t, $P(Q_t, \theta_t)$, with values on a compact support $[\underline{\theta}, \bar{\theta}]$ and distribution function F. Shocks are independently and identically distributed across periods, and demand increases with θ_t. In period t firms observe the shock before choosing their output.

Let us try to characterize the optimal cartel arrangement. To this effect it is enough to consider reversion (forever) to the Bertrand one-shot equilibrium in case of defection. This provides the most severe possible punishment because it keeps the price equal to marginal cost. The market is stationary given that demand shocks are i.i.d. Denote by $\pi_i^*(\theta)$ the current flow of profits for firm i under the collusive scheme when the demand shock takes the value θ. The flow profits from deviating from the agreement are $n\pi_i^*(\theta)$, given that the defecting firm can undercut the other firms and take the whole market. The incentive compatibility condition to sustain collusion is then

$$\pi_i^*(\theta) + \frac{\delta}{1-\delta} E\pi_i^*(\theta) \geq n\pi_i^*(\theta) \quad \text{or} \quad \frac{\delta}{1-\delta} E\pi_i^*(\theta) \geq (n-1)\pi_i^*(\theta).$$

The left-hand side of the last inequality is independent of θ, while the right-hand side is increasing in θ because so is $\pi_i^*(\theta)$. As a consequence typically in a boom phase full collusion is not sustainable, since the incentives to defect are greater. The maximal sustainable collusion typically equals the fully collusive outcome (yielding for each firm $\pi_i^*(\theta) = \pi^m(Q^m(\theta), \theta)$, where π^m is the per firm monopoly profit) for θ low, and it is somewhtat lower for high θ. In other words, there is a critical θ, say $\hat{\theta}$, above which cooperative profits are fixed at $\pi_i^*(\theta) = \pi^m(Q^m(\hat{\theta}), \hat{\theta})$.[15] As δ decreases or n increases, $\hat{\theta}$ decreases and full collusion is sustainable in a smaller range of states of demand. As usual in markets with perfect monitoring, no punishments are observed in equilibrium. The model therefore predicts that in expansionary periods collusion has to be moderated in order to preserve incentives. This is consistent with the idea that collusion tends to break down with a sudden increase in demand (e.g., when a large order arrives in an industry with fluctuating demand and infrequent orders; see Scherer and Ross 1990, ch. 8).

The cooperative model and variations of it have been used to examine the cyclical behavior of price-cost margins during the course of a business cycle. An important implication of the model in this respect is that price-cost margins may be countercyclical. For example, in a two-state demand situation $(\underline{\theta}, \bar{\theta})$ the price in the low state would be the monopoly price $p^m(\underline{\theta})$, while (unless the discount rate is very low) the price in the high state $\bar{p}$ would be below the monopoly price $p^m(\bar{\theta})$. It is possible then that $p^m(\underline{\theta}) > \bar{p}$.[16] The empirical literature is not conclusive on the issue. Rotemberg and Saloner (1986) present some evidence about the cement industry in support of their theory (i.e., that the rate of growth of GNP is negatively related to the rate of growth of cement prices),[17] but the traditional idea is that recessions induce price cutting, particularly when capacity utilization is low (see Scherer and Ross 1990, ch. 8, Domowitz, Hubbard, and Petersen 1986, and Suslow 1988 for empirical support of this view).[18]

Ellison (1994) reviewed the functioning of the Joint Executive Committee railroad cartel of the 1880s and found that price wars did occur as predicted by the Green-Porter model (although, in assuming demand to be autocorrelated, he obtained price levels that were much closer to monopoly levels than those estimated by Porter 1983b). However, Ellison did not find data to support the Rotemberg-Saloner theory (after modifying appropriately the theory to encompass imperfect observability). The notable difference is that in the Green-Porter model unanticipated low demand causes a price war episode while in the Rotemberg-Saloner model price wars are more likely when demand is high (and expected to decline).

Nevertheless, the assumptions underlying the Rotemberg-Saloner model are very strong, and alternative assumptions deliver different results. With increasing marginal costs or capacity constraints (which tend to be binding in periods of high demand), we could obtain the result that collusion tends to decrease as demand decreases (e.g., in the case of repeated capacity and price choices if the demand uncertainty is revealed after the capacity choice but before the price selection; see Staiger and Wolak 1992). When quantities are the strategic variables, it is no longer the case that an increase in demand increases the incentive to deviate (e.g., in the case of constant elasticity of demand and constant marginal costs); although there exist examples in which this is the case (with linear demand and quadratic costs.) When demand is positively autocorrelated, a high demand today indicates a high demand tomorrow, and therefore the incentive to cheat is lower. In this context it can be shown that the point in the cycle at which it is most difficult to collude is when demand is falling (see Haltinwanger and Harrington 1991 for a model with deterministic demand fluctuations). However, countercyclical pricing may still occur for some values of the discount factor (see also Kandori 1991 for a model with random fluctuations).[19]

Another debated issue is whether in an uncertain environment concentrated markets are more conducive to price rigidity. There is some empirical evidence in favor of this hypothesis (Carlton 1989 and Scherer and Ross 1990). An informal explanation is that rigid prices, nonresponsive to cost shocks, for example, help to sustain collusion because they minimize the risk of price wars being triggered.[20] Athey, Bagwell, and Sanchirico (1998) formalize the intuition in a repeated price competition model in which firms receive i.i.d., privately observed cost shocks in every period and prices are perfectly observable. The model can be seen as a dynamic extension of the static Bayesian Bertrand competition model with homogeneous product (see section 8.1.1). A rigid price scheme presents the following trade-off: On the positive side, any deviation is immediately detected as a violation of the collusive agreement. On the negative side, an efficiency cost is paid in that firms share the market despite the fact that they have different costs. A price scheme which is separating is efficient (the lowest-cost firms get to supply the market), but it carries an informational cost because higher-cost firms have to be prevented from posing as low-cost firms and set low prices. A consequence is that if firms are to improve on the static Bayesian Bertrand equilibrium, they have to introduce some price rigidity. In fact the authors show that if demand is inelastic and firms are sufficiently patient, in the optimal collusive scheme no price wars on the equilibrium path are needed. Furthermore, if the distribution of cost types is log-concave, firms choose the reservation price of consumers independent of their cost realizations.[21]

9.1.5   Private Information, Communication, and Collusion

In the Stigler (1964) secret price-cutting story, firm i observes its own sales and controls the price charged for its product but does not observe the prices or the sales of rival firms. This means that firm i receives a private signal (its sales level) which gives information about the prices set by other firms. A firm may have low sales because of an adverse demand shock or because rivals are cheating on the price agreement by secretly cutting prices. The problem in enforcing collusion under these circumstances is that there is no public history on which to base punishments, and therefore firms typically will hold different beliefs. Secret price cutting is an instance of a repeated game with imperfect monitoring and privately observed signals. Only recently progress has been made on the front where firms discount the future, by allowing the firms to communicate (exchanging public messages) at the end of each period (Compte 1998; Kandori and Matsushima 1998).

Communication restores a public history on which to base a collusive scheme. It is possible to construct equilibria in which firms voluntarily reveal their private information (in a context in which communication entails no explicit cost and therefore is cheap talk; see section 8.4.3) in order to enforce desired outcomes. Whenever there are at least three firms and it is possible to distinguish between the deviations of the different firms, collusion can be sustained for large enough discount factors (actually, a folk theorem result holds) with firms communicating seriously every period. This is accomplished by making the future payoff of every firm independent of its communication and therefore providing a (weak) incentive to tell the truth. A firm suspected of having deviated has its future payoff "transferred" to the other players. Strict incentives to reveal information truthfully are possible if private signals are correlated. In the duopoly case or when the deviations of a player can be distinguished from the deviations of other players, as in Abreu, Milgrom, and Pearce (1991), delay in the revelation of firms' observations can increase the efficiency of enforcement of collusive outcomes. The folk theorem result now holds if the private signals of firms are independent conditional on any given price vector, as the discount factor tends to one and as the interval of delay of private information tends to infinity. Collusion could be maintained through infrequent communication.

Clearly, communication is essential to sustaining collusion. This is reflected in antitrust case studies of firms that exchanged private information on prices and quantities, in particular, which facilitated collusion. This increases the probability of secret price-cut detection. Disclosure of private information was the basis of the "open price policy" advocated by A. J. Eddy (1912) for trade associations. This practice of trade associations was ended by the U.S. Department of Justice in the late 1930s and early 1940s.[22]

Information sharing about pricing or production plans has also been under discussion for its effect on competition. Communication is important in signaling players' intentions. For example, Farrell (1987) examines how communication can help two potential entrants to coordinate entry into a natural monopoly industry. The problem for the firms is to break their ex ante symmetric roles (the payoff structure is similar to the battle of the sexes game in which lack of coordination when both firms enter or stay out at the same time is penalized). Partial coordination, but not total if there is conflict, may be achieved provided that the message of a player is "credible" if it would be optimal for the player to behave according to the sent message given that the rivals use a best response to his announced action. More precisely, the firms take the first pair of announcements which, if actually played, would constitute an equilibrium, to be true. (See exercise 9.11.)

There is some experimental evidence that cheap talk can help co-ordinate expectations on collusive equilibria in repeated oligopoly games (see Friedman 1967; Daughety and Forsythe 1987a, b). However, there is also evidence that the effect is transitory (Holt and Davis 1990).[23] The conclusions from the experimental literature are dependent on whether communication is one or two sided and on whether desirable outcomes require "symmetry breaking" by the players (as in the entry game mentioned above).[24] If symmetry breaking is required, then one-sided communication is much more effective than simultaneous exchange. Otherwise, communication allows players to coordinate on more efficient equilibria, and best results are obtained with two-sided exchange.[25] These results accord with the antitrust idea that communication reduces firms' strategic uncertainty.

The research on the effect of communication on collusion is not yet conclusive. In repeated games, for instance, in the presence of imperfect monitoring and privately observed signals, it is not known whether full collusion is possible without communication or whether communication is even needed for collusion. However, in general, the presumption is that communication abets collusion.

9.1.6   Discussion

The theory of repeated games has been useful in explaining the sustainability of collusion but at the cost of expanding enormously the set of equilibria (with the folk theorem type results). Indeed, repeated games compound the multiplicity problem in oligopoly. It may be argued that if firms can communicate before the play of the game they will tend to choose a Pareto optimal equilibrium, but still this leaves many equilibria and is open to criticism. Other considerations like symmetry and focal points have been proposed also as a way around the problem (see the discussion in section 2.1), and some experimental evidence has shown the beneficial effects of communication in selecting among multiple equilibria (see section 1.5). Nevertheless, the issue is far from being settled.

Increasing the number of players does not guarantee a reduction in the multiplicity of equilibria in a repeated game. However, it is widely thought that collusion tends to break down when many players are involved. This was the opinion of Chamberlin, for example. This view is supported in several of the results presented above (and by the empirical literature which finds the breakdown of collusion with the entry of 5 to 10 firms). Indeed, when there are no capacity constraints, the critical discount factor above which collusion is possible has been shown to increase with the number of firms. Similarly, with imperfect monitoring and demand uncertainty, increasing the number of firms will diminish or even eliminate the collusive potential considering optimal trigger price equilibria. In the limit (as the number of firms tends to infinity) no collusion is sustainable in general provided that individual deviations cannot be detected. This is represented by a repeated Cournot game, finitely repeated or infinitely repeated with discounting, with a continuum of firms. Then, if individual deviations are not observable, the only possible equilibrium plays of the repeated game are sequences of one-shot Cournot equilibrium plays. The reason is that the output of a single firm cannot influence the price, and therefore any firm can free-ride on the cartel price without being discovered.[26]

Furthermore it may be argued that even SPEs are not "credible" or plausible, since when a defection has been discovered, "bygones are bygones," and firms have the incentive to renegotiate instead of following the punishment strategies prescribed by a SPE. A requirement may be added that there must not be incentives to renegotiate at any point in the development of the game. This reduces somewhat the multiplicity of equilibria by limiting the possible threats.[27]

Another feature that is somewhat disturbing in supergame analysis is the "complex" bootstrap property of the strategies used. Given that there are no real linkages between periods, the only reason that a firm pays attention to past history is because its rivals do so. In other words, if we were to restrict attention to "simple" strategies based on payoff-relevant variables (the Markov restriction studied in the next section), then only one-shot noncooperative equilibria would be sustained.

9.2 Dynamic Pricing and Commitment

The multiplicity of equilibria in the repeated game structure carries over to more fully dynamic games, where there are linkages between the periods. Decisions about long-run variables, typically investment decisions, affect directly future demand and costs conditions but also decisions about short-term variables just like prices and quantities affect future competition in the presence of adjustment costs. The pure repeated game framework, where periods are independent and history matters only because firms threaten it to matter, is a useful abstraction to analyze collusion possibilities, but it is not suitable to study commitment issues.

In full-fledged dynamic games, it has been proposed that one should restrict attention to strategies that depend only on state (payoff-relevant) variables of the industry. This gives rise to the concept of Markov strategy, a strategy that depends only on (state) variables that condense the direct effect of the past on the current payoff. For example, in the simple two-stage investment-pricing game which we analyzed in section 7.4.3, the investment variable is a state variable that conditions pricing at the second stage. More generally consider a dynamic game in which the payoff to player i in period t is given by $\pi_i^t(a^t, x^t)$, where a^t is the vector of current actions of the players and x^t a vector of state variables. The action space in any period can be affected also by the current state of the system. The state x^t evolves according to $x^t = f^t(a^{t-1}, x^{t-1})$, and players maximize the discounted sum of period profits. In this context it should be obvious that, by construction, the only payoff-relevant aspect of history is embodied in the state, and therefore a Markov strategy for player i in period t should depend only on the current state of the system x^t.

Markov strategies can be identified with "closed-loop no-memory" or "feedback" strategies in the terminology of difference/differential game theory. In a difference/differential game, state variables and the law of their evolution are given in the description of the game as stated above (see section 9.2.3 below for continuous time games; see also Basar and Olsder 1982).

In dynamic games the payoff-relevant states are generally not given exogenously. Fortunately, for games with observable actions (where at any period t the sequence of actions chosen by the players before t is known to everyone), Markov strategies can be defined in a consistent way (Maskin and Tirole 1997). The idea is that if two histories lead to subgames that are strategically equivalent (in terms of actions spaces available to the players from then on and preferences over future actions), then they should be put in the same equivalence class defining a state of the system. A Markov strategy depends only on the state of the system, and a Markov perfect equilibrium (MPE) is a subgame-perfect equilibrium in Markov strategies. In other words, an MPE is a set of strategies that is optimal for any firm, and for any state of the system, given the strategies of the rivals.[28] An MPE corresponds to a "closed-loop no-memory" or "feedback" equilibrium in the difference/differential game jargon.

The state-space approach rules out the bootstrapping typical of repeated games and allows the analysis to concentrate on the commitment issues at stake. The concept that bygones are bygones is embodied in the Markov restriction by lumping together all subgames that are strategically equivalent. This allows the analysis to isolate the effect of the state variables on pricing behavior. Markov strategies have the advantage of being "simple." In fact it can be shown that players use them in a learning context in which it is costly to increase the complexity of a strategy (Maskin and Tirole 1997). This simplicity implies that the Markov restriction proves useful when estimating or simulating dynamic models.[29] An added benefit of the Markov approach is that by eliminating conditioning on not directly payoff-relevant history, it helps in reducing—but by no means eliminates—the multiplicity of equilibria problem in dynamic games.

In this section we study pricing games both in discrete and continuous time, testing the ideas developed in the simple two-stage models. A basic issue is how commitment possibilities affect dynamic pricing and how, and whether, the character of static competition (strategic substitutability or complementarity) has an intertemporal translation. Section 9.2.1 covers commitment in simple alternating move games displaying a variety of dynamic behavior and presents more formally the concept of MPE. Section 9.2.2 provides a taxonomy of strategic behavior in the presence of adjustment costs, extending the analysis of section 7.4.3. Section 9.2.3 contains an introduction to differential games and a complete characterization of duopolistic competition in the linear-quadratic case.

9.2.1 Alternating Move Duopoly Games

Maskin and Tirole (1987, 1988) studied alternating move price and quantity games following an early model by Cyert and DeGroot (1970). For simple contexts (linear demand, constant marginal costs, and homogeneous products) they showed the existence of a unique (subgame-perfect) equilibrium in the quantity game, but they found multiple equilibria in the pricing game. In the quantity game the equilibrium is more competitive than a Cournot equilibrium. Its competitiveness is due to intertemporal strategic substitutability which yields downward-sloping dynamic reaction functions. In the pricing game they find multiple equilibria, including equilibria of the kinked demand curve type and cycles à la Edgeworth. For sufficiently low discount rates, it turns out that the only equilibrium that is robust to renegotiation attempts is a kinked demand curve price at the monopoly level. The root of the multiplicity of equilibria lies in the lack of monotonicity of dynamic reaction functions with price competition (intertemporal strategic substitutability holds for some price pairs while intertemporal strategic complementarity holds for others). Let us examine the model and results with more detail.[30]

Consider a duopoly game in which the payoff to firm i, $i = 1, 2$, is $\pi_i(a_1, a_2)$ and the action set available to the firm is a compact interval. Firms take turns in moving, and the action of firm i, to be interpreted as price or quantity, for example, is fixed for one period. Firms interact repeatedly, $t = 0, 1, 2, \ldots$, with an infinite horizon with firm 1 moving in the odd periods ($t = 1, 3, \ldots$) and firm 2 in the even periods ($t = 0, 2, \ldots$). The state variable for firm i is therefore the action taken in the previous period by firm j. A (pure) Markov strategy for firm i is a function $R_i(\cdot)$ that maps the past action of firm j into an action for firm i. This is truly a dynamic reaction function in contrast with the best-response functions derived in the static games considered in chapters 2 through 6 (in which best-response functions are useful in finding the equilibria and characterizing their stability properties).

Suppose that firms discount the future according to a discount factor δ. A Markov perfect equilibrium (MPE) is a pair of dynamic reaction functions $(R_1(\cdot), R_2(\cdot))$ such that for any state a firm maximizes its present discounted profits given the strategy of the rival. Using a dynamic programming approach, we have that the pair $(R_1(\cdot), R_2(\cdot))$ is an MPE if and only if there exist value functions $(V_1(\cdot), V_2(\cdot))$ such that

$$V_1(a_2) = \max_x \{\pi_1(x, a_2) + \delta[\pi_1(x, R_2(x)) + \delta V_1(R_2(x))]\}, \quad \text{with}$$

$$R_2(a_1) \in \arg\max_y \{\pi_2(a_1, y) + \delta[\pi_2(R_1(y), y) + \delta V_2(R_1(y))]\},$$

and similarly for firm 2. That is, given the state variable a_2 (the current action of firm 2) for firm 1, $V_1(a_2)$ gives the present discounted profits when it is the turn of firm 1 to move and both firms use the dynamic reaction functions $(R_1(\cdot), R_2(\cdot))$.[31]

It is worth noting that the dynamics at an MPE are identical to a sequential Cournot tatônnement (with player 2 moving first) replacing the static best-response functions with the dynamic reaction functions $(R_1(\cdot), R_2(\cdot))$. The dynamics at an MPE are also similar to the simultaneous Cournot tatônnement with the difference that at the "initial condition" at the MPE firm 1 must be at its reaction curve, while at a Cournot tatônnement initial conditions are unrestricted.[32]

It follows easily that when MPE dynamic reaction functions exist, they will be monotone increasing (decreasing) if the underlying one-shot simultaneous move game is strictly supermodular (submodular). Indeed, according to theorem 2.3 (and 2.4), if the payoff function $g_2(a_1, y) \equiv \pi_2(a_1, y) + \delta[\pi_2(R_1(y), y) + \delta V_2(R_1(y))]$ has strictly increasing differences in (a_1, y), then the set of maximizers of $g_2(a_1, y)$ with respect to y is strongly increasing in a_1. This means that any selection $R_2(\cdot)$ of the set of maximizers will be increasing. It is immediate that $g_2(a_1, y)$ has strictly increasing differences in (a_1, y) if and only if the same is true for $\pi_2(a_1, y)$ (indeed, $\pi_2(R_1(y), y) + \delta V_2(R_1(y))$ is independent of a_1). If $g_2(a_1, y)$ has strictly decreasing differences in (a_1, y), then any selection $R_2(\cdot)$ will be decreasing. If the profit function is smooth, then the payoffs display strictly increasing (decreasing) differences if $\partial^2 \pi_i / \partial a_i \partial a_j > (<) 0, j \neq i$.

A consequence of the monotonicity of the dynamic reaction functions is that the actions of the firms converge as t tends to infinity to $(R_1(\hat{a}_2), \hat{a}_2)$, where $\hat{a}_2$ is a fixed point of the composite reaction function map: $R_2 \circ R_1$. (Note that this map is increasing whenever the dynamic reaction functions are both increasing or decreasing; see exercise 2.11 and Dana and Montrucchio 1986.) These authors also show that if the payoff to each firm is continuous and strictly concave (in own action), if the dynamic MPE reaction functions exist and are continuous, and if the associate value functions are upper semicontinuous, then R_i tends to the static best reply r_i as the discount factor δ tends to zero.[33]

It is also possible to characterize differentiable (and strictly monotone) dynamic MPE reaction functions from the FOC of the optimization problem in the dynamic programming equations (when payoffs are differentiable and smooth equilibria exist). Some algebra yields then an implicit expression for the slope of the dynamic reaction function of firm 2,

$$\frac{dR_2}{da_1} = \frac{-(\partial \pi_1(a_1, R_1^{-1}(a_1)/\partial a_1)) - \delta(\partial \pi_1(a_1, R_2(a_1)/\partial a_1))}{\delta(\partial \pi_1(a_1, R_2(a_1)/\partial a_2)) + \delta^2(\partial \pi_1(R_1(R_2(a_1)), R_2(a_1)/\partial a_2))},$$

and a similar equation for the slope of R_1.

Let us consider two linear duopoly examples: Cournot with homogeneous products, with inverse demand $p = \alpha - Q$, and Bertrand with differentiated products, with demand for product i, $q_i = a - bp_i + cp_j, i \neq j$. We can assume, for simplicity, that firms can produce at zero cost. It can be shown that for any δ there is a unique linear MPE that is symmetric and (globally) stable and that the steady state action is increasing in δ and equals the static Nash equilibrium when $\delta = 0$. (See Maskin and Tirole 1987 for the Cournot case and exercise 9.12 for the Bertrand case.)

In the Cournot case the MPE (symmetric) dynamic reaction function is given by $R(q_j) = A - Bq_j$, where $A = (1 + B)\alpha/(3 - \delta B)$ and B is the root in the interval $(0, \frac{1}{2})$ of the equation $\delta^2 B^4 + 2\delta B^2 - 2(1 + \delta)B + 1 = 0$. The steady state output is $A/(1 + B) = \alpha/(3 - \delta B)$, is increasing in δ, and equals the Cournot output $\alpha/3$ when $\delta = 0$.

In the Bertrand case, the dynamic reaction function is given by $R(p_j) = D + Ep_j$, where $D = (1 - E)a/(2b - (1 + \delta E)c)$ and E is the root in the interval $(0, \frac{1}{2})$ of the equation $\delta^2 E^4 + 2\delta E^2 - 2(1 + \delta)bc^{-1}E + 1 = 0$. The steady state price is $D/(1 - E) = a/(2b - (1 + \delta E)c)$, is also increasing in δ, and equals the Bertrand price $a/(2b - c)$ when $\delta = 0$.

This is how to find the unique linear MPE. First, we observe that the necessary conditions of the optimization problem (summarized above by the implicit expressions for dR_2/da_1 and dR_1/da_2) are sufficient when the payoffs are quadratic and the dynamic reaction functions monotone (both downward or both upward sloping). Then the coefficients of the linear strategy are found by substituting the posited linear strategy in the equations for the slopes dR_2/da_1 and dR_1/da_2. One of the roots of the equation determining the slope of the dynamic reaction function is discarded because it leads to unstable behavior inconsistent with an MPE. The stable root yields slopes strictly less than one, and therefore the dynamic process determined by $(R_1(\cdot), R_2(\cdot))$ is stable (as in a Cournot tatônnement; see section 2.6.2).

If we were to consider games with a finite horizon (e.g., Cyert and DeGroot 1970), we would see immediately, using backward induction, that they have a unique subgame-perfect equilibrium (and therefore it has to be an MPE because the game admits an MPE).[34] With some more work we can show also that the SPE dynamic reaction functions of the finite horizon (linear) game converge (uniformly) to their infinite horizon counterpart. (See exercise 9.12 for the differentiated product case.)

With a quadratic adjustment cost of production and quantity competition, as the adjustment cost parameter grows, the MPE steady state output tends to the Cournot output. Adjustment costs in this case lessen rivalry. Indeed, a higher adjustment cost means that a firm will respond less aggressively to a decrease of output by the rival. It is not difficult to see then that when the adjustment cost is very high, it is very costly to move away from the Cournot output.

In the Cournot case the strategic incentives for a firm are to increase its output to reduce the output of the rival, and in the Bertrand case (with product differentiation) to increase price to induce the rival to be softer in pricing. Thus, in the Cournot (Bertrand) case, the static strategic substitutability (complementarity) translates into intertemporal strategic substitutability (complementarity). In other words, in the Cournot (Bertrand) case, both static and dynamic reaction functions are downward (upward) sloping. An increase in the weight firms put into the future (a larger δ) increases the strategic incentives with the result of a higher output (price) in the Cournot (Bertrand) market. In any case the equilibrium action is larger than the static equilibrium when $\delta > 0$.

When Maskin and Tirole (1988b) consider Bertrand competition in a homogeneous product duopoly market (with constant marginal cost) in which firms can choose from a finite price grid, they find multiple equilibria, including equilibria of the "kinked demand curve" type and price cycles.

For sufficiently high discount factor, it turns out that the only equilibrium that is robust to renegotiation attempts is a kinked demand curve price at the monopoly level. (An MPE is renegotiation-proof if at any price there is no other MPE that dominates it in the Pareto sense.) The strategies at this kinked demand type equilibrium are as follows: The steady state is the monopoly price. Starting at this price, if a firm raises its price, the other firm does not follow, but if the firm undercuts the monopoly price and sets $p > \underline{p}$, for some appropriate $\underline{p} > 0$, the rival responds by setting a price equal to p engages in a price war). On the other hand, if the price is below (or equal to) $\underline{p}$, the response is to raise the price to the monopoly price. The defined dynamic reaction functions are the only ones that yield average profits close to the monopoly outcome for high-discount factors. This property implies that this is the unique (symmetric) renegotiation-proof MPE for δ close to 1. Indeed, starting at any price, we cannot find any other MPE that will yield Pareto superior profits to the firms. The implied price dynamics at this MPE are somewhat different from the original kinked demand curve version of Sweezy (1939) where price cuts are matched.[35] The alternating move price game with homogeneous products provides an explanation of collusive pricing which is different from the repeated game story. In fact, under the renegotiation-proofness restriction, collusion is the only (symmetric) equilibrium outcome of the dynamic pricing game.[36]

There are also equilibria in which prices cycle. For example, it is possible to construct MPE where firms undercut each other until the competitive price is reached, then firms randomize and with some probability jump to a high price, and then another price war episode starts. Again, each firm would like the rival to be the firm that raises the price first. Equilibrium price cycles exist for a large enough discount factor and a fine grid of possible prices. Edgeworth also considered the possibility of cycles with price competition in his model with capacity constraints (where pure-strategy equilibria need not exist; see section 5.2).[37] The cycles in the Maskin-Tirole model are obtained without capacity limits.

At the root of the multiplicity of equilibria in these price games lies the lack of monotonicity of the dynamic reaction functions in the homogeneous product market. This happens because with a homogeneous product the marginal profit of a firm is sometimes increasing and some other times decreasing depending on the price charged by the rival. For example, if the rival sets a (strictly) lower price than firm i, then firm i's marginal profit (of changing its price) is zero, and if the rival sets a (strictly) larger price, then firm i's marginal profit is positive (provided that its price is below the monopoly price). However, if the prices of both firms are equal, the marginal profit is negative. In other words, the underlying static duopoly game is neither submodular nor supermodular. This contrasts with the Cournot or with the Bertrand case with product differentiation in which the monotonicity of dynamic reaction functions yields a unique linear equilibrium.

In the MPE of the alternating move price duopoly games, profits are bounded away from the competitive level because the average price is bounded away from the competitive level. Thus, in contrast to the outcome with the infinitely repeated game, where with little discounting we have the folk theorem, the multiplicity of equilibria is somewhat bounded in the alternating move game.

The effect of the discount rate on the competitiveness of the market depends on the character of the underlying static game. For Cournot competition (Bertrand with product differentiation) a larger δ yields a more (less) competitive outcome because it exacerbates the strategic incentives of a firm to reduce (increase) the output (price) of the rival. In the price game with homogeneous products a larger discount may make it possible to support collusive pricing with a kinked demand equilibrium. In any case the mechanism of δ influence is different from the supergame where the competition mode would affect only the critical δ above which collusion is sustainable.

The alternating move game provides very interesting insights but may be criticized for being somewhat artificial (although some progress has been made in endogenizing the timing of the moves of firms).[38] We turn now to dynamic games with simultaneous moves at every stage.

9.2.2   A Taxonomy of Strategic Behavior with Adjustment Costs

A taxonomy of strategic incentives in dynamic games can be obtained by extending the one developed for two-stage games (see section 7.4.3). This is done by Lapham and Ware (1994) in analyzing the MPE of the discrete time infinite horizon version of the adjustment cost model considered in section 7.4.3 (and exercise 7.11). The exercise provides a robustness test of the insights derived in two-stage models with respect to the steady states of the corresponding infinite horizon model.

Consider an infinite horizon linear-quadratic duopoly game in which in each period firms move simultaneously, the actions taken in the past are observable and firms discount the future with factor δ. The action vector in period t is given by $x^t = (x_1^t, x_2^t)$, with x_i^t denoting the action of player i in period t. Let $x = (x_1, x_2)$ denote the current vector of actions and $y = (y_1, y_2)$ the choices made in the past period. The one-period payoff to firm i is given by $G_i(x, y) = \pi_i(x) + \lambda_i F_i(x, y)$. The function π_i yields the current profit in the period and is assumed to be quadratic. The function $F_i(x, y) = -(f_i(x) - f_i(y))^2$ determines the adjustment cost in going from past (y) to current actions (x), and f_i is assumed to be linear. We have that $F_i(x, x) = 0$, $i = 1, 2$; that is, when actions are not changed, there is no adjustment cost. The parameter λ_i determines the size of the adjustment cost. When $\lambda_i = 0$, the game is just a repeated game. The vector y is the state variable.

Our aim is to characterize the MPE of the infinitely repeated game when the adjustment costs are small and firms discount the future according to the factor δ. It is known that in a linear-quadratic discrete time finite horizon dynamic game, there is a unique SPE (and it is an MPE), and the equilibrium strategies are linear (Kydland 1975). In our infinite horizon game it is possible to show that in a neighborhood of $\lambda_i = 0, i = 1, 2$, there exist linear MPE and that these equilibria are continuous functions of the adjustment parameters λ_i. This is the way to check it.

The value function associated to the dynamic programming problem of firm i is given by $V_i(y) = \max_{x_i} \{G_i(x, y) + \delta V_i(x)\}$. Positing linear strategies $x(y)$ and quadratic value functions, the FOC of the above problem, $\partial G_i/\partial x_i + \delta(\partial V_i/\partial x_i) = 0$, $i = 1, 2$, are linear and can be solved for a (linear) contemporaneous Nash equilibrium $x^*(y)$. Plugging back the solution in the value functions and differentiating with respect to the state variables y, we obtain expressions that can be equated with the posited derivatives of the value function. Identifying coefficients this yields (in this case) ten nonlinear equations in the ten unknown parameters involved in the derivatives of the (candidate) quadratic value functions. When $\lambda_i = 0$, $i = 1, 2$, the solution is the repeated Nash equilibrium. However, the Jacobian of the nonlinear system of equations is nonsingular when evaluated at $\lambda_i = 0$, $i = 1, 2$, and therefore a solution exists in a neighborhood of $\lambda_i = 0$, $i = 1, 2$. Indeed, the coefficients of the derivative of the value functions are continuously differentiable functions of λ_i, $i = 1, 2$ in a neighborhood of $\lambda_i = 0$, $i = 1, 2$.

At the steady state, $x = y = \bar{x}$, the adjustment cost is zero and the valuation for firm i is $\bar{V}_i = \pi_i(\bar{x})/(1 - \delta)$. In a neighborhood of $\lambda_i = 0$, $i = 1, 2$, a steady state MPE will exist and will be continuously differentiable with respect to λ_1 and λ_2.

We will consider the cases of symmetric and asymmetric commitment capacities, $\lambda_1 = \lambda_2 = \lambda$, and $\lambda_1 > 0$ and $\lambda_2 = 0$, respectively, to provide a taxonomy of strategic behavior at MPE for λ small. Strategic incentives will be given by the derivative (evaluated at $\lambda = 0$) of the steady state equilibrium levels with respect to λ in the symmetric case and with respect to λ_1 in the asymmetric one.

Consider the asymmetric case first. It is possible to show that

$$\frac{\partial \bar{x}_1}{\partial \lambda_1} = -\delta \left[\frac{\partial^2 \pi_1}{(\partial x_1)^2} \right]^2 \frac{\partial^2 \pi_2}{\partial x_1 \partial x_2} \frac{\partial \pi_1}{\partial x_2} \left(\frac{\partial^2 F_1}{\partial x_1 \partial y_1} + \frac{\partial^2 F_1}{\partial x_1 \partial y_2} \right) \bigg/ D^2, \quad \text{and}$$

$$\frac{\partial \bar{x}_2}{\partial \lambda_1} = \delta \frac{\partial \pi_1}{\partial x_2} \left[\left(\frac{\partial^2 \pi_1}{\partial x_1 \partial x_2} \right)^2 \frac{\partial^2 F_1}{\partial x_1 \partial y_1} + \left(\frac{\partial^2 \pi_1}{(\partial x_1)^2} \right)^2 \frac{\partial^2 F_1}{\partial x_1 \partial y_2} \right] \bigg/ D^2,$$

where

$$D = \frac{\partial^2 \pi_2}{(\partial x_2)^2} \frac{\partial^2 \pi_1}{(\partial x_1)^2} - \frac{\partial^2 \pi_1}{\partial x_1 \partial x_2} \frac{\partial^2 \pi_2}{\partial x_1 \partial x_2} > 0$$

(this is just the static equilibrium stability condition; see chapter 4).[39]

Strategic behavior, as in the two-stage case, will depend on whether competition is of the strategic complements, $\partial^2 \pi_2 / \partial x_1 \partial x_2 > 0$, or substitutes, $\partial^2 \pi_2 / \partial x_1 \partial x_2 < 0$, variety and to whether "investment" makes firm 1 tough, $(\partial \pi_1 / \partial x_2)[(\partial^2 F_1 / \partial x_1 \partial y_1) + (\partial^2 F_1 / \partial x_1 \partial y_2)] < 0$, or soft, $(\partial \pi_1 / \partial x_2)[(\partial^2 F_1 / \partial x_1 \partial y_1) + (\partial^2 F_1 / \partial x_1 \partial y_2)] > 0$. "Investment" is to be understood here as the change in the state variables. The term $\partial^2 F_1 / \partial x_1 \partial y_1$ reflects the effect of y_1 on the marginal cost of changing the action x_1. Investment by firm 1 makes firm 1 tough if $(\partial \pi_1 / \partial x_2)(\partial^2 F_1 / \partial x_1 \partial y_1) < 0$. The term $\partial^2 F_1 / \partial x_1 \partial y_2$ reflects the effect of the change in the rival's position y_2 on the marginal cost of changing action x_1. If this term is not zero, the action of player 2 affects also the incentives of player 1. Investment by firm 2 makes firm 1 tough if $\partial \pi_1 / \partial x_2)(\partial^2 F_1 / \partial x_1 \partial y_2) < 0$.

We can classify strategic behavior as in the simple two-stage game considered in table 7.1, section 7.4.3. When $\partial \bar{x}_1 / \partial \lambda_1 > 0$, there is an incentive to overinvest, and this occurs with strategic substitutes (complements) when investment makes player 1 tough (soft). When $\partial \bar{x}_1 / \partial \lambda_1 < 0$, there is an incentive to underinvest, and this occurs with strategic substitutes (complements) when investment makes player 1 soft (tough). For firm 2 a similar classification is possible, but now the character of competition (strategic substitutes or complements) is not relevant.

The effect on the steady state valuation of each player is straightforward:

$$\frac{\partial \bar{V}_i}{\partial \lambda_1} = \frac{1}{1-\delta} \frac{\partial \pi_i}{\partial \bar{x}_j} \frac{\partial \bar{x}_j}{\partial \lambda_1}, \qquad i \neq j,$$

with all derivatives evaluated at $\lambda = 0$. As usual, what matters is the effect on the (steady state) action of the rival and how the latter affects the profits of the firm.

In the symmetric case we have that $\lambda_1 = \lambda_2 = \lambda$, and we perform a comparative static analysis on λ. It is possible to show that for $i = 1, 2$,

$$\frac{\partial \bar{x}_i}{\partial \lambda} = -\delta \left[\frac{\partial^2 \pi_i}{(\partial x_i)^2} - \frac{\partial^2 \pi_i}{\partial x_i \partial x_j} \right] \frac{\partial \pi_j}{\partial x_i} \left[\frac{\partial^2 \pi_i}{\partial x_i \partial x_j} \frac{\partial^2 F_j}{\partial x_j \partial y_j} - \frac{\partial^2 \pi_i}{(\partial x_i)^2} \frac{\partial^2 F_j}{\partial x_j \partial y_i} \right] / D^2,$$

where D is as before. In consequence

$$\text{sign} \left\{ \frac{\partial \bar{x}_i}{\partial \lambda} \right\} = \text{sign} \left\{ \frac{\partial \pi_j}{\partial x_i} \left(\frac{\partial^2 \pi_i}{\partial x_i \partial x_j} \frac{\partial^2 F_j}{\partial x_j \partial y_j} - \frac{\partial^2 \pi_i}{(\partial x_i)^2} \frac{\partial^2 F_j}{\partial x_j \partial y_i} \right) \right\}.$$

Similarly as before, we have that

$$\frac{\partial \bar{V}_i}{\partial \lambda} = \frac{1}{1-\delta} \frac{\partial \pi_i}{\partial \bar{x}_j} \frac{\partial \bar{x}_j}{\partial \lambda}, \qquad i \neq j,$$

with all derivatives evaluated at $\lambda = 0$.

We can illustrate the same results with linear Cournot and Bertrand models by introducing production or price adjustment costs. If we add production adjustment costs, we have that $F_i(q_i, \hat{q}_i) = -(q_i - \hat{q}_i)^2$, where $\hat{q}_i$ is firm i's last period output. If we add price adjustment costs, we have that $F_i(p_i, \hat{p}_i) = -(p_i - \hat{p}_i)^2$, where $\hat{p}_i$ is

Table 9.1
Asymmetric adjustment costs ($\lambda_1 > 0, \lambda_2 = 0$)

	Quantity	Price
Cournot	$\dfrac{\partial \bar{q}_1}{\partial \lambda_1} > 0$	$\dfrac{\partial \bar{q}_1}{\partial \lambda_1} > 0$
	$\dfrac{\partial \bar{q}_2}{\partial \lambda_1} < 0$	$\dfrac{\partial \bar{q}_2}{\partial \lambda_1} < 0$
Bertrand	$\dfrac{\partial \bar{p}_1}{\partial \lambda_1} > 0$	$\dfrac{\partial \bar{p}_1}{\partial \lambda_1} > 0$
	$\dfrac{\partial \bar{p}_2}{\partial \lambda_1} > 0$	$\dfrac{\partial \bar{p}_2}{\partial \lambda_1} > 0$

Table 9.2
Symmetric adjustment costs ($\lambda_1 = \lambda_2 = \lambda$)

	Quantity	Price
Cournot	$\dfrac{\partial \bar{q}_i}{\partial \lambda} > 0$	$\dfrac{\partial \bar{q}_i}{\partial \lambda} < 0$
Bertrand	$\dfrac{\partial \bar{p}_i}{\partial \lambda} < 0$	$\dfrac{\partial \bar{p}_i}{\partial \lambda} > 0$

firm i's last period's price (if the product is homogeneous, then $p_i = p_j = p$). Tables 9.1 and 9.2 show the results. Cournot competition with production adjustment costs is the classic case of overproduction (overinvestment top dog incentive). The firm with a larger adjustment cost (firm 1) will produce more in the steady state. Firm 1 will profit from its commitment capacity to increase its production and reduce the production of the rival. In the symmetric case this makes both firms worse off because output is increased. Bertrand competition with price adjustment costs generates softer pricing (overinvestment fat cat incentive). Each a firm now has an incentive to raise its price to induce softer behavior by its rival. In both the asymmetric and symmetric cases, each firm is better off by the presence of adjustment costs.

The mixed cases show more variety of strategic incentives. The adjustment cost of firm i depends also on the actions of its rival firm. Under Cournot competition and costly price adjustment, the firm that faces the adjustment cost (in the asymmetric case) manages to raise its output and depress the output of the rival (top dog incenive). With symmetric commitment capacities the outcome is a reduced output (a puppy dog incentive), and firms are better off. Bertrand competition with the costly quantity adjustment yields fat cat strategic incentives in the asymmetric case but lean and hungry incentives in the symmetric one. Thus in the asymmetric case the firms are made better off by the presence of the adjustment cost and in the symmetric case worse off.

The taxonomy of strategic behavior has been derived when the dynamics come from adjustment costs. However, other sources of dynamics can be explained that appeal to the same taxonomy. Let us review briefly switching costs, the learning curve, and competition for market share.

Beggs and Klemperer (1992) study a Markov price competition duopoly model with product differentiation where consumers bear the switching costs of changing products. At every period new consumers enter the market, and after any period a fraction of the extant consumers leaves the market. It is assumed that old consumers cannot switch brands. The state variables are the two firms' stocks of old consumers. At the (symmetric linear) MPE prices are raised from the no-switching-cost benchmark. The tension between exploiting the current customer base with high prices and attracting new customers with low prices (when the firm cannot discriminate among the two groups) is resolved in favor of the first. Firms discount the future and therefore prefer to exploit market power today (indeed, the steady state price decreases with the discount factor of the firms). Furthermore a firm has an incentive to raise its price to increase the market share of the rival and induce the rival to price more softly in the future (the game thus has a fat cat flavor). (The incentive to cut prices is also diminished because consumers are farsighted and realize that a price cut today by a firm will imply higher prices tomorrow.) If firms start from an asymmetric position, the initial dominance decreases and eventually market shares are equalized. The reason is that the larger firm gains relatively more from charging a high price, in order to exploit its customer base, than from charging a low price, in order to increase the share of captured new consumers. Finally convergence to the steady state is monotonic (e.g., with the firm with an initial market share larger than the steady state losing monotonically market share).

Markets subject to a learning curve display incentives similar to
the presence of production adjustment costs. Suppose that the marginal cost of a firm is decreasing in its own production (and there are
no spillovers). With Cournot competition a firm has an incentive to
overproduce because raising its output today decreases its marginal
cost in the future (as when production is costly to adjust). With Bertrand competition (and product differentiation) a firm, by lowering
its price today, raises its own output and decreases the output of the
rival, thus lowering its marginal cost and raising the marginal cost of
the rival tomorrow. Because own effects tend to dominate cross
effects the total effect of lowering the price today is to raise the price
of the rival tomorrow (as with symmetric production adjustment
costs).[40]

Budd, Harris, and Vickers (1993) study the evolution of competition for "market share" m in a continuous time stochastic duopoly
model. A technological competition illustration is the following.
Firms compete à la Cournot in a homogeneous product market, and
the level of the (constant) marginal cost of firm i, c, depends on its
technological level $z, c = c_0 e^{-z}$. Then the instantaneous profit of firm
is proportional to $(1 + e^{-m})^{-2}$, where $m = z_i - z_j$ is the technology gap
between the firms. The authors find, among other effects, that competition tends to evolve in the direction in which joint payoffs are
maximized. This is reminiscent of the "efficiency effect" found in
patent races according to which a monopolist has more incentive to
innovate than an entrant because, if he wins, it will stay a monopoly
on the other hand, if the entrant wins, the industry will be a duopoly
(unless the innovation is drastic). The differential incentives follow
because monopoly profits are larger than total industry profit under
duopoly. (A "replacement effect," however, works in favor of the
entrant making more effort because typically the incumbent, and not
the entrant, earns profits as innovation efforts progress.)[41]

9.2.3 Commitment and Pricing in Continuous Time

Modeling competition in continuous time allows the use of the machinery developed by differential games. Those are games in continuous time where at every instant players choose simultaneously
actions and state variables that follow a law of motion depending on
the position of the system and the actions taken. Differential games
provide a convenient tool to analyze dynamics restricting strategies

to payoff-relevant variables. In this section we provide an overview of the theory of differential games with an application to the duopoly case and a full characterization of the linear-quadratic specification.[42] Let us start by describing the basic elements of a differential game.

Consider a game in continuous time, $t \in [0, T]$ with $T \leq \infty$, where player $i, i = 1, \ldots, n$, has available a set of possible actions, "controls" in the usual terminology, $u_i(t) \in U_i$ with $u_i(t)$ being the action of player i at date t and U_i a subset of Euclidean space (which to simplify notation we assume to be one dimensional). A state variable $x(t) \in X$, for some subset X of R^K, denotes the position or payoff-relevant history of the game at date t. The state variable evolves according to the law of motion[43]

$$\dot{x}_k(t) = f_k(t, x(t), u(t)) \qquad \text{with } x_k(0) = x_k^0, \quad k = 1, \ldots, K.$$

The payoff to player i (assuming discounting at the rate r) is given by

$$J_i(u) = \int_0^T \pi_i(t, x(t), u(t))e^{-rt} \, dt + g_i(x(T)),$$

where π_i is the instantaneous payoff and g_i is the terminal payoff. The solution to the law of motion differential equation describes the state trajectory or path.

In principle, one could analyze general strategies in the formulated game. These strategies depend on the entire history of the game ("closed-loop" strategies). For example, we could consider punishment-type strategies like the ones considered in repeated games (see section 9.1) to enforce cooperative outcomes as subgame-perfect equilibria. However, a potential problem is that these strategies do not need to lead to a well-defined outcome path for the game even imposing regularity conditions.[44]

Differential game analysis has concentrated attention on certain classes of strategies: Open-loop and feedback or Markov strategies. These strategies can be understood as corresponding to different information structures of the game.

Open-loop strategies are just functions of time. This obtains in the case in which the players do not observe the state variables after the game has started (though they observe the initial condition x_0). The open-loop strategies are those in which the firms commit to an action path for the game. Typically they are restricted to be piecewise continuous functions of time $(u_i(t))$. An open-loop equilibrium

(OLE) is just a Nash equilibrium in the game with open-loop strategy spaces.

In contrast, closed-loop strategies depend not only on time but potentially on the whole history of the state variables. They correspond to the (general) case of observable state history. Feedback or Markov strategies depend only on the current state variables and time ($u_i(t,x)$), and in stationary games[45] the direct time dependence can be dropped.

Typically the strategies are restricted to be continuous and almost everywhere differentiable functions.[46] The idea is to restrict attention to equilibria in which payoffs are continuous and almost everywhere differentiable functions of the state variables. Then the tools of optimal control theory can be used. However, even in this case the characterization of MPE is difficult, and some headway has been made mostly in linear-quadratic games. An n-tuple of Markov strategies forms an MPE if it induces a Nash equilibrium (in fact an MPE) starting at any date and feasible state (initial condition). At a Markov perfect equilibrium, strategies are optimal for a firm for any state of the system given the strategies of the rivals. An MPE can therefore capture the strategic incentives that firms face.

At an MPE, player i chooses $u_i(\cdot)$ to maximize the discounted sum of profits, $J_i(u_i, u_{-i})$ given $u_j(t,x)$, $j \neq i$, with $\dot{x}(t) = f(t, x(t), u(t, x(t)))$ and $x(0) = x^0$ for any possible initial condition x^0. Necessary conditions at smooth (MPE) equilibria are given as follows: Define the (current value) Hamiltonian of player i by

$$H_i(t, \mu_i, x, u) = \pi_i(t, x, u) + \mu_i f(t, x, u),$$

where μ_i is the vector of co-state variables with dimension equal to the number of state variables, $\mu_i = (\mu_{i1}, \ldots, \mu_{iK})$.[47] Then necessary conditions for the strategies $u_i(t, x)$, $i = 1, \ldots, n$, to form an MPE are

$$u_i(t, x(t)) \in \arg\max_{v_i} H_i(t, \mu_i(t), x(t), v_i, u_{-i}(t, x(t))),$$

and for $k = 1, \ldots, K$,

$$\dot{\mu}_{ik} = r\mu_{ik} - \frac{\partial H_i}{\partial x_k} - \sum_{j \neq i} \frac{\partial H_i}{\partial u_j} \frac{\partial u_j}{\partial x_k},$$

where $\mu_{ik}(T) = \partial g_i(x(T))/\partial x_k$ for $T < \infty$ and $\dot{x}_k(t) = f_k(t, x(t), u(t))$ with $x(0) = x^0$.

At an OLE, the term $\sum_{j \neq i}(\partial H_i/\partial u_j)(\partial u_j/\partial x_k)$ disappears. This represents the "strategic effect" of the state variables on the strategies of the rivals of firm i and is not present in the OLE. Because of this term μ_{ik} evolves according to a system of partial differential equations at an MPE.

The former conditions are necessary only. To obtain sufficient conditions, the concavity of π_i and f_k in x and u_i must be included as well as an appropriate transversality condition for the infinite horizon game. The latter is given by $\lim_{t \to \infty} e^{-rt}\mu_{ik}(t)x_k(t) = 0$, $k = 1, \ldots, K.$[48]

A sufficient condition for the n-tuple of strategies $u(t, x)$ to form an MPE is that there exist (continuously differentiable) value functions V_i, $i = 1, \ldots, n$, where

$$V_i(t,x) = \max_{\{u_i(\tau), \tau \geq t\}} \left\{ \int_t^T \pi_i(\tau, x(\tau), u_i(\tau), u_{-i}(\tau, x(\tau)))e^{-r\tau}\, d\tau + g_i(x(T)) \right\},$$

with the state variable following the law of motion with initial condition $x(t) = x$ and V_i fulfilling the (Hamilton-Jacobi) partial differential equations,

$$-\frac{\partial V_i(t,x)}{\partial t} = \max_{u_i} H_i\left(t, \frac{\partial V_i(t,x)}{\partial x}, x, u_i, u_{-i}(t,x)\right)e^{-rt},$$

and the transversality condition

$$V_i(T,x) = g_i(x) \quad \text{for } T < \infty$$

(or for $T = \infty$, $\lim_{t \to \infty} e^{-rt}\mu_{ik}(t)x_k(t) = 0$, $k = 1, \ldots, K$, where $\mu_{ik}(t) = \partial V_i(t, x(t))/\partial x_k$).

In the infinite horizon stationary case the strategies are given by $u_i(x)$, and we have that $rV_i(x) = \max_{u_i} H_i(\partial V_i(x)/\partial x, x, u_i, u_{-i}(x)).$[49]

A Stationary Duopoly

Consider a stationary infinite horizon duopoly with product differentiation and adjustment costs.[50] Firm i has a one-dimensional action set (e.g., the rates of change of prices or quantities) and discounts the future at rate r. The law of motion of the system is given by $\dot{x}_i(t) = u_i(t)$, $i = 1, 2$ with $x(0) = x^0$. This means that the state variable x_i is under the control of player i. The instantaneous profit of firm i is given by the (smooth) function $\pi_i = R_i(x_1, x_2) - F_i(u_1, u_2)$, where R_i stands for revenue net of production costs, and F_i is the adjustment cost, which is a function of the controls (u_1, u_2). It is assumed that $F_i(0,0) = 0$, F_i is convex with $\partial F_i(0,0)/\partial u_j = 0$, $i, j = 1, 2$. This implies that adjustment costs are minimized when there is no adjustment. Assume also that R_i is concave in x_i. Under standard boundedness conditions then a Nash equilibrium of the static frictionless game with payoffs R_i exists (see chapter 2, section 2.1).

With this formulation we can accommodate both quantity or price competition and quantity or price adjustment costs. Suppose, without loss of generality, that production costs are zero. We obtain Cournot competition with $R_i = P_i(q_1, q_2)q_i$ and $u_i = \dot{q}_i$; that is, the control equals the rate of change of output for firm i. We have Bertrand competition with $R_i = p_i D_i(p_1, p_2)$ and $u_i = \dot{p}_i$, the rate of change of price for firm i. With production adjustment costs, F_i is a function only of $\dot{q}_i$, and with price adjustment costs, F_i is a function only of $\dot{p}_i$. The "mixed" cases where adjustment costs are not borne by the strategic variable can be considered also. For example, we can have price competition with production costly to adjust. In the mixed cases the adjustment cost of a firm depends also on the control of the rival firm.

The current Hamiltonian for firm i is given by $H_i = R_i(x_1, x_2) - F_i(u_1, u_2) + \mu_{ii} u_i + \mu_{ij} u_j$, where $\mu_i = (\mu_{ii}, \mu_{ij})$ is the vector of co-state variables of firm i. Note that under our assumptions, H_i is concave in u_i. The necessary conditions for (u_1, u_2) to form an MPE pair are

$$\frac{\partial H_i}{\partial u_i} = -\frac{\partial F_i}{\partial u_i} + \mu_{ii} = 0,$$

$$\dot{\mu}_{ii} = r\mu_{ii} - \frac{\partial H_i}{\partial x_i} - \frac{\partial H_i}{\partial u_j}\frac{\partial u_j}{\partial x_i} = r\mu_{ii} - \frac{\partial R_i}{\partial x_i} + \left(\frac{\partial F_i}{\partial u_j} - \mu_{ij}\right)\frac{\partial u_j}{\partial x_i},$$

$$\dot{\mu}_{ij} = r\mu_{ij} - \frac{\partial H_i}{\partial x_j} - \frac{\partial H_i}{\partial u_j}\frac{\partial u_j}{\partial x_j} = r\mu_{ij} - \frac{\partial R_i}{\partial x_j} + \left(\frac{\partial F_i}{\partial u_j} - \mu_{ij}\right)\frac{\partial u_j}{\partial x_j},$$

and

$$\dot{x}_i(t) = u_i(t), \qquad i = 1, 2 \quad \text{with } x(0) = x^0.$$

At the steady state we will have that $u_i = \dot{\mu}_{ij} = 0$ for $i, j = 1, 2$, and therefore $\mu_{ii} = 0$ (because $\partial F_i(0,0)/\partial u_j = 0, i, j = 1, 2$). Solving for μ_{ij} in the necessary conditions for firm i, we obtain for $i, j = 1, 2, j \neq i$, $r - \partial u_j/\partial x_j \neq 0$ and

$$\frac{\partial R_i}{\partial x_i} + \frac{(\partial R_i/\partial x_j)(\partial u_j/\partial x_i)}{r - (\partial u_j/\partial x_j)} = 0.$$

It follows that in the OLE the steady state necessarily must be an interior static Nash equilibrium (defined by the FOC, $\partial R_i/\partial x_i = 0$). At an OLE, firms do not take into account the effect of variations of the state variables on the strategies; that is, there is no "feedback" and $\partial u_j/\partial x_i = 0$, $i, j = 1, 2$. In short, adjustment costs are minimized when there is no adjustment. At a stationary state the strategy of the rival firm j is not to change the current action. Given the rival firm's strategy and the fact that firm i can make the marginal cost of adjustment arbitrarily small by choosing u_i small enough, not changing is a best response only if $\partial R_i/\partial x_i = 0$. This holds only at the static Nash equilibrium.

In summary, stationary states of open-loop equilibria of the dynamic duopoly game are in one-to-one correspondence with interior Nash equilibria of the static duopoly game.

At an MPE, in general, there is feedback, and the steady state differs from the stationary OLE. Despite the difficulty in characterizing MPE in differential games, it is possible to determine the effects of strategic incentives at locally stable steady states. Consider a market with a symmetric structure (in terms of action sets $U_1 = U_2$, and payoffs; that is, $\pi_1(x_1, x_2; u_1, u_2) = \pi_2(x_2, x_1; u_2, u_1)$). Let $u_i(x_1, x_2)$ be a symmetric MPE (i.e., $u_1(x_1, x_2) = u_2(x_2, x_1)$), and $x_1 = x_2 = x^*$ a symmetric steady state of the dynamical system $\dot{x}_j = u_j(x_1, x_2)$, $j = 1, 2$. We will say that (x^*, x^*) is regular if, $\partial u_i(x^*, x^*)/\partial x_i \neq \partial u_i(x^*, x^*)/\partial x_j \neq 0$, $j \neq i$, $i = 1, 2$. Let $B \equiv \partial u_i(x^*, x^*)/\partial x_i$ and $C \equiv \partial u_i(x^*, x^*)/\partial x_j$. If (x^*, x^*) is locally stable, then $B < 0$ and $B^2 - C^2 > 0$.[51] From the necessary conditions for the steady state of an MPE, we have then that sign $\{(\partial R_i(x^*, x^*)/\partial x_j)C\} = \text{sign}\{-\partial R_i(x^*, x^*)/\partial x_i\}$ because $r - B > 0$. Given that the static game is symmetric, if there is a unique Nash equilibrium, then it will be symmetric also; denote it by (x^N, x^N). Say that (x^N, x^N) is strongly regular if it is interior, and at the equilibrium, $[\partial^2 R_i/(\partial x_i)^2]^2 - [\partial^2 R_i/\partial x_j \partial x_i]^2 \neq 0$. In this case, from the index approach to uniqueness (see section 2.5), $[\partial^2 R_i/(\partial x_i)^2]^2 - [\partial^2 R_i/\partial x_j \partial x_i]^2 > 0$, and sign$\{x^* - x^N\} = \text{sign}\{-\partial R_i(x^*, x^*)/\partial x_i\}$. The latter equality follows because $\partial R_i(x^N, x^N)/\partial x_i = 0$; x^N is the unique solution to the equation $\phi(z) \equiv \partial R_i(z, z)/\partial x_i = 0$, and $\phi'(x^N) < 0$.

The above argument has shown the following: Assume that the dynamic game is symmetric (both the net revenue function and adjustment costs are symmetric), and suppose that there is a unique strongly regular Nash equilibrium of the static game, (x^N, x^N). Consider a locally stable, regular, and symmetric steady state, (x^*, x^*), of a given symmetric MPE of the dynamic game, $u_i(x_1, x_2)$, $i = 1, 2$. Then $\text{sign}\{x^* - x^N\} = \text{sign}\{(\partial R_i(x^*, x^*)/\partial x_j)(\partial u_j(x^*, x^*)/\partial x_i)\}$.

The interpretation of the result, which extends the Fudenberg-Tirole taxonomy to the infinite horizon differential game, is straightforward. Whenever an increase in the state variable that firm i controls, x_i, decreases the action of the rival $(\partial u_j/\partial x_i < 0)$ and a decrease in the state variable of the rival x_j has a positive effect on profit $(\partial R_i/\partial x_j < 0)$, then the steady state of the MPE is larger than the static one. Both firms have incentives to "overinvest" in its state variable with respect to the open-loop benchmark. This is also the case if $\partial u_j/\partial x_i > 0$ and $\partial R_i/\partial x_j > 0$. Whenever $(\partial u_j/\partial x_i)(\partial R_i/\partial x_j) < 0$, both firms have incentives to "underinvest" in its state variable. In the Cournot case we have that $\partial R_i/\partial x_j < 0$, and in the Bertrand case that $\partial R_i/\partial x_j > 0$. In the linear quadratic model we will see that intertemporal strategic substitutability $(\partial u_j/\partial x_i < 0)$ arises when production is costly to adjust, while intertemporal strategic complementarity $(\partial u_j/\partial x_i > 0)$ arises when price is costly to adjust.

The Linear-Quadratic Model

Given the difficulty in analyzing the MPE of differential games, the study of linear equilibria of linear-quadratic models has received attention. In the linear-quadratic differential game instantaneous payoffs π_i (as well as the terminal payoff g_i) are quadratic (and assumed strictly concave in the controls), and the law of motion $f(\cdot)$ is linear in the state and the controls. In this context a linear solution for strategies and co-state variables is sought. Substituting the candidate linear solution in the necessary Hamilton-Jacobi conditions, one obtains a system of equations, the *Riccati equations*, whose solution yields the coefficients of the linear solution. In other words, if the Riccati equations have a solution, then the system of partial differential equations admits a quadratic solution for the value functions. A solution to the Riccati equations will yield an MPE if the appropriate transversality condition is fulfilled.[52] In practice, in infinite horizon games the procedure described above is used to get to the Riccati equations. Typically there are multiple solutions for the coefficients. Among those, with luck, a stable one is identified (i.e., where state variables converge to a steady state starting from any feasible initial condition). This solution then is shown to fulfill the (sufficient) transversality condition and constitutes an MPE.

In a linear-quadratic differential finite horizon game the linear solution can be shown to be unique in a class of strategies that are analytic functions of the state variables.[53] Therefore linear equilibria of the infinite horizon game can be seen as limits of the finite horizon equilibria. However, other equilibria may exist, even restricting attention to Lipschitz-continuous strategies. For example, Tsutsui and Mino (1990) show that in the infinite horizon sticky price model of Fershtman and Kamien (1987; see exercise 9.13), there are multiple (nonlinear) MPE and that as the discount factor tends to one, the collusive outcome can be approximated with Lipschitz-continuous strategies.[54]

Consider the following specification of the linear-quadratic model. For a symmetric static payoff we have that $R_i = (\alpha - \beta x_i - \gamma x_j)x_i$ with $\beta > |\gamma| \geq 0$. The unique (and symmetric) Nash equilibrium of the static game is given by $x^N = \alpha/(2\beta + \gamma)$. If the adjustment costs are borne by the strategic variable of the firm (e.g., production in a Cournot model or price in a Bertrand model), then $F_i(u_1, u_2) = \lambda_i(u_i)^2/2$, $\lambda_i > 0$. In a mixed model, $F_i(u_1, u_2) = \lambda_i(\beta u_i - \gamma u_j)^2$. For example, with quantity competition and price adjustment costs, we have $R_i = (\alpha - \beta q_i - \gamma q_j)q_i$ and $F_i = \lambda_i(\dot{p}_i)^2/2$, where $\dot{p}_i = -\beta\dot{q}_i - \gamma\dot{q}_j$.[55] We will concentrate attention mostly in the case of symmetric adjustment costs, $\lambda_i = \lambda$, $i = 1, 2$. It is worth noting that for Cournot competition the case of homogeneous product and increasing marginal cost can be accommodated. Indeed, let $\gamma > 0$, and note that then $R_i = (\alpha - \gamma(q_i + q_j))q_i - (\beta - \gamma)(q_i)^2$. The slope of marginal cost is $(\beta - \gamma)/2$.

Let us illustrate the derivation of a linear MPE (LMPE). Let (u_i^*, u_j^*) be an LMPE. The value function for firm i, $V_i(x_1, x_2)$, is the present discounted value of profits at the MPE with initial conditions $(x_1(0), x_2(0)) = (x_1, x_2)$ and law of motion $\dot{x}_j = u_j^*$, $j = 1, 2$. Given u_j^* the Hamilton-Jacobi-Bellman equation for firm i, $i = 1, 2$, is given by

$$rV_i(x_1, x_2) = \max_{u_i} H_i(x_1, x_2, u_i),$$

where the maximand on the right-hand side is the current Hamiltonian

$$H_i = \pi_i(x_1, x_2, u_i) + \frac{\partial V_i}{\partial x_i}(x_1, x_2)u_i + \frac{\partial V_i}{\partial x_j}(x_1, x_2)u_j^*(x_1, x_2),$$

$\pi_i = R_i(x_1, x_2) - F_i(u_i, u_j^*(x_1, x_2))$ is the instantaneous profit, and $\partial V_i / \partial x_k$ is the shadow value of state variable x_k for firm i. The Hamilton-Jacobi-Bellman equation has to hold for any state level vector (due to the perfection requirement). Since u_i^* is a maximizer of the current Hamiltonian, the first-order condition

$$-\frac{\partial F_i}{\partial u_i}(u_i^*, u_j^*) + \frac{\partial V_i}{\partial x_i}(x_1, x_2) = 0$$

must hold for $i = 1, 2$ and $j \neq i$. This defines firm i's instantaneous best response. The first-order condition is also sufficient for a maximum given the concavity of H_i with respect to u_i. Given that $\partial F_i(u_i^*, u_j^*)/\partial u_i$ is linear, we can derive the equilibrium of the instantaneous game given x_1 and x_2 : $(u_1^*(x_1, x_2), u_2^*(x_1, x_2))$. The strategies will be linear in $\partial V_i / \partial x_k$. We have then $rV_i(x_1, x_2) = H_i(x_1, x_2, u_1^*(x_1, x_2), u_2^*(x_1, x_2))$. If V_i is quadratic, then H_i will also be quadratic in (x_1, x_2). Positing a generic quadratic form for V_i (and a symmetric one for V_j), taking derivatives with respect to the state variables, and substituting the result in H_i, we can find the coefficients of the quadratic function V_i by identifying coefficients. Typically there are multiple solutions. Equilibria are of the form $u_i = A + Bx_i + Cx_j$, $i, j = 1, 2$, $j \neq i$. A solution will be (globally) stable if the stability condition is fulfilled: $B < 0$ and $B^2 - C^2 > 0$.[56] In this case it is easy to see that the appropriate sufficient transversality condition will be fulfilled and the stable solution will yield an MPE.[57]

Following the procedure described above, it is possible to show that in the symmetric linear-quadratic duopoly model there exists a unique LMPE that stabilizes the state. This follows from the results of Reynolds (1987), Driskill and McCafferty (1989), and Jun and Vives (1998). Reynolds (1987) and Driskill and McCafferty (1989) deal with the case of Cournot competition with homogeneous product, quadratic production costs $(\gamma > 0)$, and production adjustment costs. As we have seen, this is equivalent to the product differentiation model. The authors find that $C < 0$. Using the duality between price and quantity competition in the duopoly model with product differentiation,[58] we can extend the results to price competition with price adjustment costs. The model is formally identical to the one before, but with $\gamma < 0$. Now at the unique stable LMPE, the rate of change of prices of each firm is increasing in the price of the rival $(C > 0)$. In Jun and Vives (1998) the "mixed" case in which there is price competition $(\gamma < 0)$ and production is costly to adjust is considered. It is shown that there is a unique LMPE that is stable. At this equilibrium the rate of change of price of each firm is decreasing in the price of the rival ($C < 0$). A duality argument gives the results for Cournot competition ($\gamma > 0$) with costly price adjustment. Now at the unique stable LMPE, the rate of change of production of each firm is increasing in the output of the rival ($C > 0$).

It is immediate then that the steady state is given by $x^* = \alpha/(2\beta + \gamma(1 - C(B - r)^{-1}))$, and we know that sign$\{x^* - x^N\} =$ sign$\{-\gamma C\}$.[59] Obviously the equilibrium parameters B and C depend on the exogenous parameters of the model (β, γ, λ, and r; α is a scale parameter and does not affect B or C).

In summary, in the symmetric linear-quadratic duopoly model there is a unique symmetric LMPE that is (globally) stable. The strategies are given by $u_i = A + Bx_i + Cx_j$, $i, j = 1, 2$, $j \neq i$, where $B < 0$ and $|B| > |C| > 0$. The steady state is symmetric and given by $x^* = \alpha/(2\beta + \gamma(1 - C(B - r)^{-1}))$. When production (price) is costly to adjust, $C < 0$ ($C > 0$) and x^* is more (less) competitive than the static Nash equilibrium $\alpha/(2\beta + \gamma)$.

It is worth noting that the exhibited LMPE remains an equilibrium when the law of motion of the system is subject to additive shocks with mean zero. This allows the modeling of demand uncertainty with an intercept that follows a Brownian motion. The equilibrium of the stochastic game is independent of the variance of demand increments.

What determines the competitiveness of a market is whether the (symmetric) adjustment costs are supported by prices or quantities. With price adjustment costs, intertemporal strategic complementarity ($C > 0$) prevails and this pushes prices up. With production adjustment costs, intertemporal strategic substitutability ($C < 0$) prevails and this pushes prices down. For example, in the quantity-setting model with costly production adjustment, the steady state outcome is more competitive than that of Cournot. The reason is the presence of intertemporal strategic substitutability. A larger output by firm i today leads the firm to be more aggressive tomorrow. With symmetric adjustment costs both firms are in the same situation, and quantities are pushed beyond the Cournot level. Similarly, with price competition and price adjustment costs, the steady state price is larger than the Bertrand static price (since $-C\gamma > 0$). The economic force behind the results is intertemporal strategic complementarity. A firm pricing high today will elicit high prices from the rival tomorrow. In both cases in which the adjustment cost is borne by the control of the firm, the strategic character of static competition (strategic substitutability or complementarity) is extended to intertemporal competition (strategic substitutability or complementarity).

In mixed cases where the adjustment cost is not borne by the control of the firm, the character of competition is inverted in going from the static to the dynamic model. For example, with price competition $(C < 0)$ and production costly to adjust, the steady state price is lower than the Bertrand static price because $-C\gamma < 0$. Here a firm has to cut its price in order to induce the rival to price softly in the future, so intertemporal strategic substitutability prevails (though there is static strategic complementarity in the price game). This case can be interpreted as rationalizing the "Stackelberg warfare point" (see chapter 1). Now the attempt by each duopolist to obtain an advantageous position, and soften the pricing of the rival, is self-defeating, and fierce price competition follows. The basic force behind the result is that a firm by cutting its price today will make the rival smaller, and therefore less aggressive, in the future because the rival's short-run marginal cost will have increased. A smaller output today means that tomorrow it is more difficult to increase output because production is costly to adjust. However, a countervailing force has to be considered. When a firm cuts its price, it also increases its own output and therefore lowers its short-run marginal costs, so it will be more aggressive in the future. However, the first effect, the direct effect on the rival's cost, will dominate this second indirect effect, which comes via an increased aggressiveness of the original firm, in the determination of the price of the rival. When firms face symmetric (or not too asymmetric) production adjustment costs, the strategy is self-defeating, and firms are locked into a price war.[60]

It is possible to characterize some limiting results on B and C when λ or r change. This is relevant because the discrepancy between the steady state x^* and the static Nash action x^N is governed by $|C|/(r - B)$. The result is that as r tends to infinity, x^* tends to x^N, and as λ tends to zero, x^* does not converge to x^N. It is intuitive that as r increases, the future matters less, and the strategic incentive diminishes. The result for λ is more surprising. As λ tends to zero, both $|B|$ and $|C|$ tend to infinity. However, $|C|/|B|$, and therefore $|C|/(r - B)$, tend to a number between 0 and 1. One effect is that when λ is low, the strategic incentive, as measured by $|C|$, should be larger. The reason is that for low λ it will be less costly for the rival firm to change its action, and therefore firm i has more incentive to change its state variable to influence the behavior of the rival. Nevertheless, a low λ should also increase the response to the own state variable, $|B|$. The outcome is that for λ small the strategic incentive is significant, and $x^* - x^N$ does not tend to zero as λ tends to zero.[61]

Asymmetries in adjustment costs may modify the strategic incentives. For example, with production adjustment costs and price competition, if the adjustments costs are asymmetric enough, intertemporal strategic complementarity can be restored. However, if the strategic variable is the one bearing the adjustment costs (e.g., with Cournot competition and production adjustment costs, and with Bertrand competition and price adjustment costs), strategic incentives in the asymmetric model are similar to the symmetric case. In the first instance there is intertemporal strategic substitutability, and in the second intertemporal strategic complementarity. Hanig (1986) shows that in a Cournot model with asymmetric production adjustment costs, when the adjustment cost of firm 2 is very small, the LMPE steady state is close to the Stackelberg outcome with firm 1 as leader. Similarly the emergence of the price Stackelberg equilibrium can be shown when firms compete in prices in a differentiated product market and face a price adjustment cost as the adjustment cost of firm 2 (the "follower") tends to zero. In both cases at the steady state firm 2 will necessarily be very close to its static best-response function because the firm faces almost no adjustment cost (and has almost no commitment power). Firm 1 will optimize accordingly and consequently will price very close to its Stackelberg level. We have thus the Stackelberg outcome (see section 7.4.1) as the outcome of a fully dynamic game. The leader is the firm for which its strategic variable is costly to adjust and therefore has commitment power.

Summary

The chapter has analyzed repeated interaction and dynamics in pricing games. Repeated games and the concept of subgame-perfect equilibrium (SPE) provide the appropriate analytical tool for examining the stability of collusive agreements. The main results include a number of so-called folk theorems that rationalize collusive equilibria among a plethora of SPE in the infinitely repeated game. We have available folk theorems for games with perfect and with imperfect monitoring, as well as for games with imperfect monitoring and privately observed signals. The theory provides strategies that support collusive equilibria with simple trigger mechanisms and grim punishments, as well as optimal penal codes with a stick and carrot structure. It can be used to explain price wars, the mechanisms necessary to avoid secret price cutting, and, in general, the factors that tend to hinder or foster collusion. Among them the discount factor, reaction lags, market concentration (in terms of number of firms and asymmetries among them), capacity constraints, product differentiation, multimarket contact, and the phase of the business cycle. In fully dynamic games, in which there are "material" links between periods, attention has concentrated on the study of commitment issues using the concept of Markov perfect equilibrium (MPE). This approach alleviates the multiplicity of equilibria problems encountered in the repeated game framework. The main results include the characterization of pricing patterns in the MPE of alternating move duopoly games, a taxonomy of strategic incentives in discrete time dynamic games with adjustment costs, and the study of competition in continuous time. Strategic incentives are isolated in comparing open-loop equilibria with MPE. It is demonstrated that incentives depend crucially on whether the game displays strategic intertemporal substitutability or complementarity. In the context of a linear-quadratic specification, it is found that the competitiveness of a market is governed not by the type of competition, Cournot or Bertrand, but by what variable bears the adjustment costs.

Exercises

9.1. Characterize the set of symmetric Nash equilibria of a two-period repeated symmetric Cournot game (with no discounting) that has a unique one-stage equilibrium. Compute the set explicitly for the case of linear demand and constant marginal costs. Which ones are subgame-perfect? Suppose now that the one-stage game has multiple equilibria. Do your conclusions change?

9.2. Consider a T-period repeated n-firm Cournot market with linear demand $p = a - Q$. Firms face no production costs and maximize average (per period) profit. Suppose that the continuation payoff of a strategy in a subgame is the average of the profits of the firm in all the remaining periods. Show now how a cartel supported by trigger strategies in an ε-SPE may break down close to T. Provide a condition that guarantees that the cartel will be supported in $k (\leq T)$ periods. (See Radner 1980).

9.3. Consider a infinitely repeated game with a unique Nash equilibrium in the one-stage component game, with payoff $\hat{\pi}_i$ for firm i (see section 9.1.2). Show that the stationary path with action profile a can not be sustained using Nash reversion if $\pi_i(a) < \hat{\pi}_i$ for all i.

9.4. Consider the infinitely repeated Bertrand duopoly example of section 9.1.2. Show that if $\delta < \frac{1}{2}$, prices must equal marginal cost at any period for any SPE outcome path.

**9.5. Consider the symmetric linear product differentiation model of section 6.1 (example 1) with m substitute products. Firms produce at zero cost, and there is infinitely repeated competition with discounting.

a. Suppose first that there is a duopoly, $m = 2$, and each firm produces one product. Show that for low (high) levels of substitutability the critical discount factor to sustain collusion with quantity competition is lower (higher) than with price competition. Show also that the critical discount factor is monotone (nonmonotone) in the degree of substitutability with quantity (price) competition. Explain your results. (See Deneckere 1983.)

b. Suppose now that there are n firms, $i = 1, \ldots, n$, and that firm i produces k_i products (we have that $\Sigma_i k_i = m$). Firms compete repeatedly in prices. Explore the incentives for firms to deviate from a collusive agreement using (multiproduct) Bertrand reversion. Give sufficient conditions for the smallest firm to have the largest incentive to deviate from the cartel agreement. (See Motta 1998.) (*Hint:* With price competition when a firm deviates, two cases must be considered according to whether the firm drives other firms out of the market or not.)

9.6. Consider two identical firms with constant marginal costs of production which meet in two identical markets and compete in prices. Examine whether a multimarket contact can help sustaining collusion. (*Hint:* The answer is no; see Bernheim and Whinston 1990.)

**9.7. Characterize the optimal trigger price equilibrium $(q^*, T^*, \bar{p}^*)$ in the Green-Porter model of tacit collusion with n identical firms when both demand and costs are linear, and demand uncertainty is distributed with compact support according to a smooth and convex distribution function. When is it optimal to have Cournot reversionary episodes of infinite length $(T^* = \infty)$? Which case, $T^* = \infty$ or

$T^* < \infty$, do you think is more likely to arise? Perform a comparative static analysis of the optimal trigger price equilibrium $(q^*, T^*, \bar{p}^*)$ with respect to the exogenous parameters n, the level, and the slope of demand when $T^* < \infty$. Interpret the results. (See Porter 1983a and Abreu, Pearce, and Stacchetti 1986.)

9.8. Argue how in an infinitely repeated Cournot market with a continuum of firms collusion can be sustained provided that individual firm deviations are observed. (See Green 1980.)

*9.9. Reexamine the conclusions of the Rotemberg-Saloner model for firms that are quantity setters. Consider a general specification of demand and costs, and provide results for the cases of constant elasticity demand and constant marginal costs, as well as the case of linear demand and quadratic costs. Explain the trade-offs involved.

*9.10. Draw a parallel between the mechanism design approach to collusion (section 8.4) and the repeated game analysis under private information. Identify the incentive compatibility constraints, participation constraints, and transfers in the repeated game analysis. (See Athey, Bagwell, and Sanchirico 1998, Compte 1998, and Kandori and Matshushima 1998.)

*9.11. Reexamine the simultaneous entry model of exercise 7.10 with two potential entrants and $a - 1 > c > a - 2$. Suppose that if one firm enters and the other stays out, then the latter receives an ε profit spillover. Suppose also that there is one round of preplay communication in which if a firm says "in" and the other "out," then this is what happens at the entry stage. If both say "in" or both say "out," then they play the symmetric mixed-strategy equilibrium at the entry stage. Find the symmetric mixed-strategy equilibrium in announcements. What has happened to the probability of a coordination failure with respect to the situation of no communication? Extend the analysis to T periods of preplay communication. What happens as T tends to infinity? (See Farrell 1987.)

**9.12. Consider a dynamic alternating move Bertrand duopoly with differentiated products. Demand for product i is given by $q_i = a - bp_i + cp_j$, $i \neq j$. Firms can produce at zero cost and discount the future with factor δ.

a. Suppose that the horizon is infinite. Show that for any δ there is a unique linear MPE given by $R(p_j) = D + Ep_j$, where $D = (1 - E)a/(2b - (1 + \delta E)c)$ and E is the root in the interval $(0, \frac{1}{2})$ of the equation $\delta^2 E^4 + 2\delta E^2 - 2(1 + \delta)bc^{-1}E + 1 = 0$. Show that the steady state price is increasing in δ. How do the dynamic reaction functions compare with the static Bertrand best responses?

b. Suppose now that the horizon T is finite. Characterize the SPE of the game. Explore what happens to the SPE dynamic reaction functions as the horizon T lengthens. (*Hint:* See Maskin and Tirole 1987 for the Cournot case.)

**9.13. Consider an infinite horizon differential duopoly game with sticky prices. Firm i controls its output rate q_i and faces a cost of production of $C(q_i) = (q_i)^2/2$. The change in the market price is governed by $\dot{p}(t) = \lambda(\alpha - (q_1(t) + q_2(t)) - p(t))$ with $p(0) = p_0$, where $\lambda > 0$ denotes the speed of adjustment of the price to its theoretical level in the inverse demand $\alpha - (q_1(t) + q_2(t))$. Firms discount the future at rate r. Show that at the unique steady state open-loop equilibrium for the game the strategies for the firms are given by $q_i = \alpha(\lambda + r)/(\lambda + 3(\lambda + r))$, while the Cournot outputs are given by $\alpha/4$. (The two coincide as r tends to 0 or λ to infinity.) Using the method proposed in section 9.2.3 show that there is a linear symmetric MPE yielding a stable trajectory given by the strategies $q_i^*(p) = \max\{0, (1 - \lambda\kappa_1)p + \lambda\kappa_2\}$ where $\kappa_1 > 0$ and $\kappa_2 < 0$ are appropriate constants with $(1 - \lambda\kappa_1) > 0$. The MPE steady state price is given by $p^* = (\alpha - 2\lambda\kappa_2)/(2(1 - \lambda\kappa_1) + 1)$. Show that as r tends to infinity, the price converges to the marginal cost, and that as λ tends to infinity, p^* converges to a limit strictly between the Cournot and the competitive prices. Explain intuitively all the results. (See Fershtman and Kamien 1987.)

10   Epilogue

So far we have reviewed several advances made in oligopoly theory and related them to the contributions of the founders of the field. However, we have been selective and focused mostly on short-run pricing issues.

From the extensive application of game theory to industrial organization, we have learned quite a bit about oligopoly pricing. Indeed, our knowledge of the characterization of different types of equilibria has advanced considerably. This has been so in terms of establishing the existence, uniqueness, stability, and comparative static properties of equilibrium. In chapters 4 to 7 we have examined the models associated with the classical thinkers Cournot, Bertrand, Edgeworth, Chamberlin and Robinson, and Stackelberg with the tools provided by game theory. In chapters 8 and 9 we applied the developments in incomplete information and dynamic games in order to study pricing in environments with asymmetric information and repeated interaction.

In general, game theory has imposed discipline in our thinking about strategic situations and has allowed the rigorous analysis of a range of business practices. In short, game theory has raised in an important way the standards by which oligopoly models are judged. Internal consistency is a necessary (but not sufficient!) condition for a model to be considered acceptable.

The classical debate between Cournot and Edgeworth on the determinacy of prices in oligopolistic conditions is still ongoing. Indeterminacy is very much at the center stage in oligopoly. Our understanding of strategic competition has been advanced enormously, but a large region of indeterminacy in outcomes has remained. From a *static equilibrium* perspective, pricing is "determinate" once a simple strategy space (e.g., prices or quantities) is chosen (supposedly given a detailed knowledge of the market under study).[1] A static equilibrium approach matters even in situations of repeated interaction whenever one-shot equilibria can be viewed as steady states of the dynamic competition process.

A plethora of outcomes emerge from a less restrictive *nonequilibrium* approach (e.g., as rationalizability). However, the application of the theory of supermodular games to oligopoly, for example, to price competition with differentiated products, or to duopolistic quantity competition has provided bounds for the indeterminacy of market outcomes. Indeed, in a supermodular game extremal equilibria (in pure strategies) exist, have desirable stability and comparative static properties, and bound rationalizable behavior.

From a *dynamic equilibrium* perspective, the multiplicity of outcomes is overwhelming. This is particularly true in repeated games as the folk theorems show. Attempts to limit the multiplicity of equilibria have been only partially successful. The restriction to Markov strategies has helped to alleviate the multiplicity problem by focusing on the effect of payoff-relevant variables.

With large numbers of firms the degree of indeterminacy is reduced. In general, the existence of equilibrium (in pure strategies) is not a problem, and in homogeneous product models the competitive outcome obtains (approximately). With product differentiation a monopolistically competitive outcome may obtain, and then Cournot and Bertrand equilibria coincide. If we depart from equilibrium analysis, and require dominance solvability, for example, we restrict the class of cases for which the indeterminacy is reduced in large markets. In dynamic games, although increasing the number of players is no guarantee of a reduction in the vast number of equilibria, several models indicate that under plausible circumstances collusion is more difficult to sustain with many players.

The plethora of equilibria points to a problem for oligopoly theory. Everything can be explained. Results depend on what equilibrium is selected in a dynamic game and/or on what specific game form (strategy space, sequencing of decisions, information structure, etc.) is used to model strategic interaction. In this sense the theory is too successful in explaining the different behavioral patterns of pricing and therefore loses predictive power. On the positive side it can be said that the diversity of theories matches the great variety of strategic behavior in actual markets. Evidence to this effect is provided for example, in the industry studies by Sutton (1991). Furthermore we can interpret the theories as providing a rich variety from which to choose, using a detailed knowledge of the industry under study, and a framework for empirical analysis (Pakes 1998).

In applied work the use of the models of Cournot and Chamberlin-Robinson has been pervasive in all fields of economics. Imperfect competition has become the norm rather than the exception in many analyses in international trade, macroeconomics, growth, and public economics.[2] The models of quantity competition with homogeneous products and price competition with differentiated products (the latter in its oligopoly and monopolistic competition versions) have established themselves as building blocks of more complex models. The success of these models is due to several factors. Chief among them are their tractability and the delivery of intuitive and plausible results, which is not inconsistent with the available empirical evidence. In this respect the Bertrand-Edgeworth model is less tractable and has become suspect because of the use of mixed strategies as a technical device to obtain existence of equilibrium.

The debate about which is the "right" oligopoly model has been settled by pointing at the structure of the market in order to see which strategic variable, price or quantity, provides a better reduced form description of competition. Indeed, even if firms set prices, the Cournot model turns out to be the appropriate tool of analysis in many circumstances. To ascertain the prevalent mode of competition, the analyst must look at the basic conditions of the market (demand, cost, technology, relationship with customers, etc.). Auctions provide a paradigmatic example of a case where the organization of the market determines the game form and the type of competition (the "rules of the game"). Furthermore data have been more readily available than for other market forms. The result is that auction theory has been successfully empirically implemented in terms of predicting behavior, measuring "deep" economic parameters, and testing the theory. The distinction between Cournot-type and Bertrand-type competition has proved crucial in applications, not only in industrial organization but also in international trade and macroeconomics. Indeed, the effect of policies or the incentives for certain practices are typically reversed when considering one type of competition or another. This poses a challenge for empirical work, lagging behind the theoretical input, to distinguish empirically between different types of competition and alternative game forms.

A typical methodology starts from the pioneering work of Bresna-han and tries to build an econometric specification that encompasses different game forms and tests different static theories of oligopoly behavior.[3] Sutton (1990, 1991) advocated the derivation of robust implications from the theory of industrial structure in a reduced form way to determine bounds on observable behavior (e.g., relating concentration and market size).[4] Precision in the predictions is sacrificed then in favor of breadth in the applications.

Recent work has concentrated on the measurement of the degree of product differentiation under the maintained assumption of Bertrand (one-shot) multiproduct competition (Berry 1994 and Berry, Levinsohn, and Pakes 1995 for the automobile industry). The estimates of patterns of elasticities and cross-elasticities of substitution among products are derived building on discrete choice theory, advanced econometric techniques, and the static pricing assumption. This is reasonable if it is thought that the major source of market power in some industries is product differentiation itself. However, in an industry where dynamic elements are important, the estimates of the degree of substitutability of the products, based on static Bertrand competition, will typically be biased. This follows from the analysis of section 9.2.3, for example, if production is costly to adjust and price is the only strategic variable. Then a low margin would be misinterpreted as a high degree of substitutability of the products when in fact the presence of production adjustment costs makes the market very competitive for strategic reasons.[5] The analysis of Ericson and Pakes (1995) and Pakes and McGuire (1994) incorporate explicitly the dynamics of entry and exit using a Markov restriction on strategies, but pricing is determined with one-shot Nash behavior.

Another line of work tries to test the dynamic implications of oligopoly theory, mainly the existence of a pattern of collusive behavior with regime switches. The leading example is the study of the railroad cartel of the 1880s (Porter 1983b; Ellison 1994). The outcome of the studies is that even when appropriate data are available, it is difficult to provide compelling evidence of collusive behavior. However, as argued by Bresnahan (1997), there is more success in the measurement of market power or closeness to monopoly, and this matters for welfare analysis. Perhaps because of these difficulties, recent empirical work does not make intensive use of the latest developments of oligopoly theory and tends to focus more on the measurement of relevant parameters than in the testing of the theory.

Experimental evidence provides another way to test the theory, and even to uncover empirical regularities. It allows the economist to observe the functioning of a market under controlled conditions.[6] Early experiments in industrial organization were conducted by Chamberlin (1948).[7] The robust result of experimental work is that trading institutions and contractual provisions (posted prices, different types of auctions, decentralized negotiations, etc.) matter and can affect market outcomes. This means that a study of pricing must include a study of market microstructure. Other results show that with few players, market power is prevalent in a range of trading mechanisms, including posted prices, and that increases in the number of sellers tend to yield more competitive outcomes.[8] Although it is still too early to fully assess the contribution of experimental evidence, oligopoly theory can inform the experimental design and be used as a guide in interpreting the results.

Recent developments in oligopoly theory and industrial organization analysis alternate between empirical and theoretical perspectives. The structure-conduct-performance (SCP) paradigm of the 1950s and 1960s was implemented with little theoretical guidance. The introduction of game theory in the 1970s and 1980s pushed the field in a theoretical direction. In recent years there has been a renewal of interest in the empirical approach.[9] Despite some effort at integrating theory and empirics there is the danger that the lesson of the SCP paradigm will be overlooked, and again it will be empirics without theory. This will affect policy making because without a theoretical perspective a welfare analysis of empirical regularities cannot be performed.

The question is, has oligopoly theory failed? Or maybe the idea that there can be theory here is hopeless. Indeed, the cycling of theory and empirics in the development of the field may be inherent to the profession, but this cannot be the whole story. Oligopolistic business patterns have lacked a benchmark model of dynamic price formation. A benchmark model could provide a counterpart to well-established static models and some insight toward resolving dynamically the issue of an appropriate game form. The model should be tractable and based on plausible assumptions, and firms should use "simple" strategies so that the model can deliver relatively robust predictions. Such a result is not possible with the repeated game model, which has probably received too much attention.[10] Experimental evidence and the theories of bounded rationality could also be used in justifying appropriate modeling restrictions. The best shot in this direction seems to be to develop a tractable model based on a sufficient array of strategic instruments using the Markov restriction. Although simulations could help in the characterization of equilibria, at least simple versions of the model should be capable of delivering analytical results.

In summary, more empirical and experimental work is needed. It seems unlikely, however, that real progress will be made unless there is a satisfactory integration with theoretical developments.

Notes

Chapter 1

1. This chapter is based partially on Vives (1989a, 1993). For a general basic reference on the theory of oligopoly, see Friedman (1977), relevant chapters in the *Handbook of Industrial Organization* (Schmalensee and Willig, eds., 1989), and Tirole's textbook on industrial organization (1988). For an overview of imperfect competition in general equilibrium, see Mas-Colell (1982).

2. This theme has been developed further recently by Singh and Vives (1984; see also section 7.2.2).

3. Edgeworth is credited with introducing the general functional form for the utility function. The assumption $\partial^2 U / \partial x \partial y < 0$ appeared for the first time in *Mathematical Psychics* (1881); later Auspitz and Lieben (1889) defined it to imply substitutability (see the entry on Edgeworth by Newman in the *New Palgrave* 1988, p. 95).

4. This duopoly model constitutes a partial equilibrium benchmark to analyze oligopolistic competition with differentiated products. See sections 3.1 and 6.1.

5. Quotations are from Edgeworth (1925). See Edgeworth (1925, pp. 124–26) for a full account of the moves of Nansen and Johansen.

6. In the context of the price game with complementary products, the foreseeing firm optimizes by taking into account the reaction curve of the rival, which is downward sloping (as we will see in section 6.3, price competition with complementary products may be understood as the dual of quantity competition with substitute products, which typically involves downward-sloping reaction curves).

7. See section 2.2 for an exposition of the theory and the papers by Topkis (1979), Vives (1985b, 1990a), and Milgrom and Roberts (1990).

8. Similarly the actions x and y are strategic *substitutes* if $\partial^2 U / \partial x \partial y < 0$. This terminology was coined by Bulow, Geanakoplos, and Klemperer (1985a).

9. Marshall in his *Principles of Economics* stated that under increasing returns the monopoly outcome was the only equilibrium possibility (Marshall 1920).

10. See section 9.2.3 for a dynamic equilibrium story rationalizing the Stackelberg warfare point.

Chapter 2

1. A more thorough treatment of some of the topics covered in this chapter may be found in several textbooks. See, for example, Fudenberg and Tirole (1991), Myerson (1991), and Osborne and Rubinstein (1994). For an excellent brief introduction to noncooperative game theory, see the second part of Mas-Colell, Whinston, and Green (1995).

2. A consistency condition is fulfilled at each information set: At every node within an information set, a player must have the same set of possible actions.

3. This interpretation of equilibrium points was advanced by von Neumann and Morgenstern in 1944. See the Nobel Seminar published in the *Journal of Economic Theory* (vol. 69, pp. 153–85, 1996) for reflections on the work of Nash and interpretations of his equilibrium concept.

4. In Aumann's game (in which communication is one-way by means of signals in the form of written messages), coordination is generally achieved provided that the messages are received before the actions are chosen (Charness 1998). This supports the supposition that communication helps in attaining efficiency (Farrell and Rabin 1996). See sections 8.3.4 and 9.1.5 for an analysis of the effects of cheap talk (nonbinding nonverifiable communication) and more experimental evidence.

5. A correspondence ϕ from a set S to a set T is a function from S to the set of nonempty subsets of T; that is, for every x in S, $\phi(x)$ is a nonempty subset of T.

6. In general, when we talk about equilibrium, it is to be understood in pure strategies. Whenever the equilibrium is in mixed strategies (with players randomizing over their pure-strategy sets), the text will say so.

7. Let $S \subset R^m$, T be a compact subset of R^k, and ϕ be a correspondence from S to T. Let x^n be a sequence in S and y^n a sequence in T. Then ϕ is *upper hemicontinuous* at the point x if $x^n \underset{n}{\to} x$, $y^n \in \phi(x^n)$ and $y^n \underset{n}{\to} y$, implies that $y \in \phi(x)$.

8. Baye et al. (1993) explore conditions weaker than quasiconcavity that ensure existence of pure-strategy Nash equilibria. By imposing conditions on an aggregator function of individual payoffs, the authors characterize the existence of equilibria following the approach of Nikaido and Isoda (1955). Other results are provided by Nishimura and Friedman (1981).

9. This section follows basically Vives (1985b, 1990a).

10. A binary relation is antisymmetric if $x \geq y$ and $y \geq x$ implies that $x = y$.

11. The order $\geq^p$ is transitive on nonempty sets (the empty set is both lower and higher than any other set), but it does not need to be reflexive. In fact $B \geq^p B$ if and only if B is a sublattice of S.

12. A *selection* from the correspondence ϕ from S to T is a function f from S to T such that for every x in S, $f(x) \in \phi(x)$.

13. That is, neither $x \geq y$ or $y \geq x$ holds.

14. When working in R^n, we can replace *sup* and *inf* by *max* and *min*, respectively. For x and y in R^n, we let $\max(x, y) = (\max(x_1, y_1), \ldots, \max(x_n, y_n))$ and similarly for $\min(x, y)$.

5. Consider $x \geq x'$ and $t \geq t'$. Let $a = (x', t)$ and $b = (x, t')$, then $\inf(a, b) = (x', t')$ and $\sup(a, b) = (x, t)$. Apply the supermodularity definition to a and b.

6. See Athey (1997a) for a survey of results of monotone comparative statics under uncertainty.

7. This property is closely related to the Spence-Mirrlees single crossing condition. A decision maker with a continuously differentiable utility function in R^2 parametrized by its type t, $U(x, y; t)$, and with $\partial U / \partial y \neq 0$ satisfies the (strict) Spence-Mirrlees condition if the marginal rate of substitution $(\partial U / \partial x)/(\partial U / \partial y)$ is (strictly) increasing in t for any (x, y).

8. The condition $\partial^2 g / \partial x \partial t > 0$ is sufficient for strict monotonicity of $\phi(t)$ for interior solutions without the quasiconcavity assumption. More precisely we have that $x > x'$ for x in $\phi(t)$ and x' in $\phi(t')$ if $t > t'$ and x' is interior (see Edlin and Shannon 1998).

9. The function g is upper semicontinuous on X if $\limsup_n g(x_n) \leq g(x)$ whenever x_n tends to a point x in X.

0. For general, not necessarily Euclidean, strategy spaces the lattice A_i must be compact in a topology finer than its interval topology.

1. The a_{ih} denotes action h of player i.

2. See also d'Orey (1995) for results on fixed points of increasing correspondences in partially ordered sets.

3. Suppose that an asymmetric equilibrium $(a_1, a_2, \ldots, a_{n-1}, a_n)$ exists. Without loss of generality, say that a_1 is the largest and a_n the smallest strategy where, by assumption, $a_1 > a_n$. Given symmetry of the game, the n-tuple $(a_n, a_2, \ldots, a_{n-1}, a_1)$ is also an equilibrium. Let Ψ be the common best-response correspondence of players. Then $a_1 \in \Psi(a_2, \ldots, a_{n-1}, a_n)$ since $(a_1, a_2, \ldots, a_{n-1}, a_n)$ is an equilibrium, and $a_n \in \Psi(a_2, \ldots, a_{n-1}, a_1)$, since $(a_n, a_2, \ldots, a_{n-1}, a_1)$ is an equilibrium. Since the game is strictly supermodular, Ψ is strongly increasing, and therefore $a_1 > a_n$ implies that $a_n \geq a_1$, a contradiction. We conclude that $a_1 = a_n$ and that the equilibrium is symmetric. Note that the argument does not depend on the one-dimensional strategy set being a subset of the real line.

4. Some evidence is starting to be accumulated on the supermodularity of the profit function of the firm in some of the available actions. Miravete and Pernías (1998) provide empirical results in this respect for product and process innovating activities.

5. As usual, $x < y$ means that $x \leq y$ and $x \neq y$.

6. Milgrom and Roberts (1994) also state and prove the theorem with $S = [0, 1]$.

7. Alternatively, symmetric equilibria are given by the intersection of the graph of $= \Psi_i(\sum_{j \neq i} a_j)$ with the line $a_i = (\sum_{j \neq i} a_j)/(n - 1)$.

8. Let $\hat{a}'_{-i} < \hat{a}_{-i}$, $a'_i \in \Psi_i(\hat{a}'_{-i})$ and $a_i \in \Psi_i(\hat{a}_{-i})$. The requirement states that $(a'_i - a_i)/(\hat{a}'_{-i} - \hat{a}_{-i}) > -1$ which is equivalent to $\hat{a}'_{-i} + a'_i < \hat{a}_{-i} + a_i$.

9. See, however, the comments on firms having random sales in section 5.2.6. See also the discussion in Osborne and Rubinstein (1994, sec. 3.2).

0. See the contribution of Weibull in the Nobel Seminar published in the *Journal of Economic Theory* (vol. 69, pp. 153–85).

31. In a metric space (X, d) the function $f: X \to X$ is a *contraction* if there is a number $c < 1$ such that $d(f(x), f(y)) \le cd(x, y)$, for any x and y in X. The contraction principle asserts then that if X is a complete metric space (e.g., Euclidean space with the usual metric), it has a unique fixed point.

32. *Poincaré-Hopf Index Theorem:* Let $f: A \to R^k$ be a smooth vector field on a compact cube $A \subset R^k$. Suppose that f has only a finite number of zeros $x_1, \ldots, x_n$ and that it points in on the boundary of A. Then $\sum_{i=1}^{n} I(x_i) = 1$, where $I(x_i)$ is the index of x_i. $I(x_i) = +1$ if $\det[-Df(x_i)] > 0$, $I(x_i) = -1$ if $\det[-Df(x_i)] < 0$, and $I(x_i)$ equals an integer depending on further topological conditions if $\det[-Df(x_i)] = 0$ (e.g., see Gillemin and Pollack 1974, p. 134).

33. Dana and Montrucchio (1986) show that the trajectories generated by the Markov perfect equilibrium of an alternating move game are very close to those generated by the Cournot tatônnement when the discount factor is close to zero. (See section 9.2.1 for a description of this class of games and of the concept of Markov perfect equilibrium.)

34. However, in two-player games a mixed strategy is a best response (to some strategy of the rival) when it is not strictly dominated. Then the sets of rationalizable and serially undominated strategies coincide.

35. In supermodular games undominated pure-strategy Nash equilibria exist (a pure-strategy Nash equilibrium is undominated if for no player an equilibrium strategy is weakly dominated by another pure strategy). In fact all undominated mixed-strategy equilibria must lie between the greatest and the least undominated equilibria (see Kultti and Salonen 1997).

36. $Dr_i = -D_{i1}^{-1}D_{i2}$, where D_{i1} is the Jacobian of $\nabla_i \pi_i$ with respect to a_i and D_{i2} is the Jacobian of $\nabla_i \pi_i$ with respect to a_{-i}. The spectral radius of a square matrix M is the maximal modulus of its eigenvalues. A Nash equilibrium a^* is regular if it is interior and $D_{i1}(a^*)$ is negative definite for all i.

37. The evolutionary approach views equilibrium as resulting from a process of natural selection in a population of agents identified with their strategies. This is akin to animals identified (genetically) with their strategies. Strategies that do better against the current distribution of strategies in the population will tend to grow faster than others. See Vega-Redondo (1996) and Weibull (1995) for accounts of evolutionary games and applications to economics.

38. Another adjustment process is fictitious play in which players respond myopically to the average play of the other players (see Brown 1951, Robinson 1951, and Miyazawa 1961). Shapley (1964) provided an example of a (non-zero-sum) two-player game (with three strategies for each player) with a unique equilibrium that does not converge. Rate of convergence results for fictitious play have been established by Krishna and Sjöström (1994) and Harris (1994).

39. Krishna (1992) shows that in two-player supermodular games with completely ordered finite-strategy spaces in which payoffs satisfy a diminishing marginal returns property, fictitious play converges (even if the game has multiple equilibria).

40. The convention holds, for example, if, to change strategy, players require to strictly increase their payoffs.

41. DeGraba (1995) presents a technique to locate bounds on equilibrium points by looking at first derivatives at disequilibrium points which is related to the stability analysis presented in theorem 2.10.

2. As usual, $x \gg y$ means that $x_i > y_i$ for all i.

3. That is, trajectories with forward orbits ($\{x(t; x^0) : t \geq 0\}$) with compact closure in X. If X is not an open set, then extend the dynamics to a neighborhood V of X and make sure that they point inward in V minus X.

4. The $n \times n$ matrix A is irreducible if for all pairs of indexes $p \neq q$, $a_{pq} \neq 0$, or there is some set of indexes $i_1, \ldots, i_r$, such that $a_{pi_1} \neq 0, a_{i_1 i_2} \neq 0, \ldots, a_{i_{r-1}, i_r} \neq 0, a_{i_r, q} \neq 0$, where the indexes $p, i_1, \ldots, i_r, q$ are all different.

5. Recall that in a strict supermodular game with one-dimensional strategy sets, E is ordered if $n = 2$ or 3 (Vives 1985b).

6. For example, if $g(x, y, \theta)$ is supermodular in (x, y) for any θ, then $\Sigma_i g(x, y, \theta_i)$ is supermodular in (x, y).

7. The proof of this second result is immediate using the definition of (μ-almost everywhere) log-supermodularity; that is, $((g(\min\{z, z'\}, \min\{\theta, \theta'\})) (g(\max\{z, z'\}, \max\{\theta, \theta'\})) \geq (g(z, \theta)) (g(z', \theta'))$ for μ-almost all (z, θ) and (z', θ'), and letting $f_1(\theta) = (z, \theta), f_2(\theta) = g(z', \theta), f_3(\theta) = g(\min\{z, z'\}, \theta)$, and $f_4(\theta) = g(\max\{z, z'\}, \theta)$. (See Athey 1997a.) Karlin and Rinott (1980) termed log-supermodularity "multivariate total positivity of order 2."

8. Log-supermodularity (almost everywhere) of the (joint) density of a vector of random variables coincides with the concept of affiliation introduced by Milgrom and Weber (1982) when studying auctions. For example, multivariate gamma or logistic and symmetric positively correlated normal distributions have log-supermodular densities.

9. Early work and basic results along these lines are Karlin (1968) and the work of Jewitt (1987) on risk aversion and comparative statics.

10. Furthermore, if one of the two conditions fails, then the conclusion must fail somewhere that the other condition is fulfilled (see Athey 1997a).

11. The MLRP implies first-order stochastic dominance (FOSD), but the converse is not true. See Milgrom (1981b).

12. For a good introduction to the subject, see Laffont (1989, ch. 4).

13. To simplify notation, we will not distinguish between a random variable and its realization.

14. It is also possible to redefine the set of states of the world Θ to define "finer" in the standard sense using partitions.

15. See De Groot (1970, p. 434).

16. According to the projection theorem for normal random variables, $\text{cov}(s - E(s|\theta), E(s|\theta)) = 0$, and therefore for an unbiased signal, $\text{cov}(s - \theta, \theta) = 0$.

17. The more appropriate term is "affine" instead of "linear," but we will not use that term here even when the function considered has a nonzero intercept.

18. Consider the n-dimensional random vector $x \sim N(\mu, \Sigma)$ partitioned ($n = k_1 + k_2$) according to $\begin{pmatrix} x_1 \\ x_2 \end{pmatrix}$ with $\mu = \begin{pmatrix} \mu_1 \\ \mu_2 \end{pmatrix}$ and $\Sigma = \begin{pmatrix} \Sigma_{11} & \Sigma_{12} \\ \Sigma_{21} & \Sigma_{22} \end{pmatrix}$ where the dimension of Σ_{ij} is $k_i k_j$. Then (1) marginal distributions are normal $x_i \sim N(\mu_i, \Sigma_{ii})$; (2) Conditional dis-

tributions are normal: $x_1|x_2 \sim N(\mu_1 + \Sigma_{12}\Sigma_{22}^{-1}(x_2 - \mu_2), \Sigma_{11} - \Sigma_{12}\Sigma_{22}^{-1}\Sigma_{21})$. For $k_1 = k_2 = $
we have $x_1|x_2 \sim N(\mu_1 + \rho(\sigma_1(x_2 - \mu_2))/\sigma_2, \sigma_1^2(1 - \rho^2))$, where $\Sigma = \begin{pmatrix} \sigma_1^2 & \sigma_{12} \\ \sigma_{12} & \sigma_2^2 \end{pmatrix}$ ar
$\rho = \sigma_{12}/(\sigma_1\sigma_2)$.

59. See Ericson (1969).

60. We know that for random variables x and y $\operatorname{var} x = E\operatorname{var}(x|y) + \operatorname{var}(E(x|y)$
Because s is unbiased, we obtain $E\operatorname{var}(s|\theta) = \operatorname{var} s - \operatorname{var}\theta$. Plugging $E(\theta|s) = A + $
into $E\operatorname{var}(\theta|s) = \operatorname{var}\theta - \operatorname{var}(E(\theta|s))$, we obtain $E\operatorname{var}(\theta|s)) = (\tau_\theta + r)^{-1}$.

61. Indeed, $\operatorname{cov}(s - \theta, \theta) = Es\theta - E\theta^2$, and by the law of iterated expectations, $Es\theta$
$E(E(s\theta|\theta)) = E(\theta E(s|\theta)) = E\theta^2$ if $E(s|\theta) = \theta$. We have then $\operatorname{var}\varepsilon = \operatorname{var} s - \operatorname{var}\theta$
$E\operatorname{var}(s|\theta))$ given that $E(s|\theta) = \theta$.

62. See DeGroot (1970), Ericson (1968), and Li et al (1987).

63. $\operatorname{var}(s|\theta) = \theta(1 - \theta)/n$ and $r^{-1} = E\operatorname{var}(s|\theta) = (E\theta - E\theta^2)/n = ((\alpha + \beta)\operatorname{var}\theta)/n$.

64. See Ericson (1968) and Li (1985).

65. See, for example, Li (1985).

66. A perfect information game is one where every player, when he has to mov
knows the moves of the players that have played before. A game is of perfect infc
mation if all information sets are singletons. A game is of imperfect information if
least a player has one information set that is not a singleton.

67. This is all the relevant information that is not common knowledge to all the pla
ers: Information about the payoff function, beliefs about the rivals' payoff functio
beliefs about beliefs, and so on. Obviously this can yield a very complex space. Tl
insight of Harsanyi is to assume that it is common knowledge that the beliefs of play
i are in some set T_i which is "operational" in relation to the potential belief space. S
Mertens and Zamir (1985) for the foundations of such representation.

68. T_i is a complete separable metric space, and therefore it is a Borel space (i.e., the
is a one-to-one map between T_i and some Borel subset of $[0, 1]$ which is Borel measu
able in both directions). T_{-i} is also a Borel space and consequently there exists a reg
lar conditional distribution on T_{-i} given t_i. (See Ash 1972, p. 265.)

69. For ease of notation, we will drop the dependence of Σ_i on μ_i. With a finite numb
of types mixed strategies can be accommodated easily. Indeed, $\sigma_j(t_j)$ may denote tl
possibly mixed strategy of player j when his type is t_j. With a continuum of types son
measurability issues have to be taken care of (see Milgrom and Weber 1985).

70. This formulation can be reduced easily to the previous one where the payoff of
player depends only on actions and the types of the players. Just let $\pi_i(a; t)$
$E\{U_i(a; t_0, t)|t\}$.

71. See Royden (1968, ch. 11) for the definition and characterization of absolu
continuity.

72. Mas-Colell (1984) treats the case of games with a continuum of players.

73. This follows easily from Fatou's lemma; see Royden (1968).

74. Note also that a pointwise increase in σ_{-i} will induce a first-order stochastic dox
inance change in the distribution of realized actions a_{-i}, and therefore we will have

conditional expected payoff that is supermodular in (a_i, σ_{-i}) provided that $\pi_i(a; t)$ is supermodular in (a_i, a_{-i}).

75. A function of bounded variation can be expressed as the difference between two monotone functions (Royden 1968, p. 100).

76. This is in accordance with Helly's selection theorem (e.g., see Rudin 1976, p. 167).

Chapter 3

1. There is an important literature on general equilibrium with imperfect competition, for example, Gabszewicz and Vial (1972), Novshek and Sonnenschein (1978), Roberts (1980), and Mas-Colell (1982).

2. See, for example, Vives (1985a).

3. If income I is small enough, then the consumer consumes nothing of the numéraire good, and he solves the usual program $\max_q U(q)$ subject to $pq \leq I$.

4. This would contradict the fact that the indirect utility function is homogeneous of degree 0 in prices and income. As a result λ is homogeneous of degree -1 in prices and income (recall that the Lagrange multiplier in question is just the income derivative of the indirect utility function).

5. In the static context we can make a conceptual experiment of increasing the number of goods and income to arrive at significant demand for any good. In the intertemporal context we could think of the consumer living for n periods; in each period he receives a unit of income and can borrow or lend at a zero interest rate. Thus more periods, more income, and more goods are added.

6. The income effect would necessarily dissipate as n grows if prices tend to zero, even if expenditure shares were $1/n$ and demand was bounded. For example, if prices were restricted to be in the simplex, we would have, with n goods, $p^n = 1/n$ (since by assumption all are equal). If income were fixed at I, then demand for good i would equal I, and the income derivative of demand would equal one.

7. Formally, there exist decreasing functions ϕ and $\bar{\phi}$ from R_{++} to R_{++}, with $\phi \leq \bar{\phi}$, $\phi(z) \xrightarrow[z \to 0]{} \infty$, $\bar{\phi}(z) \xrightarrow[z \to \infty]{} 0$, such that $\phi(q_i) \leq \partial U(q)/\partial q_i \leq \bar{\phi}(q_i)$ for all $q \in R_{++}^n$ and for all i

8. Examples of this are the assumptions in the representative consumer models of Spence (1976) and Dixit and Stiglitz (1977), or the "no neighboring goods" assumption in Hart's Chamberlinian model (Hart 1985). See also Pascoa (1997).

9. More technically, let $D(p, I)$ solve $\max U(z)$ subject to $pz = I$, $z \in R_+^n$, and let $S(p, I)$ be the associated Slutsky matrix $S(p, I)$. It is well known that $S(p, I)$ is negative semidefinite and negative definite on $T_p = \{v \in R^n : v^\tau p = 0\}$. Let $I = n$. The Slutsky matrix $\{S(p, n)\}$ is *nondegenerate* if the absolute values of its eigenvalues restricted to $T_p = \{v \in R^n : v^\tau p = 0\}$ are bounded above and away from zero (uniformly in n).

10. Results about downward-sloping *market* demand have been obtained, among others, by Hildenbrand (1983), Chiappori (1985), and Novshek and Sonnenschein 1979). Further results on demand aggregation are reported in Freixas and Mas-Colell 1987) and Jerison (1984). Hildenbrand (1983) shows that if all individuals have a common demand function (which satisfies the weak axiom of revealed preference) and if the distribution of income is given by a decreasing density, then all partial market

demand curves are decreasing. Novshek and Sonnenschein (1979) consider a differentiated commodities model and decompose price-induced demand changes into three aggregate effects: substitution, income and change of commodity. They show that even if individual demand functions are upward sloping the change-of-commodity effect guarantees that market demand for a commodity must slope downward whenever there are differentiated commodities close to the given commodity.

11. For simplicity we have taken the number of goods in any group to be the same.

12. See also Bewley's formulation of the permanent income hypothesis (Bewley 1977).

Chapter 4

1. A weaker regularity assumption on inverse demand sufficient for most applications is that $QP(Q) - C_i(Q) < 0$ for all Q large enough and all i.

2. The theorem is usually stated with the assumption that $P'(Q) + QP''(Q) < 0$ for all $Q \geq 0$ (i.e., the elasticity of the slope of inverse demand strictly less than one, $E = -QP''(Q)/P'(Q), E < 1$). This is equivalent to $P'(q_i + Q_{-i}) + q_i P''(q_i + Q_{-i}) < 0$ for all $q_i, Q_{-i} \geq 0$ when $P' < 0$.

3. A function f is *log-concave* (convex) if $\log f$ is concave (convex). With constant marginal costs log-concavity of the net price $P(\cdot) - c_i$ in the appropriate range (from the smallest monopoly output to the competitive supply of firm i) is sufficient for decreasing best replies.

4. A sufficient condition for $\log(P(\cdot) - c_i)q_i$ to display increasing differences in (q_i, Q_{-i}) is that $\log(P(\cdot) - c_i)$ be convex. Some remarks about the result are in order: (1) It is not required that $P(\cdot)$ be decreasing; (2) with no capacity limits, log-convexity of $P(\cdot) - \max_i\{c_i\}$ only holds when $\lim_{Q \to \infty} P(Q) > \max_i\{c_i\}$ (and this is plausible only for $\max_i\{c_i\} = 0$).

5. The price derived from inverse demand need not be zero for large output as long as total revenue remains bounded or firms face a capacity constraint.

6. Kukushkin (1992) extends the result to accommodate different capacity constraints for firms.

7. The result can be shown checking that the correspondence $Q_{-i} + \Psi_i(Q_{-i})$ is strongly increasing.

8. The monotonicity of demand can be dispensed with if costs are linear (see Amir 1996). This latter result may prove important for general equilibrium analysis with imperfect competition, since in this context, in contrast to the partial equilibrium environment (see chapter 3), downward-sloping demand cannot be guaranteed.

9. The inverse demand function $P(Q) = e^{-aQ}$, for $a > 0$, is log-linear and therefore satisfies both.

10. See, for example, exercise 4.3; increase c_1 from 0 to $c_1 \geq (4a)^{-1}$. By letting $c_i = c > 0$ for all i, it is easily seen that the net inverse demand function $P(\cdot) - c$ cannot be log convex on the relevant domain (up to the competitive output: $[0, P^{-1}(c)]$), and that the effective strategy space of firm i, $[0, P^{-1}(c) - Q_{-i}]$ is not increasing in Q_{-i} but in $-Q_{-i}$. Both factors go against increasing best responses (see Amir 1996; and also exercise 4.4).

1. This follows since $\partial^2\pi_i/(\partial q_i)^2 = P' + q_iP'' + P' - C_i'' < 0$.

2. A sufficient condition for the contraction condition to hold is that $(P(\cdot))^{-1/n}$ and $C_i(\cdot)$ be convex (Amir, personal communication).

3. See Thorlund-Petersen (1990) for an analysis of fictitious play in the Cournot model.

4. $\varnothing_i$ is well-defined for $Q \geq r_i(0)$.

5. $\Sigma_{i=1}^n \varnothing_i$ is well-defined for $Q \geq \max_i r_i(0)$.

6. In our smooth market, $P(\cdot)$ is log-concave if and only if $P''P - 2(P')^2 \leq 0$. From the first-order condition $q_i = -(P - C_i')/P'$. Substituting q_i in $P' + q_iP''$ and using the above inequality, we obtain that $P' + q_iP'' \leq 0$ provided that $\partial\pi_i/\partial q_i = 0$. This means also that $\pi_i/\partial q_i = 0$ implies that $\partial^2\pi_i/(\partial q_i)^2 < 0$ when $C_i'' - P' > 0$ for all i. It follows then that π_i strictly quasiconcave in q_i.

7. The last condition ensures that $(n-1)|r_i'| < 1$ for all i (and equivalently, that the best-reply map is locally a contraction). It is worth noting that the contraction condition on payoffs $(\partial^2\pi_i/(\partial q_i)^2 + (n-1)|\partial^2\pi_i/\partial q_i\partial Q_{-i}| < 0$ for all i) implies that (4.1) holds (to see this, use the fact that $P' - C_i'' = \partial^2\pi_i/(\partial q_i)^2 - \partial^2\pi_i/\partial q_i\partial Q_{-i}$). For further stability results, see Al-Nowaihi and Levine (1985), Okuguchi (1976), and Dixit (1986).

8. For relationships between concentration and welfare, see also Cowling and Waterson (1976) and Dansby and Willig (1979). For results about mergers in a Cournot setting, see Salant et al. (1983), Perry and Porter (1985), Farrell and Shapiro (1990a), and Faulí-Oller (1996).

9. Seade's work (1980, 1987) provides good examples of counterintuitive results when stability conditions are met.

10. See Seade (1980a, 1980b, 1987) for the local stability result. Note that at a symmetric equilibrium, either $P' + qP'' > 0$ or $P' + qP'' \leq 0$ for all firms. In both cases the equilibrium is (locally) stable. This result is easily derived considering the continuous adjustment gradient process (which changes strategies according to marginal profitability, see section 2.6.2). Linearizing the dynamical system around a symmetric equilibrium q^* for local stability, the (symmetric) Jacobian of marginal profitability must be negative definite (have negative eigenvalues). Now, the determinant of minus marginal profits, $|J| = -(\beta - \alpha)^{n-1}(\alpha + (n-1)\beta)$, where $\alpha = P'(nq^*) - C''(q^*) + P'(nq^*) + q^*P''(nq^*))$ and $\beta = P'(nq^*) + q^*P''(nq^*))$, is positive for any n (more precisely, for all the principal minors of J) if and only if conditions (4.1), $\alpha - \beta < 0$, and (4.2), $\alpha + (n-1)\beta < 0$, hold. It is worth remarking that the uniqueness and stability conditions are not the same. Indeed, if equilibrium in a smooth symmetric Cournot market is unique (regular and interior), then it will be symmetric, and we know (from section 2.2) that $|J| - (\beta - \alpha)^{n-1}(\alpha + (n-1)\beta) > 0$. This implies that (4.2) holds (given that < 0), while (4.1) does not. Then equilibrium will be unique but not stable. However, it is clear that this cannot happen if n is even! (see Dastidar 1998). Demange (1985) shows that if demand is downward sloping and concave, and *marginal* cost is convex, then there is a unique symmetric equilibrium for any n (assuming no fixed costs), but the equilibrium may not stable if costs are concave.

11. See also Dierickx et al. (1988) for further results on the effect of value added and excise taxes in the Cournot model.

22. With $P' < 0$ and $C'' \geq 0$, the required conditions are fulfilled if $E < n$ (decreasing best replies). For a general oligopoly game the condition that price must remain above marginal cost for any n is added. Suzumura and Kiyono (1987) obtain a similar excess entry result with respect to the first-best benchmark in which the planner not only controls the number of firms but also pricing.

23. Novshek considered that any firm would choose simultaneously whether to enter and the level of output. The outcomes of this simultaneous decisions game are closely related, but not identical, to the sequential decision entry/output game considered in section 4.3.2.

Chapter 5

1. See Spulber (1989).

2. At the unique Bertrand duopoly equilibrium firms use (weakly) dominated strategies. However, if firms have to choose prices from a finite price grid, then equilibrium (with firms naming the lowest possible price strictly above c) does not involve (weakly) dominated strategies.

3. Formally this is a two-stage game, and we restrict attention (as in the Cournot case, see section 4.3) to (pure-strategy) subgame-perfect equilibria. See section 7.4 for a detailed analysis of two-stage games.

4. See Dastidar (1995, 1997) for a formal analysis.

5. For example,

$$\frac{d\underline{p}_n}{dn} = \frac{p - C'}{(p - C')\dfrac{D'}{n} + \dfrac{D}{n}} \frac{D}{n^2} < 0,$$

since at

$$\underline{p}_n : p = \frac{C(D(p)/n)}{D(p)/n} < C'\left(\frac{D(p)}{n}\right).$$

6. In the smooth case a sufficient condition for strict concavity of π_n is $L_n E_{D'} > -2$ where

$$L_n \equiv \frac{p - C'(D(p)/n)}{p} \quad \text{and} \quad E_{D'} \equiv \frac{pD''}{D'}.$$

7. The interval is determined as follows: Let $\pi_i(p) = pD(p) - C_i(D(p))$ and $\phi_i(p) = px_i - C(x_i)$ with $x_i = D(p)(S_i(p)/S(p))$. Let $\bar{p}_i = \{p \in [0, \bar{p}) : \pi_i(p) = \phi_i(p)\}$ and $\underline{p}_i = \{p \in [0, \bar{p}) : \phi_i(p) = 0\}$. Then $\bar{p} = \min_i\{\bar{p}_i\}$ and $\underline{p} = \max_i\{\underline{p}_i\}$.

8. This assumes that when the lowest-cost firm prices at the next to the lowest cost, it obtains the whole market. With this assumption the "open set problem" of the lowest cost firm trying to price epsilon below the next to the lowest cost is avoided.

9. Nevertheless, if when firms quote the same price they split demand *randomly*, then in any Bertrand-Edgeworth equilibrium each firm can be taken to choose the profit maximizing supply that corresponds to its announced price. This implies that we are back to the Edgeworth case of nonexistence in pure strategies.

10. In the mixed-strategy region industry (expected) profits increase with the capacity share of the larger firm (Ghemawat 1990).

11. As argued, for example, by Tirole (1988).

12. This equals the Stackelberg follower profit for firm i. See section 5.2.3 and exercise 5.6.

13. For example, with constant elasticity elastic demand $P(Q) = Q^{-1/\eta}, \eta > 1$, and convex costs, the profits of a firm, are quasiconcave in production.

14. Friedman (1988) considers a product differentiation context and two classes of games according to whether the quantity choice or the price choice comes first. He shows that the variable that is chosen first determines the strategic character of the game.

15. However, introducing service reliability considerations and search costs residual demand for a high-priced firm can be shown to be less than under the efficient (surplus-maximizing) rationing rule (provided that consumers are approximately risk neutral with respect to service reliability and demand is rationed "first come, first served" as in proportional rationing). In this case Cournot behavior arises as the unique SPE equilibrium of the two-stage capacity-pricing game (Herk 1993).

16. A dynamic model with sales behavior supported by mixed-strategy equilibria is given in Sobel (1984).

Chapter 6

1. If the Jacobian of D, J_D, has a dominant negative diagonal it will be negative definite.

2. The results follow from the fact that if the symmetric square matrix A is negative definite with nonnegative off-diagonal elements, then all the elements of A^{-1} are nonpositive and the diagonal elements negative (see McKenzie 1959). If J_D (J_P) is indecomposable then $\partial P_i/\partial q_j > 0$, $j \neq i$ ($\partial D_i/\partial p_j < 0$, $j \neq i$).

3. When $n = 2$, then $\partial D_i/\partial p_j = -(\partial^2 U/\partial q_i \partial q_j)/(\det H_U) \geq 0$ for $\partial^2 U/\partial q_i \partial q_j \leq 0$, $j \geq i$, since $\det H_U > 0$.

4. Indeed, $\partial^2 \pi_i/(\partial q_i)^2|_{\partial \pi_i/\partial q_i = 0} = (\partial P_i/\partial q_i) - C_i'' + (\partial P_i/\partial q_i)^{-1}\{(\partial P_i/\partial q_i)^2 - (p_i - C_i') \cdot \partial^2 P_i/(\partial q_i)^2]\} < 0$ whenever $p_i[\partial^2 P_i/(\partial q_i)^2] - (\partial P_i/\partial q_i)^2 \leq 0$ given that $\partial P_i/\partial q_i - C_i'' < 0$ note that the desired inequality holds either for $\partial^2 P_i/(\partial q_i)^2$ positive or negative).

5. See Caplin and Nalebuff (1991). The condition is equivalent to concavity of the revenue function in terms of quantities ($1/D_i(p)$ convex in p_i is equivalent to $P_i(q)q_i$ concave in q_i.) To see that $1/D_i(p)$ convex in p_i implies that π_i is quasiconcave in p_i, consider an argument that, as in the Cournot case, assumes smooth demand and strict convexity of $1/D_i(p)$ in p_i. If π_i is monotone, then it is quasiconcave. Otherwise, evaluating $\partial^2 \pi_i/(\partial p_i)^2$ at a critical point of π_i for which $\partial \pi_i/\partial p_i = 0$, we find that $\partial^2 \pi_i/(\partial p_i)^2 = (\partial D_i/\partial p_i)^{-1}\{2(\partial D_i/\partial p_i)^2 - [\partial^2 D_i/(\partial p_i)^2]D_i\}$. The second term in curly brackets is strictly positive, since $1/D_i(p)$ is strictly convex in p_i. Therefore $\partial^2 \pi_i/(\partial p_i)^2 < 0$ for $\partial \pi_i/\partial p_i = 0$, and π_i is (strictly) quasiconcave in p_i.

6. Let us recall that a nonnegative function on a convex domain is ρ-concave if f^ρ is concave for $\rho > 0$ and $-f^\rho$ is concave for $\rho < 0$ (if there are multiple solutions to

$f''(x) = y$, then take the unique positive root). A ρ-concave function is also ρ'-concave for $\rho > \rho'$. The three important cases are as follows: $\rho = 1$ (concavity), $\rho = 0$ (log-concavity) and $\rho = -\infty$ (quasiconcavity). Now $1/D_i(p)$ convex in p_i is equivalent to $D_i(p)$ being -1-concave in p_i, and therefore $D_i(p)$ log-concave (or 0-concave) implies that $1/D_i(p)$ is convex (both in p_i).

7. See Friedman (1977, ch. 4).

8. In the constant elasticity example P_i is log-supermodular in (q_i, q_{-i}) irrespective of whether the goods are substitutes or complements. Furthermore P_i is log-convex in q_i if the goods are substitutes.

9. Milgrom and Shanon (1994) extend the result and show that the game is ordinally supermodular if costs are convex. In this instance, and with substitute goods, π_i satisfies the single crossing property in (p_i, p_{-i}). For goods that are complements, the property is fulfilled if costs are concave (exercise 6.3; see exercise 6.4 for a smooth version of the result).

10. The analysis that follows is based in Singh and Vives (1984) and Vives (1985a). See also Cheng (1985) and Okuguchi (1987).

11. It is easy to see that the result also holds if products are separated in two groups with intragroup substitutability and intergroup complementarity (see Okuguchi 1987).

12. The results are immediate. For the Cournot equilibrium, note that $-\partial \pi_i / \partial p_i$ has the same sign as $((p_i - C_i')/p_i) - 1/\eta_i$ and at the Cournot solution $(p_i - C_i')/p_i = \varepsilon_i \geq 1/\eta_i$. For the Bertrand equilibrium an analogous argument establishes the result, noting that $\partial \pi_i / \partial q_i$ has the same sign as $((p_i - C_i')/p_i) - \varepsilon_i$. See Vives(1985a) and Okuguchi(1987).

13. The result follows from the Jacobian of the demand system D, J_D, being negative definite, from the fact that at symmetric price solutions $\partial D_i / \partial p_i$ are equal for all i, say $\partial D_i / \partial p_i = -b$; also $\partial D_i / \partial p_j$ are all equal for i different than j, say $\partial D_i / \partial p_j = c$. If J_D is negative definite, then $-J_D$ is positive definite, and its determinant is positive $(b + c)^{n-1}(b - (n - 1)c) > 0$. It follows then that $(-b + (n - 1)c) < 0$ as desired.

14. With more than two firms it is possible that the Cournot output of one firm is larger than its Bertrand output even though every firm faces positive demand when prices equal marginal costs. This may happen in an oligopoly with symmetric product differentiation. See Jin (1996) and exercise 6.12.

15. With complementary products $\hat{\alpha}_i = \alpha_i - m_i > 0$ ensures that $\hat{a}_i > 0$, $i = 1, 2$. However, if there are more than two firms, the price of a firm may be lower under Cournot competition (see exercise 6.12).

16. The Allen-Hicks elasticity of substitution between goods i and j is given by $\sigma_{ij} = I s_{ij}/q_i q_j$, where s_{ij} is ij term of the Slustky matrix and I the income of the consumer.

17. If the goods are independent, $\gamma = 0$, then there is no convergence, since each firm has a monopoly of its own good.

18. The (direct) elasticity of substitution between goods i and j is given by $\partial \log (q_i/q_j)/\partial \log MRS_{i,j}$, with $MRS_{i,j} = (\partial U/\partial q_j)/(\partial U/\partial q_i)$. Note also that $\varepsilon_{ij} \leq 0$ and $\varepsilon_i \geq 0$.

19. Benassy (1989) assumes that demands come from a representative consumer with utility function $U(q_0, q)$, where q is the vector of differentiated commodities and q_0 is the numéraire. U is symmetrical in q. Substitution between the numéraire good and

e differentiated goods is bounded. All goods are normal and gross substitutes. The
sts of the firms are smooth, strictly convex, symmetric, and with bounded second
rivative.

. As the goods become perfect substitutes (i.e., as γ tends to β), the contingent
mand tends to the residual demand with the surplus-maximizing rule.

. Canoy (1996) also provides a parametrized example that yields existence of a
rtrand-Edgeworth equilibrium for sufficiently differentiated products and non-
istence for sufficiently close products.

. Some models with the above features are Spence (1976b), Dixit and Stiglitz (1977),
umar and Satterthwaite (1985), Hart (1985), Pascoa (1993), and Vives (1990b).

. The result follows by the identity $p_i = P_i(D_i(p_i, \bar{p}), \bar{q})$ and differentiating with
spect to p_i. We obtain $1 = (\partial P_i / \partial q_i)(\partial D_i / \partial p_i)$ because the individual action of a firm
nnot affect market aggregates.

. Another issue is whether with free entry, as the size of the market increases (or the
xed cost to produce a variety decreases), the number of entering firms tends to
finity. Exercise 6.15 provides a robust example where this is the case. However, if
mpetition is mostly in fixed outlays, like advertising or product enhancement, that
crease the market share of a firm, and if market share is very sensitive to this type
f expenditure, then the market could be a "natural oligopoly." That is to say, even if
ie size of the market expands or the fixed setup cost to produce a variety decreases,
iere may a finite upper bound to the number of entering firms. The reason is that
mpetition in the market share enhancing expenditures may be so tough that a larger
iarket just means that all the incumbent firms expend more and there is no room left
r entrants. (See Shaked and Sutton 1983, 1987; Sutton 1991; and exercise 6.15 for a
mple example of this phenomenon.)

. This is in contrast with results for a family of utility functions presented in Dixit
nd Stiglitz (1977). However, in this family, once properly normalized so that $f(0) = 0$,
is not continuous at zero (see Pettengill 1979 and Dixit and Stiglitz 1979).

. Namely there exist positive constants ρ and κ such that $\lim_{q \to 0}[(v(q) - v(0))/q^\rho] =$
. This means that $v(q) - v(0)$ has an asymptotic expansion at $q = 0$ with a leading term
f the constant elasticity type. See assumption 2 and lemma A5 in Kühn and Vives
1999). We denote the elasticity of function $g(x)$ by $\eta_g = xg'(x)/g(x)$.

. Consider the HARA class of functions f (e.g., see Ingersoll 1987, p. 39) with $f(0) =$
. That is $f(q) = ((d + hq)^\gamma - d^\gamma)/\gamma$, and to ensure that f is increasing and concave, $h > 0$
nd $\gamma < 1$. This provides a large parametrized class of functions that is widely used in
pplied work. When $d = 0$, we are in the constant elasticity case. When $\gamma = d = 0$, f is
garithmic. Letting $h = ad/(1 - \gamma)$, with $a > 0$, and letting γ tend to $-\infty$, we obtain the
egative exponential (CARA) case, $f(q) = 1 - e^{-aq}$. The inverse elasticity ε is (strictly)
icreasing in q if and only if $d > 0$. In this case, when $\gamma < 0$, it is immediate that $\rho' < 0$,
ince $\rho = \gamma(1 + d/hq)^{-1}(1 - (d/(d + hq))^\gamma)^{-1}$. This is also true for $0 < \gamma < 1$. In conse-
uence, recalling that $v' = \rho'$, we find that there is strictly increasing preference for
ariety, $v' > 0$, if f is of the HARA class and ε is strictly increasing ($d > 0$).

. The fact that n^* is decreasing in F follows immediately, since by our assumptions
he variable profits of a firm are decreasing in the mass of firms present in the market.
herefore a larger F means that fewer firms can survive.

29. The first-order conditions are sufficient under our assumptions.

30. In the case of the structural second best, the constraint $dn^{\Psi}/dq < 0$ can be shown to hold globally.

31. This decomposition is akin to the one presented in Mankiw and Whinston (1986).

32. Mankiw and Whinston (1986) explain the business-stealing effect and the surplus effect by differentiating welfare with respect to the number of firms subject to the structural constraint $n = n^S(q)$:

$$\left.\frac{dW}{dn}\right|_S = \pi + n(p - c)\left.\frac{dq}{dn}\right|_S + G'fv.$$

The term

$$n(p - m)\left.\frac{dq}{dn}\right|_S, \quad \text{with } \left.\frac{dq}{dn}\right|_S < 0,$$

is negative for prices above marginal cost and represents the business-stealing effect. The term $G'fv$ represents the incomplete appropriation of surplus. In equilibrium $\pi = 0$, and there is excessive or insufficient entry depending on what effect dominates. With homogeneous products there is no preference for variety ($v = 0$), and there is always excessive entry (as in section 4.3.2). In the approach followed in the text, the same result is obtained because, when $v = 0$, we have that $Gf'q = G'f$ and therefore at the free entry equilibrium $G'f - mq - F = 0$.

Chapter 7

1. See Bresnahan (1981). Other refinements and extensions of the conjectural variation approach have been proposed by Laitner (1980) and Ulph (1983). Comparative static results are derived in Dixit (1986). See Daughety (1985) and Makowski (1987) for a critique.

2. If we abandon the Nash solution concept and we require only that the strategies of firms be rationalizable, then many other outcomes are possible.

3. That is, D is smooth, with $D' < 0$ and $D'' \leq 0$, whenever demand is positive and C is also smooth, with $C' > 0$ and $C'' > 0$. We also assume, without loss of generality, that $C'(0) = 0$.

4. However, Kühn (1997) shows that supply function equilibria can be a reduced form of competition among manufacturers in vertically related markets that compete in setting wholesale price schedules and then retailers compete in quantities. In this case manufacturers can only observe the sales volumes of their retailers who have private information about the uncertain demand parameter. Then the equivalence between supply function equilibria and competition in vertically related markets requires additive uncertainty with unbounded support.

5. As before, if there is no unique market-clearing price $p(\theta)$, let $\pi_i = 0$.

6. Provided that the elasticity of V'' is less than $(1/n)$ times the elasticity of V'. V concave is sufficient but not necessary for the condition to hold.

7. See Kalai and Satterthwaite (1986).

8. Cooper (1986) and Holt and Scheffman (1987) provide analyses along these lines. These are similar to best-price policies other than usual business practices and price

policies that offer discounts or coupons to customers and thus alter price competition among firms by creating endogenous switching costs for consumers and sometimes enable collusive outcomes. See Banerjee and Summers (1987), Caminal and Matutes (1990), von Weizsäcker (1984), and Klemperer (1987, 1995) for studies of the effects of exogenous switching costs.

9. However, in the price (Bertrand) game with homogeneous products and increasing marginal costs (section 5.1), it is possible to obtain the collusive outcome in the continuum of Bertrand equilibria.

10. This seems to have happened in the 1950s in the U.S. electrical equipment industry (Scherer 1980, pp. 170–1). Sellers dealt in sealed bid competitions sponsored by government by assigning shares of business and coordinating bids, sometimes according to a "phases-of-the-moon" system. Each firm was a low bidder just enough times to gain its predetermined share of the market.

11. Specifically, in a duopoly the (regular) Nash equilibrium $(\bar{a}_1, \bar{a}_2)$ can be locally improved upon by correlation if

$$\frac{\partial^2 \pi_1}{\partial a_1 \partial a_2}(\bar{a}) \frac{\partial^2 \pi_2}{\partial a_1 \partial a_2}(\bar{a}) > \frac{\partial^2 \pi_1}{(\partial a_1)^2}(\bar{a}) \frac{\partial^2 \pi_2}{(\partial a_2)^2}(\bar{a}).$$

If the inequality is reversed, the equilibrium cannot be locally improved by correlation. (See also exercise 7.3.)

12. The equivalence between Nash and rationalizable strategies turns out to depend on the stability properties of Nash equilibria with respect to the Cournot tâtonnement. Let us recall that in the example considered, there is always a unique Cournot equilibrium that is globally stable for $n = 2$ but unstable otherwise. See sections 2.6 and 4.2.

13. See, for example, Rapoport (1974) and Guth et al. (1982).

14. A sample of the literature includes Ellison (1994), Harrington (1995), Kandori (1992a), and Okuno-Fujiwara and Postlewaite (1995).

15. See Amir and Grilo (1999).

16. The concept of subgame-perfect equilibrium is due to Selten (1965).

17. See also Gal-Or (1985) and Dowrick (1986).

18. However, Cournot competition with substitute products may fall also under case 2. This happens when the Cournot game is (ordinally) supermodular (with the natural order in the action spaces; see section 4.1). It may also happen that the slopes of best replies have different signs; then we are in case 3 (see exercise 7.4).

19. Gal-Or (1985) shows that if firms are identical with downward- (upward-) sloping best responses, then there is a first- (second-) mover advantage.

20. With uncertainty the advantage of waiting to produce in the second period is that by then uncertainty is realized. The second period cost could also be lower due to discounting (Robson 1990).

21. We will follow Vives (1988a) closely. For other models of sequential entry, see Prescott and Visscher (1977), Schmalensee (1978), Judd (1980), and Bernheim (1984).

22. Think of an agricultural market where different producers plant the seeds at different times, perhaps because of the diverse weather conditions to which they are

subject. A farmer knows the amount planted by previous farmers and tries to forecas. the amount planted by those who follow. Once the output is obtained, the producer bring it to an auctioneer who clears the market according to the demand schedule That is, firms choose capacities of production first, and then a competitive, market clearing stage follows.

23. It can be shown that $Z_k = \max\{(2Y - (1 + \Delta_k)a)/(1 - \Delta_k), 0\}$, $k = 0, 1, \ldots, n$, with $\Delta_k = \sqrt{1 - 1/2^k}$. Furthermore $Z_{k+1} + r(Z_{k+1}) < Z_k$. (See exercise 7.8 and Vives 1988a fo proofs.)

24. We have stated that Z_n is the cumulated output that makes a firm facing n poten tial entrants indifferent between allowing and preventing entry. Therefore the entry preventing output which makes the incumbent indifferent between allowing and pre venting entry is the Y that solves $(2Y - (1 + \Delta_n)a = 0$. The solution (which is large than $a/2$ for $n \geq 1$) is $Y_n = (1 + \Delta_n)a/2$.

25. There are many more nonperfect Nash equilibria. For example, let $n = 1$, and suppose that $(1 + \sqrt{\frac{1}{2}})a > Y > a/2$. In this case the unique SPE is for the incumbent to set Y and the entrant to use $q(\cdot)$ where $q(Z) = r(Z)$ if $Z < Y$ and 0 otherwise. Therefore the incumbent prevents entry. However, the incumbent producing zero and the en trant using $\tilde{q}$, with $\tilde{q}(0) = a/2$, and $\tilde{q}(Z) = a$ for $Z > 0$ is a Nash equilibrium where the incumbent does not produce anything and the entrant produces the monopoly output The threat of producing up to a if the incumbent produces a positive output is clearly not credible.

26. The critical entry-preventing output Y_n increases with n, converging to a as n tend: to infinity. Therefore the region where entry is allowed shrinks as n grows. The critica n solves $Y_n = Y$.

27. Samuelson (1984) argues that expected total surplus is decreasing in n when n i. larger than the optimal number. (See exercise 7.9.) Dixit and Shapiro (1984) examine entry dynamics with mixed strategies and find in simulations with a linear deman model that the expected profits of incumbents tend to rise with the number of potentia entrants.

28. A similar point has been raised by von Weizsäcker (1980).

29. We have that $\bar{Y}_{m,n} = m[m + (1 - \Delta_n - 1)/(1 + \Delta_n)]^{-1}a$, and $\underline{Y}_{m,n} = a(m + \Delta_n)/(m + 1)$, where $\Delta_n = \sqrt{1 - \frac{1}{2^n}}$.

30. $\underline{Y}_{m,n}$ and $\bar{Y}_{m,n}$ are both increasing in n, and they converge to a as n goes to infinity

31. $\bar{n}$ solves in n, $\underline{Y}_{m,n} = Y$, and $\bar{n}$ solves $\bar{Y}_{m,n} = Y$. We have that $\bar{n} = \underline{n}$ when $m = 1$, and otherwise,

$$\bar{n} = -\frac{\log(1 - ((m + 1)(Y/a) - m)^2)}{\log 2}$$

and

$$\underline{n} = -\frac{\log(1 - (((m + 1)(Y/a) - m)/(m - (m - 1)Y/a))^2)}{\log 2}.$$

32. In Waldman (1991) the presence of several potential entrants is viewed as crucia. to obtaining underivestment results.

33. Excess capacity may arise in equilibrium if best responses are upward sloping (see Bulow et al. 1985b).

4. Ware (1984) gives and explicit solution when there is only one potential entrant. If the variable cost production (set to zero in our case for simplicity) is small enough with respect to the cost of capacity c, in the case of entry the equilibrium production of incumbent and potential entrant are the same than in the quantity commitment model, $\bar{a}/2$ and $\bar{a}/4$, respectively, where $\bar{a} = a - c$.

5. With several potential entrants an incumbent may also try to "delegate" the burden of entry deterrence to a second entrant if it finds the task too costly (McLean and Riordan 1989).

6. See Schmalensee (1978) and Judd (1985) for product positioning, Matutes and Regibeau (1988) for an analysis of the strategic effect of product compatibility decisions, and Klemperer (1992) for an analysis of the strategic effect of switching costs. See D'Aspremont et al. (1979) and Shaked and Sutton (1982) on the use of product differentiation to relax price competition.

7. Note that the term $(\partial \pi_1 / \partial x_1)(\partial x_1^* / \partial k)$ equals 0 due to the usual envelope condition

$$\frac{\pi_1}{x_1}(x_1^*, x_2^*; k) = 0.$$

8. See Brander and Spencer (1983) and Okuno and Suzumura (1993).

9. See Ponssard (1991) for another application of forward induction reasoning to oligopoly.

10. See exercise 7.11 for a formalization of the analysis taken from Lapham and Ware 1994).

Chapter 8

1. Not surprisingly, a similar methodology can be used to show existence of a Bayesian equilibrium (in pure strategies) for certain types of auctions with risk averse bidders like the "mineral rights" auction (Milgrom and Weber 1982).

2. $D_i(p_i, p_{-i}(\theta_{-i}))$ is log-supermodular in (p_i, θ_{-i}) if $D_i(p_i, p_{-i})$ is log-supermodular and $p_j(\cdot)$, $j \neq i$, is increasing. The conditional density $f(\theta_{-i}|\theta_i)$ is log-supermodular in (θ_{-i}, θ_i) if the joint density of $(\theta_1, \ldots, \theta_n)$ is log-supermodular. It follows then that $E(D_i(p_i, p_{-i}(\theta_{-i}))|\theta_i) = \int D_i(p_i, p_{-i}(\theta_{-i})) f(\theta_{-i}|\theta_i)) d\theta_{-i}$ is log-supermodular in (p_i, θ_i). Recall from section 2.7.1 that if g is a nonnegative function log-supermodular in (z, θ) μ almost everywhere, then $\int g(z, \theta) d\mu(\theta)$ is log-supermodular in z. Now let $z = (p_i, \theta_i)$, $g = D_i(p_i, p_{-i}(\theta_{-i})) f(\theta_{-i}|\theta_i))$, and identify θ with θ_{-i}. Here g is log-supermodular because the product of log-supermodular functions is log-supermodular.)

3. Adapted from Raith (1996). Asymmetric versions of the model could be developed easily.

4. The restrictions on the coefficients can be derived from the maximization of a quadratic concave utility function for n goods as in example 1, section 6.1, and exercise 6.9. Positive definiteness of the coefficient matrix of the demand systems implies the restriction on the coefficients because own effects are given by δ and cross effects by λ.

5. Recall that we denote by τ_z the inverse of the variance of z, $1/\sigma_z^2$.

6. The assumption of normality is very convenient analytically but has the drawback that prices and quantities may take negative values. However, the probability of this

phenomena can be controlled by controlling the variances of the random variable. Furthermore, as we have seen in section 2.7.2, there are pairs of prior-likelihood that yield the convenient linear conditional expectation property and avoid the mentioned drawback.

7. This method of showing uniqueness of BNE in normal (or more generally, with linear information structures) linear-quadratic models has been used by Basar and Ho (1974) and Vives (1988b).

8. For existence results in this context, see Mas-Colell (1984).

9. See, for example, Leland (1972), Weitzman (1974), and Browning (1987).

10. See Vives(1990b) for an analysis of the general model.

11. The vector $(\theta_i, \tilde{\theta}, s_i)$ is normally distributed with $E\theta_i = E\tilde{\theta} = Es_i = 0$ and variance covariance matrix

$$\sigma_\theta^2 \begin{pmatrix} 1 & \rho_\theta & 1 \\ \rho_\theta & \rho_\theta & \rho_\theta \\ 1 & \rho_\theta & t^{-1} \end{pmatrix}.$$

This can be justified as the continuum analog of the n-firm market. Then, under the assumptions, the average parameter $\tilde{\theta}_n$ is normally distributed with mean 0 and variance $\mathrm{var}\,\tilde{\theta}_n = (1 + (n-1)\rho_\theta)\sigma_\theta^2/n$, and $\mathrm{cov}(\tilde{\theta}_n, \theta_i) = \mathrm{var}\,\tilde{\theta}_n$.

12. See Vives (1988b) for a justification of the continuum approach in terms of approximating large finite replica economies.

13. This section is based mostly on Vives (1984) and Raith (1996). The literature on information sharing in oligopoly has grown substantially from the early work of Ponssard (1979) and Novshek and Sonnenschein (1982). See Khün and Vives (1995) for references.

14. It is worth noting that $E\pi_i$ are decreasing in t_j, the precision of the information of the rival, even if we keep constant the correlation of the signals, $\rho_s = (d_1 d_2)^{1/2}$. This is so because increasing t_j to keep constant ρ_s, d_j must be increased and t_i decreased, and therefore the slope of the strategy of firm i, $B_i t_i = (2\delta - \lambda d_j)t_i/(4\delta^2 - \lambda^2 d_1 d_2)$, decreases.

15. For example, in a Cournot duopoly with random (constant) marginal costs firm 1 does not want to (ex ante) disclose its costs to firm 2 if costs are highly correlated and firm 2 does not know his own cost to start with. (Note that this specification does not correspond to our private values/perfect signals case because firm 2 does not know his own cost. See Sakai 1985.)

16. With quadratic costs and quantity setting (as in the example at the end of section 8.1.2) the expected profits of the monopolist are given by $E\pi = (1 + \delta')[(\beta^2/4(1 + \delta')^2) + (t/4(1 + \delta')^2)\sigma_\theta^2]$. They are increasing in σ_θ^2 provided that the firm receives a signal with positive precision, $t > 0$. With price setting (and constant marginal costs, equal to zero for simplicity) we have that the same expression holds for $E\pi$, letting $\delta' = 0$.

17. The same is true for the strategic substitutes case, with complementary goods, and any number of firms n.

18. The result is dependent, however, on the distributional assumptions made (with the error terms of the signals positively correlated and yielding linear conditional expectations); see Nalebuff and Zeckhauser (1986), Malueg and Tsutsui (1997), and exercise 8.9.

19. As opposed to the claim made by Clarke (1983) arguing from a Cournot homogeneous product model.

20. If the goods are independent, $E\pi_i$ are increasing with λ_j and unaffected by λ_i, $j \neq i, i = 1, 2$.

21. This section is based on Vives (1990b).

22. See Vives (1984, 1990b) and Kühn and Vives (1995) for a an extension of the arguments presented here.

23. See Vives (1990b, sec. 5) for the monopoly results (and set there $\delta = \gamma = 0$), and Kühn and Vives (1995) for a development of the argument.

24. See exercise 8.8 for a precise statement of the results.

25. Li, McKelvey, and Page (1987) in a Cournot homogeneous oligopoly context (also with common value uncertainty) show that expected total surplus is larger with information sharing.

26. To ensure positive outputs in any circumstance, assume that $a > \max(2\bar{c}_i - \underline{c}_j, 2\bar{c}_j - \underline{c}_i)$.

27. In the literature the defined equilibrium concept is sometimes referred to as "weak perfect Bayesian equilibrium" (Mas-Colell et al. 1995, ch. 9). The term "perfect Bayesian equilibrium" is then reserved to some refinement that imposes some restrictions on beliefs at information sets out of the equilibrium path. The beliefs must be determined by Bayes's rule whenever possible, even out of the equilibrium path. For example, after a probability zero event occurs because player i has deviated when player j has not, then the beliefs about j are formed according to Bayes's rule. Similarly one can require that if the types are independent, then they cannot become correlated in the posterior beliefs of players and that the beliefs about a player are shared by all the other players (see Fudenberg and Tirole 1991, ch. 8). In sections 8.5.2 and 8.5.3 further developments and applications to signaling games are provided.

28. Consideration of such refinements would take us too far afield. For a good summary of possible refinements starting from the concept of sequential equilibrium by Kreps and Wilson (1982a), see Fudenberg and Tirole (1991, chs. 8 and 11).

29. See Gibbons (1992, sec. 4.3.A) and Crawford (1998) for short introductions to cheap talk games.

30. See also Green and Stokey (1980).

31. The multiplicity of equilibria in cheap talk games is not even reduced with traditional refinements of PBE because those refinements are defined in terms of payoffs and not messages. Farrell (1993) develops a refinement for cheap talk games with a common language.

32. See Grossman (1981b) and Milgrom (1981b). The results are generalized by Seidmann and Winter (1997).

33. That is, the distribution function associated to b_i is uniformly below the one associated to b_i'.

34. The assumption can be weakened to the firm always strictly preferring (disliking) to be taken as being of the highest (lowest) type of the support of the reported set.

35. This would be the case, for example, in a Bertrand duopoly with independent costs (see section 8.3.1).

36. Given the assumption $a > \max(2\bar{c}_i - \underline{c}_j, 2\bar{c}_j - \underline{c}_i)$, it is easy to see that $r_i'(c_i) < 0$.

37. As usual in signaling games there are many other equilibria including a continuum of Pareto rankable pooling equilibria and partially pooling equilibria (see Kühn 1993).

38. Note that $e_i(m_i)$ is convex and differentiable.

39. See Myerson (1985) and Fudenberg and Tirole (1991, ch. 7) for an introduction to mechanism design.

40. In the United States agricultural cooperatives and export associations are partially exempted from antitrust laws (the first according to the Cooper-Volstead Act of 1922 and the Agricultural Marketing Act of 1937; the second according to the Webb-Pomerene Act of 1918). Examples of agricultural cooperatives are Sunkist (California citrus growers) and the large Associated Milk Producers (AMPI). These cooperatives or committees of cooperatives can agree on prices or regulate industry sales through contractual agreements enforced by the courts or by the federal government. Membership in a cooperative is voluntary. In some cases, like the milk market, inter-cooperative agreements to limit competition have been established through a side payment system. (See Madhavan et al. 1990 and Cave and Salant 1987.) Profit pooling arrangements in rationalization cartels, where firms agree on the market price and the distribution of production and profits, provide another instance of collusion supported by side payments condoned by public authorities. (See Howard 1954 for an analysis of rationalization cartels in Britain in the 1950s; see also Scherer and Ross 1990.)

41. The analysis in this section and the next follows closely Kihlstrom and Vives (1992).

42. As usual we do not distinguish notationally between the random variable c_i and its realization.

43. See d'Aspremont and Gérard-Varet (1979, thm. 1).

44. See Postlewaite and Roberts (1977).

45. However, because of the capacity constraint $\hat{q}(c)$ should be redefined for non-truthful report functions c. We have that when k belongs to the interval $(Q^m(\theta_1)/\mu_1, P^{-1}(\theta_1)/\mu_1)$ and the supply of the two lowest types results in a price no larger than $\theta_2(P^{-1}(\theta_2) \leq (\mu_1 + \mu_2)k)$, then the cartel outcome, with only type 1 firms producing, is IC and IR type I if k is not too large or $|\theta_2 - \theta_1|$ is small.

46. It is possible to extend the results to cover industries with general cost structures and to consider random mechanisms where firms are instructed to produce or not according to a probability distribution.

47. The claim follows immediately noting that sign $\{B\} = \text{sign}\{\partial A/\partial \lambda\} = \text{sign}\{C\}$. We have that when $C = 0$, $B = 0$, and A is independent of σ_u^2.

48. When $\lambda = 0$, there are also other symmetric solutions. Among them, $A = 0$ and $B = 1$. That is, firms conditioning only on the shared information M. All solutions involve zero expected profits.

49. This may seem surprising since, when $\rho > 0$, the average market action is random and the aggregate information received by firms, M, should help in its estimation.

How can an agent not respond to the information contained in M? Notice first that M gives information about $\bar{y}$ and about θ_i, since the θ's are correlated. When the actions are strategic substitutes, a high M is good news to agent i because this means that θ_i is likely to be high, but it is at the same time bad news because it means that $\bar{y}$ is also likely to be high; this tends to hurt the payoff to the agent. For certain parametric configurations ($C = 0$) it so happens that the two forces exactly balance out, and it is optimal not to respond to changes in M. Clearly, this cannot happen if the actions are strategic complements, in which case a high M is good news on two counts: It means that θ_i and $\bar{y}$ are likely to be high, so the agent wants to take a high action. It is never optimal then not to respond to the information contained in M.

50. When $C \equiv \rho(2(1 - t)\omega_1 - (1 - \rho)\omega_2) = 0$, then $\pi(\lambda)$ is independent of λ, and therefore any amount of garbling yields the same expected profits. Comparing $\pi(0)$ and $\pi(\infty)$ in the strategic substitutes case, three regions in the parameter space $(\rho, \sigma_\varepsilon^2) \in ([0, 1] \times [0, \infty))$ can be distinguished. Fixing ρ, for low and for high values of σ_ε^2, we have that $\pi(0) > \pi(\infty)$, and for intermediate values, $\pi(0) < \pi(\infty)$. The boundary of the first and second regions is given by $\rho = 1 - (2\sigma_\varepsilon^2\omega_1)/(\omega_2\sigma_\theta^2)$ and corresponds to the case $C = 0$ where information sharing is irrelevant. The (explicit) equation for the boundary of the second and third regions is more complex.

51. See Appelbaum and Lim (1985) for a formalization of this argument.

52. In this discussion we follow closely Vives (1989b).

53. The single-crossing condition amounts to $E(\pi_1|s_1)$ displaying strictly increasing differences in q_1 and s_1: $\partial^2 E(\pi_1|s_1)/\partial s_1 \partial q_1 = \partial E(\theta|s_1)/\partial s_1 > 0$.

54. When $\sigma_{\varepsilon_1}^2 = \infty$, the leader selects the perfect information Stackelberg output, and when $\sigma_{\varepsilon_2}^2 = \infty$, the separating equilibrium breaks down because the follower reacts very intensely to the output of the leader forcing him to contract output drastically.

55. The condition $\sigma_{\varepsilon_2}^2/\sigma_{\varepsilon_1}^2 > \frac{1}{2}[\sigma_\theta^2/(\sigma_\theta^2 + \sigma_{\varepsilon_1}^2)]$ is necessary and sufficient for the equilibrium output of firm 2 to be positive restricting attention to distributions for the signals with positive support.

56. Why this is so is subtle, and the explanation relies on the intricacies of the concept of strategic stability (see Fudenberg and Tirole, 1991, sec. 11.1 to learn about this refinement).

57. Caminal (1990) analyzes the same two-period price competition model but with known costs and idiosyncratic shocks to demand (with a two-point support distribution). He finds that there are a continuum of both separating and pooling (sequential) equilibria. However, expected profits at any of those equilibria are larger than in the complete information case. Incentives again point toward increasing first period prices.

58. See also Tirole (1988, sec. 9.4).

59. However, if the incumbent faces an infinite number of potential entrants, there is a SPE in which any attempt to enter the market is met by predation. (See exercise 9.9.)

60. See Keller and Rady (1999) for an analysis in continuous time of optimal experimentation by a monopolist facing a changing demand with two possible states. In this case the reward function is not fixed but changes randomly over time.

61. See also Mirman et al. (1994) for a model of competing firms learning about demand.

62. The analysis can be extended to continuous time and infinite horizon (Keller and Rady 1998). See also Bolton and Harris (1999) for an analysis of strategic experimentation in continuous time.

Chapter 9

1. A complete treatment of repeated and dynamic games is outside the scope of the present monograph. The reader is referred to Fudenberg and Tirole (1991, part II) for a broad introduction to the subject.

2. An individually rational payoff for player i is a payoff above its security or minmax level. This represents the lowest payoff to which rivals can hold player i in the stage game (and therefore in the repeated game in terms of average payoffs) when this player anticipates the actions played by rivals. Restricting attention to pure strategies, the minmax payoff of player i is given by $\min_{a_{-i}} \max_{a_i} \pi_i(a_i, a_{-i})$ (allowing for mixed strategies, it can be lower in general). In the statement of the theorem, the security level is defined by the pure-strategy minmax level.

3. The dimensionality condition ensures that it is possible to reward a player without rewarding a deviant.

4. For a Nash equilibrium it would be enough to test optimality with the history produced by the strategy profile $(\sigma_i)_{i=1}^{n}$.

5. The Friedman construction can be extended to support nonstationary outcome paths. Let v_i be the discounted payoff associated to a certain outcome path for player i and $(1 - \delta)v_i$, $i = 1, \ldots, n$, the corresponding average payoff. Then any feasible average payoff strictly above the one-shot Nash can be supported as a SPE with Nash reversion when δ is close to one. The key idea to extend the result is to note that in alternating among actions, the set of attainable payoffs becomes convex.

6. See Scherer and Ross (1990, chs. 7, 8) for a perspective on applications of the conditions fostering or hindering collusion.

7. For δ large (small) the maximal number of firms consistent with cartel stability is also smaller (larger) in Bertrand than in Cournot.

8. See also the analysis in Harrington (1991) on sustaining collusion with cost differentials among firms.

9. See Deneckere (1983), Wernerfelt (1989), Ross (1992), Häckner (1994), and Motta (1998).

10. Fernández and Marín (1998) provide evidence from the Spanish hotel industry in support of the facilitating role of multimarket contact.

11. A punishment is credible if itself generates a SPE outcome path.

12. As in the finitely repeated game, care must be taken not to reward the original deviant firm when rewarding the punishing firms (this observation is at the base of the dimensionality condition in the statement of the theorem).

13. This is what Fudenberg and Tirole (1991, sec. 5.5.3) term a "perfect public equilibrium." Note that in the game considered the subgame perfect equilibrium refinement has no bite because the only subgame is the game itself.

14. See Fudenberg, Levine, and Maskin (1994) for a folk theorem in supergames with imperfect monitoring.

15. The critical $\hat{\theta}$ is determined by the condition $(n-1)\pi^m(Q^m(\hat{\theta}),\hat{\theta}) = \delta E\pi_i^*(\theta)/(1-\delta)$, where $E\pi_i^*(\theta) = \int_\theta^{\hat{\theta}} \pi^m(Q^m(\theta),\theta)\,dF(\theta) + (1 - F(\hat{\theta}))\pi^m(Q^m(\hat{\theta}),\hat{\theta})$. Note that $\pi^m(Q^m(\theta),\theta)$ is increasing in θ.

16. See Klemperer (1995) and Chevalier and Scharsftein (1996) for other models that can deliver countercyclical markups.

17. See also Rotemberg and Woodford (1992).

18. Measurement problems can also bias the empirical results. For example, if marginal cost is approximated by average variable cost (including essentially labor and materials), it could be that the margin over average variable cost increases in expansionary periods when in fact the margin over marginal cost decreases if part of the labor cost is fixed.

19. Still Bagwell and Staiger (1997) consider a model in which demand alternates between a fast-growth and a low-growth phase, and they show that the most collusive price may be procyclical (countercyclical) when growth rates are positively (negatively) correlated through time.

20. A static formal theory of price rigidity is provided by the kinked demand curve (Sweezy 1939). However, the theory suffers the same problem as with conjectural variations (see section 7.1): It tries to compress a dynamic story into a static model. See section 9.2.1 for a dynamic version of the kinked demand curve story.

21. The authors restrict attention to equilibria in which (1) firms condition only on the realized past prices and not on their private information and/or their price schedules, and (2) the continuation value is symmetric across firms for each vector of current prices. The result is a "symmetric perfect public equilibrium."

22. See Vives (1990) and Kühn and Vives (1995). See also Genesove (1998) for a detailed description of how the practices of the Sugar Institute, the trade association of the sugar industry in the United States at the end of the 1920s and beginning of the 1930s, were conducive to collusion by making price cuts transparent. The role of trade associations in sustaining collusive agreements in industries with a large number of firms has been emphasized in the literature (e.g., see Hay and Kelley 1974 and Fraas and Greer 1977).

23. See the discussion by Holt in Kagel and Roth (1995, sec. 5.VII.D).

24. See Cooper et al. (1989a, b) and Crawford (1998).

25. However, Van Huyck et al. (1990) show that strategic uncertainty in coordination games may make difficult the emergence of the Pareto dominant equilibrium.

26. For this and related "anti-folk" theorems, see Green (1980), Kaneko (1982), Dubey and Kaneko (1984), and Massó and Rosenthal (1989). See exercise 9.8 for a counterpoint.

27. See Fudenberg and Tirole (1991, sec. 5.4) for a discussion of these issues, alternative definitions of "renegotiation-proofness," and results. Abreu, Pearce, and Stacchetti (1993) propose a notion of renegotiation-proofness based on an idea of "equal bargaining power." Interestingly, they find that in the Cournot repeated game with perfect monitoring, the severest punishments turn out to involve Cournot reversion for a number of periods followed by a return to (constrained) maximal collusion.

28. An MPE is indeed a subgame-perfect equilibrium without restricting the strategies used by the players. This is so because if the rivals of a firm use Markov strategies, the firm will always have a best response in the class of Markov strategies.

29. See Ericson and Pakes (1995) and Pakes and McGuire (1994) for a computation and simulation of Markov perfect equilibria in entry and exit industry models. Pakes, Gowrisankaran, and McGuire (1993) provide a computer code for the algorithm to find MPE and make it available to the Internet user. See Olley and Pakes (1996) for an empirical application.

30. For the basic model the exposition follows Maskin and Tirole (1987).

31. Note that to ensure the optimality of the strategies $(R_1(\cdot), R_2(\cdot))$, as usual, it is enough to check for one-period deviations.

32. See Dana and Montrucchio (1986).

33. Any pair of continuous functions constitutes an MPE of some game if the discount factor is small enough.

34. See Maskin and Tirole (1997).

35. At other kinked demand curve equilibria, when a firm undercuts the monopoly price by some amount, the rival cuts prices or randomizes. The reason is that in this situation firms would like the price to go up again, but each firm would like the rival to be first to raise the price and in this way to gain market share. The outcome is a mixed strategy where, with some probability, a firm continues the price war and, with the complementary probability, raises its price.

36. Eaton and Engers (1990) extend the Maskin-Tirole alternating price model to a specific product differentiation context, do not restrict prices to belong to a finite grid, and show how cooperative equilibria with high prices can be sustained depending on the degree of product differentiation. The one-shot version of their model with simultaneous price setting, typically, does not have a pure strategy equilibrium.

37. Dudey (1992) builds a dynamic Bertrand-Edgeworth model with unique SPE payoffs, for given capacities of the firms, supported by pure strategies.

38. See Maskin and Tirole (1987, 1988a, 1988b), and Bhaskar and Vega-Redondo (1998) for a bounded rationality approach based on memory costs.

39. All derivatives are evaluated at $\lambda = 0$, although in the linear quadratic model this only matters for $\partial \pi_j / \partial x_i$ because the other derivatives are just constants.

40. See Fudenberg and Tirole (1983) and Dasgupta and Stiglitz (1988) for models of the learning curve. Cabral and Riordan (1994) provides conditions for increasing dominance to occur in the market.

41. See Gilbert and Newbery (1982) and Reinganum (1983).

42. See Basar and Olsder (1982) for a general reference to differential games. The duopoly analysis is based on Jun and Vives (1998).

43. A dot over a variable indicates a time derivative. For example, $\dot{x}(t) \equiv dx(t)/dt$.

44. See Fudenberg and Tirole (1991, sec. 13.3.4) for a discussion of the issues involved.

45. A game is stationary when both π_i and f_k do not depend directly on time, for any i and k.

46. Or, more in general, u_i is Lipschitz continuous in the state variables. The function $u_i(x)$ is Lipschitz continuous on X if $|u_i(x) - u_i(y)| \le M|x - y|$ for some constant M and all x and y in X.

47. Note that we have expressed the co-state variables as current and not present discounted value shadow prices of the state variables.

48. When any solution to the system defined by the law of motion is bounded, then $\lim_{t \to \infty} e^{-rt} \mu_{ik}(t) = 0$ is sufficient. In a stationary game at an MPE, we have that $\lim_{t \to \infty} e^{-rt} H_i(t) = 0$. In addition, when $\pi_i \ge 0$, and under some regularity conditions on f, the condition $\lim_{t \to \infty} e^{-rt} \mu_{ik}(t) = 0$ is also necessary at the equilibrium. (See Takayama 1993, chs. 9 and 10, and Michel 1982.)

49. In the infinite horizon stationary case, $V_i(t, x) = e^{-rt} V_i(0, x)$. Let $V_i(x) \equiv V_i(0, x)$.

50. We follow the analysis in Jun and Vives (1998).

51. Note that the stated conditions are necessary and sufficient for a linear system to be stable.

52. Papavassilopoulos et al. (1979) show that for $T = \infty$ a sufficient condition for an MPE to obtain is that some appropriately defined matrices fulfill a stability condition.

53. Papavassilopoulos and Cruz (1979) show in a differential finite horizon duopoly game that if the law of motion, the payoffs, and the strategies are analytic functions of the state and time, then the (MPE) equilibrium is unique if it exists. In a linear-quadratic differential finite horizon duopoly game, there is a unique linear equilibrium (Papavassilopoulos and Olsder 1984).

54. Fudenberg and Tirole (1983) show also that cooperative outcomes can be supported as subgame-perfect equilibria in the continuous time Spence (1979) irreversible investment model. At those cooperative outcomes value functions are discontinuous.

55. We could consider more general formulations of adjustment costs, including a linear term in the adjustment, for example, but nothing substantive would change in the analysis.

56. For stability the characteristic roots of the matrix $\begin{pmatrix} B & C \\ C & B \end{pmatrix}$ must have negative real parts. This is true if and only if the trace $2B$ is negative and the determinant $B^2 - C^2$ is positive. This is equivalent to ($C < 0$ and $B - C < 0$) or ($C > 0$ and $B + C < 0$).

57. It is sufficient that $\lim_{t \to \infty} e^{-rt} \mu_{ij}(t) = 0$, where $\mu_{ij} = \partial V_i/\partial x_j$. This will hold at a stable solution because $\partial V_i/\partial x_j$ is linear in the state variables and those converge.

58. See Singh and Vives (1984) and section 6.3.

59. This follows from the steady state condition

$$\frac{\partial R_i}{\partial x_i} + \frac{(\partial R_i/\partial x_j)(\partial u_j/\partial x_i)}{r - (\partial u_j/\partial x_j)} = 0$$

by noting that $\partial R_i(x, x)/\partial x_j = -\gamma x$, $\partial u_j/\partial x_i = C$, $\partial u_j/\partial x_j = B$, and $\partial R_i(x, x)/\partial x_i = \alpha - (2\beta + \gamma)x$.

60. As we have seen in section 9.2.2, a similar mechanism is present when there is a learning curve (with no industry spillovers) in a differentiated price competition market. Casual observations of the fierce competition in industries like car and aircraft

manufacturing suggest it to be consistent with the described mechanism. Benkard (1997) provides an empirical analysis of dynamic competition in aircraft production.

61. However, when $\lambda = 0$ there does not exist a linear MPE, but there is an MPE in discontinuous strategies yielding x^N (firm i jumps to x^N if its state variable is not at the Nash level and stays put otherwise). There is thus a discontinuity of linear MPE as the friction in the market disappears (this result was also found by Fershtman and Kamien 1987, Reynolds 1987, and Driskill and McCafferty 1989). As we saw in section 9.2.2, the comparative statics results of the steady state with respect to λ in a discrete time game are very different. Then for $\lambda = 0$, the steady state is the static Nash equilibrium, but there is no discontinuity as λ is increased. That is, as λ tends to zero, the steady state tends to x^N.

Chapter 10

1. Determination is up to a probability distribution with mixed-strategy equilibria.

2. This has been observed more recently in transition and development economies.

3. For progress on this front, see Bresnahan (1989, 1997). See also Appelbaum (1979, 1982), Roberts (1984), Gasmi, Laffont and Vuong (1990, 1992), and Slade (1990).

4. A related approach is followed by Bresnahan and Reiss (1990).

5. We are abstracting, however, other potential relevant factors like inventories. Adjustment costs, particularly in changes of the production run, are important in a number of industries. For instance, Karp and Perloff (1989, 1993) have found significant adjustment factors in the rice and coffee export markets.

6. Obviously it is arguable that the conditions of real markets can be reproduced in the laboratory. However, in principle, abstract theory could be tested in the laboratory setting as long as the experiment is designed carefully.

7. See also Hoggat (1959), Sauermann and Selten (1959, 1960), Siegel and Fouraker (1960), and Fouraker and Siegel (1963).

8. See Holt (1995).

9. This is true mostly in the United States; Europe seems to be more active on the theory front.

10. One possible instance of overextension of the collusive repeated game model is its application to explain price cost margins in the industrial sector of large economies like the United States. Indeed, it is hard to believe that a collusive pricing pattern prevails in most of the U.S. industries.

References

Abreu, D. 1986. Extremal equilibria of oligopolistic supergames. *Journal of Economic Theory* 39: 191–225.

Abreu, D. 1988. On the theory of infinitely repeated games with discounting. *Econometrica* 56: 383–96.

Abreu D., P. Milgrom, and D. Pearce. 1991. Information and timing in repeated partnerships. *Econometrica* 59: 1713–33.

Abreu, D., D. Pearce, and S. Stacchetti. 1986. Optimal cartel equilibria with imperfect monitoring. *Journal of Economic Theory* 39: 251–69.

Abreu, D., D. Pearce, and S. Stacchetti. 1993. Renegotiation and symmetry in repeated games. *Journal of Economic Theory* 60: 217–40.

Aghion, P., P. Bolton, Ch. Harris, and B. Jullien. 1991. Optimal learning by experimentation. *Review of Economic Studies* 58: 621–54.

Aghion, P., M. Espinosa, and B. Jullien. 1993. Dynamic duopoly with learning through market experimentation. *Economic Theory* 3: 517–39.

Al-Nowaihi, A., and P. L. Levine. 1985. The stability of the Cournot oligopoly model: A re-assessment. *Journal of Economic Theory* 35: 307–21.

Allen, B., and M. Hellwig. 1986a. Bertrand-Edgeworth oligopoly in large markets. *Review of Economic Studies* 53: 175–204.

Allen, B., and M. Hellwig. 1986b. Price-setting firms and the oligopolistic foundations of perfect competition. *American Economic Review* 76: 387–92.

Allen, B., and M. Hellwig. 1989. The approximation of competitive equilibria by Bertrand-Edgeworth equilibria in large markets. *Journal of Mathematical Economics* 18: 103–27.

Allen, B., R. Deneckere, T. Faith, and D. Kovenock. 1995. Capacity precommitment as a barrier to entry: A Bertrand-Edgeworth approach. Federal Reserve Bank of Minneapolis. Research Department Staff Report 187.

Amir, R. 1995. Endogenous timing in two-player games: A counterexample. *Games and Economic Behavior* 9: 234–37.

Amir, R. 1996. Cournot oligopoly and the theory of supermodular games. *Games and Economic Behavior* 15: 132–48.

Amir, R., and I. Grilo. 1999. Stackelberg vs. Cournot equilibrium. *Games and Economic Behavior* 26: 1–21.

Amir, R., and V. Lambson. 1996. Quasi-competitiveness and profitability in symmetric Cournot oligopoly. Mimeo.

Anderson, S. P., A. de Palma, and J.-F. Thisse. 1992. *Discrete Choice Theory of Product Differentiation*. Cambridge: MIT Press.

Anderson, S. P., A. de Palma, and Y. Nesterov. 1995. Oligopolistic competition and the optimal provision of products. *Econometrica* 63: 1281–1301.

Appelbaum, E. 1979. Testing price taking behavior. *Journal of Econometrics* 9: 283–94.

Appelbaum, E. 1982. The estimation of the degree of oligopoly power. *Journal of Econometrics* 19: 287–99.

Appelbaum, E., and Ch. Lim. 1985. Contestable markets under uncertainty. *Rand Journal of Economics* 16: 28–40.

Ash, R. 1972. *Real Analysis and Probability*. New York: Academic Press.

Athey, S. 1995. Characterizing properties of stochastic objective functions. MIT Working Paper 96-1.

Athey, S. 1997a. Comparative statics under uncertainty: Single crossing properties and log-supermodularity. MIT Working Paper 96-22.

Athey, S. 1997b. Single cross properties and the existence of pure strategy equilibria in games of incomplete information. Mimeo. MIT.

Athey, S., K. Bagwell, and Ch. Sanchirico. 1998. Collusion and price rigidity. Mimeo.

Auerbach, A. J. 1985. The theory of excess burden and optimal taxation. In Auerbach, A. J. and Feldstein, M., eds., *Handbook of Public Economics*, vol. 1. Amsterdam: North Holland.

Aumann, R. 1974. Subjectivity and correlation in randomized strategies. *Journal of Mathematical Economics* 1: 67–96.

Aumann, R. 1976. Agreeing to disagree. *Annuals of Statistics* 4: 1236–39.

Aumann, R. 1987. Correlated equilibrium as an expression of Bayesian rationality. *Econometrica* 55: 1–18.

Aumann, R. 1990. Nash equilibria are not self-enforcing. In J. J. Gabszewicz, J. F. Richard, and L. A. Wolsey, eds., *Economic Decision-Making: Games, Econometrics and Optimization*, Amsterdam: Elsevier.

Aumann, R., and L. Shapley. 1976. Long term competition: A game theoretic analysis. Mimeo.

Aumann, R., Y. Katznelson, R. Radner, R. Rosenthal, and B. Weiss. 1982. Approximate purification of mixed strategies. *Mathematics of Operations Research* 8: 327–41.

Auspitz, R., and R. Lieben. 1889. *Untersuchungen über die Theorie des Preises*. Leipzig: Duncker and Humblot. (French trans. in 2 vols. Paris: Giard, 1914.)

Axelrod, R. 1984. *The Evolution of Cooperation*. New York: Basic Books.

Bagwell, K. 1995. Commitment and observability in games. *Games and Economic Behavior* 8: 271–80.

Bagwell, K., and G. Ramey. 1991. Oligopoly limit pricing. *Rand Journal of Economics* 22: 55–72.

Bagwell, K., and G. Ramey. 1996. Capacity, entry, and forward induction. *Rand Journal of Economics* 27: 660–80.

Bagwell, K., and R. Staiger. 1997. Collusion over the business cycle. *Rand Journal of Economics* 28: 82–106.

Bain, J. 1956. *Barriers to New Competition*. Cambridge: Harvard University Press.

Bamon, R., and J. Fraysee. 1985. Existence of Cournot equilibrium in large markets. *Econometrica* 53: 587–97.

Banerjee, A., and L. Summers. 1987. On frequent flyer programs and other loyalty-inducing arrangements. HIER Discussion Paper 1337.

Basar, T., and V. C. Ho. 1974. Informational properties of the Nash solutions to two stochastic nonzero-sum games. *Journal of Economic Theory* 7: 370–87.

Basar, T. S., and G. T. Olsder. 1982. *Dynamic Noncooperative Game Theory*. London: Academic Press.

Baumol, W., J. Panzar, and R. Willig. 1982. *Contestable Markets and the Theory of Industry Structure*. San Diego: Harcourt Brace Jovanovich.

Baye, M. R., and J. Morgan. 1996. Necessary and sufficient conditions for existence and uniqueness of Bertrand paradox outcomes. Mimeo.

Baye, M. R., G. Tian, and J. Zhou. 1993. Characterizations of the existence of equilibria in games with discontinuous and non-quasiconcave payoffs. *Review of Economic Studies* 60: 953–48.

Beckmann, J. M. 1965. Edgeworth-Bertrand duopoly revisited. In R. Henn, ed., *Operations Research Verfahren III*. Meisenhein: Verlag Anton Hain, pp. 55–68.

Beggs, A., and P. Klemperer. 1992. Multi-period competition with switching costs. *Econometrica* 60: 651–66.

Benassy, J. P. 1989. Market size and substitutability in imperfect competition: A Bertrand-Edgeworth-Chamberlin model. *Review of Economic Studies* 56: 217–34.

Benassy, J. P. 1991. Monopolistic competition. In W. Hildenbrand and H. Sonnenschein, eds., *Handbook of Mathematical Economics*, vol. 4. Amsterdam: Elsevier, ch. 37.

Benkard, L. 1997. Dynamic equilibrium in the commercial aircraft market. Mimeo. Yale University.

Benoit, J. P., and V. Krishna. 1985. Finitely repeated games. *Econometrica* 53: 890–904.

Benoit, J. P., and V. Krishna. 1987. Dynamic duopoly: Prices and quantities. *Review of Economic Studies* 54: 23–35.

Bergemann, D., and J. Valimaki. 1996. Learning and strategic pricing. *Econometrica* 64: 1125–49.

Bergemann, D., and J. Valimaki. 1997. Market diffusion with two-sided learning. *Rand Journal of Economics* 28: 773–95.

Bernheim, B. D. 1984. Rationalizable strategic behaviour. *Econometrica* 52: 1007–28.

Bernheim, B. D., and M. D. Whinston. 1990. Multimarket contact and collusive behavior. *Rand Journal of Economics* 21: 1–26.

Bernheim, B. D., B. Peleg, and M. Whinston. 1987. Coalition-proof Nash equilibria Concepts. *Journal of Economic Theory* 42: 1–12.

Berry, S. T. 1994. Estimating discrete choice models of product differentiation. *Rand Journal of Economics* 25: 242–62.

Berry, S. T., J. Levinsohn, and A. Pakes. 1995. Automobile prices in market equilibrium. *Econometrica* 63: 841–90.

Bertrand, J. 1883. Review of "Théorie mathématique de la richesse sociale" and "Recherche sur les principes mathématiques de la théorie des richesses." *Journal d Savants*: 499–508.

Bewley, T. 1977. The permanent income hypothesis: A theoretical formulation. *Journal of Economic Theory* 16: 252–92.

Bhaskar, V., and F. Vega-Redondo. 1998. Asynchronous choice and Markov equilibria Theoretical foundations and applications. Mimeo.

Birkhoff, G. 1967. *Lattice Theory*, 3rd. ed. American Mathematical Society 15. Providence, RI: Colloquium Publications.

Blackwell, D. 1951. The comparison of experiments. In *Proceedings, Second Berkeley Symposium on Mathematical Statistics and Probability*. Berkeley: University of California Press, pp. 93–102.

Bolton, P., and Ch. Harris. 1999. Strategic experimentation. *Econometrica* 67: 349–74.

Bolton, P., and D. Scharfstein. 1990. A theory of predation based on agency problems in financial contracting. *American Economic Review* 80: 94–106.

Börgers, R., and M. C. Janssen. 1995. On the dominance solvability of large Cournot games. *Games and Economic Behavior* 8: 297–321.

Börgers, T. 1992. Iterated elimination of dominated strategies in a Bertrand-Edgeworth model. *Review of Economic Studies* 59: 163–76.

Bowley, A. 1924. *The Mathematical Groundwork of the Economics*. Oxford: Oxford University Press.

Brander, J., and B. Spencer. 1983. Strategic commitment with R&D: The symmetric case. *Bell Journal of Economics* 14: 225–35.

Bresnahan, T. F. 1981. Duopoly models with consistent conjectures. *American Economic Review* 71: 934–45.

Bresnahan, T. F. 1989. Empirical studies of industries with market power. In R Schmalensee and R. Willig, eds., *Handbook of Industrial Organization*, vol. 2. New York Elsevier Science, pp. 1011–57.

Bresnahan, T. F. 1997. Testing and measurement in competition models. In D. Kreps and K. Wallis eds., *Advances in Economics and Econometrics: Theory and Applications*, Seven World Congress, vol. 3.

Bresnahan, T. F., and P. Reiss. 1990. Entry in monopoly markets. *Review of Economic Studies* 57: 531–53.

Brock, W., and J. Scheinkman. 1985. Price-setting supergames with capacity contraints. *Review of Economic Studies* 52: 371–82.

Brown, G. W. 1951. Iterative solutions of games by fictitious play. In T. C. Koopmans, ed., *Activity Analysis of Production and Allocation*. New York: Wiley pp. 374–76.

Browning, M. 1987. Prices vs. quantities vs. laissez-faire. *Review of Economic Studies* 54: 91–94.

Browning, M., A. Deaton, and M. Irish. 1985. A profitable approach to labor supply and commodity demands over the life-cycle. *Econometrica* 53: 503–43.

Budd, C., C. Harris, and J. Vickers. 1993. A model of the evolution of duopoly: Does the asymmetry between firms tend to increase or decrease? *Review of Economic Studies* 60: 543–73.

Bulow, J., J. Geanakoplos, and P. Klemperer. 1985a. Multimarket oligopoly: Strategic substitutes and complements. *Journal of Political Economy* 93: 488–511.

Bulow, J., J. Geanokoplos, and P. Klemperer. 1985b. Holding idle capacity to deter entry. *Economic Journal* 95: 178–82.

Cabral, L., and M. Riordan. 1994. The learning curve, market dominance, and predatory pricing. *Econometrica* 62: 1115–40.

Caminal, R. 1990. A dynamic duopoly model with asymmetric information. *Journal of Industrial Economics* 38: 315–33.

Caminal, R., and C. Matutes. 1990. Endogenous switching costs in a duopoly model. *International Journal of Industrial Organization* 8: 353–73.

Caminal, R., and X. Vives. 1996. Why market share matters: An information-based theory. *Rand Journal of Economics* 27: 221–39.

Caminal, R., and X. Vives. 1999. Price dynamics and consumer learning. *Journal of Economics and Management Strategy* 8: 95–131.

Campos, J., and A. J. Padilla. 1996. On the limiting behavior of asymmetric Cournot oligopoly: A reconsideration. CEMFI, Working Paper 9607.

Canoy, M. 1996. Product differentiation in a Bertrand-Edgeworth duopoly. *Journal of Economic Theory* 70: 158–79.

Caplin, A., and B. Nalebuff. 1991. Aggregation and imperfect competition: On the existence of equilibrium. *Econometrica* 59: 25–69.

Carlton, D. W. 1989. The theory and the facts of how markets clear: Is industrial organization valuable for understanding macroeconomics? In R. Schmalensee and R. D. Willig, eds., *Handbook of Industrial Organization*, vol. 1. Handbooks in Economics 10. Amsterdam: North Holland, pp. 909–46.

Cave, J., and S. Salant. 1987. Cartels that vote: Agricultural marketing boards and induced voting behavior. In E. Bailey, ed., *Public Regulation: New Perspectives on Institutions and Policies*. Cambridge: MIT Press, pp. 255–83.

Chamberlin, E. H. 1929. Duopoly: Value where sellers are few. *Quarterly Journal of Economics* 43: 63–100.

Chamberlin, E. H. 1933. *The Theory of Monopolistic Competition*. Cambridge: Harvard University Press.

Chamberlin, E. H. 1948. An Experimental Imperfect Market. *Journal of Political Economy* 56: 95–108.

Charnes, G. 1998. Pre-play communications and credibility: A test of Aumann's conjecture. Working Paper 293. Universitat Pompeu Fabra.

Cheng, L. 1985. Comparing Bertrand and Cournot equilibria: A geometric approach. *Rand Journal of Economics* 16: 146–52.

Chevalier, J. A., and D. S. Scharsftein. 1996. Capital market imperfections and countercyclical markups: Theory and evidence. *American Economic Review* 86: 703–35.

Chiappori, P. A. 1985. Distribution of income and the "law of demand." *Econometrica* 53: 109–27.

Chipman, J. S., and J. C. Moore. 1976. The scope of consumer's surplus arguments. In A. M. Thang et al., eds., *Evolution Welfare and the Time in Economics: Essays in Honor of Nicholas Georgescu-Roegen*. Lexington, MA: Lexington Books.

Chipman, J. S., and Moore, J. C. 1980. Compensation variation, consumer's surplus and welfare. *American Economic Review* 72: 933–49.

Clarke, R. 1983. Collusion and the incentives for information sharing. Working Paper 8233. University of Wisconsin-Madison.

Compte, O. 1998. Communication in repeated games with imperfect private monitoring. *Econometrica* 66: 597–626.

Compte, O., F. Jenny, and P. Rey. 1997. Capacity constraints, mergers and collusion Mimeo.

Cooper, R., and A. John. 1988. Coordinating coordination failures in Keynesian models. *Quarterly Journal of Economics* 103: 441–63.

Cooper, R., D. DeJong, R. Forsythe, and T. Ross. 1989a. Communication in the battle of the sexes game: Some experimental results. *Rand Journal of Economics* 20: 568–87.

Cooper, R., D. DeJong, R. Forsythe, and T. Ross. 1989b. Communication in Coordination Games. Working Paper Series 89-16. College of Business Administration, University of Iowa.

Cooper, T. E. 1986. Most-favored-customer pricing and tacit collusion. *Rand Journal of Economics* 17: 377–88.

Corchón, L., and Mas-Colell, A. 1996. On the stability of best reply and gradient systems with applications to imperfectly competitive models. *Economic Letters* 51: 59–65.

Cournot, A. 1838. *Recherches sur les principes mathematiques de la theorie des richesses* English edition (ed. N. Bacon): *Researches into the Mathematical Principles of the Theory of Wealth*. New York: Macmillan, 1987.

Cowling, K., and Waterson, M. 1976. Price cost margins and market structure. *Economica* 43: 267–74.

Cramton, P., and T. Palfrey. 1990. Cartel enforcement with uncertainty about costs. *International Economic Review* 31: 1.

Crawford, V. 1998. A survey of experiments on communication via cheap talk. *Journal of Economic Theory* 78: 286–98.

Crawford, V., and J. Sobel. 1982. Strategic information transmission. *Econometrica* 50: 1431–52.

Cyert, R. M., and M. DeGroot. 1970. Multiperiod decision models with alternating choice as a solution to the duopoly problem. *Quarterly Journal of Economics* 84: 410–29.

D'Aspremont, C., J. J. Gabszewicz, and J. F. Thisse. 1979. On Hotelling's stability in competition. *Econometrica* 47: 1145–50.

D'Aspremont, C., and L.-A. Gérard-Varet. 1979. Incentives and incomplete information. *Journal of Public Economics* 11: 25–45.

D'Orey, V. 1995. Fixed point theorems for correspondences with values in a partially ordered set and extended supermodular games. Working Paper 252. Universidade Nova de Lisboa.

Dana, R.-A., and L. Montrucchio. 1986. Dynamic complexity in duopoly games. *Journal of Economic Theory* 40: 40–56.

Dansby, R. E., and R. Willig. 1979. Industry performance gradient indexes. *American Economic Review* 69: 249–60.

Dasgupta, P., and E. Maskin. 1986. The existence of equilibria in discontinuous economic games II: Applications. *Review of Economic Studies* 53: 1–41.

Dasgupta, P., and J. Stiglitz. 1988. Learning by doing, market structure and industrial and trade policies. *Oxford Economic Papers* 40: 246–68.

Dastidar, K. G. 1995. On the existence of pure strategy Bertrand equilibrium. *Economic Theory* 5: 19–32.

Dastidar, K. G. 1997. Comparing Cournot and Bertrand in a homogeneous product market. *Journal of Economic Theory* 75: 205–12.

Dastidar, K. G. 1998. Is a Cournot equilibrium locally stable? In *Games and Economic Behavior*, forthcoming.

Daughety, A. F. 1985. Reconsidering Cournot: The Cournot equilibrium is consistent. *Rand Journal of Economics* 16: 368–79.

Daughety, A., and R. Forsythe. 1987a. Industrywide regulation and the formation of reputations: A laboratory analysis. In E. Bailey, ed., *Public Regulation: New Perspectives on Institutions and Policies*. Cambridge: MIT Press, pp. 347–98.

Daughety, A., and R. Forsythe. 1987b. Regulatory-induced industrial organization. *Journal of Law, Economics, and Industrial Organization* 3: 397–434.

Davidson, C., and R. Deneckere. 1986. Long-run competition in capacity, short-run competition in price, and the Cournot model. *Rand Journal of Economics* 17: 404–15.

Davidson, C., and R. Deneckere. 1990. Excess capacity and collusion. *International Economic Review* 31: 521–41.

Debreu, G. 1952. A social equilibrium existence theorem. *Proceedings of the National Academy of Sciences* 38: 886–93.

DeGraba, P. 1995. Characterizing solutions of supermodular games: Intuitive comparative statics, and unique equilibria. *Economic Theory* 51: 181–88.

DeGroot, M. 1970. *Optimal Statistical Decisions*. New York: McGraw-Hill.

Demange, G. 1985. Free entry and stability in a Cournot model. Technical Report 463, Institute for Mathematical Studies in the Social Sciences, Stanford University.

Deneckere, R. 1983. Duopoly supergames with product differentiation. *Economics Letters* 11: 37–42.

Deneckere, R., and D. Kovenock. 1992. Price leadership. *Review of Economic Studies* 59: 143–62.

Deneckere, R., and M. Rothschild. 1992. Monopolistic competition and preference diversity. *Review of Economic Studies* 59: 361–73.

Diamond, P. 1982. Aggregate demand management in search equilibrium. *Journal of Political Economy* 90: 881–94.

Diamond, D., and P. Dybvig. 1983. Bank runs, deposit insurance, and liquidity. *Journal of Political Economy* 91: 401–19.

Dierickx, I., C. Matutes, and D. Neven. 1988. Indirect taxation and Cournot equilibrium. *International Journal of Industrial Organization* 6: 385–99.

Dierker, E. 1991. Competition for customers. In W. A. Barnett, B. Cornet, C. d'Aspremont, J. J. Gabszewicz, and A. Mas-Colell, eds., *Equilibrium Theory in Applications*. Cambridge: Cambridge University Press, pp. 383–402.

Dixit, A. 1980. The role of investment in entry deterrence. *Economic Journal* 90: 95–106.

Dixit, A. 1986. Comparative statics for oligopoly. *International Economic Review* 27: 107–22.

Dixit, A., and C. Shapiro. 1984. Entry dynamics with mixed strategies. In L. G. Thomas, ed., Strategic Planning. Lexington, MA: Lexington Books. pp. 63–79.

Dixit, A., and J. Stiglitz. 1977. Monopolistic competition and optimum product diversity. *American Economic Review* 67: 297–308.

Dixit, A., and J. Stiglitz. 1979. Monopolistic competition and optimum product diversity: Reply. *American Economic Review* 69: 961–63.

Dixon, H. 1985. Strategic investment in an industry with a competitive product market. *Journal of Industrial Economics* 33: 483–99.

Dixon, H. 1987. Approximate Bertrand equilibria in a replicated industry. *Review of Economic Studies* 54: 47–62.

Dixon, H. 1990. Bertrand-Edgeworth equilibria when firms avoid turning customers away. *Journal of Industrial Economics* 49: 131–46.

ixon, H. 1992. The competitive outcome as the equilibrium in an Edgeworthian price-
quantity model. *Economic Journal* 102: 301–309.

omowitz, I., R. G. Hubbard, and B. C. Petersen. 1986. Business cycles and the rela-
onship between concentration and price-cost margins. *Rand Journal of Economics* 17:
-17.

owrick, S. 1986. Von Stackelberg and Cournot duopoly: Choosing roles. *Rand Journal
Economics* 17: 251–60.

riskill, R. A., and S. McCafferty. 1989. Dynamic duopoly with adjustment costs: A
fferential game approach. *Journal of Economic Theory* 49: 324–38.

ubey, P., and M. Kaneko. 1984. Information patterns and Nash equilibria in extensive
ames: I. *Mathematical Social Sciences* 8: 111–39.

udey, M. 1992. Dynamic Edgeworth-Bertrand competition. *Quarterly Journal of Eco-
mics* 107: 1461–77.

upuit, J. [1944] 1969. On the Measurement of the Utility of Public Works. In K. J.
rrow and T. Scitovsky, eds., *Readings in Welfare Economics*, Homewood: Irwin.

ybvig, P., and Ch. Spatt. 1983. Adoption externalities as public goods. *Journal of
blic Economics* 20: 231–47.

asley, D., and N. Kiefer. 1988. Controlling a stochastic process with unknown
arameters. *Econometrica* 56: 1045–64.

aton, C., and R. Ware. 1987. A theory of market structure with sequential entry. *Rand
urnal of Economics* 18: 1–16.

aton, J., and M. Engers. 1990. Intertemporal price competition. *Econometrica* 58: 637–
.

dgeworth, F. 1881. *Mathematical Psychics: An Essay on the Application of Mathematics to
e Moral Sciences*. Reprints of Economic Classics. New York: Augustus M. Kelley
ublishers.

dgeworth, F. 1922. The mathematical economies of Professor Amoroso. *Economic
urnal* 32: 400–407.

dgeworth, F. 1925. The pure theory of monopoly. In *Papers Relating to Political Econ-
my*, vol. 1, pp. 111–42.

dlin, A. S., and Ch. Shannon. 1998. Strict monotonicity in comparative statics. *Journal
Economic Theory* 81: 201–19.

eckhoudt, L., and C. Gollier. 1995. Demand for risky assets and the monotone prob-
bility ratio order. *Journal of Risk and Uncertainty* 11: 113–22.

lison, G. 1994. Cooperation in the prisoner's dilemma with anonymous random
atching. *Review of Economic Studies* 61: 567–88.

ricson, W. 1969. A note on the posterior mean of a population mean. *Journal of the
yal Statistical Society* 31: 332–34.

ricson, J., and A. Pakes. 1995. Markov-perfect industry dynamics: A framework for
mpirical work. *Review of Economic Studies* 62: 53–82.

Farrell, J. 1987. Cheap talk, coordination, and entry. *Rand Journal of Economics* 18: 34–39.

Farrell, J. 1993. Meaning and credibility in cheap-talk games. *Games and Economic Behavior* 5: 514–31.

Farrell, J., and M. Rabin. 1996. Cheap talk. *Journal of Economic Perspectives* 10: 103–18.

Farrell, J., and G. Saloner. 1986. Installed base and compatibility: Innovation, product preannouncements, and predation. *American Economic Review* 76: 940–55.

Farrell, J., and C. Shapiro. 1990a. Horizontal mergers: An equilibrium analysis. *American Economic Review* 80: 107–26.

Farrell, J., and C. Shapiro. 1990b. Asset ownership and market structure in oligopoly. *Rand Journal of Economics* 21: 275–92.

Faulí-Oller, R. 1996. Mergers for market power in a Cournot setting and merger guidelines. Mimeo. University of Alicante.

Faulí-Oller, R., and M. Giralt. 1995. Competition and cooperation within a multidivisional firm. *Journal of Industrial Economics* 43: 77–99.

Fellner, W. 1949. *Competition among the Few.* New York: Knopf.

Fernández, N., and P. Marín. 1998. Market power and multimarket contact: Some evidence from the Spanish hotel industry. *Journal of Industrial Economics* 46: 301–15.

Fershtman, Ch., and E. Muller. 1984. Capital accumulation games of infinite duration. *Journal of Economic Theory* 33: 322–39.

Fershtman, Ch., and K. Judd. 1987. Equilibrium incentives in oligopoly. *American Economic Review* 77: 927–40.

Fershtman, Ch., and M. Kamien. 1987. Dynamic duopolistic competition with sticky prices. *Econometrica* 55: 1151–64.

Fouraker, L., and S. Siegel. 1963. *Bargaining Behavior.* New York: McGraw-Hill.

Fraas, A., and D. Greer. 1977. Market structure and price collusion: An empirical analysis. *Journal of Industrial Economics* 26: 21–44.

Fraysse, J., and M. Moreau. 1985. Collusive equilibria in oligopolies with long but finite lives. *European Economic Review* 27: 45–55.

Frayssé, J. 1986. *Equilibres de Cournot dans les grands marchés.* Monographies d'Econométrie. Paris: CNRS.

Freixas, X., and A. Mas-Colell. 1987. Engel curves leading to the weak axiom in the aggregate. *Econometrica* 55: 515–31.

Friedman, J. W. 1967. An experimental study of cooperative duopoly. *Econometrica* 35: 379–97.

Friedman, J. W. 1971. A noncooperative equilibrium for supergames. *Review of Economic Studies* 38: 1–12.

Friedman, J. 1977. *Oligopoly and the Theory of Games.* Amsterdam: North-Holland.

Friedman, J. 1983. *Oligopoly Theory.* Cambridge: Cambridge University Press.

Friedman, J. 1985. Cooperative equilibria in finite horizon noncooperative supergames. *Journal of Economic Theory* 35: 390–98.

Friedman, J. 1988. On the strategic importance of prices versus quantities. *Rand Journal of Economics* 19: 607–22.

Frink, O. 1942. Topology in lattices. *Transactions of the American Mathematical Society* 51: 569–82.

Fudenberg, D., D. Levine, and E. Maskin. 1994. The folk theorem in repeated games with imperfect public information. *Econometrica* 62: 997–1039.

Fudenberg, D., and D. Levine. 1998. *Theory of Learning in Games.* Cambridge: MIT Press.

Fudenberg, D., and E. Maskin. 1986. The folk theorem in repeated games with discounting and incomplete information. *Econometrica* 54: 533–54.

Fudenberg, D., and J. Tirole. 1983. Capital as a commitment: Strategic investment to deter mobility. *Journal of Economic Theory* 31: 227–56.

Fudenberg, D., and J. Tirole. 1984. The fat cat effect, the puppy dog ploy and the lean and hungry look. *American Economic Review, Papers and Proceedings* 74: 361–68.

Fudenberg, D., and J. Tirole. 1986. Fundamentals of pure and applied economics. In A. Jacquemin, ed., *Dynamic Models of Oligopoly.* vol. 3. New York: Harwood.

Fudenberg, D., and J. Tirole. 1991. *Game Theory.* Cambridge: MIT Press.

Gabay, D., and H. Moulin. 1980. On the uniqueness and stability of Nash equilibrium in non cooperative games. In A. Bensoussan, P. Kleindorfer, and C. Tapiero, eds., *Applied Stochastic Control in Econometric and Management Science.* Amsterdam: North-Holland.

Gabszewicz, J., and J. P. Vial. 1972. Oligopoly "à la Cournot" in a general equilibrium analysis. *Journal of Economic Theory* 4: 381–400.

Gabszewicz, J. J., and J.-F. Thisse. 1992. Location. In R. J. Aumann and S. Harts eds., *Handbook of Game Theory with Economic Applications.* Amsterdam: North Holland.

Gal-Or, E. 1985. First mover and second mover advantages. *International Economic Review* 26: 649–53.

Gal-Or, E. 1986. Information transmission—Cournot and Bertrand equilibria. *Review of Economic Studies* 53: 85–92.

Gal-Or, E. 1987. First mover disadvantages with private information. *Review of Economic Studies* 54: 279–92.

Gal-Or, E. 1988. The advantages of imprecise information. *Rand Journal of Economics* 19: 266–75.

Gale, D., and H. Nikaido. 1965. The Jacobian matrix and global univalence of mappings. *Mathematische Annalen* 159: 81–93.

Gasmi, F., J.-J. Laffont, and Q. H. Vuong. 1990. A structural approach to empirical analysis of collusive behavior. *European Economic Review* 34: 513–23.

Gasmi, F., J.-J. Laffont, and Q. H. Vuong. 1992. Econometric analysis of collusive behavior in a Soft-Drik market. *Journal of Economics and Management Strategy* 1: 277–311.

Genesove, D. 1998. Narrative evidence on the dynamics of collusion: The Sugar Institute case. Mimeo.

Gérard-Varet, L. A., and H. Moulin. 1978. Correlation and duopoly. *Journal of Economic Theory* 19: 123–49.

Ghemawat, P. 1990. The snowball effect. *International Journal of Industrial Organization* 8: 335–51.

Gilbert, R., and D. Newbery. 1982. Preemptive patenting and the persistence of monopoly. *American Economic Review* 72: 584–26.

Gilbert, R., and X. Vives. 1986. Entry deterrence and the free rider problem. *Review of Economic Studies* 172: 71–83.

Gillemin, V., and A. Pollack. 1974. *Differential Topology*. Englewood Cliff, NJ: Prentice Hall.

Gliksberg, I. L. 1952. A further generalization of the Kakutani fixed point theorem with application to Nash equilibrium points. *Proceedings of the American Mathematical Society* 38: 170–74.

Green, E. 1980. Noncooperative price taking in large dynamic markets. *Journal of Economic Theory* 22: 155–82.

Green, R. J., and D. Newbery. 1992. Competition in the British electricity spot market. *Journal of Political Economy* 100: 929–53.

Green, E., and R. Porter. 1984. Non-cooperative collusion under imperfect price information. *Econometrica* 52: 87–100.

Green, R. J., and N. Stokey. 1980. A two-person game of information transmission. Discussion Paper 751. Harvard Institute of Economic Research.

Grossman, S. 1981a. Nash equilibrium and the industrial organization of markets with large fixed costs. *Econometrica* 49: 1149–72.

Grossman, S. 1981b. The informational role of Walrasian and private disclosure about the product quality. *Journal of Law and Economics* 24: 461–83.

Guth, W., R. Schmittberger, and B. Schwarze. 1982. An experimental analysis of ultimatum bargaining. *Journal of Economic Behavior and Organization* 3: 367–88.

Häckner, J. 1994. Collusive pricing in markets for vertically differentiated products. *International Journal of Industrial Organization* 12: 155–77.

Hadar, J., and W. R. Russell. 1978. Applications in economic theory and analysis. In G. Whitmore and M. Findlay, eds., *Stochastic Dominance*. Lexington, MA: Lexington Books, ch. 7.

Hahn, F. 1962. The stability of the Cournot oligopoly solution concept. *Review of Economic Studies* 29: 329–31.

Haltinwanger, J., and J. Harrington. 1991. The impact of cyclical demand movements on collusive behavior. *Rand Journal of Economics* 22: 89–106.

Hamilton, J., and S. Slutsky. 1990. Endogenous timing in duopoly games: Stackelberg or Cournot equilibria. *Games and Economic Behavior* 2: 29–46.

Hanig, M. 1986. Differential gaming models of oligopoly. PhD dissertation. Massachusetts Institute of Technology.

Harrington, J. 1986. Limit pricing when the potential entrant is uncertain of its cost function. *Econometrica* 54: 429–37.

Harrington, J. 1987. Oligopolistic entry deterrence under incomplete information. *Rand Journal of Economics* 18: 211–31.

Harrington, J. 1991. The determination of price and output quotas in a heterogeneous cartel. *International Economic Review* 32: 767–92.

Harrington, J. 1995. Cooperation in a one-shot prisoners' dilemma. *Games and Economic Behavior* 8: 364–77.

Harris, Ch. 1994. On the rate of convergence of continuous-time fictitious play. ISP Discussion Paper 52. Boston University.

Harsanyi, J. C. 1967–1968. Games with incomplete information played by Bayesian players. *Management Science* 14: 159–182, 320–334, 486–502.

Harsanyi, J. C. 1973. Games with randomly disturbed payoffs: A new rationale for mixed-strategy equilibrium points. *International Journal of Game Theory* 1: 1–25.

Harsanyi, J. C., and R. Selten. 1988. *A General Theory of Equilibrium Selection in Games.* Cambridge: MIT Press.

Hart, O. 1982. Reasonable conjectures. Discussion Paper. Suntory Toyota International Centre for Economics and Related Disciplines, London School of Economics.

Hart, O. 1985. Monopolistic competition in the spirit of Chamberlin: A general mode. *Review of Economic Studies* 52: 529–46.

Hart, S., and K. Schmeidler. 1989. Existence of correlated equilibria. *Mathematics of Operations Research* 14: 18–25.

Hausman, J. 1981. Exact consumer's surplus and deadweight loss. *American Economic Review* 71: 662–76.

Hay, G., and D. Kelley. 1974. An empirical survey of price fixing conspiracies. *Journal of Law and Economics* 17: 13–38.

Hendricks, K., and R. Porter. 1988. An empirical study of an auction with asymmetric information. *American Economic Review* 78: 865–83.

Hendricks, K., and R. Porter. 1989. Collusion in auctions. *Annales d'Economie et de Statistique* (15–16): 217–30.

Hendricks, K., and Porter, R. 1993a. Bidding behaviour in OCS drainage auctions: Theory and evidence. *European Economic Review* 37: 320–28.

Hendricks, K., and Porter, R. 1993b. Optimal selling strategies for oil and gas leases with an informed buyer. *American Economic Review* 83: 234–39.

Hendricks, K., and Porter, R. 1994. Auctions for oil and gas leases with an informed bidder and a random reservation price. *Econometrica* 62: 1415–44.

Herk, L. F. 1993. Consumer choice and Cournot behavior in capacity constrained duopoly competition. *Rand Journal of Economics* 24: 399–417.

Hicks, J. R. 1941. The rehabilitation of consumer's surplus. *Review of Economic Studies* 9 108–16.

Hicks, J. R. 1946. *Value and Capital*. Oxford: Oxford University Press.

Hildenbrand, W. 1983. On the law of demand. *Econometrica* 51: 997–1019.

Hirsch, M. 1985. Systems of differential equations that are competitive or cooperative II: Convergence almost. SIAM, *Journal of Mathematical Analysis* 16: 423–39.

Hirsch, M. 1988. Stability and convergence in strongly monotone dynamical system *Journal für diereine and angewandte mathematik* 383: 1–53.

Hoggatt, A. 1959. An experimental business game. *Behavioral Science* 4: 192–203.

Holt, C. 1995. Industrial organization: A survey of laboratory research. In J. Kagel and A. Roth, eds., *The Handbook of Experimental Economics*. Princeton: Princeton University Press, pp. 349–443.

Holt, C., and D. Davis. 1990. The effects of non-binding price announcements in posted-offer markets. *Economics letters* 34: 307–10.

Holt, C., and D. Scheffman. 1987. Facilitating practices: The effects of advance notice and best-price policies. *Rand Journal of Economics* 18: 187–97.

Hotelling, H. 1929. Stability in competition. *Economic Journal* 39: 41–57.

Hotelling, H. 1969. The general welfare in relation to problems of taxation and the railway and utility rates. In K. L. Arrow and T. Scitovsky, eds., Homewood, IL Irwin.

Howard, J. 1954. Collusive behavior. *Journal of Business* 27: 196–204.

Ingersoll, J. 1987. *Theory of Financial Decision Making*. Rowman and Littlefield Studies in Financial Economics. Totowa, NJ: Littlefield, Adams; Rowman and Littlefield.

Jerison, M. 1984. Aggregation and pairwise aggregation of demand when the distribution of income is fixed. *Journal of Economic Theory* 33: 1–31.

Jewitt, I. 1987. Risk aversion and the choice between risky prospects: The preservation of comparative statics results. *Review of Economic Studies* 54: 73–85.

Jin, J. Y. 1996. Comparing Cournot and Bertrand equilibria revisited. WZB, Working Paper.

Judd, K. L. 1985. Credible spatial preemption. *Rand Journal of Economics* 16: 153–66.

Jun, B., and X. Vives. 1998. Dynamic price competition and Stackelberg warfare. Discussion Paper 1838. Harvard University.

Kagel, J., and A. Roth. 1995. *The Handbook of Experimental Economics*. Princenton Princeton University Press.

Kalai, E., and M. A. Satterthwaite. 1986. The kinked demand curve, facilitating practice, and oligopolistic competition. Northwestern Center for Mathematical Studies in Economics and Management Science. Working Paper 677. Northwestern University.

Kandori, M. 1991. Correlated demand shocks and prices wars during booms. *Review of Economic Studies* 58: 171–80.

Kandori, M. 1992a. Social norms and community enforcement. *Review of Economic Studies* 59: 63–80.

Kandori, M. 1992b. The use of information in repeated games with imperfect monitoring. *Review of Economic Studies* 59: 581–93.

Kandori, M., and H. Matsushima. 1998. Private observation, communication and collusion. *Econometrica* 66: 627–52.

Kaneko, M. 1982. Some remarks on the folk theorem in game theory. *Mathematical Social Sciences* 3: 281–90.

Karlin, S. 1968. *Total Positivity*, vol. 1. Stanford: Stanford University Press.

Karlin, S., and Y. Rinott. 1980. Classes of orderings of measures and related correlation inequalities: A multivariate totally positive distribution. *Journal of Multivariate Analysis* 10: 467–98.

Karp, L., and J. Perloff. 1993. A dynamic model of oligopoly in the coffee export market. *American Journal of Agricultural Economics* 75: 448–57.

Karp, L., and J. Perloff. 1989. Dynamic oligopoly in the rice export market. *Review of Economics and Statistics* 71: 462–70.

Katz, M., and C. Shapiro. 1986. Technology adoption in the presence of network externalities. *Journal of Political Economy* 94: 822–41.

Keller, G., and S. Rady. 1999. Optimal experimentation in a changing environment. *Review of Economic Studies* 66: 475–507.

Keller, G., and S. Rady. 1998. Market experimentation in a dynamic differentiated-goods duopoly. Mimeo.

Kihlstrom, R. 1984. A Bayesian exposition of Blackwell's theorem on the comparison of experiments. In M. Boyer and R. Kihlstrom, eds., *Bayesian Models in Economic Theory*. New York: Elsevier Science.

Kihlstrom, R., and X. Vives. 1992. Collusion with asymmetrically informed firms. *Journal of Economics and Management Strategy* 1: 371–96.

Klemperer, P. 1987. The competitiveness of markets with switching costs. *Rand Journal of Economics* 18: 137–50.

Klemperer, P. 1995. Competition when consumers have switching costs: An overview with application to industrial organization, macroeconomics, and international trade. *Review of Economic Studies* 62: 515–40.

Klemperer, P., and M. Meyer. 1986. Price competition versus quantity competition: The role of uncertainty. *Rand Journal of Economics* 17: 618–38.

Klemperer, P., and M. Meyer. 1989. Supply function equilibria in oligopoly under uncertainty. *Econometrica* 57: 1243–77.

Kohlberg, E., and J.-F. Mertens. 1986. On the strategic stability of equilibria. *Econometrica* 54: 1003–38.

Kolstad, Ch., and L. Mathiesen. 1987. Necessary and sufficient conditions for uniqueness of a Cournot equilibrium. *Review of Economic Studies* 54: 681–90.

Kovenock, D., and S. Roy. 1995. Free riding in non-cooperative entry deterrence with differentiated products. Mimeo. Purdue University.

Kreps, D., and J. Scheinkman. 1983. Quantity pre-commitment and Bertrand competition yield Cournot outcomes. *Bell Journal of Economics* 14: 326–37.

Kreps, D., and R. Wilson. 1982a. Sequential equilibrium. *Econometrica* 50: 863–94.

Kreps, D., and R. Wilson. 1982b. Reputation and imperfect information. *Journal of Economic Theory* 27: 253–79.

Kreps, D., P. Milgrom, J. Roberts, and R. Wilson. 1982. Rational cooperation in the finitely repeated prisoner's dilemma. *Journal of Economic Theory* 27: 245–52.

Krishna, V. 1992. Learning in games with strategic complementarities. Working Paper 92-073. Harvard Business School.

Krishna, V., and T. Sjöström. 1994. On the rate of convergence of fictitious play. Mimeo. Pennsylvania State University and Harvard University.

Kühn, K.-U. 1997. Nonlinear pricing in vertically related duopolies. *Rand Journal of Economics* 28: 37–62.

Kühn, K.-U., and X. Vives. 1995a. Information exchange among firms and their impact on competition. European Commission Document.

Kühn, K.-U., and X. Vives. 1995b. Excess entry in monopolistic competition revisited. Mimeo. Institut d'Anàlisi Econòmica.

Kühn, K.-U., and X. Vives. 1999. Excess entry, vertical integration and welfare. *Rand Journal of Economics*, forthcoming.

Kukushkin, N. 1992. An existence theorem for Cournot equilibrium. Mimeo. Russian Academy of Sciences, Moscow.

Kultti, K., and H. Salonen. 1997. Undominated equilibria in games with strategic complementarities. *Games and Economic Behavior* 18: 98–115.

Kumar, R., and M. Saterthwaite. 1985. Monopolistic competition, aggregation of competitive information and the amount of product differentiation. *Journal of Economic Theory* 37: 32–54.

Kydland, F. 1975. Noncooperative and dominant player solutions in discrete dynamic games. *International Economic Review* 16: 321–35.

Laffont, J.-J. 1989. *The Economics of Uncertainty and Information*. Cambridge: MIT Press.

Laffont, J.-J., and E. Maskin. 1979. On the difficulty of attaining distributional goals with imperfect information about consumers. *Scandinavian Journal of Economics* 81: 227–37.

Laffont, J.-J., and Q. Vuong. 1993. Structural econometric analysis of descending auctions. *European Economic Review* 37: 329–41.

Laffont, J.-J., H. Ossard, and Q. Vuong. 1995. Econometrics of first-price auctions. *Econometrica* 63: 953–80.

Laitner, J. 1980. Rational duopoly equilibrium. *Quarterly Journal of Economics* 95: 641–62.

ambson, V. E. 1987. Optimal penal codes in price-setting supergames. *Review of Economic Studies* 54: 385–97.

ambson, V. E. 1994. Some results on optimal penal codes in asymmetric Bertrand upergames. *Journal of Economic Theory* 62: 444–68.

ambson, V. E. 1995. Optimal penal codes in nearly symmetric Bertrand supergames vith capacity constraints. *Journal of Mathematical Economics* 24: 1–22.

ancaster, K. J. 1966. A new approach to consumer theory. *Journal of Political Economy* 4: 132–57.

ancaster, K. J. 1971. *Consumer Demand: A New Approach.* New York: Columbia University Press.

ancaster, K. J. 1979. *Variety, Equity and Efficiency.* New York: Columbia University ress.

apham, B., and R. Ware. 1994. Markov puppy dogs and related animals. *International urnal of Industrial Organization* 12: 569–93.

eland, H. 1972. Theory of the firm facing uncertain demand. *American Economic Review* 62: 278–91.

evitan, R., and M. Shubik. 1972. Price duopoly and capacity constraints. *International conomic Review* 13: 111–22.

i, L. 1985. Cournot oligopoly with information sharing. *Rand Journal of Economics* 16: 21–36.

i, L., R. D. McKelvey, and T. Page. 1987. Optimal research for Cournot oligopolists. urnal of Economic Theory 42: 140–66.

ippman, S., J. Mamer, and K. McCardle. 1987. Comparative statics in non-cooperative ames via transfinitely iterated play. *Journal of Economic Theory* 41: 208–303.

iu, L. 1996. Correlated equilibrium of Cournot oligopoly competition. *Journal of Economic Theory* 68: 544–48.

Madden, P. 1995. Elastic demand and the Kreps-Scheinkman extension of the Cournot model. Discussion Paper 9518. University of Manchester.

Madhavan, A., R. Masson, and W. Lesser. 1990. Cooperation or retaliation: An empirical analysis of cartelization. Mimeo.

Maggi, G. 1996. Endogenous leadership in a new market. *Rand Journal of Economics* 27: 41–59.

Maggi, G. 1997. The value of commitment with imperfect observability and private nformation. Mimeo.

Mailath, G. 1989. Simultaneous signaling in an oligopoly model. *Quarterly Journal of conomics* 104: 417–27.

Mailath, G. 1993. Endogenous sequencing of firm decisions. *Journal of Economic Theory* 9: 169–82.

Makowski, L. 1987. Are "rational conjectures" rational? *Journal of Industrial Economics* 6: 35–47.

Malueg, D., and S. Tsutsui. 1998. Distributional assumptions in the theory of oligopoly information exchange. *International Journal of Industrial Organization* 16: 785–97.

Mankiw, G. N., and M. D. Whinston. 1986. Free entry and social inefficiency. *Rand Journal of Economics* 17: 48–58.

Marshall, A. 1920. *Principle of Economics*. London: Macmillan.

Mas-Colell, A. 1975. A model of equilibrium with differentiated commodities. *Journal of Mathematical Economics* 2: 263–95.

Mas-Colell, A. 1982. The Cournotian foundations of Walrasian equilibrium theory: An exposition of recent theory. In W. Hidenbrand, ed., *Advances in Economic Theory*. Cambridge: Cambridge University Press.

Mas-Colell, A. 1984. On a theorem of Schmeidler. *Journal of Mathematical Economics* 13: 201–206.

Maskin, E. 1986. The existence of equilibrium with price-setting firms. *American Economic Review, Papers and Proceedings*, 76: 382–86.

Maskin, E., and J. Riley. 1984. Optimal auctions with risk averse buyers. *Econometrica* 52: 1473–518.

Maskin, E., and J. Tirole. 1987. A theory of dynamic oligopoly, III: Cournot competition. *European Economic Review* 31: 947–68.

Maskin, E., and J. Tirole. 1988a. A theory of dynamic oligopoly I: Overview and quantity competition with large fixed costs. *Econometrica* 56: 549–69.

Maskin, E., and J. Tirole. 1988b. A theory of dynamic oligopoly II: Price competition kinked demand curves, and Edgeworth cycles. *Econometrica* 56: 571–99.

Maskin, E., and J. Tirole. 1997. Markov perfect equilibrium, I: Observable actions. Discussion Paper 1799. Harvard University.

Mason, C. F., O. R. Philips, and C. Nowell. 1992. Duopoly behavior in asymmetric markets: An experimental evaluation. *Review of Economic and Statistics* 74: 662–70.

Massó, J., and R. W. Rosenthal. 1989. More on the "anti–folk theorem." *Journal of Mathematical Economics* 18: 281–90.

Matutes, C., and P. Regibeau. 1988. Mix and match: Product compatibility without network externalities. *Rand Journal of Economics* 19: 221–34.

Matutes, C., and X. Vives. 1998. Imperfect competition, risk taking and regulation in banking. *European Economic Review*, forthcoming.

Mckenzie, L. 1959. Matrices with dominant diagonals and economic theory. In K. Arrow, S. Karlin, and P. Suppes, eds., *Mathematical Methods in the Social Sciences*. Stanford: Stanford University Press, pp. 47–62.

McLennan, A. 1984. Price dispersion and incomplete learning in the long run. *Journal of Economic Dynamics and Control* 7: 331–47.

McLean, R., and M. Riordan. 1989. Industry structure with sequential technology choice. *Journal of Economic Theory* 47: 1–21.

McManus, M. 1962. Numbers and size in Cournot oligopoly. *Yorkshire Bulletin of Social and Economic Research* 14.

McManus, M. 1964. Equilibrium, numbers and size in Cournot oligopoly. *Yorkshire Bulletin of Social Science and Economic Research* 16.

Mertens, J. F., and S. Zamir. 1985. Formulation of Bayesian analysis for games with incomplete information. *International Journal of Game Theory* 10: 619–32.

Michel, P. 1982. On the transversality condition in infinite horizon optimal problems. *Econometrica* 50: 975–86.

Milgrom, P. 1981a. An axiomatic characterization of common knowledge. *Econometrica* 49: 219–22.

Milgrom, P. 1981b. Good news and bad news: Representation theorems and applications. *Bell Journal of Economics* 12: 380–91.

Milgrom, P., and R. Weber. 1982. A theory of auctions and competitive bidding. *Econometrica* 50: 1089–1122.

Milgrom, P., and R. Weber. 1985. Distributional strategies for games with incomplete information. *Mathematics of Operation Research* 10: 619–32.

Milgrom, P., and C. Shannon. 1994. Monotone Comparative Statics. *Econometrica* 62: 157–80.

Milgrom, P., and J. Roberts. 1982a. Limit pricing and entry under incomplete information: An equilibrium analysis. *Econometrica* 50: 443–59.

Milgrom, P., and J. Roberts. 1982b. Predation, reputation and entry deterrence. *Journal of Economic Theory* 27: 280–312.

Milgrom, P., and J. Roberts. 1986. Price and advertising signals of product quality. *Journal of Political Economy* 94: 796–821.

Milgrom, P., and J. Roberts. 1990. Rationalizability, learning, and equilibrium in games with strategic complementarities. *Econometrica* 58: 1255–77.

Milgrom, P., and J. Roberts. 1994. Comparing equilibria. *American Economic Review* 84: 441–59.

Milgrom, P., and J. Roberts. 1996. Coalition-proofness and correlation with arbitrary communication possibilities. *Games and Economic Behavior* 17: 113–28.

Miravete, E., and J. Pernías. 1998. Innovation complementarity and scale of production. Economic Research Reports 98–42. New York University.

Mirman, L., L. Samuelson, and E. Schlee. 1994. Strategic information manipulation in duopolies. *Journal of Economic Theory* 62: 363–84.

Miyazawa, K. 1961. On the convergence of the learning process in a 2×2 nonzero-sum two-person game. Economic Research Program, Research Memorandum 33. Princeton University.

Modigliani, F. 1958. New developments on the oligopoly front. *Journal of Political Economy* 66: 215–32.

Mohring, H. 1971. Alternative welfare gain and loss measures. *Western Economic Journal* 9: 349–68.

Motta, M. 1998. Does symmetry help collusion? Mimeo.

Moulin, H. 1982. *Game Theory for the Social Sciences*. New York: New York University Press.

Moulin, H. 1984. Dominance solvability and Cournot stability. *Mathematical Social Sciences* 7: 83–102.

Myerson, R. 1985. Bayesian equilibrium and incentive compatibility: An introduction. In L. Hurwicz, D. Schmeidler, and H. Sonnesnschein, eds., *Social Goals and Social Organization: Essays in Memory of Elisha Pazner*. Cambridge: Cambridge University Press.

Myerson, R. 1991. *Game Theory: Analysis of Conflict*. Cambridge: Harvard University Press.

Myerson, R., and M. Satterthwaite. 1983. Efficient mechanisms for bilateral trading. *Journal of Economic Theory* 29: 265–81.

Nalebuff, B., and R. Zeckhauser. 1986. The ambiguous antitrust implications of information sharing. Kennedy School of Government, Discussion Paper 147D. Harvard University.

Nash, J. F. 1950a. Equilibrium points in *n*-person games. *Proceedings of the National Academy of Sciences* 36: 48–49.

Nash, J. F. 1950b. Non-cooperative games. PhD dissertation. Mathematics Department Princeton University.

Nash, J. F. 1950c. The bargaining problem. *Econometrica* 18: 155–62.

Nash, J. F. 1951. Non-cooperative games. *Econometrica* 18: 155–62.

Nash, J. F. 1953. Two-person cooperative games. *Econometrica* 21: 128–40.

Nikaido, H., and K. Isoda. 1955. Note on noncooperative convex games. *Pacific Journal of Mathematics* 5: 807–15.

Nishimura, K., and J. Friedman. 1981. Existence of Nash equilibrium in *n* person games without quasi-concavity. *International Economic Review* 22: 637–48.

Novshek, W. 1980. Cournot equilibrium with free entry. *Review of Economic Studies* 47: 473–86.

Novshek, W. 1985a. On the existence of Cournot equilibrium. *Review of Economic Studies* 52: 86–98.

Novshek, W. 1985b. Perfectly competitive markets as the limits of Cournot markets. *Journal of Economic Theory* 35: 75–82.

Novshek, W., and H. Sonnenschein. 1978. Cournot and Walras equilibrium. *Journal of Economic Theory* 19: 223–66.

Novshek, W., and H. Sonnenschein. 1979. Marginal consumers and neoclassical demand theory. *Journal of Political Economy* 87: 1368–76.

Novshek, W., and H. Sonnenschein. 1982. Fulfilled expectations Cournot duopoly with information acquisition and release. *Bell Journal of Economics* 13: 214–18.

Okuguchi, K. 1976. *Expectations and Stability in Oligopoly Models*. Berlin: Springer Verlag.

Okuguchi, K. 1987. Equilibrium prices in the Bertrand and Cournot oligopolies. *Journal of Economic Theory* 42: 128–39.

Okuno-Fujiwara, M., and A. Postlewaite. 1995. Social norms and random matching games. *Games and Economic Behavior* 9: 79–109.

Okuno-Fujiwara, M., and K. Suzumura. 1993. Symmetric Cournot oligopoly and economic welfare: A synthesis. *Economic Theory* 3: 43–59.

Okuno-Fujiwara, M., A. Postlewaite, and K. Suzumura. 1990. Strategic information revelation. *Review of Economic Studies* 57: 25–47.

Olley, S., and A. Pakes. 1996. The dynamics of productivity in the telecommunications equipment industry. *Econometrica* 64: 1263–97.

Ormiston, M., and E. Schlee. 1992. Necessary conditions for comparative statics under uncertainty. *Economic Letters* 40: 429–34.

Ormiston, M., and E. Schlee. 1993. Comparative statics under uncertainty for a class of economic agents. *Journal of Economic Theory* 61: 412–22.

Osborne, M. J., and C. Pitchnik. 1986. Price competition in a capacity constrained duopoly. *Journal of Economic Theory* 38: 238–60.

Pakes, A. 1998. A framework for applied dynamic analysis in I.O. Invited lecture at the Annual Meeting of the European Economic Society, Berlin.

Pakes, A., and P. McGuire. 1994. Computing Markov perfect equilibria: Numerical implications of a dynamic differentiated product model. *Rand Journal of Economics* 25: 555–89.

Pakes, A., G. Gowrisankaran, and P. McGuire. 1993. Code for implementing the Pakes-McGuire algorithm for computing Markov perfect equilibrium. Mimeo. Yale University.

Pal, D. 1991. Cournot duopoly with two production periods and cost differentials. *Journal of Economic Theory* 55: 441–49.

Papavassilopoulos, G. P., and J. B. Cruz. 1979. On the uniqueness of Nash strategies for a class of analytic differential games. *Journal of Optimization Theory and Applications* 27: 309–14.

Papavassilopoulos, G. P., J. V. Medanic, and J. B. Cruz. 1979. On the existence of Nash strategies and solutions to coupled Riccati equations in linear-quadratic games. *Journal of Optimization Theory and Applications* 28: 49–76.

Papavassilopoulos, G. P., and G. J. Olsder. 1984. On the linear-quadratic, closed-loop, no-memory Nash game. *Journal of Optimization Theory and Applications* 42: 551–60.

Pascoa, M. 1993. Noncooperative equilibrium and Chamberlinian monopolistic competition. *Journal of Economic Theory* 60: 335–53.

Pascoa, M. 1997. Monopolistic competition and non-neighboring goods. *Economic Theory* 9: 129–42.

Pearce, D. 1984. Rationalizable strategic behavior and the problem of perfection. *Econometrica* 52: 1029–50.

Perry, M. K. 1984. Scale economies, imperfect competition and public policy. *Journal of Industrial Economics* 32: 313–30.

Perry, M. K., and R. Groff. 1985. Resale price maintenance and forward integration into a monopolistically competitive industry. *Quarterly Journal of Economics* 100: 1293–1311.

Perry, M. K., and R. H. Porter. 1985. Oligopoly and the incentive for horizontal merger. *American Economic Review* 75: 219–27.

Pettengill, J. 1979. Monopolistic competition and optimum product diversity: Comment. *American Economic Review* 69: 957–60.

Ponssard, J. P. 1979. The strategic role of information on the demand function in an oligopolistic environment. *Management Science* 25: 243–50.

Ponssard, J. P. 1981. Forward induction and sunk costs give average cost pricing. *Games and Economic Behavior* 3: 221–36.

Porter, R. H. 1983a. Optimal cartel trigger price strategies. *Journal of Economic Theory* 29: 313–38.

Porter, R. H. 1983b. A study of cartel stability: The Joint Executive Committee, 1880–86. *Bell Journal of Economics* 14: 301–13.

Postlewaite, A., and J. Roberts. 1977. A note on the stability of large cartels. *Econometrica* 45: 1877–78.

Postlewaite, A., and X. Vives. 1987. Bank runs as an equilibrium phenomenon. *Journal of Political Economy* 95: 485–91.

Prescott, E. C., and M. Visscher. 1977. Sequential location among firms with foresight. *Bell Journal of Economics* 8: 378–93.

Radner, R. 1962. Team decision problems. *Annals of Mathematical Statistics* 33: 857–81.

Radner, R. 1980. Collusive behavior in non-cooperative epsilon equilibria of oligopolies with long but finite lives. *Journal of Economic Theory* 22: 121–57.

Radner, R., and R. Rosenthal. 1982. Private information and pure-strategy equilibria. *Mathematical Operations Research* 7.

Raith, M. 1996. A general model of information sharing in oligopoly. *Journal of Economic Theory* 71: 260–88.

Rand, D. 1978. Exotic phenomena in games and duopoly models. *Journal of Mathematical Economics* 5: 173–84.

Rapoport, A. 1974. Prisioner's dilemma—Recollections and observations. In A. Rapoport, ed., *Game Theory as a Theory of Conflict Resolution*. Dordrecht: Reidel.

Reinganum, J. 1983. Uncertain innovation and the persistence of monopoly, *American Economic Review* 73: 741–48.

Reinganum, J. 1989. The timing of innovation: Research, development and diffusion. In R. Schmalensee and R. Willig, eds., *Handbook of Industrial Organization*. Amsterdam: North Holland.

Reynolds, S. 1987. Capacity investment, preemption and commitment in an infinite horizon model. *International Economic Review* 28: 69–88.

Reynolds, S. 1991. Dynamic oligopoly with capacity adjustment costs. *Journal of Economic Dynamics and Control* 15: 491–514.

Riordan, M. 1985. Imperfect information and dynamic conjectural variations. *Rand Journal of Economics* 16: 41–50.

Roberts, J., and H. Sonnenschein. 1976. On the existence of Cournot equilibrium without concave profit functions. *Journal of Economic Theory* 13: 112–17.

Roberts, J., and H. Sonnenschein. 1977. On the foundations of the theory of monopolistic competition. *Econometrica* 45: 101–13.

Roberts, K. 1980. The limit points of monopolistic competition. *Journal of Economic Theory* 22: 256–78.

Roberts, K. 1983. Self-agreed cartel rules. IMSSS Technical Report 427. Stanford University.

Roberts, K. 1985. Cartel behavior and adverse selection. *Journal of Industrial Economics* 33: 401–13.

Roberts, M. 1984. Testing oligopolistic behavior. *International Journal of Industrial Organization* 2: 367–83.

Robinson, J. 1933. *The Economics of Imperfect Competition*. New York: Macmillan.

Robinson, J. 1951. An iterative method of solving a game. *Annals of Mathematics* 54: 296–301.

Robson, A. J. 1990. Duopoly with endogenous strategic timing: Stackelberg regained. *International Economic Review* 31: 263–74.

Rosen, J. B. 1965. Existence and uniqueness of equilibrium points for concave N-person games. *Econometrica* 33: 520–34.

Ross, T. W. 1992. Cartel stability and product differentiation. *International Journal of Industrial Organization* 10: 1–13.

Rotemberg, J., and G. Saloner. 1986. A supergame-theoretic model of price wars during booms. *American Economic Review* 76: 390–407.

Rotemberg, J. J., and G. Saloner. 1986. A supergame-theoretic model of price wars during booms. *American Economic Review* 76: 390–407.

Rotemberg, J. J., and M. Woodford. 1992. Oligopolistic pricing and the effects of aggregate demand on economic activity. *Journal of Political Economy* 100: 1153–1207.

Rothschild, M. 1974. A two-armed bandit theory of market pricing. *Journal of Economic Theory* 9: 185–202.

Royden, H. L. 1968. *Real Analysis*. New York: Macmillan.

Rubinstein, A. 1979. Equilibrium in supergames with the overtaking criterion. *Journal of Economic Theory* 21: 1–9.

Rudin, J. 1976. *Principles of Mathematical Analysis*. New York: McGraw-Hill.

Ruffin, R. J. 1971. Cournot oligopoly and competitive behaviour. *Review of Economic Studies* 38: 493–502.

Sakai, Y. 1985. The value of information in a simple duopoly model. *Journal of Economi* *Theory* 36: 36–54.

Salant, S., S. Switzer, and R. Reynolds. 1983. Losses due to merger: The effects of an exogenous change in industry structure on Cournot-Nash equilibrium. *Quarterly Jour* *nal of Economics* 98: 185–99.

Saloner, G. 1987. Cournot duopoly with two production periods. *Journal of Economi* *Theory* 42: 183–87.

Salop, S. 1979. Monopolistic competition with outside goods. *Bell Journal of Economic* 10: 141–56.

Salop, S. 1986. Practices that credibly facilitate oligopoly coordination. In J. Stiglitz and F. Methewson, eds., *New Developments in the Analysis of Market Structure*. Cambridge MIT Press.

Samuelson, P. A. 1947. *Foundations of Economic Analysis*. Cambridge: Harvard Univer sity Press.

Samuelson, P. A. 1967. The monopolistic competition revolution. In R. E. Juenne, ed. *Monopolistic Competition Theory*. New York: Wiley.

Samuelson, W. 1984. Potential entry and welfare. Working Paper 12–84. Boston Uni versity, School of Management.

Sauermann, H., and R. Selten. 1959. Ein Oligolpolexperiment. *Zeischreft für die Gesante Staatswissenschaft* 115: 427–71.

Sauermann, H., and R. Selten. 1960. An experiment in oligopoly. *General Systems Yearbook of the Society for General Research* 5: 85–114.

Schelling, T. 1960. *The Strategy of Conflict*. New York: Oxford University Press.

Scherer, F. M. 1980. *Industrial Market Structure and Economic Performance*. Chicago Rand McNally.

Scherer, F. M., and D. Ross. 1990. *Industrial Market Structure and Economic Performance* 3d ed. Boston: Houghton Mifflin.

Schmalensee, R. 1978. Entry deterrence in the ready to eat breakfast cereal industry *Bell Journal of Economics* 9: 305–27.

Schmalensee, R. 1992. Sunk costs and market structure: A review article. *Journal of Industrial Economics* 40: 125–34.

Schmalensee, R., and R. Willig. 1989. *Handbook of Industrial Organization*, vols. 1–2 Amsterdam: North Holland.

Seade, J. 1980a. The stability of Cournot revisited. *Journal of Economic Theory* 23: 15–27

Seade, J. 1980b. On the effects of entry. *Econometrica* 48: 479–89.

Seade, J. 1987. Profitable cost increases and the shifting of taxation: Equilibrium responses of markets in oligopoly. Mimeo.

Seidmann, D., and E. Winter. 1997. Strategic information transmission with verifiable messages. *Econometrica* 65: 163–69.

Selten, R. 1965. Spieltheoretische Behandlung eines Oligopolmodells mit Nachfrageträgheit. *Zeitschrift für die gesamte Staatswissenschaft* 12: 301–24.

Selten, R. 1970. *Preispolitik der Mehrproduktenunternehmung in der Statischen Theorie.* Berlin: Springer-Verlag.

Selten, R. 1975. Re-examination of the perfectness concept for equilibrium points in extensive games. *International Journal of Game Theory* 4: 25–55.

Selten, R. 1978. The chain-store paradox. *Theory and Decision* 9: 127–59.

Shaked, A., and J. Sutton. 1982. Relaxing price competition through product differentiation. *Review of Economic Studies* 49: 3–14.

Shaked, A., and J. Sutton. 1983. Natural oligopolies. *Econometrica* 51: 1469–84.

Shaked, A., and J. Sutton. 1987. Product differentiation and industrial structure. *Journal of Industrial Economics* 36: 131–46.

Shapiro, C. 1986. Exchange of cost information in oligopoly. *Review of Economic Studies* 53: 433–46.

Shapiro, C. 1989. Theories of oligopoly behavior. In the R. Schamlensee and R. Willig, eds., *Handbook on Industrial Organization.* Amsterdam: North Holland.

Shapley, L. S. 1964. Some topics in two-person games. In M. Dresher, L. S. Shapley, and A. W. Tucker, eds., *Advances in Game Theory.* Annals of Mathematic Studies 52, pp. 1–28.

Shapley, L. S., and M. Shubik. 1969. Price strategy oligopoly with product variation. *Kyklos* 1: 30–43.

Shilony, Y. 1977. Mixed pricing in oligopoly. *Journal of Economic Theory* 14: 373–88.

Shubik, M. 1959. *Strategy and Market Structure.* New York: Wiley.

Shubik, M., and R. Levitan. 1971. *Market Structure and Behavior.* Cambridge: Harvard University Press.

Siegel, S., and L. Fouraker. 1960. *Bargaining and Group Decision Making: Experiments in Bilateral Monopoly.* New York: McGraw-Hill.

Simon, L. K. 1987. Games with discontinuous payoffs. *Review of Economic Studies* 54: 569–97.

Singh, N., and X. Vives. 1984. Price and quantity competition in a differentiated duopoly. *Rand Journal of Economics* 15: 546–54.

Sklivas, S. 1987. The strategic choice of managerial incentives. *Rand Journal of Economics* 18: 452–58.

Slade, M. E. 1990. Strategic pricing models and interpretation of price-war data. *European Economic Review* 34: 524–37.

Sobel, J. 1984. The timing of sales. *Review of Economic Studies* 51: 353–68.

Sobel, M. 1988. Isotone comparative statics in supermodular games. Mimeo. State University of New York, Stony Brook.

Sonnenschein, H. 1968. The dual of duopoly is complementary monopoly: Or, two of Cournot's theories are one. *Journal of Political Economy* 76: 316–18.

Spady, R. H. 1984. Non-cooperative price-setting by asymmetric multiproduct firms. Mimeo. Bell Laboratoires.

Spence, M. 1976a. Product Differentiation and Welfare. *Papers and Proceedings of the American Economic Review* 66: 407–14.

Spence, M. 1976b. Product selection, fixed costs and monopolistic competition. *Review of Economic Studies* 43: 217–35.

Spence, M. 1977. Entry, capacity, investment and oligopolistic pricing. *Bell Journal of Economics* 10: 1–19.

Spence, M. 1979. Investment strategy and growth in a new market. *Bell Journal of Economics* 10: 1–19.

Spulber, D. 1989. *Regulation and Markets*. Cambridge: MIT Press.

Spulber, D. 1995. Bertrand competition when rivals' costs are unknown. *Journal of Industrial Economics* 53: 1–13.

Stackelberg, H. 1934. *Marktform und Gleichgewicht*. Vienna: Springer.

Stackelberg, H. 1952. *The Theory of the Market Economy*. New York: Oxford University Press.

Staiger, R., and F. Wolak. 1992. Collusive pricing with capacity constraints in the presence of demand uncertainty. *Rand Journal of Economics* 23: 203–20.

Stigler, G. 1964. A theory of oligopoly. *Journal of Political Economy* 72: 44–61.

Suslow, V. Y. 1988. Stability in international cartels: An empirical survey. Working Paper in Economics, E-88-7. Hoover Institution.

Sutton, J. 1990. Explaining everything, explaining nothing? Game theoretic models in industrial economics. *European Economic Review* 34: 505–12.

Sutton, J. 1991. *Sunk Costs and Market Structure: Price Competition, Advertising, and the Evolution on Concentration*. Cambridge: MIT Press.

Suzumura, K., and K. Kiyono. 1987. Entry barriers and economic welfare. *Review of Economic Studies* 54: 157–67.

Sweezy, P. 1939. Demand under conditions of oligopoly. *Journal of Political Economy* 47: 568–73.

Sylos-Labini, P. 1962, *Oligopoly and Technical Progress*. Cambridge: Harvard University Press.

Szidarovszky, F., and K. Okuguchi. 1997. On the existence and uniqueness of pure Nash equilibrium in rent-seeking games. *Games and Economic Behavior* 18: 135–40.

Szidarovszky, F., and S. Yakowitz. 1977. A new proof of the existence and uniqueness of the Cournot equilibrium. *International Economic Review* 18: 787–89.

Takayama, A. 1993. *Analytical Methods in Economics*. Ann Arbor: University of Michigan Press.

Tarski, A. 1955. A lattice-theoretical fixpoint theorem and its applications. *Pacific Journal of Mathematics* 5: 285–308.

The New Palgrave Dictionary of Economics. 1988. Edited by J. Eatwell, M. Milgray and D. Newman. New York: Macmillan, vol. 2.

Thisse, J., and X. Vives. 1988. On the strategic choice of price policy in spatial competition. *American Economic Review* 78: 122–37.

Thisse, J., and X. Vives. 1992. Basing point pricing: Competition versus collusion. *Journal of Industrial Economics* 40: 249–60.

Thorlund-Petersen, L. 1990. Iterative computation of Cournot equilibrium. *Games and Economic Behavior* 2: 61–75.

Tirole, J. 1988. *The Theory of Industrial Organization*. Cambridge: MIT Press.

Topkis, D. 1978. Minimizing a submodular function on a lattice. *Operations Research* 26: 2.

Topkis, D. 1979. Equilibrium points in nonzero-sum n-person submodular games. *SIAM Journal of Control and Optimization* 17: 773–87.

Topkis, D. 1995. Comparative statics of the firm. *Journal of Economic Theory* 67: 370–401.

Tsutsui, S., and K. Mino. 1990. Nonlinear strategies in dynamic duopolistic competition with sticky prices. *Journal of Economic Theory* 52: 131–61.

Ulph, D. 1983. Rational conjectures in the theory of oligopoly. *International Journal of Industrial Organization* 1: 131–54.

Ushio, Y. 1983. Cournot equilibrium with free entry: The case of decreasing average cost functions. *Review of Economic Studies* 50: 347–54.

Ushio, Y. 1985. Approximate efficiency of Cournot equilibria in large markets. *Review of Economic Studies* 52: 547–56.

Van Damme, E., and S. Hurkens. 1996. Commitment robust equilibria and endogenous timing. *Games and Economic Behavior* 15: 290–311.

Van Huyck, J., R. Battalio, and R. Beil. 1990. Tacit coordination games, strategic uncertainty, and coordination failure. *American Economic Review* 80: 234–48.

Varian, H. 1980. A model of sales. *American Economic Review* 70: 651–59.

Vega-Redondo, F. 1996. *Evolution, Games, and Economic Behavior*. Oxford: Oxford University Press.

Vettas, N. 1997. On the informational role of quantities: Durable goods and consumers' word-of-mouth communication. *International Economic Review* 38: 915–44.

Vickers, J. 1985. Delegation and the theory of the firm. *Economic Journal Supplement* 95: 138–47.

Vickers, J. 1995. Entry and competitive selection. Mimeo. Oxford University.

Vives, X. 1984. Duopoly information equilibrium: Cournot and Bertrand. *Journal of Economic Theory* 34: 71–94.

Vives, X. 1985a. On the efficiency of Bertrand and Cournot equilibria with product differentiation. *Journal of Economic Theory* 36: 166–75.

Vives, X. 1985b. Nash equilibrium in oligopoly games with monotone best responses. CARESS Working Paper 85-10. University of Pennsylvania.

Vives, X. 1986a. Rationing rules and Bertrand-Edgeworth equilibria in large markets. *Economics Letters* 21: 113–16.

Vives, X. 1986b. Commitment, flexibility and market outcomes. *International Journal of Industrial Organization* 4: 217–29.

Vives, X. 1987. Small income effects: A Marshallian theory of consumer surplus and downward sloping demand. *Review of Economic Studies* 54: 87–103.

Vives, X. 1988a. Sequential entry, industry structure and welfare. *European Economic Review* 32: 1671–87.

Vives, X. 1988b. Aggregation of information in large Cournot markets. *Econometrica* 56: 851–76.

Vives, X. 1989a. Cournot and the oligopoly problem. *European Economic Review* 33: 503–14.

Vives, X. 1989b. Technological competition, uncertainty and oligopoly. *Journal of Economic Theory* 48: 386–415.

Vives, X. 1990a. Nash equilibrium with strategic complementarities. *Journal of Mathematical Economics* 19: 305–21.

Vives, X. 1990b. Trade association, disclosure rules, incentives to share information and welfare. *Rand Journal of Economics* 21: 409–30.

Vives, X. 1993. Edgeworth and modern oligopoly theory. *European Economic Review* 37: 463–76.

von Neumann, J., and O. Morgenstern. 1944. *Theory of Games and Economic Behavior.* Princeton: Princeton University Press.

von Weizsäcker, C. C. 1980. A welfare analysis of barriers to entry. *Bell Journal of Economics* 11: 399–420.

von Weizsäcker, Ch. 1984. The cost of substitution. *Econometrica* 52: 1085–1116.

Waldman, M. 1987. Noncooperative entry deterrence, uncertainty, and the free rider problem. *Review of Economic Studies* 54: 301–10.

Waldman, M. 1991. The role of multiple potential entrants/sequential entry in noncooperative entry deterrence. *Rand Journal of Economics* 22: 446–53.

Ware, R. 1984. Sunk costs and strategic commitment: A proposed three-stage equilibrium. *Economic Journal* 94: 370–78.

Weibull, J. 1995. *Evolutionary Game Theory.* Cambridge: MIT Press.

Weitzman, M. 1974. Prices vs. quantities. *Review of Economic Studies* 41: 477–91.

Wernerfelt, B. 1989. Tacit collusion in differentiated Cournot games. *Economics Letters* 29: 303–306.

Willig, R. 1976. Consumer's surplus without apology. *American Economic Review* 66: 589–97.

Wold, H., and L. Juréen. 1953. *Demand Analysis*. New York: Wiley.

Zhou, L. 1994. The set of Nash equilibria of a supermodular game is a complete lattice. *Games and Economic Behavior* 7: 295–300.

Ziv, A. 1993. Information sharing in oligopoly: The truth-telling problem. *Rand Journal of Economics* 24: 455–65.

Index